THE HISTORY OF AMERICAN FOREIGN POLICY FROM 1895

THE HISTORY OF AMERICAN FOREIGN POLICY FROM 1895

• Fourth Edition •

Jerald A. Combs

Routledge
Taylor & Francis Group

LONDON AND NEW YORK

First published 2012 by M.E. Sharpe

Published 2015 by Routledge
2 Park Square, Milton Park, Abingdon, Oxon OX14 4RN
711 Third Avenue, New York, NY 10017, USA

Routledge is an imprint of the Taylor & Francis Group, an informa business

Notices
No responsibility is assumed by the publisher for any injury and/or damage to
persons or property as a matter of products liability, negligence or otherwise,
or from any use of operation of any methods, products, instructions or ideas
contained in the material herein.

Practitioners and researchers must always rely on their own experience and
knowledge in evaluating and using any information, methods, compounds, or
experiments described herein. In using such information or methods they should
be mindful of their own safety and the safety of others, including parties for
whom they have a professional responsibility.

Product or corporate names may be trademarks or registered trademarks, and
are used only for identification and explanation without intent to infringe.

Library of Congress Cataloging-in-Publication Data

Combs, Jerald A.
  The history of American foreign policy from 1895 / by Jerald A. Combs. — 4th ed.
    p. cm.
  Includes bibliographical references and index.
  ISBN 978-0-7656-3349-1 (hardcover : alk. paper)—ISBN 978-0-7656-3350-7 (pbk. : alk. paper)
1. United States—Foreign relations. I. Title.

E183.7.C6562 2012
327.73—dc23   2011049950

ISBN 13: 9780765633507 (pbk)
ISBN 13: 9780765633491 (hbk)

CONTENTS

LIST OF MAPS

PREFACE

Anyone who has experienced the bitter debates over U.S. policy toward Iraq, El Salvador, or Vietnam understands that American foreign policy inevitably generates controversy. Yet most people expect a history of American foreign policy to be a simple narrative of the "truth" about the past. They seem unaware that events of the distant past created just as much controversy as those of the present day. They also seem to assume that historians will be unaffected by past controversies, let alone by present ones.

Unfortunately, historical study cannot provide a final truth about the past. Historians can approach the truth by close study of the documents surrounding critical events in America's diplomatic history, but their accounts are still affected by their own experiences, judgments, and predilections. These differences have given rise to several opposing views of the history of American foreign policy.

Some historians see American diplomacy as a fairly successful blend of democratic idealism and realistic concern for American national interests. They generally assume that American values of liberty, democracy, and free enterprise are worthy goals that, if encouraged throughout the world by American diplomacy, will benefit all the people of the earth as well as the United States. They portray most of America's wars as justified resistance to foreign aggression. For instance, they see the American Revolution and the War of 1812 as necessary battles against British tyranny. They look upon westward expansion as the spread of liberty and civilization over reactionary colonial regimes and tragic but doomed Indians. They emphasize the aggressiveness of the Mexicans leading to the Mexican War and the tyranny of Spain in Cuba and the Philippines prior to the Spanish-American War of 1898. They regard the two world wars as gallant crusades to save Europe from the tyranny of Kaiser Wilhelm's Germany and then from Hitler's Nazis. They tend to see the events of the Cold War, including the conflicts in Korea and Vietnam, as part of a noble if occasionally inept resistance to the expansion of Soviet and Communist plans for world domination. Finally, they believe that the invasion of Iraq was necessary both to eliminate a terrorist threat to the United States and to make the world more secure by establishing a peaceful democracy in the Middle East.

This view—which I call the nationalist interpretation of American foreign policy—represents the outlook of many secondary school texts, politicians, newspapers, and television commentaries. It also continues to have strong support in the academic world. It can lead to blatant, superpatriotic flag-waving, as in the speeches of some politicians, but also it can be the sophisticated conviction of scholars who have examined the realistic alternatives available to American statesmen at various times and concluded that in most circumstances America's leaders chose properly.

For the most part, those who hold the nationalist view are politically conservative. Among politicians, Ronald Reagan and George W. Bush are good examples. A recent general history of American foreign policy written from this point of view is Robert Kagan's *Dangerous Nation: America's Place in the World from Its Earliest Days to the Dawn of the 20th Century* (2006). The classic nationalist textbook is *A Diplomatic History of the United States* (4th ed., 1955) by the dean of American diplomatic historians, Samuel Flagg Bemis.

A second and more critical interpretation of the history of American foreign policy is the so-called realist view. This has probably been the dominant interpretation among diplomatic historians since World War II. Realists insist that American foreign policy generally has been too naive, idealistic, and moralistic. They believe that Americans, regarding their own nation as more peaceful and moral than others because of America's democratic form of government, have oscillated foolishly between a policy of isolation, designed to insulate themselves from evil foreigners and their meaningless wars, and a policy of crusading internationalism, designed to eliminate foreign evils by making nations over in America's image. For instance, realists argue that America's devotion to total victory over Nazi Germany and its unconditional surrender destroyed Central Europe and left a vacuum of power that naturally tempted the Soviets to expand. Instead of meeting that expansion with a realistic negotiating stance, the United States first hoped to deter it by peaceful intentions and goodwill, and then overreacted to the failure of this naive approach by embarking on an excessive military buildup and an anti-Communist crusade. Realists believe that the United States must follow a steadier policy based on national interests rather than grandiose democratic ideals, seeking peace through a balance of power rather than some utopian vision of a world without conflict. They urge that the nation balance its goals with the power available to reach them.

Although many American diplomatic historians share this realist outlook, they often divide over its application to particular events. Hard realists emphasize the need for the United States to protect its national interests and the world balance of power by dealing with adversaries from a position of unassailable strength. Where there is an imbalance between America's goals and its power, they generally favor increasing the nation's power. They believe that America must be willing to take significant risks, including major military action, to prevent the expansion of its adversaries even in morally ambiguous situations or in areas others might see as unimportant to America's most vital interests. Thus, they favor a very activist American foreign policy. Henry Kissinger, who favored the Iraq war for strategic rather than idealistic, democratic reasons, is a good example of a contemporary politician and historian who operates from this perspective, as set forth in his classic analysis of the history of American foreign policy, *Diplomacy* (1994). The most popular American diplomatic history textbook for decades was also written from this point of view, Thomas A. Bailey's *A Diplomatic History of the American People* (10th ed., 1980).

There are a number of soft or restrained realists, however, who argue that a proper analysis of America's national interest, the balance of power, and the limited ability of military action to accomplish worthwhile policy goals should have led the United States to greater restraint in its relations abroad. As opposed to the hard realists, the soft realists, when faced with an imbalance between America's goals and power, would usually favor reducing the nation's goals rather than increasing its military power. They would also emphasize that power should be measured not strictly by military force, but also by what political scientist Joseph Nye has called "soft power," the persuasive power of ideological consistency, respect for the cultures and opinions of others, and the importance of multinational cooperation. Soft or restrained realists generally think that greater patience and more expert diplomacy might have saved the United States from some of its wars, such as those in Vietnam and Iraq. The most prominent advocates of this view among writers on diplomatic history have been George Kennan, Walter Lippmann, and Hans Morgenthau. Several recent surveys of American foreign policy also operate generally from this view. They include George Herring, *From Colony to Superpower: U.S. Foreign Relations since 1776* (2008); Michael H. Hunt, *The American Ascendancy: How the United States Gained and Wielded Global Dominance* (2007); and Richard Immerman, *Empire for Liberty: A History of American Imperialism from Benjamin Franklin to Paul Wolfowitz* (2010). In general, soft realism is the view to which I subscribe and from which I have written this account.

While realists have chastised American foreign policy for excessive idealism and moralism, another group of critics known as revisionists argue that American diplomacy instead has been realistic and self-interested to the point of rapaciousness. Revisionists regard the primary theme of American diplomatic history not as an oscillation between isolationism and interventionism, but as continuous aggressive expansion. They see American imperialism beginning with the westward movement, extending through America's attempts to protect its markets and capitalist economy in the first and second world wars, and culminating in recent efforts to preserve American economic interests in Vietnam, the Middle East, and Central America.

The most radical of these revisionists believe that American imperialist foreign policy will not change unless the United States becomes a socialist nation. They agree with Lenin's theory that imperialism is the product of capitalism's intrinsic need to expand its markets and sources of raw materials. Capitalist nations must continually expand their economies by acquiring either formal or informal colonies, because only in this way can the elite who monopolize the internal wealth of the nation find new resources to buy off the masses, whose exclusion from the benefits of their labor would otherwise lead to a revolutionary redistribution of the nation's goods. Radicals believe that this redistribution of goods would enhance the purchasing power of the vast majority of the people, augment economic demand, and thus increase production and jobs. America's prosperity would no longer depend on overseas expansion and aggression, and the major motive behind imperialism and war would be gone. Failing this, the United States and the other capitalist nations would continue to expand, inevitably clash in their competition for markets and resources, and bring war and destruction on the earth. You will not find many American politicians who hold this point of view; they have difficulty being elected in the United States. But you will find a strong statement of this perspective in Gabriel Kolko's *The Roots of American Foreign Policy* (1969). Moderate revisionists also criticize America's foreign policy as rapacious expansionism and imperialism, but, stressing the economic factor in foreign policy somewhat less than do the radicals, imply that domestic reform rather than revolution might be adequate to change the nation's approach to foreign relations. They see American diplomacy as the product of bureaucratic as well as economic elites, of ideological, cultural, and psychological factors such as racism and fear of communism as well as capitalist expansion, and of well-intentioned error as well as malevolence. They also find some leaders and episodes in American history with which they sympathize, especially Franklin Roosevelt's attempts to accommodate the Soviet Union during World War II. An excellent text on American diplomacy from this moderate revisionist point of view is *American Foreign Policy: A History* (6th ed., 2005) by Thomas G. Paterson, J. Garry Clifford, Deborah Kisistaski, Shane J. Maddock, and Kenneth J. Hagan.

This viewpoint has received a boost in the last decade or so from the increased emphasis in the discipline of history on cultural, ideological, and social matters. Rather than concentrating on the issues of power and national interest, recent histories of American foreign policy have often focused on the culture and ideology that led Americans to believe that they were different from and superior to nations and peoples with whom they were in conflict. By analyzing the texts of U.S. culture and diplomacy, these historians have plumbed the depths of American racism and paternalism; although some also see the cultural biases of America's enemies as contributing to the nation's conflicts, to a large extent their cultural histories illustrate the imperialistic nature of the American approach to foreign policy. Three excellent general surveys that illustrate this approach are Walter L. Hixon, *The Myth of American Diplomacy: National Identity and U.S. Foreign Policy* (2008); Walter Nugent, *Habits of Empire: A History of American Expansionism* (2008); and William O. Walker III, *National Security and Core Values in American History* (2009). For a general cultural history of American foreign policy, see Carlos Rowe's *Literary Culture and U.S. Imperialism: From the Revolution to World War II* (2000). For an excellent application of this approach to specific American policies, see Odd Arne Westad's *The Global Cold War: Third World Interventions and the Making of Our Times* (2007).

In the following work, I, like the authors of all the other texts mentioned above, have tried to write a balanced account of the history of American foreign policy. But like them, I cannot help but be affected by my own experiences and point of view. I have tried to compensate for this by ensuring that even when the narrative expresses strong opinions about an episode, it presents other interpretations as well. The reader will also find detailed reviews of conflicting interpretations in the historiographical discussions at the end of each chapter. These essays trace the development of the major schools of historical thought outlined in this introduction—schools I think affect not only histories of past American diplomacy, but the making of present policy as well.

THE HISTORY OF AMERICAN FOREIGN POLICY FROM 1895

CHAPTER 1

THE SPANISH-AMERICAN WAR AND THE DECISION FOR EMPIRE

The Imperial Surge, 1895–1917

It is doubtful that many Americans living in the early 1890s realized that they stood on the threshold of a new age in American diplomacy. National politics still revolved around internal questions. Americans regarded the economic issues stemming from industrialization and immigration as essentially domestic, despite rising concerns about foreign trade. The warnings of the founders against foreign entanglements, military establishments, and colonial oppression still dominated popular attitudes toward foreign policy. Little of the nation's economic strength had been translated into the military or diplomatic power necessary for large-scale overseas intervention, and most Americans would have been aghast at any suggestion that the United States should involve itself in a major way in Europe or Asia. The balance of opinion was more tenuous on acquisitions closer to home, however, especially if they might be annexed without much fuss or expense. Rejections of treaties or petitions for the annexation of Santo Domingo, Cuba, Haiti, and Hawaii had been somewhat accidental, involving political partisanship, personalities, and fortuitous events that swung the balance against territorial expansion. The balance against overseas annexations and involvements was becoming increasingly precarious, ready to be altered by a major crisis or opportunity that could give it a substantial push.

The forces inclining the United States toward overseas expansion and intervention had developed rapidly in the post–Civil War period. Most important of these was America's growing power. The nation's population increased from 39 million in 1870 to 63 million in 1890. By the 1890s, America had surpassed all nations in the production of coal, oil, and steel, the sinews of modern power until the atomic age. Popular writers and politicians made clear to the American people the strategic and economic benefits of acquiring Caribbean naval bases, an isthmian canal, and Hawaii. They helped translate hazy inclinations into systematic thought patterns.

The Spanish-American War supplied the catalyst to create a new national majority ready to intrude into the realm of great power politics and accept an overseas empire. The original rationale of the Spanish-American War, intervention to free Cuba from Spain, did not stretch the old diplomacy too much, especially when Congress declared its intention not to annex Cuba. But the thrill of military combat and victory broke down many of the barriers to overseas intervention and annexation. The United States took Puerto Rico, the Philippines, Guam, and Wake Island, completed the annexation of Hawaii, and asserted a protectorate over Cuba. It then acquired the Panama Canal route, undertook wholesale military interventions in Central America and the Caribbean, and increased its diplomatic activity in Asia.

Even in this imperial aftermath of the Spanish-American War, Americans remained wary of European entanglement. They defended their Latin American interventions as necessary to ward off European expansion and consequent conflict with the interests of the United States. They offered the Open Door in Asia as an alternative to European attempts to carve China further into spheres of interest, a process that might entangle the United States in European balance-of-power politics. Finally, however, World War I dragged the United States into the European arena. Americans became thoroughly enmeshed in global politics.

The Diplomatic Revolution of the 1890s

Foreign nations seemed no more aware that the United States was on the verge of adopting a new diplomatic posture in the 1890s than Americans themselves. When the Turkish sultan sought to cut expenses in 1880, he decided to eliminate the diplomatic missions in several minor powers, including Sweden, Belgium, the Netherlands, and the United States. The German envoy in Washington offered to take a pay cut if his superiors would transfer him to Madrid. Russia neglected to send a minister to the United States for two years after the previous one had left.

These nations failed to realize that the Industrial Revolution had increased American strength tremendously. By the 1890s, the United States was manufacturing almost as much as Great Britain, Germany, and France combined. This output gave the United States the means to expand its diplomatic role from a regional to a global power. Industry also provided a motive for such a change in American foreign policy, creating more need for overseas markets. By the 1890s, manufactures had surpassed agricultural products as America's main exports. Of all the nations in the world, only Great Britain outstripped the United States in the total value of its exports, and Britain's lead was clearly temporary. America's increasing desire for overseas markets naturally led to calls for a more active diplomacy.

Throughout the post–Civil War period there had been no lack of voices calling for a more aggressive military and diplomatic policy to accompany America's increasing economic strength and expanding foreign trade. Naval officers like Admiral Stephen Luce extolled the benefits of a larger, more modern navy. In the 1880s these officers succeeded in beginning a naval building program that produced long-range, steam-driven, steel-clad battleships. Otherwise, as we have seen, the United States pursued overseas markets, coaling stations, and strategically located colonies sporadically and ineffectually. Then, in the 1890s, advocates of an aggressive foreign policy took advantage of several traumatic events to propel America into a policy of global intervention and the acquisition of an overseas empire.

The economic panic of 1893, initiating a four-year depression more severe than any

America faced until 1929, did much to turn influential Americans toward a more active pursuit of foreign markets. Fifteen thousand businesses failed in 1893, including several major railroads. Hundreds of banks went under. Three million people were left jobless, some 20 percent of the workforce. Farm production and prices plummeted. Violent strikes occurred in coal mines and railroads, and federal troops were called in to break up the great Pullman strike. Discontented farmers flocked into the Populist Party. They demanded currency inflation by unlimited coinage of silver, advocated a graduated income tax, and urged government control of railroads and utilities. Some leaders of government and industry feared that America stood on the brink of revolution.

The depression highlighted other disturbing trends that had seemed less ominous when the country was more prosperous. Large combinations of capital were becoming increasingly dominant in American business, threatening the older America of smaller competitive enterprises. Cities expanded tremendously, undercutting the power and prestige of the countryside and the older prototypical American, the yeoman farmer. Immigrants flowed into these cities at a staggering rate; over 500,000 arrived in America every year. Most of these newcomers were from southern and eastern Europe, bringing with them cultural mores and religious practices that clashed with the Protestantism and Anglo-Saxon culture of the dominant elite.

In addition to the problems posed by immigration, historian Frederick Jackson Turner startled the nation by publicizing the fact that the census of 1890 no longer recognized the existence of a frontier line in the West. Turner warned that the disappearance of this frontier would mean declining opportunities for internal territorial and economic expansion. Since he thought that much of America's democracy had stemmed from the frontier, he feared its disappearance would have political as well as economic consequences.

All these trends produced in America what historian Richard Hofstadter called a "psychic crisis." Powerful and wealthy as the United States was, many Americans seem to have feared that the nation was close to blowing up or at least entering a decline in wealth and political well-being. For some, this fear led to gloom and apathy, but others sought to deny their own failure of confidence by embarking on a frantic crusade, motivated by the hope that if they could convince others of their virtue and strength, they could convince themselves as well.

The economic, political, and psychic crisis brought on by the depression of 1893 caused some soul-searching among leading figures in the Cleveland administration, Congress, and business. They argued that the depression resulted from a glut of American agricultural and industrial products. Since America's factories and farms were producing more than domestic markets could consume, the United States needed to pursue overseas markets more aggressively. Yet at the same time that exports came to seem increasingly important to many American leaders, foreign markets seemed to be closing against American trade. European nations were carving up Africa and, in the wake of Japan's victory over China in the Sino-Japanese War of 1895, were seeking to increase their spheres of influence in Asia as well. These European colonial powers generally erected discriminatory tariff barriers in their newly acquired territories. Even in Great Britain, the trend seemed to be toward closing markets to foreign competition. The British colonial secretary, Joseph

Chamberlain, advocated preferential tariff structures throughout the British Empire, which formerly had been relatively open to exports from the United States.

American Culture and the Rise of U.S. Imperialism

While the depression frightened the United States into a more interventionist policy abroad, intellectual, religious, and cultural currents provided a moral rationale for expansion. The surge of European imperialism in the 1880s and 1890s led to a wealth of literature praising the beneficence of European colonial government. Writers such as Frederick Fabri and James Anthony Froude spread these ideas to the attentive and cosmopolitan portion of the American public that was aware of and concerned for national policy.

Influential politicians also propagated the imperial gospel among Americans. Theodore Roosevelt, for instance, argued that peace could not be had "until the civilized nations have expanded in some shape over the barbarous nations. This means the cooperation of the civilized peoples of the earth to that end, whatever the cost or time." Naturally, Roosevelt thought the United States the best of such civilized nations, but in areas outside America's interests, he was willing to support the imperialism of other European powers. For instance, he thought England would be doing "her duty as a civilized nation" by colonizing the Sudan. He also said it was in the interest of civilization that the English-speaking race be dominant in the Western Hemisphere.

Roosevelt did not believe such colonialism ran contrary to the traditions of the founders expressed in the Declaration of Independence and President Washington's Farewell Address. In his best-selling book, *The Winning of the West*, he pointed out that the founders had conquered and colonized the Indians. This action had been perfectly justified, he thought, for it had been impossible "to avoid conflicts with the weaker race, unless we were willing to see the American continent fall into the hands of some other strong power" or "willing that the whole continent west of the Alleghenies should remain an unpeopled waste, the hunting-ground of savages."

A still more influential propagator of the imperial vision of the 1890s was Roosevelt's friend, Admiral Alfred Thayer Mahan. His world-famous book, *The Influence of Sea Power upon History*, extolled the benefits of Christianity and Western civilization and noted the role the British navy had played in establishing the British Empire for the mutual benefit of the British economy and these barbaric natives. He urged that the United States likewise build a strong, two-ocean navy, acquire bases and coaling stations in the Caribbean and the Pacific, build an isthmian canal, and thus extend protection to the extensive commerce that would carry American civilization to Asia and Latin America while enriching the United States. He pointed out that modern technology had brought within reach lands that the founders had considered far beyond the realm of vital American interests. Conversely, he warned that the United States now was also within easier reach of foreign powers and would become increasingly vulnerable militarily if it did not build its navy and take a more active interest in overseas affairs.

American missionaries reinforced the inclination of the followers of Mahan and Roosevelt to seek a more activist foreign policy. Josiah Strong embodied this missionary spirit. His best seller, *Our Country*, proclaimed that the Anglo-Saxon race in America, "a race of unequaled energy, with all the majesty of numbers and the might of wealth behind it—the representative, let us hope, of the largest liberty, the purest Christianity, the highest civilization—having developed peculiarly aggressive traits calculated to impress its institutions upon mankind, will spread itself over the earth. If I read not amiss, this powerful race will move down upon Mexico, down upon Central and South America, out upon the islands of the sea, over Africa and beyond. And can anyone doubt that the result of this competition of races will be the 'survival of the fittest'?" Strong emphasized that this expansion need not be a "war of extermination" for "the contest is not one of arms, but of vitality and of civilization." Nonetheless, his description of international affairs as a competition of races culminating in the survival of the fittest could not help but contribute to a more aggressive American foreign policy.

"The survival of the fittest" was a catchword of the 1890s and a powerful intellectual support for the "large policy" of people like Roosevelt and Mahan. It derived from Charles Darwin's pathbreaking work on biological evolution that portrayed natural selection as the means by which species had evolved from primitive forms to their present status. An Englishman, Herbert Spencer, adapted Darwin's idea of biological evolution to the realm of human social affairs. Spencer theorized that civilizations, like biological species, progressed by natural selection and the survival of the fittest. Spencer's social Darwinism was translated by many imperialists into a formula for international relations. Nations and races competed with one another; the strong survived, the weak succumbed. Thus civilization progressed.

Some Americans found the Darwinian emphasis on survival of the fittest a convenient rationale for their own desire to participate in a glorious fight. Most of the generation alive in the 1890s had not experienced the blood and terror of the Civil War. That war appeared to them in retrospect as a great adventure fought for profound principles. It seemed far more exciting than the dreary economic concerns that dominated their own industrial America of the 1890s. They were like adolescents desperate to test their new power in a fight with an evil bully. Some even agreed with Theodore Roosevelt that "this country needs a war."

Roosevelt epitomized the emphasis on manliness and contempt for effeminacy that dominated American attitudes in the 1890s and pointed the nation toward war and imperialism. Roosevelt had transformed himself from a teenage weakling into a vigorous athlete who prided himself on strenuous and dangerous activities. He urged Americans to follow his example. In a famous address to the Hamilton Club of Chicago in 1899, he condemned "the timid man, the lazy man, the man who distrusts his country, the over-civilized man, who has lost the great fighting, masterful virtues. . . . These are the men who fear the strenuous life, who fear the only national life which is really worth leading."

Popular Culture and U.S. Imperialism

The attitudes of American and white superiority, manliness, and survival of the fittest permeated mass culture in the United States. Popular literature, such as tales of the Old West, and mass spectacles, such as world fairs and circuses, portrayed the United States as rising over primitive conditions and peoples to reach a new apex of civilization. For instance, Buffalo Bill Cody's Wild West show—which played to 50 million people throughout the United States and the world and required eighteen railroad cars to transport its entourage of cowboys, Indians, animals, and wagons—illustrated the progress from primitivism to civilization by moving from scenes of "The Primeval Forest" through "The Prairie," "The Cattle Ranch," and "The Mining Camp." In most of these scenes, Buffalo Bill and other cowboys rescued white settlers from Indians. Thus, the Wild West show represented the imperial ethic of Anglo-Saxons taming nature and triumphing over savagery, although the message was somewhat less straightforward when Cody added Custer's Last Stand as the culminating episode of the show.

Another American popular cultural spectacle that embodied the message of American superiority in the 1880s and 1890s was baseball. As one journalist put it, baseball was "a great sport, representative and typical of the people who practice it . . . one that stimulates all the faculties of the mind . . . keenness, invention, perception, agility, celerity of thought and action, adaptability to circumstances—in short, all the qualities that go to make the American man the most highly-organized, civilized being on earth." Thus, baseball celebrated the American values of self-reliance, individualism, competition, and survival of the fittest.

A.G. Spalding, manufacturer of baseball equipment and owner of the Chicago White Stockings in the National League, imitated Buffalo Bill by taking his own team and a mix of other players on a world tour in 1888–1889. His goal was to promote the sport, the United States, and his own products. Spalding told the Australians during his time down under that his teams, composed entirely of white players with a single black mascot who entertained audiences with "plantation dances," embodied "all those essentials of manliness, courage, nerve, pluck and endurance characteristic of the Anglo-Saxon race." After touring New Zealand, Australia, and Ceylon (now Sri Lanka), the tour stopped in Egypt, where the game was played in the shadow of the pyramids and the players shocked the audience by trying to throw balls over the tombs. It culminated in Europe with games in Italy, France, England, Ireland, and Scotland. As with Buffalo Bill's show, the baseball tour had only mixed success in convincing foreign audiences of American superiority. The British, for instance, refused to accept Spalding's insistence that baseball was superior to cricket and instead mocked baseball as much closer to their children's game of rounders.[1]

Opposition to Imperialism

The depression, the psychic crisis, the increased need for foreign markets, the rapid development of modern communications and transportation, the surge of European imperialism, and the development of powerful, cultural rationales for overseas expansion set the stage for the Spanish-American War and its imperial aftermath. But there were still strong voices for restraint, even among those who might have been expected to be in the vanguard of imperialism.

Two of America's most prominent social Darwinists, William Graham Sumner and John Burgess, were nonetheless strong opponents of overseas expansionism. So was the historian James Schouler, who had written paeans to earlier continental expansion. Such people could agree that the United States housed a superior race and civilization, yet oppose overseas acquisitions. Like the older generations of Americans, who had an equally fervent if not so systematic belief in American superiority, they were convinced the United States best fulfilled its missionary impulse by serving as a model for foreigners rather than as a conqueror and reformer.

James Schouler demonstrated how racists could also be anti-imperialists in an article opposing the annexation of Hawaii. He thought Americans did not "wish these islands thrown upon them, under a race conquest, like that of Cortes over the Astecs [sic] in Mexico, but must feel well assured that the Hawaiians themselves come toward us with open arms and of their own free accord, as well as resident foreigners who undertake to pledge their consent." For "notwithstanding our innate and earnest desire to diffuse the blessings of freedom which we enjoy over the rest of the globe, one would think that, with Indians not yet reclaimed, negroes emancipated only by the bloodiest and costliest of civil strifes, and, as the latest factor, Chinese disturbing our national peace of mind—not to speak of the refuse of European nations cast lately upon us so constantly by the Atlantic tides—this Union had enough of the problem of amalgamating races into one brotherhood to last at least for the rest of this century." Schouler thought America's present Hawaiian trade ties and coaling stations satisfied the national interest and that the United States should avoid territorial annexation and overt political rule.

The Venezuelan Boundary Dispute

The Venezuela crisis of 1895 demonstrated the delicate balance between the conflicting impulses for an aggressive and a restrained foreign policy. Grover Cleveland, the president who precipitated the crisis with his belligerent claims of American rights abroad, was the same man who had rejected a Hawaiian annexation treaty two years before. He was also the man who had risked war with his strong nationalist stands against Germany in a quarrel over Samoa and against the British in a controversy over sealing in the waters off Alaska. Thus, he embodied within himself the competing urges for an aggressive and a restrained foreign policy. Still, Cleveland's conduct in the Venezuelan crisis puzzles most historians.

Venezuela and the British colony of Guiana had never agreed on the boundary between them. For many years the conflict had been muted because the boundary ran through uninhabited and seemingly valueless land. Still the issue had the potential for serious conflict. Venezuela claimed that its proper border included nearly two-thirds of the territory Britain already ruled as Guiana, while the British insisted that the true boundary was a line favorable to Guiana established by Robert Schomburgk in a survey commissioned by the British in 1840.

The United States had expressed mild concern about the border controversy from time to time since the Civil War, but the issue heated up in 1894 when an American agent paid by Venezuela, William L. Scruggs, published a vitriolic pamphlet accusing the British of open aggression and defiance of the Monroe Doctrine. Congress responded with a unanimous vote on behalf of a resolution, drafted largely by Scruggs himself, urging Venezuela and Great Britain to submit the dispute to arbitration. Venezuela wanted arbitration rather than direct negotiations with Great Britain because it knew that its large delinquent debt to Britain could be used as leverage against Venezuela's border claims in an open negotiation. Arbitration would supposedly limit the issue to the border alone.

The United States probably did have sufficient interest in the dispute to justify a call for arbitration. The largest gold nugget ever discovered came from the disputed area. Great Britain also was trying to bend the Schomburgk Line to include Point Barima, with its access to the mouth of the Orinoco River. This would give Great Britain a chance to control what some regarded as a vital trade artery into the heart of South America. The claim to Point Barima, which Britain made formally in 1895, came on the heels of several other international conflicts involving British territorial claims. The most important of these resulted when British marines temporarily occupied the Nicaraguan town of Corinto, close to the potential canal site. Because Cleveland had stayed aloof from these disputes, denying in particular that the British-Nicaraguan clash involved the Monroe Doctrine, he was roundly criticized by the Republicans for his "weakness."

Cleveland believed he had already lost one election for his supposed softness toward the British, an impression created by the British minister to the United States, Lionel Sackville West, who wrote a letter in 1888 recommending Cleveland over his Republican opponent in the presidential election of that year. Facing the backlash from the Corinto incident as well as the fallout from the depression of 1893, he may have thought it salutary for the national as well as his own political interest to call a loud halt to Britain's creeping advance in South America. In any case, he proved receptive to a blustering note his new secretary of state, Richard Olney, proposed to send to Great Britain. Olney and Cleveland decided to end the Venezuelan boundary dispute once and for all and in the process defend the Monroe Doctrine. Thus they hoped to dash any ideas European nations might have entertained of extending their competition for colonies from Asia and Africa to the Western Hemisphere.

Although Richard Olney was not a particularly warlike man, he was impatient, blunt, rigid, and self-righteous. (He banished his daughter from his home for unknown reasons and refused to see her for thirty years even though she lived in the same town.) With Cleveland's approval, Olney told the British that the Monroe Doctrine was well-established public law in America and that Britain was violating it by seeking to expand its territory in the Western Hemisphere at the expense of Venezuela. The United States had a right to demand that Britain submit the entire matter to arbitration, since "distance and three thousand miles of intervening ocean make any permanent political union between a European and an American state unnatural and inexpedient. . . . To-day the United States is practically sovereign on this continent, and its fiat is law upon the subjects to which it confines its interposition."

The British did not realize how gravely Cleveland and Olney viewed what seemed

Venezuela-British Guiana Boundary Dispute

to be a remote border quarrel. Olney's inflated language no doubt made the crisis seem a political ploy aimed at domestic voters rather than a serious diplomatic initiative. Besides, the British cabinet was preoccupied with the massacre of Armenians in Turkey and Russian pressure for Chinese concessions in Manchuria, both of which held the potential for a general European war. As a consequence, Prime Minister Lord Salisbury delayed the British answer to Olney's note for four months. Cleveland was especially irritated by the delay because he wanted to announce a resolution of the issue in his State of the Union message. He was even more irritated when the British response, handed to Olney a few days after Cleveland's congressional message, rejected out of hand any suggestion that the Venezuela dispute was covered by the Monroe Doctrine or that the doctrine was international law. Salisbury also said Britain could not risk arbitration of any territory that might result in the transfer of "large numbers of British subjects . . . to a nation of different race and language, whose political system is subject to frequent disturbance, and whose institutions as yet too often afford very inadequate protection to life and property."

Cleveland's response was to threaten war. In a sensational message to Congress, Cleveland asserted that the Monroe Doctrine was indeed international law and that it covered the Venezuelan dispute. He announced that the United States would commission a study of the proper boundary that, when approved by the American government, would obligate the United States "to resist by every means in its power, as a willful aggression upon its rights and interests, the appropriation by Great Britain of any lands or the exercise of government jurisdiction over any territory which after investigation we have determined of right belongs to Venezuela."

For a few days war seemed imminent. Congress unanimously accepted Cleveland's recommendation for a border survey. But opposition quickly arose and dampened the flames, reasserting the balance between the urges for aggression and restraint. The famous Harvard philosopher William James said Cleveland had committed a political crime. Charles Francis Adams Jr., the elder brother of the great historian Henry Adams, joined James's opposition, causing Henry to wail that Charles had aligned himself with "all the other Harvard college 'mokes,' the professors of history, by talking out loud" against Cleveland's action. Businessmen joined the outcry against war with Britain when stock market prices plunged, while farmers expressed fears of losing their export markets in a war with England.

Britons also recoiled from war. Thousands signed petitions urging their government to arbitrate. Sentiment was so strong in both countries that the two nations agreed not only to arbitrate the Venezuela-Guiana border dispute, but also to negotiate a general arbitration treaty that would cover almost all future Anglo-American disputes. Ironically, in the euphoria of their reconciliation, the United States and Great Britain excluded Venezuela from any part in the arbitration of its own border. Venezuela protested and opposed the arbitration agreement. Relenting, the United States and Great Britain allowed Venezuela to choose one member of the panel, although they stipulated that the member could not be Venezuelan. Reluctantly accepting the modified arbitration agreement, Venezuela selected an American to serve as its representative.

The arbitration panel decided substantially in favor of the British position. It established the Venezuela border close to the Schomburgk Line, excluding only the mouth of the Orinoco and several thousand miles of trackless interior. The Venezuelans were outraged.[2] The United States and Britain, however, hailed the Venezuela arbitration with enthusiasm. Even though the Senate later rejected the general Anglo-American arbitration treaty, giving it three votes less than the two-thirds necessary for consent, the incident had clearly shocked the United States and Great Britain into a new recognition of their mutual interests.

The Anglo-American Rapprochement

In January 1896, while the Venezuela incident still endangered the peace between Great Britain and the United States, the German kaiser sent a note of congratulation to the president of the Boer Republic of South Africa on the failure of a raid into the Transvaal by a band of Englishmen led by Dr. Leander Jameson. This "Jameson telegram" dramatized for the British the growing challenge Germany presented to their preeminent position as a world empire and helped turn them away from the impending confrontation with the United States. Unified only two decades before the Jameson incident, Germany had rapidly become the greatest land power in Europe. The German army had beaten Austria and France in quick succession in 1866 and 1870. In the 1890s, Germany began planning a navy that would threaten Britain's traditional supremacy on the seas. As a latecomer to the ranks of great powers, Germany felt left out of the earlier scramble for colonies and therefore began abrasively asserting new claims in Africa, the Pacific, and even to some extent in the Western Hemisphere.

Russia, a giant nation of immense population and potential, also was awakening to challenge British interests in eastern Europe, Turkey, and the Mediterranean. The Russians were active in Afghanistan, which bordered British India, and they looked covetously toward China, where Britain had long been supreme. In addition, Japan demanded entrance into the exclusive club of world powers. With its policy of industrialization after the Meiji Restoration, Japan had leaped miraculously into the modern age, dramatizing its arrival as a great power by defeating China handily in the Sino-Japanese War of 1894–1895. Afterward, it too demanded a share in the exploitation of continental Asia. Russia, Germany, and France intervened, forcing Japan to give up a portion of its conquests, especially the Liaotung Peninsula of China. Then they began their own scramble for new concessions from the rotting hulk of the Chinese empire. These European powers and Japan thus threatened the British position in Asia at about the same time Cleveland hurled America's challenge on Venezuela and the Western Hemisphere.

Watching the rise of these new powers and the dangers they posed to the stability of the Pax Britannica, the British leaders decided it was foolish to provoke the United States. Of all the rising powers, the United States posed the least danger to Britain's vital interests. The United States no longer agitated for the annexation of Canada, and the expansion of its power and interest in the rest of the Western Hemisphere did not pose an intolerable threat to Britain's growing trade and investment in Latin America. In any case, Latin America was far less important to the British than Europe, East Asia, or the eastern Mediterranean, with its Suez link to India. As Britain's policy of "splendid isolation" began to look less and less splendid, British leaders contemplated the benefits of having the United States as a friend, if not an outright ally.

Other recent events had helped pave the way for this sudden turn toward Anglo-American friendship. The British had reformed their electoral system, broadened the franchise, and brought their politics more into line with the democracy of the United States. At the same time, the new immigration into the United States had emphasized to the old-stock elites of America the kinship they felt with the culture of their British cousins, as opposed to the teeming masses of Catholic Italians, Irish, and southern Europeans who threatened to displace the old-stock Protestants in the cities. The racial attitudes of the day drew attention to the shared Anglo-Saxon heritage of the two nations, and the American elites began to find attractive even the British aristocratic attitudes they had formerly so resented. They hailed the many trans-Atlantic marriages between American daughters and such British luminaries as Joseph Chamberlain, Lord Randolph Churchill, and the Duke of Marlborough. Practical economics reinforced sentimental ties. Great Britain took more than half of America's exports and supplied more imports and capital than any other nation. The United States provided nearly a quarter of Britain's imports and bought more than 10 percent of its exports.

Consequently, Great Britain began to withdraw from its dominant position in the Western Hemisphere and entrust the remainder of British interests in the area to American hegemony. The submission of the Venezuelan border dispute to arbitration was only the first step in a retreat that continued through the next decade. As the British turned the Western Hemisphere over to the United States, they also sought to draw American power into East Asia. They saw in the United States a potential ally in the struggle to keep Russia, Japan, and Germany from carving China into exclusive spheres of interest that would be closed to the trade and investment of other foreigners. Britain then dominated the China trade and left its own sphere of China relatively open to foreign trade because it was strong enough to tolerate competition. The United States was not anxious to acquire a sphere of its own, and the establishment of closed foreign spheres would hurt American trade. Noting the harmony of interests between the two nations, the British approached the United States in 1898 on a joint policy to hold the Chinese markets open. Cleveland's successor, William McKinley, refused Britain's offer.

McKinley's rejection of a limited British alliance did not stop the American movement toward cooperation with Great Britain as the United States moved toward world power. The British continued their transformation from chief rivals to best friends. Those nations that had helped America challenge British supremacy on the high seas in earlier days, such as Russia and Germany, went from friends to enemies. The United States thus played a key role in the world diplomatic revolution of the 1890s.

The Spanish-American War

The Cuban rebellion against Spain in 1895 furnished the major catalyst for America's own diplomatic revolution. The endemic chaos on the island, which had endured nine separate rebellions since 1823, worried American leaders throughout most of the nineteenth century. Americans had long coveted Cuba, and the abolition of slavery in both countries following the American Civil War eliminated the major roadblock to intervention. America's desire for Caribbean naval bases to protect an isthmian canal added to Cuba's attractiveness.

When rebellion broke out in Cuba in the 1870s, President Ulysses S. Grant came to the brink of intervention. Congressional opposition to the annexation of a tropical province of a different race and culture thwarted Grant for the moment, but even Grant's opponents had no wish to see a major power replace the moribund Spanish rule. Americans of both parties feared that increasing chaos in Cuba would provide an incentive for Spain to request military aid from other European powers, and the intrusion of a new European nation in Cuba would be a direct challenge to the Monroe Doctrine. The United States publicly warned Germany against acquisition of Cuba in the 1880s after rumors circulated that Germany was seeking a pretext for intervention.

By the time a new revolution erupted in Cuba in 1895, American sentiment was far more ready for intervention than it had been in Grant's era. The Venezuela incident of that same year had been too ambiguous to upset the close balance between restraint and assertiveness in American foreign policy. The Cuban revolution, on the other hand, was dramatic and popular enough to swing the balance toward an aggressive, interventionist diplomacy and to help America sustain that posture for at least two decades.

Cuba certainly had enough reason to revolt against Spain. The Spanish army and civil service in Cuba were inefficient, corrupt, and arrogant. Spaniards occupied almost all positions of power and wealth. They confined most of the 800,000 white Cubans to menial labor and left the 600,000 recently emancipated blacks in conditions little better than their previous slavery. Spain monopolized Cuba's trade, and the United States compounded the problems this created by placing high duties on Cuban sugar in the Wilson-Gorman Tariff of 1894.

Americans sympathized thoroughly with the Cubans. They had regarded Spain with dislike and contempt since the early days of America's westward movement. One railroad magnate wrote to his senator that "Spain is and always has been an impudent, arrogant, and barbarous nation. . . . It is quite time she was booted out of Cuba . . . and nine out of every ten of our citizens without regard to party will agree with me." Newspapers of the time, which were just then becoming instruments of mass circulation, played on these anti-Spanish sentiments. In their battle for circulation in New York, the Pulitzer and Hearst papers tried to outdo each other with titillating horror stories about the war in Cuba. The most sensational episode in this battle of the "yellow press" was the rescue of the daughter of a former Cuban official from her Spanish cell by a Hearst reporter, who naturally made the most of his scoop. Local newspapers were perhaps even more important than the big-city yellow press in stirring American emotions. Desperate for copy, they often printed verbatim the handouts from the Cuban junta's headquarters in New York.

While the general public was enthusiastically for the rebels, the Cleveland and McKinley administrations were more interested in seeing the war come to an end regardless of the victor. They feared Spain might call in another major power to help put down the rebellion. The war was also hurting American trade and investments in the island. American exports to Cuba dropped from $20 million in 1894 to half of that in 1898. The fighting endangered some $50 million worth of American investments in Cuba. Most of these were in sugar plantations sold by frightened Spaniards during the previous revolution of the 1870s. The rebellion's impact on American business could not help but concern America's political leaders, even though most businessmen opposed military intervention in Cuba because they feared that war with Spain would threaten their far more valuable trade with Europe.

Cleveland had responded at first to the 1895 rebellion by invoking America's neutrality laws. These laws forbade organizing or recruiting men in the United States. They did not specifically bar the sale of arms, but Cleveland sought to discourage this traffic as well. Nominally this neutrality policy helped Spain more than the rebels, since only the rebels needed men and arms from the United States. Actually, neither American nor Spanish patrols could halt the aid that flowed to the revolutionaries from Cuban exiles and other sympathetic Americans, a situation that brought howls of protest from Spain.

Congress urged Cleveland to do more for the rebels. Congressional Democrats and Republicans alike saw in the Cuban issue a popular cause around which they could unite their parties. By outdoing each other in professions of sympathy for the oppressed Cubans, they hoped to paper over the deep divisions within their parties brought about by the free silver issue. Over Cleveland's protests, Congress passed a resolution urging recognition of the Cubans' status as belligerents. Refusing to offer that recognition, Cleveland asserted that he would not use the American army in Cuba even if Congress authorized him to do so. But the situation in Cuba was deteriorating. The revolution was rapidly evolving from an issue the American political parties could use for their own purposes to one they could not escape even if they wished.

The revolution simply demolished Cuba. The rebels saw their best chance for victory in the ruin of the Cuban economy and with it the island's value to Spain. They burned crops and sugar refineries, tore up railroads, and destroyed many American-owned plantations. They knew that if the United States intervened in Cuba to protect American property, it would never intervene on the side of Spain. Meanwhile, in early 1896, the Spanish appointed General Valeriano Weyler, nicknamed "Butcher" Weyler by the Hearst press, as the new commander in Cuba. Toward the end of the year, Weyler initiated the *reconcentrado* policy. People living in the countryside were concentrated in camps where they could be defended against the rebels and also prevented from supplying or supporting them. The army assumed that all people outside these camps were rebels and would shoot them on sight.

The Spanish army had no way to supply adequate food and sanitation for these camps. By 1898, newspapers estimated that nearly 400,000 Cubans, one-quarter of the island's entire population, had died during the revolution. Later studies have shown this number to be an exaggeration. The true figure was probably somewhere between 100,000 and 200,000, but that was bad enough, and the Spaniards themselves actually believed that the number of deaths had been close to 400,000.

As reports of destruction and atrocity multiplied, even Cleveland came to believe that American intervention might be necessary. In a lame-duck message to Congress, he proposed that Spain grant Cuba greater autonomy and warned that if the war dragged on it would be the duty of the United States to halt it. His successor, William McKinley, had similar opinions. He too wished for an early end to the revolution to avoid the need for American intervention. But McKinley seems to have been somewhat more pro-rebel than Cleveland. Cleveland might have forced the rebels to accept a Spanish offer of limited autonomy; McKinley would not require the rebels to accept a settlement they thought unfavorable. Since the rebels wanted nothing less than independence and Spain was adamantly against that, the prospects for securing an early end to the war were minimal.

Despite the obstacles, McKinley hoped that through diplomatic pressure he might bring both sides to settle. He instructed America's minister to Spain, Stewart L. Woodford, to inform Spain that the United States expected notice of an "early and certain peace" by November 1, 1897. Otherwise the United States would do whatever was necessary to procure that peace. McKinley reasoned that the Spanish were at the peak of their strength in Cuba during the 1897–1898 campaign season. If they were unable to settle the war by the time the tropical rains forced a halt to the fighting, the prospect was for an interminable and bloody stalemate. Perhaps an American ultimatum would force Spain to offer concessions that, along with military pressure, could bring the rebels to a settlement. Meanwhile, McKinley induced Congress to appropriate $50,000 for aid to the suffering Cubans and got Spain to admit these supplies duty-free. He personally contributed $5,000 to the Cuban relief fund.

Coincidentally, just as McKinley began to apply pressure, a new liberal Spanish government succeeded that of the assassinated conservative prime minister, Antonio Cánovas. The liberals recalled General Weyler, alleviated the reconcentration policy, released American citizens imprisoned for rebel activity, and offered considerable autonomy to Cuba within the Spanish empire. Although these concessions were made as a result of Spain's domestic politics rather than American diplomacy, McKinley could portray them as a partial response to his initiative. He used his supposed success to keep Congress from demanding immediate intervention and hoped he still could force both sides into agreement.

The slim chance that Spain and Cuba could work out an agreement was shattered, however, when riots broke out among Spanish loyalists in Cuba against the recall of Weyler and the offer of Cuban autonomy. Many army personnel who were supposed to suppress the riots joined them instead. Opposition rose in Spain as well as in Cuba. Queen Christina and her government feared they might be overthrown if they surrendered Cuba voluntarily. McKinley and other Americans wondered whether the Spanish government could come to an agreement with the Cuban rebels even if Spain negotiated in good faith. When the Americans read an intercepted letter written by the Spanish minister to the United States, Enrique Dupuy de Lôme, they had to wonder whether the government was negotiating in good faith in any case. De Lôme characterized McKinley as "weak and a bidder for the admiration of the crowd, besides being a would-be politician who tries to leave a door open behind himself while keeping on good terms with the jingoes of his party." Then de Lôme suggested negotiating with the Americans "even if only for effect."

Shortly after the de Lôme letter, the American battleship *Maine* exploded in Havana harbor in February 1898. McKinley unwisely and hastily had sent the *Maine* to Havana during the Weyler riots to show America's desire for order in Cuba. When it sank, killing 266 of the 350 crew members aboard, it made American intervention in the Cuban revolution almost inevitable.

While a naval board investigated the cause of the *Maine* explosion, McKinley tried one last time for a diplomatic solution. At his request, Congress appropriated $50 million for a defense fund that McKinley could use at his own discretion. Woodford said the appropriation stunned the Spanish government, and McKinley seemed to have considerable leverage to force a settlement. He lost much of his room to maneuver, however, when Redfield Proctor, a highly respected senator from Vermont, made an extraordinary speech on his return from an inspection of Cuba. In a calm, dispassionate voice, he recounted the horrendous scenes he had witnessed and confirmed the rumors that 200,000 Cubans had died in the reconcentration camps. His speech convinced many that the Spanish had simply lost control of Cuba; Spain could never win the struggle, but only draw out the bloody stalemate.

The report of the American naval board on the sinking of the *Maine* reinforced the assumption that Spain had lost control; the board concluded that an external rather than an internal explosion had destroyed the ship. A floating mine was a more likely culprit than a boiler room accident. Although some of the more lurid newspapers and excitable politicians of the time implied that the Spanish had sunk the *Maine*, neither the naval board nor most American leaders accused the Spanish of deliberate sabotage. Yet Spain was responsible for the safety of ships in its harbors, and the *Maine* incident convinced almost all Americans of Spain's impotence to control the colony over which it claimed sovereignty.

McKinley was under terrible pressure to do something dramatic. Failure would open the door for the Democrats to proclaim themselves the true advocates of Cuba and portray the Republicans as cowardly betrayers of freedom. The powerful Republican senator Henry Cabot Lodge warned McKinley: "If the war in Cuba drags on through the summer with nothing done we shall go down in the greatest defeat ever known. . . . I know that it is easily & properly said that to bring on or even to threaten war for political reasons is a crime & I quite agree. But to sacrifice a great party & bring free silver upon the country for a wrong policy is hardly less odious."

McKinley had known for a week the results of the naval board's investigation. He could imagine the public reaction, so he tried to force a quick settlement of the Cuban revolution. Bypassing his senile secretary of state, John Sherman, McKinley communicated with Spain through his close friend, Acting Secretary of State William Day. On March 26, 1898, McKinley composed and Day signed a telegram to the American minister, Woodford, informing the Spanish that it was essential peace be made within a month. Spain should revoke the reconcentration order and offer the Cubans "full self-government, with reasonable indemnity." Woodford asked if this actually meant Cuban independence. Day responded that it did.

But after Woodford reported that Spain had made some tentative inquiries about an armistice in Cuba, McKinley and Day sent another telegram that clouded their earlier ultimatum. McKinley and Day told Woodford to get Spain to offer the rebels an armistice under American good offices until October 1, along with revocation of the reconcentration order, and to add "if possible: Third. If terms of the peace not satisfactorily settled by October 1, President of the United States to be final arbiter between Spain and insurgents."

A careful reading of this final telegram indicates that McKinley was still demanding Cuban independence. The rebels would never agree to a settlement before October 1 because they understood that McKinley, arbitrating after that date, would grant Cuba independence. Still the telegram said that the third demand was to be added only "if possible." A confused Woodward asked what the demand for full self-government and an indemnity actually meant. William Day responded with a telegram that should have ended all doubt. He said it meant "independence." That issue is important because Spain ultimately conceded the unequivocal first two demands of McKinley's final telegram. Spain revoked the reconcentration order and offered a cease-fire to the rebels. However, Spain offered the armistice only after refusing until the last minute, then claiming to make the offer because the pope had requested it, and finally asserting that the length and extent of the armistice would be up to the Spanish commander in Cuba. Spain said nothing of American arbitration or Cuban independence.

Woodford reported these concessions as the prelude to further Spanish surrenders and, despite Day's information that McKinley was demanding Cuban independence, urged the president to delay the use of force. McKinley, however, regarded the concessions as too little, too late, and given with insufficient grace to indicate that Spain was willing to go still further and grant Cuba independence. He sent a long-contemplated message to Congress requesting authority to intervene with force if necessary to end the war in Cuba. He noted the last-minute Spanish concessions only as an afterthought.

There was no doubt Congress would grant McKinley the authority he wanted. The vast majority in Congress and the country were in favor of war, and many were criticizing the president for his procrastination. Even the business community, long opposed to armed intervention in Cuba, had come to feel that anything was preferable to the current lingering uncertainty. Thus, McKinley led a united and enthusiastic nation to war. After the war, however, when McKinley's telegrams and Woodford's advice that Spain would submit without war became public, they triggered a debate over the intervention that still continues among historians. Most concluded that the war indeed had been unnecessary, that a weak and vacillating president had bowed to partisan advantage and the war frenzy whipped up by an unscrupulous press. Like Theodore Roosevelt, historians portrayed McKinley as a man with no more backbone than a chocolate éclair. Echoing Representative "Uncle Joe" Cannon, they said the president kept his ear so close to the ground that it had grasshoppers in it.

Some historians made more sinister accusations. They argued that imperialists like Assistant Secretary of the Navy Theodore Roosevelt and Senator Henry Cabot Lodge had manipulated McKinley into an unnecessary war to give the United States a chance to acquire a colonial empire. Supposedly, Roosevelt and Lodge had arranged the appointment of Commodore George Dewey to the command of the Pacific squadron. Then, in the temporary absence of the secretary of the navy, Roosevelt had ordered Dewey to attack the Spanish fleet in Manila harbor. Dewey's victory would allow the United States to acquire the Philippines and gain access to the China markets.

The charge that Roosevelt and Lodge had maneuvered McKinley into an unnecessary war in order to acquire the Philippines is quickly enough dismissed. An attack on the Spanish fleet in Manila had long been part of the plan for war with Spain. That fleet was one of the two major Spanish naval forces, and its existence would threaten America's Pacific coast as well as any expedition to Cuba. Manila's harbor defenses had been investigated by an American naval officer in civilian clothes as early as 1876, and an attack on the fleet was made part of the formal plan for a war with Spain in 1896. Roosevelt's telegram to Dewey was approved by McKinley himself.

President William McKinley, whose diplomacy leading up to the Spanish-American War still stirs controversy among historians. *(Courtesy of the National Archives)*

The attack on the fleet, however, was not part of a concerted plan to conquer the Philippines. No troops were sent with Dewey to occupy Manila in the event he defeated the Spanish fleet. McKinley made preparations to send troops only after he received news of Dewey's victory and amid fears that Spain was sending another fleet to the Philippines. McKinley and the American navy did decide quickly that they wanted to keep Manila's great harbor as a window to the China market, but this was a consequence of Dewey's victory, not a motive for the attack in the first place.

It is also extremely doubtful that Spain was ready to relinquish its hold on Cuba, despite Woodford's opinion that it would do so. The Spanish government faced riots over declaration of the armistice, let alone Cuban independence. Queen Christina feared she would be overthrown if she freed Cuba without a fight. While the Spanish government offered an armistice, it also looked about Europe in the hope of getting other powers to intervene against Cuba and the United States. Thus there is little chance that Spain's compliance with American demands for revocation of the reconcentration order and an armistice presaged a grant of independence. It was more likely a delaying tactic. So long as America insisted on Cuban independence, war was probably inevitable.

Nevertheless, many historians continue to criticize McKinley for failing to pursue the slim chance for peace by making his demand for Cuban independence clearer and then delaying a while to see if Spain would extend its concessions. McKinley's defenders (and their number has increased substantially in the past few decades) argue that the Spanish understood perfectly well that Cuban independence was necessary to prevent American intervention and that McKinley could not risk a categorical demand because the proud Spanish would have been sure to reject it. They see McKinley's diplomacy as the product not of weakness and vacillation, but of strength, subtlety, and realism. The evidence does seem to support their claim that McKinley was in full control of his policy and was not the spineless creature portrayed in earlier accounts, but it is still difficult to see why he avoided a clear statement of his purposes to Spain. Since war resulted anyway, it could not have made matters worse.

Even after war was imminent and McKinley had announced the goal of Cuban independence to the American people, he studiously ignored the wishes of the Cuban rebel forces and avoided recognizing them as the successor government of the island. The Cuban rebels were strongly against an armistice because they were afraid their army would disintegrate if there were a substantial pause in the fighting, so McKinley probably would not have been able to fulfill his side of the bargain he had proposed to Spain anyway. Moreover, the rebel leaders did not welcome U.S. military intervention because they rightly feared that American forces would not leave the governing of Cuba to them. During the *Maine* crisis, the rebels had told McKinley: "We do not ask you to go to war; we only ask you for your neutrality, for the recognition of Cuban belligerent rights." McKinley rejected this plea. He did not think the rebels could win the war quickly without American assistance, he had no doubt Spain would decree war immediately if he recognized Cuban independence or belligerence directly, and he did not think the Cuban government was yet "capable of performing the duties and discharging the functions of a separate nation." While he implied that he might recognize Cuba later, he decided to try to stop the war as a neutral, and he asked Congress to authorize him to use force to do so.

The House of Representatives gave him the authorization he requested. But the Senate insisted on pushing him further than he wanted to go. It passed resolutions directing rather than authorizing McKinley to use force in Cuba, recognized Cuban independence and the rebels as the legitimate government (the Turpie-Foraker Amendment), and disavowed any intention of annexing Cuba (the Teller Amendment).

McKinley threatened to use his veto if the House accepted the Senate version. He insisted at least that recognition of the rebel government be dropped. A joint House-Senate resolution did so amid charges that McKinley and his followers opposed recognition because they feared this would invalidate Spain's Cuban bonds, some of which allegedly had been purchased by Americans. When McKinley signed the resolution on April 20, Spain broke diplomatic relations. Two days later, McKinley imposed a naval blockade on Cuba, and Spain declared war on the United States.

The Acquisition of an Overseas Empire

John Hay, who became McKinley's last secretary of state, called the Spanish-American conflict "a splendid little war." The United States, which had clear military superiority over Spain, won a quick, decisive victory. Nevertheless, the war could have been far bloodier and more prolonged had it not been for considerable luck and Spanish incompetence. Dewey's fleet steamed into Manila harbor past the fortress island of Corregidor without suffering a single effective shot. The Spanish fleet fatalistically anchored in shallow water so its crews could get to shore when the ships were sunk. These shallows were located out of reach of the shore guns in Manila that could have helped fight the Americans. Dewey won the battle with the loss of only a single man, and he to a heart attack.

The Americans were equally lucky in their invasion of Cuba. The ill-planned amphibious operation began only after a long wait in tropical Florida camps by soldiers clothed in winter woolens. The scramble to the ships was chaotic. Artillery and cavalry went aboard one ship, ammunition and horses aboard another. Fortunately, the invasion force landed unopposed on Cuban beaches because the Spanish foolishly abandoned their coastal defenses for inland positions. The American army cooperated tenuously with the Cuban rebels and together they moved toward Santiago, where the Spanish fleet had taken refuge. The famous charge up San Juan Hill put the Americans and their Cuban allies in a commanding position above Santiago, so the Spanish fleet made a forlorn dash from the harbor. The American blockading vessels pursued and sank them one by one. Americans won the war while losing only 379 men in combat.[3]

While American troops were occupying Manila and Cuba, McKinley and his administration moved to expand and consolidate their hold on other territories in the Pacific and the Caribbean. McKinley finally secured the formal annexation of Hawaii, partly by claiming that the islands were vital for getting troops and supplies to Dewey in the Philippines. Even so, to overcome Democratic opposition, McKinley had to resort to a joint resolution of Congress rather than the formal treaty procedure. American forces also took Spain's lesser colony of Puerto Rico without a fight, and no Teller Amendment required the United States to forgo annexation of this Caribbean island.

It was an obvious conclusion by the end of hostilities with Spain that the United States would have an overseas empire. The only question was how big that empire would be. Should the United States keep the Philippines as well as Puerto Rico and Hawaii?

McKinley seems to have decided shortly after Dewey's victory to keep at least Manila. It was a fine port and naval base that provided access to China and the rest of Asia. McKinley also ordered seizure of the uninhabited Wake Islands and the Spanish island of Guam as stepping-stones from Hawaii to Manila. He found it difficult, however, to decide what to do about the rest of the Philippines. It seemed intolerable to leave them in the hands of Spain after seeing Spanish misrule of Cuba. He did not want to see Great Britain, Germany, or Japan acquire them and use them to gain supremacy in the China trade.

He might have left them to the Philippine rebels, whose leader, Emilio Aguinaldo, had returned to the islands aboard an American ship. But McKinley did not think the rebels capable of governing the Philippines any more than he thought the Cuban rebels prepared

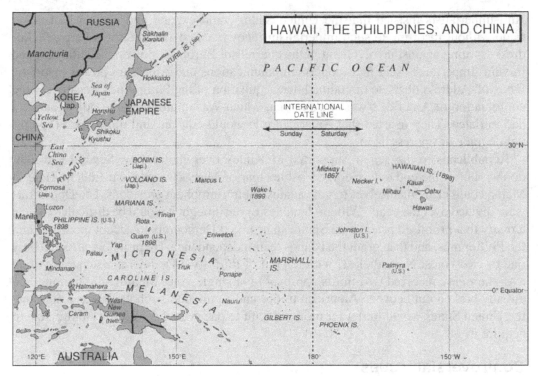

U.S. Expansion into the Pacific, 1867–1899

to govern their island. He believed the Philippines would fall into anarchy and then into the hands of one of the other great powers. While America might throw a protectorate over the islands to prevent this fate, the difficulties and frictions of dealing with an indigenous government in such a situation had already been made clear in Samoa. Besides, McKinley's military advisers told him that Manila was indefensible without control of the entire island of Luzon.

McKinley's inclination to keep the entire archipelago was confirmed by a campaign swing through Middle America, where mention of taking the islands drew cheers from the crowds. He returned to Washington to instruct the American peace commission negotiating with the Spaniards in Paris to insist on keeping the Philippines. After the United States assuaged Spanish protests with an offer to pay $20 million, the peace treaty was signed.

The thrill of victory brought most Americans to accept the acquisition of Puerto Rico and Hawaii, but a substantial number of influential Americans thought the Philippines were too distant, too alien, and too hostile to be annexed. Grover Cleveland, Andrew Carnegie, and Mark Twain joined the campaign against annexation organized by the newly formed Anti-Imperialist League. They argued that America could never bring the Philippines into the Union as an equal state; the United States would have to rule the Philippines as a colony at the point of a bayonet. The precedent of bayonet rule would be as dangerous to American domestic liberty as it would be harmful to the Filipinos.

Anti-imperialists insisted that the United States could expand and protect its foreign trade without resorting to such imperialism. They recalled Washington's Farewell Address warning against involvement in the quarrels of European powers. But they argued in vain. Imperialists said that modern communications and American power made the Farewell Address obsolete or claimed that acquisition of the Philippines was merely the continuation of America's westward march, which Washington and the other founders had initiated. They insisted that American rule would educate and uplift the Filipinos, not degrade or oppress them.

Republicans in the Senate supported McKinley overwhelmingly. Several had their doubts, but in the end only George Frisbie Hoar of Massachusetts and Eugene Hale of Maine could bring themselves to vote against their triumphant president. The Democrats were divided over the treaty. William Jennings Bryan thought it would be difficult to defeat a treaty that promised peace with Spain, so he urged Democrats to accept the treaty and the Philippines, and then grant the islands their independence. He probably affected only one or two votes. Nevertheless, with ten out of thirty-two Democratic senators voting aye, the treaty received two-thirds approval by a single vote. Meanwhile, fighting had already broken out between American troops and Aguinaldo's rebels. It was a sign that the United States would find it far more difficult to pacify and govern its empire than to acquire it.

Controversial Issues

The United States entered the Spanish-American War with little popular dissent. Contemporaries quarreled over the later decision to take the Philippines far more than they did over the decision to expel the Spanish from Cuba.[4] However, when the diplomatic correspondence leading to the war was published in 1901, revealing Woodford's opinion that Spain would have been willing to make more concessions without war, it did generate some criticism.

Most early historical criticism of the war came from conservatives. They feared that overseas colonialism endangered American liberty at home and entangled the United States needlessly abroad, but they did not worry much about the negative impact of American rule on Cubans or Filipinos. They disliked the Cuban rebels as terrorists and thought the Filipinos would be better off under American rule. These authors did not argue that the war was the product of an imperialist plot led by Theodore Roosevelt and Henry Cabot Lodge. Instead, they saw it as the result of the yellow press, ignorant popular enthusiasm, and McKinley's weakness.[5] Even Admiral French Ensor Chadwick, a member of the naval commission that investigated the sinking of the *Maine* and the author of an encyclopedic defense of the war, moderated his stance in light of this critique.[6] But until the post–World War I era, most historians continued to justify America's forcible intervention in Cuba.[7]

Disillusion after World War I brought with it a reaction against the imperial and interventionist policies initiated in the 1890s. Defenders of the Spanish-American War were few. The conservative critique of the war continued in the works of such prominent historians as James Ford Rhodes and Samuel Flagg Bemis.[8] But now liberal and socialist historians joined in condemning the war. Walter Millis, a prominent journalist, wrote a best seller that popularized the view that Roosevelt, Lodge, and other imperialists maneuvered America into a needless war to get the Philippines. Millis was very critical of the annexation of the Philippines, but less so of America's intervention in Cuba.[9] Socialists Scott Nearing and Joseph Freeman were unsparing of the Cuban intervention as well. In a popular book titled *Dollar Diplomacy*, Nearing and Freeman blamed big business and economic interests along with imperial thinkers like Roosevelt, Lodge, and Mahan for America's imperialism.[10] A still influential book by Julius Pratt tried to absolve business and economic interests of the charge that they had sought war to gain an empire by showing that business had generally opposed the war. It was the imperial-minded intellectuals like Roosevelt, Lodge, and Mahan who were responsible for the needless war, Pratt implied. Business became converted to the cause of imperialism during the war, however, and played a major role in the decision to annex the Philippines and other territories in the imperial aftermath of the war, he said.[11]

World War II cast U.S. interventionism in a better historical light than had World War I. Many realist historians began to praise the Spanish-American War as initiating America's necessary involvement in world affairs. Nevertheless, historians remained somewhat ambivalent about the way the United States had entered the war and the imperialism that had resulted. Richard Hofstadter and William Leuchtenberg wrote as though the war had been a needless consequence of neurotic belligerence on the part of liberals as well as conservatives, while Foster Rhea Dulles perpetuated the idea that Roosevelt and Lodge had manipulated America into the war to get the Philippines.[12]

In the 1960s, two historians discovered in U.S. naval records that the Navy Department had devised plans as early as 1896 to attack the Spanish fleet at Manila if war broke out over Cuba. This undercut the idea that Roosevelt and Lodge had ordered the attack against the wishes of their superiors.[13] Meanwhile, a new biography of McKinley by H. Wayne Morgan led many historians to revise their estimate of McKinley's supposed weakness and gullibility by arguing that McKinley was purposeful and in complete command of his administration throughout the events leading to war and the acquisition of the Philippines.[14] Historian Ernest May was not fully convinced of McKinley's competence, but his *Imperial Democracy* (1961) argued that Spain had been fully aware of America's demand for Cuban independence and had purposely delayed while trying to get European help against the United States. May was not sure that Spain's actions justified war, but said that McKinley, while operating out of a cowardly fear for the fate of the Republican Party, still "conceived he had some justification for demanding a final end to the violence in Cuba."

Revisionists, of course, were far more critical of the war. Walter LaFeber's highly influential *The New Empire* (rev. ed., 1998) argued, contrary to Julius Pratt, that business had not only been favorable to the war, but that its influence had been the primary one in McKinley's final decision to intervene in Cuba as well as take the Philippines. In the wake of Vietnam, historian Philip Foner argued an even more radical thesis. Using Cuban documents, Foner claimed that the rebels had actually opposed American intervention and had wanted only arms and munitions. McKinley had intervened not to help them, but to expand the American empire. Thus, Foner said, McKinley had purposely omitted a demand for Cuban independence in his ultimatum, refused to recognize the rebel government, and meant from the outset to use the war to take the Philippines. He intended his delays merely to provide time for military preparations. When he was ready, he sent the *Maine* to Havana to create an incident that would justify war.[15]

Louis A. Perez carried Foner's revisionist argument further by asserting that the Cuban rebels were on the brink of victory and that McKinley intervened not to help the Cubans but to prevent them from achieving independence.[16] John L. Offner responded to the revisionist argument by conceding that McKinley disregarded the wishes of much of the Cuban rebel leadership. But Offner pointed out that the Cuban leadership was actually divided on the issue of U.S. intervention and he insisted that McKinley and other American leaders believed not that the Cubans were close to victory but that the war was a stalemate that would grind on with continued suffering and threats to American interests.[17]

Further Reading

A recent and vividly written popular account of the diplomacy and war, though not as broadly researched as the works of Offner and Perez, is Ivan Musicant, *Empire by Default: The Spanish-American War and the Dawn of the American Century* (1998). A good book on the military aspects of the war is Joseph Smith, *The Spanish American War: Conflict in the Caribbean and the Pacific, 1895–1902* (1994).

Four broad surveys of the whole spectrum of events covered in this chapter are Walter LaFeber, *The American Search for Opportunity* (1993); David Pletcher, *The Diplomacy of Trade and Investment: American Economic Expansion, 1865–1900* (1998); Charles S. Campbell, *The Transformation of American Foreign Relations, 1865–1900* (1976); and Robert L. Beisner, *From the Old Diplomacy to the New* (1975). In addition to these books, the Venezuelan crisis can be studied in Dexter Perkins, *The Monroe Doctrine, 1867–1907* (1937); Gerald Eggert, *Richard Olney* (1973); and Richard E. Welch Jr., *The Presidencies of Grover Cleveland* (1988). On the subsequent Anglo-American rapprochement, see Bradford Perkins, *The Great Rapprochement* (1968); Charles S. Campbell, *From Revolution to Rapprochement* (1974); and Robert G. Neale, *Great Britain and the United States, 1895–1903* (1960). On the rise of imperialism and the anti-imperialist countermovement, see Warren Zimmermann, *First Great Triumph: How Five Americans Made Their Country a World Power* (2002); David Healy, *U.S. Expansionism: The Imperialist Urge in the 1890s* (1970); William Appleman Williams, *The Roots of the Modern American Empire* (1969); Ernest May, *American Imperialism* (1968); Frank A. Ninkovich, *The United States and Imperialism* (2001); Robert L. Beisner, *Twelve Against Empire* (1968); and Richard Welch, *Response to Imperialism: The United States and the Philippine-American War, 1899–1902* (1979). A fascinating book on the role of gender in the imperialist movement is Kristin Hoganson, *Fighting for American Manhood: How Gender Politics Provoked the Spanish-American and Philippine American Wars* (1998). For an argument that the culture of cosmopolitan elites in America was not as racist or pessimistic about the progress of nonwhite peoples in the world, see Frank Ninkovich, *Global Dawn: The Cultural Foundation of American Internationalism, 1865–1890* (2011).

Notes

1. Robert W. Rydell and Rob Kroes, *Buffalo Bill in Bologna: The Americanization of the World, 1869–1922* (2005); Thomas W. Zeiler, *Ambassadors in Pinstripes: The Spalding World Baseball Tour and the Birth of the American Empire* (2006); Peter Levine, *A.G. Spalding and the Rise of Baseball: The Promise of American Sport* (1986).

2. They became even more disturbed in 1949 when they discovered that the American members of the arbitration panel had made the award unanimous only because otherwise the neutral member, chosen and agreed to by both the American and British delegations to ensure there would not be a stalemate, threatened to vote for the British position. The border issue is still open and sensitive between Venezuela and the now independent state of Guiana.

3. However, some 3,000 died from malaria and yellow fever. Spain lost between 5,000 and 6,000 men in combat and some 50,000 to disease. Cuban casualties are not known.

4. John Holladay Latané, *Diplomatic Relations of the United States and Spanish America* (1900); James Morton Callahan, *Cuba and International Relations* (1899).

5. Horace Edgar Flack, *Spanish-American Diplomatic Relations* (1906); Elbert Jay Benton, *International Law and the Diplomacy of the Spanish-American War* (1908). Both books emerged from a Johns Hopkins seminar given by W.W. Willoughby.

6. French Ensor Chadwick, *The Relations of the United States and Spain: Diplomacy* (1909).

7. See Albert Bushnell Hart, *The Monroe Doctrine* (1916); John Holladay Latané, *America as a World Power* (1907); and John Bassett Moore, *The Principles of American Diplomacy* (1918).

8. James Ford Rhodes, *The McKinley and Roosevelt Administrations* (1922); Samuel Flagg Bemis, *A Diplomatic History of the United States* (1936).

9. Walter Millis, *The Martial Spirit* (1931).

10. Scott Nearing and Joseph Freeman, *Dollar Diplomacy: A Study in American Imperialism* (1925).

11. Julius Pratt, *The Expansionists of 1898* (1936).

12. Richard Hofstadter, "Manifest Destiny and the Philippines," in *America in Crisis*, ed. Daniel Aaron (1952), and *Social Darwinism* (1944); William Leuchtenberg, "The Needless War with Spain," in *Times of Trial*, ed. Allan Nevins (1958), and "Progressivism and Imperialism: The Progressive Movement and American Foreign Policy, 1898–1916," *Mississippi Valley Historical Review* (1952); Foster Rhea Dulles, *America's Rise to World Power, 1898–1954* (1955).

13. J.A.S. Grenville and George Berkeley Young, *Politics, Strategy, and American Diplomacy* (1966).

14. H. Wayne Morgan, *William McKinley and His America* (1963). See also Morgan's *America's Road to Empire* (1965); Margaret Leech, *In the Days of McKinley* (1959); and Lewis L. Gould, *The Spanish-American War and President McKinley* (1982).

15. Philip S. Foner, *The Spanish-Cuban-American War and the Birth of American Imperialism, 1895–1902* (1972).

16. Louis A. Perez, *Cuba Between Empires, 1878–1902* (1983), and *The War of 1898: The United States and Cuba in History and Historiography* (1998). See also his *Cuba in the American Imagination: Metaphor and the Imperial Ethos* (2008).

17. John L. Offner, *An Unwanted War: The Diplomacy of the United States and Spain over Cuba, 1895–1898* (1992).

CHAPTER 2

THE SURGE INTO ASIA
EMPIRE IN THE PHILIPPINES AND
THE OPEN DOOR IN CHINA

The Suppression of the Philippine Revolution

Admiral Dewey's fleet sailed into the Philippines during a recess in a revolution that was already two years old, the first modern colonial revolution in Asia. In August 1896, the small, educated Filipino middle class led an open rebellion against the Spanish. The rebels were especially angry at the Catholic friars' economic control of much of the islands' arable land. Not only did the friars hold huge feudal estates, but they maintained political control of many Filipino barrios.

As the Spanish authorities and the rebels drew near to a pitched battle that would have been bloody and costly to both sides, they agreed to compromise. The rebels were not seeking outright independence; they merely wanted to reduce the power of the church, open the economy to greater participation by the middle class, and introduce more islanders into the higher echelons of government. When Spain offered a series of reforms and a payment of $800,000 for an end to the rebellion, rebel leader Emilio Aguinaldo accepted and went into exile.

Spain never did carry out its promised reforms, and the insurrection broke out again. Aguinaldo had banked Spain's first payment of $400,000 against future contingencies, and he drew on this money to supply arms and matériel to the rebels from his exile in Hong Kong. The Americans helped him because Dewey decided that Aguinaldo and his rebels could furnish the troops Dewey lacked to give ground support to his fleet. Dewey even had Aguinaldo brought to Manila on the fleet's flagship. Aguinaldo maintained ever after that Dewey and his representatives had promised him an independent Philippine nation. Dewey swore he had made no such commitment.

When American troops finally arrived in the Philippines months after Dewey's victory, conflict quickly flared between them and the Filipino rebels. Dewey and the American army commander, General Elwell Otis, refused to permit Aguinaldo's troops to join the attack on the city of Manila, which was still held by the Spanish garrison. The Americans arranged with the Spanish defenders to stage a short and harmless firefight for the salvation of Spanish honor, whereupon the surrender would be offered and accepted. The battle for Manila became a bit more realistic than intended when some Filipino troops joined the mock attack without authorization. Afterward, the Americans forced the Filipinos to camp outside the city, and resentment smoldered between the two occupying armies.

While American troops took Manila, Aguinaldo and his sympathizers gained control of much of the rest of the Philippines. Aguinaldo declared the Philippines independent, set up a government, and established a capital at Malolos. Nevertheless, William McKinley ignored the Filipinos. He ordered the American peace commission to demand Spanish cession of the islands to the United States. Then, before the Senate even ratified the treaty, he issued an executive order establishing American military government throughout the Philippines. This meant that the American army would have to wrest control of all but Manila from the Aguinaldo government and troops already in place. General Otis tried to disguise the full import of McKinley's order from the Filipinos by judiciously editing McKinley's proclamation before publishing it. This only made matters worse when the deception was exposed by a subordinate's inadvertent publication of the unexpurgated version.

Aguinaldo and his lieutenants were rightly suspicious, tensions heightened, and inevitably an American patrol clashed with the Philippine troops dug in around Manila. The clash came only forty hours before the Senate vote on the treaty and probably contributed to the Senate's narrow consent to it, since few senators wanted to be seen as refusing to back America's soldiers in a foreign land. The convenient timing of this incident outside Manila has led to suspicions on the part of several historians, American as well as Filipino, that McKinley provoked the incident. But there is no evidence of this, and the poor communication between McKinley and his military commanders makes it unlikely he could have contrived the incident even if he had so desired.

The war for the Philippines lasted more than three years and cost the Americans nearly 5,000 lives. The Filipinos suffered even more. The war cost them the lives of 20,000 soldiers and at least 200,000 civilians, probably many more if one counts those dead from starvation and diseases tied directly to the conflict. It was a savage war marked by atrocities and racial hatreds. American soldiers expressed their feelings in a song that was so offensive that the American commanders tried to ban it:

> Damn, Damn, Damn the Filipinos
> Cross-eyed kakiak ladrones,
> Underneath our starry flag,
> Civilize them with a Krag,
> And return us to our own beloved homes.

(A *ladrone* is a thief; a Krag was the army-issue rifle of the United States. *Kakiak* may have been a slurring reference to Native Americans [Inuit/Eskimos], with whom some soldiers believed Filipinos shared common racial characteristics.)

The Americans, expecting a quick triumph over people they regarded as inferiors, were exasperated by the protracted war. Exasperation turned to brutality when the Filipinos refused to surrender after a series of American victories and instead dispersed to fight as guerrilla bands. "Water cures" and other forms of torture became commonplace as ways to gain information from villagers or captives about guerrilla locations and identities. Guerrillas also fought savagely. After one especially brutal attack on unarmed American troops in a chow line, the American commander promised to make the entire surrounding area a "howling wilderness."

Ultimately the United States had to station 70,000 men on the islands to control them. The troops converted Philippine villages into garrisons in order to cut off supplies to the guerrillas, tactics reminiscent of Butcher Weyler's reconcentration policy that Americans had found so objectionable in Cuba. Finally, a daring raiding party captured Aguinaldo, the Filipino middle class lost heart, other Filipino commanders surrendered their forces, and the official war ground to a bitter, anticlimactic end in 1902. Hostilities in the Muslim southern islands continued until 1913, however.

The war generated much controversy in America. Prominent members of the Anti-Imperialist League publicized the case against American rule in the islands. The Democratic Party tried to make an issue of imperialism in the election of 1900, but other issues muddled the election and it never served as the referendum on imperialism that William Jennings Bryan proclaimed it would be. Imperialism was potentially divisive in both parties, so political leaders tended to downplay it. Only after the election did news of American as opposed to Filipino atrocities make headlines in a couple of sensational courts-martial. By that time the war was nearly over, and no great political movement against the occupation developed.

The relative success of America's colonial government also muted criticism in America and the Philippines. The governors and civil servants sent by the United States to the Philippines were imbued with the spirit of American progressivism, a political movement that emphasized clean government produced by an enlightened, rational electorate choosing educated, disinterested elites who would promote economic and social progress, thus displacing corrupt, self-interested political bosses who relied on bribes, empty promises, and ethnic sympathies to manipulate the ignorant masses. These Progressive American governors and civil servants not only promised but actually delivered better schools, cleaner cities, more roads and factories, and improved agriculture.

The American colonial government also promoted democratic self-government for the Filipinos, although under American guidance and protection. The Americans sought to educate the Filipino elites so they could replicate the Progressive view of self-government, including an educated, enlightened electorate choosing between competing political parties and resulting in honest, progressive, disinterested political leaders.

The Filipino elites largely accepted this American promise of democratic self-government, but only because they used their patronage and influence to ensure that they themselves were elected and thus were able to use the taxes they collected to maintain their own status as patrons of their agricultural tenants and constituents. Thus, the American occupation failed to truly transform the Spanish colonial heritage or compensate for the brutalities of the war. Nevertheless, the occupation reforms succeeded in quieting the islands and enabling American rule.

Despite the relative success of the American colonial government in the Philippines, the residual effect of the Philippine war and colonial aftermath left many Americans un-settled. Even Theodore Roosevelt came to believe that the acquisition of the Philippines was a mistake. He concluded that the islands were a strategic Achilles heel: they invited attack from other powers in Asia and could not be defended. Consequently, although the United States undertook several more military interventions in the next two decades, popular acceptance of such intervention was reluctant rather than buoyant.

The Open Door Notes

Acquisition of the Philippines naturally prompted greater American interest in Asia. The dream of a great China market, one of the primary reasons the McKinley administration decided to annex the Philippines, now beckoned even more invitingly. American Christian missionaries sponsored by U.S. churches also began concentrating their efforts on China. Before the 1890s most missionaries were stationed in the Mediterranean; only 200 were active in China. By 1900 there were over 1,000 American missionaries in China. By 1905, when the Chinese government began to offer more protection to foreigners, that figure rose to 3,000, more than 80 percent of all American missionaries abroad. The missionaries, of whom a slight majority was women, joined with American merchants and diplomats in China to form what one historian called an "Open Door constituency" that agitated for greater U.S. government involvement in Asia.

Consequently, the McKinley administration regarded the increasing pace of European imperialism in China with greater concern after the Spanish-American War. The accelera-tion of European imperialism had begun after the Japanese victory in the Sino-Japanese War of 1895. First the European powers had forced Japan to limit its spoils to the island of Formosa (Taiwan), the nearby Pescadores, and a sphere of influence in the strategic peninsula of Korea. After checking Japan, the European powers proceeded to carve their own concessions in China. Germany took financial control of the Shandong peninsula and a naval base in the port of Jiaozhou. The Russians leased a naval base at Port Arthur on the Liaoning peninsula, which they had forced Japan to disgorge. Russia also secured the right to control railroads through Chinese territory to connect its Trans-Siberian Railroad with Port Arthur and Vladivostok. France extorted a naval base at Kwangchowan.

Great Britain had been no happier with these imperial ventures than the United States. Britain already controlled most of China's trade and one-third of the foreign investments in that beleaguered country. Since Great Britain was becoming increasingly preoccupied with the rising strength of Germany in Europe and wished to concentrate more of its power there, it would have been happier with the earlier status quo in China. Britain did successfully request a new concession at Weihai on the Shandong peninsula, from which it could keep an eye on the Russians. Britain also made China promise not to alienate any part of the Yangtze Valley to other foreigners. But Britain expended its primary diplomatic effort in trying to get the other imperial powers to maintain the Open Door for the trade of all nations in their spheres of interest, and it warned against further dismemberment of sovereign Chinese territory.

The British knew the Americans were not in the market for their own sphere of inter-

China and the Imperialists, 1899

est in China and so had a similar interest in restricting the imperial scramble. Prior to the Spanish-American War, the British had approached McKinley about a joint declaration in favor of the Open Door and the territorial integrity of China, but McKinley had turned them down. Then the victory over Spain and the acquisition of the Philippines changed McKinley's attitude. The continuing European intrusions in China brought him to accept the suggestion of a limited initiative in pursuit of America's East Asian interests.

The suggestion for the initiative came from William Rockhill, acknowledged at the time as one of the few American experts on China. He had gained the ear of John Hay, McKinley's last secretary of state. Rockhill feared that the collapse of China would set off a scramble among the imperial powers that might not only close out American trade, but also bring world war. He knew that Hay and McKinley would balk at any American engagement to protect China's territorial integrity, but one of his acquaintances, an Englishman named Alfred Hippisley, recommended a more limited course that Hay and McKinley might find acceptable. Hippisley was an official of China's semiautonomous Imperial Maritime Customs Service, which was responsible for collecting the customs duties owed China. These tariffs constituted the major reliable source of income for the moribund Chinese government. If the European powers in China insisted on a monopoly of trade and investment in their new spheres of interest, they might prevent the Imperial Maritime Customs Service from operating there as well. Such a ban would destroy the financial underpinnings of China's government.

To forestall this possibility, Hippisley drafted a statement for Rockhill that Hay sent off almost unchanged in September 1899 as the first Open Door note. (The British government by this time had drifted away from its earlier advocacy of the Open Door and had no role in Hippisley's initiative.) In it, the United States requested each imperial power to keep its spheres of interest in China open to trade from foreign nations. This note did not challenge acquisition of those spheres of interest or demand equality of investment along with trading rights in them.

None of the great powers was terribly anxious to accept such an Open Door to trade, but Russia and Japan were not nearly as concerned with the commerce in their spheres as they were with investments in such strategic enterprises as railroads and mines. Rather than offend the Americans over what they perceived as a minor issue, they and the other powers gave tentative and carefully hedged endorsements of Hay's suggestion. Hay ignored the qualifications and announced that the Open Door was now international policy. None of the nations wanted to contradict him, and his statement passed for an accepted principle among the uninitiated. Many Americans praised Hay's coup as a brilliant stroke that demonstrated America's new prestige and influence in international affairs, along with its shrewdness and idealism in protecting China against predatory powers.

The following year, Hay burnished that image even further with his second Open Door note. Hay sent this one in the midst of a crisis in China known as the Boxer Rebellion. The Society of Righteous and Harmonious Fists, or Boxers, as westerners called them, was a secret organization dedicated to eradicating foreign influence from China. At first the society also opposed the dowager empress Cixi and her Manchu court. The empress diverted the Boxers' efforts exclusively toward the Europeans by quietly throwing her influence behind them and supplying them with arms. She believed the Europeans were trying to restore her son to the throne after she had imprisoned him and exiled or executed many of his advisers for excessive reformist zeal. With the secret encouragement of the empress, the Boxers murdered hundreds of Christian missionaries and their Chinese converts and laid siege to the foreign embassies and compounds in the capital of Beijing (Peking).

Hay and McKinley sent 2,500 American troops from the Philippine war to join the forces of the other European powers in an expedition that set off from the China coast to rescue the besieged foreigners in Beijing. The combined force plundered its way to the capital, with the American troops only somewhat less brutal than their allies. Almost every hut and village on the path of the expedition was destroyed. (Kaiser Wilhelm of Germany encouraged his troops to make themselves as fearsome to the Chinese as Attila the Hun had been to the ancient world. His army obeyed, and his unfortunate turn of phrase earned the Germans the unwanted nickname "Huns" that would plague them throughout World War I.)

McKinley and Hay quite naturally feared that some of the expedition's participants might be reluctant to remove their troops once their mission had been accomplished. To encourage their withdrawal, Hay sent a second Open Door note urging not just the Open Door for trade, but also respect for the territorial and administrative integrity of China. He uttered no threats, asked no commitments, and made none on the part of the United States. The note was simply a statement of American interests and wishes. Meanwhile, Hay worked cleverly to bolster Chinese provincial authorities who were suppressing the Boxers in the southern districts of China. He then pointed to the stability being restored there as good reason for the other powers to refrain from carving out further spheres. Once a satisfactory settlement to the Boxer Rebellion had been achieved, the United States withdrew its own troops.

Again Hay and McKinley won plaudits for what seemed a successful intervention on behalf of China. The relief of the besieged legations made a sensational story that entranced many Americans who had never given a thought to foreign policy. After Hay's death in 1905, his friends enshrined the Open Door policy alongside the Monroe Doctrine as a seemingly beneficent if vague foreign policy commandment demonstrating both America's strength and its idealism. Naive Americans portrayed the United States as the protector of China, and the Chinese as grateful protégés.

While America's decision makers did believe they were doing China a good turn in issuing the Open Door notes, their primary concern had been America's interests in the potential trade offered by China's markets. They also understood the limitations of that interest; only 2 percent of America's exports found their way to China at the time, whatever the potential for the future. Hay and McKinley intended no major commitment to China. America's army was bogged down in the Philippines, its fleet was concentrated in the Caribbean against an imagined German threat to Latin America, and despite the defeat of the anti-imperialist campaign in the United States, the Philippine war had taken its toll on public opinion toward foreign adventures. A single expedition to China in pursuit of the traditional goal of protecting American lives and property might be popular; a significant military commitment on behalf of the Open Door or in pursuit of America's own sphere of influence in China, on the other hand, would be very risky politically as well as strategically. Consequently, Hay and McKinley were willing to support the concept of the Open Door verbally, but they had no intention of risking war.

Recognizing that the call for the territorial integrity of China in the second Open Door note had no teeth and could well be brushed aside by the major powers in China, Hay prepared an alternative plan. He sent a discreet feeler to China about the possibility of America's acquiring a coaling station at Samsah Bay in Fukien Province. The request was just as tentative and toothless as the Open Door notes themselves. Hay withdrew the request without even waiting for a Chinese reply when the Japanese, who already had a paramount interest in Fukien, pointedly reminded Hay of his own principles. The imperial powers thus were fully aware of the limitations of American interest in and commitment to the Open Door. They were careful of American sensitivities only because the power balance was so delicate in East Asia that for the moment even mild American action might tip the situation in favor of one side or another.

China's leaders also understood the limits of the American commitment and the essentially self-interested character of the Open Door policy. Hay never consulted the Chinese themselves about American decisions affecting their affairs. However much the principles of the Open Door and American hopes for Chinese territorial integrity may have corresponded to China's own interests, it was difficult to maintain that the Chinese should have felt much gratitude. American merchants and diplomats dealing directly with China generally urged forceful policies against supposed Chinese duplicity. Even American missionaries, idealistic as their motives may have been, were subversive of China's own culture and contemptuous of Chinese authority; their presence was made possible only by the gunboat patrols and diplomatic threats that lay behind the unequal treaty system.

Also, at the very time the United States was proclaiming the Open Door and pressing for the rights of its merchants and missionaries residing in China, Congress was making full use of its treaty right to "suspend" Chinese immigration. Meanwhile, the Immigration Bureau harassed Chinese students, merchants, and travelers in the United States, subjecting them to humiliating oral and physical examinations to ensure they were not laborers who might try to maintain permanent residence in the United States and compete for local jobs. Congress also proceeded to prohibit Chinese immigration into Hawaii and the Philippines when the United States acquired those islands. The Chinese government was too weak to retaliate for the fact that America was demanding an Open Door in Asia while maintaining a closed one at home, but the Chinese people noticed and resented it.

Theodore Roosevelt, Japan, and the Limits of the Open Door

Theodore Roosevelt, who succeeded the assassinated McKinley in September 1901, was under no illusions about the extent and nature of America's commitment to the Open Door policy. Occasionally he would bluster, as he did after the Boxer Rebellion when Russia refused to withdraw its troops from Manchuria and then erected trade barriers against

American cotton exports to that area. At that time Roosevelt said he would not mind "going to extremes" with the Russians, but his actual instructions to Hay were far more restrained. Hay put the matter in perspective when he commented privately that both the Chinese and Russians knew the U.S. position was only moral. Hay suspected that neither country would pay much attention since moral force was "mere flapdoodle."

The British also decided that America's posturing in East Asia was mere flapdoodle. Turning to Japan instead for help in restraining Russia in China, they negotiated the Anglo-Japanese Alliance of 1902. The Japanese were aching to confront the Russians. They resented Russia's role in ousting them from the Liaoning Peninsula and Port Arthur. They regarded Russia as a grave threat to their strategic interests in Korea and to their economic interests in the resources and railroads of Manchuria. Japan feared only that France might come to the aid of its Russian ally. The Anglo-Japanese Alliance protected against that contingency by pledging Great Britain to aid Japan if Japan found itself at war with more than one power. Thus fortified, Japan launched a surprise attack on Russia's Asiatic fleet and sank it while it lay at anchor at Port Arthur. The Russians immediately sent their European fleet into Asian waters, and the Japanese sank it too. Meanwhile, Japanese land forces conquered Port Arthur and Mukden after long, bloody sieges. The world looked on in astonishment as supposedly backward, inferior Asians beat a major European power.

Theodore Roosevelt was gleeful as well as astonished. Japan was doing "our work" in China, he said, and it was "bully" the way the Japanese had started the war with a surprise attack. Yet the extent of the Japanese victory gave him some pause. He did not believe it likely that the United States and Japan would ever go to war, but an increasingly powerful Japan could pose a threat to the nearly indefensible Philippines and Hawaii, perhaps even to the Pacific coast of the United States. Japan might issue its own challenge to the Open Door in China as well. Roosevelt thought America's interest in China was relatively negligible and actually hoped Japan could be induced to spend its energies on the Asian continent rather than in the Pacific, where the United States was more involved. Still, he thought it desirable that Russia remain at least strong enough to keep some semblance of a balance of power in northern Asia.

With these interests in mind and perhaps even more motivated by his unquenchable thirst for adventure and personal glory (Roosevelt's daughter said he wanted to be the bride at every wedding and the corpse at every funeral), Roosevelt agreed to mediate the Russo-Japanese War. He immediately found himself in difficulties. Russia was willing to make concessions in Korea and Manchuria in exchange for peace, but Japan wanted more. Unknown to most, Japan was nearly bankrupt and desperately needed money. It demanded a large financial indemnity and the cession of Sakhalin Island. Russia was ready to break off negotiations rather than submit to these additional demands; only Roosevelt's pressure kept the bargaining from breaking down. Russia finally conceded the southern portion of Sakhalin, and Japan gave up its demand for the indemnity. Peace was made. Roosevelt won the Nobel Prize for his success, but he paid a price. The Japanese government was hard-pressed to explain to the Japanese people, who had been told that their enormous sacrifices had won a great victory, why there was no indemnity to relieve their financial suffering. Naturally, the government blamed the financial hard times on Roosevelt.

Nonetheless, the Japanese and the Roosevelt administration were able to compromise their respective positions in Asia. Roosevelt's special envoy to Japan, William Howard Taft, agreed to a memorandum with Japanese prime minister Taro Katsura in 1905 that Japan would not challenge the U.S. position in the Philippines, while the United States would recognize Japanese predominance in Korea. This Taft-Katsura Memorandum said nothing about Manchuria, but it was no coincidence that a few months later Japan opened Manchuria to American trade.

In 1906 this accommodation faltered when San Francisco demonstrated its resentment of Japanese and Chinese laborers by segregating Japanese along with Chinese students in the school system. The Japanese were mortally offended. Unlike earlier Chinese governments, which had been apathetic about discriminatory practices in America, Japan encouraged its people to emigrate abroad. The Japanese islands were overcrowded, and the government saw emigration to the Pacific islands, the United States, and South America as a chance not only to relieve this population pressure, but also to create markets for Japanese goods. Prior to Japan's victory over China in 1895, Japanese leaders had preferred this expansion by Pacific emigration to military and political expansion on the Asian continent. The Sino-Japanese and Russo-Japanese Wars had shifted Japan's emphasis toward Asia, but Pacific emigration remained a significant goal of Japan's foreign policy.

The United States had already spiked some of these ambitions by closing the Philippines and Hawaii to Japanese immigrants and forbidding contract labor. Then riots and the segregation controversy in San Francisco led to a movement in Congress to extend the 1904 law prohibiting Chinese immigration to include Japan. Japan protested vehemently. Some American politicians and writers panicked and warned that Japan, with its fierce military traditions and sense of honor, might declare war.

Roosevelt recognized that despite the depth of Japan's anger, the chance of war was remote, but he still thought it important to resolve the immigration and discrimination issues. When he found sentiment for excluding the Japanese too strong to be countered, he decided his only hope of avoiding a direct insult was to strike a deal. San Francisco would end its educational segregation and Congress would abandon its attempts to prohibit Japanese immigration; Japan itself would take the responsibility for preventing its citizens from emigrating to the United States. Roosevelt brought San Francisco mayor Eugene Schmitz and the entire city school board to Washington, a major feat since Schmitz was free on bail after being charged with five counts of extortion. Roosevelt got the board to give up segregation, and a skeptical Congress dropped the bill to prohibit Japanese immigration. Japan, as its part of this so-called Gentleman's Agreement, quietly and reluctantly stopped issuing passports to laborers emigrating to the United States.

When anti-Japanese riots continued in California, Roosevelt reversed himself and concluded that war with Japan might indeed be a possibility. He decided to strengthen America's navy not only to deter Japan, but also because Britain's construction of a monster battleship, the HMS *Dreadnought*, had set off a new European naval race. To stir public support for his expensive expansion of the American navy, Roosevelt sent the existing fleet on a highly publicized voyage to the Pacific coast. Then, to impress the Japanese, he ordered the Great White Fleet to continue around the world.

President Theodore Roosevelt *(center)* with the Russian and Japanese delegations at Portsmouth, New Hampshire, where he helped negotiate an end to the Russo-Japanese War. *(Courtesy of the National Archives)*

Fortunately for this exposed naval task force, Japan's leaders did not contemplate war as feverishly as some American military leaders and newspaper pundits feared. A new Japanese cabinet made a formal decision to turn away from expansion by Pacific emigration and to concentrate instead on Japan's continental interests in Korea, Manchuria, and China. In this way Japan assumed that it would avoid conflict with America's domestic racism and its possessions in the Pacific. Rather than objecting to the Great White Fleet's voyage of intimidation, the Japanese cabinet invited the American ships to visit Japanese ports. The fleet received a tumultuous welcome.

Roosevelt and the Japanese moved quickly to publicize their détente and dampen war speculation. In November 1908, Ambassador Takahira Kogoro and Hay's replacement as secretary of state, Elihu Root, exchanged notes reaffirming respect for each other's Pacific possessions, the Open Door, and the territorial integrity of China. In private conversations, the Japanese told Root and Roosevelt that they considered Manchuria, Taiwan, and Korea among the Pacific possessions that the United States must respect. Root and Roosevelt made no objection.

The Chinese were not nearly so pleased with Roosevelt's East Asian policies. The Chinese had hoped to make use of America's commitment to the Open Door policy to help them resist Japanese and Russian encroachments in Manchuria. The Chinese had long subscribed to the stratagem of manipulating barbarians to protect China's interests against other barbarians. By the time Roosevelt became president, China's officials were under more than usual pressure to redeem Chinese interests because a national spirit was beginning to rise among some urban and student groups. In 1905 a few Chinese nationalists even organized a boycott against American goods in response to the Chinese Exclusion Act of 1904. No longer would they permit their officials to look with indifference upon the treatment of Chinese in barbarian lands.

Roosevelt sympathized with the boycotters' anger at the indignity of Chinese exclusion. Yet he could do nothing about the law. He could only issue orders for government officials to deal fairly with the Chinese already in America. Then, unwilling to see the Chinese boycott humiliate American businessmen before the merchants of other powers, he insisted that the Chinese government suppress it. He even had America's Asiatic fleet anchor at Shanghai. Chinese officials mildly supported the boycott for a few months, fearful that the boycotters might turn their energies against the regime if it moved against them. When Chinese businessmen began to lose interest, the Chinese government finally responded to American pressure and suppressed the boycott. Roosevelt told Congress afterward that the United States had been much to blame for the conflict because "grave injustices and wrong have been done by this nation to the people of China."

Despite Roosevelt's tentative sympathy for rising Chinese nationalism, he did not make any other dramatic gestures on China's behalf. He protested vigorously when, during the boycott, the Chinese government sought to regain control of a concession it had granted the American China Development Company to build a railroad from Hankou to Guangzhou (Canton). The stockholders of the company included such financial powerhouses as E.H. Harriman, Jacob Schiff, and the presidents of National City Bank, Chase National Bank, and Carnegie Steel. Yet by 1903, eight years after receiving its concession, the company had built only ten miles of railroad. Disturbed at the ineptitude and lethargy of the company, China took advantage of the anti-American atmosphere to try to buy back the concession from J.P. Morgan, who had assumed control after the company had passed through the hands of a Belgian consortium. Morgan was perfectly willing to sell, but Roosevelt regarded the Chinese offer as a slap at American prestige.

Only after a long meeting with Morgan did Roosevelt abandon his protests and allow the financier to sell the concession back to China.

William Howard Taft and Dollar Diplomacy in Asia

Roosevelt had little compunction about putting pressure on the hapless Chinese over Morgan's railroad in southern China, but he and Root were very cautious about American activities in northern China, where Japan had its interests. Roosevelt's successor, William Howard Taft, was not so fastidious. He and his secretary of state, Philander Knox, were determined to help China. They devoutly believed that American investment in "backward" countries would aid them at the same time it fulfilled America's own interest in international stability. Taft's emphasis on financial intervention contrasted sharply with Roosevelt's greater concentration on power politics, and the newspapers began to call Taft's foreign policy "dollar diplomacy."

A group of young, vigorous American diplomats urged Taft and Knox toward financial intervention in Manchuria. These diplomats, Willard Straight, Huntington Wilson, and William Phillips, had served in East Asia and were busily and self-consciously replacing William Rockhill as the recognized American experts on the area. When the State Department was reorganized at the end of Roosevelt's administration, they formed the staff of the new Bureau of Far Eastern Affairs. In the course of their earlier duties abroad, all of them had learned to detest the Japanese. They believed it was America's mission to support China against Japan, a policy Rockhill condemned as foolhardy. Their displacement of Rockhill had little impact on such determined leaders as Roosevelt and Root, but they and their attitudes had considerable influence on the administration of Taft and Knox.

The staff of the Bureau of Far Eastern Affairs secured the support of Taft and Knox for a project of railroad baron E.H. Harriman that deeply worried the Japanese. Harriman cherished ambitions to build a round-the-world railway and was eager to acquire a Manchurian route as one link in this grandiose dream. He even induced Willard Straight to resign from the State Department and become his agent. Joining the Taft administration in supporting Harriman, China offered him a concession to build a railroad between Jinzhou (Chinchow) and Aihun (Aigun). The Chinese hoped that such a railroad would drain business and influence from Japan's Southern Manchurian Line. When Japan objected angrily, however, the Chinese quickly aborted the project. They knew that the Americans could not protect them from Japan and that the British would not be drawn into a scheme against their Japanese allies. Undeterred, Knox proposed the neutralization of all Manchurian railways so that no foreign nation would control them and suggested that eventually China be permitted to buy control of them with a loan from the great powers. To Japan's great relief, this scheme also failed.

Taft did succeed in wedging American capitalists into a consortium formed by British, French, and German bankers to float a loan to China. Taft and the Chinese both thought this loan might give China some strength to resist Japan. The Japanese foiled that plan by compelling the consortium to invite them and the Russians to participate as well. This ensured that the consortium would do nothing to imperil the various foreign spheres of

President William Howard Taft brought about a significant shift in U.S. diplomacy toward Japan and China. *(Courtesy of the National Archives)*

influence in China. Yet Taft continued to cooperate; he even accepted the consortium's request to delay recognition of the Chinese Nationalist government that overthrew the Manchu dynasty in 1912. Taft's inconsistency only succeeded in making China as angry as Japan.

Although the president's dollar diplomacy offended Japan, Taft and Knox were not truly anti-Japanese. They did their best to protect Japanese rights in the United States. In 1911 they gave up America's rights under the unequal treaty system to control Japanese tariffs on American products, and they renewed the Gentlemen's Agreement. They simply did not understand that Japan would regard their policies as a threat to its vital interests. They did nothing to prepare America's naval or coastal defenses in the Pacific, and they were taken by surprise when Japan drew closer to its old enemy Russia to resist the American drive on Manchuria. Theodore Roosevelt warned Taft and Knox against challenging Japan, but Knox replied that China needed Manchuria as much as Japan did and he accused Roosevelt of abandoning America's historic Open Door policy.

Woodrow Wilson and Missionary Diplomacy in Asia

Roosevelt was not the only critic of Taft's dollar diplomacy in East Asia. Many liberals refused to believe that Taft's cooperation with Wall Street bankers and European imperial powers could possibly be intended to help China. His acceptance of Japanese participation in the consortium and his delay in recognizing China's new government confirmed their suspicions. In contrast to Theodore Roosevelt, these idealistic liberals thought America should do more to help China. American missionaries in China, encouraging such help, greatly influenced the thinking of Woodrow Wilson and his minister to China, a former college professor named Paul Reinsch.

When Wilson became president, he abruptly withdrew government support for the consortium. This caused the participating American bankers to pull out, because the government would no longer guarantee to collect the consortium's loans. Wilson had consulted none of the other nations involved in the consortium when he made his decision; he had not consulted China; he had not even consulted his own State Department. Huntington Wilson resigned in protest. But President Wilson, convinced of the righteousness of his position, announced that the United States would recognize the revolutionary government of China.

Japan argued against recognition by pointing out that the revolutionary government was on the verge of civil war. That government was an unstable coalition between the Nationalists, who had risen to control southern China in 1911, and the commander of the Manchu empire's army, Yuan Shi-kai. Yuan controlled much of northern China; by taking him into the government, the Nationalists had hoped to avoid civil war. After Yuan persuaded the last Manchu emperor to abdicate in 1912, Sun Yat-sen, whom the Nationalists had made their provisional president, stepped aside in favor of Yuan as president of the new Republic of China. Yuan secured recognition and a loan from the European powers in 1913, but many of the Nationalists disliked the terms of the loan and feared that Yuan was using the money to finance the army on which his power depended.

The Nationalists raised a second revolution against Yuan. Yuan put it down easily, and Sun and many of his followers fled to Japan. Yuan then outlawed their Guomindang party and suspended the national and provincial parliaments. He even contemplated making himself emperor. Open civil war broke out a month after Wilson recognized the new regime. It kept China divided because Yuan could not conquer the Nationalists in the south, and the Nationalists, having no army, could not defeat Yuan in the north. To add to the chaos, Yuan lost control of his own lieutenants, who proceeded to set themselves up as independent warlords in various regions.

Meanwhile a much larger war had broken out in Europe. World War I diverted the attention of Europe and America from the Asian theater, and Japan saw an open field in a weak, divided China. Japan extorted from the European Allies the right to conquer Germany's colonies in China and the Pacific as the price for its entry into the war. Quickly

THE SURGE INTO ASIA   43

Japan took Shandong and Germany's Pacific islands north of the equator (Australia and New Zealand got those south of the equator). Then, in early 1915, Japan presented China with a document that became known as the Twenty-One Demands. China was to ratify Japanese control of Shandong; extend Japanese concessions in Manchuria and central China; permit no further acquisition of harbors or islands on the China coast by other foreigners; purchase half its armaments from Japan; accept Japanese advisers for all its political, military, and economic affairs; and permit Japanese police to share control of critical points throughout China. In short, China would become a Japanese colony.

The Japanese told China to keep the Twenty-One Demands secret. But the Chinese leaked them to the American missionary community. Paul Reinsch clamored from China for Wilson to do something. Initially Wilson left the affair to the State Department while he concentrated on the European war, and the State Department reacted rather coolly to China's request for help. State Department counselor Robert Lansing said it would be "quixotic in the extreme" for the United States to entangle itself in the affair. Secretary of State William Jennings Bryan issued a statement recognizing the legitimacy of Japanese concerns in Shandong and Manchuria and expressed only mild concern for the Open Door and the territorial integrity of China. Nevertheless, other voices in the State Department, led by Reinsch, warned Wilson that China's very existence was in danger.

Wilson told Bryan he wanted the United States to be the champion of China. He wrote a stern note warning that the United States would not recognize any agreement between Japan and China that impaired American rights, Chinese political and territorial integrity, or the Open Door. Great Britain joined the protest because the Twenty-One Demands infringed on its sphere in the Yangtze and Hubei areas. This opposition, along with some internal dissent within Japan, caused the Japanese to abandon the most far-reaching of the demands. But Japan forced the Chinese to accept the rest of its ultimatum, and the Japanese now resentfully regarded the United States as their primary obstacle in Asia.

With Japan operating almost unchecked in China, Wilson swallowed hard and agreed to a new consortium to loan money to the Chinese. Japan would be a member of the consortium, but at least Wilson thought Japanese influence might be diluted if America furnished some of the loan money. In this way Wilson established a measure of superficial cooperation with Japan. As the United States entered the war in Europe in 1917, Wilson thought it important to cool the Japanese-American rivalry still further. Neither Wilson nor Japan was willing to make substantial concessions, so Robert Lansing and Japanese special minister Ishii Kikujiro agreed to a set of notes papering over the disagreements. Japan would respect the Open Door and the territorial integrity of China, while the United States would accept Japan's "special interests" there. Just what constituted Japan's special interests was left to the imagination, although a secret protocol pledged both sides to respect the status quo in China for the duration of the war.

Japanese-American relations remained strained despite the Lansing-Ishii Agreement of 1917. When Japan insisted on sending an expeditionary force into Siberia following Russia's withdrawal from World War I, a reluctant Wilson dispatched an American force to Siberia as well, in large part to keep an eye on the Japanese. Then, at the Paris Peace Conference, Wilson tried unsuccessfully to get the Allies to withdraw their cession of the Shandong Peninsula to Japan. He was also instrumental in defeating a clause Japan sought to insert into the peace treaty that proclaimed the equality of all races, a clause Wilson opposed personally and feared would prevent Senate consent. Japanese-American relations remained distrustful and contentious for the next twenty-five years.

Controversial Issues

The Open Door policy in Asia was immensely popular in the United States after John Hay enunciated it at the turn of the century. Newspapers, popular magazines, and politicians praised Hay for devising a clever diplomacy that supposedly saved China from predatory imperialists while protecting American interests, all without entangling the United States in foreign alliances or war.[1] Hay knew how little influence his declaration of policy had had in the absence of any disposition on the part of the United States to enforce it. Nevertheless, he and his successors did nothing to stop the popular portrayal of the Open Door as the savior of China. Consequently, the Open Door notes rapidly acquired an aura of sanctity approaching that of the Monroe Doctrine. This popular image proved tenacious through the years, especially in those sectors of the public influenced by the reports of American missionaries in China. Even today, many Americans continue to see the United States as having been the friendly protector of China, fighting Japan in the 1940s to save China's independence, only to be betrayed by the triumph of Mao Zedong and the Communists in 1949.

Academic historians have never been so enamored of the Open Door or America's actions in East Asia, though differing strongly about their effect. The first group of historical critics in the 1920s and 1930s was isolationist. Those critics saw the Open Door as having entangled the United States in European imperial rivalries. Then, when the Europeans pulled back, the United States was left standing alone as the primary obstacle to Japan's ambitions. Isolationists thought the United States should have avoided foreign entanglements in both Asia and Europe, confining its military power to the defense of North America or perhaps at most the Western Hemisphere. They particularly condemned the United States for supposedly defending the interests of the British Empire by declaring the Open Door in China.[2] One great pre–World War II historian of American policy in East Asia, Tyler Dennett, wrote his major works to demonstrate that the United States should have allied itself with Great Britain and been willing to use force rather than mere words and diplomacy to ensure the Open Door and the survival of China. But by the 1930s he had come around to the isolationist view.[3]

After World War II, realist historians joined the chorus condemning America's interventionist policy in Asia, but they did not denounce American intervention in World War II in Europe, as the isolationists did. Instead, they thought the United States should have tried to stay out of the war with Japan so it could concentrate its efforts against the greater threat of Hitler's Germany. These historians pointed out that the China market never amounted to anything, that American interests in Asia were too few and unimportant to justify taking any risks for them, and that the United States would have been better off if it had allowed Japan to exert some control over China. Perhaps if the Japanese had not been threatened by American obstruction, they would have been more moderate in China and never attacked Pearl Harbor. The realists argued that the war with Japan endangered the effort against Hitler without doing China any good and without winning any real loyalty from the Chinese. China soon went Communist anyway, and the United States began its equally ineffective attempts to control communism in Asia, leading to the wars in Korea and Vietnam.

The primary quarrel among realist historians has been over which actions and leaders were most to blame for the tragic policy in Asia. Some have seen it as stemming inevitably from the decision to keep the Philippines and then issue the Open Door notes.[4] But most realists argue that John Hay and Theodore Roosevelt were well aware of the limitations of American interest in Asia, were quite willing to accommodate Japan, and confined their activities to diplomacy and verbal expressions of American desires. Their only fault was their failure to explain their policies adequately to their successors and the general public. These realist historians blame William Howard Taft, Woodrow Wilson, and pro-Chinese State Department officials rather than Roosevelt and Hay for America's supposedly blind and excessive attachment to China, the Open Door, and confrontation with Japan.[5]

As realist historians dated America's overcommitment in Asia from the accession of Taft to the presidency in 1909, naturally John Hay's Open Door notes lost much of their previous significance. The significance of the notes was further undermined by historians of Chinese-American relations who pointed out that Hay did little more than confirm policies America had been supporting since its first contacts with China in the eighteenth century. Certainly Americans did not need the British to dupe them into adoption of the Open Door, especially since Great Britain was in the midst of changing its policy when Hippisley was approaching the Americans without British government authorization.[6]

Historians who have concentrated on China have generally been less sympathetic to Japan than those realists or other historians who have concentrated on Japanese relations with the United States. Most historians of China have argued that the United States never supported China to the point of risking war with Japan or seriously threatening Japanese interests until 1940, when Japan allied itself with Germany and truly menaced American security. These historians agreed that the United States could have followed a more enlightened Japanese policy before 1940, but, unlike some realists, they had little conviction that a better policy would have avoided Pearl Harbor. Meanwhile, they pointed out that American diplomats and businessmen condescended to China and exploited it, while the missionaries, however good their intentions, undermined China's culture and national self-confidence. And while Americans mistreated the Chinese in China, they also mistreated Chinese immigrants in the United States. The regrets of most historians of China have not been for the war against Japan, but for America's self-delusion about the supposed benevolence of its policy toward China, its sense of outrage and betrayal at the Communist revolution, and the consequent refusal of recognition of the new Chinese government and the ultimate war with Mao's China over Korea.[7]

Revisionists have dissented even more strongly from the realists who wished America had appeased Japan. Revisionists think the United States should have been far more supportive of China. They have regarded the Open Door as simply a policy of informal empire and economic exploitation. They have argued that Americans were as confident of their industrial dominance as to believe the United States could control the Chinese economy and, through the economy, China itself if given a chance to compete openly in the China market. Americans had no real interest in China's territorial integrity or general well-being, only in the opportunity for profits. If the United States had been truly eager to help China, it would have joined the Soviets in supporting the Chinese Nationalists. This would have created a strong China capable of withstanding Japan and therefore deterring it prior to Pearl Harbor.[8]

According to a fascinating book by historian Bruce Cumings, a revisionist who incorporates cultural as well as economic motives into his interpretation, American policy toward the Philippines and the rest of Asia was the natural outgrowth of the culture spawned by America's westward movement. The American westward movement was not the product of democratic, egalitarian frontier farmers so beloved of Thomas Jefferson and Andrew Jackson, according to Cumings. The democratic, egalitarian farming frontier was in reality a quick casualty of urbanization, industrialization, and ethnic diversity emanating first from Chicago and then from the urban centers of the Pacific Coast, particularly Los Angeles and San Francisco, but also Seattle, Portland, and San Diego. The white immigrants to the West were not the virtuous democrats of mythology but instead energetic entrepreneurs who were also narrow, rapacious, racist, and often Christian fundamentalists. For these frontier immigrants, land was not so much a sacred fount of economic and political independence as it was an economic commodity—real estate. The keys to the wealth of that real estate were water and railroads, the domination of which created fabulous fortunes for the few along with the urban and suburban consumer culture that came to be the model not only for the United States but also for the world. Ironically, Cumings notes, the supposedly individualistic frontier entrepreneurs relied on the big government they scorned in their political rhetoric. The railroad fortunes depended on government land grants. The real estate fortunes depended on government organization and control of water and other infrastructure. Moreover, the labor on which these wealthy titans depended was a multiethnic mix of Mexicans, Chinese, and Japanese whom they disdained as inferior peoples.

The culture of this expanding westward movement turned its back on Europe, acted unilaterally, and crushed those people who stood in its way. It disdained the eastward-looking elites who were more willing to cooperate with and draw closer to the Old World of Europe and who were consequently somewhat more restrained in Asia and toward Asians. But the westward-looking American culture also disdained other expansionists who sought to avoid European entanglements yet were more patient and peaceful in their expansionism, statesmen like Thomas Jefferson, John Quincy Adams, and William Seward. Instead, American culture came to reflect the aggressiveness, militarism, and racism of James K. Polk. Thus, according to Cumings, American policy in the Pacific, including the acquisition of Hawaii and the Philippines and the devastation of their peoples in the late 1800s; the subsequent treatment of China, Japan, and Korea; and especially the persecution of Asians in the United States, partook more of Polk than of Jefferson. And, except for the period of World War II and the Cold War, when eastern elites temporarily dominated American foreign policy and fashioned a fairly multilateral Europe-centered policy, Cumings believes that the western foreign policy outlook has dominated U.S. diplomacy.[9]

Further Reading

For information on the Philippine war and occupation, see Brian McAllister Linn, *The Philippine War, 1899–1902* (2000); Glenn Anthony May, *Battle for Batanga* (1991); Ken de Bevoise, *Agents of Apocalypse: Epidemic Disease in the Colonial Philippines* (1995); Richard Welch, *Response to Imperialism: The United States and the Philippine-American War, 1899–1902* (1979); Stuart Creighton Miller, *"Benevolent Assimilation": The American Conquest of the Philippines, 1899–1903* (1982); Peter W. Stanley, *A Nation in the Making: The Philippines and the United States, 1899–1921* (1974); and for a strong revisionist denunciation, William J. Pomeroy, *American Neo-Colonialism: Its Emergence in the Philippines and Asia* (1970). A profound recent cultural analysis of America's early occupation of the Philippines is Julian Go, *American Empire and the Politics of Meaning* (2008).

Notes

1. See, for example, A.L.P. Dennis, *Adventures in American Diplomacy, 1896–1906* (1928).

2. See, for example, A. Whitney Griswold, *The Far Eastern Policy of the United States* (1938); and Samuel Flagg Bemis, *A Diplomatic History of the United States* (1936).

3. See Tyler Dennett, *Americans in Eastern Asia* (1922), *Roosevelt and the Russo-Japanese War* (1925), and *John Hay* (1933); and Dorothy Borg, "Two Historians of the Far Eastern Policy of the United States: Tyler Dennett and A. Whitney Griswold," in *Pearl Harbor as History*, ed. Dorothy Borg and Shumpei Okamoto (1973).

4. See, for example, Louis J. Halle, *Dream and Reality: Aspects of American Foreign Policy* (1959); and George F. Kennan, *American Diplomacy, 1900–1950* (1951).

5. See Raymond A. Esthus, *Theodore Roosevelt and Japan* (1966); Charles E. Neu, *An Uncertain Friendship: Theodore Roosevelt and Japan, 1906–1909* (1967), and *The Troubled Encounter: The United States and Japan* (1975); Akira Iriye, *Pacific Estrangement: Japanese and American Expansionism, 1897–1911* (1972), and *Across the Pacific: An Inner History of American–East Asian Relations* (rev. ed., 1992); and Burton Beers, *Vain Endeavor: Robert Lansing's Attempts to End the American-Japanese Rivalry* (1962).

6. R.G. Neale, *Great Britain and United States Expansion, 1898–1900* (1966); Paul A. Varg, *Open Door Diplomat: The Life of W.W. Rockhill* (1952).

7. See John King Fairbank, *The United States and China* (1958); Paul A. Varg, *Missionaries, Chinese, and Diplomats: The American Protestant Missionary Movement in China, 1890–1952* (1958), and *The Making of a Myth: The United States and China, 1897–1912* (1968); Marilyn Blatt Young, *The Rhetoric of Empire: American China Policy, 1895–1901* (1968); Warren I. Cohen, *America's Response to China* (2nd ed., 1981); Charles S. Campbell Jr., *Special Business Interests and the Open Door Policy* (1951); Roy Curry, *Woodrow Wilson and Far Eastern Policy, 1913–1921* (1957); Russell H. Fifield, *Woodrow Wilson and the Far East: The Diplomacy of the Shantung Question* (1952); Shihshan Henry Tsai, *China and the Overseas Chinese* (1984); Michael H. Hunt, *The Making of a Special Relationship: The United States and China to 1914* (1983); James Reed, *The Missionary Mind and American East Asian Policy* (1982); Key Ray Chong, *Americans and Chinese Reform and Revolution, 1898–1922*

(1984); and Daniel M. Crane and Thomas A. Breslin, *An Ordinary Relationship: American Opposition to Republican Revolution in China* (1986). Two excellent books on the role of women missionaries in China are Jane Hunter, *The Gospel of Gentility: American Women Missionaries in Turn-of-the-Century China* (1984); and Patricia R. Hill, *The World Their Household: The American Woman's Foreign Mission Movement and Cultural Transformation, 1870–1920* (1985).

8. See William Appleman Williams, "China and Japan: A Challenge and a Choice of the Nineteen Twenties," *Pacific Historical Review* 26 (1957); Charles Vevier, *The United States and China, 1906–1913* (1955); Thomas J. McCormick, *China Market: America's Quest for Informal Empire, 1893–1901* (1967); and Jerry Israel, *Progressivism and the Open Door: America and China, 1905–1921* (1971).

9. Bruce Cumings, *Dominion from Sea to Sea: Pacific Ascendancy and American Power* (2009).

CHAPTER 3

THE SURGE INTO LATIN AMERICA
VARIETIES OF AMERICAN EMPIRE

The Nature of the U.S. Empire in Latin America

Throughout its history, the United States has been wary of the idea of imperialism. Americans pride themselves on the fact that their revolution was the first successful rebellion against European colonialism. Their political ideology is based on the principle of government by consent of the governed. Although they have subscribed to other competing values—desire for national security, economic prosperity, and the prestige associated with great power status—they suffer considerable discomfort when they sacrifice the principle of democracy too easily and blatantly to those other desires. Before the Spanish-American War, Americans found it relatively easy to rationalize the contradictions between their actions and their commitment to democratic self-determination. They ignored the Indians and visualized the westward movement as expansion into "empty lands" that they would ultimately incorporate into the Union as equal states. But it was difficult for Americans to conceive of making states out of the Philippines, the South Sea Islands, Hawaii, or Puerto Rico. The Supreme Court even decided in the famous Insular Cases that the inhabitants of America's new colonies were not entitled to all the basic liberties granted American citizens by the Constitution. To add to the dilemmas the United States faced in its new colonies, many Americans thought it essential to ensure stability in still other nations that were economically or strategically important.

The United States could no longer escape the fact that it was an imperial and interventionist power. In the first flush of victory, the thrill of arrival as a great world power overrode the sense of guilt and the anti-imperialist movement that had exploited that guilt. Then, as the thrill waned amid the blood and atrocities of the Philippine revolution, Americans began to regard their colonial experiment and intervention in general with an increasingly dubious eye.

Still, intervene they did. They may not have done so enthusiastically, they may have considered intervention only the lesser of evils; yet most came to feel that the United States had no other choice, especially in Latin America. Even many politicians and historians who opposed the annexation of the Philippines or an activist policy in defense of the Open Door in Asia were ready to defend the acquisition of colonies and protectorates in Central America and the Caribbean. They reasoned that Latin American was closer to home than Asia and that controlling the isthmian canal routes was strategically vital for the United States.

By the end of the Spanish-American War, the United States was well on its way to achieving the goal of an isthmian canal. America displaced Spanish rule in two critical islands guarding the Caribbean approaches to the canal routes, Cuba and Puerto Rico. Great Britain was slowly but surely reducing its power and presence in the Western Hemisphere in order to concentrate on the European theater. The United States wanted nothing to tempt Spain or Great Britain to return to the Caribbean or Central America and hoped to deter the recently united and aggressive Germany from intruding there as well.

As the strategic interest of the United States in Latin America increased, so did its direct economic stake. Cuba was especially valuable. It supplied sugar and tobacco; it served as an important market for American manufactured goods; and Americans invested heavily there in tobacco and sugar plantations, banks, railroads, and public utilities. Mexico, where Americans were developing similar markets and investments, was equally valuable. The rest of Latin America was not, although several American corporations had substantial interests in various areas and sought protection from the U.S. government. The United States had always assumed that protection of American lives and property abroad was a proper goal of diplomacy, so the government became more inclined to intervene as its Latin American economic interests increased and the obstacles posed by major rivals decreased.

Americans naturally managed to find ideological rationales for their multiplying interventions. They convinced themselves that American rule could never be like European colonial oppression because the United States would educate the indigenous peoples for liberty. As time wore on, this anticolonial inclination took the concrete form of a decision to free the Philippines and to consider granting statehood to the largest and most compatible of the colonies. Where the United States felt compelled to intervene militarily or to exert a rather heavy-handed economic and diplomatic influence, Americans were at least half convinced that this too could work for the good of all. American trade and investments would increase the economic wealth of those nations. U.S. military power would protect Latin America against European colonial exploitation and preserve peace among the weaker nations. Political supervision could help bring stability and democracy. American influence would work against dictatorship, corruption, and the chaos that indigenous romantic nationalists or radicals might bring in their wake.

Events quickly exposed the problems and contradictions involved in colonizing or intervening in foreign areas. The clash of cultures between the native inhabitants and Americans was often bitter and ugly. Most Americans shared a condescending attitude toward non-Europeans. Even sophisticated Americans of this era generally regarded Latin Americans as racial inferiors. Those who avoided such racism nevertheless considered most Latin Americans as cultural inferiors who needed U.S. schooling to achieve political democratic maturity and economic prosperity. The image of Latin Americans that permeated all classes of U.S. society had been captured by the first American foreign aid official sent to Venezuela in 1812 with supplies to relieve the suffering caused by a massive earthquake. He called the Venezuelans "timid, indolent, ignorant, superstitious, and incapable of enterprise or exertion. From the present moral and intellectual habits of all classes, I fear they have not arrived at that point of human dignity which fits man for the enjoyment of free and rational government."

Thus, when Americans served abroad in positions of authority as factory owners, colonial officials, teachers, and missionaries, they often aroused nationalistic hostilities. American troops stationed in foreign countries caused special difficulties. Most soldiers were uneducated and unsophisticated. They regarded foreigners as strange and inferior and treated them as such. Consequently, American military intervention often created more problems than it solved.

The United States usually intervened in hope of establishing reasonably stable and democratic regimes. Nevertheless, those who were the targets of the intervention generally regarded any government established or supported by the United States as collaborationist. Such a government could not survive by democratic means. It would resort to oppression, invite rebellion and chaos, and tempt American intervention once again. The events of Theodore Roosevelt's administration exposed many of these problems. Roosevelt's successor, William Howard Taft, tried to circumvent the need for military intervention by substituting dollar diplomacy. By encouraging American investment to enrich and buttress weak economies, Taft hoped to stabilize the politics of those nations as well. But dollar diplomacy failed; American investment and trade usually enriched a few Americans and a small group of Latin Americans without raising the general standard of living.

Most Latin American countries began to concentrate on one or two cash crops or natural resources that might be exchanged in the United States for manufactured items and luxury goods. The upper classes might benefit from this trade and from the American investments and loans that made possible the railroads, port facilities, and public utilities necessary to commerce; few peasants did. The economies of these nations became almost totally dependent on the United States, whose superior economic strength permitted its citizens in large measure to control the price of both Latin American exports and imports. Latin Americans paid more for the manufactured goods they imported than they received for the agricultural products or raw materials they exported.

Woodrow Wilson recognized some of the problems with dollar diplomacy and thought they were caused by the greed of Wall Street investors. He believed that a greater dedication to democracy abroad and less concern for selfish profits in American trade and investment would resolve the difficulties. But to his chagrin, his attempt to establish just and democratic governments led to more conflict and intervention than the policies of either of his predecessors.

The dilemma Wilson, Taft, and Roosevelt faced is still with us and still generates controversy. Revisionists condemn America's historic policies toward Latin America in toto. Like the Latin American Left itself, they believe that the United States intervened in Latin America primarily for economic gain, to protect and increase American trade and investments. American interventions were not motivated by fears for national security, because no outside power posed a credible threat to Latin America after the British retreated at the turn of the century. The United States intervened instead to perpetuate the dictatorship of the Latin American upper classes, which were allied with the economic interests of the United States. It sought to protect its collaborators against indigenous revolutionaries

The Caribbean Area, 1889–1961

who had no choice but to seek nationalization of land and resources because wealth was concentrated in so few hands. In the revisionist view, the United States obviously had no interest in democracy or it would have supported such revolutionary movements.

Restrained realists also have been highly critical of U.S. policy toward Latin America, but for somewhat different reasons. They do not believe economic interests provided the primary motivation for U.S. interventions because, until the latter half of the twentieth century, U.S. economic interests in Latin America were minor compared to those in Europe. Although economics certainly provided some incentive for U.S. intervention, restrained realists think the United States intervened because of imagined threats to U.S. security in Latin America. The United States also intervened out of naive desires to bring stability and democracy to people whom U.S. citizens regarded as inferiors in need of political and economic guidance. In addition to benefiting the Latin Americans, such stability and democracy would eliminate the temptation for hostile foreign nations to intervene in America's hemisphere. But the restrained realists agree with the revisionists that most U.S. interventions in Latin America were unnecessary because U.S. security was not truly threatened. Thus, intervention generated hostility toward the United States while doing little good. On the other hand, restrained realists see it as inevitable that a powerful nation should influence and to some extent dominate its weaker neighbors, so the best the United States could hope to do was to mitigate the situation. Moreover, the realists would not hesitate to intervene if vital U.S. interests were truly at stake.

Nationalists do not regard the Latin American policy of the United States as such an unmitigated failure. Like the realists but unlike the revisionists, they do not place great emphasis on economic motivations. Nationalists also do not believe that U.S. trade and investment have done great harm. They argue that Latin America needed capital and would have been far worse off if the United States and its corporations had not furnished it. They are not so willing to discount the threats of outside nations to the Western Hemisphere, past or present. Nationalists also believe that the encouragement of democracy in Latin America was a sincere and worthy goal, even if U.S. intervention and influence failed to secure it in very many places. Blaming the failure of democracy more on the Latin Americans themselves than on the United States, nationalists refuse to equate U.S. policy there with European imperialism.

But even nationalists find it hard to deny that the United States created at least an informal empire in Central America and the Caribbean after the turn of the twentieth century. Along with annexing the formal colony of Puerto Rico, the United States made a protectorate of Cuba, acquired all but absolute sovereignty over the Panama Canal Zone, intervened militarily in several Central American and Caribbean nations, and exerted a profound economic influence over the rest of Latin America. Meanwhile, the United States successfully excluded all the military and much of the economic influence of the European powers.

Puerto Rico: Governing a Colony

The United States met little opposition in seizing Puerto Rico during the Spanish-American War. Americans conducted no land campaign at all. Puerto Rican revolutionaries in New York, cooperating to some extent with the Cuban junta, invited American intervention. Thus, Americans found their presence welcomed for the first two years of their occupation of the island. The Puerto Ricans had little reason to mourn the demise of the Spanish Empire. Puerto Rico had shared the tragic experience of the rest of the Caribbean, including European conquest, extermination of most of the Indian population, and establishment of a brutal slave system by absentee owners of large sugar plantations. Spain had finally emancipated the slaves in its Cuban and Puerto Rican colonies in 1848, but the society remained fixed in a rigid class system with a small upper class dominating a large mass of landless, racially mixed peasants. In 1898 only 21 percent of Puerto Rico's land was under cultivation. There were no banks and only two or three roads.

Nevertheless, this was no "empty land" available for mass American immigration. The island was already overpopulated as well as poverty-stricken. Americans would come to Puerto Rico as colonial officials, entrepreneurs, missionaries, or tourists, not as farmers and settlers. Some American capital did flow into the island, and Americans replaced Spaniards as absentee landlords. They shifted Puerto Rican agricultural enterprise even more toward sugar, away from the cultivation of coffee produced on the small, relatively independent farms of Puerto Rico's interior. With abundant supplies of coffee from elsewhere, the United States saw sugar as more profitable.

By 1930 American absentee owners controlled more than half of Puerto Rico's sugar, 80 percent of its tobacco, 60 percent of its banks and public utilities, and, under special government protection, 100 percent of its shipping. Some 70 percent of the profits from

Puerto Rico's large enterprises went to foreigners, including Americans. Much of the other 30 percent went to rich Puerto Ricans, who in turn spent it on manufactured and luxury goods from the United States. Lower-class Puerto Ricans had to buy food from the United States at tariff-protected prices or produce their own on small, inadequate farms. Existence was possible only at a low subsistence level. Many fled to the cities or to the United States itself to escape their dilemma, so no middle-class farming population developed. The Puerto Rican middle class was essentially a set of bureaucrats or low-level managers in the large enterprises and almost totally dissociated from the peasants.

Meanwhile, the Anglo-Calvinist civilization of the United States conflicted with the Catholic Spanish-Creole culture of the island. Puerto Ricans, themselves ambivalent and uncertain in their attitudes toward race, were shocked to find themselves considered black by their American masters. The middle and upper classes considered themselves white and looked with disdain and some alarm at what they considered the shallow, materialistic imported culture of their supposed racial superiors. This economic and cultural scenario was repeated to a lesser or greater extent throughout Central America and the Caribbean.

The impact of the United States was somewhat different on Puerto Rico than on the rest of Latin America because Puerto Rico was a formal rather than an informal colony (although it was officially titled an "unincorporated territory"). The Insular Cases dictated that the United States did not have to govern Puerto Rico and the Philippines with the expectation that they would become states, as had been the rule with previous American territories. The Organic Act of 1900 gave Puerto Rico a territorial government that allowed election of Puerto Rican representatives, but guaranteed an American governor and an American majority on the governing council. Various American administrations usually reserved these offices for loyal party workers, without regard to their knowledge of Puerto Rico or the Spanish language. Often these officials did little to disguise their patronizing attitudes.

The United States did extend citizenship to the Puerto Ricans in 1917. Americans improved sanitation, utilities, and roads, although the primary benefits of these went to the cities and large agricultural enterprises rather than to the ordinary peasant. Americans also did much for education on the island. Puerto Rico's literacy rate rose to better than 80 percent, compared to Haiti's 15 percent or the Dominican Republic's 26 percent. Still, these improvements did not offset the growing resentment of the Puerto Ricans toward their American overlords.

It was not until the early 1940s that Puerto Rico tenuously accepted its position within the American empire. During those years, a remarkable Puerto Rican leader, Luís Muñoz Marín, organized a political party that finally convinced the United States to allow Puerto Rico to elect its own governor. Muñoz Marín then gained commonwealth status for Puerto Rico, corrected some of the most glaring of the island's economic inequalities, lobbied successfully for large economic benefits from Congress, and attracted considerable private capital. Yet Puerto Rico's consent to its U.S. connection remained unstable and laced with considerable hostility. This boded ill for U.S. relations with the rest of Latin America, where the problems raised by the overwhelming North American presence were not balanced as they were in Puerto Rico by the investment of some $500 million between 1898 and 1945 and by the right of free passage to the United States.

Cuba: Shaping a Formal Protectorate

William McKinley committed the United States to abstain from annexing Cuba when he accepted the Senate's Teller Amendment that prohibited annexation (see Chapter 1 in this volume), but also he avoided recognizing the Cuban rebel government. This balancing act left him free to set the ground rules under which Cuba could remain independent. He forced the Spanish to surrender Cuba to the U.S. military, not to the Cuban rebels. The United States then established a temporary military government and managed to disband the Cuban army by making liberal payments to its commanders and soldiers. After complaints from Cubans and Americans alike that the first U.S. governor was too liberal toward the defeated Spanish, McKinley appointed General Leonard Wood to succeed him. Wood was a medical doctor who was able, confident, energetic, and sympathetic to the "large policy" of his friends, Theodore Roosevelt and Henry Cabot Lodge. Wood did much to improve sanitation, eradicate yellow fever, establish public schools, and bring a measure of efficiency to Cuba's government and public services. Yet he distrusted Cuban abilities and always put North Americans in charge of these projects. He even established a paternalistic code of discipline that prescribed public whippings for those who violated his new civic codes.

Wood and Secretary of War Elihu Root formulated the terms on which the United States would turn Cuba over to an indigenous government. Wood and Root wanted a stable Cuba that would protect U.S. trade and investment and that would welcome a U.S. military presence to defend the island, the approaches to the Caribbean, and the peninsular canal routes. To achieve this, Root circumvented a congressional prohibition against permanent economic concessions in Cuba by granting supposedly temporary ones instead. He and Wood also worked through Senator Orville Platt of Connecticut to attach the Platt Amendment to the army appropriations bill of 1901. This prohibited Cuba from granting foreign economic concessions without U.S. permission or doing anything to impair Cuban independence. The Platt Amendment required Cuba to keep its debt at a low level, grant the United States sites for military and coaling stations, and permit the United States to intervene if necessary to protect Cuban independence and maintain stability.

To persuade a Cuban constitutional convention to accept these stipulations, Root promised that the United States would intervene only in the most extreme circumstances. Wood proclaimed that the U.S. occupation force would not leave until Cuba accepted the terms of the Platt Amendment. The Cubans reluctantly acquiesced, and in 1902 Wood turned over the government to a newly elected Cuban president. U.S. troops left, but in conformance with a treaty negotiated on the basis of the Platt Amendment, the U.S. Navy moved into the strategic port of Guantánamo to establish its major Caribbean base. A reciprocal trade treaty was also part of the bargain. Cuba received tariff concessions on exports of sugar to the United States and gave U.S. products special privileges in Cuban markets. U.S. investments also increased rapidly. In 1898 U.S. citizens had some $50 million invested in Cuban sugar; by 1920 that figure was $1.25 billion.

Cuban stability did not last very long. President Tómas Estrada Palma refused to accept the verdict of the polls when he was defeated for reelection. His opponents announced a revolution, and Estrada Palma begged for U.S. support. Theodore Roosevelt sent an American warship to Havana, but decided that Estrada Palma himself was the major problem. Roosevelt appealed to the Cubans to resolve the issue fairly to avoid American intervention. No one wanted a repetition of the Philippine war. On the other hand, Roosevelt and his special envoy to the island, William Howard Taft, did not want to turn the government over to the rebels and thus reward armed insurrection. The United States preferred that Estrada Palma stay on temporarily while new and fair elections were held.

Estrada Palma and the rebels, however, refused to negotiate. They both angled for U.S. intervention in hopes that Roosevelt would support their position. Estrada Palma resigned rather than accept a new election, and Roosevelt sent Taft, supported by the landing of 5,000 American troops, to establish himself as head of a provisional government. The U.S. provisional government itself held new elections while Roosevelt warned the Cubans that "if the elections become a farce, and if the insurrectionary habit becomes confirmed in the Island, it is absolutely out of the question that the Island should continue independent." Taft's successor as governor, Charles Magoon, tried to encourage reform and strong political parties, but the parties had few roots among the people. Party leaders were mostly intent on the spoils of office. They felt little responsibility because they knew they could induce U.S. intervention in a crisis by threatening revolution and chaos.

After Taft's elections established a new government, the United States withdrew its troops in 1908, some two years after it had intervened. Nevertheless, the Cuban political system remained unstable, corruption increased, and the army set up by the new government became an expensive source of political favoritism and boodle.

In 1912 the United States intervened once again in Cuba. President Taft sent 500 marines to support the Cuban regime against a rebellion of army officers and blacks who were protesting political discrimination. Woodrow Wilson denounced such interventions, but as president he too felt compelled to threaten intervention to deter a revolt against the incumbent Cuban regime on the eve of U.S. entry into World War I. His action won the consent of a grateful Cuban government to station U.S. troops on the island to guard against any potential German threat. The crisis of World War I temporarily silenced opposition in the United States to Wilson's action, but it was increasingly clear that military intervention in Cuba was self-defeating.

The Panama Canal: Acquiring a Formal Enclave in an Informal Colony

By establishing a colony in Puerto Rico and a protectorate over Cuba, the United States took two major steps toward securing control of the Caribbean access to any canal built through Central America. The strengthened U.S. position affected Great Britain as well as Latin America. The United States had been trying for years to rid itself of its obligations under the Clayton-Bulwer Treaty of 1850 to share control of any Central American canal with Great Britain, and in December 1898, the British decided to open new negotiations on the issue.

After a year of hard bargaining, Secretary of State John Hay and British ambassador Lord Julian Pauncefote concluded a pact that gave the United States sole control of the potential canal, but ensured its neutrality by forbidding the canal's fortification. Vice-President Theodore Roosevelt and his "large policy" cohorts campaigned against this first Hay-Pauncefote Treaty because it prohibited fortification, and the Senate responded by mangling the treaty so thoroughly that it had to be renegotiated. By the time the second Hay-Pauncefote Treaty was signed in January 1902, Roosevelt himself was president and the British were ready to retreat still further from Latin America. This second treaty was silent on fortification, implicitly according to the United States the right to full military control of the canal.

All that remained was for the United States to choose between Nicaragua and Colombia's province of Panama as the canal route. The Walker Commission, appointed by McKinley, had reported in favor of Nicaragua in 1901. The commission's engineers admitted that Nicaragua's river system might be too shallow for easy construction, but the Panama route had an even more serious drawback: De Lesseps's bankrupt New Panama Canal Company demanded the exorbitant sum of $109 million for the purchase of its works and concessions. The House of Representatives accepted the Walker Commission report and authorized construction through Nicaragua.

William Nelson Cromwell, a remarkable U.S. lobbyist for the New Panama Canal Company, refused to accept this House action as final. He convinced the Panama Company to reduce its demand from $109 million to $40 million. Then he persuaded the U.S. Senate to authorize the money and to urge the negotiation of a treaty with Colombia for canal rights through Panama with the proviso that if negotiations failed, Roosevelt would return to the Nicaragua option. Cromwell got his way in Congress through liberal application of money. His allies distributed Nicaraguan stamps showing an erupting volcano to counter Nicaraguan claims that its route would be perfectly safe.

The Roosevelt administration quickly negotiated the Hay-Herrán Treaty with Colombia, which gave the United States a ninety-nine-year lease on a canal zone six miles wide in exchange for an initial payment of $10 million plus $250,000 annually. But the Colombian senate balked. It wanted an increase in payments and greater acknowledgment of Colombian sovereignty over the canal zone. Colombia had reason to stall. The New Panama Company's concessions ran out in 1904, and Colombia would then receive the money for De Lesseps's works as well.

The stall enraged Roosevelt. He might have turned to Nicaragua, but instead he resolved to get the better of the "contemptible little creatures in Bogotá." You could no more make a binding agreement with them than you could "nail currant jelly to a wall," he later complained. When an influential Panamanian suggested that Panama might rebel against its Colombian overlords and sign its own treaty with the United States, Roosevelt was ready to listen. Roosevelt knew rebellion was endemic in Panama. The United States, in its role as guarantor of transit rights across the Isthmus of Panama, had intervened four separate times in recent years to protect the railroad against rebel attacks. The man who suggested that a convenient rebellion might break out again was Philippe Bunau-Varilla, an official of the New Panama Canal Company who was desperate to strike a deal before the company's concession ran out.

Bunau-Varilla wanted the United States to protect the revolution against Colombian reconquest by using its rights as guarantor of transit to block Colombian landings or use of the Panamanian railway. Panama needed the help because its revolutionary forces consisted of a fire brigade, a few local police, and a small contingent of Colombian soldiers whose commander had been bribed. Roosevelt told Bunau-Varilla that he could not encourage revolution, but he let John Hay inform Bunau-Varilla that the American ship *Nashville* was steaming toward the isthmus. Roosevelt later commented that Bunau-Varilla would have been a very dull man not to have known what America would do in case of a revolution.

Bunau-Varilla was not dull. He delayed the revolution until the *Nashville* was lying off the Colombian port of Colón. When the revolution began, however, the commander of the *Nashville* failed to prevent the Colombians from landing an invasion force because orders to do so had been too late in arriving. A quick-thinking railroad supervisor saved the day. He had already sent almost all the rolling stock to the Pacific side of the isthmus, stranding the Colombian force. He then invited the Colombian commanders aboard one of the last available trains and sent them off also, leaving the troops leaderless. The *Nashville* landed some U.S. sailors to "keep the peace," and the revolution was secure.

Panama's new leaders gratefully authorized Bunau-Varilla to negotiate a canal treaty with the United States. They told him at the same time to protect Panama's sovereign rights over the canal, but Bunau-Varilla was so anxious to guarantee the American Senate's approval of the treaty that he gave away even more than Hay requested. Hay wanted American control of a canal zone six miles wide for ninety-nine years. Bunau-Varilla insisted the United States govern "as if it were sovereign" a ten-mile zone in perpetuity. In return, the United States would protect the sovereignty of Panama, especially against Colombia. The Panamanian leaders protested Bunau-Varilla's giveaway, but accepted it rather than face Colombia alone.

The treaty with Bunau-Varilla ran into considerable opposition in the United States from the press and Congress. The Democrats particularly denounced Roosevelt's unscrupulous tactics. They argued that America should have turned to the Nicaraguan route rather than encouraging the Panamanian revolution. The Senate could not resist the handsome concessions the president had won, however, and it accepted the treaty by a vote of sixty-six to fourteen. Roosevelt defended his actions as perfectly legal. When he asked his cabinet if he had successfully vindicated himself, Elihu Root replied that he certainly had: "You have shown that you were accused of seduction and you have conclusively proved that you were guilty of rape." Later, in 1911, Roosevelt was quoted as telling an audience at the University of California, "I took the Isthmus." His alleged comment triggered a congressional investigation, and President Woodrow Wilson subsequently apologized to Colombia while trying to get Congress to appropriate $25 million as an indemnity. Roosevelt succeeded in getting his Republican friends in Congress to defeat Wilson's move, but two years after Roosevelt's death in 1919, Congress did grant Colombia the indemnity.

Ironically, as Colombia became more mollified, Panama became less so. The United States completed the canal in 1914 and eliminated yellow fever in the process, but it established the Canal Zone as a protected enclave against the Panamanians themselves. The American flag gradually replaced the Panamanian flag. The Americans set up separate schools and commissaries. They made English the language of the zone and imported English-speaking West Indians to replace Panamanians in jobs on the canal. The United States officially segregated the Canal Zone by race, grouping the Panamanians with the West Indians as blacks. American labor bosses, often white southerners, treated the Panamanians and West Indians as they had treated blacks at home. Discrimination even extended to the currency in which laborers were paid: American citizens received gold, while the Panamanians and West Indians were paid in less valuable silver. The United States also exerted tremendous authority in Panama outside the zone. It controlled all lakes and streams necessary to the operation of the canal, it had a monopoly of all communications and utilities, and it tied Panama's economy to the American dollar.

Although the United States maintained the right of direct intervention in Panamanian politics and foreign policy, it tried to leave this sphere to the Panamanians as much as possible. Panamanian politics degenerated into a struggle for power within an economic elite of established families that considered themselves "white" and whose main goal was protection of their private interests. If this political system did little for the mass of Panamanians, it permitted efficient and uninterrupted operation of the Panama Canal by the United States.

The Roosevelt Corollary to the Monroe Doctrine: Staking Out America's Sphere of Influence

As the United States strengthened its hand in the Caribbean through acquisition of formal colonies and protectorates in Cuba, Puerto Rico, and the Panama Canal, Theodore Roosevelt reconsidered America's policies toward the other independent nations of the area. At first he did not seem to think that anything more than the traditional adherence to the Monroe Doctrine was necessary. In 1902—when Great Britain and Germany approached him with a plan to use naval power to force Venezuela to pay its long-overdue debt— Roosevelt made no objection beyond warning that the venture must lead to no territorial acquisitions by the two European powers. He even wrote the German ambassador that if any South American country misbehaved toward a European country, the European nation should "spank it." He had a change of heart, however, after Britain and Germany sank several Venezuelan gunboats, blockaded the Venezuelan coast, and bombarded several coastal forts.

When the Venezuelans offered to submit the debts to international arbitration, Roosevelt urged a reluctant Germany and a somewhat less reluctant Great Britain to accept. Roosevelt later claimed that he had not only urged Germany to accept arbitration, but had sent an ultimatum to the kaiser that had finally forced the Germans to agree. There is no record of such an ultimatum in German or American archives, but Roosevelt did indeed deploy the fleet in Latin American waters and use leaks to the press to threaten Germany. In any case, Germany and Britain ultimately did allow the case to go to arbitration.

This second Venezuelan crisis stirred some soul-searching in many nations. Financial chaos, indebtedness, and political instability were endemic throughout Latin American. Other crises like the one in Venezuela were bound to arise. Sooner or later, a major European power would acquire control of a Latin American country, either by conquest or by gaining command over its economy and finances. This would pose a direct challenge to the Monroe Doctrine, which Roosevelt and the United States took far more seriously after the Spanish-American War.

Roosevelt considered two alternatives beyond the enforcement of the traditional injunctions of the Monroe Doctrine. The first of these was suggested by the Argentine foreign minister, Dr. Luís Drago. He proposed a new international principle: public debts should not justify the use of force or territorial occupation. This Drago Doctrine, however, contradicted the European and American diplomatic tradition that a nation had the right to protect the lives and property of its citizens abroad. Roosevelt was willing to accept the Drago Doctrine, but he insisted that if a debtor nation refused to submit the issue to arbitration, then force was justified. He supported this modified Drago Doctrine in 1907 at the Hague Conference, which accepted it.

Many Latin American nations refused to sign the Hague modification of the Drago Doctrine because they rejected forcible collection of debts under any circumstances. The United States also had an incentive to ignore the Hague agreement. In the arbitration of the Venezuelan debt following the second Venezuelan crisis, the arbitrators favored the debts of the British and Germans over those of the United States. Since the British and Germans had used force to secure their debts while the United States had not, Roosevelt feared this precedent would undermine whatever authority was left to the Drago Doctrine after so many Latin American countries had refused to sign it.

Roosevelt turned to a very different alternative. He declared that if worse came to worst, the United States itself would intervene in Latin America to see that Latin American nations behaved justly toward their European creditors. U.S. intervention would eliminate any pretext for European intervention. This policy of "preventive intervention" became known as the Roosevelt Corollary to the Monroe Doctrine.

The occasion for Roosevelt's announcement was a crisis in the Dominican Republic. The Dominican Republic was the scene of continuous political and economic chaos. In seventy years, it had had nineteen revolutions and fifty-three presidents. The latest civil war had broken out in 1903, while European creditors were clamoring for payment of their debts and their war vessels sailed Dominican waters. In 1904 the harassed Dominican president asked the United States to intervene by sending arms, guaranteeing Dominican sovereignty, and paying its debts. Roosevelt had no desire for a new territory. He said he would as soon annex the island as "swallow a porcupine wrong-end-to."

He suggested that the United States take over Dominican customs collections, pay off creditors, and turn the remainder of the revenue over to the Dominican government. The suspicious Dominicans accepted out of fear of the Europeans, but the U.S. Senate recoiled after hearing Roosevelt claim that in cases of "chronic wrongdoing, or impotence" among Western Hemisphere nations, the United States "however reluctantly" would have to exercise "an international police power." Roosevelt seemed ready to extend the Platt Amendment to the whole of the Caribbean and Central America.

Roosevelt established the Dominican customs house receivership on his own authority until the balky Senate finally accepted the treaty with the Dominican Republic in 1907. Yet he hoped to keep the intervention limited and to avoid any further ones. He managed to do so until the end of his term; his successors were not so fortunate.

The Monroe Doctrine in U.S. Popular Culture

The very fact that Theodore Roosevelt associated his announcement of U.S. policy toward Latin America with the Monroe Doctrine is a tribute to the power of that doctrine in U.S. popular opinion. As John A. Kasson, a prominent Republican politician and diplomat, pointed out in 1881, the Monroe Doctrine ranked as chief among "the very few maxims which serve to guide public opinion in our country. . . . It may be said to indicate the only established idea of foreign policy which has had a permanent influence upon our national administration. It has also taken fast hold on the popular mind. A president of the United States justly appealing to it in an emergency, could not fail of unanimous following of patriotic citizens, even in the presence of a consequently impending war. It touches the instinct of national safety, and of pride in our national institutions." But because the Monroe Doctrine had such a powerful influence on popular opinion, Americans of all sorts fought over its meaning and sought to enlist it on the side of their own ambitions.

The Republican platform in 1900 tried to convince voters that Republicans were strong adherents to the Monroe Doctrine by pointing out that the McKinley administration was abstaining from interference in the European sphere even though it was intervening well outside the Western Hemisphere in the Philippines and elsewhere. "We assert our steadfast adherence to the policy announced in the Monroe Doctrine. . . . [T]he American Government must continue the policy prescribed by Washington, affirmed by every succeeding President and imposed upon us by The Hague treaty, of non-intervention in European controversies." Yet, the platform went on to assert, "No other course was possible than to destroy Spain's sovereignty throughout the West Indies and in the Philippine Islands."

The Democratic platform insisted that the Republicans were violating the Monroe Doctrine while the Democrats were the true adherents of its sacred principles, which included not just abstinence from affairs outside the Western Hemisphere and the exclusion of Europe from American affairs, but also the supremacy of the United States in the Western Hemisphere. "The declaration in the Republican platform adopted at the Philadelphia Convention, held in June, 1900, that the Republican Party 'steadfastly adheres to the policy announced in the Monroe Doctrine' is manifestly insincere and deceptive. This profession is contradicted by the avowed policy of that party in opposition to the spirit of the Monroe Doctrine to acquire and hold sovereignty over large areas of territory and large numbers of people in the Eastern Hemisphere. We insist on the strict maintenance of the Monroe Doctrine in all its integrity, both in letter and in spirit, as necessary to prevent the extension of European authority on this Continent and as essential to our supremacy in American affairs."

Before the Spanish-American War and Roosevelt's announcement of his corollary, there had been at least some leaders of opinion in the United States who tried to limit the expansive influence of the Monroe Doctrine. In an 1889 article in *Forum*, H.C. Bunts argued that it had certainly not been the intention of the doctrine's original authors "to proclaim to the World that the United States had arrogated to themselves exclusive guardianship over the entire western hemisphere." But the outlook of most people in the United States toward Latin Americans made intervention seem almost inevitable. Richard Harding Davis, author of a wildly popular novel, *Soldiers of Fortune*, about an American engineer in a mythical republic of South America, both represented and influenced that outlook. Davis's hero does more than just bring modern efficiency to a mine where the "people know [the ore] is there, but they have no knowledge of its value, and are too lazy to ever work it themselves." He also helps the people of the nation avoid takeovers by Spanish sympathizers and revolutionary dictators. As Davis advised in another of his travel narratives: "The Central American citizen is no more fit for a republican form of government than he is for an Arctic expedition, and what he needs is to have a protectorate established over him, either by the United States or by another power, it does not matter so long as it leaves the Nicaragua Canal in our hands." Theodore Roosevelt proclaimed that Davis's writings "form a text-book of Americanism."[1]

William Howard Taft and Dollar Diplomacy in Central America

Taft tried to avoid interventions under the Platt Amendment or the Roosevelt Corollary by stabilizing Latin American regimes through the infusion of private American capital. The new bureaucracy in the State Department advocated this dollar diplomacy in Latin America just as it did in China. Just as in China, the policy brought little but trouble.

Roosevelt had tried to promote stability in Central America by sponsoring a tenuous treaty arrangement among the fractious republics of the area. Taft tried to secure the area further by negotiating a customs receivership in Honduras to stave off potential British intervention. The arrangement was frustrated by the objections of the U.S. Senate and by various Honduran governments and agencies embroiled in their own civil wars.

In Nicaragua, Taft used greater force to accompany his dollar diplomacy. Nicaragua was meddling in other Central American states, including Honduras, and had contracted major loans with British institutions. Taft and Secretary of State Philander Knox threw their support to a rebellion that promised a more pliant regime. They landed U.S. Marines in rebel-held territory to protect North American property and lives, just incidentally deterring the government from reconquest. After many twists and turns, the U.S.-sponsored government took power, and it accepted an American loan and a customs receivership to guarantee repayment. The U.S. Senate delayed its consent to the arrangement, but under Knox's urging, U.S. banks funded the loan anyway. These North American financiers also established the Bank of Nicaragua and chartered a corporation for operating Nicaragua's rail and steamship lines, all in defiance of the Nicaraguan constitution, which forbade special concessions to foreigners. U.S. Marines then helped to put down another rebellion that charged the incumbent Nicaraguan regime with selling out to Wall Street. As the marines withdrew, leaving behind a 100-man legation force to keep order, Taft and Knox proclaimed their policy of stabilizing Central American economies a success.

Woodrow Wilson and Missionary Diplomacy in the Caribbean

Woodrow Wilson disagreed with Taft's proclamation that dollar diplomacy had been successful. As he had criticized such diplomacy in Asia for its selfish economic motivations and its favors to Wall Street, so he denounced the loans and customs receiverships in Nicaragua and Honduras. Wilson apologized to Colombia for Roosevelt's "taking" of Panama and tried to get Congress to appropriate $25 million as compensation. He also announced that the United States would never seek another foot of territory in Latin America.[2] Although neither Roosevelt nor Taft had sought more territory, Wilson's pledge, along with his denunciation of dollar diplomacy as unwarranted interference in the affairs of sovereign nations, implied that he would seek a less interventionist policy than his predecessors.

Yet for all Wilson's denunciations of dollar diplomacy, he still assumed that an orderly, free economy open to "legitimate" U.S. trade was a vital part of the proper democratic system every nation should enjoy. His devout belief in democratic political procedures and a free economy actually gave Wilson the incentive to intervene in the affairs of the Caribbean and Central American nations even more often than the strategic doctrines of Roosevelt or the dollar diplomacy of Taft. Critics branded Wilson's ideological interventionism "missionary diplomacy," and it quickly became clear that his inclination toward missionary diplomacy would override his initial commitment to nonintervention when he militarily occupied the two nations that shared the island of Hispaniola, Haiti and the Dominican Republic.

The most systematic and extensive of these interventions took place in Haiti. That country had had a long history of suffering and turmoil since the legendary slave revolt led by Toussaint L'Ouverture at the turn of the nineteenth century. American ships and marines had intervened there eight times between 1867 and 1900 to protect American lives and property. A thin upper class of French-speaking Creoles arbitrarily and rather contemptuously ruled a great mass of peasants. The elite was tied to France by culture, religion, and the exchange of Haitian coffee for French tobacco. An influential coterie of German merchants also resided in Haiti. U.S. economic interests were less important than those of France or Germany until 1900. Then a rapid rise of activity brought the United States control of 60 percent of Haiti's import market by 1910. With State Department support, U.S. bankers pried their way into a French and German consortium that controlled Haiti's national bank. The 50 percent share they acquired allowed the United States to dominate Haiti's customs office, since the bank was empowered to collect customs duties.

Before the Spanish-American War, Haiti's fine port at Môle St. Nicholas had given the country strategic importance, and the United States had tried to secure the harbor several times. After the United States had acquired Puerto Rico and Guantánamo in Cuba, the Haitian port seemed less important. But the United States still did not want to see Môle St. Nicholas fall into the hands of a rival European power like Germany. The continuing turmoil in Haiti thus led to considerable sentiment for intervention in the State and War Departments of the United States. American bankers also encouraged such interventionist sentiments in hopes of gaining government protection for their financial concessions.

Racial prejudices inclined American officials to think the worst of Haiti's potential for stable and humane government. These prejudices were reinforced by the fact that between 1911 and 1915, seven of Haiti's presidents were assassinated or forcibly removed from office, one of them by being blown up in his palace. The final incentive for Wilson's intervention came in 1915 when the Haitian president tortured and executed 167 political prisoners and in turn was dismembered by angry revolutionaries.

The United States had already made the decision to intervene if fighting broke out in the capital because a staunch opponent of U.S. influence seemed prepared to overturn the government. Wilson sent in marines, established martial law, and installed a hand-picked government. The marines forced this government to accept a treaty empowering the United States to supervise Haiti's customs collection and finances, establish schools, build roads, and train a National Guard. The marines and their National Guard protégés then carried on a running battle with bands of Haitians who were menacing the roads the Americans were building with conscripted labor. Americans also began buying land in Haiti after forcing repeal of Haiti's constitutional provision prohibiting foreigners from owning property.

U.S. military courts constituted the Haitian judicial system until 1929. The Americans improved government efficiency and established roads and schools, but at great cost. A rebellion in 1919 cost 3,000 Haitian lives. American racism was rampant and bred much resentment. The second U.S. commander in Haiti, U.S. Marine Colonel Littleton W.T. Waller, expressed his disgust with the necessity of "bowing and scraping to these coons." The Haitian National Guard, organized by the United States to maintain order, became a force of its own. The Guard, continuing the conscription of labor after the U.S. occupiers had formally abandoned it, waited to take control when the United States left.

A year after U.S. Marines landed in Haiti, they occupied the neighboring Dominican Republic. The United States had operated the Dominican Republic's customs since 1905, maintaining financial and political stability there while satisfying the country's European creditors. Such stability demonstrated the virtue of the customs receivership to many Americans. The United States failed to recognize how much Dominican stability owed to that nation's powerful president, Ramón Cáceres. When Cáceres was shot in 1911, the country became a revolving door for presidents, each of whom gutted the treasury before he abandoned office. The Dominican Republic was left with no public sanitation, a 90 percent illiteracy rate, only forty miles of roads, and not a single public school. Bandits roamed the interior, and even the capital city became a wasteland.

The Taft administration intervened briefly in 1912 to end one civil war by helping to install a provisional president. The civil war resumed immediately after the U.S. ship left, however, and the provisional president resigned. Pressing the Dominican factions to end the turmoil, Wilson's administration insisted that the United States be given supervisory control to ensure free elections and clean government. When even the factions most sympathetic to the United States resisted, the marines landed. After a brief effort to find a compliant government, the American military took full control. It tried to confiscate all private weapons, and it replaced the politicized National Guard with a new independent one officered primarily by Americans. Again the United States built roads, established schools, provided public sanitation, and reformed government finances, yet the occupation raised almost universal resentment against the U.S. overlords. In addition to the racism that plagued the United States' reputation everywhere it intervened, the occupation authorities established a particularly noxious press censorship. And, as in Haiti, Cuba, Panama, and Nicaragua, the National Guard established under U.S. auspices overran its bounds once the U.S. occupation ended.

Missionary Diplomacy in Mexico

Wilson's intervention in Mexico was more sensational than his interventions elsewhere, but Mexico's size and the power of its nationalist resistance also made the intervention much shorter and more embarrassing. In the thirty-five years before the Mexican Revolution of 1910, General Porfirio Díaz's dictatorship had given the United States little reason to consider intervention. Díaz's ruthlessness had provided order and rapid economic growth, and he had invited U.S. businesses to share the profits. The United States was the market for 75 percent of Mexico's exports. Europeans shared more equally in Mexico's import markets, investments, and loan portfolios, but Americans dominated the railroads and communications. Americans owned many of Mexico's mines and much of its agricultural land; after 1901 they invested heavily along with the British in the extraction of oil.

Foreign economic domination naturally roused nationalist antagonism in Mexico. Resentment was especially strong toward the United States, the most prominent foreign presence and the well-remembered despoiler of Texas, California, and the Southwest. Even Díaz, who generally welcomed foreign investment, disliked the dominance of foreign technicians and the use of English as the official language on the railroads. He began to buy out foreign investors. When his grip on the country faltered, there was a reservoir of anti-American nationalism ready to be tapped by the revolutionary contenders for his power.

A loose alliance of local leaders headed by Francisco Madero finally overthrew Díaz in 1911. Fighting then broke out between Madero and his erstwhile allies, who included Francisco "Pancho" Villa, Bernardo Reyes, and Emiliano Zapata. Madero had to rely on the regular army, led by Victoriano Huerta, to suppress these local rebellions. Huerta ultimately joined Madero's enemies, overthrew and murdered him, and then made himself provisional president.

President Taft and Secretary of State Knox followed a cautious policy toward the revolution. Madero had considerable sympathy in the United States, and Taft and Knox had no desire to get entangled in Mexican politics. On the other hand, their ambassador to Mexico, Henry Lane Wilson, had no such compunctions. He regarded Madero as a visionary and wrote urgent, distorted analyses of Madero's supposed radicalism and anti-Americanism. Before Madero's overthrow, Huerta worked out an agreement with the other rebel leaders at the American embassy under the auspices of Henry Lane Wilson. The ambassador also did nothing to prevent Madero's murder.

Henry Lane Wilson's policies and actions came under strong criticism from American liberals and certain sectors of the press, who pointed out the ambassador's connections to American investment interests that had long opposed the Madero family. Taft consequently resisted the ambassador's urging to recognize Huerta's government immediately, leaving the touchy issue to the new American president, Woodrow Wilson. Woodrow Wilson came to office with little knowledge of Mexico, but with strong liberal commitments to legitimate democratic practices at home and abroad. He decided to make Mexico an example of the virtues of democracy. He told Huerta that the United States would withhold recognition of his government until Huerta established a cease-fire and held proper elections in which he would refrain from running. When Huerta balked, Wilson dismissed Ambassador Wilson and cut off arms to Huerta's government. Huerta persuaded President Wilson to cut off arms to his opponents as well by hinting that he would not run in the coming elections. As Huerta saw his power slipping, however, he arrested most of his congressional opponents, declared the subsequent election void, and stayed on as provisional president.

Woodrow Wilson responded by trying to induce the European powers to withhold recognition and arms. Then he settled down to a policy he called "watchful waiting" as various Mexican rebel groups under the umbrella title of Constitutionalists carried on the fight against Huerta. The Republican Party ridiculed Wilson's policy and demanded vigorous military intervention in Mexico to ensure stability and protect American economic interests. As the turmoil in Mexico continued and Republican political pressure mounted, Wilson removed the embargo on arms to the Constitutionalists.

Then he found the opportunity for an even more sensational gesture. In April 1914, an American naval vessel patrolling Mexico's gulf coast sent a whaleboat ashore to purchase gasoline, only to have the crew arrested by Mexican soldiers for trespassing. The Mexican commanding officer released the eight crewmen with an apology in a couple of hours, but the American fleet commander demanded far more—a written apology, a court-martial for the arresting officer, and a twenty-one-gun salute to the American flag. President Wilson supported him and ordered the Atlantic fleet to Mexico. He did not want a confrontation, but he insisted on the twenty-one-gun salute, and he let it be known to Huerta that the United States would return the salute. When Huerta continued to hesitate, Wilson ordered the occupation of Vera Cruz, Mexico's second city.

After a bloody invasion costing 100 American and 500 Mexican casualties, Americans took the city. But Wilson did not know what to do with it. American intervention had strengthened Huerta's position in his country rather than weakened it. Wilson wanted to withdraw as quickly as possible, yet saw no way to do it gracefully. His chance came when the ABC powers—Argentina, Brazil, and Chile—offered mediation. Wilson accepted but insisted that the settlement include replacement of Huerta's government by the Constitutionalists until new elections could be held. Even the leader of the Constitutionalists, Venustiano Carranza, refused such direct interference in Mexico's internal affairs. Carranza took power on his own two weeks after the ABC mediation had offered a meaningless declaration to paper over the Mexican-American dispute. He refused to hold elections or cater to America in any way—and he left the embarrassed Wilson still with no graceful way out of Vera Cruz.

Finally, Carranza found himself in desperate need of the port at Vera Cruz to defeat the rebellions of Pancho Villa and Emiliano Zapata. He pledged to avoid reprisals against collaborators and political opponents in Vera Cruz, and with this face-saving concession in hand, Wilson withdrew the American forces. Carranza immediately arrested or fired everyone who had cooperated with the Americans in Vera Cruz.

When Carranza's forces gained the upper hand over those of Villa and Zapata in the following year, 1915, Wilson decided to recognize the Carranza government. He also cut off arms to Carranza's opponents. Pancho Villa retaliated angrily: his troops massacred seventeen Americans while robbing a Mexican train, and Villa himself led a raid across the U.S. border on the New Mexico town of Columbus in March 1916. Against the protests of Carranza, Wilson sent a military force under General John Pershing into Mexico in pursuit. Pershing found himself fighting not just Villa's forces, but Carranza's troops and the populace of several towns as well. After one particularly fierce fight with Carranza's troops at Carrizal, open war between Mexico and the United States seemed probable. Perhaps it was prevented only by the growing conflict with Germany that ultimately led the United States into World War I. In February 1917, the distracted Wilson withdrew Pershing's troops unilaterally.

Relations between Mexico and the United States remained strained in the succeeding years. Germany even proposed an alliance to Mexico if the United States entered World War I on the Allied side. Germany offered the reconquest of Texas and the Southwest as a reward. Mexico did not consider the offer seriously, but when the famous Zimmermann telegram proposing the alliance came to light, it reemphasized the tenuous state of Mexican-American relations. The constitution adopted by Carranza's revolutionary government damaged relations even further. It established a liberal labor code to be enforced against foreign as well as Mexican employers. The constitution also gave the Mexican government the right to expropriate any property necessary for the good of the Mexican society. Carranza could take over foreign investments in Mexico's mines, agricultural land, and oil fields. He began by imposing a royalty tax on oil drillers. Thus he directly challenged America's commitment to protect the property of its citizens abroad.

Wilson protested but kept a low profile to avoid war, since the United States was deeply involved in the European conflict and needed Mexican oil. Wilson's dilemma in Mexico illustrated the basic issues that would bedevil American relationships with the third world in the twentieth century. America's interest in foreign trade and investment would often conflict with indigenous economic interests, beget dislike of economic dependence on the United States, and lead to conflict if the United States adhered to its historic belief in the right of a nation to protect the property of its citizens abroad. American insistence on stability and to a lesser extent on democratic procedures in nations of strategic or economic importance would lead to military interventions. American racial and cultural prejudices, borne by its military forces, merchants, missionaries, and travelers, further aroused nationalist resentments.

Some of these difficulties were no doubt inevitable. Relationships of weak to strong nations cannot help but be tinged with a degree of dependency and consequent resentment. Even the most enlightened nations and peoples tend to radiate a degree of cultural smugness and disdain for foreign ways. Regardless, many people will agree that a serious threat to vital national strategic and economic interests may justify forcible intervention. Yet it seems clear in retrospect that Germany, Great Britain, and Japan did not really jeopardize vital American interests in East Asia and Latin America. With the possible exception of the isthmian canal, it is difficult to find interests in East Asia and Latin America that the United States could rightly consider vital. Neither the strategic threats nor the economic trade and investments in those areas were significant enough to justify the extent and forcefulness of America's interventions in this pre–World War I era. A more restrained diplomacy could have protected most American interests without breeding the resentment that America's imperial surge did.

Controversial Issues

American historians writing after the Spanish-American War almost unanimously supported American intervention in Central America and the Caribbean as necessary to national security. Although they were not very enthusiastic about it, they could not bring themselves to oppose it outright. They often demonstrated their reluctance by accompanying their defense of the Roosevelt Corollary or dollar diplomacy with ironic asides about the self-righteousness of Americans in denying their imperialistic tendencies.[3] Their reluctance also could show up in partisanship. Democratic historians often limited their criticisms of intervention to those undertaken by Republicans, especially Roosevelt's "taking" of Panama. Republicans, on the other hand, praised Roosevelt's interventions while ridiculing Woodrow Wilson for trying to remove the problems of Latin American republics by "removing their independence."[4] Still, historians were clearly in the interventionist camp.[5] Some even condemned Wilson for being too restrained in his policy toward Mexico.[6] The author of the only full condemnation of American intervention written in this period, Hiram Bingham, recanted only a few years later by saying that the United States owed it "to the progress of the world . . . to see to it that the republics of Tropical America behave."[7]

Following World War I, there was a general acknowledgment in the United States that military interventions in Latin America were undesirable and in many cases had been mistaken. This trend would culminate in the Good Neighbor Policy of the 1930s. Among historians, it would lead to a widespread belief that restraint toward Latin America was necessary, but significant divisions remained over the reasons for such restraint and over evaluations of America's past and present policies.

Nationalist historians generally defended America's past interventions as necessary under existing conditions to prevent the chaos that would have invited intervention by Germany or other European powers. Nationalists were ready to show more restraint following World War I because they said that the Latin American nations themselves were becoming more stable and capable of self-defense. This made U.S. intervention less necessary. Nationalist historians implied, however, that if instability were again to invite intervention by outside powers hostile to the United States, strategic interests would require the United States to resume its interventionist policy.[8]

Most historians since World War I have been more critical of America's military interventions. They have argued that neither Germany nor any other power posed a serious threat to American security in the Western Hemisphere in the early twentieth century. Therefore American interventions were generally mistaken overreactions to imaginary threats that did great harm to the image of the United States in the minds of Latin Americans. But most historians also implied that if ever there had been or were to be a true threat to American security, however remote the possibility, the United States would have to intervene. Liberal internationalists hoped the unpleasant necessity might be mitigated by making intervention a cooperative enterprise through international or regional organizations like the Organization of American States or the United Nations.[9] Realists urged that the United States simply face up to the fact that although it needed to use far more restraint in Latin America, "a nation which has tremendous economic strength and worldwide strategic concerns must develop a political philosophy which will take account of unavoidable dependency, whether it be economic or strategic, or as it sometimes must, political as well."[10]

As in the case of historians of U.S. Asian policy, these realist historians are generally less critical of Theodore Roosevelt's frankly power-oriented interventions than of Taft's idealistic dollar diplomacy or Wilson's even more idealistic missionary diplomacy. Also they do not believe American interventions were much motivated by narrow economic interests, but harshly condemn the few instances they find.[11]

Although some of these realist analyses of U.S.–Latin American relations can be quite critical of American intervention, revisionist analyses are generally more so. Revisionists do not regard American policy as having been motivated by benevolent if mistaken liberalism or concerns for imaginary security threats. They see it as intentional rapine motivated mostly by economic greed.[12]

Further Reading

The best recent surveys of U.S. relations with Latin America are Lars Schoultz, *Beneath the United States: A History of U.S. Policy Toward Latin America* (1998), and Mark T. Gilderhus, *The Second Century: U.S.–Latin American Relations Since 1889* (2000), both written from a critical realist viewpoint; and Greg Grandin, *Empire's Workshop: Latin America, the United States, and the Rise of the New Imperialism* (2006), written from a revisionist viewpoint.

Notes

1. Gretchen Murphy, *Hemispheric Imaginings: The Monroe Doctrine and Narratives of U.S. Empire* (2005).

2. Apparently he did not regard purchasing the Virgin Islands from Denmark under threat of seizure (as he did in 1916) to be in violation of this pledge.

3. See, for example, Archibald Cary Coolidge, *The United States as a World Power* (1918).

4. For criticism of Roosevelt's intervention, see John Holladay Latané, *America as a World Power* (1907). For defenses of Roosevelt accompanied by criticisms of Wilson, see Albert Bushnell Hart, *The Monroe Doctrine: An Interpretation* (1916).

5. Chester Lloyd Jones, *Caribbean Interests of the United States* (1916).

6. See, for example, Frederick A. Ogg, *National Progress, 1907–1917* (1918).

7. Hiram Bingham, *The Monroe Doctrine: An Obsolete Shibboleth* (1913). For his recanting, see Thomas L. Karnes, "Hiram Bingham and His Obsolete Shibboleth," *Diplomatic History* (Winter 1979).

8. The classic work of this genre is Samuel Flagg Bemis, *The Latin American Policy of the United States: An Historical Interpretation* (1943). Another broad text with a similar outlook is J. Lloyd Mechem, *A Survey of United States–Latin American Relations* (1965). Works in this vein restricted to the Caribbean are Chester Lloyd Jones, *The Caribbean Since 1900* (1916); and Howard C. Hill, *Roosevelt and the Caribbean* (1927). On Cuba, see Russell Fitzgibbon, *Cuba and the United States, 1900–1935* (1935); and two later works that argue that the United States abandoned its occupation too soon, Allan R. Millet, *The Politics of Intervention: The Military Occupation of Cuba, 1906–1909* (1968); and James Hitchman, *Leonard Wood and Cuban Independence, 1898–1902* (1971). Not many historians since World War II have been willing to defend America's post–Spanish-American War interventions, but Julius W. Pratt's survey *America's Colonial Experiment: How the United States Gained, Governed, and in Part Gave Away a Colonial Empire* (1950) is considerably more sympathetic to the occupations than one might have expected from his earlier books.

9. See, for example, Dexter Perkins, *A History of the Monroe Doctrine* (1963); and J. Fred Rippy, *The Caribbean Danger Zone* (1940).

10. Whitney T. Perkins, *Denial of Empire: The United States and Its Dependencies* (1962), p. 351.

11. Broad surveys that criticize the United States from a realist outlook are Lars Schoultz, *Beneath the United States: A History of U.S. Policy Toward Latin America* (1998); Mark T. Gilderhus, *The Second Century: U.S.–Latin American Relations Since 1889* (2000); and Lester D. Langley, *The United States and the Caribbean in the Twentieth Century* (1989). See also Thomas J. Leonard, *Central America and the United States: A Search for Stability* (1991). The classic survey of U.S. policy toward the Caribbean is Dana G. Munro, *Intervention and Dollar Diplomacy in the Caribbean, 1900–1921* (1960). Another excellent work emphasizing the political aspects of American intervention is Whitney Perkins, *Constraints of Empire: The United States and Caribbean Interventions* (1981). For Theodore Roosevelt's policies, see Richard H. Collin, *Theodore Roosevelt, Culture, Diplomacy, and Expansion: A New View of American Imperialism* (1985); and Howard K. Beale, *Theodore Roosevelt and the Rise of America to World Power* (1956). For Taft's dollar diplomacy, see Walter V. Scholes and Marie V. Scholes, *The Foreign Policies of the Taft Administration* (1970). For Wilson's missionary diplomacy, see Arthur Link's multivolume biography, *Woodrow Wilson* (1947–). For Mexico, see Jurgen Buchenau, *In the Shadow of the Giant: The Making of Mexico's Central American Policy, 1876–1930* (1996); Josefina Zoraida Vasquez and Lorenzo Meyer, *The United States and Mexico* (1985); Karl M. Schmitt, *Mexico and the United States* (1974); P. Edward Haley, *Revolution and Intervention: The Diplomacy of Taft and Wilson with Mexico, 1910–1917* (1970); Kenneth J. Grieb, *The United States and Huerta* (1969); and Robert E. Quirk, *An Affair of Honor: Woodrow Wilson and the Occupation of Vera Cruz* (1962), an excellent book. For Cuba, see Lester D. Langley, *The Cuban Policy of the United States* (1968).

12. One of the oldest of these analyses is that of Scott Nearing and Joseph Freeman, *Dollar Diplomacy: A Study in American Imperialism* (1925). A somewhat milder book, and an excellent one, is Leland H. Jenks, *Our Cuban Colony: A Study in Sugar* (1928). Critical surveys of U.S.–Latin American relations that emphasize the economic dimension are Greg Grandin, *Empire's Workshop: Latin America, the United States, and the Rise of the New Imperialism* (2006); Cole Blasier, *Hovering Giant: United States Responses to Revolutionary Change in Latin America* (1978); and Gordon Connell-Smith, *The*

United States and Latin America: An Historical Analysis of Inter-American Relations (1974). For a look at Cuba from the revisionist point of view, see Jules Robert Benjamin, *The United States and Cuba: Hegemony and Dependent Development, 1880–1934* (1977); and Louis A. Perez Jr., *Cuba Under the Platt Amendment, 1902–1934* (1986). A milder revisionist account is David F. Healy, *The United States in Cuba, 1898–1902: Generals, Politicians, and the Search for Policy* (1963). The best revisionist work on Panama is Walter LaFeber, *The Panama Canal: The Crisis in Historical Perspective* (updated ed., 1989).

For other works on Panama, see J. Michael Hogan, *The Panama Canal in American Politics* (1986); Julie Greene, *The Canal Builders: Making America's Empire at the Panama Canal* (2009); and Alexander Missal, *Seaway to the Future: American Social Visions and the Construction of the Panama Canal* (2008). For Haiti, see Mary A. Renda, *Taking Haiti: Military Occupation and the Culture of U.S. Imperialism* (2001); and Hans Schmidt, *The United States Occupation of Haiti, 1915–1934* (1971). For Santo Domingo, see Bruce J. Calder, *The Impact of Intervention: The Dominican Republic during the U.S. Occupation of 1916–1924* (1984). For Mexico, see Robert F. Smith, *The United States and Revolutionary Nationalism in Mexico, 1916–1932* (1972); and Friedrich Katz, *The Secret War in Mexico: Europe, the U.S. and the Mexican Revolution* (1981). For Puerto Rico, see Gordon Lewis, *Puerto Rico* (1963); Arturo Morales Carrion, *Puerto Rico: A Political and Cultural History* (1983); Ronald Fernandez, *The Disenchanted Island: Puerto Rico and the United States in the Twentieth Century* (2nd ed., 1996); and Julian Go, *American Empire and the Politics of Meaning* (2008).

To view the U.S. surge into Latin America through the eyes of the Latin Americans themselves, see Warren Dean, ed., *Diplomatic Claims: Latin American Historians View the United States* (1985).

CHAPTER 4

EUROPE, AMERICA, AND WORLD WAR I

Germany Disrupts the European Balance of Power

The rise of the United States and Japan at the end of the nineteenth century challenged the stability of the international system and resulted in three potentially disruptive conflicts: the Sino-Japanese, Russo-Japanese, and Spanish-American Wars. But at least the United States and Japan intruded into areas relatively remote from the existing major powers of Europe. No similar power vacuums cushioned the rise of Germany in the late nineteenth and early twentieth centuries. When Germany joined the roster of world powers, it threatened the heart of Europe and disturbed the precarious balance that had been the basis of peace since the defeat of Napoleon.

In 1860 Germany had been little more than a geographical expression, thirty-nine principalities sharing a heritage of German language and culture but little sense of political or economic unity. The central plain of Europe offered few natural boundaries, and Germans were mixed liberally into surrounding areas such as Schleswig-Holstein (Denmark), Alsace-Lorraine (France), Luxembourg (Holland), Switzerland, Austria, Poland, and the Baltic fringes of Russia.

The architect of modern Germany was the chancellor of Prussia, Otto von Bismarck. Using the small but efficient Prussian army, he combined with Austria to seize Schleswig-Holstein from Denmark. Then he turned on his Austrian ally in a contest for influence over the numerous principalities that lay between the two Germanic rivals. Bismarck won this war at the Battle of Sadowa in 1866, but he refrained from occupying Vienna and managed to avoid alienating Austria permanently.

Five years later, Bismarck's rising Germany shocked Europe by attacking and defeating France. Bismarck was not as successful in reconciling France to its defeat as he had been in pacifying Austria. His military commander, the great Prussian general Helmuth von Moltke, refused to accept the easily defended Rhine River as Germany's western border. Instead, he insisted on annexing Alsace-Lorraine, with its large French population, in order to secure the province's resources of iron ore and a defensive perimeter in the Vosges Mountains. The annexation all but guaranteed permanent Franco-German enmity. To sustain the memory of its lost territory, France draped black veils over the statues in Paris's Place de la Concorde that represented the capital cities of Alsace and Lorraine.

Following the Franco-Prussian War, Bismarck set out to protect his new Germany by juggling the balance of power among the major European states. After winning an alliance with Austria in 1879, he lured Russia into the arrangement by emphasizing the common interest of the emperors of Germany, Austria, and Russia in resisting France. Although France had lost most of its revolutionary fervor domestically, it continued to advocate liberalism and nationalism in the rest of Europe. The nationalism that France encouraged in Poland worried the three empires especially, since they had divided Poland among them in the previous century.

Bismarck had to work mightily to hold the Three Emperor Alliance together. Russia and Austria could agree on Poland and France, but they were bitter antagonists in the Balkans. There Russia encouraged the rebellions of its kindred Orthodox Slavs against the rule of Ottoman Turkey, "the sick man of Europe," in order to extend the czar's sway through the Balkan Slavs to the Dardanelles. These straits would give the Russian navy access from the Black Sea into the Mediterranean. Austria feared that the independence movements Russia was encouraging would spread to Slavic groups within the Austro-Hungarian Empire and rip that multiethnic state to shreds. Bismarck dampened some of this Balkan rivalry between his allies by acting as an "honest broker" in the area and by encouraging Russia to direct its expansion toward China and India, where it would not conflict with the interests of Austria or Germany.

Bismarck's convoluted policy began to unravel when Kaiser Wilhelm II came to the German throne in 1888. Wilhelm found Bismarck's policy too conservative and constraining. He dismissed the Iron Chancellor and permitted the treaty of alliance with Russia to lapse. France leaped at the chance to end its isolation in Europe, loaned money to the czar, and in 1898 began a series of contracts and agreements that led to a military entente. Europe looked on aghast as the autocratic czar of Russia bared his head at the playing of the "Marseillaise," the anthem of revolutionary France. Kaiser Wilhelm naturally drew closer to Austria. Then both Germany and France began casting half-apprehensive, half-inviting glances at Great Britain.

Great Britain stood aloof from most of this maneuvering. So long as no European nation threatened the British Isles directly, Great Britain preferred to concentrate on its overseas imperial interests, especially the Suez Canal, India, China, and southern Africa. These interests brought the British more frequently into conflict with France and Russia than with Germany or Austria. France, whose citizens had built the Suez Canal, challenged Britain for control of Egypt and the Mediterranean, Britain's lifeline to India. France and Great Britain came dangerously close to war in 1898 when rival military expeditions confronted each other at the small Egyptian-Sudanese outpost of Fashoda. France, finding itself at a military disadvantage, withdrew, but the Fashoda Incident was almost enough to make France forget Alsace-Lorraine and turn to Germany for help against Britain. France's ally Russia also posed a major threat to Britain. Russia's push toward the Dardenelles made Britain fear for its control of the Mediterranean and Suez. Russian pressure on Persia and Afghanistan threatened the British colony of India. Russian movement into Manchuria, Korea, and northern China challenged the British position in southern China as well.

Compared to Britain's problems with France and Russia, Bismarck's cautious probes for colonies in Africa and the Pacific (such as Samoa) seemed minor, temporary irritants. Neither Bismarck nor Kaiser Wilhelm looked on Great Britain with any special enmity, although both German statesmen found it necessary to protect the imperial throne and the aristocratic class structure against rising German liberalism by appealing to German nationalism with bold foreign policy adventures that challenged the position of Britain and its empire.

Bismarck had managed to limit his expansionist initiatives enough to avoid provoking a permanent alliance of offended powers against him. The kaiser did not. He angered London by demanding that it leave railroad concessions in Turkey to Germany, and he began to build a railroad to Baghdad. He sent his flamboyant Jameson telegram of support to the Boers of South Africa, denying British claims to the Transvaal. To support his push for overseas colonies, he began a huge naval building program in 1897 and extended it in 1900. The fleet he built in his North Sea ports seemed aimed particularly at Great Britain's traditional naval supremacy. At the instigation of the kaiser's chief naval adviser, Grand Admiral Alfred von Tirpitz, Germany constructed battleships capable of taking on the British fleet, rather than fast cruisers that might raid colonial commerce. The kaiser and Tirpitz drummed up domestic support for their heavy naval expenditures with shrill anti-British rhetoric.

A surge of German industrial and military growth accompanied all these developments. For two centuries France had been the major continental power, but by 1910 Germany towered over its rival. Germany led France in population by 65 to 39 million, in coal production by 222 to 38 million tons, in steel by 14 to 3 million tons. The German army also replaced that of France as the most powerful in Europe. Germany pioneered the efficient general staff system, the development of elaborate contingency war plans, and the use of masses of trained civilian reserves to supplement professional troops. After 1910 Germany sought to improve on its advantages by doubling its military appropriation. None of its neighbors could afford to match this expenditure.

Even before 1910, the British began to fear that Germany could overrun France and the Low Countries, which would make possible a successful invasion of England. Since Germany's industrial output surpassed that of Great Britain as well as France and since Germany's navy seemed intent on challenging British supremacy, Britain grew nervous about its policy of "splendid isolation" and its emphasis on imperial affairs. To counter Germany's threat to the European balance of power, Britain sought to resolve its conflicts with the United States. Great Britain accepted a secondary status in the American sphere and returned its Western Hemisphere fleet to home waters to guard against the German threat from the continent. It concluded an alliance with Japan in 1902 to protect British interests in East Asia, thus enabling it to bring home major elements of its Asian fleet as well. It began a bitter internal debate over the possibility of abandoning its open market policy in the British Empire to protect British commerce from the rising economic power of Germany. Finally, in 1904, Great Britain and France determined to put aside the bitterness of the Fashoda Incident and move toward a closer understanding. France traded its claims in Egypt for British support of the French colonial position in the rest of North Africa.

The United States and the European Balance of Power: The Algeciras Conference

The reconciliation between Great Britain and France shocked Germany. Leading German diplomats wanted to disrupt the Anglo-French entente before it could be extended from a minor colonial agreement to a continental alliance aimed against Germany. They believed that if they challenged French control of Morocco, where Germany also had some treaty claims, Great Britain would back away, exposing the hollowness of its support for France. The German army approved the timing of this challenge because France's ally, Russia, had been at least temporarily shattered by its humiliating defeat in the Russo-Japanese War of 1904 and the subsequent abortive revolution of 1905. The German navy, however, opposed the Moroccan maneuver because its fleet was not ready to confront Great Britain. Even the kaiser was reluctant to trigger a crisis at that moment. Nevertheless, his foreign policy advisers bullied him into a visit to Morocco, where he delivered a speech encouraging the sultan to resist French supervision and make an independent agreement with Germany. Caught between the great powers, the sultan appealed for an international conference to resolve the issue.

Although the United States had stood apart from these European struggles, Kaiser Wilhelm sought the support of Theodore Roosevelt for the German position on Morocco. Wilhelm appealed to America's time-honored dislike of European colonialism and desire for open doors for trade by insisting that Germany sought nothing more than equality of treatment for all nations in Morocco. He warned that war might result if France disregarded German rights and interests in North Africa and that the victors might then partition China to America's disadvantage. The German ambassador to the United States, Roosevelt's personal friend Speck von Sternburg, tried to give further emphasis to the kaiser's goodwill toward the United States by writing Roosevelt that the kaiser would accept any advice Roosevelt chose to give him for a settlement. (Sternburg had been authorized only to say that the foreign ministry would urge the kaiser to abide by Roosevelt's suggestions.)

Roosevelt responded to this extraordinary expression of Germany's respect with much flattery and words of sympathy. But after the Venezuela crisis, Roosevelt harbored some concern about the growth of German power and intentions in the Western Hemisphere. He was more favorably disposed toward Great Britain because the British had removed the last barrier to Anglo-American friendship in 1903 by accepting the decision of an American-stacked commission on the disputed border between Canada and Alaska. So Roosevelt determined to use the influence Sternburg's indiscreet letter had given him to back France and preserve the Anglo-French entente in the face of German threats. He persuaded France to accept the call for a conference by promising that the United States would participate and support France against any German demands that Roosevelt considered unreasonable. Roosevelt hoped the conference would avoid war and at the same time maintain the balance of power against Germany's growing strength.

America's official delegates to the Algeciras Conference in Spain in 1906 operated strictly as observers. Behind the scenes, however, Roosevelt persuaded a reluctant Kaiser Wilhelm to accept French dominance in Morocco by threatening to publish Sternburg's letter, which supposedly committed the kaiser to abide by Roosevelt's advice. Afterward, Roosevelt ingenuously congratulated the kaiser on a diplomatic triumph. Thus Roosevelt helped avert war and maintain the Anglo-French entente. But, to his great frustration, he had to keep the full extent of his role in the outcome secret because he knew he had no support from the American people for meddling in European politics.

The Issue of Neutral Rights on the Eve of War

Roosevelt did not have to be so secretive about his role in the Second Hague Peace Conference of 1907. Like the First Hague Conference of 1899, the second conference was called by the Russian czar to discuss means of preventing or limiting war, and the American public approved of such efforts; but the results were disappointing. The conferees could not agree on military budget limitations, restrictions on the size of ships, reduction of army enlistment terms, or the composition and powers of a world court. They did agree on a modified version of the Drago Doctrine prohibiting forcible debt collection unless the debtor state refused arbitration, but most Latin American nations refused to sign.

In the Second Hague Conference's one concrete accomplishment, the conferees managed to set up an International Prize Court of Appeals to judge cases involving the rights of neutrals on the high seas. Unfortunately, they could not agree on the neutral rights that the court was supposed to enforce. They scheduled a conference to devise such a code in London the following year, when surprisingly Britain reversed its naval policy of centuries to agree to a broad range of neutral rights. The resultant formulation of international law, embodied in the Declaration of London of 1909, seemed to eliminate the issue that had driven Great Britain and the United States to war in 1812 and had hung over Anglo-American relations ever since.

But the Declaration of London masked internal disagreements over maritime issues in both nations, disagreements that would play a vital role in America's entry into World War I. Just as American diplomats were winning the long struggle for neutral rights at the Hague and London conferences, Alfred Thayer Mahan and some other important naval officers changed their views of America's interest in that struggle. Since the United States had become a major naval power, they wanted to avoid restrictions on its navy's operations and adopt the old British view of the rights of belligerents. (Some of these officers had the inflated notion that the Union navy had won the Civil War for the North by invoking the doctrine of continuous voyage to prevent neutrals from trading with the Confederacy through Mexico and thus circumventing the Union blockade.) For once Theodore Roosevelt ignored such strategic balance-of-power arguments and nonchalantly instructed his delegates to the London conference, including Mahan, to continue their traditional advocacy of neutral rights. The other delegates, overcoming Mahan's obstructionism, negotiated the London agreement.

The British delegation endorsed the Declaration of London amid almost equal confusion. The British navy supported the declaration's provisions on neutral rights because the admirals no longer thought it necessary to stop all neutral trade with Europe in wartime. If war broke out with Germany, the British navy planned only a limited blockade sufficient to draw the German battle fleet out of port so it could be destroyed. Thus Great Britain would not need to invoke the doctrine of continuous voyage to stop neutral trade from reaching Germany through nonbelligerent neighbors like the Netherlands. The British navy also was willing to restrict the contraband list, for the British Isles were far more dependent on imported food than they had been in Napoleonic times, and the declaration would prohibit the confiscation of food shipments as contraband.

A number of British leaders, however, challenged this strategy. These leaders, who came to be known as Continentalists, worried that the French might abandon the entente if the navy strategy were followed because it would leave France the entire burden of fighting the Germans on land. Besides, most Continentalists assumed that any potential war would be over quickly, like the Austro-Prussian, Franco-Prussian, and Russo-Japanese Wars. (They assumed that the only exception to the rule of short wars in the previous half-century, the American Civil War, had degenerated into a lengthy war of attrition only because American military men were inept amateurs.) In a short land war, a naval blockade, which took a long time to be effective, would be irrelevant.

Thanks to this disagreement, the naval strategists and the Continentalists never fully rationalized British strategy. The Continentalists, with their assumption that the next war would be too brief for a blockade to be effective, had little more objection to the neutral rights protected by the Declaration of London than their naval rivals. But the bickering between the two groups made it possible for those outside either clique to make their voices heard. Many of these outsiders in Parliament and the press denounced the declaration for giving up too many belligerent rights, while others condemned it for placing too few restrictions on the capture of food as contraband. Even politicians who considered such objections silly had difficulty resisting the political gains to be made by attacking the declaration. Consequently, Parliament deferred ratification time and again. When war finally came in 1914, the British still had not formally ratified the declaration, and as the war dragged on they once again turned to a rigid blockade that violated the neutral rights the Americans and Germans had both assumed would be universally accepted.

The Outbreak of World War I

While the Second Hague Conference and London Conference were seeking international agreement, Great Britain came to its own private arrangement with its longtime antagonist, Russia. Great Britain had believed it necessary to find some common ground with the ally of its entente partner. Russia, after its defeat at the hands of the Japanese, was ready to forgo the Asian ambitions that clashed with British interests and return its attention to European questions, particularly the Balkans. In this atmosphere, the British successfully urged the reconciliation of the interests of their Japanese ally with Russia, reached an accommodation with Russia on the Persian approaches to India, and tabled their historic opposition to Russian ambitions for the Dardanelles. This Anglo-Russian Entente of 1907 quickly brought cries of "encirclement" from Kaiser Wilhelm and his allies.

But the two great European alliances were not yet facing each other with unalloyed enmity. Russia and Austria even worked out a secret Balkan deal. Russia would stand by while Austria annexed Bosnia; Austria would not object when Russia took the Dardanelles. Suddenly, Austria double-crossed its rival in the Balkans by annexing Bosnia before Russia was ready to move. This betrayal added to the legacy of bitterness between the two nations. Tensions increased during the Second Balkan War of 1912–1913 in which Serbia, a Russian client and the chief Balkan instigator of the Slavic nationalism that threatened to destroy the Austro-Hungarian Empire, acquired another great bite of Turkey's territory. When the heir to the Austro-Hungarian throne, the Archduke Franz Ferdinand, and his wife were assassinated in Bosnia's capital city of Sarajevo by Bosnian Serbs who had entered Sarajevo with help from the Serbian secret police, the stage was set for calamity.

Austria used the occasion to send an ultimatum to Serbia with demands for control over its internal affairs. Austria purposely made the demands harsh enough to force a Serbian rejection and provide a reason for war. Foolishly, Kaiser Wilhelm promised support for whatever action Austria thought necessary in the wake of the assassination of the Hapsburg heir. Russia, having already been humiliated once by Austria in the Bosnian annexation affair, believed it could not afford to stand by again while Austria swallowed Russia's Serbian protectorate. Russia mobilized its troops along the Austrian border and then extended the mobilization along its German border as well.

Mobilization in that era constituted a threat almost guaranteeing war, for a mobilized nation using modern transportation could conquer an immobilized nation before any resistance could be mounted. So Germany mobilized against Russia. But Germany's plan for war with the entente, the so-called Schlieffen Plan, called for a holding action on the eastern front, where Germany thought the backward Russians would be very slow in bringing their potential force to bear, while an all-out invasion would quickly conquer a more formidable France. Consequently, Germany mobilized against the French as well as the Russians, and the French responded with their own mobilization.

As the continent plunged toward war, Great Britain wavered. The British cabinet appealed desperately for a mediated peace. It had forsworn British interests in the Balkans and might have stayed out of the war entirely if the conflict had remained limited to that area. But when the German armies slashed through neutral Belgium, threatening the conquest of France and the destruction of the continental balance of power, Great Britain honored its treaty obligations, declared war, and sent its expeditionary force to France.

The French and British finally managed to stop Germany's westward drive in the great Battle of the Marne. In turn, Germany thwarted a Russian invasion of Prussia. The war settled into a long and bloody stalemate. At the outset, the British had launched their long-planned attempt to draw the German fleet into battle by instituting a limited blockade of Germany. Then, as World War I degenerated into a prolonged war of attrition, Britain's allies pressed for a total blockage of trade to their enemies. The British never declared an official blockade. That would have required them to station ships directly at

Alignment of the European Powers in World War I, 1914–1918

the mouth of German harbors, a suicidal action after the invention of long-range artillery and submarines. But the British found other ways to stop almost all trade to the Central Powers of Germany, Austria, and Turkey.

The British turned away the United States' request that all belligerents abide by the unratified Declaration of London. They extended the contraband list to include such American exports as copper, oil, lead, rubber, aluminum, and ultimately cotton. They declared food contraband on the pretext that the German government had nationalized all food distribution, even though the rumor of nationalization proved false. They used the doctrine of continuous voyage to extend their blockade to neutral Holland, arguing that food sent to the Netherlands was destined for Germany. The British navy even sowed mines northward from Scotland into the open ocean to block the approaches to the North Sea. These actions did more than contravene the unratified Declaration of London; they violated doctrines of international law that even Britain had accepted over the past two centuries.

Wilsonian Neutrality

Woodrow Wilson watched in surprise and horror as the world around him exploded into war. The first inkling that the Sarajevo crisis might bring general war did not reach him from his ministers abroad until the very day the shooting started. He had remarked on his accession to the presidency how ironic it would be if he, with all his preparation for presiding over domestic reforms, were called upon to lead the United States in a foreign war. Like all Americans, he was determined to stay out of the conflict. He told his countrymen to remain neutral in deed as well as name, impartial in thought as well as action.

Wilson's call for neutrality and his sincere desire to stay out of the war did not mean that he was personally impartial, however. He was a profound admirer of Great Britain's parliamentary tradition, and he regarded Germany as militaristic, brutal, and a threat to civilization. A German victory, he feared, would "change the course of our civilization and make the United States a military nation." He told the British ambassador to the United States, "Everything that I love most in the world is at stake." These sentiments were not strong enough to push Wilson into immediate war with Germany, but they certainly determined him to avoid a clash with Great Britain over neutral rights. He did not want conflict between American exporters and the British fleet to bring the United States into the war on the wrong side, as Wilson believed had happened when America's declaration of war against Britain in 1812 had in effect supported France. Wilson did not suspect that the United States could be drawn into the war in any other way than challenging British restrictions on neutral trade. Germany had neither the fleet nor the geographical proximity to clash with American interests or retaliate for America's tolerance of the British blockade. Wilson saw a conciliatory policy toward the British as the best way to gratify his desire to check the ambition of militaristic Germany and keep America out of the conflagration.

Despite Wilson's strong feelings about Great Britain and Germany, he did not immediately take full charge of American policy toward the war. His wife died a day after Great Britain declared war on Germany, and he spent much of the energy that remained to him shepherding his domestic reform program through Congress. He did not think it necessary to worry about the intricacies of neutral rights under international law in any case. He assumed, along with the Europeans, that the war would be over before the posture of the United States could have serious consequences.

With Wilson preoccupied, the task of shaping American policy fell largely to William Jennings Bryan, the ill-prepared secretary of state, and Robert Lansing, a narrow and somewhat devious international lawyer who served as the chief legal adviser to the

State Department. Leaving the technicalities of international law to Lansing, Bryan set out to restore peace in Europe. He offered immediate American mediation between the belligerents. Bryan either did not understand or did not think it important that immediate mediation would enable Germany to demand large concessions from France, Britain, and Russia, since the German invasion force had occupied much of Belgium and northern France in its march toward Paris. The shocked Allies rejected Bryan's mediation proposal and held their breath. If the Central Powers accepted, Germany might appear to the United States as the advocate of peace and win American public opinion.

Fortunately for the Allies, the German chancellor, Theobold von Bethmann-Hollweg, rejected Bryan's offer. Bethmann would have been happy to accept and escape from the war with minimal annexations, but his country was split. The right wing, buoyed by the early German victories, demanded that the war be pursued until the Allies conceded Belgium, Poland, the Baltic states, parts of France, and the dismemberment of much of the British Empire. The German left wing, having debated furiously within itself whether its duty to the international laboring class and peace outweighed its duty to support the fatherland, had assuaged its conscience after deciding for war by insisting that the conflict was purely defensive and should end with no annexations. Bethmann tried to pacify the two sides with a "diagonal policy," contriving to agree with both and remaining silent on war aims until the progress of the war brought some hope of agreement between the factions. His rejection of Bryan's mediation proposal bought him some time, but at the cost of sacrificing his best chance to ensure that the most powerful of all noncombatant nations did not come into the war against Germany.

If Bryan did not understand the significance of his actions, another of Wilson's entourage did. "Colonel" Edward M. House held no official position in Wilson's administration, but he was the president's closest confidant and adviser. He was a wily, soft-spoken man who flattered the strong-willed president by listening well, never contradicting, and suggesting ideas that he insinuated were mere rephrasings of Wilson's own. He played on Wilson's idealism and vanity with great virtuosity. This honorary Texas colonel felt even more strongly than Wilson that the Allies were fighting a war for civilization. He was not anxious to see Germany totally defeated and the balance of power in Europe destroyed, but he certainly did not want to see a German victory of any sort. He warned Wilson against Bryan's mediation approach, and Wilson privately agreed to entrust Colonel House with any further attempts at mediation. House henceforth would be sure to clear all diplomatic initiatives with the Allies before presenting them to the Central Powers. This would ensure that the United States would never be lined up with Germany, pressing the Allies to accept unwanted peace terms.

Meanwhile, Robert Lansing was trying to devise a response to Great Britain's announcement that it intended to ignore or revise parts of the Declaration of London in order to stop German commerce. Lansing composed a rather stiff note of protest. Colonel House told Wilson that the note was exceedingly undiplomatic, and Wilson decided to pursue private negotiations with the British in order to remove any possible contention. During a month of quiet contacts, Wilson and his advisers tried to induce the British to make at least sufficient gestures to America's neutral rights to avoid raising a popular outcry among the American people that might force the government into a hostile posture. The British refused to do anything that might restrict their naval warfare, so Wilson and Lansing finally issued a blunt official protest against Britain's policies. But the American leaders made clear in subsequent contacts that they would not push a general protest to the breaking point. Instead, they would protest each individual case of interference with American ships or goods as it came up and would be willing to accept a settlement after the war.

The relieved British continued to tighten their blockade and to funnel all American goods to themselves and their allies. Wilson's protests were muted, and so were those of American shippers and exporters. Accelerated trade with Great Britain more than offset the loss of potential trade with Germany. Vast exports of food, raw materials, and arms to the British revived an American economy that had been in a recession since 1911.

Meanwhile, Wilson made several other decisions that encouraged the growth of this one-sided trade with the Allies. At the outset of the war, Wilson and Bryan had decided to forbid private citizens from making loans to the belligerents. Soon it became clear that Great Britain would not have the ready cash to continue its volume of purchases. Without credits from American suppliers and banks, the booming trade that was lifting the United States out of recession would dry up. Wilson, with Bryan's reluctant consent, quietly removed the ban on private loans. There was nothing legally unneutral about the decision; international law did not forbid loans to belligerents from neutrals. Germany itself agitated for removal of the ban, unaware as yet that the Allied blockade would be effective enough to prevent supplies Germany might buy on credit from reaching the Central Powers.

In another significant decision concerning his nation's neutral stance, Wilson refused to prohibit exports of arms to the nations at war. Again, this was no violation of neutrality; all belligerents would have the right to purchase American arms, and Germany did not argue with the decision at first. Only after it became clear that the British blockade would ensure that the Allies alone benefited from neutral armaments did Germany object. Wilson refused to change his mind. He believed that a ban on arms shipments would encourage militarism, since the neutral arms trade would benefit primarily nations that had not made prewar preparedness a fetish. Wilson also argued that to revise America's neutral stance in midwar after the course of combat had made it disadvantageous to one or the other of the belligerents would itself be unneutral.

Finally, Wilson refused to order a strong protest against the British mining of the North Sea approaches. Since American ships preferred the English Channel route, the mines did little or no harm to American trade, and Wilson did not think the issue warranted the risk of conflict with Britain.

The German Response: Submarine Warfare

Throughout the last months of 1914, the Germans protested long and loud against Great Britain's illegal interference with neutral trade to the Central Powers and against Wilson's refusal to enforce those rights at the risk of conflict with the Allies. The German navy was particularly frustrated. Its battle fleet was too weak to meet the British navy head-on; it had to remain in port and watch helplessly as the British fleet swept up German merchant ships and then proceeded to stop neutral vessels headed for Germany or any other nation that might trade with the Central Powers. The only ships in the German navy that did anything at all in the early days of the war were a few submarines that, through a combination of luck and British carelessness, managed to sink four aged British warships. The German navy formerly had regarded U-boats as experimental and auxiliary craft, but these early successes seemed to promise a chance for the navy to help win the war. The submarines might turn the tables on Great Britain and blockade the British Isles. Great Britain was far more dependent on overseas commerce than Germany, and an effective blockade would be devastating to the Allied cause.

Unfortunately for Germany, an attempt to blockade England with submarine warfare inevitably would run afoul of international law. International law permitted enemy war-ships to be sunk on sight, but required that merchant or passenger ships be warned and safety provided for their crew and passengers before they were sunk. Submarines were unable to fight under such rules. Even small weapons could penetrate their thin hulls, and a merchant or passenger ship was perfectly capable of ramming a U-boat if the submarine surfaced to give warning.

Germany could afford to ignore such niceties in its dealings with the British, since the British already were doing as much harm to Germany as they could. But Germany could not afford to offend the United States to the point that it joined the Allies. Submarine warfare had the potential to do just that. Under international law, citizens of neutral nations had the right to work or travel aboard belligerent merchant or passenger vessels. If Germany violated international law by failing to warn civilian belligerent ships and provide for the safety of passengers and crew, it might kill American citizens as well as British subjects. Germany also had to fear that submarines, operating under conditions that made visibility very difficult, might sink American ships by mistake. British ships often used the ruse of sailing under an American flag, which increased the chances of mistaken sinkings.

Chancellor Bethmann-Hollweg thought these were reasons enough to avoid the use of submarines against British commerce. He believed that American entry into the war would be fatal to Germany's hope for victory. And he did not think Germany's fleet of submarines could effectively blockade the British Isles in any case. In early 1915, Germany possessed a grand total of twenty-one submarines, of which only about half could be on station at any one time. This was far too few to sink the hundreds of ships carrying goods to the Allies. Germany had estimated before the war that it would take 221 submarines to mount an effective blockade. But German naval officers maintained that a U-boat campaign could frighten ships from even attempting to reach Great Britain. These officers ignored the disparity between the force they previously had insisted would be necessary and the U-boat fleet they actually had. They wanted to get the German navy into the war. Admiral von Tirpitz warned his fellow officers, "If we come to the end . . . without the fleet having bled and worked, we shall get nothing more for the fleet, and all the scanty money that there may be will be spent on the army."

Tirpitz orchestrated a colorful newspaper campaign on behalf of submarine warfare, raising considerable support among the right and center parties in the German Reichstag. The admiral also made use of his privilege as a military leader to carry his argument directly to Kaiser Wilhelm without having to go through the civilian chancellor. Tirpitz finally won over the emperor to a declaration of U-boat warfare in February 1915. That declaration established a war zone around Great Britain in which enemy merchant ships would be sunk without warning. Germany suggested that neutrals keep their citizens and goods off belligerent vessels and also warned that neutral ships might be sunk in cases of mistaken identity. Germany acknowledged that its new policy went beyond the customary rules of warfare, but justified it as reprisal against Great Britain's flagrant violations of international law and neutral rights.

Wilson's Temporary Victory: "He Kept Us Out of War"

President Wilson had several options when he realized that Germany's declaration of submarine warfare would endanger American citizens and ships. William Jennings Bryan urged him to do nothing that would endanger America. He advised Wilson to treat Germany as he treated Great Britain—protest, but reserve settlement until after the war. He further asked Wilson to warn American passengers and sailors away from belligerent vessels and to couple his protest to Germany with one to Great Britain against its violations of neutral rights. Thus, Wilson would be able to retreat from his protests by claiming that both belligerents violated American rights and that neither was worthy of American sacrifice.

Although none of Wilson's advisers suggested it, later critics of Wilson and American entry into World War I have argued that there was a better way to avoid the war. Wilson could have forced Great Britain to respect American neutral rights and to abandon much of the blockade by embargoing supplies and credits to the Allies or convoying neutral ships and goods to Germany. Internal British cabinet reports and memos indicate that the British probably would have backed down rather than face a confrontation with American convoy escorts or loss of American matériel.[1] But wartime emotions made the British response unpredictable, and an embargo or convoys could have led to war with Great Britain. It also is doubtful that enforcing neutral rights would have deterred Germany's decision for submarine warfare. Germany did not embark on submarine warfare in retaliation for the British blockade or American lack of neutrality; it did so because German leaders gambled that the submarine could win the war. Only the threat of war with the United States kept the German navy from sinking any ships sailing toward Great Britain. To avoid confrontation with Germany, Wilson would have had to keep all American vessels and citizens away from the waters around Great Britain or to overlook attacks by German submarines.

Wilson was not willing to do that. He regarded submarine warfare on civilian vessels as a drastic and barbaric challenge to international law and humanity. He sent a stiff note to Germany warning that the United States would take "any steps necessary to safeguard American lives and property" and would hold Germany to a "strict accountability" for the actions of its U-boats.

Wilson's "strict accountability" note bristled like an ultimatum but it fell short of one. It did not say whether Germany would be held accountable during or after the war, and Bryan signed the note thinking it meant afterward. Wilson encouraged Bryan's hopes that "strict accountability" did not presage war when he sent a parallel protest to Great Britain, albeit a far weaker one, warning against the use of the American flag as a ruse by British ships. His policy in the weeks following issuance of the note cast further doubt that Wilson was prepared to enforce his protest at the risk of war. The United States sent a note to Germany suggesting that the Germans trade their submarine warfare on merchant ships for a British promise to permit foodstuffs to reach Germany. As Wilson and the State Department wrestled with the new and complex issues surrounding the use of undersea weapons, protests against German sinkings that affected American ships or property were delayed and muted. During a brief period of German fright at the "strict accountability" note, Bethmann urged revocation of the submarine order to prevent American entry into the war. But the Germans soon concluded that Wilson was not prepared to fight. The kaiser then instructed submarine commanders to stop risking their own ships in the attempt to identify the nationality or nature of potential target vessels.

Sinkings increased. The British steamer *Falaba* went down, taking an American citizen with it. Another German submarine mistakenly torpedoed the American ship *Gullflight*. Wilson waited three weeks before protesting the *Falaba* incident and was still wrestling with the *Gullflight* issue when the destruction of the *Lusitania* abruptly ended his hesitation.

The *Lusitania* was a giant British passenger liner carrying more than 1,900 people from New York to England. On May 7, 1915, a German submarine torpedoed it off the coast of Ireland; the ship sank within twenty minutes. Nearly 1,200 passengers drowned, including 124 Americans. The Germans had posted signs in New York warning people not to sail on the ship, and they correctly claimed that the vessel carried some arms and ammunition. Germany thus felt the sinking was justified, and some Germans even celebrated it by declaring a school holiday.

Wilson and America, not yet accustomed to the routine killing of civilians in war, were horrified at the deaths of over a thousand civilians. The British enhanced the shock of the *Lusitania* attack by releasing a report signed by the respected British commentator on American life, Lord Bryce, which detailed and exaggerated German atrocities during the "rape" of Belgium.

At first Wilson reacted somewhat tentatively. He announced that America was a nation "too proud to fight." But then he sent a protest note to Germany harshly condemning the sinking of the *Lusitania* and calling for an end to submarine warfare against civilian ships. To strengthen the note even more, he deleted an indication that the United States might defer compensation until after the war. When Germany delayed its response, he sent a second and still harsher note. He rejected Bryan's advice to couple his notes with parallel protests against the British, even though the British had exploited the period of outrage against the sinking of the *Lusitania* to tighten their blockade drastically. Wilson also refused the suggestions of his secretary of state that he order Americans off belligerent ships and out of the war zone. Bryan refused to sign the second *Lusitania* note and resigned on June 8, complaining, "Colonel House has been Secretary of State, not I. I have never had your full confidence."

Wilson's reaction to the *Lusitania* convinced Bethmann that Germany had to stop torpedoing passenger ships or it would face a new, powerful enemy on the battlefield. The chief of staff of the German army, General Erich von Falkenhayn, agreed that the danger of American intervention outweighed the benefits of U-boat warfare, and he refused to support the adamant naval officers in a ferocious debate before the kaiser. The kaiser finally permitted Bethmann to prohibit submarine attacks on large passenger liners and to order greater caution against sinking neutral vessels, but Wilhelm insisted that the order be kept secret so Germany would not be seen as retreating. Since Wilson could not know that his protests had had some effect, he continued to press the case and relations remained tense. Then a German U-boat mistakenly sank the British passenger liner *Arabic*, killing two Americans. Wilson could only see this attack as an obdurate refusal to heed his warnings. Failure to take strong action would expose his protests as hollow, destroying both American prestige and his own.

Still, as in the *Lusitania* crisis, Wilson was willing to exert some patience. Rather than issue an immediate public ultimatum, he had his new secretary of state, Robert Lansing, privately inform the German ambassador that the United States would sever relations with Germany if it did not stop submarine attacks against innocent ships and passengers. The German ambassador, Count Johann von Bernstorff, violated his orders by informing Lansing of the earlier secret instructions against attacks on large passenger liners. Stating that the *Arabic* sinking was a mistake, Bernstorff promised compensation. After some confusion and hesitation in confirming his promises, caused by another struggle between the navy and Bethmann for the mind of Kaiser Wilhelm, on September 1, 1915, the German government gave a further public pledge that no passenger liners of any kind would be sunk. Beyond this *Arabic* pledge, Bethmann also issued secret orders to withdraw all submarines from the west coast of England, where passenger liners most commonly traveled. Temporarily, Bethmann had managed to stifle the threat of American intervention. But the German navy and its political allies were merely biding their time. Winter weather and the shortage of U-boats would have rendered submarine warfare relatively ineffective for the following months anyway. The return of operational weather and the growth of the U-boat fleet would inevitably bring new pressures on the German chancellor.

Wilson could not know of the debates within the German hierarchy, but he was aware of how fragile America's peace was. He had staked the prestige of the nation on his warnings against illegal submarine warfare. If Germany embarked again on all-out U-boat warfare, he would face a choice between humiliating retreat and measures almost sure to bring the United States into the war. Britain added its own reminder of possible future conflict with America: it placed cotton on the contraband list. Waiting as usual until a German-American crisis could divert attention from the blow, the British issued the order immediately after the sinking of the *Arabic*. Britain also signed a contract to purchase large amounts of U.S. cotton to support the market price and pacify American farmers. Still, Wilson and Lansing felt they had to respond with a long, detailed protest against British policies toward neutral trade.

Such tensions convinced Wilson that the only sure way the United States could stay out of the hostilities and maintain its honor was to end the war. He approved a plan offered to him by Colonel House that involved an enormous gamble to bring the war to an end through American mediation. Wilson would call for a peace conference and threaten war against whichever side refused. But first House would consult with the Allies and, by promising that American mediators at the conference would be sympathetic to Allied war aims, ensure that they would not be the ones to refuse. House went to London and induced British Foreign Minister Sir Edward Grey to accept this plan, as embodied in the so-called House-Grey Memorandum.

Under the terms of the House-Grey Memorandum, Wilson would wait until the Allies informed him that the military situation was propitious. Then he would issue a call for a peace conference. If Germany refused, the United States *probably* would join the Allies in the war. If Germany agreed to the conference but then rejected reasonable terms of peace, the United States *probably* would leave the conference a belligerent on the side of Great Britain. (Wilson personally added the "probablies" to this memorandum of understanding, the first before House negotiated it with the British, and the second afterward.) Meanwhile, House tried to tempt the Germans to accept the call for a peace conference by telling them that Great Britain was unlikely to accept. At the same time, he assured the Allies that the peace conference was nothing but a gimmick to pave the way for American intervention on the side of Britain and France.

Wilson's wait for the British signal to call the conference and mediate a peace was interminable. The British never did decide the time was propitious. David Lloyd George, the new British prime minister, later claimed that Wilson's "probablies" undermined the whole plan. No doubt he worried even more that Wilson's ideas of reasonable terms could never satisfy the war aims the Allies had developed during a year of bloody warfare. France would not be satisfied without moving Germany out of Alsace-Lorraine and all other lands west of the Rhine. Great Britain would insist on the reduction of the German fleet. Both would want Germany weakened so it could not attack through Belgium again. Russia insisted on concessions in the Balkans. Only a complete Allied victory, not a Wilson-mediated peace, could achieve those goals.

Wilson became desperate for Britain to give him the signal to call the conference, because by the time House returned to America in February 1916, the danger of American intervention had increased drastically. On February 10, Germany had announced resumption of submarine warfare against armed merchant ships. Bethmann thought he could get away with this ploy because while House had been bouncing around Europe, Secretary of State Lansing had been trying to work out a modus vivendi between Germany and Great Britain. Lansing wanted the British to cease arming merchant ships in return for Germany's promise to abandon submarine sinkings of unarmed ships without warning. The British rejected this trade of a practice long sanctioned by international law for a submarine warfare they regarded as totally illegal. Bethmann thought this British rejection would dispose Wilson and Lansing to accept resumption of U-boat attacks on armed merchants.

But German U-boats "mistakenly" sank many neutral merchants and one Dutch passenger liner. It was only a matter of time before another ship went down with American passengers or a submarine sank an American merchant vessel. Many members of Congress tried to forestall the crisis by promoting the Gore-McLemore Resolutions, warning Americans off armed merchant ships or ships carrying contraband. Wilson defused this movement with a letter to the chair of the Senate Foreign Relations Committee refusing to accept a single abatement of American rights. Then, on March 24, a submarine attacked the French channel steamer *Sussex*. The *Sussex* did not sink, but eighty people died and four of the twenty-five Americans aboard suffered serious injury.

Wilson sent the Germans a public ultimatum: the United States would break relations if Germany did not halt all submarine attacks on passenger and freight-carrying ships, armed or unarmed. Anticipating such a crisis, Bethmann had convinced the kaiser that since the German navy did not possess enough U-boats to blockade Great Britain effectively, continuation of submarine warfare was not worth the risk of war with the United States. Bethmann also had maneuvered the resignation of Admiral von Tirpitz. This enabled him to answer Wilson's protest with amazing concessions. The German note conceded that the attack on the *Sussex* had been wrong and promised no further sinkings without warning. This *Sussex* pledge was a remarkable victory for Wilson's diplomacy. Wilson campaigned for and won the presidency in 1916 with the slogan, "He kept us out of war."

America Enters the War

In the euphoria that followed the *Sussex* pledge, few noticed that Germany's *Sussex* note claimed the right to resume submarine warfare if the United States did not compel Great Britain to respect international law. No one in America could know that the German navy was continuing to build U-boats with the intention of reopening the issue when it had enough to enforce an effective blockade of Great Britain. Nor could Americans know that Bethmann was losing his power to resist the naval campaign. General Paul von Hindenburg had replaced Falkenhayn in command of the German armies, and he and his chief subordinate, General Erich Ludendorff, had enough influence with the kaiser to override Bethmann on the U-boat issue if they chose. The Centre party also gave up its opposition to the submarine campaign, depriving Bethmann of his parliamentary majority in the Reichstag. Bethmann decided his only chance to prevent all-out submarine warfare in the near future was to make peace.

Bethmann had at least a slim chance to succeed in getting American support for a peace conference. Once the *Sussex* pledge seemingly ended the crisis with Germany, Wilson had turned harshly on Great Britain. He was disillusioned by Britain's refusal to ask him for mediation in line with the House-Grey Memorandum, and he was increasingly angered by British contempt for American neutral rights. He was prepared to offer neutral mediation and call for peace terms from both sides without preconditions, a dangerous course for the Allies so long as Germany had the military advantage and occupied Allied territory.

This danger caused Wilson to hesitate, especially after Germany began to deport Belgian civilians to work in German factories. In the interim, Bethmann asked the neutral powers, including the United States, to communicate to Great Britain an offer of a peace conference. Wilson proposed his own mediation as a substitute. Claiming that the objects for which each side said it was fighting were "virtually the same," he invited the belligerents to send him their peace terms. Bethmann refused to take this last chance to split America and the Allies. Distrustful of Wilson and the Americans, he refused Wilson's mediation offer and insisted on talking directly to the Allies.

The British did not make the same mistake. They were greatly offended that Wilson could equate their objectives with those of the German militarists and they feared that Wilson's mediation offer was part of a German plot, but they were coaxed to give an answer by Secretary of State Lansing. Lansing had no desire to see the British refuse to answer and cast themselves as the enemy of Wilson's ambition to be a peacemaker. Lansing believed the true policy of the United States should be to "join the Allies as soon as possible and crush the German Autocrats." He assured the British and French that Wilson's mediation offer was not part of the German proposal and that the president preferred the democracies enough to support any demands they might devise. Lansing even encouraged the Allies to make their peace terms as extreme as they wished. Lansing's unauthorized maneuvers convinced Great Britain to spell out its war aims, and it was even more encouraged to do so when Germany refused to state its own terms.[2]

The Allies insisted on restoration of all territories conquered by the Central Powers, by which it turned out they meant Alsace-Lorraine as well as Belgium, Serbia, Montenegro, and parts of France, Russia, and Rumania. They also demanded liberation of the nationalities dominated by the Austro-Hungarian Empire and Turkey, along with reparations for war damages. Wilson considered these demands a bluff and continued private negotiations with the belligerents. He added pressure to his peace initiative by making a dramatic speech to the U.S. Senate in which he appealed brilliantly for "peace without victory," a peace that would replace the balance of power with a community of power. The peace settlement would be based on the concepts of national self-determination, government by consent of the governed, arms limitations, and freedom of the seas. He promised that the United States would contribute its power to a league of nations designed to maintain this peace.

Wilson did not know that his great appeal for mediation and peace was doomed before he set foot in the Senate. The British believed that there could be no return to the prewar status quo and that only an Allied victory could produce the world Wilson desired. They also feared they might lose the war unless the United States intervened soon on their side. They essentially ignored Wilson's initiative and hoped it would go away. The Germans too believed that the war must end in a victorious rather than a compromise peace, and they too feared they would lose the war if it continued much longer. But they knew the United States would not enter on their side to save them. They put their faith instead in their submarines.

By January 1917, Germany had nearly 100 U-boats, which the navy claimed could, if given free rein, reduce Great Britain to starvation in six months. Germany's leaders realized that renunciation of the *Sussex* pledge would mean American intervention, but they gambled that they could win the war before the United States could do much to help the Allies. The choice seemed to be between winning the war quickly with the submarine or losing without it. The kaiser secretly decided on January 9, nearly two weeks before Wilson's "peace without victory" speech, to launch unrestricted submarine warfare. On February 1, the German government announced that its U-boats would sink without warning all ships sailing in the war zone around Great Britain, including neutral vessels. This was the first time Germany had declared it would sink American ships purposely. The United States would have to fight or back down ignominiously from the stand it had taken since the sinking of the *Lusitania*.

Wilson immediately broke relations with Germany and demanded that the Germans go back to the *Sussex* pledge. But he did not ask Congress for a declaration of war; he told the Senate he would wait for "overt acts" before taking extreme measures. Three weeks later, the British turned over to the United States a telegram to Mexico from the German foreign secretary, Arthur Zimmermann. Zimmermann proposed an alliance between Germany, Mexico, and Japan against the United States if America joined the war, and he offered to help Mexico regain the territory it had lost in the Mexican War. This Zimmermann telegram convinced Wilson that Germany preferred war to abandonment of its submarine campaign. Two days later, Wilson asked Congress for permission to arm American merchant ships to resist German attacks. A Senate filibuster by what Wilson condemned as "a little group of willful men" blocked the measure. So Wilson ordered this interim step toward war on his own authority. He hoped arming American merchant vessels might be enough to protect American ships and avoid full-scale war. But within two weeks he received news that German submarines had sunk three American ships with the loss of fifteen lives. After two more days of mental agony and soul-searching, he accepted the advice of his cabinet and asked Congress for a formal declaration of war.

Wilson accepted that tragic alternative with immense sorrow, but with one great consolation. If the United States were an active and powerful participant in the war, the president would have great influence over the peace settlement. He would have the opportunity to create a just peace that would promote democratic government and eliminate the causes of war that had plagued the Old World for so long. Since the February Revolution in Russia had just overthrown the czar and installed a democratic socialist government, Wilson could portray the war against Germany to himself and the American people as pitting free nations against militaristic tyrannies. In ringing tones he asked Congress to enlist the United States in a crusade to "make the world safe for democracy."

Opposition to War: The Culture of Dissent

Although a majority of Americans had supported Wilson's attempt to avoid joining the war, once the President and Congress decided to enter the conflict, the people responded with great unity and enthusiasm. Only a small but active minority continued to oppose it. That minority was increasingly reviled as the war went on, especially because it was composed of easily marginalized gender, ethnic, and political groups.

Women were especially powerful in the peace movement. Jane Addams, who had led prominent campaigns on behalf of the poor and homeless in America's major cities, helped build the Women's Peace Party in the United States and then went on to become the first president of the Women's International League for Peace and Freedom in May 1919. Ethnic minorities also represented a large part of the antiwar movement. Recent immigrants from Germany were torn in their loyalties. Irish nationalists who hated the British Empire opposed joining the war on behalf of their oppressors, especially in the wake of the uprising that began in Dublin on Easter in 1916 and culminated in Irish independence after World War I. Immigrants from Ireland, Germany, and other nations in Europe, 5 million of whom had arrived in the United States in the four years before America entered the war, joined millions of other recent immigrants as working-class residents of America's largest cities and often brought with them strong beliefs in labor unions and socialist politics. These immigrants formed large majorities of radical unions and parties that opposed the war as a capitalist and imperialist enterprise.

As war fever mounted in the United States, the governments and private vigilantes attacked pacifists, radicals, and ethnic minorities whom they regarded as "the enemy within." Even before the war, Theodore Roosevelt had sneered at the Irish-Americans, German-Americans, and other minority ethnic groups who were reluctant to prepare for war as "hyphenated Americans." Once America was in the war, mobs descended on the offices of one of the women's peace organizations in Washington, DC, and told the women to "beat it" or they would be "raided and raped." Several German-speaking immigrants were lynched. The Department of Justice rounded up more than 150 people in the offices of the radical union, the International Workers of the World, and held them for mass trials. Fifteen of the leaders received sentences of twenty years in prison under the terms of the recently passed Espionage Act. Strikes or protests of any sort were often seen as hindrances to the war effort. Thus, vigilantes rounded up 1,200 European and Mexican workers who had gone on strike against mine owners in Bisbee, Arizona, piled them into twenty-four railroad cars, and dumped them in New Mexico. After the war, the pent-up rage against political radicals and minorities who had been insufficiently supportive of the war culminated in the Red Scare of 1919, during which Wilson's administration deported many recent immigrants.[3]

Controversial Issues

The vast majority of historians of Wilson's day, like the vast majority of Congress and Americans at large, approved Wilson's decision for war and had no doubts about the reasons behind it. They agreed that Wilson had tried to be neutral. They approved Wilson's refusal to do more than protest British illegalities, for to do more might have made Americans participants in the war on the side of Germany. This was unthinkable; Germany's violation of Belgian neutrality, its subsequent atrocities in that unhappy country, and its brutal submarine campaign confirmed for many that Germany was "a horrible menace to civilization" that, if it won the war, would form a great empire that would "dominate Europe and imperil the safety of the Americas."[4] Historians who criticized Wilson argued only that he had not entered the war soon enough. Frederick A. Ogg censured the president for leading Americans to believe that they were unconcerned with the causes and objects of the Great War "until he and the country were rudely awakened by what had become clear to many much earlier—that this was a contest between democracy and autocracy" and that the United States would have to fight imperialistic Germany alone if "the Teutonic powers" were victorious. John Holladay Latané shuddered to think that if Germany had not violated international law so flagrantly with its submarines, Wilson would have permitted a German victory with its grave consequences for the security of the Americas.[5]

Within five years after the end of the war, historical opinion began to change. The refusal of the European powers at the Paris Peace Conference to abandon the more self-interested of their war aims in the interest of America's ideas of a just peace undermined the conviction that America had joined a crusade for democracy. Revelations from the historical archives of the defeated powers destroyed the Allies' accusation that Germany and Austria had purposely plotted world war. This raised further questions about why the United States should have intervened. Early critics of American intervention took a rather conspiratorial view of Wilson's decision for war. They accused munitions makers of pushing the Wilson administration into conflict as a means of increasing their war profits. Critics charged that Wall Street bankers had maneuvered America into war to prevent the Allies from losing and defaulting on the vast loans granted them by American financial institutions. Critics also claimed that a vicious British propaganda campaign had twisted facts, created Germany atrocities out of whole cloth, and made use of Britain's control of the single communications cable to the United States to delude American opinion into supporting intervention on the side of the Allies.[6]

Later World War I revisionist critics returned a broader indictment. Charles Beard pointed out that America's high volume of trade with the Allies and the loans that encouraged it tied the prosperity of all Americans, not just big business, to the survival of the Allies. The original mistake of encouraging this trade gave the United States no choice but to intervene to save the British and French from defeat. Charles Tansill was not so ready to absolve big business in the most extensive of these revisionist studies. He argued that big business had influenced Wilson to encourage trade with the Allies in the first place and to violate America's neutral duties by refusing to make an effective challenge to Britain's illegal blockade. An embargo or convoy system would have broken the blockade easily and without danger of war with the dependent Allies. Germany would not have used the submarine, and America could have continued neutral.[7]

These World War I revisionist histories had a great impact on American opinion in the years before World War II. They influenced Congress to pass a series of neutrality acts to prevent the United States from being drawn into World War II in the ways revisionist historians claimed it had been drawn into World War I.

But Wilson had many defenders among historians as well as the population at large. These defenders argued that Wilson was the last person to have been influenced by big bankers or munitions makers. Wilson had defended neutral rights with no initial expectation that this stance would bring war and then felt the United States could not abandon its stand in midwar without itself being less than neutral. They agreed with Wilson that Germany's offenses were more heinous than Britain's since submarine warfare destroyed people as well as property. If Wilson had instituted an embargo or convoy system, destroying American prosperity while risking war with Britain on the side of Germany, he would have provoked a revolt against his administration. Nothing Wilson could have done would have kept Germany from resorting to submarine warfare anyway. Germany had to stop all British trade to win the war, and this required either sinking or terrorizing neutral ships as well as Allied ones.

Yet even Wilson's defenders in this pre–World War II era no longer asserted, as the wartime historians had, that the United States had had to intervene to protect itself from invasion by a ruthless Germany bent on world conquest. They agreed that Wilson had intervened not to protect American security, but to defend American neutral rights and prestige against submarine warfare. All agreed that Wilson had tried to maintain American neutrality and had joined the war only reluctantly. But one of his most prominent defenders, his official biographer and former press secretary Ray Stannard Baker, accused Wilson's advisers House and Lansing of disloyally trying to maneuver the president into the war.[8]

World War II, reviving American fears of Germany as a menace to civilization, made the next generation of historians more willing to believe that American intervention in World War I had been essential. Walter Lippmann wrote a highly influential book during World War II in which he bewailed the naïveté he had shared with the American people and urged a return to a realistic foreign policy based on national interest and power politics. In the course of his argument, he claimed that Wilson had intervened in World War I on these realistic grounds, recognizing that unlimited submarine warfare would cut Atlantic communications, starve Great Britain, and leave the United States to face a "new and aggressively expanding German empire which had made Britain, France, and Russia its vassals, and Japan its ally."[9]

Other realist historians like George Kennan and Robert Osgood accepted the contention that Wilson should have intervened in the war to protect Britain and the balance of power. But they did not believe that Wilson or the American people had done so for that reason. Osgood conceded that House and Lansing might have thought intervention necessary to American security, but pointed out that Wilson paid his advisers little heed. In any case, most American interventionists, including the leaders of the preparedness campaign, had not thought of security in terms of the subtle interest the United States had in the European balance of power. They spoke instead of the chimerical threat of a direct German invasion of the United States or the Western Hemisphere.

Neither Wilson nor most Americans took the threat of a direct invasion seriously. Osgood pointed out that at the time Wilson and Congress made their decision for war, no one in the United States believed the U-boat campaign would break the great stalemate and defeat the Allies. It was only months later, when Great Britain was weeks from running out of food, that the prospect of German victory became imminent. Thus, Wilson had chosen war because he was offended by German conduct, not because he thought it posed a threat to American survival. Wilson's failure to understand and explain America's self-interest in joining the war to preserve the European balance of power left the American people open to the suggestion that the United States had fought for no good reason at all, that it had been duped into rescuing the Allies by British propaganda and international bankers.

Psychohistorians bolstered these contentions as they attempted to explain the strange quirk of character that had led Wilson to deal in rigid moralistic and legalistic terms with matters he should have handled pragmatically in terms of power and self-interest.[10]

A plausible defense of Wilson against this realist onslaught was slow to emerge. Even Arthur Link, most prominent of all Wilsonian scholars and defenders, at first accepted the realist contention that Wilson had ignored the hardheaded advice of Lansing and House and had gone to war because submarine warfare violated American neutral rights. Link differed only in that he believed this reason was good and sufficient.[11] But Edward Buehrig noted Wilson's subtle recognition of the European balance of power in the president's hopes for a negotiated peace that would avoid total defeat of either the Allies or the Central Powers. Buehrig thought this showed Wilson was realistic, even though Wilson often said the peace should transcend balance-of-power considerations.[12] Link, seizing on Buehrig's point, admitted that Wilson might have contented himself with armed neutrality after Germany's declaration of unlimited submarine warfare if Germany had avoided sinking American ships. Thus he might have permitted a German victory. Yet his decision for war when German submarines did sink American ships represented more than just a defense of neutral rights; Wilson knew that failure to react strongly to the German provocation would have sacrificed America's prestige and leverage abroad, giving him no chance to influence the peace. With what Link called a "higher realism," Wilson intervened at least in part to ensure that the peace would be a just one that did not sow the seeds of future war by inciting revenge or disrupting the balance of power.[13]

Since the 1970s, most historians have accepted Link's formulation of Wilson's motivation.[14] Their differences are subtle ones, except in their evaluations of Wilson's advisers. Some historians praise House and Lansing for their realism. Most follow Link (and Ray Stannard Baker of the earlier era) in arguing that House and Lansing were disloyal and devious.[15]

Revisionist historians have concentrated their criticism of Wilson on his opposition to revolutions rather than his entry into World War I, so they have not done much to revive the earlier critiques of Beard, Tansill, et al.[16] John W. Coogan, however, revived at least one part of the older critique even though he does not adhere to most of the precepts of the New Left revisionist school. Coogan argued that Wilson never was truly neutral by proper standards of international law, that he undermined the entire system of international relations by his favoritism toward Great Britain, and that even though it may have been to America's interest to prevent Germany from defeating the Allies, it was even more to America's interest to defend American neutrality, prevent a crushing victory by either side, and maintain both the balance of power and the prewar structure of international law. Coogan also presented interesting new information on negotiations and strategic planning in Europe prior to World War I.[17]

Further Reading

For further information on the plunge of Europe into the war and on the war itself, the best survey is James Joll, *The Origins of the First World War* (2nd ed., 1992). See also Niall

Ferguson, *The Pity of War* (1999), which argues provocatively that Britain should have stayed out of the war, which of course would have meant that the United States would have stayed out also. Other important books on this topic are Bernadotte E. Schmitt and Harold C. Vadaler, *The World in the Crucible, 1914–1919* (1984); David Stevenson, *The First World War and International Politics* (1988); Paul Kennedy, *The Rise of Anglo-German Antagonism* (1980); A.J.P. Taylor, *The Struggle for Mastery in Europe* (1954); Laurence Lafore, *The Long Fuse* (1965); Dwight E. Lee, *Europe's Crucial Years: The Diplomatic Background of World War I, 1902–1914* (1974); Samuel R. Williamson, *The Politics of Grand Strategy: Britain and France Prepare for War, 1904–1914* (1969); and Gerhard Ritter, *The Schlieffen Plan* (1979).

On American-European relations prior to the Wilson administration, see Howard K. Beale, *Theodore Roosevelt and the Rise of America to World Power* (1956); Raymond Esthus, *Theodore Roosevelt and International Rivalries* (1970); Frederick Marks, *Velvet on Iron: The Diplomacy of Theodore Roosevelt* (1979); and Calvin Davis, *The United States and the First Hague Peace Conference* (1962) and *The United States and the Second Hague Peace Conference* (1975). Richard Challener investigated American military planning and influence in *Admirals, Generals, and American Foreign Policy, 1898–1914* (1973), while Holger Herwig wrote of German planning for war with the United States in *The Politics of Frustration: The United States in German Naval Planning, 1889–1914* (1976).

Notes

1. This argument is made most persuasively by Robert W. Tucker, *Woodrow Wilson and the Great War: Reconsidering America's Neutrality, 1914–1917* (2007).

2. Historians still debate why Lansing wrote such strong protest notes against the British blockade early in the war if he was so pro-Allied. Charles Tansill and other opponents of American entry have speculated that Lansing, in hopes of furthering his own career, changed his policy to conform to the opinion of Colonel House. Other historians, like Daniel Smith, argue that Lansing's initial response was simply that of a narrow legal mind confronted with violations of international law.

3. Frances H. Early, *A World Without War: How U.S. Feminists and Pacifists Resisted World War I* (1997); Akan Dawley, *Changing the World: American Progressives in War and Revolution* (2003). For an excellent analysis of the intellectual arguments between pacifists, Wilsonians, and so-called Atlanticists like Theodore Roosevelt and Henry Cabot Lodge, see Ross A. Kennedy, *The Will to Believe: Woodrow Wilson, World War I, and America's Strategy for Peace and Security* (2009).

4. John Bach McMaster, *The United States in the World War* (2 vols., 1918–1920). See also John Spencer Bassett, *Our War with Germany* (1919); Christian B. Gauss, *Why We Went to War* (1920); and Carleton J.H. Hayes, *A Brief History of the Great War* (1920).

5. Frederick A. Ogg, *National Progress, 1907–1917* (1918); John Holladay Latané, *From Isolation to Leadership: A Review of American Foreign Policy* (1918). There was only one significant book criticizing Wilson for entering the war at all, socialist Scott Nearing's *The Great Madness* (1917).

6. John Kenneth Turner, *Shall It Be Again* (1922); Harry Elmer Barnes, *The Genesis of the World War* (1927); Frederick Bausman, *Let France Explain* (1922) and *Facing Europe* (1926).

7. Charles A. Beard, *The Devil Theory of War* (1936); Charles C. Tansill, *America Goes to War* (1936). See also Walter Millis, *The Road to War: America 1914–1917* (1936); and C. Hartley Grattan, *Preface to Chaos* (1936). These World War I revisionists, as opposed to the later revisionists writing in the Cold War era, were very diverse politically. Turner and Grattan were socialists; Barnes, Beard, and

Millis were disillusioned liberals; Tansill and Bausman were right-wing conservatives who detested the British Empire, partly because of their nineteenth-century American nationalism and, in Tansill's case at least, ethnic sympathies with the Irish and Germans. But their books did not reflect these political divisions. The socialists and liberals denounced British propaganda and America's pro-British bias as ardently as the conservatives, and the conservative Tansill denounced the influence of big business on intervention as thoroughly as those historians on the Left.

8. Ray Stannard Baker, *Woodrow Wilson: Life and Letters* (6 vols., 1927–1937). See also Charles Seymour, *Woodrow Wilson and the World War* (1921), *American Diplomacy During the World War* (1934), and *American Neutrality, 1914–1917* (1935); and Newton D. Baker, *Why We Went to War* (1936).

9. Walter Lippmann, *U.S. Foreign Policy: Shield of the Republic* (1943).

10. Robert E. Osgood, *Ideals and Self-Interest in American Foreign Policy: The Great Transformation* (1953); George Kennan, *American Diplomacy, 1900–1950* (1951). The best of the psychohistorical biographies is Alexander L. George and Juliette L. George, *Woodrow Wilson and Colonel House: A Personality Study* (1956). The least accurate and most tendentious is by Sigmund Freud himself, with William C. Bullitt, *Thomas Woodrow Wilson: A Psychological Study* (1966). See also John M. Blum, *Woodrow Wilson and the Politics of Morality* (1956).

11. Arthur S. Link, *Woodrow Wilson and the Progressive Era, 1910–1917* (1954).

12. Edward H. Buehrig, *Woodrow Wilson and the Balance of Power* (1955).

13. Arthur S. Link, *Wilson: The Struggle for Neutrality, 1914–1915* (1960), *Wilson: Confusions and Crises, 1915–1916* (1964), *Wilson: Campaigns for Progressivism and Peace, 1916–1917* (1965), and *Wilson the Diplomatist: A Look at His Major Foreign Policies* (1957), revised as *Woodrow Wilson: Revolution, War, and Peace* (1970).

14. One exception is Lloyd E. Ambrosius, who has adhered firmly to the realist criticisms of Wilson in his *Wilsonian Statecraft: Theory and Practice of Liberal Internationalism during World War I* (1991).

15. Favorable to House and Lansing are Ernest May, *The World War and American Isolation, 1914–1917* (1957), still the best one-volume history of American intervention; and Daniel S. Smith, *Robert Lansing and American Neutrality, 1914–1917* (1958), and *The Great Departure: The United States and World War I, 1914–1920* (1965). Closer to Link's view of House, Lansing, and Ambassador Walter Hines Page are Patrick Devlin, *Too Proud to Fight: Woodrow Wilson's Neutrality* (1975), which agrees that Wilson fought primarily to protect America's prestige but regards this motive with a more jaundiced eye than Link; Ross Gregory, *The Origins of American Intervention in the First World War* (1970); Julius W. Pratt, *Challenge and Rejection* (1967); and three books by John Milton Cooper: *The Vanity of Power: American Isolationism and World War I, 1914–1917* (1969), *Walter Hines Page: The Southerner as American, 1855–1918* (1977), and *The Warrior and the Priest: Woodrow Wilson and Theodore Roosevelt* (1983). Defensive of Wilson's realism but on the basis of his use of military force rather than his "higher realism" is Frederick S. Calhoun, *Power and Principle: Armed Intervention in Wilsonian Foreign Policy* (1986). Kendrick A. Clements has also written a book favorable to Wilson's diplomacy, *Woodrow Wilson: World Statesman* (1987), along with a good study of Wilson's first secretary of state, *William Jennings Bryan: Missionary Isolationist* (1982).

16. One exception, Sidney Bell's *Righteous Conquest: Woodrow Wilson and the Evolution of the New Diplomacy* (1972), is rather ham-handed and has generally been disregarded by recent historians.

17. John W. Coogan, *The End of Neutrality: The United States, Britain, and Maritime Rights, 1899–1915* (1981).

CHAPTER 5

THE UNITED STATES AND THE PEACE OF VERSAILLES

America and the Allied Victory

The European Allies welcomed America's entry into World War I with a sigh of relief. American intervention seemed to ensure their victory. They turned out to be correct, but by a far closer margin than they or the United States expected. The German submarine campaign proved frighteningly successful. U-boats sank one out of every four British merchant ships that left harbor. At one point in the early summer of 1917, Great Britain had on hand only a six-week supply of food. After much anguished debate, the British decided to change their naval tactics. They abandoned their attempts to sneak widely dispersed ships past the U-boats and instead concentrated them in convoys protected by destroyers. This convoy system, enhanced by America's contribution of destroyers, merchant vessels, and supplies, broke the back of the German submarine campaign.

In declaring war on Germany, the United States had expected to play a role as supplier, financier, and naval adjunct to the Allies. It had not expected to send large numbers of troops to fight the land war in Europe. At the time the United States intervened, the Allies seemed to have a comfortable edge in manpower over the Central Powers. The British and French armies on the western front commanded more than 2.5 million men against only 1.5 million Germans. That ratio changed, however, when the Bolsheviks took power in Russia in November 1917 and shortly afterward abandoned the war. The peace treaty Germany forced on Russia at Brest-Litovsk not only gave Germany access to the wheat fields of the Ukraine and the oil fields of the Caucasus to supply the continuing war against the western Allies, but also permitted the Germans to transfer 1 million soldiers from the eastern to the western front.

With these reinforcements, the German commanders Paul von Hindenburg and Erich Ludendorff launched an all-out offensive to conquer France and win the war. The United States poured men into Europe to stop it. While many of the 2 million Americans ultimately sent to Europe got there too late to be part of the major campaigns, their imminent arrival permitted France and Great Britain to throw their reserves into the final battles with confidence that replacements were on the way. Those Americans who arrived early fought valiantly in the battle that stopped the German offensive just short of Paris; they then joined the counteroffensive that broke the German lines.

As the German armies reeled back toward their own territory, Ludendorff panicked. He beseeched the German government to negotiate an armistice immediately and save his army from disaster. Shortly thereafter, the Allied attack outran its supplies and communications, the counteroffensive bogged down, and Ludendorff realized he had time to establish a new line of defense. He did an abrupt about-face and demanded that the German government call off its peace initiative. But it was too late: the German armies and the home front were demoralized. A moderate socialist government took control of Germany to make peace. In all probability, the continuing Allied blockade and American buildup would have forced a German surrender in a few more months anyway. Ludendorff and the army, however, insisted they could have prevented defeat had they not been sold out by socialist and Jewish peace-mongers at home. The German army shelled its own peace delegation as it returned from signing the armistice. The bitterness spawned within German ranks by the myth of the Jewish and socialist "stab in the back" held ominous implications for the future.

Conflicting Plans for Peace: Wilson's "New Diplomacy" Versus Europe's "Old Diplomacy"

When the Germans sued for an armistice, they did not approach their old enemies, the British and the French; they turned instead to Woodrow Wilson. They quite rightly believed that President Wilson would be willing to give them better terms. Before the war, Wilson had made himself the supreme symbol of the idea of peace without victory, a peace of justice rather than revenge. To emphasize the distinction between the purposes of the United States and those of the Allies (as well as to cater to the historic American aversion to alliances), Wilson insisted that America was merely an "associate power" rather than one of the formal Allies.

Wilson reinforced his idealistic stance when the Bolsheviks announced that they were going to publish the secret territorial treaties the czar and the Allies had made among themselves. Publication promised to be a terrible blow to the domestic unity of the Allies, since many liberals in Great Britain, France, Italy, and the United States had supported the war only because they believed the Allies represented the ideals of democracy and peace against the aggressiveness and autocracy of the Central Powers. Thinking it essential to restore Allied idealism, Wilson asked the Allies to abandon their secret treaties and territorial demands. The Allies refused despite the threat by Wilson's negotiator, Colonel Edward House, that the United States might make a separate peace. Consequently, on January 8, 1918, Wilson unilaterally issued a lofty statement of war aims, the Fourteen Points.

The Fourteen Points and Wilson's later elaborations on them galvanized liberal opinion in America and the world. Wilson appealed for an end to the practices liberals believed were the basic causes for war—secret diplomacy, barriers to free international trade and navigation of the seas, arms races, and colonialism that took no account of the desires of the indigenous populations. Wilson also called for territorial adjustments in Europe designed not to cripple Germany, but to honor the wishes of the many different peoples of Europe for national self-determination. Under the rubric of self-determination, Wilson specified the return of Alsace-Lorraine to France, German evacuation of Belgium and Russia, adjustment of Italy's frontier with Austria according to nationality, autonomy for the peoples of eastern Europe long ruled by the Austro-Hungarian, Russian, German, and Ottoman Turkish empires, and the establishment of an independent Poland with access to the sea.

Most important, Wilson called for an international organization of nations to supervise the settlement. This League of Nations could provide a peaceful means of revising the final war settlement if that proved necessary. If some discontented nation tried to overthrow the treaty settlement by force, the League would provide an international alliance of powers to protect the independence and territorial integrity of the victim. No aggressor would ever be able to stand against such a force. Collective security would eliminate the need for secret treaty arrangements, contests for strategic borders, and all the other accoutrements of balance-of-power politics.

Wilson had a negative as well as a positive reason for seeking a generous policy toward the defeated Central Powers. He feared that a harsh peace would so demoralize the beaten Germans, Austrians, and Hungarians that they would be easy prey for Bolshevik revolutionaries. Wilson thought the best way to prevent Bolshevik revolutions in the ravaged nations of Europe was to eliminate the conditions that drove people to such desperate measures. He urged the Allies to lift the blockade during the armistice and get food to the starving people of the Central Powers. Meanwhile, the Allies would offer a generous peace on the condition that the defeated nations replace their militaristic governments with democratic ones. Wilson firmly believed that liberal democratic institutions and national self-determination offered the world the best protection against the war and suffering produced by the imperialism of the old aristocratic orders and against the revolutionary tyranny of the Bolsheviks.

Georges Clemenceau, the premier of France, came to symbolize European opposition to Wilson's "new diplomacy." Clemenceau remarked cynically, "God gave us the Ten Commandments, and we broke them. Wilson gives us the Fourteen Points. We shall see." He told Colonel House, "I can get on with you. You are practical. I understand you, but talking to Wilson is something like talking to Jesus Christ!" Clemenceau was not willing to trust the League of Nations or the United States to prevent Germany from launching another attack on France. He wanted Germany weakened to the point that it could not break the peace even if it wished to. He called not only for the return of Alsace-Lorraine to France, but also for a buffer state along the Rhine under French domination and French control of the Saar Valley.

These acquisitions would give France Germany's most productive iron and coal mines, along with much of its industrial capacity. French occupation of the Rhine would prevent the Germans from fortifying that natural barrier to a French invasion. Clemenceau also demanded huge reparation payments from Germany, both to weaken that nation and to help pay for the enormous destruction France had suffered. All the fighting on the western front had taken place on French rather than German soil, and since the Germans had flooded the French coal mines before retreating, Clemenceau had no doubt that France was justified in compensating itself at the expense of the enemy.

Clemenceau was all the more determined to weaken Germany because the Bolshevik Revolution in Russia had removed a major prop from the old balance of power. Without a Russian ally to threaten Germany from behind, France could not afford to have Germany return to its previous strength. France wanted forcibly to overthrow the Bolshevik regime and bring Russia back into the family of Western nations. Unfortunately for Clemenceau, only the United States had enough troops and resources left to make intervention in Russia successful. Clemenceau tried to inveigle the United States into providing the wherewithal, but when Wilson proved reluctant, the French decided their best alternative was to support and enlarge the tier of new nations in eastern Europe that were emerging out of former German, Austrian, and Russian territories.

The French could expect American help in this enterprise because Wilson saw nations such as Poland, Czechoslovakia, Rumania, Yugoslavia, Latvia, Lithuania, and Estonia as embodying his principle of national self-determination. Thus, France hoped to erect a cordon sanitaire against the spread of bolshevism from Russia and to build an alliance of eastern European nations to contain and oppose Germany from behind. When Wilson warned that such a punitive peace might drive Germany, Austria, and Hungary to bolshevism, Clemenceau argued that the best way to prevent this was not food and generosity, but bayonets.

Clemenceau's approach to peace found substantial support from the Allies, whose war aims could be satisfied only by stripping the Central Powers. Great Britain was not as concerned about the continental territorial settlement as was France, but it wanted many of Germany's colonies, and it especially wanted to confiscate the German navy. Italy had entered the war because the Allies had promised to revise its boundaries with Austria. Italy would acquire the Brenner Pass and with it a strategically defensible border at the crest of the Alps. It also would get the important Adriatic port of Trieste. Italy insisted that these commitments be fulfilled even though the new border violated the principle of national self-determination and incorporated the German-speaking Tyrol. Later, the Italians went even further to demand the port cities and strategic islands of the Dalmatian coast that were to have been vital outlets to the Adriatic Sea for the new nation of Yugoslavia. Italy could justify its desire for such ports, especially the city of Fiume, on the grounds that many Italians lived there, surrounded by the Slavic inhabitants of the interior. However, Italy's major purpose was absolute control of the Adriatic.

Japan too insisted on its pound of flesh from Germany. The Allies had promised to give the Japanese control of the German colony on the Shandong peninsula of China, along with Germany's Pacific island colonies north of the equator (those south of the equator would join Australia and New Zealand in the British Empire). Great Britain, Italy, and Japan also largely agreed with Clemenceau that the spread of revolution in Russia and Central Europe should be countered by force rather than generosity.

Intervention in Russia

The old diplomacy of Clemenceau and the new diplomacy of Wilson fought a preliminary battle before the peace conference as Wilson and the Allies heatedly debated the proper approach to the revolution in Russia. The French and Italians, with support from many prominent Britons like First Lord of the Admiralty Winston Churchill, wanted a full-scale intervention to overturn the Bolsheviks. Their primary goal was to restore the eastern front.

In the spring of 1917, a moderate socialist government originally had taken power in Russia after the overthrow of the czar, and it had obliged the Allies by pursuing the war. But it had lost thousands of men in an abortive campaign on the Austrian front, bringing total Russian deaths in the war to 1.7 million. The Bolsheviks then denounced the war and came to power in the autumn of 1917 on a wave of popular disgust with the suffering and fruitless slaughter incurred by the inept leaders of both imperial and postimperial Russia. The Bolsheviks kept their promise to end the war by accepting the costly peace of Brest-Litovsk in March 1918 and abandoning Estonia, Latvia, Lithuania, Finland, Poland, and the Ukraine to German control or influence. Since Lenin had arrived in Russia after the czar's overthrow aboard a sealed German train, some Allied officials feared the Bolsheviks not only as a menace in their own right, but also as potentially active contributors to the German war effort.

The European Allies sent economic aid, weapons, and some military advisers to the scattered anti-Bolshevik forces in Russia, but only the Americans and perhaps the Japanese could supply the troops necessary for full-scale intervention. Wilson opposed such an effort. The European Allies nonetheless cajoled him into sending American troops to participate in the occupation of Murmansk and Archangel, the two northern Russian ports through which the Allies had sent supplies while Russia was still in the war. Because of the inefficiency of the railroads that connected those ports to the Russian interior, some 160,000 tons of supplies furnished on credit to the Russians had piled up in Archangel, and the Allies feared that the Russians would turn them over to Germany. The Allies planned to take back the supplies and keep the ports out of German hands. Some 5,000 American troops moved into northern Russia under orders to protect the ports. World War I ended three months later, but winter trapped the occupying forces until they could be withdrawn in 1919. After they left, the Bolsheviks shot between 10,000 and 30,000 collaborators.

Wilson and the Allies occupied a third major Russian port as well, the Pacific harbor of Vladivostok, which served as the eastern terminus of the Trans-Siberian Railroad and housed an Allied stockpile four times greater than Archangel's. Again Wilson was reluctant. But the Japanese were not, and Wilson feared that a unilateral Japanese intervention on the heels of Japan's Twenty-One Demands on China would result in Japanese control of Manchuria and the Trans-Siberian Railroad.

The plight of the Czech Legion, 40,000 Czech soldiers who had fought on the eastern front alongside the Russians and had been trapped there when Russia left the war, also influenced Wilson. The Czechs were riding the Trans-Siberian Railroad to the Pacific, where they expected to be ferried back to Europe to join the war on the western front. They were bitterly anti-Bolshevik and were busily fighting various Bolshevik units along the way. A portion of the Czechs reached Vladivostok and occupied the city, but a Bolshevik force blocked the railroad and stranded the remainder 2,000 miles up the line in Siberia.

Wilson got the idea that nearly 1 million German and Austrian prisoners of war held in Siberia had been released by the revolutionaries and were attacking the Czech Legion. The Allies had long feared that the Germans might use these prisoners to take control of eastern Russia. Wilson sent an American contingent of 7,000 American troops to join the Japanese in occupying Vladivostok.

In joining the Siberian intervention, Wilson did not understand the intentions of the Allies. They intended not to withdraw the Czechs, but to encourage them to stay and fight. The Czechs in Vladivostok actually linked up with their compatriots on the Trans-Siberian Railroad two days before the Americans arrived. The Americans then stayed in Vladivostok while the Japanese occupied the Manchurian portion of the railroad. A British unit of 1,000 soldiers helped clear the railway and then took up garrison duty in the Urals in support of the anti-Bolshevik effort of Russian admiral A.V. Kolchak.

As had been the case at Murmansk and Archangel, the Americans stayed on in Vladivostok for a year and a half, even though the war ended a few weeks after their arrival. Wilson did not want to withdraw them during the peace conference. But he did hope to find means other than force to combat bolshevism in Russia and elsewhere.

During the peace conference, Wilson and British prime minister David Lloyd George wanted to invite the Bolsheviks and their leading domestic opponents to Paris to try to work out an arrangement under the guidance of the major Western powers. Clemenceau refused to have the Bolsheviks in France, but consented to such a meeting on the island of Prinkipo in the Turkish Sea of Marmara. Clemenceau's consent was deceptive, however, for he successfully encouraged the Russian Whites to reject the invitation to meet with the Bolshevik Reds.

Surprisingly, the Bolsheviks had expressed a willingness to come to Prinkipo even though it meant sitting down as mere equals with numerous Russian factions that could not compare in power and influence with the Bolshevik government. Since the Prinkipo meeting was off, Colonel House thought the Bolsheviks' positive response made it worthwhile to send a mission to talk with Lenin. With Britain's silent approval, House delegated Assistant Secretary of State William Bullitt to explore the possibility of exchanging Allied withdrawal from Russia for amnesty toward those who had collaborated with the Whites and the Allies. Lenin, who evidently was fearful of a major Allied offensive in the spring, offered Bullitt a truce with all sides continuing to occupy their present positions; but he insisted on a reply within two weeks.

The excited Bullitt met a wall of apathy on his return to Paris. Lloyd George, under heavy attack from conservatives at home for even considering recognition of the Bolsheviks, denied ever endorsing the Bullitt mission. Wilson evidently regarded the mission as a mere fact-finding expedition; he had no more interest than Lloyd George in according recognition to the Bolsheviks. He turned instead to a plan offered by Herbert Hoover, the former director of the American relief effort in German-occupied Belgium, to undertake a food distribution program in Russia designed to wean the Russian people away from bolshevism.

Hoover thought Lenin might be desperate enough to accept a truce, turn over Russian railroads to a neutral commission for distribution of the food, allow local elections to choose the domestic distributors, and all this without any commitment to Allied withdrawal. Lenin was not that malleable. In any case, Clemenceau and other conservatives considered the Wilson and Hoover plan appeasement and stalled it because Kolchak's Whites seemed for a short time to be winning.

In the end, however, the scattered White contingents failed to coordinate their efforts, alienated many Russians with their forced conscription of troops, and fell apart before the Red onslaught. The Allies withdrew ignominiously, having done far too little to overturn the Bolsheviks, but more than enough to confirm them in their hatred and distrust of the capitalist West.

Pressures on the Peace from Left and Right

During the peace conference in Paris, Wilson, Clemenceau, and the Allies had to deal with Communist revolutions in the defeated Central Powers as well as in Russia. Since defeat in the war had discredited the old orders in Germany, Austria, and Hungary, politics swung to the left. In Hungary a moderate socialist government displaced the old Hapsburg Empire. But Czech and Rumanian troops took much of Transylvania from the helpless Hungarians, while the Yugoslavs appropriated Hungary's last anthracite mines. This demonstration of Wilson's inability to keep his promises of a just peace, along with the food shortage produced by the continuing Allied blockade, undermined Hungary's successor government just as the military defeat had undermined the old imperial regime. The moderates, giving up, turned the government over to the Communists, headed by Béla Kun. Kun's government lasted only 133 days, but it threw a major fright into the peacemakers in Paris.

To add to Allied concern, a Communist government took power briefly in Bavaria. Even Vienna trembled on the brink of revolution. Most critical, the moderate socialist government in Germany, facing the harsh demands of the Allies, found itself under siege from the radical Left and its charismatic Sparticist leaders Karl Liebknecht and Rosa Luxemburg. But Hindenburg and the German army, remaining loyal to the government, threw their weight against the radical Left. The Freicorps, unofficial organizations of returning soldiers, crushed a radical-led general strike in Berlin and summarily executed Liebknecht and Luxemburg. Ultimately the moderate government survived, but it continually pointed to the danger of revolution as reason for the Allies to moderate the peace terms.

Clemenceau refused to be deterred by such considerations. As he had urged intervention in Russia, so he insisted that the Allies should take what they wanted from the Central Powers and forcibly quell any radical attempt to exploit the situation. His approach found increasing support throughout the Allied nations. As defeat turned the Central Powers to the left, victory turned the domestic politics of the Allied nations to the right. French military commander Marshal Ferdinand Foch and France's president, Raymond Poincaré, demanded that Clemenceau be even harder on the defeated enemy. England's prime minister, Lloyd George, won reelection on the eve of the conference by promising to squeeze the Germans "until the pips squeak" and thus encouraged the British Right to demand that he secure large reparations from Germany. The moderate premier of Italy, Vittorio Orlando, was under immense pressure for annexations from his foreign minister, Baron Sonnino, and from populist right-wing groups led by the noisy demagogue Benito Mussolini.

Even Wilson faced a rising rightist tide at home. During the off-year election of 1918, Wilson had appealed for the election of more congressional Democrats to support his program. The Republicans, denouncing Wilson for breaching the bipartisan approach to foreign policy that ostensibly had prevailed during the war, won narrow victories in both houses of Congress. With their two-seat margin in the Senate, the Republicans were able to reorganize that body's entire committee structure. This included the Senate Foreign Relations Committee, to which Wilson would have to submit his peace treaty. The most likely candidate for chair of the committee was the president's worst political enemy, Henry Cabot Lodge. Just as Wilson left for the peace conference, Lodge proclaimed that the Allies should be permitted to dismember Germany and exact heavy reparations from it. In effect, he and his fellow Republicans told the Allied leaders they could afford to ignore Wilson's grandiose plans because Wilson had been repudiated by his own people in the election of 1918.

Negotiating the Treaty of Versailles

The electoral defeat of 1918 was not the only factor that undercut Wilson's position; the terms of the armistice agreement weakened Wilson's bargaining power as well. Wilson personally handled the first stage of the negotiations when the Germans approached him rather than the other Allies with an offer to make peace based on the Fourteen Points. Wilson spent the month of October 1918 clarifying the terms of the armistice in the face of steady complaints from Republicans like Theodore Roosevelt that peace should be made by hammering guns rather than clicking typewriters. Wilson let the Germans know that a democratically governed Germany might receive better terms than the kaiser's militaristic regime, and the German Reichstag dutifully installed a democratic government. The kaiser abdicated and fled to Holland, where, according to a popular gibe, he lived for twenty-three years "unwept, unhonored, and unhung."

When the British and French objected that Wilson was conducting these preliminary negotiations unilaterally and expressed reservations about the Fourteen Points, Wilson secured German approval for Britain's rejection of the point concerning freedom of the seas and for France's insistence on specific recognition of its right to reparations for civilian damages. Then, on the assumption that the Fourteen Points with these minor reservations would serve as the basis for a final peace, Wilson turned the negotiations over to the Allied military command.

Marshal Foch, with the full support of America's General John Pershing, insisted on terms that would ensure the Germans could not resume the war. He demanded that the Germans turn over half their machine guns, a third of their artillery, and all of their battle fleet. The Germans also had to permit the Allies to occupy bridgeheads over the Rhine. The Germans bridled at the terms, but by this time felt incapable of further resistance. The British interned the German fleet at Scapa Flow, its major naval base, where the

The U.S. delegation to the Paris Peace Conference *(left to right):* "Colonel" Edward House, Secretary of State Robert Lansing, President Woodrow Wilson, Henry White, and General Tasker Bliss. *(Courtesy of the National Archives)*

German crews ultimately scuttled their own ships. The Allies left the blockade in force until seven months later, when the final peace had been concluded. The Allied ground forces improved their position with each periodic renewal of the armistice, leaving the Germans with no geographical position to defend even if they had had the weapons to do so. Thus Germany could exert no military leverage to ensure a just peace; pointing to the moral obligation of the Allies to live up to Wilson's prearmistice agreement, the Germans could only threaten to collapse into Bolshevik arms.

Although the disarming of Germany and the defeat of the Democratic Party in the U.S. midterm elections of 1918 undermined Wilson's bargaining power, his reception on his arrival in Europe seemed to restore it. The president received a tumultuous welcome in the cities he visited on his way to Paris and the peace conference. Wilson assumed that the people in these huge emotional crowds sympathized with his peace plans. No doubt many did, but many others welcomed him as another victor, rather than an angel of mercy. Wilson was wrong to assume that the nationalistic demands of the European leaders at the conference went beyond the sentiments of their constituencies.

Wilson did have another element of strength. Before his departure for Paris, he had had Colonel House assemble a group of academic experts, dubbed The Inquiry, to investigate the various territorial, ethnic, political, and economic issues that would come up in the negotiations. The Inquiry helped make the American delegation the best informed at the conference. But the makeup of the negotiating delegation itself was not nearly so strong. Wilson, of course, was the chief delegate. Colonel House, who held no official position in the government and was heartily disliked by almost all except Wilson, was a second delegate. Secretary of State Lansing, who was not in full sympathy with Wilson and was seldom consulted by the president, was the third. General Tasker Bliss served competently as a military representative, although his liberal Wilsonian outlook was far out of line with that of General Pershing and much of the rest of the military establishment. Finally, Wilson ignored William Howard Taft and Elihu Root, the two most powerful Republican Party advocates of an international peacekeeping organization, and chose Henry White instead as a Republican representative on the delegation. White was a career diplomat with no influence whatever over the congressional Republican regulars who stood in the way of Wilson's peace objectives. One periodical portrayed the delegates as follows:

Name	Occupation	Representing
Woodrow Wilson	President	Himself
Robert Lansing	Secretary of state	The executive
Henry White	None	Nobody
Edward M. House	Scout	The executive
Tasker H. Bliss	Soldier	The commander in chief

The Paris Peace Conference, which began meeting in January 1919, was a huge affair, with twenty-seven national delegations forming some fifty commissions and holding over 2,000 separate meetings. One observer described it as a "riot in a parrot house." The Allies did not invite Germany to join the deliberations; they decided to negotiate terms among themselves and then present them as a fait accompli to the Central Powers. Russia did not participate in the treaty making either. It remained to be seen whether a peace settlement could be maintained when two of the six major world powers were not party to it.

Great Britain moved quickly to secure the German colonies it wanted, supported by the Japanese, French, and Italians, who also received parts of the German Empire. Wilson, in conformity with the strictures against colonialism in the Fourteen Points, tried to moderate the colonial partition and succeeded at least in getting the German colonies nominally assigned as wards of the League of Nations, to be administered by the colonial powers as temporary mandates.

The League of Nations itself was Wilson's great passion. He used his prestige to make it the first order of business and got himself appointed chair of the commission assigned to draw up the League charter. Driving himself and the commission mercilessly, he managed to formulate a draft in only ten days. The League of Nations would consist of an Assembly, in which all members would have one vote, and a Council, composed of the Big Five (the United States, Great Britain, France, Italy, and Japan) as permanent members, with several temporary elected nations. Under Article X of the League covenant, the organization would provide united international action to preserve the independence and territorial integrity of all its members. The League also would be an integral part of the peace treaty. Wilson proudly proclaimed, "a living thing is born." Then, on February 24, 1919, he boarded his ship for a three-week return to the United States to sign pending congressional bills and prepare domestic public opinion for participation in the new international organization.

The president quickly ran into trouble. Many members of Congress resented Wilson's failure to consult them or keep them informed of the important proposals he was making to the peace conference. The Senate and House committee members Wilson summoned to discuss the League with him greeted the president's advocacy with sullen silence. Senator Henry Cabot Lodge circulated what came to be known as the Round Robin Petition, which harshly criticized the League, and thirty-nine members of the recently elected Senate signed it. This was more than enough senators to prevent Wilson from getting the two-thirds vote necessary to consent to the treaty. Wilson responded defiantly that the League of Nations covenant would come back to the United States so intertwined with the rest of the peace treaty that it could not be removed without ruining the entire structure of the settlement. Evidently he never dreamed the Senate might reject the entire treaty in order to rid itself of the League.

Despite Wilson's bold response, he knew he had to modify the League covenant if he expected to win the approval of two-thirds of the Senate. Even some senators friendly to the idea of a League of Nations worried that the covenant did not specifically recognize the Monroe Doctrine, exempt domestic issues like immigration and tariffs from its purview, or provide a means for a nation to withdraw from the organization. Wilson would have to make concessions to the other Allies to win their consent to these changes.

Wilson returned to Paris in mid-March to find his bargaining position even weaker than he had expected. He had left Colonel House in charge of the American side of the negotiations and had told House he did not want the work of the conference held up by his own absence. But he did not expect that Colonel House actually would try to speed up the conference and bring many matters close to settlement before Wilson returned. In House's haste to get a settlement, he consented to a French plan to include some substantive peace issues in a temporary military settlement, thus providing immediate relief from uncertainty and chaos in large areas of Europe, while leaving only the more controversial issues to the lengthy negotiations that would lead to a final treaty. In the discussion over this temporary military settlement, House tentatively had implied American willingness to concede some of France's territorial and reparations demands. Worse, from Wilson's point of view, this preliminary settlement would not include the League of Nations. Since Wilson had fought France to get the covenant included in the peace treaty itself, he assumed that House had fallen for a European plot to kill the League. Publicly announcing that the League of Nations would be an inextricable part of the treaty, Wilson set about trying to retrieve the ground he blamed House for losing.

He faced a tough battle. Clemenceau inspired a virulent French press campaign against Wilson, accusing the president of delaying the peace treaty so as to invite the Bolsheviks

The Big Four at the Paris Peace Conference *(left to right):* Vittorio Orlando of Italy, David Lloyd George of Great Britain, Georges Clemenceau of France, and Woodrow Wilson of the United States. *(Courtesy of the National Archives)*

to take advantage of the resulting chaos. During this time of extreme stress, Wilson fell seriously ill and had to conduct his campaign from a sickbed. At one point he ordered his ship to be ready to take him back to America and threatened to sign a separate peace with Germany if the Allies continued to demand harsh terms. In the end, however, he compromised more than his adversaries.

Lloyd George extorted a commitment from Wilson that the United States would not build up its navy to rival that of the British. In exchange, the British consented to an amendment to the League covenant recognizing the Monroe Doctrine. Lloyd George also joined Clemenceau in pressing for a huge reparations settlement, and ultimately they got Wilson to turn the question over to a reparations commission. Wilson wanted to put a limit on the amount the commission could award, but under Allied pressure he left the sum open. In addition to this blank check for the reparations commission, Wilson agreed to the French demand that veterans' pensions be considered civilian war damages and added to the reparations bill, a serious distortion of the prearmistice discussions Wilson had conducted with Germany.

Since Lloyd George already had won Britain's major goals, he joined Wilson to secure a compromise on French territorial demands. France recovered Alsace-Lorraine. The French also would occupy the strategic Rhineland for fifteen years, after which it would become a demilitarized zone of Germany. The League of Nations would administer the Saar Valley, while France took over the area's coal mines. After fifteen years the inhabitants of the Saar would conduct a plebiscite to determine whether they would rejoin Germany. All assumed they would vote to do so. In exchange for Clemenceau's agreement not to remove the Saar and Rhineland from Germany permanently, Great Britain and the United States signed a separate security treaty with the French in which they promised to intervene if a revived Germany attacked France. (The Senate ultimately declined this security pact as well as the Treaty of Versailles. The French felt betrayed, since they received neither the Rhineland nor the security treaty.)

The reparations and western border settlements were not the only ways in which the peace settlement weakened Germany. The Allies gave Poland a corridor through East Prussia so it could have access to the sea. As a concession to the German character of the port city of Danzig (now Gdansk), which lay at the corridor's terminus, the Allies made Danzig a free city rather than a formal part of Poland. Czechoslovakia acquired the Sudetenland, with its German minority of some 3 million. The Treaty of Versailles reduced German armed forces to what was essentially a police constabulary, a provision accompanied with a vague promise that the Allies would soon disarm. The settlement prohibited any German tie to Austria. Wilson and the Allies also reluctantly permitted Italy to take full advantage of its wartime treaty to acquire Austria's southern Tyrol, with its strategic Brenner Pass and its German population.

Italy was not so fortunate in its drive to acquire Fiume and the other Adriatic ports the Allies had promised to Yugoslavia. Wilson even appealed over the heads of the Italian delegation to the Italian people, asking them to repudiate the demands of their leaders. Orlando and Sonnino left the conference huffing that Wilson was trying to restore his lost virginity at Italian expense. To Wilson's great chagrin, the Italians gave Orlando tumultuous support for his stand on Fiume. But Wilson remained adamant, and Italy ultimately regarded the loss of its demands as reason to join Germany and other dissatisfied powers in their drive to revise the Treaty of Versailles.

If Wilson's stand on Fiume did not endear him to the Italians, it did temporarily revive his prestige among liberals in the United States and the rest of Europe. But his support quickly dissipated when Wilson, backing away from another confrontation with Japan, conceded Japanese control of Germany's former Chinese leasehold, the Shandong Peninsula. Japan in turn abandoned its drive to include a specific recognition of racial equality in the treaty, a provision Wilson knew would make ratification that much more difficult at home. The Japanese also promised to return the Shandong Peninsula to nominal Chinese sovereignty in the future and keep for themselves only the railroads and other economic concessions in the area. (This they did in 1923.) China objected to this arrangement and refused to sign the treaty. Wilson's liberal supporters despaired at yet another violation of the principle of national self-determination. Conservatives meanwhile found in the unpopularity of Wilson's decision to favor the Japanese over America's beloved China another weapon to use against Wilson's treaty.

Colonialism and Self-Determination in the Treaty of Versailles

The conflict between Wilson's popular commitment to self-determination and the territorial demands of the Allies, as illustrated in the Shandong, Fiume, and Tyrol situations, plagued the Paris negotiators throughout the conference. The failure of the peacemakers to deal with the issues of colonialism would come back to haunt the Allies, including the United States, from that day to this. Wilson's calls for self-determination brought swarms of petitions and petitioners to Paris from all over the globe. Vladimir Lenin and the Bolsheviks had been much more specific and passionate in their calls for the end to colonialism than Wilson, and in fact Wilson had issued his Fourteen Points and anticolonial statements in part to counter the appeal of the Russian Revolution. But in 1919 many anti-colonial leaders turned to Wilson because he appeared to have a real chance to win their autonomy, if not outright independence, while the Bolsheviks seemed a localized and rather sinister movement. Some of the petitioners for independence, including the Poles, Czechs, Serbs, Arabs, and Jewish Zionists, received invitations to the conference. All of these were seen by the Allies as friendly or malleable peoples whose autonomy would weaken the former Central Powers. Most European petitioners and almost all non-European seekers of self-determination were ignored.

Sinn Fein petitioned in vain for Irish independence from Great Britain even as British and Irish soldiers returning from World War I were using artillery to put down rebellions in Dublin. Catalans centered on Barcelona petitioned for independence from Spain. Armenians, reeling from massacres at the hands of Turks and Kurds in eastern Turkey, called for redress and nationhood. Their cries for independence were joined by Georgians, Syrians, Lebanese, and Assyrian Christians. Koreans begged for independence from the Japanese Empire. Ho Chi Minh, a young kitchen assistant in Paris, submitted a petition for the independence of Vietnam from France. Mohandas Gandhi joined other Indian nationalists in petitioning for independence from Great Britain. Egyptian nationalists led by Sa'd Zaghlul, still revered today in Egypt as the father of the nation, led a delegation to demand that the Allies free them from British rule. The African-American scholar and reformer W.E.B. DuBois organized a Pan-African Congress to represent Africans before the peacemakers.

The Allied dismissal of almost all these petitions reverberated through the years and culminated in the collapse of the European colonial system after World War II. Those leaders who had petitioned for mere autonomy rather than outright independence moved toward more radical calls for independence. Gandhi organized the Indian National Congress to demand independence rather than mere self-rule within the British Empire. Sa'd Zaghlul formed the Wafd Party in Egypt to call for independence from Great Britain. And many other leaders turned away from Wilsonian toward Leninist ideology. In the wake of the May Fourth movement in China, a huge protest in Tiananmen Square against the Shandong settlement, Mao Zedong wrote that not only China's interests had been dismissed, but also those of the Indians and Koreans. "So much for national self-determination! I think it is really shameless!"[1]

One of the failures of Wilsonian self-determination occurred in the disposition of Germany's colonies. The Allies had agreed in the wartime secret treaties to divide Germany's colonies between them. Wilson, however, insisting he would not stand for "dividing the swag," argued that "if the process of annexation went on, the League of Nations would be discredited from the beginning." On the other hand, even Wilson believed that many peoples were not yet fit for self-government. Thus, he did not challenge the right of the Allies to continue holding their own colonies, as Ho Chi Minh found out when he received no answer to his petition for Vietnamese independence from France. Wilson argued only that the Allies should not annex the colonies of Germany directly, but instead hold and govern them temporarily as "mandates" of the League of Nations while the peoples were prepared for self-government. Wilson considered this a major shift away from colonialism, but in reality the Allies divided Germany's colonies between them with no consultation whatever of the people of those colonies, and the only real difference between those mandates and annexed colonies was that the countries holding mandates had to make an annual report to the League of Nations. In this fashion, Japan acquired Germany's island colonies in the Pacific north of the equator (including the Marshall, Mariana, Caroline, Yap, and Palau Islands, which the United States would invade in its island-hopping campaign of World War II). The British and their Commonwealth would take the German Pacific colonies south of the equator, including southern New Guinea for Australia and Samoa for New Zealand.

The Allies also divided Germany's colonies in Africa to hold as mandates. Again, no one consulted the inhabitants of those areas. France got Togoland, the Camaroons, and full control of Morocco. Great Britain got Tanganyika (later Tanzania) in East Africa. Belgium got mandates for Rwanda and Burundi. South Africa got German South West Africa (later Namibia), its representatives claiming that South Africans understood the natives better than the cruel Germans. After World War II, these mandates would pass from the defunct League to the United Nations and would be freed in the general African revolt against colonialism. None of those mandates had been governed with any consideration of the interests of their inhabitants, and the borders established by the colonialists cut across ethnic boundaries in ways that made the resulting nations very unstable. The new African nations suffered mightily as a consequence once they secured their independence.

The peacemakers extended their system of mandates to the Turkish as well as the German empire. Britain, France, and Russia had made a preliminary agreement in 1916 whereby Russia would get access to the Dardanelles while Britain and France would divide between them the Arab portions of the empire. In the Sykes-Picot agreement of 1916, Britain and France proceeded to make that division; Britain staked its claim to Palestine and Mesopotamia (Iraq) while France would get Syria and Lebanon. When the peace conference began in 1919 and Wilson began pushing for self-determination, France and Britain quickly agreed that these areas would be mandates rather than colonies, but, after a great deal of bickering, took them over with little provision for the rising Arab nationalism that would ultimately bring the colonialists to grief in the Middle East.

As for the rest of Turkey's territory, the Russians had sacrificed their claim to the Dardanelles because of the Bolshevik Revolution, but Turkey's neighbors, with the support of Britain, France, and the United States, who disdained Turkey because of its wartime atrocities against the Armenians, threatened to dismember the defeated state and leave it with a mere rump of territory. France, Britain, Italy, and even the United States considered taking a mandate for a portion of Turkey. Greece especially sought to regain its ancient glory at Turkey's expense. Using the presence of Greek residents in and around Istanbul (Constantinople) and Asia Minor as evidence that it was implementing self-determination, Greece secured the backing of Wilson, Clemenceau, and Lloyd George to occupy the primary port of the Anatolian coast, Smyrna (Izmir), and then attacked into the interior of Turkey. Meanwhile, after signing the Treaty of Versailles with the Germans, the Allies imposed the Treaty of Sèvres on Turkey in 1920, not only giving Greece much of Anatolia but also providing for an independent Armenia and Kurdistan and for Greek control of Turkish territory up to the Dardanelles (exempting Istanbul and a bit of its surrounding territory). The threat to dismember Turkey, however, aroused Turkish nationalism, which was organized and led by a military officer named Mustafa Kemal Ataturk. Ataturk restored Turkey's homeland by occupying Kurdistan and most of Armenia, forcing the retreat of British, French, and Italian occupying forces, and attacking the overextended Greek forces in Anatolia. The Turkish conquest of the Greeks in Smyrna was accompanied by killing, looting, and the burning of the city. The many Greeks in Anatolia fled their homes of centuries. The Turks in Greece fled in turn for the safety of Turkey. The bitterness caused by this mutual ethnic cleansing has extended to this day even though both Greece and Turkey became NATO allies of the United States after World War II.

Even in those areas where the Allies sought not mandates but true self-determination in independent and self-governing nations, the peacemakers had great difficulties because of competing nationalist, ethnic, and religious identities, especially where those populations were mixed. In the Balkans, the Allies consented to a united Yugoslavia against the territorial claims of Italy, Hungary, and Rumania. They did so in part because the leaders of the area presented a fait accompli after they broke away from the defeated Austrian Empire, but also because the various ethnic and religious groups spoke a common language: Serbo-Croatian. Despite that common language, however, the groups that made up the South Slav (Yugoslav) region—Serbian Orthodox Christians, Croatian and Slovenian Roman Catholics, and Bosnian Muslims—generally detested each other and in many cases had opposed each other in the war, with Catholics generally supporting Austria-Hungary while Orthodox Christians fought on the side of Serbia and its patron, Russia. Not only did the Allies consent to a new unified Yugoslavia, but also they extended the borders of the new nation so that all its neighbors except Greece regarded the fragile country as an aggressive nuisance. Thus it was plundered by its neighbors and ravaged by internal warfare during World War II, was temporarily restored to unity after 1945 under Marshal Tito, and then disintegrated into atrocious ethnic cleansing after the Cold War.

In 1919—while the Bolshevik Revolution and the innumerable conflicts over the remnants of the Turkish Empire still raged—the Allies completed their bundle of compromises over Germany and called the Germans to the Palace of Versailles to receive the completed treaty. The Germans balked at the terms and especially at a clause that admitted Germany's guilt for starting the war. They also complained that since they had not surrendered but only agreed to an armistice, they should be permitted to negotiate the peace instead of having it imposed on them. The Allies made a few minor adjustments in response to Germany's complaints. For instance, they allowed a plebiscite in Upper Silesia instead of awarding the province outright to Poland. But then the Allies threatened to march on Berlin unless Germany signed. On June 23, 1919, the Germans grudgingly accepted the Treaty of Versailles.

The Senate, the League of Nations, and the Treaty of Versailles

Wilson returned home to a barrage of criticism. Henry Cabot Lodge, recently appointed chair of the Senate Foreign Relations Committee, made the committee a forum for every variety of denunciation available. Disillusioned liberals like William Bullitt testified against the treaty on the grounds that Wilson had betrayed the Fourteen Points and imposed a "Carthaginian" peace on Germany. Liberals worried that the crushing reparations imposed on Germany along with the fragmentation of eastern Europe would make Central Europe's economic recovery impossible. Disillusioned liberals also opposed American participation in a League of Nations whose purpose, according to Article X, would be the preservation of boundaries and territorial entities that were products of an unjust peace. Why should the United States protect Italy against the natural resentments of Germans and Slavs, or Japan against a rightfully offended China? Irish-Americans joined the chorus against the League. They feared it would require American support of Britain's territorial integrity against the legitimate aspirations of the oppressed Irish, whose Easter Uprising the British had crushed in 1916.

Lodge also encouraged the testimony of conservative opponents of the League. Conservatives did not concern themselves much about the harsh treatment of the Central Powers, whom they would just as soon have beaten into total surrender and impotence. Conservatives worried instead that the League of Nations would threaten America's historic tradition of independence, isolation, and unilateralism. On this issue they were joined by a few senators whose liberalism took the form of isolationism rather than Wilsonian internationalism.

Wilson and other defenders of the League pointed out that Article X of the League covenant was a moral rather than a legal commitment. They reminded Americans that some concessions to the desires of the Allies had been inevitable. They insisted that at least Wilson's presence and persistence had moderated Allied goals. Germany had lost only about 13 percent of its territory and 10 percent of its population, and much of both had historically been French or Polish.

At first a clear majority of both the Senate and the American people at large favored the treaty and the League of Nations. But Lodge managed the opposition very adroitly. Six of the ten Republicans he appointed to the Foreign Relations Committee were irreconcilably against the treaty, and he struck a deal with them whereby they would support his attempts to attach amendments and reservations to the treaty before voting against the whole package. At first, the majority of the committee attached forty-five amendments and four reservations. When it became apparent that the Senate would reject such a package, in part because the amendments would require Wilson to renegotiate the entire settlement, Lodge fell back on a set of fourteen reservations. Three of the four great powers—Britain, France, Italy, and Japan—would have to accept these reservations, but there would be no need to renegotiate the treaty itself. The most significant of Lodge's reservations disavowed the obligation to defend victims of aggression unless Congress approved. Many of the other reservations were irrelevant or redundant.

Wilson regarded Lodge's proposals as dire threats to the integrity of the League of Nations. Ignoring his doctor's warnings following his bout with illness in Paris, Wilson embarked on a cross-country train tour to drum up support for the League.[2] After a speech in Pueblo, Colorado, he collapsed. He was rushed back to Washington, but several days later a massive stroke paralyzed half his body and left him an invalid, confined to his bedroom. His second wife, Edith, guarded his time and privacy so he could not aid in the battle for the League of Nations or keep his finger on the pulse of public opinion. The stroke also seemed to drain his small store of political flexibility. Even though he constructed four reservations of his own for possible use by the Democrats to counter Republican opposition in an emergency, he refused to compromise at all with Lodge. Insisting that the Lodge reservations "emasculated" the League of Nations, he ordered Democrats to vote against the treaty if those reservations were attached. Democrats joined the irreconcilables to defeat the treaty with the attached Lodge reservations, thirty-nine senators voting for it to fifty-five against. Then the irreconcilables and Republicans defeated the Democrats' attempt to pass the treaty without reservations, thirty-eight to fifty-three.

Public outcry and the fact that four-fifths of the Senate supported the League in some form forced Lodge and the Senate to reconsider. Lodge actually began to meet with some Democrats and Republican "mild reservationists" to work out a compromise. But the irreconcilables threatened to disrupt both Lodge's career and the Republican Party, and he abandoned the discussions. Wilson proved no more cooperative. He continued to insist that his loyal Democratic followers reject the treaty if the Lodge reservations were attached. In the final vote on the Peace of Versailles, twenty-one Democrats who realized that the choice was between the treaty with reservations and no treaty at all deserted Wilson and voted for it. But twenty-three Democrats joined the irreconcilables, and the treaty fell seven votes short of the two-thirds majority necessary to consent to ratification.

Wilson, despite his perilous physical condition, hoped to run again for president in 1920 and make the election a referendum on the treaty. A public mandate might still make it possible to bring the United States into his beloved League of Nations. But the Democratic Party nominated Governor James Cox of Ohio. Cox and his running mate, Franklin Delano Roosevelt, campaigned on a platform that supported the League of Nations, but they did not make the League the centerpiece of their effort. The Republican nominee, Warren G. Harding, purposely muddied the issue. Many prominent Republicans, including Elihu Root and Herbert Hoover, insisted that a vote for Harding was a vote for a modified League. Irreconcilables insisted that Harding opposed the peace settlement. Harding, uttering vacuous platitudes that could be interpreted either way, won the election by promising to return the country to quiet and "normalcy." He made no attempt to revive the League during his administration; he said it was dead as the dodo. In 1921 he signed a separate peace with Germany and left the shrunken League of Nations to its own devices.

Controversial Issues

In the wake of the Senate's defeat of the Treaty of Versailles, participants and historians rushed to assess the blame for the failure of the peace. Even those who defended the treaty did so tepidly and spent most of their time discussing who was to blame for its shortcomings.

Although the greatest opposition to Wilson's League of Nations came from conservatives, there were very few published critiques of Wilson's diplomacy from that point of view. Henry Cabot Lodge's own memoirs of the Senate fight, *The Senate and the League of Nations* (1925), constituted the most thorough conservative analysis. Lodge insisted that Wilson should have told the Allies that "the boundaries to be fixed in Europe were nothing to us, that we wanted a peace which would put it beyond Germany's power for many years to attempt again to destroy the peace of the world and the freedom and civilization of mankind." He blamed Wilson's rigidity for the Senate's rejection of the League, but admitted he did not regret the League's ultimate defeat.

The memoirs of Wilson's secretary of state, Robert Lansing, also contributed to the conservative critique, even though Lansing favored ratification of the treaty with all its defects. Lansing criticized Wilson's attempt to make Europe's borders conform to the principle of popular self-determination because that principle often conflicted with strategic and economic interests and imperiled national safety, "always the paramount consideration in international and national affairs." Lansing pronounced himself favorable to the League of Nations only if it preserved America's right to a unilateral foreign policy. He believed Wilson was wrong to reject the treaty with the Lodge reservations. He reproved Wilson for attending the conference personally when the other nations had sent ministers rather than their heads of state and further argued that Wilson should have paid more attention to the advice of his fellow delegates. All these criticisms would become subjects of later historiographical disputes.[3]

These conservative criticisms probably had more impact on general popular opinion than the complaints of the disillusioned liberals, but the disillusioned liberals had more influence than the conservatives on historians and intellectuals. Most historians in the post–World War I era followed the liberals, bewailing Wilson's failure to achieve his aims rather than criticizing the aims themselves. John Maynard Keynes, the prominent English economist and a member of the British delegation to Paris, published a famous book called *The Economic Consequences of the Peace* (1920). In it he called Wilson's supposed negotiating collapse "one of the decisive moral events of history." Although he characterized most of Wilson's advisers as "dummies," he wished that Wilson had heeded Colonel House, who Keynes claimed had far more knowledge and wisdom than the president. Keynes especially flayed Wilson for refusing to admit the shortcomings of

CENTRAL EUROPE AND
THE BALKANS, 1925

TERRITORIAL CHANGES 1914–1925

Lost by Germany

Lost by Russia

Retained by Germany

Austria-Hungary, 1914

0   300 miles

DENMARK

SWEDEN

North Sea

Copenhagen

Baltic S

Schleswig Plebiscite

Heligoland — Wilhelmshaven

HOLSTEIN

Kiel Canal

POMER

UNITED KINGDOM

London

Amsterdam

NETHERLANDS

OLDEN-BURG

HANNOVER

Bremen

Hamburg

Elbe R.

MECKLEN-BURG

N

Berlin

BRANDENBURG

SILESIA

The Ruhr

Leipzig

Weimar

Dresden

Bre

Brussels

Lille

BELGIUM

Cologne

Rhineland Demilitarized

SAXONY

THÜRINGIA

Prague

HULTSCI

Eupen and Malmédy

Coblenz

LUX.

RHINELAND

Rhine R.

HESSE

Main R.

BOHEMIA

Brü

MOR

Compiègne

Paris

Versailles

Verdun

Marne R.

Seine R.

Alsace-Lorraine

Meuse R.

Saar Plebiscite, 1935

Nuremberg

BAVARIA

WÜRTTEMBERG

BADEN

Danube R.

Munich

Bra

Vienn

F R A N C E

Orléans

Loire R.

Belfort

Basel

Bern

AUSTRIA

Sopr

Klagenfurt Plebiscite

Clermont-Ferrand

Lyons

Geneva

SWITZERLAND

Rhône R.

Rhine R.

Locarno

TYROL

Drave R.

Burge Plebi

SAVOY

South Tyrol

Trentino

VENETIA

Piave R.

SLAV

Milan

Adige R.

Trieste

Venice

Fiume

Agram

Save R.

BO

Genoa

Istria and Fiume

HERZE

FINLAND

SOVIET UNION

ESTONIA

LATVIA

LITHUANIA

POLAND

BESSARABIA

TERRITORY LOST BY RUSSIA, 1914–1920

0   300 miles

Florence

Corsica (Fr.)

Ancona

Adriatic Sea

DALMA

ITALY

Rome

Sardinia (It.)

Naples

Lagos

English Channel

L'ATVIA

Memelland   Memel

LITHUANIA

Vilna District

Danzig Free City

Smolensk

Nieman R.   Kovno

Vilna

EAST PRUSSIA   SUWALKIE

RANIA

Polish Corridor

Allenstein Plebiscite

WHITE RUSSIA

Dnieper R.

Vistula R.   Bug R.

Warsaw

Brest-Litovsk

Pripet R.

P O L A N D

S O V I E T
U N I O N

Lodz

Curzon Line

Upper Silesia Plebiscite

eslau

Kiev

Dnieper R.

Cracow

GALICIA

Lvov (Lemberg)

Territory lost by Russia

CHIN

ünn

TESCHEN   SPIS

ORAVA

U K R A I N E

RAVIA

CZECHOSLOVAKIA

SLOVAKIA

CARPATHO-RUTHENIA

Dniester R.

atislava

na

ron

BUKOVINA

Pruth R.

BESSARABIA

Budapest

Tisza R.

MOLDAVIA

Jassy

Odessa

HUNGARY

Klausenburg

Transylvania

enland
biscite

Arad

RUMANIA

ONIA

BANAT

AUSTRIA-HUNGARY, 1914

Bucharest

DOBRUJA

Constantsa

OSNIA

Belgrade

Morava R.

Black Sea

EGOVINA

Sarajevo

S E R B I A

Danube R.

Varna

MATIA

YUGOSLAVIA

Nish

Sofia

BULGARIA

sta
(ft.)

MONTENEGRO

Serma R.

EAST RUMELIA

Skoplje

R U M E L I A

Adrianople

Vardar R.

Monastir

Istanbul

Tirana

GREECE

Western Thrace

GALLIPOLI

Dardenelles

TURKEY

ALBANIA

MACEDONIA

Salonika

the treaty and claimed that the sanctimonious Presbyterian president had tried to disguise his sellout by using the "subtlest sophisters and most hypocritical draftsmen" to clothe the pact with insincere language.

Wilson's chief defender in the two decades after World War I was his aide and press officer, Ray Stannard Baker, whom Wilson authorized to publish the presidential papers. Even Baker, however, began his defense by admitting the shortcomings of the peace settlement. His primary argument was that others were to blame for them. The Europeans had refused to abandon the precepts of the "old diplomacy." Secretary of State Robert Lansing had given aid and comfort to the treaty's adversaries because of his dislike of the principle of national self-determination and his continuing belief in an isolated America devoted to its own "selfish development." The pliable Colonel House, caving in to the pressure of the Europeans during Wilson's absence, had advanced a long way toward a preliminary peace that conceded many of the Allies' unjust demands while leaving out the League covenant. Wilson temporarily saved the League from this "plot" by making his "bombshell" announcement that the League would be tied inextricably to the treaty, but never had been able to regain the ground House had lost.[4]

Colonel House cooperated with Yale historian Charles Seymour to defend himself against the charges that he had been responsible for Wilson's concessions at Paris. House and Seymour insisted that the concessions were inevitable. Not only had Wilson's insistence on the League of Nations made it necessary to defer to the Allies on other issues, but Wilson had undermined his domestic position by rejecting House's advice to avoid a partisan appeal during the election of 1918 and refusing to add more prominent Republicans like Elihu Root or William Howard Taft to the negotiating delegation. The need to make concessions had "suddenly appeared" during Wilson's absence, but House committed Wilson to no concessions and certainly had not been part of a plot to sidetrack the League. Throughout his book, House spoke of "Wilson's compromises" and professed himself distraught that Wilson had made them.[5]

Meanwhile, Wilson's defenders turned their fire on Henry Cabot Lodge and the Senate. D.F. Fleming claimed that Lodge deliberately sabotaged the treaty. First Lodge undermined Wilson's bargaining position by forcing the president to seek amendments to the League covenant on his return to Paris. Then Lodge conspired with the irreconcilables to defeat the treaty in the Senate. Fleming rejected Lodge's claim that he had favored the League so long as reservations were attached to it. Fleming saw the attachment of the reservations strictly as a partisan maneuver to kill the peace. Fleming's analysis brought agreement from W. Stull Holt, whose study of the Treaty of Versailles and other treaties defeated by the Senate led him to argue that the Senate's role in making treaties should be reduced.[6]

In 1933 another Englishman turned his attention to Wilson at Versailles. Harold Nicolson, who had served as a minor functionary in the British delegation, echoed Keynes's argument that Wilson was a fanatical, obsessed Presbyterian true believer who convinced himself that he had not compromised his principles. Nicolson agreed that Wilson's peace program was better than continued dependence on the dangerous and provocative balance of power in the European system. But unlike Keynes, Nicolson concluded that Wilson's hopes had been impossible from the beginning. Neither Wilson's domestic opponents nor the European Allies would permit a generous peace. That being the case, Nicolson said, perhaps a Carthaginian peace would have been better than the hypocritical compromise that emerged. If the peace was not to be generous, better that it crush Germany rather than wound it and leave it powerful enough to act on its resentment.[7]

Nicolson's analysis had a tremendous impact in the United States. The rise of Hitler and the outbreak of World War II seemed to validate his argument. Many popular pronouncements in Europe and the United States blamed the Treaty of Versailles for World War II. But no major historian in the United States concluded that the treaty should have been harsher toward Germany. All influential books on the peace settlement assumed that a generous peace gave a better promise of avoiding war, and all argued that the Treaty of Versailles was not that bad. Paul Birdsall's *Versailles: Twenty Years After* (1941) pointed out that despite the concessions to the Europeans, which Birdsall blamed primarily on Colonel House, the treaty established at least some degree of international responsibility for colonial possessions and provided much self-determination for Europe. If boundaries were not fully compatible with ethnic loyalties or economic rationality, there was little Wilson or the other powers could have done about it. The collapse of Germany and Russia allowed the eastern European nations to occupy boundaries that could have been altered by the peace conference only through the use of force. Thomas A. Bailey's *Woodrow Wilson and the Lost Peace* (1944) and *Woodrow Wilson and the Great Betrayal* (1945) treated Wilson's decisions and concessions more caustically than Birdsall, but still said the treaty was worthy of ratification. Birdsall and Bailey saw World War II more as the consequence of the League's failure to enforce the Treaty of Versailles than as a product of the treaty provisions themselves.

Robert Osgood incorporated the views of Birdsall and Bailey into the realist critique of the post–World War II era. Accepting the argument that the Treaty of Versailles was not a bad peace settlement, Osgood blamed Wilson for raising popular expectations with excessive appeals to idealism, leading people to imagine that no deviations from American desires would be necessary. Wilson also foolishly presented the League "as a substitute for the balance-of-power system, not as a supplementation or extension of it." In the absence of any explanation of the nation's self-interest in the League, the American people's enthusiasm waned rapidly. Without American participation, Europe could not enforce the peace terms against Germany, and Hitler could march Germany toward World War II.[8]

Several prominent historians defended Wilson against the realist charges that he had negotiated unrealistically and had raised excessive expectations in the American people. David Trask studied Wilson's war strategy and concluded that the president understood the connections between military dispositions and the settlement that would follow, while Lawrence Gelfand's study of The Inquiry led him to believe that Wilson was more realistic than his advisers.[9]

Generally, however, realists and Wilsonians moved toward a loose consensus. The realists admitted that Wilson's negotiations and the treaty terms were not so bad as the previous era had asserted, while the Wilsonians admitted that Wilson had conducted himself too rigidly in the battle to get Senate consent for the League.[10] Meanwhile, the debate continued over why Wilson had been so rigid in the Senate fight over the treaty. Alexander and Juliette George published a highly influential psychoanalytical account of Wilson that traced the president's lack of flexibility to his relationship with an overbearing father. Other historians claimed that Wilson's rigidity was a consequence of the physical impairment connected with several strokes.[11] In any case, as historians came to agree that Wilson had mismanaged the Senate fight, the reputation of Wilson's opponents, especially Henry Cabot Lodge, tended to revive.[12]

Even as the realists and Wilsonians approached their consensus, revisionists began to shift the focus on Wilsonian diplomacy. They portrayed Wilson's plan for a moderate peace and the League of Nations as a conservative attempt to combat Russian bolshevism, the radical European Left, and revolutionaries in general rather than as an altruistic step toward forgiveness of past enemies and the spread of democracy. They saw Wilson's program as expansionist—a search for an open-door world that would permit American economic and cultural expansion and forestall the advance of the rival Leninist system.[13] While Wilsonians and realists admitted some aspects of the revisionist view, they resisted this inversion of Wilson's priorities from a benevolent peace toward Germany to combating Russian bolshevism. They pointed to studies of Wilson's reluctant participation in the Russian intervention as evidence of his opposition to a crusade against communism abroad.[14]

Further Reading

All these years of study and argument culminated in a great work that describes the peacemaking with verve, humor, great learning, and compassion: Margaret MacMillan's *Paris 1919: Six Months That Changed the World* (2001). See also the recent definitive biography of Wilson, John Milton Cooper, *Woodrow Wilson: A Biography* (2009).

Notes

1. Erez Manela, *The Wilsonian Moment: Self-Determination and the International Origins of Anticolonial Nationalism* (2007); Mao's quotation is on p. 194.

2. J. Michael Hogan, *Woodrow Wilson's Western Tour: Rhetoric, Public Opinion, and the League of Nations* (2006).

3. Robert Lansing, *The Peace Negotiations* (1921).

4. Ray Stannard Baker, *What Wilson Did at Paris* (1919), and *Woodrow Wilson and World Settlement* (3 vols., 1922).

5. Charles Seymour, ed., *The Intimate Papers of Colonel House* (4 vols., 1926–1928).

6. D.F. Fleming, *The United States and the League of Nations, 1918–1920* (1968; originally published 1932); and W. Stull Holt, *Treaties Defeated by the Senate* (1933).

7. Harold Nicolson, *Peacemaking, 1919* (1933).

8. Robert Osgood, *Ideals and Self-Interest in America's Foreign Relations: The Great Transformation* (1953). George Kennan's realist tract, *American Diplomacy, 1900–1950* (1951), was more critical of the peace, but the trend was against him.

9. David F. Trask, *The United States in the Supreme War Council: American War Aims and Inter-Allied Strategy, 1917–1918* (1961); Lawrence E. Gelfand, *The Inquiry: American Preparations for Peace, 1917–1919* (1963).

10. Robert H. Ferrell, *Woodrow Wilson and World War I, 1917–1921* (1985); Klaus Schwabe, *Woodrow Wilson, Revolutionary Germany, and Peacemaking, 1918–1919* (1985). Lloyd E. Ambrosius, *Woodrow Wilson and the American Diplomatic Tradition* (1987), remained strongly critical of Wilson in the realist tradition, while Frederick S. Calhoun, *Power and Principle: Armed Intervention in Wilsonian Foreign Policy* (1986), maintained that Wilson was much more realistic in his use of military force than most historians have recognized.

11. Alexander L. George and Juliette L. George, *Woodrow Wilson and Colonel House: A Personality Study* (1956); Edwin Weinstein, *Woodrow Wilson: A Medical and Psychological Biography* (1981); Arthur Link, introduction to Inga Floto, *Colonel House in Paris* (1973). For a medical view contrary to the stroke theory as the main factor in Wilson's rigidity, see Michael F. Marmor, "Wilson, Strokes, and Zebras," *New England Journal of Medicine* (August 1982).

12. See Warren F. Kuehl, *Seeking World Order: The United States and International Organization to 1920* (1969); Ralph A. Stone, *The Irreconcilables* (1970); William C. Widenor, *Henry Cabot Lodge and the Search for an American Foreign Policy* (1980).

13. David S. Foglesang, *America's Secret War Against Bolshevism: U.S. Intervention in the Russian Civil War, 1917–1920* (1995); Lloyd C. Gardner, *Safe for Democracy: The American Response to Revolution, 1913–1923* (1987); Arno J. Mayer, *Politics and Diplomacy of Peacemaking: Containment and Counterrevolution at Versailles, 1918–1919* (1967); N. Gordon Levin Jr., *Woodrow Wilson and World Politics: America's Response to War and Revolution* (1968). William Appleman Williams opened discussion of some of these themes as early as 1952 in his *American-Russian Relations, 1781–1947* (1952).

14. Among the studies documenting Wilson's reluctance to intervene in Russia are Donald E. Davis and Eugene P. Trani, *The First Cold War: The Legacy of Woodrow Wilson in U.S.-Soviet Relations* (2002); Georg Schild, *Between Ideology and Realpolitik: Woodrow Wilson and the Russian Revolution, 1917–1921* (1995); Norman E. Saul, *War and Revolution: The United States and Russia, 1914–1921* (2001); David W. McFadden, *Alternative Paths: Soviets and Americans, 1917–1920* (1992); George F. Kennan, *Russia Leaves the War* (1956), *The Decision to Intervene* (1958), and *Russia and the West Under Lenin and Stalin* (1960); Betty Miller Unterberger, *America's Siberian Expedition* (1956) and *The United States, Revolutionary Russia, and the Rise of Czechoslovakia* (1989); John Thompson, *Russia, Bolshevism, and the Versailles Peace* (1966); and Benjamin D. Rhodes, *The Anglo-American Winter War with Russia, 1918–1919: A Diplomatic and Military Tragicomedy* (1988). A book that condemns Wilson for not strangling bolshevism in its crib is Ilya Somin, *The Stillborn Crusade: The Tragic Failure of Western Intervention in the Russian Civil War, 1918–1920* (1996).

CHAPTER 6

U.S. FOREIGN POLICY BETWEEN THE WORLD WARS

Was World War II Inevitable?

Many Europeans and Americans who witnessed the creation of the Treaty of Versailles predicted that its provisions would make a second world war inevitable. Those critics who survived until 1939 no doubt felt vindicated in their judgment. They saw Germany use the Polish corridor that the Allies had carved out of East Prussia as the excuse for the invasion of Poland that triggered World War II. Germany already had raised international tension to an intolerable pitch by successfully sweeping aside the other hated provisions of the Versailles settlement—reparations, disarmament, the demilitarization of the Rhineland, the prohibition against German-Austrian union, and the border with Czechoslovakia.

Yet most modern historians wonder whether the admitted instability produced by the Versailles settlement might have been overcome had it not been for the Great Depression of 1929. The Depression drastically exacerbated the despair and fanaticism already present in Germany, paving the way for Adolf Hitler. The moderate governments that preceded Hitler sought treaty revision, just as Hitler did. Like Hitler, the moderates agitated for rectification of Germany's eastern borders with Poland and Czechoslovakia and the right to have German armed forces. But their tactics were cautious and peaceful. Europe could have accommodated them without war. Hitler, on the other hand, pursued treaty revision ruthlessly, using it to enlist domestic support for such grandiose ambitions that he indeed made war inevitable.

A similar situation existed in Japan. The Japanese had insisted throughout World War I that they had to have secure access to the resources and markets of Manchuria and China. After the war, however, a series of moderate Japanese governments willingly pursued Japan's goals in conjunction with the Western imperialists. These governments sought especially to avoid a clash with the United States because American trade was extremely valuable to Japan. Moderates restrained the young Japanese military officers who, emboldened by their unbroken string of victories in the Sino-Japanese War, Russo-Japanese War, and World War I, believed Japan should take what it needed in Asia by military force without regard to the desires of the West, let alone of the Chinese. When the Depression cut off much of Japan's trade with the West, it removed a major rationale for the moderate approach. The military and its allies took power and began to move along the way toward Pearl Harbor.

These developments led historians to wonder whether the West could have propped up the moderate German and Japanese regimes in the 1920s to the point that they might have survived the political and economic impact of the Depression. It would have been no easy task. The moderate governments in Germany had a very tenuous credibility with the German people. These successor regimes, rather than the kaiser's government and army, bore the onus of Germany's defeat because Wilson and the Allies had invited democratically inclined Germans to overturn the kaiser, then made them responsible for signing the harsh Versailles Treaty. The combined votes of the extreme nationalists and Communists in the German Reichstag always outnumbered those of the centrist parties. If the extremists of Right and Left could forget their hatred of each other long enough to vote together, as they did after the Depression, they could topple any moderate regime whenever they pleased. Likewise, an increasingly extremist military could thwart the moderates in Japan because the Japanese constitution gave the army and navy ministries direct access to the emperor and the right to full and independent control of all matters pertaining to high strategy.

Yet there was still some slight chance that an enlightened, determined policy on the part of France, Great Britain, and the United States might have enabled moderate governments to survive in Germany and Japan. The United States especially had the leverage to influence the course of events. It emerged from World War I with extraordinary economic power. At the outset of the war, the United States had owed other nations $3.7 billion; at the end of the war, other nations owed the United States $12.5 billion. (By 1930 they would owe America $21 billion.) In 1919 the United States produced nearly half the world's manufactured goods, sent out one-sixth of the world's exports, and took one-eighth of its imports. By 1929 the U.S. gross national income was greater than that of Great Britain, France, Germany, Canada, Japan, and the next eighteen wealthiest nations combined. The American army demobilized rapidly after World War I, but the American navy was second only to that of Great Britain. At the peace conference, Wilson had promised to slow America's naval building program in exchange for Lloyd George's promise to amend the League covenant so as to recognize the Monroe Doctrine. But since the United States had refused to ratify the Treaty of Versailles, it was theoretically free to resume naval building.

Ever since World War II, historians and the general public have regretted that the United States did not use its economic, military, and political power to support its former allies in restraining German and Japanese aggression. For decades after World War II, historians blamed the isolationism of the Republican administrations that succeeded Wilson for doing so little to prevent the rise of aggressive fascist dictators. The administrations of Warren Harding, Calvin Coolidge, and Herbert Hoover seemed to be the natural successors of Senator Henry Cabot Lodge and the other despoilers of Wilson's League of Nations.

Harding refused to resubmit the Treaty of Versailles to Congress. He also went along with the earlier rejection of the separate French security treaty Wilson had negotiated in Paris. For a while Harding declined even to recognize the existence of the League of

Nations, going to the absurd length of refusing to open League mail addressed to the American government. More important, the Republicans rejected several chances to give the president the power to suspend America's neutral right to trade with an aggressor nation in wartime. Such a measure might have encouraged the British to a firmer support of French security against a revanchist Germany, since the British would not have had to fear another conflict with American neutrality policy. (Democratic president Franklin Roosevelt abandoned a similar initiative early in his administration.)

Warren Harding and the Republicans were determined to avoid any further political entanglements with Europe. When they finally agreed to send observers to meetings of the League and its various committees, they carefully insisted that these observers were unofficial. Yet, as recent historians have pointed out, the Republican administrations of Harding, Coolidge, and Hoover used those private envoys to give vigorous support to many aspects of Wilsonian internationalism. In no way did the Republicans return to the degree of isolationism that had pervaded U.S. foreign policy in the nineteenth century. Those who most affected Republican foreign policy between the wars, including elder statesman Elihu Root, Secretary of State Charles Evans Hughes, and Hoover himself, were progressives who accepted much of Wilson's internationalism. Although they rejected the political and military commitments Wilson would have made to Europe, they used American political influence and economic power to goad European governments into moderating the Versailles peace terms, induce the Europeans to settle their quarrels peacefully, secure disarmament agreements, and strengthen the European capitalist economies in order to provide prosperity for them and their American trading partners.

This unofficial internationalist diplomacy had some notable successes during the 1920s. Although U.S. rejection of the Treaty of Versailles had left the Americans with no official representation on the reparations commission that set the amount Germany owed for its aggression, unofficial U.S. influence ensured that the final sum of $33 billion was much closer to the U.S. suggestion of $30 billion than to the $120 to $200 billion the French and British had wanted. Later in the 1920s, American bankers served as unofficial delegates to reparations conferences that further moderated the settlement. Those bankers also arranged loans to Germans to help them pay their reparations.

Despite the successes of the Republicans' unofficial economic diplomacy, such internationalism unsupported by the political and military involvement that Wilson sought in his League of Nations proved unequal to the task of preventing Europe's plunge into World War II. The reparations settlement hung like a black cloud over Europe. Germany probably had the capacity to pay the $33 billion. By the late 1930s it had spent far more than that on armaments alone. But German industrialists complained about the exorbitance of the reparations even as they avoided the taxes that would have paid them, while many ordinary Germans, reeling from the drastic inflation of the mark in 1923 and again from the Depression of 1929, naturally looked upon the drain of reparations from the German economy as the cause of their ruin.

Meanwhile, France and England relied on German reparations to pay French and British war debts to the United States. Whenever the Americans asked for a reduction of the German reparations bill, the French and British demanded that the United States compensate by reducing Allied war debts. After all, France and Great Britain had made far greater contributions in blood and suffering than the United States. America ought to regard the loans as its own contribution to the war and forgive the debts. But Wilson had refused to link war debts and reparations in the Paris conference, and the Republican administrations of the 1920s followed suit. Calvin Coolidge allegedly remarked, "They hired the money, didn't they?"[1] Congress howled whenever there was a hint that the war debts might be linked to reparations. The Europeans would simply spend the money they saved on armaments, Americans complained.

Hughes, Hoover, and the other internationalists serving in the Republican administrations of the 1920s actually wanted to reduce the war debts. But they bowed to the domestic political pressure and, instead of forgiving the debts, urged American bankers to float huge loans to Germany to help it restore its economy while paying out reparations. In effect, the United States loaned money to Germany, which Germany paid in reparations that came back to the United States as war debt payments. This revolving money machine functioned so long as Germany's economy continued to expand and give promise of an eventual ability to pay off both reparations and American loans. But when the German economy faltered in 1928 and 1929, American bankers stopped loaning money, Germany stopped paying reparations, and Great Britain, France, and the other ex-Allied countries with the exception of Finland stopped paying American war debts. This was a major cause of the collapse of the world economy in 1929.

The Republicans' refusal to make any political commitments in support of French security and their rejection of any linkage between war debts and reparations were not their only contributions to the undermining of European prosperity and moderate governments. They also insisted on a high tariff to protect American manufacturers and farmers against foreign competition. The Fordney-McCumber Tariff of 1922 and the Hawley-Smoot Tariff of 1930 effectively closed the American market to the very countries that needed to sell products to enable them to pay war debts or reparations.

While postwar America would undertake no political and only informal private economic commitments abroad, it participated vigorously and publicly in efforts to reduce armaments. Certainly Americans were right to believe that arms races contributed to international tension and war. But Wilson's successors did not pay sufficient attention to the need for better political understandings to go hand in hand with arms reductions. America's reliance on the idea that disarmament alone might produce peace ultimately boomeranged. By 1939 the poorly prepared Western democracies faced rearmed and aggressive totalitarian regimes determined to rule or ruin.

The Republican regimes that permitted this state of affairs deserve a large measure of blame, but there were important mitigating circumstances. Wilson's unsuccessful, bitter fight with the Senate over the Treaty of Versailles had left a sour political atmosphere in which statesmanlike conduct was very difficult. Congressional Democrats vied with their Republican colleagues in denouncing the slightest move toward linking war debts and reparations. The United States turned inward in its search for domestic prosperity and gave little thought to the effects abroad of a creditor nation, untouched by the devastation of war, closing its markets to foreign products. Historical revisionism in the 1920s, which disproved the Allied theory that Germany alone was guilty of starting World War I, left disillusioned Americans with little justification for sacrificing their comforts to protect foreigners from the consequences of their own greed and cynicism. Of course, Americans operated without foreknowledge of the militaristic regimes that would emerge in Germany and Japan in the 1930s. But when those regimes did take power, the first response of Americans was even greater withdrawal.

The pattern of partial withdrawal in the 1920s and 1930s extended beyond the United States' relations with Europe and Asia to its relations with Latin America as well. In the case of Latin America, however, historians have praised this partial withdrawal as vociferously as they have denounced it in Europe. Most historians have wondered not whether the United States should have retreated in Latin America, but whether it retreated far enough.

The United States and Attempts at Disarmament

The stunningly successful Washington Naval Conference of 1921–1922 epitomized much of the postwar Republican approach to foreign policy. Although many Republicans, including President Harding, wanted to complete Wilson's naval building program and make the United States the world's leading sea power before considering naval limitations, a British suggestion for a conference to discuss naval and East Asian affairs offered a tempting opportunity to achieve several goals. The British at the time indicated a willingness to accept American naval parity, and for the United States to gain parity while still reducing government expenditures would be a great political triumph. The British also indicated a willingness to modify their alliance with Japan if that could be done gracefully. A naval limitation conference might enable the United States to strip Japan of its British support and ensure American naval supremacy over Japan at the same time. If the United States could achieve all those goals while avoiding political entanglements, the Washington Conference could serve as a worthy Republican alternative to Wilson's League of Nations.

An agreement with the British and Japanese seemed all the more attractive in 1921 because tensions with both countries were high. The British were excluding American oil companies from their recently acquired League mandates in Iraq and Palestine. The British navy was determined on a naval arms race if the United States, freed from Wilson's pledge to slow American naval building by the Senate's rejection of the Treaty of Versailles, resumed the building program Congress had authorized in 1916 and 1918. British association with Japan in the alliance of 1902 created much anger in the United States because Japan's relations with the United States had become quite hostile during and shortly after World War I.

In the wake of the Wilson administration's stand against Japan's Twenty-One Demands on China and Wilson's opposition at the Paris Peace Conference to Japan's desire for the Shandong peninsula, a new wave of anti-Asian agitation swept the American West. Both the Democrats and the Republicans adopted Japanese exclusion planks in their 1920

Charles Evans Hughes *(center)* with delegates to the Washington Naval Disarmament Conference.

party platforms. Japan also contributed to U.S.-Japanese estrangement by increasing the number of its occupation troops in Manchuria from the expected 7,000 to 72,000 and by keeping control of eastern Siberia after the United States withdrew its contingent from Vladivostok on April 1, 1920. Finally, a dispute over American rights to establish a cable station on Yap Island led the United States to agitate against all the Pacific mandates Japan had acquired at the Paris conference. The American navy believed rumors that Japan was building fortifications on the Pacific islands, contrary to the terms of its mandates, and worried that those fortifications, combined with Japan's accelerated naval building program in 1920, might give Japan control of Asia.

Harding's secretary of state, Charles Evans Hughes, after extending invitations for the Washington Naval Conference to all the major nations of the world except the Soviet Union, startled the diplomats with a dramatic and very specific proposal for naval limitation. After a period of hard bargaining, the powers agreed to freeze the tonnage of their capital ships (battleships, large cruisers, and aircraft carriers) for ten years at the following ratio: the United States and Great Britain 5, Japan 3, France and Italy 1.75. At Japanese insistence, the United States agreed not to increase fortifications in Guam and the Philippines, knowing Congress probably would refuse appropriations for them anyway. In exchange, the Japanese gave up any further fortifications of their outlying island mandates. The Japanese assumed that the limitations on American fortifications in the western Pacific, along with America's need to spread its superior navy over two oceans, would permit Japanese naval supremacy in East Asian waters.

Fearing that Britain would refuse to fight the United States regardless of the provisions of the Anglo-Japanese Alliance, the Japanese also agreed to terminate that treaty. A Four Power Treaty between the United States, Japan, Great Britain, and France replaced the Anglo-Japanese Alliance, with the four signatories merely promising to consult each other if any of their possessions were endangered. A supplementary Nine Power Treaty committed the powers to respect China's territorial integrity and the Open Door policy. None of the signatories would seek special concessions at the expense of the citizens of other nations. In addition, Japan gave the United States the right to establish its cable station on Yap, withdrew Japanese forces from Siberia, and promised to return Shandong to Chinese sovereignty.

The Washington Naval Conference was a remarkable step toward world peace and stability. But it was just a first step; it left some major questions and dissatisfactions. Only continued progress toward political amicability would allow it to hold up. Moderates in Japan, for instance, assumed that the dictum in the Nine Power Treaty against infringement of any nation's rights in China validated Japan's existing special position in Manchuria and northern China. The United States, on the other hand, regarded the dictum as the beginning of a new Open Door order in Asia. The Japanese armed forces bridled at the inferior naval status granted them by the Washington Conference and remained ready to attack the moderates if the West's policies endangered Japanese hegemony in Manchuria.

The French were even more disturbed than the Japanese. They felt they had given up much of their naval security and then been denied an agreement on land armaments that would solidify their position on the continent. The French believed that since their navy had to defend coastlines on both the Atlantic and the Mediterranean, France should have received parity with Japan rather than Italy. Italy required only a Mediterranean fleet, and France's need to station some of its ships in the Atlantic would give Italy an edge in the Franco-Italian rivalry over North Africa. As a consequence, France had opposed extending the Washington Naval Limitation Agreement beyond capital ships to smaller cruisers, destroyers, and submarines. Great Britain found reason to avoid such limitations as well. Thus the treaty covered only capital ships, and the race for supremacy in auxiliary ships continued.

The naval race over auxiliary ships especially strained relations between Great Britain and the United States. In 1927 the powers met again at Geneva to try to extend the Washington agreement to auxiliary ships, but the conference foundered. France and Italy boycotted the meeting because they refused to separate the issue of naval disarmament from that of land armaments. The Japanese demanded that their ratio of auxiliary ships be raised above the ratio they had received for capital ships to compensate for their earlier concessions. The British and Americans could not agree whether the treaty should be slanted to allow a few large ships with long cruising ranges, which the United States needed to defend its wide-spaced possessions and to break any potential British blockade, or to allow more and smaller ships, which the British wanted to defend their more numerous colonies and to enforce a blockade.

The British, the Japanese, and the Americans tried again for agreement at the London Naval Conference of 1930, and this time they succeeded. Ramsay MacDonald, the British Labour government's new prime minister, defied his admirals and declared to the United States, "What is this bother about parity? Parity? Take it, without reserve, heaped and flowing over." The British and Americans agreed to accord Japan the higher ratio on auxiliary ships it had demanded, and all seemed well. But Japanese militants assassinated their prime minister who had made the agreement, and the Japanese military prepared to take charge of the government in order to secure Japanese power in Asia.

Meanwhile, the European powers failed to make any progress toward reductions in land armaments. Germany was especially distressed, protesting that it had accepted disarmament under the Treaty of Versailles only because other powers had promised they would soon join Germany in disarming. France wanted some guarantee of joint military action against aggression before it would consent to arms reductions, but the United States objected. The United States had already rejected participation in the Geneva Protocol of 1924 that would have required joint military action against any nation that refused to submit a quarrel to arbitration. Secretary Hughes even claimed the United States might regard the League of Nations as a potential enemy if it took action in the Western Hemisphere under the Geneva Protocol. A full-scale land disarmament conference did not meet in Geneva until 1932. President Herbert Hoover tried to duplicate Hughes's dramatic Washington Naval Conference coup by proposing that all nations reduce their arms by one-third. Germany welcomed the proposal, but France insisted on security guarantees before reducing its military edge, and the conference stalled.

In 1933 British prime minister Ramsay MacDonald proposed a new plan to the Geneva Conference. European nations would equalize the size of their armies and, along with the United States, pledge to consult with each other to identify any aggressor who broke the peace. The new U.S. president, Franklin Roosevelt, agreed that the United States would join the consultations and would not insist on its neutral right to trade with the aggressor if America agreed with the outcome of the consultations. The new German chancellor, Adolf Hitler, welcomed Roosevelt's initiative. But the old irreconcilable senators William Borah and Hiram Johnson opposed any economic discrimination against aggressors. They attached to a neutrality bill pending before Congress an amendment prohibiting any discriminatory embargoes. The preoccupied Roosevelt accepted the amendment, only to have Secretary of State Cordell Hull point out that it violated Roosevelt's pledge to the Geneva Disarmament Conference. Without the right to enact discriminatory embargoes, the United States would not be able to stop neutral trade with an aggressor. Roosevelt then sidetracked the entire neutrality act. Hitler, who was pledged to German rearmament anyway, cynically denounced the negotiations and withdrew Germany from both the Geneva Conference and the League of Nations.

Economic Diplomacy Toward Europe

By the time Hitler pulled out of the Geneva meeting and the League of Nations, he and the Depression had destroyed more than America's hopes for disarmament; they also destroyed the Republican belief that the United States could maintain a stable, peaceful Europe through unofficial economic diplomacy without political or military commitments.

Although rejecting the League and the World Court, Republicans had participated eagerly if unofficially in European economic negotiations. The first major flurry of Republican unofficial economic diplomacy occurred in the early 1920s. This was a time of severe economic and political crisis in Europe. Germany was challenging the terms of the Versailles Treaty; it published great volumes of documents to disprove its war guilt and urged reduction of its reparations bill. When France, feeling itself vulnerable and betrayed by America's rejection of the League and of the supplementary security treaty, insisted that Germany obey every provision of the Treaty of Versailles, Germany turned to another outcast nation, the Soviet Union. The governments of Germany and Soviet Russia detested each other, but they saw a rapprochement as a means of frightening their common adversaries. The Treaty of Rapallo that they signed in 1922 restored diplomatic relations between them and promised consultation on economic matters. Russia was already secretly permitting Germany to train soldiers with heavy weapons on Russian territory, thereby circumventing the Versailles strictures against German rearmament.

The French saw the Treaty of Rapallo as part of a dangerous trend toward German militarism. Freicorps toughs operated freely in Bavaria under the protection of the right-wing Bavarian government that had overthrown the short-lived Communist regime. The Nazi Party of Adolf Hitler, then rising in Bavaria, encouraged Freicorps activities. Armed bands assassinated two moderate German leaders, Matthias Erzberger and Foreign Minister Walter Rathenau, in 1921 and 1922. Amid the economic and social chaos that still pervaded Germany three years after the war, the German government fell into the hands of business owners who were profiting from the inflation by extending their businesses in Germany, salting away their money in foreign currency and banks, and refusing to pay taxes for reparations.

Germany defaulted on reparations payments, and France, in the absence of support from its former allies, took matters into its own hands. In January 1923, the French army marched into the Ruhr to take over the mines and factories there and collect France's own reparations. The German workers laid down their tools and sabotaged French collections by passive resistance. The German government paid the striking workers out of government funds and inflated the currency to the point that Germans rushed to buy goods whose prices might triple during the time they were standing in line. The British protested the French action, and the United States withdrew its last troops from the occupied Rhineland as a sign of disfavor.

As inflation wiped out the savings of most of the German middle class and ravaged the economy, a new moderate government under Gustav Stresemann took power and moved to end the crisis. He called off the passive resistance campaign in the Ruhr and put down revolts from right and left, including Hitler's abortive Beer Hall Putsch. The

French, whose own currency was being undermined by the German economic collapse, consented to a conference on reparations. Secretary of State Hughes decided the United States should try to help in this crisis. Although he still adamantly refused to link reparations and war debts, he sent two prominent American business leaders, Charles G. Dawes and Owen D. Young, to serve as unofficial American delegates to the conference. Because Americans could provide the loans to make a reparations plan work, Dawes and Young played a prominent role. They helped formulate the Dawes Plan, which supplied loans from the former Allies to stabilize the German currency, temporarily scaled down German reparation payments, and secured French withdrawal from the Ruhr.

France left the Ruhr convinced of the futility of occupying Germany to force reparations payments. The French economy required at least a minimally healthy German economy, and every time France threatened to strangle Germany, Germany threatened to die. So France cast around for other ways to maintain its security against a reviving Germany.

Through the League of Nations, France proposed a treaty that would require all signatories to give armed support to any victim of aggression on their continent. The British balked because they had possessions on almost every continent and conceivably could be required to fight anywhere in the world. The United States warned that it would not tolerate interference with its right as a neutral to trade with any nation at war. As this hope for a collective security treaty collapsed, France, Germany, and Great Britain turned to a more limited form of security guarantee. They signed the Treaty of Locarno in 1925.

All agreed to guarantee the French-German border, thus confirming Alsace-Lorraine to France. They also agreed that the Rhineland would be demilitarized permanently. Germany became part of the League of Nations and promised to solve its problems peacefully. But the treaty gave no guarantee of Germany's eastern borders, and Stresemann made clear Germany's intention to rectify them sometime in the future. France could only console itself that Stresemann usually advocated peaceful means of treaty revision and had demonstrated his sincerity by giving tacit consent for France to sign new security treaties with Czechoslovakia and Poland. At the same time, however, Germany signed a neutrality treaty with Russia, demonstrating that it was not abandoning the leverage of Rapallo.

By 1927 France had given up all hope of getting the United States to sign an official security treaty. Yet Aristide Briand, the French foreign minister who had been one of the architects of the Treaty of Locarno, thought he might at least involve the United States unofficially. He proposed that the United States and France sign a pact outlawing war between the two nations. He hoped that such a treaty would deter the United States from clashing with France and its League allies if they applied sanctions against an aggressor. Perhaps the pact would also relieve British fears of a conflict with the United States and encourage Britain to consider more favorably potential sanctions against Germany. President Calvin Coolidge and the irreconcilable Senator William E. Borah expressed some interest in the idea. Borah, however, soon retreated to the idea of a pact that would include all nations and would say nothing that might deny American neutral rights to trade with an aggressor. Secretary of State Frank Kellogg agreed. Although Briand had no interest in such a watered-down pact, he decided there would be no harm in signing a treaty renouncing war. In July 1928, all the great powers except Russia signed the Kellogg-Briand Pact, outlawing all wars but those of self-defense.

In the wake of this emotional paean to peace, the new Republican administration of Herbert Hoover sent Owen Young, one of the American negotiators who had shaped the Dawes Plan of 1924, back to Europe to negotiate a new and more permanent reparations settlement. The Young Plan of 1929 reduced German reparations still further. But neither the Young Plan nor the paper promises of the Kellogg-Briand Pact could survive the tumultuous emotions and events brought about by the depression that struck late in 1929.

At first Hoover and the Republicans tried to cope with the Great Depression by using strictly domestic means, including raising tariff rates with the Hawley-Smoot Tariff of 1930. But the drastic economic situation in Germany and Great Britain as well as the United States brought Hoover in mid-1931 to suggest a one-year moratorium on both reparations and war debt payments, thus finally making the link that Washington had tried so hard to avoid.

Unfortunately, the Depression proved too powerful for Hoover's initiative to lead to a permanent solution. France, which got more in reparations than it paid out in debts, refused to accept the moratorium unless Germany diverted money from armaments to its reparations bill. France also insisted that the United States reduce its debt demands. Germany refused to make political concessions unless the Treaty of Versailles was revised. The United States would not reduce its debt demands unless France, which of all the major powers was the least affected by the Depression, proved its incapacity to pay. Finally, at Lausanne in Switzerland, the European powers agreed to reduce Germany's reparations by 90 percent if the United States would make a similar concession on war debts. Hoover was furious because this politically explosive proposal came on the eve of the presidential election. He refused, but he went down to defeat at the hands of Franklin Roosevelt anyway.

In his lame-duck period, Hoover gingerly tried to get Roosevelt to join him in accepting the linkage of debts and reparations along with the inevitable political flak that would result, but Roosevelt dodged his requests. Hoover therefore demanded that Great Britain and France make their 1932 debt payments on time. When the French government tried to do so, the French Assembly overturned the measure. One by one the other European nations followed France in defaulting. Shortly afterward, German president Paul von Hindenburg invited Adolf Hitler to accept Germany's chancellorship.

The United States, Japan, and the New Order in Asia

In Asia as well as in Europe, the postwar Republican administrations tried to maintain a stable, peaceful environment without drastic action or political commitments. They found in Japan, as they had in Germany, a moderate government that maintained only tenuous control over militant and dissatisfied elements of its population. Japanese moderates were willing to defend Japan's interests in China in cooperation with the other imperial powers, as they did at the Washington Naval Conference, rather than resort to such provocative measures as the Twenty-One Demands. Ironically, however, the moderates tried to cooperate with the European imperial system just as that system was crumbling.

The Washington Conference nominally replaced the cooperative imperial system with America's long-sought Open Door. Japan signed the Nine Power Treaty, thus recognizing the principles of the Open Door, but insisted that its existing rights in China were not affected. Instead, the Lansing-Ishii Agreement of 1917, by which the United States recognized Japan's special position in Manchuria, remained in force. Harding and Hughes, on the other hand, argued that the Nine Power Treaty superseded the Lansing-Ishii Agreement and invalidated Japan's special position.

Hughes told the Japanese that if they insisted that the Lansing-Ishii Agreement still pertained, the United States would have to publish the agreement's secret protocol. That protocol pledged both powers not to seek privileges in China that would abridge the rights of other nations. Japan had insisted it be kept secret for fear of arousing its own militants. The Japanese finally agreed to renounce the Lansing-Ishii Agreement, but went on to proclaim that their special rights in China existed without need for express recognition in diplomatic documents. Hughes replied he was happy that the Japanese did not claim special rights prejudicial to China or the other imperial powers. Just as in the past, the United States and Japan talked past each other when discussing the Open Door and Japan's special position in East Asia.

Perhaps, as the Republicans hoped, time would resolve the Japanese as well as German issues peacefully. In the case of Asia, these Republican hopes were thwarted not only by the Depression, but by another powerful agent as well—the rise of nationalism in China.

The emergence of Chinese nationalism dealt a far greater blow to the imperial system and Japan's special position in China than America's mild attempts to implement the Open Door. Chinese nationalism made itself felt at the Washington Conference when a Chinese delegation showed up with ten demands, including an end to extraterritoriality and the elimination of foreign control over China's tariff. But the Washington conferees were more concerned with eliminating the rivalry between the imperial powers than in accommodating China. At the instigation of the Americans, the powers promised to hold future conferences on the tariff and extraterritoriality. For the present, however, they would only return control of the postal service to China, and that with strings attached. Regarding China as too chaotic to provide adequate security for the lives and interests of foreigners, the powers refused to abandon the unequal treaties until order could be guaranteed.

China was indeed a chaotic land of warring factions. The authority of the government extended only to those provinces controlled by semiloyal warlords. The Beijing government's primary opposition came from Sun Yat-sen's Guomindang or Nationalist Party, which controlled portions of South China from its capital of Guangzhou (Canton). Sun Yat-sen demanded that the imperial powers recognize him as the ruler of China and revise the unequal treaty system. When the powers refused, he turned to the one nation that had offered to give up its special privileges in China—the Soviet

Union. At the urging of his major military leader, Chiang Kai-shek, Sun accepted Soviet advisers and merged the Chinese Communists with his Guomindang. Then he embarked on a campaign to unite China under Nationalist rule and at the same time force the imperial powers to give up their unequal treaty system. When Sun died of cancer in 1925, Chiang took over and marched his armies northward to try to unite China by military force.

The Nationalists' northern campaign brought several clashes with the citizens of the treaty powers. The British insisted that their subjects should be protected against the fighting and in one instance bombarded the city of Wanxian, killing many civilians. The Americans opposed the use of force but sent 5,000 marines to join the British in defending foreign nationals in Shanghai. Fortunately, the Nationalists took Shanghai without incident. In Nanjing, however, Nationalist soldiers killed several foreigners, including the American vice president of Nanjing University and a Japanese officer.

Throughout these clashes, the United States, remaining relatively aloof, continued to offer concessions to the Chinese. In 1925, a year before the northern campaign, the United States, Great Britain, and Japan had agreed that China would have tariff autonomy as of 1929. During the northern campaign, the United States and Great Britain offered to make further concessions if the Chinese developed a government with which the Western powers could negotiate. The Americans and British became even more conciliatory when Chiang Kai-shek turned against Russia and his Communist allies in the bloody purge of 1927. The Americans and British saw Chiang as a moderate who might restrain the most militant anti-Westerners in his party. Chiang confirmed their view by marrying an American-educated wife and converting to Christianity later in 1927. When Chiang consolidated his hold on China in 1928, the United States quickly recognized his government. Many American observers warned, however, that the Guomindang had lost its ideals and maintained only a fragile control over China through bribery, corruption, and alliances with various warlords and large landowners.

The Japanese were not so accommodating. They regarded American policy as "hypocritical humanism" and denounced it for undermining the prestige of the Japanese and other foreigners in China. The Japanese had much more at stake than the United States: more than 40 percent of their trade and investments depended on Manchuria and Inner Mongolia, and they believed that their Manchurian railroad and mining concessions and their cotton textile mills in China were vital to Japan's existence. They disliked the idea of Chinese tariff autonomy because tariff revision might make Chinese-owned cotton mills competitive with their own. Nationalist-inspired strikes and riots also threatened the Japanese mills and railroads in China. Before Chiang purged his Communist allies, those Communists had added fuel to the Nationalist strikes, while Chiang's link to Russia had posed a strategic threat to the Japanese position in Manchuria and Inner Mongolia.

The Japanese responded to the Nationalist threat by trying to induce the warlord who controlled Manchuria, Chang Tso-lin, to separate himself from China and accept Japanese tutelage. But Chang resisted, so when Chiang Kai-shek turned against the Communists, the Japanese government decided to try to work out an arrangement in harmony with the other imperial powers. Even when former general Giichi Tanaka took over as Japanese prime minister and pledged a more "positive" policy in Manchuria, he continued to try to work with Chiang's government.

The Japanese army in Manchuria was not as sanguine as the civilian government. Both the army and navy considered a major war in Asia inevitable and believed that Japan had to secure a self-sufficient empire that would include Manchuria. The army saw Chiang's northern campaign as a threat to Japan's position in Manchuria despite Chiang's protestations to the contrary. When Prime Minister Tanaka ordered Japanese army units to march from Manchuria to the Shandong peninsula to protect Japanese citizens and interests there from Chiang's troops, one of the officers exceeded instructions and occupied the town of Jinan, directly in the path of the advancing Nationalists. After a clash between Japanese and Chinese soldiers, the Japanese military decided to use the opportunity to make war. With the support of Tanaka, Japanese officers formulated an ultimatum too harsh for the Chinese to accept, then expelled the Chinese army from the Jinan area and ruled by terror for a year. Meanwhile, Japanese officers in Manchuria assassinated Chang Tso-lin, the Manchurian warlord, in hopes of creating chaos that would require full military occupation of Manchuria.

This was going too far even for Tanaka. While he still pressed Chang Tso-lin's son to maintain a degree of autonomy from the rest of China, Tanaka recognized Chiang Kai-shek's government as the ruler of all China, including Manchuria, and resigned when the army refused to court-martial Chang's assassins. A more moderate government succeeded Tanaka's. It moved toward greater cooperation with the imperial powers at the London Naval Conference of 1930 and in negotiations to modify extraterritoriality in China. But the Depression destroyed this process. The silk market in the United States dried up, and silk prices plummeted 75 percent. The level of Japanese exports to the United States sank 40 percent and the Hawley-Smoot Tariff of 1930 reduced them still more. As the incentives for cooperation with the West declined, many of the people hardest hit by the Depression in Japan sided with the military's desire for a stronger policy in China. They denounced the concessions made at the London Naval Conference and fanatics decided to assassinate the prime minister, who died of his wounds six months later.

With rising public support and continuing problems in China, the Japanese army decided to act on its own. In September 1931, officers in Manchuria blew up some of the railroad track on the Japanese-controlled South Manchurian Railroad north of Mukden, blamed the explosion on Chinese dissidents, and used this so-called Mukden Incident to justify military occupation of all of Manchuria. The Japanese civilian government, accepting the fait accompli, formed the puppet state of Manchukuo with the heir to the old Manchu dynasty as regent.

The Stimson Doctrine

The United States responded cautiously. Herbert Hoover's secretary of state, Henry Stimson, told the Chinese that the Americans were "playing no favorites." He thought the Chinese were partly at fault for violating their treaties with Japan. He also hoped that the incident was just another military mutiny and that if the West avoided sanctions against the Japanese that might strengthen the fanatics, the civilian government might get the army officers to crawl "back into their dens." The Japanese did consent to an investigation by a neutral commission headed by the Earl of Lytton, but they continued to seize strategic points in Manchuria.

Stimson reluctantly and belatedly associated the United States with a League of Nations initiative that reminded Japan and China of their obligations under the Kellogg-Briand Pact and requested that the Japanese withdraw in one month. But he withheld endorsement of the Lytton Commission investigation even though the Japanese had consented to it. Only after Japan continued to consolidate its hold on Manchuria did Stimson take action. He announced that the United States would recognize neither infringements on American rights, the Open Door, or China's territorial integrity, nor any changes brought about by force in violation of the Kellogg-Briand Pact. This nonrecognition statement came to be known as the Stimson Doctrine.

Japan disregarded the Stimson Doctrine and, in response to a Chinese boycott of Japanese trade, sent its navy to bombard Shanghai. The indiscriminate slaughter outraged public opinion in the West: the United States and Great Britain sent troops to Shanghai to protect their own nationals; the League of Nations adopted a resolution similar to the Stimson Doctrine that refused to recognize Japanese gains in Manchuria. But both Hoover and the British rejected Stimson's suggestion of economic or military sanctions. Stimson could only state that Japan's violation of the Washington Conference agreements freed the United States from its pledge not to fortify its Pacific possessions.

This empty threat did nothing to deter Japan. When the League of Nations adopted the Lytton Commission report, which mildly condemned the Manchurian invasion while blaming China for some of the actions that provoked it, Japan announced its withdrawal from the League. Japan also continued to fortify and expand its control of all Chinese territory north of the Great Wall. It even forced China to accept a broad demilitarized zone south of the wall. Japan's attempts to cooperate with China or the other imperial powers were over.

The Good Neighbor Policy in Latin America

The American post–World War I reaction against military intervention took effect more slowly in Latin America than it did in Europe and Asia. Secretary of State Charles Evans Hughes, to whom Harding delegated control over Latin American policy, made no such dramatic initiative in Latin American affairs as he had with the Washington Naval Conference. This might seem surprising because World War I devastated the military strength of many participants and ended for a time whatever very small chance there had been of a major European intervention in Latin America. Not only was Europe weaker, but also many Latin American countries had grown stronger. The United States could no longer invoke the Roosevelt Corollary to cover its own interference in Latin America. It was too obvious that postwar interference would be designed not to prevent European intervention, but to protect U.S. economic and political interests. For as European economic interest in Latin America waned, that of the United States increased. British investments in Central America, for instance, peaked in 1913 at about $115 million. But $40 million of that was invested in nearly worthless government bonds and the remaining $75 million concentrated in railroad holdings in Guatemala and Costa Rica. Meanwhile, investments by U.S. citizens drew even with the British during World War I, and U.S. money went not into worthless bonds but into the more profitable and influential sectors of the economy, such as bananas and mining.

By the turn of the twentieth century, Latin Americans had come to fear U.S. intervention far more than any possible European invasion. The Harding and Coolidge administrations failed to change the interventionist policies of Theodore Roosevelt, Taft, and Wilson. Hughes withdrew American troops from the Dominican Republic in 1924, but kept the customs house and therefore Dominican finances in U.S. hands. The Dominican Republic remained an American protectorate ruled by the dictatorial Trujillo family, whose power stemmed from the U.S.-trained National Guard. Coolidge and his new secretary of state, Frank Kellogg, withdrew American marines from Nicaragua in 1925, but sent them right back in the following year when civil war broke out. In response to criticism of America's continuing presence, Coolidge proclaimed: "We are not making war in Nicaragua any more than a policeman on the streets is making war on a passerby." In 1932 Herbert Hoover and his secretary of state, Henry Stimson, embarrassed by the comparison of America's position in Nicaragua with Japan's conquest of Manchuria, finally decided to withdraw the marines permanently. Stimson ordered the Nicaraguans to hold an election under the supervision of the 400 U.S. Marines who remained in the country, and on the election of Juan Sacasa as president, the United States withdrew its last marine contingent. Unfortunately, as in Santo Domingo, American withdrawal left Nicaragua and its new president subject to the power of the National Guard. The guard commander, General Anastasio Somoza, asserted his authority by intercepting and assassinating the guerrilla leader, Augusto Cesar Sandino, who was on his way from a peace meeting with the new president. Although Sandino had been a nuisance to the American occupying forces for five years and although Somoza said that he had received approval for the assassination from the U.S. minister in Nicaragua, Arthur Bliss Lane, it seems clear that neither Lane nor the U.S. government had approved. Nevertheless, when Somoza pushed aside the government and took full control of Nicaragua in 1936, his lying and brutality did not keep the United States from accepting his government as a client state.

Wilson's Republican successors faced an even more dangerous and delicate situation in Mexico. Under Article 17 of Mexico's 1917 constitution, the Mexican government claimed all rights to subsoil resources in its territory. It also restricted surface land ownership to Mexican nationals except under special conditions, and any foreigners permitted to own land would have to subscribe to the Calvo Doctrine by promising not to appeal to their home governments for diplomatic assistance. Under these constitutional provisions, Mexican president Venustiano Carranza threatened to confiscate American oil company holdings. This threat gave new impetus to the estrangement between the United States and Mexico that had nearly led to hostilities prior to World War I. The United States protested on behalf of the oil companies, and Carranza gave none-too-credible assurances that the law would not be used retroactively against the companies. Meanwhile, he used the law to tax the companies in ways the companies thought were punitive.

In 1920 Álvaro Obregón overthrew Carranza, but the dispute with the United States continued. The United States withheld recognition of Obregón because he would not sign a treaty guaranteeing the property rights of U.S. citizens. Finally, in 1923, Obregón agreed to an informal understanding rather than a public treaty on property rights, and the United States recognized his government. But expropriations continued under Article 17. Mexico also imposed harsh restrictions and punishments on the Catholic Church and clergy, raising a strong outcry from American Catholics. To strain relations even further, Mexico extended aid to opponents of American occupation in Nicaragua. Kellogg went so far as to denounce Mexico for abetting a Bolshevik plot on Latin America. But public opposition in the United States to intervention in Mexico and Central America remained high, and ultimately Coolidge backed away from confrontation. He sent Dwight Morrow to Mexico as ambassador with instructions to avoid war. With the aid of Mexican judicial decisions that sided to some extent with the oil companies and with a diminution of the Mexican government's anticlerical policies, Morrow managed to smooth relations. Many historians pointed to his success as the beginning of the Good Neighbor Policy.

Herbert Hoover took several additional steps toward a more cooperative and less interventionist policy in Latin America. He made a tour of Latin America in 1928 as president-elect and emphasized his wish to avoid further interventions. He abandoned to a large extent the manipulation of U.S. recognition policy to force changes on Latin American governments. After considerable hesitation, he endorsed a memorandum by Undersecretary of State Reuben Clark that repudiated the Roosevelt Corollary. Secretary of State Stimson explained Hoover's decision by pointing out that "the Monroe Doctrine was a declaration of the United States versus Europe—not the United States versus Latin America." But Hoover coupled his repudiation with a defense of the right of the United States to intervene in order to counter actual European threats or protect American lives and property. He also signed, albeit reluctantly, the Hawley-Smoot Tariff, whose high rates were a formidable blow to Latin American economies. Thus Latin Americans were not too impressed by Hoover's professed friendliness, even when he withdrew American marines from Nicaragua, accelerated marine withdrawal from Haiti, and avoided further intervention into the tumults that followed the Depression in Panama, Honduras, and Cuba.

Franklin D. Roosevelt was far more successful than Hoover in convincing the Latin Americans that the United States had retreated from interventionism. He made the Good Neighbor Policy his own in the eyes of most people, South and North American alike. In a 1928 article for *Foreign Affairs*, Roosevelt had denounced unilateral intervention by the United States in Latin America, although he endorsed joint intervention with other American powers. After his election as president in 1932, he appointed Cordell Hull, an ardent supporter of reciprocal tariff reductions, as secretary of state.

Roosevelt's turn toward nonintervention did not start auspiciously. A series of coups in Cuba in 1933 resulted in a leftist government headed by Dr. Ramón Grau San Martín. Roosevelt sent his personal friend, Undersecretary of State Sumner Welles, to Cuba as ambassador and troubleshooter, and Welles suggested sending troops to overthrow Grau. Roosevelt refused, but he did send several naval ships to Havana harbor and he withheld recognition from Grau. Welles then encouraged Fulgencia Batista, the military strongman behind Grau, to withdraw his support. Batista did, Grau was overthrown, and the United States recognized the new government in five days.

In the midst of this Cuban imbroglio, Cordell Hull met with the leaders of other countries of the Western Hemisphere at the Montevideo Conference of 1933. Under strong criticism for America's interference in Cuba, Hull surprised the conference by accepting a pledge against any nation interfering in the internal affairs of another Western Hemisphere country. Hull inserted a reservation that the United States did not give up its right to protect the lives and property of its citizens abroad. He also narrowly defined intervention as military rather than economic or diplomatic interference. But the pledge seemed to many at the time a substantial step forward.

The Roosevelt administration followed the Montevideo pledge with further symbols of its good faith. In 1934 it abrogated its right to intervene in Cuba under the Platt Amendment. Roosevelt said nothing, however, of the right of the United States to intervene under other provisions of international law. Also in 1934, Roosevelt withdrew the U.S. Marines from Haiti three months ahead of Hoover's schedule, although the United States kept control of Haitian finances. In 1936 Roosevelt signed a new treaty with Panama that ended America's special rights of intervention. Unfortunately, the Senate refused consent until 1939, when an exchange of notes guaranteed the right of American intervention in an emergency. In 1940 Roosevelt relinquished the right to intervene unilaterally (but not jointly) in Santo Domingo.

As all the qualifications to these treaties and pledges suggest, the Good Neighbor Policy did not mark a wholesale abandonment of U.S. intervention in Latin America. Not only did Roosevelt insist on the United States' continuing right to intervene to protect American lives and property, he also sought mechanisms to permit joint intervention with other Latin American countries. Thus, at the Buenos Aires Conference of 1936, he accepted a new pledge that broadened the prohibition against intervention to "direct and indirect" interference, but saw to it that this prohibition extended only to intervention by "any one state," not a combination of countries. Roosevelt coupled this qualified commitment to yet another pledge that required all Pan American nations to consult with one another if there were a threat to peace.

Shortly afterward, in 1937 and 1938, Bolivia and Mexico tested Roosevelt's noninterventionist intentions by expropriating American oil companies. Roosevelt deferred the issue in Bolivia by requiring Standard Oil to exhaust all Bolivian court remedies before seeking U.S. government assistance. The Mexican situation was more difficult. Roosevelt feared that Mexican president Lázaro Cárdenas might invite Germany, Italy, or Japan to help run the confiscated oil equipment and resources. Josephus Daniels, ambassador to Mexico, still urged Roosevelt to be accommodating. Daniels had the ear of the president, for he had been secretary of the navy while Roosevelt was assistant secretary, and they both had come to regret their part in Woodrow Wilson's occupation of Vera Cruz. Roosevelt urged Mexico to submit the oil companies' claims of $450 million to arbitration. Cárdenas refused, but his more conservative successor agreed with Roosevelt to submit the claims to a two-man mixed arbitration commission. When the commission awarded the oil companies $24 million, Roosevelt accepted the decision and refused to back the companies in further action.

World War II brought further attempts by the United States to tighten its ties to Latin America and increase U.S. security. The Pan American foreign ministers, at U.S. instigation, issued the Declaration of Panama in September 1939. It established a neutrality zone 300 miles into the Atlantic from all coasts in the Western Hemisphere where belligerent ships were prohibited to sail. All the belligerents ignored it. In Havana in the following year, 1940, the foreign ministers endorsed the no-transfer principle. This prohibited Germany from acquiring French and Dutch colonies in the Western Hemisphere after it had conquered the mother countries. Since Germany never attempted to take the colonies, that declaration too was a dead letter. Even more illustrative of the growing Pan American cooperation on hemispheric defense, the Havana Conference of 1940 agreed that an attack by a non-American state on an American nation would be regarded as an attack on all.

There remained much contention in the Western Hemisphere, however, despite the Good Neighbor Policy and the threat of World War II. Argentina sympathized with the Nazis, while many other nations wanted no part of the European war. Many countries resented the attempts of the Federal Bureau of Investigation to ferret out subversives in Latin America. Many also resisted American desires to place troops in strategic areas of Latin America, remembering all too well past U.S. military interventions. The United States nonetheless stationed some 100,000 troops in Latin America during World War II, most of them in Central America and the Caribbean to guard the Panama Canal.

The United States also sent $475 million in lend-lease aid to Latin America and supported Export-Import Bank loans to strengthen the Latin American economies, making available more strategic materials from those nations to help the war effort. Since the Depression devastated the economies of Latin America, this wartime aid and trade, along with the few reciprocal trade treaties Hull managed to negotiate, tied Latin American finances even more tightly to the United States. In addition, the war closed many of Latin America's alternative markets. The U.S. wartime demand for raw materials thus distorted Latin American economies, which faced major difficulties when the end of the war reduced U.S. demand. Meanwhile, the U.S. leaders most responsible for the relative restraint of Roosevelt's policy toward Latin America left the stage one by one. Sumner Welles, an important architect of the Good Neighbor Policy once he had returned from his aggressive embassy in Cuba, had to resign when political enemies threatened to publicize an alleged incident of homosexual solicitation on a railroad train. Cordell Hull, an adversary of Welles but a supporter of the Good Neighbor approach, left office shortly before Franklin Roosevelt died of a stroke on the eve of victory in Europe. The faltering steps that the United States had taken under the Good Neighbor Policy toward cooperation and less intervention in Latin America would be undone by new leaders facing the challenge of the Cold War.

The Good Neighbor Policy in Action: Fordlandia

The intentions, limitations, and ultimate failure of U.S. attempts to be a good neighbor to Latin America can be seen in the history of one of the most bizarre episodes in U.S.–Latin American relations: the attempt by Henry Ford to establish a rubber plantation on a huge tract of land in Brazil's Amazon which would be modeled not only on his efficient automobile factories but also on the small, rural, Protestant towns of Ford's childhood.

Ford had built his fortune and reputation in the United States by designing assembly production lines that reduced the costs of an automobile so that middle-class Americans could afford them, and also by paying wages to his laborers that would permit them to be among his consumers. But Ford expected his laborers to spend their high wages on worthwhile investments, such as cars, homes, and health care rather than sinful or wasteful items such as liquor, prostitutes, gambling, or luxury goods. He employed hundreds of agents in his Sociological Department to check up on his workers and make sure they had bank accounts, low debts, and steady family lives. His benevolence also had other limitations. He hated unions and labor organizers to the point that he once mounted machine guns on top of his factories to confront strikers. He detested Roosevelt's New Deal and any government intrusions into his business on behalf of workers. Thus, when Ford sought to establish a model U.S. economic and social enterprise in the Amazon, it would be a model based on a specific and narrow set of U.S. ideals.

Rubber for tires, gaskets, and hoses was the one natural resource Ford did not control in his production line of the 1920s and he was fearful that the near-monopoly of rubber production by the British Empire in Southeast Asia might result in a spike in prices. He decided to produce his own rubber in the Amazon, where rubber trees had first grown exclusively before a British renegade had smuggled out seedlings to London. From London the seeds had been transplanted in Southeast Asia, which soon dominated the rubber market because there were fewer of the natural pests that limited the density of those trees in the Amazon. Ford assumed that scientific methods could overcome the obstacles to mass production of rubber in Brazil, and so in the late 1920s he purchased land along one of the tributaries to the Amazon and built plantations and towns that consisted not only of rubber trees, watering systems, and power plants, but also of Cape Cod plank houses with indoor plumbing, manicured lawns, central squares, theaters, hospitals, swimming pools, and golf courses.

Unfortunately, science could not overcome the pests and most of the rubber trees died. Moreover, many of the Brazilian workers were mistreated and Ford was forced to compromise with labor organizing and Brazilian government intrusions on behalf of those workers, just as he had to accommodate Roosevelt's New Deal in the United States. In the end, the plantations were an economic failure.

Meanwhile, however, the U.S government moved to take advantage of the resources of Fordlandia to further its Good Neighbor Policy. Laboratories and hospitals became federal experimental stations to improve the health of Amazonians, and plantation doctors cooperated with the Office of Inter-American Affairs in fighting tropical diseases such as malaria and hookworm. Ford, a bitter anti-Semite, even agreed to let the United States consider resettling Jewish refugees from Europe on his plantations. In the end, however, Fordlandia faded away along with the Good Neighbor Policy. Now, of course, the former Fordlandia stands in the path of a far more successful and destructive deforestation campaign that makes Ford's project seem tame by comparison.[2]

Controversial Issues

The primary debate between historians over this period has been whether it truly constituted a retreat from internationalism. Certainly Americans of the time thought it was, and most approved of that retreat. Historians were more divided. Many of them, keeping their Wilsonian sympathies, regretted America's lack of cooperation with the League of Nations, along with the country's refusal to be involved in European security affairs.[3]

World War II then converted Americans and their historians almost en masse into critics of what they still perceived as America's retreat from internationalism in the 1920s and early 1930s. Most historians laced their writings with harsh denunciations of the silliness and irresponsibility of the Republican administrations and the American citizens who failed to see in the 1920s that peace and disarmament had to be linked to considerations of security, politics, and the balance of power.[4]

A few historians stood outside this post–World War II consensus.[5] Especially important was William Appleman Williams's seminal revisionist article, "The Legend of Isolationism in the 1920s," published in *Science and Society* in 1954, which denied that the Republican era had been isolationist in the first place. Williams pointed especially to American economic expansion abroad, much of which he disapproved, to dispute the idea that the United States had truly retreated from internationalism after World War I.

Williams's criticism of American expansion became very influential in the 1970s and later, in part because the Vietnam War undercut much sympathy for American interventionism. At the same time, many historians studying American diplomacy in the 1920s and 1930s reinforced Williams's point when they discovered many internationalist activities of American businesses operating as surrogates for the U.S. government. These historians (often calling themselves "corporatist" historians because of their insistence that America's public diplomacy and private business interests have often reinforced each other in a single corporate policy) concluded that the supposedly isolationist Republican administrations that had opposed Wilson's League of Nations actually agreed with much of the remainder of Wilson's progressive internationalist policies. Like Wilson, these Republican progressives had sought cooperative policies with the European powers to open markets abroad for American trade. Thus, progressive Republican administrations and their corporate surrogates had led the attempt to reform the international economic system with the Dawes and Young plans for reducing reparations. They had also helped to provide loans to German and other European producers so as to create better markets for American exports. These discoveries led the corporatist historians to adopt a more ambiguous view of American foreign policy in the 1920s than Williams had. On the one hand, many of them disapproved of American economic expansionism; on the other, they approved of America's involvement in internationalist activities that had some potential for averting or opposing the rise of fascism in Europe. In any case, later historical works have been somewhat milder in their condemnations of Republican diplomacy in both Europe and Asia in the 1920s than were works on the more immediate aftermath of World War II.[6]

In contrast to historical works on American policy toward Europe and Asia, there have been few historians to argue for American interventionism in Latin America. Contemporaries welcomed the Good Neighbor Policy, and most post–World War II historians continued to praise it, arguing only whether Franklin Roosevelt deserved credit for it.[7]

Revisionists have seen the Good Neighbor Policy as a mere change of tactics rather than a retreat from American empire. They emphasize America's increasing economic penetration of the Latin American nations. Although Franklin Roosevelt did not resort to military interventions as often as his predecessors did, military intrusions were an ever-present threat and ultimately would become necessary to protect the United States' increasing economic stake in Latin American stability. For revisionists, then, the Good Neighbor Policy was no more than a blip in the continuing history of America's economic expansion.[8]

Recent American policy toward Latin America has influenced even nationalists and realists to take a harsher view of U.S. policy and the supposed successes of Good Neighbor diplomacy. Many of these historians are almost as critical of American policy as revisionists, but they place somewhat less emphasis on economic motives and are somewhat more fatalistic about the influence a great power will have over a smaller one.[9]

Further Reading

For developments in Europe, see Raymond Sontag, *A Broken World, 1919–1939* (1971); Sally Marks, *The Illusion of Peace: International Relations in Europe, 1919–1933* (1976); Patrick O. Cohrs, *The Unfinished Peace after World War I: America, Britain, and the Stabilization of Europe, 1919–1922* (2006); and Robert Boyce, *The Great Interwar Crisis and the Collapse of Globalization* (2009), which takes a very pro-French position.

On Harding, see Robert K. Murray, *The Harding Era* (1969), which is excessively favorable, and Eugene P. Trani and David L. Wilson, *The Presidency of Warren G. Harding* (1977). On Charles Evans Hughes, see Betty Glad, *Charles Evans Hughes and the Illusions of Innocence* (1966), a harsh critique. Older but milder treatments of Hughes are Dexter Perkins, *Charles Evans Hughes and American Democratic Statesmanship* (1956); and Merlo J. Pusey, *Charles Evans Hughes* (2 vols., 1951). An excellent character study is Elting E. Morison's biography of Stimson, *Turmoil and Tradition* (1960). Robert Schulzinger examines the State Department at this time in *The Making of the Diplomatic Mind: The Training, Outlook and Style of United States Foreign Service Officers, 1908–1931* (1975).

The most significant work on American-Japanese relations in this era is Akira Iriye, *After Imperialism: The Search for a New Order in the Far East, 1921–1931* (1965). See also Youli Sun, *China and the Origins of the Pacific War, 1931–1941* (1993); Dorothy Borg, *American Policy and the Chinese Revolution, 1925–1928* (1947); and Dorothy Borg and

Shumpei Okamoto, *Pearl Harbor as History: Japanese-American Relations, 1931–1941* (1973). On the various naval limitation conferences with Japan, see Richard W. Fanning, *Peace and Disarmament: Naval Rivalry and Arms Control, 1922–1933* (1995); Emily O. Goldman, *Sunken Treaties: Naval Arms Control Between the Wars* (1994); Thomas Buckley, *The United States and the Washington Conference, 1921–1922* (1970); Roger Dingman, *Power in the Pacific: The Origins of Naval Arms Limitation, 1914–1922* (1976); Gerald E. Wheeler, *Prelude to Pearl Harbor: The United States Navy and the Far East, 1921–1931* (1963); and Stephen Pelz, *Race to Pearl Harbor: The Failure of the Second London Naval Conference and the Onset of World War II* (1974). For British policy toward the United States and the Far East, see William Roger Louis, *British Strategy in the Far East, 1919–1939* (1971); and Christopher Thorne, *The Limits of Foreign Policy: The West, the League, and the Far Eastern Crisis of 1931–1933* (1972). For a Japanese view, see Saburo Ienaga, *The Pacific War: World War II and the Japanese, 1931–1945* (1978); Sadaka Ogata, *Deviance in Manchuria: The Making of Japanese Foreign Policy, 1931–1932* (1964); and Takehiko Yoshihashi, *Conspiracy at Mukden* (1963). James B. Crowley takes a harsh view of Japan in *Quest for Autonomy: National Security and Foreign Policy, 1930–1938* (1966). For American responses to the rise of nationalism in China, see Russell D. Buhite, *Nelson T. Johnson and American Policy Toward China, 1925–1941* (1968).

Notes

1. This was only one of many stories that floated around in the 1920s to illustrate the laconic Coolidge style. "Silent Cal" was famous for long naps and short statements. When one lady sitting next to him at dinner told him that she had a bet with friends that she could make him say more than two words at dinner, Coolidge told her, "You lose." When his wife asked the topic of the sermon at a church service Coolidge had attended, he supposedly said, "Sin." His wife asked what the preacher had said about it, and Coolidge replied, "He was against it."

2. The preceding section is based on a fascinating book by Greg Grandin, *Fordlandia: The Rise and Fall of Henry Ford's Forgotten Jungle City* (2009).

3. See, for example, Denna F. Fleming, *The United States and World Organization: 1920–1933* (1938). For a collection of pre–World War II opinions, see Quincy Wright, ed., *Neutrality and Collective Security* (1936).

4. See, for instance, the works of Robert Ferrell on this period: *Peace in Their Time: The Origins of the Kellogg-Briand Pact* (1952), *American Diplomacy in the Great Depression* (1957), and *Frank B. Kellogg and Henry L. Stimson* (1963). Other works on important topics that took this view were Selig Adler, *The Isolationist Impulse* (1957) and *Uncertain Giant* (1965); Alexander DeConde, ed., *Isolation and Security in Twentieth-Century American Foreign Policy* (1957); Alan Nevins, *The United States in a Chaotic World* (1950); John D. Hicks, *The Republican Ascendancy* (1960); Gordon A. Craig and Felix Gilbert, eds., *The Diplomats, 1919–1939* (1963); John Chalmers Vinson, *The Parchment Peace: The United States Senate and the Washington Conference, 1921–1922*, and *William E. Borah and the Outlawry of War* (1957); Marian C. McKenna, *Borah* (1961); L. Ethan Ellis, *Frank B. Kellogg and American Foreign Relations* (1961); Joseph Brandes, *Herbert Hoover and Economic Diplomacy: Department of Commerce Policy, 1921–1928* (1962); Raymond G. O'Connor, *Perilous Equilibrium: The United States and the London Naval Conference of 1930* (1962); Armin Rappaport, *Henry L. Stimson and the Japanese, 1931–1933* (1963); and Herbert Feis, *The Road to Pearl Harbor* (1950) and *Diplomacy of the Dollar* (1950).

5. See especially Richard N. Current's revisionist *Secretary Stimson* (1954), which condemns Stimson for his interventionism.

6. See especially the works of Joan Hoff Wilson, *American Business and Foreign Policy, 1920–1933* (1971) and *Herbert Hoover: Forgotten Progressive* (1975); Carl Parrini, *Heir to Empire: United States Economic Diplomacy, 1916–1923* (1969); Michael J. Hogan, *Informal Entente: The Private Structure of Cooperation in Anglo-American Economic Diplomacy, 1918–1928* (1977); Melvyn Leffler, *The Elusive Quest: America's Pursuit of European Stability and French Security, 1919–1933* (1979); Frank Costigliola, *Awkward Dominion: American Political, Economic, and Cultural Relations with Europe, 1919–1933* (1984); Warren I. Cohen, *Empire Without Tears: America's Foreign Relations, 1921–1933* (1987); Peter H. Buckingham, *International Normalcy: The Open Door Peace with the Former Central Powers, 1921–1929* (1983); Emily S. Rosenberg, *Spreading the American Dream: American Economic and Cultural Expansion, 1890–1945* (1982); and Neal Pease, *Poland, the United States, and the Stabilization of Europe, 1919–1933* (1986). The most recent broad survey of this period, one that leans toward a more traditional view, is Benjamin D. Rhodes, *United States Foreign Policy in the Interwar Period, 1918–1941: The Golden Age of American Diplomatic and Military Complacency* (2001). Other broad surveys of this period are L. Ethan Ellis, *Republican Foreign Policy, 1921–1933* (1968); Arnold Offner, *The Origins of the Second World War* (1975); and Henry Blumenthal, *Illusion and Reality in Franco-American Diplomacy, 1914–1945* (1986).

7. For examples of works praising the Good Neighbor Policy, see Edward O. Guerrant, *Roosevelt's Good Neighbor Policy* (1950); Bryce Wood, *The Making of the Good Neighbor Policy* (1961); Irwin F. Gellman, *Good Neighbor Diplomacy: United States Policies in Latin America, 1933–1945* (1979); Dana G. Munro, *The United States and the Caribbean Republics, 1921–1933* (1974); Kenneth J. Grieb, *The Latin American Policy of Warren G. Harding* (1976), which argues that Harding truly initiated the policy of restraint toward Latin America; Alexander DeConde, *Herbert Hoover's Latin American Policy* (1951); and Donald Dozer, *Are We Good Neighbors?* (1959), which sees World War II as bringing an increase in U.S. intervention and undermining the restraint of the Good Neighbor Policy.

8. Lars Schoulz, *Beneath the United States: A History of U.S. Policy Toward Latin America* (1998); David F. Schmitz, *Thank God They're on Our Side: The United States and Right-Wing Dictatorships, 1921–1965* (1999); David Green, *The Containment of Latin America: A History of the Myths and Realities of the Good Neighbor Policy* (1971); Jules Robert Benjamin, *The United States and Cuba: Hegemony and Dependent Development, 1880–1934* (1977); Robert F. Smith, *The United States and Revolutionary Nationalism in Mexico, 1916–1932* (1972); Dick Steward, *Trade and Hemisphere: The Good Neighbor Policy and Reciprocal Trade* (1975); Lloyd C. Gardner, *Economic Aspects of New Deal Diplomacy* (1964); Joseph Tulchin, *Aftermath of War: World War I and U.S. Policy Toward Latin America* (1971); Walter LaFeber, *Inevitable Revolutions: The United States in Central America* (1983).

9. See, for instance, Mark Gilderhus, *The Second Century: U.S.-Latin American Relations Since 1889* (2000); Gordon Connell-Smith, *The United States and Latin America* (1974); Cole Blasier, *The Hovering Giant: U.S. Responses to Revolutionary Change in Latin America* (1976); Michael Grow, *The Good Neighbor Policy and Authoritarianism in Paraguay* (1981); William Kamman, *A Search for Stability: United States Diplomacy Toward Nicaragua, 1925–1933* (1968); Hans Schmidt, *The United States Occupation of Haiti* (1971); Stanley E. Hilton, *Brazil and the Great Powers, 1930–1939* (1975); Stephen J. Randall, *The Diplomacy of Modernization: Colombian-American Relations, 1920–1940* (1977); John D. Findling, *Close Neighbors, Distant Friends: United States–Central American Relations* (1987); Helen Delpar, *Enormous Vogue of Things Mexican: Cultural Relations Between the United States and Mexico, 1920–1935* (1992); Eric Paul Roorda, *The Dictator Next Door: The Good Neighbor Policy and the Trujillo Regime in the Dominican Republic, 1930–1945* (1998); and Michel Gobat, *Confronting the American Dream: Nicaragua under U.S. Imperial Rule* (2005).

CHAPTER 7

FRANKLIN D. ROOSEVELT AND THE COMING OF WORLD WAR II

Appeasement, 1932–1939

Franklin Roosevelt had been a champion of the League of Nations while serving as President Woodrow Wilson's assistant secretary of the navy and again when running for vice president on the Democratic ticket in 1920. But as public opinion recoiled from Wilson's vision in the 1920s, Roosevelt grew more cautious. During his campaign for the presidency in 1932, Roosevelt bowed to the pressure of the powerhouse Democratic publisher William Randolph Hearst and actually went so far as to renounce the League of Nations.

Nonetheless, Roosevelt's internationalist opinions occasionally peeked through during his first administration. In November 1933, Roosevelt broke with the U.S. policy of nonrecognition of the Soviet Union. Wilson, his Republican successors, and the American Congress had held aloof from the Soviets in part because the Bolsheviks had repudiated over $600 million in debts Russia owed to the United States and in part out of revulsion against the Soviet Communist system. Ironically, American business had not stayed so aloof from the Soviets. Several large American corporations, including General Electric, DuPont, and International Harvester, had contracts in the 1920s to provide technological aid to the Soviet Union. Henry Ford, the archcapitalist, spent millions setting up a factory in Russia to produce Model A cars and trucks. Thus, Roosevelt could count on support from much of the American business community for his decision to formally recognize the Soviet government. Roosevelt also hoped that the Soviets might be of aid in resisting Japanese expansion on the Asian continent.

Roosevelt showed other internationalist proclivities in early 1934 when he contemplated the desirability of an international trade boycott against Nazi Germany. Two years later, when Hitler marched his troops into the demilitarized Rhineland, Roosevelt confided to a British visitor that he thought the choice was between war immediately or five years later. But Roosevelt would not pursue any internationalist action that posed the slightest threat to the domestic consensus he needed to pull the United States out of the Great Depression. He demonstrated this determination in two sensational 1933 decisions.

The first of these decisions, mentioned in the preceding chapter, was to accept the attachment of an amendment prohibiting discretionary embargoes to the pending neutrality bill. As we have seen, this contradicted Roosevelt's pledge to the Geneva Disarmament Conference that the United States would avoid challenging collective economic actions against an aggressor. Even more sensationally, Roosevelt disrupted the London Economic Conference of 1933 by choosing domestic over international priorities. The European delegates to the London Conference wanted the United States to forgive the war debts, lower its tariffs, and agree to a plan that would stabilize the exchange rates between national currencies. Roosevelt refused from the outset to permit any discussion of war debts. (In the Johnson Act of 1934, Congress went further and prohibited new loans to any nation that had defaulted on its debts.) Roosevelt also refused to permit Cordell Hull, secretary of state and leader of the American delegation, to pursue his cherished program of reciprocal tariff reductions. Roosevelt feared lower duties would undermine his hopes to raise domestic prices.

The president initially remained vague about the third European goal, monetary stabilization. But when White House adviser Raymond Moley, whom Roosevelt had sent to London in midconference amid a splash of publicity and wounded outcries from Hull, recommended a stabilization agreement, Roosevelt sent the assembly what the press at the time termed a "bombshell" message. The United States would accept no stabilization agreement whatever. Like tariff reduction, stabilization would interfere with his desire to raise domestic prices.

Roosevelt's priorities remained the same even as Europe and Asia marched toward war. He believed he had little choice, for most Americans regarded the approach of a foreign war as reason for further withdrawal rather than intervention to prevent it. Roosevelt was very sensitive to public opinion; he commissioned poll after poll to test it. He commented once in the late 1930s that it was a "terrible thing to look over your shoulder when you are trying to lead—and to find no one there."

The apathetic public mood in the United States was a compound of events and personalities—not only the reaction to the sacrifices of World War I, the Senate defeat of the League of Nations and the Treaty of Versailles, the Depression, and the rise of totalitarian governments, but also the highly publicized activities and opinions of isolationist politicians, historians, and activists. In 1934 Senator Gerald P. Nye conducted hearings on the causes of American entry into World War I that publicized the idea that munitions makers, bankers, and British propagandists had maneuvered the United States into the conflagration. Revisionist historians like Harry Elmer Barnes, Walter Millis, and Charles A. Beard reinforced the idea that intervention had been a mistake, if not an evil plot.

A strong pacifist movement supported isolationist sentiments. Uncompromising organizations like the National Society for the Prevention of War and the Women's International League for Peace and Freedom condemned the League of Nations and any sort of international sanctions on the grounds that disarmament was the only road to peace. They challenged the older peace organizations, such as the World Peace Foundation and the Carnegie Endowment for International Peace, which had supported the League and collective security.

This groundswell of isolationist opinion had a powerful impact on Congress and the president. In 1935 isolationist senators William Borah, Hiram Johnson, George Norris, and Robert LaFollette engineered the congressional defeat of an innocuous proposal for the United States to join the World Court. At the same time, Roosevelt suggested that Congress formulate a new neutrality act to prohibit U.S. citizens from engaging in the activities that Americans believed had dragged them into World War I: loaning money and shipping arms to belligerents and traveling aboard belligerent vessels. Unfortunately, this suggestion immediately raised the issue that had sidetracked the neutrality bill of 1933: should an arms embargo extend to all belligerents or just to the aggressors?

Roosevelt and the internationalists wanted to be able to embargo arms to an aggressor while supplying them to the victim. They argued that the best way for the United States to stay out of a war was to prevent it in the first place by joining collective security agreements. Isolationists, on the other hand, insisted on an impartial arms embargo against all belligerents, without any discretion for the president to punish a supposed aggressor. Senator Nye successfully filibustered against the discriminatory clause, and the Senate finally included an impartial arms embargo in the Neutrality Act of 1935. Roosevelt got a six-month limit put on the bill, announced it was entirely satisfactory to him, and then warned while signing it that it might do more to push the United States into war than to avoid it.

Behind Roosevelt's vacillation there seems to have lain a hidden agenda. He accepted the Neutrality Act for six months because he saw how he might manipulate it to punish Italy for its aggression toward Ethiopia. Benito Mussolini, whose Fascist regime had taken power in Italy in 1922, had been agitating to incorporate Ethiopia into Italy's existing North African empire for more than a year. Immediately after Roosevelt signed the Neutrality Act of 1935, Mussolini followed up his bluster with an invasion, complete with tanks, artillery, and poison gas ranged against spear-carrying Ethiopian warriors on horseback. Roosevelt immediately invoked the Neutrality Act. He embargoed arms to the nations at war, warned Americans off belligerent ships, and announced that Americans traded with Italy and Ethiopia at their own risk. As Roosevelt had foreseen, the supposedly impartial Neutrality Act worked entirely against the Italian aggressors. Ethiopia had no passenger vessels and no submarines to threaten Italian liners. Roosevelt's decree affected only Italian ships. Likewise, Ethiopia had no way to get trade from the United States, so the act affected only trade with Italy. Hull, who favored a more cautious policy, pointed out to Roosevelt that invoking the Neutrality Act was a "gratuitous affront" to Italy.

Roosevelt's circuitous attempt to punish Italian aggression presented a golden opportunity for the League of Nations and the United States to align their policies. Tragically, they missed their chance. The League condemned Mussolini's invasion and embargoed a long list of goods to Italy. But it omitted oil from the embargo list, the one commodity that might have made Mussolini reconsider. Great Britain and France feared that embargoing oil might lead Italy to declare war and fall into Hitler's waiting arms. Roosevelt also moved cautiously. He would not risk joining the League embargo formally, especially since the omission of oil made it ineffective. He did ask American business voluntarily to observe a "moral embargo" on trade with Italy, but despite his request the volume of Italian-American trade went up rather than down.

Meanwhile, in December 1935, British foreign secretary Sir George Hoare and French foreign minister Pierre Laval decided to offer Mussolini control of most of Ethiopia if he would end his invasion. Public outcry aborted this Hoare-Laval deal and forced Hoare's resignation, but Mussolini completed his conquest without further interference. England, France, and the United States drew still further apart with mutual recriminations over who was at fault for the collapse of resistance to Italy.

This situation precipitated further American withdrawal from European affairs. Congress extended the Neutrality Act into 1937 and added to it a ban on private loans to belligerents, a provision that had fallen out of the original act in the 1935 revision. In the debates over extension of the Neutrality Act, Roosevelt asked once again for some presidential discretion. He wanted to be able to bar trade in strategic materials to aggressors while continuing such trade, excepting arms, with the victims. Once again he failed. This time Congress members who wanted an impartial embargo found allies among those who wanted no embargoes on strategic materials at all. These latter members of Congress insisted on vigorous and impartial enforcement of America's neutral right to trade with all belligerents. They thought truly impartial trade rather than abstention was the proper means to keep America out of war. In the face of this opposition, Roosevelt dropped his request for flexibility and signed the bill without comment. One week later, on March 7, 1936, Hitler's troops marched into the demilitarized Rhineland.

Hitler's move was an enormous gamble. It violated both the Treaty of Versailles and the Treaty of Locarno. It posed a grave strategic threat to France, for it put German troops in a position to attack France once again through Belgium. Such a move would outflank the elaborate Maginot Line the French had been building on the German border since 1929. France had not only an incentive to resist the German move, but also the capability. Germany's army was just rebuilding, and the French had an enormous military superiority. They easily could have forced a German retreat, and Hitler's government would probably not have survived the fiasco. The French general staff, however, advised against resistance. The British, having already signed a treaty with Hitler recognizing Germany's right to a navy so long as it did not exceed 35 percent of the British navy, told the French they could expect no help from Great Britain if they attacked. The beleaguered French did nothing but strengthen the Maginot Line.

The German occupation of the Rhineland demonstrated the bankruptcy of British and French foreign policy. Hitler's bold success made his political position in Germany unassailable, and he began immediately to fortify Germany's west wall. This confirmed the French in their defensive strategy. They ignored the advice of General Charles de Gaulle to build offensive weapons such as tanks, airplanes, and submarines. Instead, they relied on the defensive weapons of fortifications, machine guns, heavy artillery, and infantry to make themselves invulnerable to another German attack. They also counted on their eastern European allies to force a two-front war on Germany if Germany attacked France. By adding 30 million Poles and 12 million Czechs to France's own population of 40 million, the Allies would outnumber Germany's population of 65 million.

Unfortunately, the French did not anticipate that Germany, adopting modern offensive weaponry and blitzkrieg (lightning war) tactics, would so easily sweep aside their defensive preparations. Even more inexcusably, they failed to anticipate that Germany might attack eastward and eliminate Polish and Czech resistance before invading France. France had no way to respond to an invasion of its allies because of its defensive posture. Great Britain, with its navy, might have had the capacity to land an expeditionary force to aid Poland and Czechoslovakia, but the British were unwilling to defend the eastern borders created by the Treaty of Versailles against what they believed was inevitable German revision. Great Britain's commitment to France was limited to joining it in a *defensive* war. That meant that if Germany attacked Poland or Czechoslovakia and France responded by attacking Germany from the rear, Great Britain would regard it as an *offensive* war and feel under no obligation to aid the French.

Roosevelt also remained aloof in the Rhineland crisis. He refused the French plea for a moral condemnation of Germany and declined to send observers to the League discussion of Germany's challenge to the Versailles system. With the Europeans themselves rejecting a strong stand against Germany, Roosevelt saw no reason for the United States to leap into the fray. After all, Germany did not seem to pose an immediate threat to the United States. France was strong behind the Maginot Line, Britain maintained naval supremacy in European waters, and those two nations with their Czech and Polish allies still far outnumbered the Wehrmacht in troops. Besides, Italy was not yet firmly allied to Germany, and the Soviet Union seemed to be a permanent and determined enemy of the Nazis. The chance seemed very remote that Hitler's remilitarization of the Rhineland could lead to the unification of all of Europe into a hostile German empire capable of challenging the United States across the Atlantic moat.

On the heels of the Rhineland crisis, civil war broke out in Spain. Royalist general Francisco Franco and the Spanish army launched a campaign to overthrow Spain's republican government. Great Britain and France asked the United States and other nations to deny arms to both sides and thus prevent the war from spreading. Roosevelt heeded their plea. But Germany and Italy provided invaluable support for Franco. When the Spanish navy refused to ferry Franco's troops from North Africa to Spain to join the fight, German planes did the job. The Soviet Union tried to counter the Fascist support for Franco by sending arms and advisers to the Spanish government, and American liberals emotionally demanded that the United States join the Russians in aiding the Loyalists. After all, they pointed out, the Neutrality Act did not prevent the United States from sending arms to a legitimate government for use against rebels. Roosevelt personally favored the Loyalists, but pressure from American Catholics in support of Franco along with the desire to cooperate with Britain and France froze Roosevelt's policy until Franco's triumph in 1939.

The Spanish Civil War triggered renewed discussion of the Neutrality Act, the provisions of which were due to expire in 1937. Many members of Congress expressed fear that ordinary trade with nations at war could drag the United States into a war as easily as trade in armaments. They suggested extending the arms embargo to all commerce with belligerents. Others argued that this policy abandoned too many of America's neutral rights and would threaten American economic recovery from the Depression. Financier and sometime presidential adviser Bernard Baruch suggested an alternative that could save American trade and avoid war at the same time. He would permit belligerents to buy American goods, but require them to use their own ships to transport the goods home. Thus, if the ships and goods were attacked, the United States would have no stake in them and would not be obliged to fight in defense of American lives or property. Roosevelt supported this cash-and-carry provision because he saw it would aid Great Britain and France to the exclusion of Germany. British control of the sea would ensure that the Germans would not be able to get their ships to America to take advantage of cash-and-carry purchases. The British were disturbed that the impartial arms embargo remained in the Neutrality Act of 1937, but they were grateful for the opportunity to obtain other goods.

Cash-and-carry did not work so conveniently in Asia. A few weeks after Congress passed the Neutrality Act of 1937, the Japanese army clashed with Chinese soldiers at the Marco Polo Bridge just south of Beijing, and Japan immediately took the opportunity to embark on a war of conquest into southern China. If Roosevelt recognized the state of war and invoked the Neutrality Act, as he was expected to do, Japan would benefit because it had the navy to take advantage of cash-and-carry. Again Roosevelt showed his ingenuity in using isolationist laws to benefit interventionist causes. He refused to recognize the state of war and thus permitted American trade with China to continue. Still, the volume of trade with Japan, especially in critical matériel such as oil and scrap iron, far exceeded trade with Japan's victim: China took only 13 percent of America's trade with Asia while Japan took 36 percent.

Japanese aggression seemed all the more ominous because Japan was moving toward an alliance with Germany and Italy. Germany and Italy had signed a treaty eliminating obstacles to cooperation between them in October 1936, during their joint venture in the Spanish Civil War. A month later, Japan signed the Anti-Comintern Pact with Germany, which promised mutual aid if either were attacked by the Soviet Union. Italy joined the Anti-Comintern Pact the following year, 1937. Roosevelt began to contemplate some sort of gesture against what he privately called these "bandit nations."

He made a sensational splash in late 1937 when he spoke publicly of "quarantining" aggressors. He also joined Great Britain and France in condemning Japan's war with China as a violation of the Washington Conference treaties and agreed to send an American delegate to a meeting in Brussels to discuss the conflict in China. But nothing came of any of these gestures. Roosevelt had no firm plan in mind when he gave his quarantine speech, and neither he nor any other Western leader was prepared to risk being dragged into the war in Asia. When Japanese planes attacked the American gunboat *Panay* on the Yangtze River in late 1937, Roosevelt accepted the Japanese apology and let the matter drop.

The president was too weak domestically in 1937 and 1938 to do much more than make gestures on foreign policy. His attempt to pack the Supreme Court with new justices who would support his New Deal had failed amid charges that he was becoming a dictator on the model of the European Fascists. His refusal to break several prolonged sit-down strikes in 1937 cost him considerable support among middle-class voters. Most devastating of all, the economy plunged downward in 1937 to destroy much of the painfully slow recovery that had been made under the New Deal. Conservative Democrats in Congress deserted the New Deal coalition and joined the Republicans to try to defeat further reform legislation and deter Roosevelt from seeking a third term in 1940. One group of congressmen told Roosevelt, "For God's sake, don't send us any more controversial legislation." Roosevelt tried to improve his position in the 1938 elections, but his attempts to replace conservative Democrats with liberals in the primaries failed, and the Republicans picked up eighty-one seats in the House along with eight in the Senate during the subsequent general elections.

With the strengthened bipartisan conservative coalition stalemating most of Roosevelt's political initiatives, the president could do little more than watch as Hitler forced Austria to select a Nazi prime minister and then got him to invite German troops across the border to prevent violence and bloodshed. Hitler then demanded that Czechoslovakia turn over the Sudetenland. The Sudetenland contained 3.5 million Germans whom Hitler had encouraged to make extortionate demands on the Czech government. Roosevelt briefly considered encouraging France and Great Britain to support the Czechs by offering to join them in confronting Germany. But the British and French were desperate to avoid war and successfully pressed Czechoslovakia to agree to give the territory eventually to Germany, so Roosevelt lost heart. When Hitler arrogantly demanded that Czechoslovakia cede the territory immediately or he would march, Roosevelt made public appeals for peace. He wired British prime minister Neville Chamberlain, "Good man!" when Chamberlain arranged a meeting with Hitler at Munich to head off the crisis, although privately he thought Chamberlain was "taking very long chances." At Munich, Chamberlain, French prime minister Edouard Daladier, Mussolini, and Hitler agreed that Germany would occupy the Sudetenland in exchange for Hitler's promise that he would seek no further territory in Europe. The relief of the world was short-lived, for six months later Hitler flagrantly broke his promise and occupied the remainder of Czechoslovakia.

The shock of Czechoslovakia stirred Roosevelt to try once again to revise the Neutrality Act. He wanted to be able to lift an arms embargo against the victim of aggression while leaving it on the aggressor. But the Senate stalled and the House defeated the discriminatory provision by four votes. Roosevelt called the Senate leaders to the White House to try to reverse the defeat. After his emotional appeal, Vice President John Nance Garner polled the group and told Roosevelt, "Well, Captain, we may as well face the facts. You haven't got the votes, and that's all there is to it." Not until Europe was actually at war would the United States begin to abandon its isolationist course.

America's March Toward War in Europe

After Hitler completed his invasion of Czechoslovakia, he quickly revealed further ambitions in Eastern Europe. First he occupied Memel at the expense of Lithuania. Then he demanded that Poland turn over the free city of Danzig and permit a German railroad across the corridor to East Prussia. Great Britain already had begun a substantial arms-building program after Hitler's betrayal of his Munich promises. Then, when Hitler made his demands of Poland, Neville Chamberlain responded by making a defensive alliance with the beleaguered Poles and other eastern European states. Hitler was shocked. He had hoped to seize eastern Europe without interference from the West. France seemed sufficiently intimidated, but Hitler told his commanders that he wanted to avoid war with Great Britain at least until 1943.

The key to the situation was the Soviet Union. After Great Britain made its guarantees to Poland and Poland's neighbors, Chamberlain and the French approached Russia for a pact that might further deter Germany's eastward march. But the Soviet dictator Joseph Stalin distrusted the British and the French. He professed to believe that Britain and France purposely had conceded Hitler's demands on Czechoslovakia to keep Hitler pointed eastward and ultimately embroil Germany and Russia in a war. Stalin demanded that any pact with the West should involve a guarantee of the independence of eastern Europe's regimes even if they did not want such a guarantee. He also insisted that a military pact precede a political agreement and that the military pact should include the stationing of Russian troops in Poland and elsewhere to meet invading German troops well short of the Soviet border.

Poland was adamant against Russian troops on its soil, and other nations were reluctant as well. The British were especially suspicious of Stalin's purposes after the Russian leader told Estonia that any concession Estonia might make to Germany would result in an end to Russia's nonintervention pledge. Stalin's program seemed to be a prelude to Soviet occupation of eastern Europe. This realization made the British and French hesitant and vacillating in their negotiations with the Soviets.

Hitler showed no such hesitation. As often as he had railed against Russia and communism, he was ready to make a nonaggression pact with the Soviets. He believed this would not only prevent Soviet opposition to his intended conquest of Poland, but also demoralize the Western powers and deter their intervention as well. To achieve the stunning Russo-German Non-Aggression Pact of August 1939, Hitler conceded eastern Poland, Finland, Estonia, Latvia, and the Bessarabian portion of Rumania to the Soviet sphere of influence. (The Russians added Lithuania to their sphere a month later.)

Freed of the fear of Russian intervention, Hitler sent his armies plunging into Poland on September 1, 1939. To his surprise and chagrin, the British and French declared war even though they had no means to resist Germany's advance into eastern Europe. While Germany's blitzkrieg tactics demolished and conquered western Poland, the Soviets moved into eastern Poland to claim their share and then turned to attack Finland. The Finns put up a surprising battle. This Russo-Finnish War absorbed American attention for several months because the Germans paused after conquering Poland. Having denuded his western borders of troops in order to concentrate them in Poland, Hitler had to return them before striking at France. But France did not exploit the opportunity to attack. After a minor sally into the Saar Valley, most of the French army hunkered down in defensive positions along the Maginot Line to await a German offensive. Hitler used this opportunity to capture Denmark and Norway. Then he ended the period of "phony war" or *sitzkrieg* with a surprise attack through the Ardennes Forest that broke the French lines, forced France's surrender in little more than a month, and sent the British Expeditionary Force scurrying back across the Channel from the collapsing pocket around Dunkirk.

Hitler's invasion of Poland stirred deep anger in the United States. Roosevelt invoked the Neutrality Act with the comment that he regretted ever signing it. In contrast to Woodrow Wilson's appeal on the outbreak of World War I, Roosevelt asked for neutrality in action but not in thought. He then called for repeal of the arms embargo. Roosevelt knew repeal would favor Britain and France, but he portrayed it simply as a return to traditional international law. Although this tactic failed to avert a terrific debate between isolationists and internationalists in Congress, repeal finally passed.

The fall of France then shocked Congress into a still more vigorous response. Under Roosevelt's urging, Congress increased the military budget for 1940 from $2 billion to $10.5 billion. Public opinion also changed drastically. Before France's collapse, 82 percent of Americans expected the Allies to win the war and thus saw no particular reason for the United States to aid them. After Germany had swatted aside French resistance, a majority of Americans polled feared that Germany would win the war. Therefore 80 percent favored extending aid to Great Britain, even though 65 percent expected this to lead to American involvement. And yet 82 percent still opposed American military intervention.

Roosevelt read the message these polls delivered. Americans wanted Britain to win the war and were willing to aid it, but they did not want to enter the war themselves. Consequently, Roosevelt portrayed every action he took to aid Great Britain as designed to prevent American intervention by helping the British to win on their own. Roosevelt undoubtedly realized that Britain would require American military intervention to win, but he never said that directly to the American people. He would not take a divided nation into a major war. Instead, he urged aid to the Allies in hopes either that a miracle would allow them to win or that Hitler would retaliate and galvanize Americans into a united determination to fight and defeat the Nazis.

Roosevelt was anxious to prevent a Nazi conquest of Europe because he knew this would give Hitler the resources to threaten the United States. He especially worried that Hitler might capture the British navy intact. He had no doubt that once Hitler had the capability to extend his power to the Western Hemisphere, he would have no trouble finding a rationale for doing so.

Despite Roosevelt's deviousness and proclamations that he would never send Americans to fight a foreign war, polls showed that Americans had few illusions about what the president was doing. In fact, most historians who have criticized Roosevelt have accused him of moving too cautiously toward intervention. They argue that the polls show Roosevelt to have been behind public opinion rather than ahead of it. Hitler seemed to understand Roosevelt's intentions as well. He refused to respond to Roosevelt's provocations by creating an incident that would bring America into the European war. He remembered too vividly the miscalculation Germany had made in World War I. In hopes of diverting the United States from Europe, he encouraged the Japanese to expand. Even if this led to war with the United States, America would have to fight on two fronts, and Hitler could continue his triumphant march of conquest.

Once Hitler had defeated France, he began to soften up England for an amphibious invasion. His air force bombed port facilities and Royal Air Force bases, and then foolishly switched to terror bombing of English cities in order to break British morale. At the same time, German submarines began sinking vast numbers of British cargo ships. The cash-and-carry provisions of America's Neutrality Acts prevented Roosevelt from using American ships to carry the goods. But after three months of hesitation, Roosevelt responded to British prime minister Winston Churchill's pleas by giving Great Britain fifty destroyers to guard the convoys. Roosevelt softened the impact of this "destroyer deal" by trading the overage destroyers for leases on British naval bases in the Western Hemisphere and Britain's promise not to let its navy fall into German hands. The British regarded this as a hard bargain, but it permitted Roosevelt to portray the deal as strengthening American defenses rather aiding the Allies. Public opinion polls showed wide support for Roosevelt's action, but still he took no chance of congressional interference. He concluded the destroyer deal as an executive agreement rather than as a treaty that would require the consent of two-thirds of the Senate.

Roosevelt remained cautious as he approached the election of 1940, in which he sought a third term as president. He stayed aloof from the battle in Congress for a Selective Service Act and signed it without fanfare in September 1940, the same month he announced the destroyer deal. When the Republicans rejected isolationist Robert Taft and nominated Wendell Willkie, a fervent supporter of aid to Britain, Roosevelt thought he would be permitted to continue his ambiguous course. On the eve of the election, however, Willkie succumbed to temptation and attacked Roosevelt for secretly maneuvering the United States toward war. Roosevelt responded by promising an Irish isolationist crowd in Boston, "I have said this before, but I shall say it again and again and again: Your boys are not going to be sent into any foreign wars." His advisers had warned against this unqualified pledge, reminding him that the Democratic platform promised to stay out of war "except in the case of attack." Roosevelt blithely disregarded this advice with the remark, "Of course we'll fight if we're attacked. If somebody attacks us, then it isn't a foreign war, is it?" Willkie was not so blithe. "That hypocritical son of a bitch! This is going to beat me," he complained. He was right; Roosevelt won 55 percent of the vote.

A month after his electoral victory, Roosevelt faced another crisis. Britain's Royal Air Force had won the Battle of Britain by defeating the German air campaign and forcing Hitler to call off his invasion. But Hitler accelerated submarine wolf-pack attacks on British convoys to starve the British into submission. Churchill informed Roosevelt that Great Britain was running out of money to buy American supplies and ships to carry them. He asked Roosevelt to find a way to expand the American supply effort.

The Neutrality Acts prohibited loans of money to belligerents. The Johnson Act of 1934 prohibited loans to any nation that had defaulted on its war debts. Roosevelt decided to circumvent these prohibitions with the ingenious program he called lend-lease. America would loan Britain war matériel rather than money, and Great Britain would return it after the war. It was like lending a neighbor a garden hose to put out a fire, he told the American people. It was far more like loaning chewing gum, one of his opponents said. After the neighbor had used it, you did not want it back. Senator Burton Wheeler claimed that lend-lease was another Agricultural Administration Act—it would plow under every fourth American boy. Roosevelt called this the rottenest remark made during his political life. He argued that the United States had to become the "arsenal of democracy." The lend-lease program was a serious risk, for if Great Britain lost, American equipment needed for the defense of the United States would fall into German hands. Nevertheless, the Senate and House, following changing public opinion, passed the Lend-Lease Act by overwhelming majorities.

Winston Churchill called lend-lease the most unsordid act in history but, as with the destroyer deal, the United States demanded a quid pro quo. The British had to exhaust their financial holdings in the United States to demonstrate to the American people their need for aid. The British also had to reduce the barriers to outsiders trading with Britain's colonies.

At this time, Roosevelt permitted British and American military officials to plan strategy for joint operations if America entered the war. These officials decided that the Allies would concentrate their primary efforts to defeat Hitler in Europe while maintaining a holding operation in Asia, where the less powerful Japanese posed much less of a threat to Western security and vital interests. Roosevelt also moved to extend American naval protection to British convoys near American shores. At the outset of the war, the United States and Latin America had proclaimed a neutrality zone of 300 miles from their coasts. In April 1939, Roosevelt extended that zone to incorporate Greenland. American ships patrolled the defense area and radioed the position of German submarines to both convoys and British sub-hunting planes. But American ships could not fire at the German submarines, so the German wolf-pack war remained a grave danger to Britain's North Atlantic supply route.

While Hitler was expanding his submarine war, he also was expanding his effort on land. He sent troops to the Balkans and North Africa to rescue his floundering Italian allies. Then he launched an invasion of Russia. Roosevelt's advisers, claiming that the Soviet Union could survive for only a few months, urged the president to increase aid to Great Britain while Germany was tied up in Russia. At first Roosevelt seemed to move in that direction. After maneuvering an invitation from Iceland, Roosevelt occupied that nation. Then he prepared to escort British vessels with the American convoys supplying Iceland. But he backed away from those convoys at the last minute. Then, as the USSR proved more resilient than anyone had expected after its inept performance in Finland, Roosevelt decided to gamble and extend lend-lease to Russia. He found surprising support for this move. While Americans hated communism, they did not yet fear Russian power and admired Russia's brave stand against the Nazis. They hoped that Russian resistance just might help defeat Hitler without the United States having to join the fight. Their reluctance to fight showed up in the close congressional vote to extend the terms of men serving in the military under the Selective Service Act; it passed the House by a single vote in August 1941.

That same month, Roosevelt took another step toward intervention by meeting Winston Churchill in Argentia Bay off Newfoundland. In addition to issuing the Atlantic Charter, a joint declaration on the purposes of the war to defeat fascism, Roosevelt and Churchill agreed that the United States should finally begin convoying British ships as far as Iceland. Despite this agreement, Roosevelt hesitated until a German submarine attacked the American destroyer *Greer*. Roosevelt did not reveal that the *Greer* had been trailing the submarine and radioing its position to a British patrol plane, but announced that this "unprovoked" attack was indicative of Germany's plan for world conquest by force, terror, and murder. He announced that American ships would protect convoys in the neutrality zone as far as Iceland and would fire on German submarines to do so. A subsequent attack on the American destroyer *Kearney* provided the impetus for repeal of the Neutrality Act's prohibition against arming merchant ships and sending them into combat zones. The United States now was free to escort convoys all the way to Great Britain.

Hitler still did not order attacks on American ships. He told Admiral Erich Raeder, commander in chief of Germany's navy, that such incidents would have to be avoided at least until October. Probably he was waiting to be sure that the Japanese would fight and force the United States to face a two-front war.

The March Toward War in Asia

The Manchuria incident of 1931–1932 turned out to be the beginning rather than the end of militant Japanese actions aimed at dominating China and Asia. In 1934 Japan formally renounced the Washington Treaties of 1922 and their naval ratios. In 1935 the Japanese delegates walked out of the London Naval Conference when the other powers refused to give Japan full naval parity with Great Britain and the United States. Meanwhile, the Japanese infiltrated China's northern provinces and made plans for severing them entirely from China. The Japanese military steadily increased its power over more moderate politicians who wished to achieve Japanese hegemony in Asia by pressure diplomacy rather than war.

Military rebels assassinated three high cabinet officials in 1936 for lack of militancy, and they missed the prime minister only because they killed his brother-in-law by mistake. The Japanese army put down the rebels, but it informed the prime minister that henceforth it would make full use of an 1895 rule that only high-ranking military officers could serve as ministers of war and the navy. This gave the military the power to bring down any government. The war and navy ministers could threaten to resign with the assurance that no other officer would accept the positions, thus preventing the formation of a new cabinet. In 1936 Japan also signed the Anti-Comintern Pact with Nazi Germany. Although ostensibly an agreement to combat Communist subversion and propaganda, secret protocols made it a defensive alliance, and the rest of the world suspected as much.

Despite these signs of increasing Japanese militancy, the United States and the League of Nations were shocked in 1937 when Japan escalated a clash with Chinese soldiers at the Marco Polo Bridge into a full-scale war. The Japanese were responding not only to the Marco Polo Bridge incident, but also to a bizarre agreement between Chiang Kai-shek and the warlord Chang Hsueh-liang, whom the Japanese had expelled from Manchuria. Chiang had visited the Manchurian warlord to arrange for another campaign against the Chinese Communists. Chang then kidnapped the Nationalist leader and insisted that he concentrate his efforts against the Japanese rather than the Communists. Chiang Kai-shek agreed, and Chang not only freed him, but also accompanied him back to Nanjing as his prisoner.

The Japanese heartily disliked this alliance. They made use of the incident at the Marco Polo Bridge to reinforce their armies, occupy Beijing, and seize most of northern China. Chiang Kai-shek broadened the war by attacking the Japanese garrisons in the southern city of Shanghai, perhaps hoping to force the Western nations to intervene to protect their own nationals and interests. But the United States and the League of Nations were preoccupied with the crisis in Europe. Roosevelt briefly raised Chinese hopes by delivering his quarantine speech, but dashed them again by rejecting sanctions. The most he would do was make use of Japan's unwillingness to declare a formal state of war to avoid invoking the Neutrality Act. This permitted American-owned companies to ship weapons and supplies to China without the restrictions of an arms embargo or cash-and-carry provisions. The League of Nations met in Brussels to consider the China situation, but its members also refused sanctions and chose appeasement.

Japan stirred another flurry of anger when its planes sank the American gunboat *Panay* and damaged several other American and British boats during a rapacious siege of the Nationalist capital at Nanjing. Even when it became apparent that the Japanese pilots had deliberately attacked the boats and that it was not a case of mistaken identity, the United States and Great Britain accepted Japanese apologies, and the incident blew over.

Japan, seeing that China would receive no support from the Western powers, continued its relentless advance. By 1938 it controlled all the railroads, industries, and major cities of northern and central China. In November, it announced that the war would not end until a reformed China accepted a New Order in Asia. China would have to accept Japanese troops wherever necessary to combat communism. China also would have to coordinate its military, economic, and cultural life with Japan. Outside powers would no longer have an Open Door, but would have to recognize Japan's special position in China. Hitler withdrew his aid and military advisers from China and in effect gave his blessing to the New Order. It soon became public knowledge that Germany and Japan were discussing an expansion of the Anti-Comintern Pact into a general military alliance.

Still, Roosevelt and his advisers hoped that Japanese moderates might resume control and restrain Japan's expansion within tolerable limits. Roosevelt made gestures against the Japanese advance in China, but he did not interfere with the extensive American trade to Japan in scrap iron and oil. This matériel was vital to Japan's war machine, and an embargo would have created a crisis. Instead, Roosevelt loaned China $25 million and unofficially embargoed airplanes to Japan. As public anger against the Japanese mounted, Henry Stimson led an organized campaign to impose an embargo on all trade to Japan, including scrap iron and oil. Roosevelt circumvented the demand by giving Japan notice that the United States would terminate the Japanese-American Trade Agreement of 1911.

Japanese reaction to this notice was angry, but both Japan's anger and the American agitation for an embargo were short-circuited when Hitler invaded Poland and began World War II in Europe. Hitler's action not only turned American attention away from Asia toward Europe, but it forced Japan to reconsider its entire policy. The Nazi-Soviet Agreement of 1939 that preceded the invasion of Poland undermined Japan's Anti-Comintern Pact with Germany and shocked the Japanese army. The army, which regarded the Soviet Union as its greatest enemy in Manchuria, had suffered over 50,000 casualties in a 1939 clash with Soviet troops at Lake Nomonhan along the Manchurian border. The Japanese military dreamed of expansion into Siberia at Soviet expense once the China situation was settled. Siberian natural resources would relieve Japan of its dependence on the United

States for 80 percent of its oil products, 90 percent of its gasoline, 74 percent of its scrap iron, and 60 percent of its machine tools. But with Russia the partner of Germany, Japan turned its attention even more strongly toward Southeast Asia, especially the oil of the Dutch East Indies and the rubber, rice, and tin of French Indochina and British Malaya. These targets became all the more tempting when Germany conquered the Netherlands and France and put their colonies up for grabs.

Immediately after the French and Dutch fell to Hitler, the Japanese successfully demanded that the French stop supplies from reaching Chiang Kai-shek through Indochina. The Japanese also forced Dutch authorities in the East Indies to ensure a more rapid flow of oil and trade to Japan. Finally, they pressed the isolated British into closing the Hong Kong and Burma Road supply routes to China for three months.

On the advice of Joseph Grew, the U.S. ambassador to Japan, Roosevelt and Secretary of State Hull briefly tried to wean Japan away from Germany following Germany's betrayal of the Anti-Comintern Pact. They offered to negotiate a new commercial agreement that might accept Japanese de facto control of Manchuria and northern China. But when Japan demanded that the United States also recognize its candidate to replace Chiang Kai-shek as ruler of all China, the negotiations foundered. As Japan pressed southward, Roosevelt decided to keep the American fleet in Hawaii, where it had been on maneuvers, rather than signal weakness by withdrawing it to San Diego's better staging and repair facilities. A month later, on July 25, 1940, Roosevelt imposed an embargo on the shipment of aviation fuel and the highest grades of steel and scrap iron to Japan on the grounds that they were needed for America's own defense.

These warning gestures did not deter the hard-line Japanese cabinet that had taken power three days before Roosevelt announced his limited embargo. Japan forced the Vichy government, which nominally ruled France after Hitler's conquest, to permit the stationing of Japanese troops in France's northern Indochina colony. As Japanese troops moved across the Indochinese border, the United States also learned that Japan was about to sign a formal military alliance with Germany. Ambassador Grew, reversing his earlier advice to avoid confrontation, urged Roosevelt in what came to be called the "green light" telegram to adopt economic sanctions as a "show of force" to deter further Japanese aggression. Roosevelt responded by deciding to embargo oil and steel. When Hull warned that this move would bring war, Roosevelt modified the order to omit oil. On September 27, 1940, a day after this embargo on all grades of iron and scrap steel, Japan signed the Tripartite (or Axis) Pact with Germany and Italy.

Germany, Japan, and Italy aimed the Tripartite Pact directly at the United States by agreeing to mutually assist one another if one of the participants were "attacked by a power at present not involved in the European war or in the Sino-Japanese conflict." Since the Soviet Union was specifically exempted from the treaty, that left only the United States as a potential target. Private letters among the Axis nations undermined the commitment they made to one another in this alliance by leaving the definition of when an attack had taken place up to each individual nation, so historians have considered the pact a "hollow alliance." Nevertheless, the Axis hoped that the Tripartite Pact would intimidate the United States and prevent it from further aiding Great Britain in either Asia or Europe.

Instead, the pact had exactly the opposite effect. It stiffened American opinion by dramatizing what seemed to be a united and global totalitarian threat. Still, Roosevelt and Hull considered Germany a far greater threat than Japan, and they desperately wanted to delay war until America was better prepared. While they were not willing to make major concessions to Japan or engage in an "Asian Munich," they hoped to delay any confrontation and keep China in the war until the United States was better armed and more unified or until, by some stroke of fortune, the British finished the war in Europe. Roosevelt knew that the U.S. rearmament plan passed by Congress in the wake of France's defeat would make the American navy twice as large as the Japanese navy by 1943 and three times as large by 1944.

Thus, Roosevelt and Hull walked a narrow line. Roosevelt permitted secret joint naval planning with the British on Asia. He extended a further $100 million loan to Chiang's government in China. In his "arsenal of democracy" defense of lend-lease, he included Japan as part of the unholy alliance that sought to "dominate and enslave the human race." He privately concluded that he could not afford to let the Japanese strip the British of their colonies in Asia and thus undermine Britain's war effort in Europe, yet he was afraid to make a firm public commitment to defend the European colonies in Asia.

There was some chance that Roosevelt could have saved the colonies by conceding Japan a free hand in China. Some historians have argued that Roosevelt should have made that concession in order to avoid a two-front war and be able to concentrate on the greater threat in Europe. If such a concession had involved merely American abstention, Roosevelt might have accepted that unpleasant alternative. But the minimum demand of moderates as well as militants in Japan required the United States not just to abandon the Chinese Nationalists, but also to guarantee the flow of oil and steel necessary to supply Japan's brutal war in China. Roosevelt feared that such a betrayal would undermine the American people's moral opposition to aggressive dictators in Europe as well as Asia.

Rejecting both major concessions and confrontation, Roosevelt saw no alternative but to make small incremental additions to the embargo list, using American defense needs rather than Japanese provocations as justification. He hoped Japan would become frightened of a total interruption of American trade and draw back from its advance in Asia. But just as Japan's Axis Pact with Germany and Italy provoked stiffer American resistance, so Roosevelt's tightening of trade restrictions provoked more rather than less Japanese military expansion. Each tightening of the American trade noose brought the Japanese army to make stronger demands for the conquest of areas with the oil and metal resources that would render the Japanese Empire self-sufficient.

The Japanese navy was slightly less militant, but the navy and most Japanese politicians as well were willing to fight the United States rather than abandon the war in China and their dreams of Asian hegemony. The Japanese militants realized that the United States had the resources to win a war with Japan and that those resources would increase with time. Rather than retreat from China, however, they would take the calculated risk of a quick strike to conquer the western and southern Pacific and establish a naval defense line through the chains of Pacific islands. They hoped that the United States, faced with a fait accompli and diverted by the war in Europe, would be unable to summon the determination or accept the sacrifices necessary to destroy the Japanese Empire.

Some Japanese moderates hoped to avoid such a dangerous gamble. They made contact with Roosevelt and Hull in January 1941 through two Catholic Maryknoll missionaries serving in Japan, Bishop James E. Walsh and Father James M. Drought. Walsh and Drought, known in the interests of secrecy as the John Doe Associates, told Roosevelt and Hull that the Japanese were willing to withdraw from the Axis Pact and remove their troops from China if the United States would guarantee the flow of critical supplies. Roosevelt and Hull doubted that the Japanese government truly was willing to do this, but they asked the missionaries to continue their private contacts and get the Japanese proposal in writing. The Japanese government sent Colonel Hideo Iwakuro of the War Ministry to consult with the missionaries, and together they drew up a proposal.

Colonel Iwakuro ensured that the proposal was far more favorable to Japan than the missionaries had led Hull and Roosevelt to believe it would be. Japan would not withdraw from the Axis alliance, but it would promise not to fight the United States unless the United States were the aggressor in an attack on Germany. The United States also would have to request China to make peace and form a coalition government with the Japanese-sponsored regime. Then some Japanese troops would be removed, but others would stay behind for "joint defense against communistic activities and economic cooperation."

Hull was very disappointed. Instead of breaking off negotiations, however, he told the Japanese ambassador, Kichisaburo Nomura, a moderate admiral favorable toward the United States, that the United States would be willing to negotiate on the basis of this draft proposal if Japan would pledge itself in advance to four principles: the territorial integrity of China, noninterference in the internal affairs of other nations, equality of commercial opportunity, and the status quo in the Pacific. Unfortunately, the Japanese ambassador misunderstood Hull. In transmitting the draft agreement to the Japanese government, he not only omitted Hull's four principles, but also portrayed the Maryknoll draft as an American offer rather than an informal Japanese initiative. The Japan government naturally drafted a counterproposal that was even more favorable to Japan, and the negotiations were stalemated.

Japanese foreign minister Yosuke Matsuoka opposed negotiations with the United States anyway; he favored defying America and taking what Japan needed in Southeast Asia. Ignoring Hitler's hints that the Russo-German pact might be less than permanent, Matsuoka negotiated a nonaggression pact with the Soviets in April 1941. Thus Japan's northern flank was protected if and when it moved into Southeast Asia. But in June Hitler invaded Russia and urged Japan to take the opportunity to attack Siberia. In a momentous series of cabinet meetings in June and July, the Japanese refused the invitation. They decided to continue southward to build the Greater East Asia Co-Prosperity Sphere. They would expand from north into south Indochina preparatory to invading British Malaya and the Dutch East Indies. They specifically stated that they would not be "deterred by the possibility of being involved in a war with England and America."

The United States knew of this decision almost immediately because, in the spring of 1941, naval intelligence had broken the Japanese diplomatic codes and could now decipher messages between Tokyo and the Japanese embassy in Washington. Hull broke off his talks with Ambassador Nomura and, after Japan made public its demands on Vichy, warned against the Japanese plans. The Japanese ignored Hull and moved their troops into southern Indochina. Roosevelt then froze all Japanese assets in America. If strictly enforced, this freeze order would establish a total embargo on the Japanese by denying them the means to pay for any further purchases in the United States.

As in many instances involving the inscrutable Roosevelt, there is considerable debate over whether the president intended to enforce the freeze to the point that it completely cut off the critical supply of oil to Japan. Roosevelt did order the release of enough blocked funds for Japan to make oil purchases at the prewar level. But Dean Acheson and others in the State Department thwarted Japanese oil purchases by stalling the issuance of export licenses. The British and Dutch also froze Japanese assets and effectively embargoed oil to Japan. This left the Japanese with no further sources of petroleum and only an eighteen-month supply in reserve. Since the Japanese calculated that they would need a year to conquer the East Indies and restore the flow of oil from there, Japan had six months to accommodate the United States and restore its American supply line or conquer another source.

It is possible that Roosevelt was chagrined at Acheson's maneuver to cut off Japan's oil supply and that he sanctioned Acheson's stall after the fact only because he did not want to show weakness to Japan by retreating from the de facto oil embargo. On the other hand, it seems likely that Roosevelt would have known from the outset what Acheson was doing because the president's close friend in the State Department, Sumner Welles, would have told him. Roosevelt, then, could have stopped Acheson before any public retreat would have been necessary. The fact that he did not stop Acheson indicates that Roosevelt might have intended all along for the freeze order to embargo oil to Japan.

One historian, Waldo Heinrichs, believes Roosevelt did this purposely in order to turn Japan's aggression toward the great oil resources of the Dutch East Indies in the south and away from an attack on the Soviet Union, whose Siberian oil resources were less proven and less accessible than those of the Indies. According to Heinrichs, Roosevelt took the gamble of tempting the Japanese southward because he realized that the survival of the Soviet Union was essential to the defeat of Hitler. Of course, Roosevelt might have thought instead that the Japanese would choose to end their aggression and cooperate with the United States to restore the flow of American oil, rather than attacking either north or south. Unfortunately, just as the Japanese militants were wrong to believe that joining the Axis would intimidate the United States and make war less likely, the Americans who believed that cutting off vital supplies to the Japanese would make them less rather than more aggressive were wrong as well.

Japan's prime minister, Prince Fuminaro Konoye, decided to make one last stab at a peace settlement with the United States. He proposed a summit meeting with Roosevelt. The Japanese military consented grudgingly, but only on the condition that if Konoye failed to get the United States to accept Japanese dominance in Asia by October 1941, he would have to be prepared to lead a war against the United States, Great Britain, and the Dutch East Indies.

American ambassador Joseph Grew urged that Roosevelt accept the meeting with Konoye. He thought the prime minister would risk his own assassination to make a compromise agreement with the United States once he was out of Japan. Konoye sent a personal message to Roosevelt promising that Japan would withdraw from Indochina at the conclusion of what the Japanese referred to as "the China Incident" and would not invade Southeast Asia if the United States would cease its aid to China and assure Japan an adequate supply of raw materials. Roosevelt was anxious to meet with Konoye, but he believed that if he sold out China, it would undermine America's willingness to resist totalitarianism. Also, meeting with the prime minister of Japan, the ally of Hitler, might leave the British fearing they would have to fight alone in Asia as well as Europe. At Hull's urging, Roosevelt decided to insist on further guaranteed concessions before taking such a political risk.

Through the months of August and September, Roosevelt and Hull delivered several messages to Konoye. They insisted on Japanese acceptance of the four points Hull had communicated to Ambassador Nomura, expressed fears of Japan's obligations under the Tripartite Pact, opposed Japanese discriminatory trade policies in China, and asked for a "clear-cut manifestation" of Japan's intention to withdraw its troops from China and Indochina. They tried to string out the negotiations in order to gain time for defensive preparations. They also sent a squadron of B-17 bombers to the Philippines in hopes of intimidating the Japanese. Konoye pressed his war minister, General Hideki Tojo, to break the stalemate by acceding to the American demand for troop withdrawals from China. But Tojo, holding Konoye to the agreed October timetable for a decision on war, suggested Konoye resign. When Konoye did so, the emperor appointed Tojo to take his place.

Tojo was not absolutely bent on war. He was determined, however, to make a final decision on it. Roosevelt quickly learned through the MAGIC code-breaking operation that the United States would have to restore trade by November 25 or face a rupture of negotiations. A later message from Tojo's government to the Japanese embassy in Washington extended the deadline to November 29, after which "things would automatically begin to happen." Roosevelt assumed this meant an invasion of the Dutch East Indies or British Malaya. He suspected the Japanese might also attack the American-held Philippines. He had no idea that the automatic happening would be the departure of the Japanese fleet for an attack on Pearl Harbor in Hawaii.

The Japanese decided to present their final peace terms in two plans, A and B. Plan A would be a long-term settlement. If the United States would restore trade to Japan and force China to make peace, Japan would withdraw its troops from China and Indochina after a suitable interval. Japan also would permit equality of commercial activity in China so long as the Open Door program would be adopted in the colonies of other nations as well. The chances of an Open Door policy throughout the world were so slim as to vitiate this Japanese concession. In addition, MAGIC intercepted a message to Nomura that although Japan would agree to evacuate troops from China after peace was made, actually Japan would only shift areas of occupation. "We will call it evacuation; but . . . in the last analysis this would be out of the question." Finally, Tojo refused to cancel the Tripartite Pact. Japan expected the United States to reject this plan A offer, and it did.

Secretary of State Cordell Hull *(left)* and President Franklin D. Roosevelt. *(Courtesy of the National Archives)*

Plan B visualized a short-term truce. Japan would promise no new moves, while the United States would restore trade and end its support for China. Again MAGIC intercepted a rebuke to the Japanese negotiating team in the United States for suggesting that Tojo eliminate the requirement that the United States cease aid to China. Hull and Roosevelt had been working on a modus vivendi as an answer to plan B—a three-month truce during which the United States would sell some oil and raw materials to Japan if Japan would withdraw from southern Indochina and make no new moves while further negotiations were in progress. But Chiang Kai-shek objected "hysterically." Churchill also objected; he warned that Chiang had been on a "thin diet" and might drop out of the war.

When Hull received news that Japanese ships were moving toward Indochina and the message that "things would automatically begin to happen" after November 29, he decided it was hopeless to stall further. He and Roosevelt decided to "kick the whole thing over." They discarded the modus vivendi and sent Japan a ten-point reply essentially demanding that Japan leave China. On November 27, Washington sent "war warnings" to the American commands in the Philippines and Hawaii. On December 3, Roosevelt finally made a firm commitment to Great Britain. If the Japanese attacked the British or Dutch colonies, the United States would give "armed support." He continued to worry, however, whether he could bring a united America into a war for British colonies if the United States was not directly attacked.

He need not have worried. At that very moment, Japanese carriers were steaming through the northern Pacific toward Hawaii. Pressure rose in Washington on December 6 as MAGIC intercepted thirteen parts of what was said to be a fourteen-part message to the Japanese embassy. The message warned the embassy that nothing was to be communicated to the Americans until the fourteenth portion arrived the following morning. Roosevelt told his chief aide Harry Hopkins, "This means war."

Many Americans have wondered why, then, the Japanese were able to surprise the Pacific fleet at Pearl Harbor, killing 2,403 Americans and wounding 1,178 while destroying five battleships, four cruisers, and almost all the warplanes in Hawaii. Some isolationists and historians have suspected that Roosevelt deliberately sacrificed the fleet in order to get America into the war by "the back door" after his attempts to provoke Hitler had failed. Why had Hawaii been unprepared when the United States had broken the Japanese code and received various indications of a possible attack? Why had the fleet been lined up in such close quarters rather than dispersed? Why had the carriers been absent and obsolete battleships left in the harbor?

These questions have been answered to the satisfaction of almost all historians. MAGIC had revealed approximately when the Japanese would move, but not where. All Japanese ship and troop movements pointed to Southeast Asia. The Pearl Harbor attack fleet left Japan under radio silence and moved toward Hawaii north of regular shipping channels. American intelligence personnel assumed that radio silence from these carriers indicated they were still in home waters, using low-frequency radios that would not be picked up by long-range American monitoring equipment. The American army and navy commanders in Hawaii received war warnings on November 27, but had too little aviation fuel to mount round-the-clock aerial surveillance. The naval commander feared sabotage from local Japanese rather than a surprise air attack, so he kept his ships close together to guard against infiltration.

Scattered warnings that the Japanese might strike Pearl Harbor as well as Southeast Asia drowned in the noise of thousands of other conflicting signals. A report to Joseph Grew from the Peruvian embassy in Japan that the Japanese would attack Hawaii seemed of little worth, since no one could understand how the Peruvians would know. A warning of an attack on Pearl Harbor from a German double agent inexplicably stopped at the desk of FBI director J. Edgar Hoover. Americans observed Japanese workers burning papers at their consulate in Hawaii, but this gave no clue that the Japanese would strike Hawaii, only that war was imminent. The Americans already knew that.

Perhaps the best evidence against a Roosevelt conspiracy is that it made no political or strategic sense. If Roosevelt had wanted to galvanize American opinion to fight the Axis, he did not have to sacrifice the fleet; a Japanese attack on an empty harbor would have sufficed. No one knew at the time that the battleships and cruisers lost at Pearl Harbor would prove obsolete and that the carriers would be decisive in the naval war to come. Besides, Roosevelt did not want war in the Pacific; he wanted to fight the far greater threat of Hitler in Europe. There was no guarantee that Pearl Harbor would bring America into the European conflict. It might even have diverted American public attention to the Pacific and made a declaration of war against Germany all the more difficult. Fortunately for Roosevelt, he did not have to request war against Germany as well as Japan. Hitler cheered Pearl Harbor and declared war on the United States. He had avoided provoking conflict while Roosevelt extended aid to Britain, but evidently he had concluded that war was inevitable. Roosevelt had waited until Japan forced his hand, but now Americans were united in their commitment to World War II.

Controversial Issues

America's entry into World War II caused far less historical controversy than its entry into World War I. World War I revisionists Charles A. Beard, Charles Tansill, and Harry Elmer Barnes survived to write parallel denunciations of World War II, but historians dismissed them far more quickly than they had the earlier ones. (These World War I and World War II revisionists are to be distinguished from the more modern revisionists who have been writing since the advent of the Cold War.) Beard, Tansill, Barnes, and their revisionist compatriots denied that either Germany or Japan had posed a serious threat to American interests or security. They admitted that Hitler was a dangerous neurotic, but his major goal had been the destruction of the Soviet Union. If Roosevelt had stood aside, Hitler and Stalin would have demolished each other. If, in the process, Germany and Japan had destroyed the British Empire as well, that was no concern of the United States.

Unfortunately, the revisionists claimed, Roosevelt wanted war to ensure his reelection, preserve the British Empire, and expand American markets abroad. Thus, he supported appeasement at Munich at a time when the Allies were strong enough to defeat Hitler. Roosevelt did not want war then because the Allies would have won it too quickly to permit him to get the United States into the conflict. Only after he had helped destroy the Allied defensive potential did he support resistance to Hitler. Once combat was safely under way, he undertook to lie America into war because he could not lead it into war. He steadily and often secretly extended unneutral aid to the Allies in hopes of provoking Hitler to strike the first blow. He knew this was the only way to get the American people to support the war. But Hitler would not accommodate him. The postwar capture of German war plans demonstrated that Hitler had no plans to attack the United States and actually was trying to avoid an American conflict.

When Roosevelt failed to lure Hitler into an attack, he decided to take the "back door to war" by provoking Japan. He brushed aside reasonable offers from the Maryknoll priests, Prince Konoye, and General Tojo. He knew from the MAGIC intercepts that this meant war. Revisionists cited as proof of their contentions Hull's remark that he was washing his hands of the Japanese problem and turning it over to the military. They also quoted Secretary of War Henry Stimson's famous remark, "The question was how we should maneuver them into firing the first shot without allowing too much danger to ourselves."

Finally, World War II revisionists claimed that Roosevelt purposely invited the Japanese attack on Pearl Harbor. Roosevelt made sure only obsolete battleships were there, withheld MAGIC information from the commanders, and then, while Japanese planes butchered thousands of Americans, "in the quiet atmosphere of the oval study in the White House, with all incoming telephone calls shut off, the Chief Executive calmly studies his well-filled stamp albums while Hopkins fondles Fala, the White House Scottie. At one o'clock, Death stood in the Doorway."[1]

The conspiracy charges of the World War II revisionists naturally excited many replies, which have been convincing enough to discredit these revisionists entirely in the historical profession.[2] Other historians could not swallow the revisionists' contention that the Axis posed no threat to American security. Historians searching the German documents did not turn up a Nazi plan for the conquest of the Western Hemisphere, but they almost all concluded that Hitler would have threatened America if he had acquired the British fleet and the vast resources of Europe and Russia.[3]

Historians also recoiled from the vitriolic portraits of a scheming Roosevelt offered by the World War II revisionists, although historians admit Roosevelt was devious and a good many argue that he was far more devious than he needed to be. They maintain that public opinion was prepared for a far stronger response to the Axis than Roosevelt permitted. If he had provided clear and vigorous leadership instead of hesitant limited actions covered by uncandid remarks, the United States might have been much better prepared for war when it came and might have intervened before the Allies teetered dangerously on the brink of collapse.[4]

Many other historians have defended Roosevelt's pace and tactics in bringing America to intervention. They maintain that isolationism was far too strong and dangerous to permit the direct, rapid action that seems so necessary in retrospect.[5]

Historians discredited the plot thesis of Pearl Harbor and the back door to war as thoroughly as they discredited the World War II revisionist position on the intervention in Europe.[6] But while historians dismissed the Pearl Harbor plot thesis, they continued to debate whether Roosevelt's policy in East Asia had been wise. Roosevelt certainly had many prominent defenders who argued that the United States had little choice but to oppose Japanese expansion into Asia. The United States simply could not continue to supply war matériel that would permit Japan's conquest of China, and nothing short of that would have deterred the Japanese from conquering the European colonies in Asia that were necessary to the allied war effort against Hitler. Perhaps more flexible American diplomacy could have delayed war a few more weeks, but that was all.[7]

A good many historians, however, questioned whether war in the Pacific was necessary. These were not revisionist or isolationist historians who opposed American entry into World War II; they were realists who believed that the United States could and should have avoided war with Japan and concentrated all its effort against the greater threat to America and the world balance of power, Germany. These realists based their contention that America could have avoided war with Japan on the memoirs of Ambassador Joseph Grew.[8] Grew believed that the German attack on Russia had discredited the Japanese militarists and the Tripartite Pact. The attack gave Konoye a chance to break with Germany, galvanize moderate sentiment, and come to a dramatic settlement with the United States if only Roosevelt had met with him. Even without the meeting, Japan had signaled its willingness to abandon the march southward and to leave the European colonies intact if the United States would permit some Japanese control over China. The realists thought this a price worth paying to ensure the defeat of Hitler in Europe. Chiang Kai-shek was incapable of unifying China even with American help; elimination of the Japanese presence simply created a vacuum of power into which the Chinese Communists and the Russians could move. The diversion of resources from the European theater not only prolonged the war, but permitted the Soviet Union to move farther into Western Europe than it might have done had the Allies invaded Normandy earlier.[9]

Many other realists were not so sure actions taken as late as 1941 could have prevented war with Japan. But they sympathized with the idea of avoiding confrontation with Japan to concentrate on Europe and argued that America might have contributed to a peaceful situation in Asia with a friendlier policy toward Japan in earlier years.[10] Thus, in a conference of American and Japanese historians in the 1970s, Richard Leopold noted that American contributors to the conference "look back on the Pacific war as a mistake, one that led to many of the intractable problems confronting the United States today," while ironically the Japanese contributors see "that conflict somewhat fatalistically, as perhaps the only instrument by which the incubus of fascism and militarism could have been exorcised."[11]

The revulsion against interventionism that followed the Vietnam War had less impact on the historiography of World War II than on any other interventionist episode in U.S. history. There have been only a couple of modern revisionist accounts, and they attack America's motives for going to war rather than the intervention itself.[12] Anti-interventionism, however, has led to a lessening of the criticisms against Roosevelt's slowness to intervene as well as those leveled at his isolationist opponents.[13]

Further Reading

The only other significant trend in the historiography of the American entry into World War II has been an increased emphasis on Anglo-American rivalry, a trend encouraged primarily by the opening of diplomatic and treasury documents in Great Britain. See, for example, Arnold Offner, *American Appeasement: United States Foreign Policy and Germany, 1933–1938* (1969) and *The Origins of the Second World War: American Foreign Policy and World Politics, 1917–1941* (1975); James Leutze, *Bargaining for Supremacy: Anglo-American Naval Collaboration, 1937–1941* (1977); and David Reynolds, *The Creation of the Anglo-American Alliance, 1937–1941: A Study in Competitive Cooperation* (1982). For continued emphasis in the popular press on Anglo-American cooperation and friendship, see Joseph P. Lash, *Roosevelt and Churchill, 1939–1941: The Partnership That Saved the West* (1976). For an excellent work on lend-lease aid to the British, see Warren F. Kimball, *The Most Unsordid Act: Lend-Lease, 1939–1941* (1969).

There is also an interesting debate over U.S. policy toward the Spanish Civil War, with some claiming the United States and Roosevelt were actively hostile toward the Spanish leftist government in favor of Franco and his Axis allies while others claim Roosevelt was sympathetic to the Spanish government but hesitant to act on its behalf. See Douglas

Little, *Malevolent Neutrality: The United States, Great Britain, and the Origins of the Spanish Civil War* (1985); Dominic Tierney, *FDR and the Spanish Civil War: Neutrality and Commitment in the Struggle That Divided America* (2007).

Notes

1. The quotation is from Charles Callan Tansill, *Back Door to War: The Roosevelt Foreign Policy, 1933–1941* (1952), p. 652. Other major revisionist studies include Charles A. Beard, *American Foreign Policy in the Making, 1932–1940: A Study of Responsibilities* (1946), and Beard's more elaborate work, *President Roosevelt and the Coming of the War, 1941* (1948). Harry Elmer Barnes, ed., *Perpetual War for Perpetual Peace: A Critical Examination of the Foreign Policy of Franklin Delano Roosevelt and Its Aftermath* (1953), includes brief summary articles by many of the following authors: George Morgenstern, *Pearl Harbor: The Story of the Secret War* (1947); William Henry Chamberlin, *America's Second Crusade* (1950); Frederick C. Sanborn, *Design for War: A Study of Secret Power Politics, 1937–1941* (1951); Robert A. Theobold, *The Final Secret of Pearl Harbor: The Washington Contribution to the Japanese Attack* (1954); Husband E. Kimmel, *Admiral Kimmel's Story* (1955); and Anthony Kubek, *How the Far East Was Lost: American Policy and the Creation of Communist China, 1941–1949* (1963).

2. John Toland tried to revive the Pearl Harbor plot thesis in *Infamy: Pearl Harbor and Its Aftermath* (1982) by offering supposedly new evidence from anonymous sources that Roosevelt knew the attack was coming at Pearl Harbor, but Toland's argument was not convincing. The general antiwar atmosphere after Vietnam inspired Bruce M. Russett to reconsider the wisdom of American abstention from World War II in *No Clear and Present Danger: A Skeptical View of the United States Entry into World War II* (1972). But those are about the only flickers of World War II revisionism in recent times.

3. Gerhard L. Weinberg, *A World at Arms: A Global History of World War II* (1994); Hans L. Trefousse, *Germany and American Neutrality, 1939–1941* (1951); Saul Friedlander, *Prelude to Downfall: Hitler and the United States, 1939–1941* (1963; English translation 1967); James V. Compton, *The Swastika and the Eagle: Hitler, the United States, and the Origins of World War II* (1967); Alton Frye, *Nazi Germany and the American Hemisphere, 1933–1941* (1967).

4. Walter Lippmann made this argument during the war in *U.S. Foreign Policy: Shield of the Republic* (1943). It was made far more extensively in what is still the most complete history of the U.S. entry into the war: William L. Langer and S. Everett Gleason's *The Challenge to Isolation, 1937–1940* (1952) and *The Undeclared War, 1940–1941* (1953). For similar views, see Benjamin D. Rhodes, *United States Foreign Policy in the Interwar Period, 1918–1941: A Golden Age of American Diplomatic and Military Complacency* (2001); Robert A. Divine, *The Reluctant Belligerent: American Entry into World War II* (1965) and *The Illusion of Neutrality: Franklin D. Roosevelt and the Struggle over the Arms Embargo* (1962); Arnold Offner, *American Appeasement: United States Foreign Policy and Germany, 1933–1938* (1969) and *The Origins of the Second World War: American Foreign Policy and World Politics, 1917–1941* (1975); and Michael Leigh, *Mobilizing Consent: Public Opinion and American Foreign Policy, 1937–1947* (1976).

British historians particularly emphasize how Roosevelt's unwillingness to support the balance of power in Europe against Germany left Chamberlain and other European leaders with little choice but to appease Hitler while trying to improve their own military preparedness. See Malcolm H. Murfett, *Fool-Proof Relations: The Search for Anglo-American Naval Cooperation during the Chamberlain Years, 1937–1940* (1984); William R. Rock, *Chamberlain and Roosevelt* (1988); C.A. MacDonald, *The United States, Britain and Appeasement, 1936–1939* (1981); and especially D. Cameron Watt, *How War Came* (1989), an encyclopedic and nearly definitive account of the actions of all the important governments leading to World War II. A British historian who is somewhat kinder to Roosevelt is David Reynolds, *From Munich to Pearl Harbor: Roosevelt's America and the Origins of the Second World War* (2002).

5. Dexter Perkins made this argument during the war in *America and Two Wars* (1944). The best work from this point of view is Robert Dallek, *Franklin D. Roosevelt and American Foreign Policy, 1932–1945* (1979). See also Barbara Rearden Farnham, *Roosevelt and the Munich Crisis* (1997); Basil Rauch, *Roosevelt: From Munich to Pearl Harbor* (1950); Donald F. Drummond, *The Passing of American Neutrality, 1937–1941* (1955); William E. Kinsella Jr., *Leadership in Isolation: FDR and the Origins of the Second World War* (1978); T.R. Fehrenbach, *F.D.R.'s Undeclared War, 1939–1941* (1967); Gloria J. Barron, *Leadership in Crisis: FDR and the Path to Intervention* (1973); and John E. Wiltz, *From Isolation to War, 1931–1941* (1968). Edward M. Bennet credits Roosevelt with trying, although rather ineptly, to bring the Soviet Union to the side of the democracies against Hitler in *Franklin D. Roosevelt and the Search for Security: American-Soviet Relations, 1933–1939* (1985) and *Franklin D. Roosevelt and the Search for Victory: American-Soviet Relations, 1939–1945* (1990).

6. Samuel Eliot Morison, "Did Roosevelt Start the War—History Through a Beard," *Atlantic Monthly* (August 1948); Roberta Wohlstetter, *Pearl Harbor: Warning and Decision* (1962); Gordon W. Prange, *At Dawn We Slept: The Untold Story of Pearl Harbor* (1981) and *Pearl Harbor: The Verdict of History* (1986); Edwin T. Layton, *"And I Was There": Pearl Harbor and Midway—Breaking the Secrets* (1986); Robert Ferrell, "Pearl Harbor and the Revisionists," *Historian* (Spring 1955); Herbert Feis, "War Came at Pearl Harbor: Suspicions Considered," *Yale Review* (Spring 1956).

7. In addition to the general surveys of Roosevelt's diplomacy already cited, see Herbert Feis, *The Road to Pearl Harbor: The Coming of the War Between the United States and Japan* (1950); Robert J.C. Butow, *Tojo and the Coming of the War* (1961) and *The John Doe Associates: Backdoor Diplomacy for Peace, 1941* (1974), which deals with the Maryknoll initiative; Samuel Eliot Morison, *The Rising Sun in the Pacific, 1931–April 1942* (1948); James H. Herzog, *Closing the Open Door: American-Japanese Diplomatic Negotiations, 1936–1941* (1973); and Waldo Heinrichs, *Threshold of War: Franklin D. Roosevelt and American Entry into World War II* (1988). Accounts of the internal politics of Japan make it evident that there was almost no hope of a compromise short of war because all elements of the Japanese leadership were convinced by late 1941 that Japan could not remain dependent on the United States for resources essential to its great power status. See Michael A. Barnhart, *Japan Prepares for Total War* (1988); Ian H. Nish, *Japanese Foreign Policy* (1977); James Morley, ed., *Fateful Choice: Japan's Advance into Southeast Asia* (1980); Akira Iriye, *Origins of the Second World War in Asia and the Pacific* (1987); and Warren I. Cohen, ed., *New Frontiers in American–East Asian Relations: Essays Presented to Dorothy Borg* (1986). An excellent book on China's role in the U.S.-Japanese conflict is Youli Sun, *China and the Origins of the Pacific War, 1931–1941* (1998).

8. Joseph C. Grew, *Ten Years in Japan* (1944) and *Turbulent Era: A Diplomatic Record of Forty Years, 1904–1945* (2 vols., 1952).

9. Paul W. Schroeder, *The Anglo-American Alliance and Japanese-American Relations, 1941* (1958); David J. Lu, *From the Marco Polo Bridge to Pearl Harbor: Japan's Entry into World War II* (1961); F.C. Jones, *Japan's New Order in East Asia: Its Rise and Fall, 1937–1945* (1954); Jonathan C. Utley, *Going to War with Japan, 1937–1941* (1985).

10. See the works of such realists as Nicholas Spykman, *America's Strategy in World Politics: The United States and the Balance of Power* (1942); and George F. Kennan, *American Diplomacy, 1900–1950* (1951). See also the historiographical discussion in the Controversial Issues section of Chapter 9 in this book.

11. Richard W. Leopold, "Historiographical Reflections," in *Pearl Harbor as History: Japanese-American Relations, 1931–1941*, ed. Dorothy Borg and Shumpei Okamoto (1973).

12. Lloyd C. Gardner, *Economic Aspects of New Deal Diplomacy* (1964); Robert Freeman Smith, "American Foreign Relations, 1920–1942," in *Towards a New Past: Dissenting Essays in American History*, ed. Barton J. Bernstein (1968); Patrick J. Hearder, *Roosevelt Confronts Hitler: America's Entry into World War II* (1987).

13. Robert Divine, in the 1979 edition of his *Reluctant Belligerent*, noted that he had softened the strictures in the original 1965 edition against Roosevelt's hesitancy to intervene. For typical earlier denunciations of isolationism, see Walter Johnson, *The Battle Against Isolation* (1944); Selig Adler,

The Isolationist Impulse: Its Twentieth-Century Reaction (1957); and John E. Wiltz, *In Search of Peace: The Senate Munitions Inquiry, 1934–1936* (1963). Wayne S. Cole was more sympathetic toward the isolationists in his earlier as well as his later works, *America First: The Battle Against Intervention, 1940–1941* (1953), *Senator Gerald P. Nye and American Foreign Relations* (1962), *Charles A. Lindbergh and the Battle Against Intervention in World War II* (1974), and *Roosevelt and the Isolationists, 1932–1945* (1983). Works that sympathize at least with some of the motives of the isolationists include Justus D. Doenecke, *Storm on the Horizon: The Challenge to American Intervention, 1939–1941* (2000); Manfred Jonas, *Isolationism in America, 1935–1941* (1974); and Geoffrey S. Smith, *To Save a Nation: American Counter-Subversives, the New Deal, and the Coming of World War II* (1973).

CHAPTER 8

THE DIPLOMACY OF WORLD WAR II AND THE SEEDS OF THE COLD WAR

Roosevelt, Churchill, and Stalin: Competing Strategies for the Grand Alliance

Immediately after Pearl Harbor, British prime minister Winston Churchill arrived in Washington, DC, for the Arcadia Conference with President Franklin Roosevelt and Soviet ambassador Maxim Litvinov. With great fanfare, the three allies announced that their war goals would be the defense of "life, liberty, independence and religious freedom," along with "human rights and justice."

Even as they were preparing this United Nations Declaration, the Russians confronted Roosevelt and Churchill with a demand that was thoroughly embarrassing to the high ideals they were ready to proclaim. The Soviets wanted immediate recognition of the borders they had possessed just before the Nazi invasion. Thus the West would endorse the Soviet absorption of Latvia, Lithuania, Estonia, eastern Poland, and a portion of Rumania, areas the Soviet Union had won by virtue of its 1939 pact with Nazi Germany and its subsequent war against Finland in 1940. These provinces, which the Soviets felt had been unjustly stripped from them after World War I, were areas of intense nationalist sentiment.

The suppression of national independence in these areas would seem a cynical flouting of the principles enunciated in the United Nations Declaration. Churchill and his foreign minister, Anthony Eden, expressed some willingness to concede the Soviets a free hand in this eastern European sphere of influence, but Roosevelt and his secretary of state, Cordell Hull, refused. They saw Russia's request as too reminiscent of the secret treaties of World War I that had wrecked Woodrow Wilson's hopes for a just peace. Anything that smacked of Europe's "old diplomacy"—the acquisition of new colonies, the establishment of spheres of influence, or the cynical manipulation of the balance of power—could revive isolationist opinion in America. Not only would this undermine America's immediate war effort, but also it might destroy popular support for American participation in postwar international arrangements. Roosevelt and Hull feared that World War III then would follow World War II as surely as World War II had followed World War I.

Yet Roosevelt and Churchill also wanted to avoid offending Stalin; they needed a willing Russia in the war. Ever since Hitler had turned away from the Battle of Britain to invade Russia, the Soviets single-handedly had confronted the major portion of the German war machine. The Allies could not afford to have the Soviets make another separate peace like Brest-Litovsk or the Nazi-Soviet Pact and leave Germany free to concentrate on Western Europe. Roosevelt wanted Stalin not only to help win the European war, but to join the fight against Japan once the European phase was over.

For these reasons, Roosevelt tried to avoid controversy over Stalin's border demands. He asked Stalin to agree that the Allies would defer all territorial claims until after the war. This delay would avoid disputes that might threaten the Allied war effort. It would also give Roosevelt a chance to win Stalin's confidence. If the Soviets could see they had nothing to fear from the West, they might not feel the need to impose an iron hand on eastern Europe to guarantee their own security.

As a first step, Roosevelt and Churchill reaffirmed their earlier agreement on a "Europe First" strategy. This was the most important decision of the war, and it took some courage on Roosevelt's part to make it. Many Americans, angrier at Japan after Pearl Harbor than at Germany, demanded that the United States concentrate its war effort in Asia and the Pacific. Roosevelt realized that Germany was the far greater threat: Japan could never conquer the United States but Germany might be able to if it gained control of Europe's resources and Britain's naval fleet. Consequently, Roosevelt pledged to Churchill and Stalin that the United States would give top priority to the European theater and relegate the Pacific to a holding action until Hitler was defeated.

Roosevelt went even further than this at a meeting with Soviet foreign minister V.M. Molotov in Washington in May 1942. Against the better judgment of Churchill and some of his own American military advisers, Roosevelt promised that the United States and Great Britain would take the pressure off Russia by opening a second front in Europe as early as 1942. This was an almost impossible task; the United States had only begun to mobilize, and the Allies were very short of landing craft. Churchill refused to go along with Roosevelt's promise. He remembered too well the devastations of trench warfare in World War I and was determined to avoid a repetition. Besides, since an early European second front would be set up before full American mobilization, British ships and soldiers would bear the brunt of the effort. Even the Americans admitted that an early European landing would be "sacrificial." Churchill favored a peripheral strategy. He wanted to delay a cross-channel invasion until an air bombing campaign had softened up the Germans sufficiently to guarantee success. Meanwhile, British and American forces would attack the Mediterranean periphery of Germany's empire—first North Africa, then the Mediterranean islands, and finally the "soft underbelly of Europe," Italy and the Balkans.

Churchill claimed that such diversions would make the ultimate cross-channel invasion even more likely to succeed. They would also protect the British lifeline to India and Asia through the Mediterranean and the Suez Canal. They might even give the Allies a chance to get to the Balkans and eastern Europe before the Russians. Of course, while this strategy would mean limited fighting and casualties for Great Britain and the United States, it would increase the time the Russians would be engaged with the bulk of the German army. Stalin and the American military chiefs came to suspect that Churchill would avoid a frontal attack on France entirely if he could.

Stalin complained often and bitterly about the delay in a major second front, and generally Churchill responded with concern for Stalin's natural desire to see pressure taken off the Russian front. Churchill was anxious to aid Russia, if only to keep it in the war. He knew that the Red Army was the primary hope of defeating Hitler. But he was not ready to jeopardize the British armed forces, economy, and empire on behalf of the Russians. When Stalin became too insistent, Churchill reminded him with some asperity that the Soviets had left the British to fight the Germans alone until 1941.

The Diplomacy of the War, 1941–1943

Churchill and the American military chiefs, led by George Marshall, finally succeeded in convincing Roosevelt that an invasion of Europe in 1942 was impractical. At this point, Churchill and Marshall parted company. Churchill pressed Roosevelt to undertake a limited invasion of North Africa to help the British defend their Mediterranean-Suez lifeline, then threatened in Egypt by the army of Marshal Erwin Rommel, known as the Desert Fox. Marshall and the American military high command opposed any peripheral operations that might divert effort from a cross-channel invasion in 1943. They correctly feared that an invasion of North Africa would occupy the landing craft and troops essential to the cross-channel invasion and delay it until 1944. Roosevelt decided in favor of Churchill. He thought it politically necessary to involve American troops in the Atlantic theater immediately. Otherwise, public pressure to turn to the Pacific might become irresistible. He ordered Marshall to substitute a North African operation for the European invasion he had promised Stalin.

At almost the same time, Roosevelt and Churchill felt compelled to halt convoys bearing lend-lease aid to the Soviet Union because the Germans were sinking more than half the ships sent into the Baltic. On August 12, 1942, Churchill flew off to Moscow to inform Stalin personally of the painful North African and lend-lease decisions and to try to allay the Russian's anger. Churchill said he felt as though he was "carrying a large lump of ice to the North Pole." He emphasized to Stalin that the North African invasion would occupy at least some German troops. Stalin, only slightly mollified, expressed bitterness that the British and Americans were unwilling to accept the kind of casualties the Russians were suffering.[1]

Operation Torch, the invasion of North Africa, turned out to be a military success. The British and Americans defeated Rommel, captured many of his troops, and pushed the remainder back across the Mediterranean. Yet the operation occupied relatively few German forces, while the Russians faced massive invasions aimed at Leningrad, Stalingrad, and the Caucasus oil fields. Operation Torch also raised some serious political complications. Roosevelt and the commander of Torch, General Dwight D. Eisenhower, decided to make an arrangement with a notorious Nazi collaborator, Admiral Jean Darlan, the ranking French naval officer in North Africa. Darlan promised that the Vichy French military forces would not resist the American invasion if he were left in charge. While the Darlan deal did limit resistance in many areas, it did not keep the French from scuttling their fleet at Toulon or eliminate the fighting in Tunisia. Meanwhile, the United States was seen to be cooperating with a regime that was imprisoning Jews and hunting down French citizens opposed to the Nazis.

The Darlan deal soured relations between Roosevelt and General Charles de Gaulle, commander of the Free French. Roosevelt, refusing to believe that de Gaulle had much support in France itself, tried consistently to relegate the general to a minor role. When Darlan was assassinated, the Americans unsuccessfully tried to force de Gaulle into a subsidiary role behind General Henri Giraud. After de Gaulle cleverly maneuvered Giraud into a lesser position, it was only with great reluctance that Roosevelt permitted de Gaulle and the Free French to take a significant part in the liberation of France. Roosevelt thought de Gaulle's vision of the postwar French Empire inflated. Openly opposing any return of Indochina or Dakar (in Africa) to the French, Roosevelt hoped instead for some sort of international administration that would permit an American military presence in those areas.

Roosevelt and Churchill, 1943

The successful completion of the North African operation in early 1943 left 500,000 Allied troops unoccupied. With the number of troops and landing craft still too few to guarantee a successful cross-channel invasion, Churchill urged that they be used to invade Sicily and Italy in hopes of forcing the weakest member of the Axis out of the war. Roosevelt and Churchill met at Casablanca in January 1943 to settle these plans. The American military chiefs continued to urge an invasion of France in 1943. Since most of the ships and troops in Europe at this time were still British rather than American, however, the chiefs reluctantly accepted Churchill's plan for a limited invasion across the Mediterranean in exchange for a firm British promise to support a cross-channel invasion in 1944.

Stalin refused to join Roosevelt and Churchill at Casablanca because he feared that a decision to defer a major second front might be imposed on him. Knowing Stalin would object, Roosevelt and Churchill put off notifying him officially of the deferral until much later in 1943. In the hope of sweetening the bitter pill and counteracting the squalid aftermath of the Darlan deal, Roosevelt announced at the end of the Casablanca Conference that the Allies would demand unconditional surrender of the Axis powers. Unconditional surrender would reinforce the decision to postpone territorial arrangements until after the war by reassuring Stalin that his allies would not make a separate peace. Unconditional surrender also implied the total destruction of German power in order to avoid what was thought to have been a mistake at the time of World War I. The Russians would not need to fear future invasions from a weakened Germany, so Roosevelt hoped that Stalin might abandon his demands for a rigid security sphere in eastern Europe.

After the Casablanca Conference, dissension increased among the Allies over the second front strategy. Churchill feared that the Americans wanted to divert supplies and troops to the Pacific theater. The Americans tried to limit the Mediterranean operation in favor of building and planning the 1944 cross-channel invasion. Stalin kept up a running denunciation of the ineffective efforts of both his allies to relieve the Russian front. Meanwhile, the Allied invasion of Sicily and Italy quickly forced Italy's surrender, causing further Allied dissension. Great Britain wanted to deal with the Italian king and Marshal

Pietro Badoglio, whom the British believed were best able to keep Italy from falling apart. Roosevelt preferred to replace these Fascist collaborators with a more centrist government headed by Count Carlo Sforza. Stalin complained that the Russians were being ignored entirely in arranging the surrender. Hitler rendered much of the debate moot when he sent crack German troops to stop the Allied advance through Italy and then set up a new Italian regime with Mussolini as its nominal leader.

Great Britain and the United States faced another vital question while they were debating the second front—the development of the atomic bomb. At the beginning of the war, Great Britain had offered to share its atomic technology with the United States. Roosevelt and Churchill agreed that the bomb would be built in the United States, where the industrial capacity existed and where there was less danger of the facilities being overrun. As work on the manufacture of the bomb progressed, however, American military leaders began to withhold some information from their British partners. Although Churchill protested, Roosevelt's advisers argued that the president should share only information that could be used during the present war and hold all the rest secret. Rejecting their advice, Roosevelt ordered full collaboration on atomic weapons, but only after Churchill had once again firmly committed the British to a cross-channel attack in 1944.

Once Stalin was satisfied that Churchill and Roosevelt would invade Europe in 1944, he finally agreed to a summit meeting of the three leaders. He even gave some preliminary pledges of his own. He promised to enter the war against Japan once the European war was over. He also accepted Roosevelt's argument that China should be included with Great Britain, the Soviet Union, and the United States as one of the Big Four to police the postwar peace.

Roosevelt had boosted China for a position as one of the Big Four ever since America's entry into the war. He knew that the regime of Chiang Kai-shek was hollow, dictatorial, and corrupt and that China was far from being a major power. Nevertheless, he thought China's vast population gave it the potential to be a great power in twenty-five to fifty years, and he wanted it to be on America's side. He also wanted to appeal to the popular American image of China as a suffering, democratic, friendly protégé. Americans might be more willing to join a postwar international organization that included China. Meanwhile, China could be used as an alternative occupying power in Korea, French Indochina, and parts of the British Empire as these areas were recaptured from the Japanese. This would give the United States a chance to reduce the European empires in Southeast Asia and to stave off Russian penetration in northern Asia.

Chiang, despite Roosevelt's backing, was not very cooperative. He actually did very little against the Japanese. He employed his best troops to surround the Communist forces of his domestic rival Mao Zedong in the north at Yenan. Chiang refused to contribute to the reopening of the Burma Road through which Allied supplies might reach him, yet demanded that the Allies fly supplies to him "over the hump" of the Himalayas in ever-increasing amounts, despite the dangers involved. He so exasperated his American military adviser, General "Vinegar Joe" Stilwell, that that acerbic soldier referred contemptuously to him as "Peanut" and told Roosevelt that he should press Chiang to turn over control of China's military forces to Stilwell himself.

From left to right: Soviet premier Joseph Stalin, President Franklin D. Roosevelt, and British prime minister Winston Churchill at Teheran, 1943. *(Courtesy of the National Archives)*

Roosevelt was unwilling to push Chiang too hard, however. He saw no alternative to Nationalist rule, and he certainly did not want China to collapse. Roosevelt believed China would be essential as a launching pad for an eventual invasion of Japan. With his Europe First strategy, he could not afford to send much help to China anyway. He tried instead to pacify Chiang with morale-building gestures. He invited Chiang to meet with him and Churchill at Cairo in November 1943, immediately before he and Churchill were to meet together for the first time with Stalin at Teheran. Chiang used the opportunity to press for more supplies and less harassment from Stilwell, but his timing was poor. With Russia's pledge to enter the war against Japan, Roosevelt felt less need of China. Roosevelt put Chiang off with a few promises of support for a Burma campaign and a statement that China should regain the islands and territories Japan had seized earlier.

From Teheran to Yalta, November 1943 to February 1945

In November 1943, after the Cairo Conference, Churchill and Roosevelt flew to Teheran in Iran to meet Stalin. Roosevelt tried to charm Stalin; he even baited Churchill about the British Empire to win Stalin's approval. He joined Stalin in rejecting Churchill's desire for a Balkan invasion to supplement the invasion of Normandy. Roosevelt and Stalin also agreed in opposition to Churchill that France should not be rebuilt into a major power or its empire returned after the war. Finally, Roosevelt and Stalin discussed dividing Germany into five separate provinces after the war, while Churchill wanted to preserve some German strength by dividing it into no more than two. Churchill actually challenged Stalin directly by asking if he contemplated a postwar Europe of small, weak states.

On the other hand, Stalin and Churchill found more agreement with each other than with Roosevelt on the shape of postwar international arrangements. They were thinking in terms of regional organizations of nations. Roosevelt objected that this idea smacked too much of spheres of influence. He advocated instead one organization dominated by the Big Four to police the world at large, although he agreed that each of the Big Four would have primary responsibility in its own area of the globe. To disarm any Soviet suspicions that the United States might try to use such a world body to dominate areas critical to Russian security, Roosevelt warned that American troops would probably remain in Europe no more than a year or two after Germany's defeat and asked that the United States be given only limited occupation duties.

Ominously, however, Stalin found himself somewhat isolated on the issue of eastern Europe. Roosevelt tried to reassure Stalin by acknowledging Russia's historic and strategic interest in the area and suggesting the internationalization of the Baltic waterways so vital to the Soviet Union. He asked in return that Stalin recognize the importance to American opinion of self-determination in eastern Europe. Stalin objected bluntly. The question of self-determination had not come up when the czar had controlled the area, he said. He told Roosevelt that some propaganda work should be done to reconcile the American people to the Soviet position. Stalin was particularly adamant about Poland; he insisted that Russia should regain eastern Poland and that Poland should be compensated with portions of eastern Germany. Stalin also refused to have anything to do with the exiled Polish government in London.

The London Poles refused to acknowledge Russian demands for border adjustments and demanded a Red Cross investigation into the Katyn Forest massacre. The London Poles knew that thousands of Polish officers and members of the upper classes had been put in Soviet camps following the Russian occupation of eastern Poland in 1939. They also believed, on good evidence, that the mass graves discovered by the Germans in the Katyn Forest contained the bodies of several thousand of those Poles, executed by the Russians. (In October 1992 the Russians released a document bearing Stalin's signature that ordered the execution of 20,000 Polish prisoners.)

Roosevelt and Churchill had both tried unsuccessfully to get the London Poles to reconcile themselves to Soviet power while urging Stalin not to set up a rival Communist government. Churchill reminded Stalin that Britain had gone to war over Poland and that for the Allies to recognize different Polish governments would be a major blow to hopes for the continuing unity of the alliance. Roosevelt spoke of the importance of the Polish voters within the United States. Roosevelt and Churchill implied acceptance of most of Russia's 1941 borders, but Roosevelt said he would make no commitments until after the 1944 election, and both made clear the need for compromise on the status of the London Poles and east European elections.

Returning to the United States, Roosevelt was optimistic about the Teheran agreements. He assured the American people in a fireside chat that the United States would get along with Stalin and the Russian people "very well—very well indeed." Churchill, on the other hand, returned in a funk. He told his physician that the allies would have to do something with the "bloody Russians."

Stalin appeased Churchill's funk somewhat when he cooperated with the Normandy invasion in June 1944 by launching a simultaneous attack on the eastern front. Once the Normandy invasion forces finally broke out of the beachhead at the end of the summer and began their race across France toward Germany, victory was in sight. The imminence of victory forced the Allied diplomats to begin their own race to create a comprehensive plan for postwar Europe. The Bretton Woods Conference of August 1944 established much of the postwar economic structure. In a bucolic resort hotel at the foot of Mount Washington in New Hampshire, the United States won the endorsement of the representatives of forty-four Allied countries for measures designed to encourage world trade by stabilizing currency exchange rates, reducing tariffs, and providing reconstruction loans. The conference created the International Monetary Fund (IMF), which would use the contributions of gold and currency from its members to support the exchange rates. The IMF would loan money to nations whose deficits threatened the value of their currency, but only if the deficit countries followed policies the other members thought necessary to ensure fiscal stability. Since the United States was the major contributor to the fund, it received weighted votes that gave it the dominant voice in determining the loans the IMF would make. On the other hand, the United States did consent to rules that would require it to dispense some of the vast surplus of gold and dollars it had acquired as a result of the war. This lessened the burden of debtor and deficit states. The Bretton Woods Conference also established the World Bank to loan money to weak nations for reconstruction and development projects. Again, the United States had the dominant voice in determining World Bank loans.

The British joined these arrangements with some trepidation. Britain's political Left feared that the open world of international trade contemplated by the Bretton Woods arrangements would prevent domestic control of the British currency and tariff rates. This would make it impossible to guarantee full employment by protecting British enterprises against the competition of the powerful American economy. The British Right feared that opening the British Empire to world trade would permit the more powerful United States to replace British influence in British colonies. To allay these fears, the United States promised to help the exhausted British pay their enormous war debts and modernize their industrial plant. With this concession, the British chose to join the open and expanding system of world trade promised by Bretton Woods.

The Russians were less amenable. The Soviets ran a closed economy; the government conducted all trade and set the value of the national currency by fiat. Despite this obstacle, the Soviets attended the Bretton Woods Conference and agreed to join the IMF and the World Bank. The Roosevelt administration, seeing this step as a considerable concession on the part of the Soviets, was much encouraged. U.S. Treasury officials even began to consider a separate $10 billion loan to Russia. (In late 1945, however, the Soviet government decided not to ratify the Bretton Woods Agreement.)

A month after Bretton Woods, representatives of the Allied nations met at Dumbarton Oaks near Washington, DC, to establish the United Nations. The Soviets were far less cooperative in these negotiations, which were designed to build an international political structure to accompany the Bretton Woods economic structure. The USSR demanded sixteen votes in the General Assembly, one for each of the Soviet Socialist Republics. The Soviet Union also demanded the right of a permanent member of the Security Council to veto a discussion of any topic, not just the final decision. Despite personal appeals from Roosevelt, the Soviets refused to budge. The conference finally adjourned without resolving these critical questions. While Soviet demands at Dumbarton Oaks raised British and American hackles, Stalin's conduct toward Poland created far darker suspicions. Prior to the Bretton Woods and Dumbarton Oaks conferences, Stalin set up the Lublin Committee, a group of Poles loyal to the Soviet Union, as a potential rival to the Polish government in exile in London. Still, he did not officially recognize the Lublin Committee as the legitimate government of Poland, nor did he shut the door completely on the London Poles. Roosevelt and Churchill did not yet despair of an amicable settlement. Then, in July 1944, Soviet army radio appealed to the pro-London Warsaw underground to rise against the Nazi occupiers and aid the advancing Red Army's entrance into the city. Warsaw began its uprising on July 31, but the Russian army halted on the outskirts of the city. The Germans proceeded to slaughter the underground fighters.

It is possible that German resistance and the logistical problems of crossing the Vistula River halted the Russian advance, as Stalin claimed. Stalin raised strong suspicions of his motives, however, when he prevented the British and Americans from air-dropping supplies to the beleaguered Warsaw garrison until it was too late. Shortly afterward, Averell Harriman, America's ambassador to the Soviet Union and previously a sympathetic director of lend-lease aid to the Russians, warned Roosevelt that the Soviet Union was inclined to be a "world bully." He advised Roosevelt henceforth to demand a quid pro quo for any concessions he made to Stalin.

In this troubled atmosphere, Roosevelt met Churchill at Quebec in September 1944. He listened sympathetically to Churchill's complaints about Soviet actions in Rumania and Bulgaria and to Churchill's argument that if the war in Italy was concluded soon, American and British troops should be sent into the Balkans through Trieste in hope of beating the Russians to Vienna. Roosevelt also agreed with Churchill that they should continue to withhold atomic information from the Soviet Union. Roosevelt had known for a year that Russian spies were keeping Stalin informed of Anglo-American progress on the bomb, and he had been advised by physicist Niels Bohr that he had nothing to lose and much to gain by offering to share atomic technology with the Russians. Nevertheless, Roosevelt apparently wanted a firmer demonstration of Russian cooperation before he risked sharing atomic secrets with the Soviets, particularly since he knew Congress would be extremely hostile to the idea. He let Bohr believe he might consider sharing in the future, expecting that Bohr would get the message to the Soviets, and accepted instead Churchill's advice to withhold collaboration.

Despite this decision, Roosevelt had not given up his attempts to cooperate with the Russians. His secretary of the treasury, Henry Morgenthau, convinced him that the Soviets wanted the destruction of Germany in order to eliminate any chance of another invasion. Morgenthau devised a plan for "pastoralizing" Germany by eliminating its industrial as well as its military potential. Roosevelt abruptly and casually recommended this plan to Churchill at Quebec. Churchill said he looked upon the Morgenthau plan with as much favor as he would "chaining himself to a German corpse." He thought German productivity was necessary for the revival of Europe. Morgenthau and Roosevelt argued that Britain would prosper more when relieved of German competition. The issue was probably decided by Churchill's desperate need for American aid after the war. When Roosevelt promised to continue lend-lease, Churchill accepted the Morgenthau plan.

The agreement came unglued almost immediately after the Quebec Conference. The State Department, which considered that Morgenthau's Treasury Department had usurped the planning for a German settlement, agreed with Churchill that Europe needed the products of Germany's Saar and Ruhr valleys. Even the Russians were anxious for reparations that a pastoralized Germany could never provide. Finally, Roosevelt, admitting that Morgenthau had "pulled a boner," backed away from the Morgenthau plan. The president also heeded congressional opposition to postwar lend-lease aid for the British and reduced the level of support he had promised them.

In one final agreement at Quebec, Roosevelt and Churchill decided to send a joint note remonstrating with Stalin about his lack of cooperation. Afterward, Churchill had second thoughts and chose to meet with Stalin personally in October 1944. The British prime minister found this meeting encouraging. After he protested the ruthless Soviet conduct in Rumania and Bulgaria, Stalin agreed to a broad division of influence in the Balkans. The Russians were to have 90 percent of the authority in Rumania, 85 percent in Bulgaria, and 75 percent in Hungary, while Great Britain would have 90 percent control in Greece. They would divide influence in Yugoslavia 50–50. This agreement substantially broadened an earlier tentative arrangement reached just before D-day in which they had exchanged Russian control of Rumania for British control of Greece. Roosevelt remained wary of these spheres-of-influence agreements. He had accepted the first one only after being assured it was a temporary military measure, and he avoided commitment to the second by announcing in advance that he would not be bound by any decision made by Churchill and Stalin at their Moscow meeting.

The ambiguity in the arrangements on the Balkans might not have raised serious problems if the Allies had been able to reach agreement on the far more critical issues of Poland and Germany. Stalin was determined to have a friendly regime in Poland. It was his corridor to Germany as well as Germany's invasion route into Russia, and the Poles would be behind his lines as he undertook the final thrust into Berlin. The British also felt strongly about Poland. They had gone to war over Poland, had fought alongside the military forces commanded by the Polish government in exile, and were anxious that the Poles have some degree of self-determination. The United States, with a large number of Polish immigrants, also felt a sentimental attachment to Poland. Roosevelt acknowledged that the Soviets had a greater stake in the Polish settlement and had the troops in place to see that their will was done. But he insisted on at least enough self-determination for the Poles to pacify American public opinion.

Churchill came away from the Moscow meeting with Stalin believing progress had been made on the Polish issue. The situation fell apart, however, when the London Poles refused to accept the Russian claim to eastern Poland up to the so-called Curzon Line, causing the prime minister of the government in exile, Stanislaus Mikolajczyk, to resign in protest over his colleagues' intransigence. To the dismay of Roosevelt and Churchill, Stalin then officially recognized the Lublin Committee as the government of Poland. Although Roosevelt and Churchill were willing to encourage Poland to accept Stalin's border demands, they did not believe the Lublin Committee represented anywhere near a majority of Poles.

Fearing that Stalin's actions might trigger another American retreat to isolationism, Roosevelt called for another climactic meeting of the Big Three. Roosevelt had incentives in Asia as well as in Europe for requesting a summit conference. He naturally wanted confirmation of the date for Russian entry into the war with Japan. But he also wanted Stalin's cooperation in forcing the Chinese Communists into a coalition with Chiang Kai-shek's Nationalists. Chiang continued to resist U.S. pressure to send his best troops into battle against the Japanese. When Japanese forces attacked Nationalist-held areas containing critical American air force facilities, Chiang left their defense to inexperienced local militia totally incapable of stopping the Japanese offensive. Chiang would not contribute to the campaign to open land supply routes to China through Burma or aid the British in their defense of India against a Japanese invasion from Southeast Asia.

Roosevelt tried everything, including an ultimatum, to get Chiang to fight. He demanded that Chiang turn over command of his entire army to General Stilwell and combine with the Communists to oppose the Japanese. Chiang continued to stall. Finally, with Russia's firm commitment to enter the Pacific war and the capture of some islands close enough to serve as air bases for the bombing of the Japanese homeland, Roosevelt decided he would not need China to defeat the Japanese after all. He quit trying to force Chiang to fight and even gave in to the generalissimo's insistence that he recall Stilwell.

Some of Roosevelt's more knowledgeable advisers thought the United States might do better to aid the Chinese Communists rather than Chiang. The Nationalist regime was doomed anyway, and Mao's might be kept independent of the Russians by American cooperation. Roosevelt, however, needed a truly friendly regime in China for his postwar plans, even if he did not need Chinese help against the Japanese. He also knew that the fall of Chiang's government would raise protest in America against both Roosevelt and continued American participation in world politics. Consequently, he tried to save Chiang by arranging a truce and coalition between Chiang and Mao. With Stilwell removed, he sent General Patrick Hurley as his personal representative to negotiate between the Nationalists and the Communists.

Hurley was an ignorant blusterer who arrived in China wearing an army uniform adorned with every campaign ribbon except that for Shays's Rebellion, according to one observer. He failed totally to overcome the resistance of Chiang and Mao to a coalition. With Hurley's failure, Roosevelt turned to Stalin in the hope that he would force Mao to accept a subsidiary position in a coalition with Chiang.

The Yalta Conference, February 1945

Roosevelt, Churchill, and Stalin arranged to meet at the Russian resort town of Yalta in the Crimea. Roosevelt and Stalin came with a separate agenda of priorities. Roosevelt wanted Stalin to help defeat Japan and push Mao toward a coalition with Chiang Kai-shek. Roosevelt knew he had to agree to a settlement in Poland that would provide a regime friendly to Stalin because Russian troops occupied the country, but he still hoped to salvage something of the Poles' right to self-determination. He wanted similar settlements in the rest of eastern Europe, but these were of less public interest to the West. Most important, Roosevelt, having abandoned the Morgenthau plan completely, wanted an agreement on Germany that would permit it to remain strong enough economically to contribute to Europe's recovery and prosperity. In addition, he had accepted Churchill's argument that France should regain its position as a great power. He was ready to support France's position as a permanent member of the United Nations Security Council with a veto and to give France an area of occupation in Germany.

At Yalta, he would also abandon his attempts to dismantle the French Empire. Under pressure from Churchill, who had the fate of the British Empire in mind, Roosevelt would agree that the United Nations should be given trusteeships only over colonies of the defeated Axis powers, not over any colonies of the Allies. Thus, Roosevelt was ready to permit the French to reassume their control of Indochina once the Japanese were defeated. Finally, Roosevelt wanted to maintain cordial relations with the Soviet Union and keep it engaged with the United States in a United Nations that would be attractive to American public opinion.

Stalin's primary goal at Yalta seems to have been the guarantee of Soviet security through the establishment of friendly regimes receptive to Soviet troops in strategic areas of eastern Europe, especially Poland and Rumania. He wanted to ensure that Germany would never again be in a position to invade and devastate Russia. He also needed some source of funds to help rebuild his shattered nation. No doubt he wanted Communist regimes, or at least weak nations, in Western Europe. But whatever his future ambitions for expansion, they were subordinated to his immediate desire for security and recovery. Thus, Stalin gave no great help or encouragement to the Communist uprisings in Greece, Italy, or China, and he posed no serious objections to the revival of France.

By the time of the Yalta Conference, Roosevelt was seriously ill. He had very high blood pressure and a weak heart; he was gray with fatigue, and his hands trembled. Critics of the Yalta agreements have often argued that physical illness might have been a major reason Roosevelt supposedly gave away so much to the Russians. The members of the American delegation who attended Yalta, however, have testified that Roosevelt was alert and competent. If he tired easily, he also recovered quickly. The Yalta agreements seem to bear out Roosevelt's competence, for they were quite consistent with his priorities on the eve of the conference.

Roosevelt, Churchill, and Stalin concurred rather easily on most aspects of a settlement with Germany. They divided Germany into four occupation zones, with Stalin consenting to a French zone so long as it was carved out of the British and American territories.

Germany in Defeat, 1945

They divided Berlin, which lay deep in the Russian zone, into its own four occupation zones, with what turned out to be rather minimal guarantees of Western access to the city through Soviet-occupied Germany. The Big Three then agreed to give Poland a portion of eastern Germany in compensation for Poland's loss of some of its eastern territory to the Soviet Union. But they hedged the most critical question concerning Germany.

Stalin wanted vast reparations from Germany. Churchill and Roosevelt objected. They remembered the debacle brought about by the reparations settlement following World War I. They also feared that the size of the reparation settlement demanded by Stalin would prevent Germany's recovery and contribution to the revival of Western Europe. Despite these fears, Roosevelt finally accepted a figure of $20 billion in German reparations as the basis for future discussion, $10 billion of which was to go to the Soviet Union. Churchill

Poland After Yalta, 1945

complained that the figure was beyond reason and perhaps even beyond possibility, but he reluctantly acquiesced.

Accord on Poland was more difficult to reach. The Big Three disagreed over whether Poland's western border should be moved as far into Germany as the western branch of the Neisse River, as Russia insisted, or should go no farther than the eastern Neisse, as Roosevelt and Churchill maintained. The conferees ultimately deferred the decision until a final peace treaty conference could be held, a conference all assumed would take place in the near future. Roosevelt wanted the postponement because he feared the Senate would revolt at any territorial settlements he might make outside the regular treaty process. Churchill also thought it "would be a pity to stuff the Polish goose so full of German food that it died of indigestion." He knew that the more German territory Poland had, the more dependent Poland would be on the Soviet Union to protect it from German revanchism.

The makeup of the Polish government was even more controversial. Stalin was adamant that the Lublin Poles should form the basis of the government. He had neither objected to de Gaulle's elevation in France without an election nor interfered in Greece, he pointed out. He promised that the Polish government would be reorganized on a broader democratic basis to include other Poles from abroad and that this government would hold "free and unfettered" elections shortly after the war was over. Yet it was clear that Stalin would decide how much reorganization would take place and which Poles would be considered democratic. He rejected a proposal that an Allied commission, including representatives of the United States and Great Britain, be permitted to observe and report on the elections.

Admiral William Leahy, one of Roosevelt's aides, warned the president that the Polish settlement was "so elastic that the Russians can stretch it all the way from Yalta to Washington without ever technically breaking it." "I know, Bill," Roosevelt replied; "I know it. But it's the best I can do for Poland at this time." Roosevelt and Leahy might have expressed the same sentiments about the Declaration on Liberated Europe. In this case, the Yalta conferees publicly promised the creation of governments in occupied territories that were "broadly representative of all democratic elements in the population and pledged to the earliest possible establishment through free elections of governments responsible to the will of the people."

On the United Nations, Stalin finally reduced his demand for Russian votes in the General Assembly from sixteen to three. He also abandoned his insistence on the right of a permanent member of the Security Council to veto discussion as well as final action. In turn, the United States and Great Britain were ready to abandon their wish that the permanent members be prohibited from voting on issues that directly involved them and be allowed to veto any substantive decision. Roosevelt reserved the right to have three American votes in the General Assembly to match the Soviets if this proved necessary to win congressional approval (the United States never exercised this option). They all further agreed to hold an organizing conference for the United Nations in San Francisco in April.

The Big Three also came to a settlement on East Asia at Yalta, although this was kept secret because the Soviet Union was still officially neutral in the Pacific war. Stalin promised to enter the war against Japan within three months of the conclusion of the war in Europe. He also promised to recognize Chiang Kai-shek as the head of the Chinese government and to push Mao to join a coalition with the Nationalists. In turn, Roosevelt promised to see that the Soviet Union regained the territory and rights it had held in Asia before the Russo-Japanese War of 1904–1905. The USSR would receive southern Sakhalin Island, the Kuriles, recognition of the Soviet satellite regime in Outer Mongolia, management of China's Manchurian railroads, and control of the warm-water ports of Darien and Port Arthur. Although Roosevelt guaranteed that these conditions would "unquestionably be fulfilled," he also inserted a clause that Chiang would have to concur in those provisions that concerned Chinese territory. Thus Roosevelt made himself responsible for getting

Chiang's consent. He did not think this would be too difficult: he had plenty of leverage over Chiang, and besides he incorrectly expected that Chiang would be happy to exchange the Yalta concessions for Stalin's help with Mao.

Still, these agreements and many other aspects of the Yalta accords were fragile. Chiang might kick up a public fuss about the concessions of Chinese territory, thus raising tumultuous opposition to Roosevelt in the United States. American public opinion might also be aroused by the acceptance of an only slightly modified Lublin government in Poland if Stalin used too heavy a hand there. Finally, if Russia was to receive $10 billion in reparations from Germany, much of it would have to come from the British, French, or American zones, since they included the rich Ruhr and Saar areas.

Roosevelt might have tried to explain to the American people that the presence of Russian troops in eastern Europe and the need for Russian help against Japan had made concessions necessary. He might have pointed out that the United States and Britain had no choice but to accord the Soviet Union its sphere of interest, even though Stalin would impose arrangements that all Americans would find distressing. Candor, however, had never been one of Roosevelt's virtues. He always put on a hearty exterior, but he confided in few people, and even to those few he told contradictory things. Secretary of War Henry Stimson and Chief of Staff George Marshall complained that he spoke with the frivolity and irresponsibility of a child. General Stilwell said, more to the point, that the president was just a "bag of wind." Roosevelt often avoided issues by talking nonstop. (His advisers used to compete to join him at meals in the hope that they might get a word in when the president's mouth was full.) He could rarely bring himself to say no to anyone. Rather than disappoint, he would pretend to agree. Instead of firing officials with whom he was displeased, he would appoint parallel officers. He even had to have his wife fire his barber. When two antagonists left his office together and smiling, his secretary remarked that one would later find his throat cut.

After Yalta, Roosevelt probably feared that an open, frank acknowledgement of the differences between the Western Allies and the Soviets would be offensive to Stalin and at the same time arouse domestic opposition to further cooperation with Communist Russia. He still thought that cooperation was essential, since it required a unanimous agreement among the five major powers for the United Nations Security Council to act. For these reasons, he kept secret the arrangement for the Soviets to have three votes in the United Nations. He also kept the East Asian agreement secret, but for that he had an additional reason. The Allies did not want to warn the Japanese that the Soviets were committed to enter the war against them. Nevertheless, the effect of this secrecy was very unfortunate. Shortly after Roosevelt had reported on Yalta to Congress, the arrangement about the United Nations leaked out, causing a public outcry. Cordell Hull's successor as secretary of state, Edward Stettinius, tried to defuse the issue by telling the press that no further secret Yalta agreements remained undisclosed. Suspicions of a secret deal on East Asia remained, however, and when these agreements leaked out a year later, some opponents of Roosevelt's policies accused the late president of treason.

Roosevelt not only kept secret several of the Yalta agreements, but he also made a dramatic speech to Congress on his return in which he claimed that the Yalta accords would eliminate unilateral national action, exclusive alliances, spheres of influence, balance-of-power politics, and "all other expedients that had been tried for centuries—and have always failed." Roosevelt must have realized that the Russians would do as they pleased in their sphere. He probably hoped that Stalin would be discreet and operate with some appearance of democratic method. Perhaps if Stalin could be brought to trust his Western Allies sufficiently, he might even be satisfied with a strong influence rather than absolute control of eastern Europe.

But this was not to be. Negotiations on the reorganization of the Polish government stalled on Stalin's post-Yalta insistence that a couple of London Poles would simply be grafted onto the existing Lublin regime and no full reorganization would take place. Worse, two weeks after Yalta, Stalin sent Andrei Vishinsky, the ruthless prosecutor of Stalin's late-1930s show trials, to Rumania with an ultimatum. If the Communists were not given power within two hours, Russia would not be responsible for the continuance of Rumania as an independent nation.[2] While Stalin shattered hopes that he would abide by the Declaration on Liberated Europe, he made clearer his distrust of his allies. American and British military leaders were meeting with representatives of the German commander in Italy to try to arrange a surrender of the German army there. The Allied commanders had refused Stalin's request for a Russian observer to be present. Stalin bitterly accused Roosevelt of betraying the alliance, seeking to arrange a separate peace, and permitting Germany to shift its troops from Italy to the eastern front.

Roosevelt responded indignantly. He was increasingly disturbed by the virulence of Stalin's suspicions and by the ruthlessness of Soviet actions in Poland and Rumania. He remarked to a friend that Averell Harriman had been right: the United States could not do business with Stalin because he had broken every promise he had made at Yalta. Yet Roosevelt continued to hope. In his last cable to Churchill, he said he would minimize problems with the Soviets, since difficulties arose every day and most of them straightened out. Thus it is unclear how he would have reacted to the continuing mixture of heavy-handed oppression and occasional surprising concession that Stalin meted out over the next year. When Roosevelt died of a massive cerebral hemorrhage in the last days of the war in Europe, he left that task to his successor, Harry S. Truman. Unfortunately, Roosevelt had not explained the reasoning behind his policies to Truman any more than he had to the American people.

Controversial Issues

It was not long after Roosevelt's death that hostility between the United States and the Soviet Union rose to such a pitch that it was dubbed the Cold War. The praise Roosevelt had received for his wartime success in cooperating with the Russians quickly melted away, to be replaced by harsh critiques for his supposed lack of realism in trusting the Soviets. Memoirs of participants in wartime diplomacy emphasized his naïveté in thinking he could win Stalin over. They claimed he had disregarded the political ramifications of his military strategy. He had ignored his State Department advisers and listened only to his military chiefs, who were intent on winning the war as quickly as possible without regard to the political consequences. He had refused Churchill's plan for a Balkan invasion that might have met the Soviets farther east. He had refused to demand Russian guarantees of self-determination in eastern Europe as a price for opening the second front. He had demanded unconditional surrender from the Axis, thereby bringing about the destruction of Germany and Japan, the only two countries that might have balanced Soviet power.

Roosevelt's demand for unconditional surrender from the Japanese also eliminated any hope that Japan could be defeated without an all-out invasion of its home islands. Such an invasion required Russian help, and to get it Roosevelt had been forced to make concessions to the Soviets in eastern Europe and Asia. Some historians wondered why Roosevelt had made so many concessions to get the Soviet Union into the war against Japan when he supposedly knew that the atomic bomb would be available to force Japan's surrender without Soviet help and without an invasion. A few right-wingers decided that there had been more than naïveté involved in these concessions. They were not sure if Roosevelt himself had been treasonous, but they were convinced that advisers like Alger Hiss and Harry Dexter White had been Communist agents steering American policy toward appeasement of Russia.[3]

These criticisms of Roosevelt's diplomacy made a bigger impact on popular opinion than they did on historians. Careful historical research discredited the practicality of many of Roosevelt's supposed alternatives. Herbert Feis agreed that Roosevelt had failed to take into consideration some of the political implications of his unconditional surrender formula, but argued that it had made little difference. Popular opinion would have revolted at too many concessions to the Axis. Germany and Japan would have fought to the end anyway—the Germans because they knew that retribution awaited them if they lost, the Japanese because their culture inspired fanatical resistance. Meanwhile, military historians argued that Roosevelt had acted properly with regard to the second front. An earlier invasion of Europe would have been very difficult militarily and might well have failed. An invasion of the Balkans might have bogged down in the mountainous terrain, as had the campaign in Italy. The Red Army would then have gone over the top of the Allied penetration to occupy all of Germany and France.[4]

Finally, historians defended Roosevelt's policies at Yalta. With the Russians already occupying much of eastern Europe, Roosevelt had no leverage to get a better settlement. No one realized the atomic bomb would be as important as it later became. Scientists estimated it would be no more powerful than a single flight of conventional bombers already operating over Germany. Thus Roosevelt had needed continued Soviet cooperation in Europe and Asia and had not conceded the Soviets anything in either theater that they were unable to take on their own if they wished.[5] Most historians concurred that however desirable a more realistic attitude on the part of Roosevelt might have been, it would have made no substantial difference in the position of Russia and the Western Allies after the war.[6]

Realist historians then shifted their ground. If Roosevelt's concessions to the Russians had been a product of inescapable military necessity, then the United States should have granted the Soviets their sphere of influence and avoided fatuous efforts to promote liberty or self-determination there. It was wrenching to abandon the Poles, East Germans, and the Balkan and Baltic peoples to Soviet tyranny, but there was no alternative short of World War III. Conceding the Soviets their sphere might at least have kept East-West tensions from escalating. Meanwhile, however, the realists believed the United States should have extended political, economic, and military aid to its allies around the Soviet periphery to "contain" any Soviet hopes for further expansion.[7]

Many historians who looked with favor upon this spheres-of-influence approach to the Soviets ultimately concluded that Roosevelt had actually followed just such a policy. They pointed to his early conception of the United Nations as a big-power policing organization, quite different from the universalism of Wilson's League of Nations. They argued that he had fully intended to grant Stalin control of Poland and the rest of eastern Europe and had only wanted enough gestures from Stalin to make this concession palatable to American public opinion. They criticized Roosevelt not for naïveté, but for dissembling, for continuing to portray his foreign policy to Americans as a universalist pursuit of democracy without explaining the realistic, spheres-of-influence, balance-of-power politics that truly lay behind it. Thus the deluded American people felt betrayed when Stalin quite naturally took full control of his sphere. After Roosevelt's death, the United States overreacted to Stalin's actions and helped initiate the Cold War.[8]

Some realists, however, have argued that Roosevelt should have been firmer with Stalin at Teheran and Yalta even if he could not have prevented Stalin from acquiring an eastern European sphere of influence by withholding the second front or avoiding the unconditional surrender doctrine. These authors have insisted that Stalin was in a weak economic and political position in this period and that if Roosevelt had fully supported Churchill's remonstrances against Soviet policy in Poland and elsewhere, Stalin might well have backed down.[9] Research in Soviet archives opened as a result of the fall of the Soviet Union unfortunately has not clarified this issue. The available Soviet documents on Stalin do make clear that he hoped and expected to cooperate with the British and Americans after the war but that he thought he could do so while also solidifying his own security sphere. Perhaps the most surprising thing to emerge from the Soviet archives is that Stalin actually believed that the eastern Europeans would view the Soviet Union and communism with increasing favor and that the inevitable depressions in the capitalist West would bring many people there into the Communist camp as well. In other words, he could afford to be cooperative with the West because time was on his side. But there still seems no way to tell how he would have reacted to a more adamant stand on Poland and eastern Europe by Roosevelt and Churchill.[10]

However much these realists criticized Roosevelt for not explaining the actual motives behind his concessions to the Soviets, they still portrayed Stalin and the Soviets as the primary instigators of the Cold War, since Russian tyranny in eastern Europe had done far more to sour relations than any mistakes Roosevelt or Truman may have made. But the revisionists argued that the Americans had been more at fault for the Cold War than the Russians.

Most of the early revisionists, however, exempted Roosevelt from this blame. They argued that Roosevelt had truly cooperated with the Russians and at Yalta had indeed accorded the Soviets their sphere in eastern Europe. Then, on Roosevelt's death, Truman had gone back on Roosevelt's bargain. He had tried to force Stalin to open up eastern Europe to the economic and political influence of the United States and the West. Thus Truman was at fault for the Cold War.[11]

More radical revisionists, denying that Truman had reversed Roosevelt's course, argued that Roosevelt too had sought a world open to capitalist expansion and had done his share to initiate the Cold War. The most strident of these works, Gabriel Kolko's *The Politics of War: The World and United States Foreign Policy, 1943–1945* (1968), argued that Roosevelt and his advisers had calculated the political consequences of their actions very carefully. They had delayed the second front purposely to hurt Russia, then invaded Normandy and raced eastward because France and Germany were more important than the Balkans. Roosevelt had temporarily supported the Morgenthau plan not as a sop to the Soviets, but because he did not want Germany to be able to supply reparations to Russia. By denying Russia reparations, he would make the Soviets dependent on the United States instead. Roosevelt abandoned the Morgenthau plan only when he saw the need of the Western economies for a revived Germany. But he made sure to direct Germany's economic productivity westward rather than toward the Soviets. Then he used lend-lease and other economic leverage to try to pry the Soviet and eastern European economies open to American exploitation. Meanwhile, Roosevelt had refused to share atomic technology with the Russians, inducing still further distrust between the two powers.[12]

Kolko also attacked the image of Anglo-American cooperation during the war. Traditional accounts had noted some strain between Britain and the United States over the strategy of opening a second front and questions involving the British and French empires. But these traditional accounts had emphasized the rapport between Churchill and Roosevelt, exemplified by the unprecedented and successful merging of the two countries' military commands during the war.[13] Kolko, on the other hand, portrayed a rapacious America bent on using Britain's weakness to force that nation into economic dependency and take over its empire by breaking down imperial barriers to American trade.

Recent works, exploiting the British archives, have struck a balance between these two portrayals of Anglo-American relations, seeing essentially a cooperative relationship that was nevertheless more competitive than earlier historians had acknowledged.[14]

Further Reading

The best book on the war itself is Gerhard Weinberg, *A World at Arms: A Global History of World War II* (1994). For the war in Asia, see Ronald H. Spector, *Eagle Against the Sun: The American War with Japan* (1985); Akira Iriye, *Power and Culture: The Japanese-American War, 1941–1945* (1981); and John Dower, *War Without Mercy: Race and Power in the Pacific War* (1986), a harrowing account of the ethnic hatreds and brutality of the war. A book comparable to Dower's that details the brutalities of the war in Europe is William I. Hitchcock, *The Bitter Road to Freedom: A New History of the Liberation of Europe* (2008). For diplomacy with China during World War II, see Herbert Feis, *The China Tangle* (1953); Akira Iriye, *The Cold War in Asia* (1974); Tang

Tsou, *America's Failure in China, 1941–1945* (1963); Barbara Tuchman, *Stilwell and the American Experience in China* (1970); Warren I. Cohen, *The American Response to China* (2nd ed., 1980); Michael Schaller, *The United States Crusade in China, 1938–1945* (1979); Wesley M. Bagby, *The Eagle-Dragon Alliance: America's Relations with China in World War II* (1992); Carolle J. Carter, *Mission to Yenan: American Liaison with the Chinese Communists, 1944–1947* (1997); Xiaoyuan Liu, *A Partnership for Disorder: China, the United States, and Their Policies for the Postwar Disposition of the Japanese Empire, 1941–1945* (1996); and Jung Chang and Jon Halliday, *Mao: The Unknown Story* (2005). Other books on special topics include Raoul Aglion, *Roosevelt and de Gaulle: A Personal Memoir of Allies in Conflict* (1988); James Edward Miller, *The United States and Italy, 1940–1950* (1986); Michael S. Sherry, *The Rise of American Air Power* (1987); Richard Rhodes, *The Making of the Atomic Bomb* (1987); and Susan M. Hartman, *The Home Front and Beyond: American Women in the 1940s* (1982).

Notes

1. After the North African invasion, Cordell Hull, still worried about the potential casualties in a cross-channel invasion, mentioned to the Russians the 200,000 casualties America already had suffered. The Soviet aide to whom he was speaking replied, "We lose that many each day before lunch. You haven't got your teeth in the war yet."

2. The Soviets had some justification for this takeover because toward the end of the war they had uncovered a pro-Nazi plot that involved many of the supposedly moderate Rumanian politicians.

3. The early memoirs criticizing Roosevelt for his naïveté included those of Winston Churchill himself, *The Second World War* (6 vols., 1948–1953); see also William C. Bullitt, "How We Won the War and Lost the Peace," *Life* (August 30 and September 6, 1948); Robert E. Sherwood, *Roosevelt and Hopkins* (1948); Robert Murphy, *Diplomat Among Warriors* (1964); and Arthur Bliss Lane, *I Saw Poland Betrayed: An American Ambassador Reports to the American People* (1948). Elements of these critiques were picked up by some of the early realist historians, including Hans Morgenthau, *In Defense of the National Interest: A Critical Examination of American Foreign Policy* (1951) and *Politics Among Nations: The Struggle for Power and Peace* (1948); Hanson Baldwin, *Great Mistakes of the War* (1954); Louis J. Halle, *Civilization and Foreign Policy* (1955) and *Dream and Reality: Aspects of American Foreign Policy* (1959); and Anne Armstrong, *Unconditional Surrender: The Impact of the Casablanca Policy upon World War II* (1961). Right-wingers who took these criticisms to an extreme included William Henry Chamberlin, *America's Second Crusade* (1950); Anthony Kubek, *How the Far East Was Lost: American Policy and the Creation of Communist China, 1941–1949* (1963); Edward Rozak, *Allied Wartime Diplomacy: A Pattern in Poland* (1958); and Robert Nisbet, *Roosevelt and Stalin: The Fateful Courtship* (1988). A recent popular book in this mold is Thomas F. Fleming, *The New Dealers' War: Franklin D. Roosevelt and the War Within World War II* (2001). For good summaries of right-wing thought and activities, see George H. Nash, *The Conservative Intellectual Movement in America since 1945* (1976); and Athan C. Theoharis, *The Yalta Myths: An Issue in U.S. Politics, 1945–1955* (1970).

4. Herbert Feis, *Churchill—Roosevelt—Stalin: The War They Waged and the Peace They Sought* (1957); Kent Roberts Greenfield, *American Strategy in World War II: A Reconsideration* (1963); Maurice Matloff and Edwin M. Snell, *Strategic Planning for Coalition Warfare, 1943–1944* (1959); Forrest C. Pogue, *The Supreme Command* (1954); Samuel Eliot Morison, *Strategy and Compromise* (1958).

5. John Snell, *Illusion and Necessity: The Diplomacy of Global War, 1939–1945* (1963).

6. Gaddis Smith, *American Diplomacy During the Second World War, 1941–1945* (1965); William L. Neumann, *Making the Peace, 1941–1945* (1950).

7. George Kennan, *American Diplomacy, 1900–1950* (1951). For the shifts in the realist outlook, compare Hans Morgenthau's *In Defense of the National Interest*, especially pp. 109–112, with his essay in Lloyd D. Gardner, Arthur Schlesinger Jr., and Hans J. Morgenthau, *The Origins of the Cold War* (1970). Compare also Louis Halle's *Civilization and Foreign Policy* with his *Cold War as History* (1967), and William Neumann's *Making the Peace* with his *After Victory: Churchill, Roosevelt, Stalin, and the Making of the Peace* (1967). See also Herbert Feis, *Between War and Peace: The Potsdam Conference* (1960), p. 38. An early advocate of this spheres-of-influence strategy was William Hardy McNeil, *America, Britain, and Russia: Their Cooperation and Conflict, 1941–1946* (1950).

8. The best of these books, and the best book on Roosevelt's diplomacy in general, is Robert Dallek, *Franklin D. Roosevelt and American Foreign Policy, 1932–1945* (1979). James MacGregor Burns, *Roosevelt: The Soldier of Freedom* (1970), sees Roosevelt as somewhat less realistic. See also Raymond G. O'Connor, *Diplomacy for Victory: FDR and Unconditional Surrender* (1971); Robert A. Divine, *Roosevelt and World War II* (1969) and *Second Chance: The Triumph of Internationalism in World War II* (1967); John Lewis Gaddis, *The Cold War: A New History* (2005) and *The United States and the Origins of the Cold War, 1941–1947* (new ed., 2000); George C. Herring, *Aid to Russia, 1941–1946: Strategy, Diplomacy, and the Origins of the Cold War* (1973), dealing with lend-lease; Martin F. Herz, *The Beginnings of the Cold War* (1966), emphasizing the Polish issue; Lynn Etheridge Davis, *The Cold War Begins: Soviet-American Conflict over Eastern Europe* (1974); Lisle A. Rose, *Dubious Victory: The United States and the End of World War II* (1973); Hugh Di Santis, *The Diplomacy of Silence: The American Foreign Service, the Soviet Union, and the Cold War, 1933–1947* (1980), examining the role of the State Department; and Warren F. Kimball, *The Juggler: Franklin Roosevelt as Wartime Statesman* (1991).

9. The most important of these books is Vojtech Mastny, *Russia's Road to the Cold War* (1978), which makes good use of eastern European sources. Analyses of Stalin's weakness are in Adam Ulam, *The Rivals: America and Russia Since World War II* (1971); and William Taubman, *Stalin's American Policy* (1981). Viewing Roosevelt and Churchill from this point of view are Frederick Marks, *Wind over Sand* (1988); Steven M. Miner, *Between Churchill and Stalin: The Soviet Union, Great Britain, and the Origins of the Grand Alliance* (1988); and Keith Sainsbury, *The Turning Point* (1985), which deals with the Teheran Conference. For other books on Teheran, see Paul D. Mayle, *Eureka Summit: Agreement in Principle and the Big Three at Teheran, 1943* (1987); and Keith Eubank, *Summit at Teheran* (1985). On Yalta, see Russell D. Buhite, *Decision at Yalta* (1986).

10. Vladislav Zubok and Constantine Pleshakov, *Inside the Kremlin's Cold War: From Stalin to Khrushchev* (1996); Eduard Mark, "Revolution by Degrees: Stalin's National Front Strategy for Europe, 1941–1947," Working Paper #31, Cold War International History Project, www.wilsoncenter.org.

11. The earliest of these revisionist accounts was Denna Frank Flemming, *The Cold War and Its Origins; 1917–1960* (2 vols., 1961). See also Daniel Yergin, *Shattered Peace: The Origins of the Cold War and the National Security State* (1977). Gar Alperovitz, *Atomic Diplomacy: Hiroshima and Potsdam* (1965), argues that the atomic bomb gave Truman the confidence to reverse Roosevelt's policy and blackmail the Soviet Union. Thomas J. Paterson, *Soviet-American Confrontation: Postwar Reconstruction and the Origins of the Cold War* (1973), emphasizes economic rather than atomic blackmail as Truman's major goal. Thomas M. Campbell, *Masquerade Peace: America's UN Policy, 1944–1945* (1973), sees Truman's rejection of Roosevelt's policy coming in the United Nations. Stephen E. Ambrose, *Rise to Globalism: American Foreign Policy Since 1938* (2nd ed., 1980), surveys the whole of U.S. military and strategic policy from this moderate revisionist point of view.

12. Books agreeing with Kolko's insistence on the continuity of American economic expansionist diplomacy from Roosevelt to Truman, although usually stating it in milder terms, include Walter LaFeber, *America, Russia, and the Cold War* (6th ed., 1991); Bruce Kuklick, *American Policy and the Division of Germany: The Clash with Russia over Reparations* (1972); Diane Shaver Clemens, *Yalta* (1970), which is a bit ambiguous on this question, supporting one view in the text and another in the conclusion; Lloyd Gardner, *Architects of Illusion: Men and Ideas in American Foreign Policy, 1941–1949* (1970); Barton Bernstein, ed., *Politics and Policies of the Truman Administration* (1970); and Robert A. Pollard,

Economic Security and the Origins of the Cold War (1986). In *A World Destroyed: Hiroshima and Its Legacies* (3rd ed., 2000), Martin J. Sherwin supports the revisionist view by arguing that Roosevelt initiated the atomic policy that Truman later followed.

13. In addition to Churchill's memoirs and the military histories already cited, see Richard Gardner, *Sterling-Dollar Diplomacy* (1956); and Joseph P. Lash's later *Roosevelt and Churchill, 1939–1941: The Partnership That Saved the West* (1976).

14. See Armand Van Dormael, *Bretton Woods: Birth of a Monetary System* (1978); Alfred E. Eckes Jr., *A Search for Solvency: Bretton Woods and the International Monetary System, 1941–1971* (1981); Christopher Thorne, *Allies of a Kind: The United States, Britain, and the War Against Japan, 1941–1945* (1978); William Roger Louis, *Imperialism at Bay, 1941–1945: The United States and the Decolonization of the British Empire* (1978); D. Cameron Watt, *Succeeding John Bull: America in Britain's Place, 1900–1975* (1984); Randall Bennett Woods, *A Changing of the Guard: Anglo-American Relations, 1941–1946* (1990); Alan P. Dobson, *U.S. Wartime Aid to Britain, 1940–1946* (1986); and Henry B. Ryan, *The Vision of Anglo-America* (1987). Brian Loring Villa, "The Atomic Bomb and the Normandy Invasion," *Perspectives in American History* 11 (1977–78), argues that Roosevelt extorted final agreement on the second front by withholding atomic sharing. On the second front, see also Mark A. Stoler, *The Politics of the Second Front: American Military Planning and Diplomacy in Coalition Warfare, 1941–1943* (1977). See especially for the Anglo-American relationship, Warren F. Kimball, ed., *Churchill and Roosevelt: The Complete Correspondence* (1984) and his work utilizing that correspondence, *Forged in War: Roosevelt, Churchill, and the Second World War* (1997).

CHAPTER 9

HARRY TRUMAN AND THE ONSET OF THE COLD WAR

Truman Takes Over

If Franklin Roosevelt had survived World War II, he would have faced a monstrous dilemma of his own making. He would have had to reconcile his vague promises to Stalin of a Soviet sphere with his assurances to the American people that the Allies were fashioning an open, democratic world. Even a master politician like Roosevelt might have faltered. How much more difficult, then, was it for Harry Truman? Truman did not even understand that he faced a dilemma. He did not know that Roosevelt had all but conceded the Soviets their sphere in eastern Europe or that the United States was close to exploding its first atomic bomb. In his profound ignorance of the status of Roosevelt's diplomacy, Truman naturally turned to State Department advisers. He did not realize that Roosevelt had largely ignored them, relying instead on his military advisers or his own wits. After years of plucking fruitlessly at the sleeves of those in power, the State Department grabbed its chance to explain to Truman that Roosevelt had trusted the Russians too much.

Averell Harriman returned to Washington from his post as ambassador to the Soviet Union to tell Truman that Soviet conduct in Poland and the rest of eastern Europe posed a threat to American interests. Harriman and other advisers recounted for Truman the Soviet clampdown in eastern Europe and the betrayal of the Warsaw uprising. They warned that once the Soviet Union had control of eastern Europe, its hostility toward capitalist nations would tempt it to penetrate adjacent areas. Harriman urged Truman to be firm and use Russia's desperate need for reconstruction funds as economic leverage.

Truman accepted this advice "with an alacrity that unsettled even those who had given it."[1] When Soviet foreign minister Vyacheslav Molotov passed through Washington on his way to the United Nations (UN) organizing conference in San Francisco, Truman told him in unvarnished terms that Soviet-American relations would no longer be a one-way street. Molotov complained that he had never been talked to like that in his life. "Carry out your agreements and you won't get talked to like that," snapped Truman.

Truman loved to project this image—a quick, decisive man of plain common sense. "The buck stops here," proclaimed a plaque on his White House desk. Quick and decisive he was. One State Department official bragged that Truman had gone through fourteen problems in less than a quarter of an hour. But Truman seems to have used this air of decisiveness to cover a deep uncertainty. He often made snap decisions without much information and then had to rescind them with considerable embarrassment. When the war in Europe ended, he signed an order cutting off further lend-lease aid to the Soviet Union. This was in accordance with the letter of the lend-lease law, and many Congress members had made clear they wanted to stop the program immediately after a German surrender. But the abruptness of the cutoff, turning ships around in mid-ocean, was a gratuitous slap at an ally the Americans hoped would join the war against Japan. Stalin could not help but see Truman's lecture to Molotov and this sudden termination of lend-lease aid as an indication of a changed American policy. The Russian dictator complained bitterly and Truman lamely apologized that he had not read the lend-lease directive he had signed. He ordered the ships to turn around again and return to the Soviet Union.

Truman also had second thoughts about what he had called his straight one-two to Molotov's jaw. "Did I do right?" he plaintively asked former U.S. ambassador to Russia Joseph Davies. When Davies and others explained Russia's side of several of the questions bedeviling Soviet-American relations, Truman decided to try a more amicable approach. He and General Dwight Eisenhower, for example, refused to accept Churchill's advice to violate the Yalta agreement and hold Prague until Stalin became more cooperative. The president also sent on special missions two men who were identified with a relatively benign view of Soviet intentions. He dispatched Joseph Davies to London to explain Truman's position to Churchill, and Roosevelt's closest adviser Harry Hopkins to Moscow to deal with Stalin.

Hopkins carried out his mission even though he was suffering from terminal cancer, and Stalin appeared impressed by this demonstration of America's intent. The Soviet leader assured Hopkins that Russia would enter the war against Japan and reaffirmed his endorsement of Chiang Kai-shek in China. He and Hopkins also agreed on a list of non-Lublin Poles whom Stalin would invite to Moscow for consultations on revision of the Lublin Polish government. Stalin even claimed that Poland would be governed in a manner similar to Belgium, Holland, or Czechoslovakia. If Hopkins were inclined to believe such an exaggeration, he would have been disabused of it by Stalin's refusal to release sixteen Polish underground leaders he had already arrested. Hopkins mused at the conclusion of his mission that Stalin would never understand America's interest in a free Poland as a matter of principle. The Russian leader viewed everything in terms of power.

Stalin's attitude perplexed Truman as well. Truman's vacillation mirrored the confusion most Americans, even those high in government councils and supposedly knowledgeable about foreign affairs, felt about Soviet intentions. Were Stalin and the Soviets still Communist revolutionaries bent on world conquest, ready to use any Western concessions as stepping-stones to further aggression? Or was Stalin truly willing to give up world revolution in favor of communism in one country, seeking more traditional Russian national interests such as security from attack through eastern Europe? Truman and most Americans were ready to judge the Soviets' intentions by their conduct in eastern Europe. If Stalin were willing to compromise with the West on arrangements there, permitting a modicum of freedom as Americans understood that word, then Truman would assume that Stalin's goals were limited and defensive. Failure to compromise in eastern Europe would be seen as evidence of Stalin's aggressive intent elsewhere.

Unfortunately, such a test not only failed to take into account the fact that few freely elected regimes in eastern Europe would be friendly to the Soviet Union, but also that Stalin might be ruthless and cautious at the same time. Stalin directed his ruthlessness almost entirely toward the most strategically vital areas in eastern Europe, a sphere he may well have believed Roosevelt had conceded to him. It was true that he was merciless in Poland, Rumania, and Bulgaria, and Truman and many of his advisers naturally worried that this tyranny indicated Stalin's intentions for other areas he sought to control. Yet Stalin did permit a degree of self-determination in less strategic countries such as Hungary and Czechoslovakia so long as Communists loyal to the Soviet Union controlled key posts within those governments. Later he would be even more accommodating toward Finland and Austria, insisting only that their foreign policies be neutral rather than hostile to the Soviets.

Truman and his advisers may have been further confused about Stalin's intentions because they regarded Josip Tito's relatively independent regime in Yugoslavia as a faithful satellite of Stalin. They assumed that Tito made his militant demands for control of Trieste and the surrounding area at the head of the strategic Adriatic Sea at Stalin's instigation. They missed Stalin's subtle signals that he placed a lower priority on the Balkans. They also blamed Stalin for instigating the Communist rebellion against the British-backed regime in Greece. Actually Stalin was trying to restrain Tito from supporting the rebels and interfering in the sphere that Stalin had accorded the British.

During this early postwar period, Stalin also restrained Communists in other areas of the West. The Communist parties of Italy and France were still under orders to cooperate with the regimes established by the Western Allies. So was the American Communist Party. But when the head of the American party, Earl Browder, proclaimed that this cooperation would continue for the foreseeable future, the French Communist leader Jacques Duclos denounced this as heresy and insisted that class war was a permanent condition. In retrospect, Duclos's public rebuke to Browder in April 1945 seems to have been a reassurance to international Communists that they could continue to collaborate as Stalin was instructing them to without giving up their ideology. Many contemporary observers in the West, however, saw it as Stalin's own proclamation of the end of the cooperation with the West that the exigencies of World War II had forced upon the Soviet Union.

Amid these swirling events and conflicting signals, Truman remained confident for a time that the United States could control matters regardless of Russia's intentions. The Red Army in Europe might be larger than that of the Western Allies and its position would grow even stronger as America withdrew its troops to finish the Japanese war, but the Soviets seemed in desperate need of economic support. The USSR had lost one-quarter of its capital equipment, 1,700 towns, 70,000 villages, 100,000 collective farms, and 20 million dead. By early 1945 it was clear that Congress was not going to extend lend-lease into the postwar era, so Truman would not be able to offer that as bargaining leverage to get Russian concessions. But Secretary of the Treasury Henry Morgenthau's suggestion of a multibillion-dollar loan was still alive in the State Department, if only barely. Congress might approve the loan if Russian conduct were more reassuring. In addition, Truman could still arrange for Germany to supply reparations to the Soviets. Here certainly was something for which the Soviets would be willing to bargain. They already were busy looting the industries of their own sector of Germany, but the Western Allies controlled the great bulk of German's industrial facilities. Russia would have to win Western consent to gain access to them.

Stalin seems to have misjudged this economic situation just as he did the Western response to his suppression of liberty in eastern Europe. Stalin assumed that the capitalist world faced a postwar depression and that the West was desperate for new overseas markets for its goods. Stalin thought he was doing the United States a favor by accepting postwar aid and credits, thus furnishing an outlet for American products and postponing the inevitable crisis of capitalism. Certainly he needed and wanted Western economic assistance, but even some Western experts recognized that this was not as vital to Stalin as it appeared to most Western leaders.

Many intelligence reports claimed that American aid would speed Russian reconstruction by only a matter of months. Besides, Stalin was counting on the economic crisis of the capitalist world to permit a cautious but persistent expansion of communism in the future. Apparently he was unwilling to risk a major war or confrontation with the West, but certainly he would take what he could get cheaply, as of course would the West in the Soviet sphere. America's economic lever thus worked far less effectively in bargaining with the Soviets than Truman, Harriman, and many other American advisers expected.

Truman, however, had another reason for believing he could force Russian cooperation. The first test of an atomic explosion was nearly ready when he took office. He listened only fifteen minutes to the report on the bomb given by Secretary of War Henry Stimson and General Leslie Groves. He then appointed an interim committee to advise him on its use and accepted Stimson's recommendation to try to postpone his summit meeting with Stalin at Potsdam until a successful test demonstrated the bomb's feasibility. He would not brandish the new weapon at Potsdam or threaten the Russians directly, but he would not offer to share it either. He would inform Stalin of the explosion as casually as possible and turn aside any question of shared control. Even with sole possession of the bomb to go along with American economic leverage, Truman knew he could not get all he wanted from the Soviets. But he concluded that he should be able to get 85 percent or so.

From Potsdam to the Truman Doctrine: The Transition from Quid Pro Quo Diplomacy to Containment

News of the first successful test explosion of an atomic device near Alamagordo, New Mexico, reached Truman in the midst of the Potsdam Conference. Churchill immediately noted an increased confidence in Truman. Yet that confidence did not do the United States or Britain much good. Stalin passed over Truman's implied threat that the United States had acquired a tremendous new weapon with an offhand wish that it would be used on the Japanese. Stalin seemed even less moved by Truman's attempt prior to the meeting to conciliate him with an abrupt recognition of the slightly reorganized Polish government.

(Truman had given Churchill only a few hours' notice of his intention to recognize the Lublin government and then ignored British protests.) The little progress that was made at Potsdam seemed to be accomplished through hard bargaining and reciprocal concessions. The Big Three agreed that Germany should be administered as a single unit by a four-power control council composed of military commanders. There harmony ended. The Americans insisted that German assets and production should go first to ensuring Germany's own economic survival and that only what was left over should go for reparations. When the Soviets objected, the Americans suggested that each side should just take reparations from its own zones. The Russians protested that this arrangement would destroy the agreement to administer Germany as a single unit. Since Germany's primary assets were in the western part of the country, a division would make it impossible for the Russians to obtain their $10 billion worth of reparations.

Finally, the Big Three worked a trade. Acceding to Soviet desires, the Western Allies recognized the Polish-German border at the western Neisse River. The USSR agreed to take most of its reparations from its own zone of Germany and acquire only a small amount of additional capital equipment from the western zones deemed "unnecessary" to German recovery. The Russians were unhappy, but realized they would get nothing from the western zones if there was no agreement. Meanwhile, the Big Three established a council of foreign ministers to draw up the peace treaties with Germany's ex-allies. Again a trade was evident. Stalin made sure that the fate of the treaty with Italy was linked directly with the fate of the treaties with Rumania, Bulgaria, Hungary, and Finland.

Another proposed Potsdam "deal" did not come off. Stalin demanded military bases, territorial concessions, and other guarantees from Turkey to give the Soviets effective control over the Dardanelles, the bottleneck that controlled Russia's access to the Mediterranean from the Black Sea. Truman argued instead that the Dardanelles and the whole Danube River ought to be under international control. Stalin then proposed that the Suez and Panama Canals be treated the same way, a suggestion that several members of the American delegation to Potsdam regarded as solid evidence of Russia's aggressive, expansionist desires. That impression was reinforced by Stalin's requests for control of Japan's Hokkaido Island and portions of Italy's colonies in North Africa. The Soviet desire for part of Libya particularly disturbed those American officials knowledgeable about the atomic bomb, for they saw Libya as a stepping-stone to the Belgian Congo, the source of most of America's uranium ore.

The Potsdam Conference ended with many unsettled questions and considerable American suspicion of the Soviets. Truman told a sailor on the ship home that he thought Stalin was an "S.O.B." But then, he added, Stalin probably thought he was one too. Truman still seemed to hope he could strike a deal with Stalin on a quid pro quo basis. He also seemed to hope, however, that the bomb would make Russian participation in the war against Japan less necessary and remove the opportunity for the USSR to fulfill all its ambitions in Asia.

Truman never seems to have had a second thought about using the atomic bomb on Japan. Some of the scientists who had worked to develop the bomb urged that the United States demonstrate it to the Japanese in some uninhabited place, but Truman's interim advisory committee, headed by Stimson, rejected the idea. The committee recommended instead that the two bombs in America's arsenal be dropped on relatively untouched Japanese cities. This might eliminate the need for an invasion of the Japanese home islands, which U.S. military authorities estimated would cost tens of thousands of American lives. (Truman maintained in his memoirs that his decision to use the atomic bomb saved half a million American lives. His exaggeration may indicate that he felt some guilt about the decision despite his many statements that he had no doubts about it.)

It is clear to historians now that Japan probably would have surrendered in a short time without the bomb and probably without an invasion of the home islands. American navy and air corps officers argued that a naval blockade and continued conventional bombing might have been sufficient. Even if Truman had been inclined to discount such claims as posturing by rival armed services, there were other reasons for him to have considered the possibility. The Japanese were already extending peace feelers to the Soviets that Stalin dutifully passed on to Truman. These feelers indicated that the Japanese might be inclined to surrender if they could be assured that their emperor, Hirohito, would maintain his position, a concession that the Allies permitted Japan in the end anyway. The shock of the upcoming Soviet entry into the war in Asia would have provided even more incentive for Japan's surrender. But Truman did not even pause to consider these possibilities.

Some historians argue that Truman and Stimson, knowing full well that they did not have to drop the bomb on Japan to end the war and save American lives, used it anyway to impress Russia with the weapon's horror and thereby make the Soviets more manageable in the postwar period. Most historians grant that the American leaders considered the impact of the bomb's use on the Soviets but see the decision as motivated by bureaucratic momentum, wartime callousness, and the desire to save American lives regardless of the cost in Japanese lives. American leaders had assumed since the inception of the Manhattan Project that the bomb would be used when ready, and only a major reevaluation by Stimson or Truman could have reversed that course. Stimson was not ready to change his assumptions on the use of the bomb, and Truman was never inclined to thorough evaluations anyway. They were already inured to the horror and civilian casualties involved in modern war by the Nazi rocket-bombing of London, the suicidal Japanese stands on the Pacific islands, the kamikaze raids on American ships, and their own massive bombing raids on Dresden and Tokyo.[2] The American view of the Japanese as fanatical monsters willing to fight to the last man, woman, and child further removed any inhibitions against using a bomb that would inevitably cause massive civilian casualties. (There was, for instance, no parallel in the American image of Japan to the idea of the occasional "good German.") Besides, American intelligence intercepts showed that Japan had recently reinforced its defenses on the home island of Kyushu, the planned landing site for the American invasion of Japan, and that American casualties would inevitably be higher than previously estimated.

On August 6, 1945, the United States dropped it first atomic bomb on Hiroshima. Two days later and one day before America's second atomic bomb wiped out Nagasaki, Russia opened its attack on Manchuria. Even after the two atomic bombs, the Soviet declaration of war, the looming certainty of the destruction of more cities, and the prospect of famine,

Emperor Hirohito had to intervene personally to secure acceptance from the Japanese military of the American offer to couple surrender with permission for him to stay on the throne under the control of the American occupiers. Meanwhile, the Soviets moved quickly to occupy the areas they had been promised at Yalta, and they kept their own Yalta promise by signing a treaty with Chiang Kai-shek pledging him exclusive moral support and military aid.

Truman and his advisers may have expected that the use of the atomic bomb would make Stalin more malleable, but recently opened Soviet archives reveal that it worked in precisely the opposite way. Even with the information Stalin had been receiving from his spies on the United States' progress in building an atomic weapon, he was not impressed enough with the potential of the bomb to regard his own atomic project as urgent until after the destruction of Hiroshima. That explosion changed his mind. He may well have regarded Truman's use of the bomb as intended to end the war quickly so as to limit Soviet gains in China. He certainly regarded the bomb as a major challenge to Soviet power. He immediately put his secret police chief, Lavrenty Beria, in charge of a crash program to build a Russian bomb, thus letting his scientists know that their lives were on the line. Stalin also resolved to show the American negotiators that he was not intimidated by their bomb in the interval before the Soviets got their own atomic weapon.

As the war in the Pacific came to an end, Henry Stimson, apparently guessing how Stalin would react, reconsidered the advice he had given Truman on the use of the atomic bomb. Contemplating the lack of progress at Potsdam, Stimson concluded that carrying the bomb conspicuously on the American hip made the Soviets resentful and stubborn rather than malleable. Stimson was also mindful of the estimates of America's atomic scientists that the Russians would probably develop an atomic bomb within one to five years. An American atomic monopoly of such short duration would provide little incentive for Russia to make major concessions. Stimson advised Truman to promise not to use the bomb in the future and to share the technology for peaceful application of atomic energy with the Soviets in exchange for a Russian promise not to build an atomic bomb in the first place.

Truman's new secretary of state, James F. Byrnes, opposed such an approach. Rejecting scientific estimates of a one- to five-year monopoly, he believed instead the calculation of General Leslie Groves, head of the Manhattan Project, that the Soviets would not have an atomic bomb for fifteen to twenty years. Thus Byrnes saw the atomic "secret" as a valuable counter in negotiating with the USSR. (Actually General Groves based his estimate not on any technological secrets, but instead on a top-secret program he had undertaken during the war to monopolize the world's sources of uranium ore. He was unaware that the Russians had plentiful supplies of uranium in East Germany.)

Several members of the recently formed Joint Congressional Committee on Atomic Energy supported Byrnes in his opposition to sharing even peaceful atomic technology and advised Truman to keep the secrets of the bomb. A public opinion poll also showed the vast majority of Americans in favor of keeping the bomb secret even if the monopoly could be expected to last only one to five years. After some vacillation, Truman decided to go along with Byrnes rather than Stimson. From a speech on atomic energy, he deleted a

Secretary of State James F. Byrnes *(left)* and President Harry Truman. *(Courtesy of the National Archives)*

sentence warning that no amount of secrecy could keep foreigners from drawing abreast of American atomic technology in a "comparatively short time."

The threat of the bomb played a significant role in the London Conference of Foreign Ministers, which met from September to October 1945 to draw up the final peace treaties with Italy, Rumania, Bulgaria, Hungary, and Finland. When Byrnes pushed for more representative governments in the Soviet sphere, Molotov demanded a greater say in Japan, Italy, and the Italian colonies. In the midst of this argument, the dour Molotov asked with a studied attempt at humor if Byrnes had an atomic bomb in his side pocket. Byrnes replied with equally studied humor that he did and if Molotov did not become more cooperative he would "pull it out and let him have it." When neither side would budge, Molotov suddenly denounced the participation of the Chinese foreign minister in European questions, using it as a pretext to break up the conference.

Byrnes's highly publicized failure at the foreign ministers' conference caused him to reconsider his strategy. He decided that the Soviets would neither be intimidated by the bomb nor succumb to economic blandishments. He asked them for another foreign ministers' meeting, and this time he prepared to offer international control of the atomic bomb in order to gain Russian concessions. Republican senator Arthur Vandenberg and Democratic senator Tom Connally, members of the Congressional Committee on Atomic Energy and vital figures in Truman's hopes to conduct a bipartisan foreign policy, went to the president to protest Byrnes's secrecy and independent policy making. Truman responded by ordering Byrnes to secure safeguards before offering to share atomic technology with the Russians.

Byrnes ignored the president. He had been a more prominent senator than Truman and had expected to be selected over him for the vice presidency in 1944. Considering himself more qualified to conduct American foreign policy than this accidental president, Byrnes tended to treat Truman somewhat condescendingly. Therefore, at the Moscow Conference of Foreign Ministers in December 1945, Byrnes conceded that United Nations control of atomic energy might be lodged in the Security Council, where Russia could veto enforcement measures, rather than in the General Assembly. In return for Byrnes's concessions on atomic policy and acceptance of Russian practices in eastern Europe, the Soviets accepted American domination of occupation policy in Japan, added two non-Communists to the Bulgarian government, and agreed to new elections in Rumania. They had already permitted elections in Hungary that gave the Communists only 17 percent of the vote. Returning to the United States, Byrnes scheduled a triumphant speech to the nation even before reporting to the president.

Truman was enraged both by Byrnes's concessions and his failure to keep the president informed. Truman had just read a report on eastern Europe compiled by Mark Ethridge, a liberal newspaperman and friend of former vice president Henry Wallace, whom Byrnes had sent to check on State Department reporting in the Soviet sphere. Ethridge had surprised Byrnes by describing Soviet actions in eastern Europe as oppressive and warning that the Russians harbored aggressive intentions for Turkey and Iran as well. Byrnes withheld this report from Truman until the eve of Byrnes's departure for the Moscow Conference.

To add to Truman's increasing distrust of Byrnes and Russia, General Patrick Hurley resigned from his special mission to China with a report that Stalin was hindering Nationalist attempts to occupy Manchuria in favor of Mao's Communists. Hurley further claimed that American diplomats were abetting Soviet strategy. At the same time, Truman learned that Canada had broken up a spy ring aimed at America's atomic technology and that at least one member of the State Department was suspected of having been in league with the Canadian spies. Truman remained calm about these revelations; he knew that there was no great secret to be discovered. But the revelations no doubt made him more receptive when Senator Vandenberg denounced Byrnes's offer on atomic sharing at the Moscow Conference as "another typical American giveaway."

Meeting with Byrnes after his return from Moscow, Truman announced that he disapproved entirely of the secretary's approach. Eastern European governments would not be recognized until they had become truly representative, the president said. He bewailed Soviet pressure on Turkey and Iran and proclaimed he was "tired of babying the Soviets."

It is clear from recently opened Soviet and east European archives that, at this point, Stalin was still anxious to cooperate at least temporarily with the Allies so long as he could do so without endangering his control of his security sphere in eastern Europe and Asia. Also he was determined to build up his atomic and industrial power for the contest he believed was inevitable between the Communist and capitalist world. On February 9, 1946, he made a public speech calling for a series of five-year plans aimed at a rapid military-industrial buildup and referring to the wartime alliance as a thing of the past. This address shocked many American leaders. Supreme Court justice William O. Douglas called it a declaration of World War III. Equally alarmed, the State Department asked George Kennan, its foremost expert on Russia, for an explanation of Soviet policy. Kennan wired an 8,000-word reply from Moscow that came to be known as the Long Telegram.

Kennan told American leaders in Washington that their policy to date had been built on a false assumption. Americans assumed that Soviet conduct could be affected by outside influences. Thus Roosevelt had thought the USSR could be won to cooperation by open-handedness. Byrnes had sought to alter Soviet policies by horse-trading. Actually, Kennan said, Soviet foreign policy was dictated by internal necessities so strong that nothing but the threat of force could limit or alter Soviet ambitions. The Soviets' Marxist-Leninist persuasion made them inevitably hostile and suspicious of the West, and nothing the United States could do would alter that. More important, Russian leaders knew no other way to govern their people than by a heavy-handed dictatorship. They needed to conjure up an external threat to justify the suffering they imposed upon their people.

Kennan was not terribly clear about how the United States should deal with Soviet behavior. His program, developed over the next year, would culminate in what came to be called the doctrine of containment. But one implication stood out: the United States should cease offering concessions to win Stalin's confidence. The United States had a perfect right to resent and denounce Soviet conduct in the areas controlled by the Red Army, but neither threats nor concessions would change that conduct. All the United States could do was draw a line around the Soviet sphere and put itself in a position to resist any further Soviet penetration. The American people had to be alerted to the situation and rallied to support a long, difficult effort to contain Communist expansion.

Kennan was relatively optimistic about the outcome if this policy were followed. He would argue over the coming year that the Soviet regime was cautious and weakened by World War II. Therefore it would not challenge the American position at the risk of all-out war. If the Soviet regime could be contained for a while, it would inevitably mellow or be overthrown, for no people could sustain its intensity or bear its oppressiveness for an extended period of time. (When the Soviet Union and its empire collapsed some forty-five years later, many people congratulated Kennan on his prediction. He declined the honor with the confession that he had anticipated the collapse within just a few years.)

Kennan's Long Telegram received an enthusiastic welcome throughout much of the American government. Byrnes, already pushed toward a stronger line by Truman, abandoned his quid pro quo approach and adopted a program of "patience and firmness." Government officials began to publicize their quarrels with the Soviets for the first time. Truman invited former British prime minister Winston Churchill to the United States to speak on Soviet policy and sat on the speaker's platform at Westminster College in Fulton, Missouri, on March 5, 1946, as Churchill warned that the Russians had dropped an "iron curtain" around the territories they had conquered. Byrnes and Truman had gone over Churchill's speech beforehand, but Truman was not yet ready to associate himself fully with Churchill's draconian view of the Soviet threat or with his suggestion of an Anglo-American "fraternal association" to counter it. Consequently, Truman denied that he had known what Churchill was going to say.

Public opinion began to push Truman in Churchill's direction, however, when the Canadian spy scandal burst into the headlines. A crisis in Iran also came to a head only days after Churchill's speech. Iran had long been an arena of competition between Great Britain and Russia because it controlled access to the Persian Gulf. The discovery of oil in Iran in the early twentieth century added to that nation's value. In the 1920s, the British government obtained majority control of the Anglo-Iranian Oil Company, which monopolized exploitation of the oil fields of southern Iran. The shah of Iran, the former commander of Iran's armed forces who seized control on the eve of World War II, began to look to Germany to counter the overwhelming British presence in southern Iran and continuous Russian pressure on the northern border. When the British and the Russians became allies in 1941, they forestalled Germany by occupying Iran and deposing the shah in favor of his son. The United States joined the occupation in order to use the major Iranian railroad as a means of getting lend-lease aid into Russia. Because the Americans worried that Great Britain or the Soviet Union might try to make their occupations permanent, the United States instigated a treaty in 1942 that committed all occupying powers to withdraw their troops within six months after the end of the war.

The young shah, Mohammad Reza Pahlavi, saw the opportunity to use the United States as a permanent counterweight against Britain and Russia. The Soviets were especially troublesome. They restricted travel in their northern zone of occupation, encouraged dissident ethnic and religious groups against the new shah's central government, and hindered the movement of the Iranian army to suppress these dissidents. In hopes of checking the Russians, the shah requested the American government to send advisers to Iran and invited American oil companies to seek concessions. The United States complied, but it was more interested in keeping Iran as a strong buffer for America's existing oil concessions in Saudi Arabia than in acquiring new ones in Iran. Consequently, Roosevelt agreed to Churchill's proposal in 1944 that the United States would not make "sheep's eyes" at Iranian oil, while the British would stay away from Saudi Arabia. To check the Russians, the United States and Britain then supported the shah's decision to defer any new Iranian concessions until after the war. All occupation troops would be withdrawn by then, and the shah would be able to resist demands for concessions from Iran's near and feared neighbor to the north.

The Russians accepted the deferment of oil concessions with bad grace. Ominous troop movements and heavy-handed propaganda roused Iranian, British, and American fears that the Soviet army would not leave Iran as it had promised. These fears were justified. The British and Americans withdrew their troops before the March 2 deadline, except for a few American advisers asked to stay by the Iranian government. The Soviets, however, announced that their troops would remain "pending examination of the situation." Even more frightening, these troops were deployed for full-scale combat. Byrnes angrily decided to give it to the Soviets "with both barrels." He personally joined the Iranian delegation at the United Nations to denounce the Soviet deployment in northern Iran. The Russian ambassador indignantly walked out of the UN deliberations, but the Soviet government did finally withdraw its troops.

Truman and many American leaders now believed they had the key to dealing with Russia—firmness. Acting on this assumption, Truman took a hard line in 1946 when Russia sent an ultimatum to Turkey demanding joint control of the Dardanelles. "We might as well find out whether the Russians are bent on world conquest, now as in five or ten years," he declared. As in the Iranian crisis, the Americans registered a harsh protest. More important, they dispatched a naval task force to the eastern Mediterranean that quickly became a permanent presence in the area. Again the Soviets failed to follow up their threats.

Meanwhile, the Americans moved to shore up their line in Western Europe. At a meeting of foreign ministers in Paris, Byrnes tried one more test of Russian intentions by offering a four-power treaty that would guarantee German demilitarization for twenty-five years. If the Russians truly were motivated by security rather than ambition, Byrnes assumed they would accept this, because it would eliminate the fear of another German invasion and the need for a security zone in eastern Europe; but Molotov turned it down. The United States then began to unite the western zones of Germany and integrate them into the Western European economy. The commander of the American occupation troops had halted reparation payments from the American zone in May 1946, although he had aimed his action more at France than at the Soviets. Byrnes extended the ban on reparations and approved a merger of the American and British zones to take effect on January 1, 1947. Since this so-called Bizonia was expected to establish its own economic rules and currency, it was a significant move away from joint control with the USSR over a unified Germany. At the same time that Byrnes consolidated the western sphere, he moved toward acceptance of Russian domination over its own sphere. Byrnes and his advisers thought there might be less contention between the Soviets and Americans if they disengaged from as many common problems and joint enterprises as possible. At the foreign ministers' conference in Paris in October 1946, Byrnes signed the final peace treaties that recognized the legitimacy of the governments of Rumania, Bulgaria, Finland, and Hungary, while Molotov did the same for Italy. Truman made it clear, however, that he did not intend this recognition to signify a softer line toward Russia. After this Paris peace conference, he accepted Byrnes's resignation. He had already fired Henry Wallace from his position as secretary of commerce for making a speech critical of the hard line toward Russia, a speech that Truman had inexplicably approved before Wallace delivered it.

Throughout 1946, the United States was also trying to devise a safe plan for international control of atomic energy. American leaders recognized the dangers of a nuclear arms race. They were ready to give up the American atomic monopoly if they could be assured that a peaceful, stable world would result, but they were increasingly distrustful of Soviet goals. If the Soviets really intended to take over Western Europe, there was little in the way of conventional military forces to stop them. The U.S. Army, which had consisted of 12 million men at the end of the war, had dwindled to 3 million by mid-1946 and would be down to 1.5 million a year later. Western Europe was devastated and nearly bankrupt. Even though Stalin was reducing the size of his Red Army, the West was demobilizing even faster and could not provide the forces necessary to balance the Soviet forces in or near eastern Europe. World War II had already demonstrated to the satisfaction of most American leaders that American security was dependent upon a balance of power in Europe. What but the atomic bomb stood in the way of the Russian forces?

The American government's scientific advisers tried to counter such strategic thinking. Led by J. Robert Oppenheimer, they placed first priority on avoiding a nuclear arms race rather than defending Europe against what might turn out to be a nonexistent threat. They knew that the USSR could not be far from developing its own bomb, so they drew up a simple, direct plan for turning atomic energy over to the United Nations. Dean Acheson and David Lilienthal, who were in charge of devising an American plan for international control of atomic energy, were less sanguine. They wanted the turnover to go through four stages, with inspections after each one to ensure that no nation was concealing a potential nuclear threat. In this process, the UN would survey all sources of radioactive ores and atomic industrial facilities before the United States would actually turn over its bombs and technology. The Americans realized that these inspections might deter Soviet acceptance of the plan because the United States could wait until the survey had been completed and all Russia's military secrets had been exposed, and then find an excuse to refuse to turn over the bomb itself. Regardless, Acheson and Lilienthal thought inspection was necessary. Besides, if the Soviets were willing to make such concessions, it would indicate that they did not really have aggressive intentions in Western Europe or elsewhere so the United States would be justified in abandoning its atomic monopoly.

After Acheson and Lilienthal had formulated their plan, Byrnes and Truman appointed Bernard Baruch to present it to the United Nations. Baruch had an inflated reputation as an astute, experienced adviser to past presidents, and Byrnes counted on Baruch's clout to win public and congressional approval for atomic sharing. Baruch agreed with General Leslie Groves that America's atomic monopoly would be long-lasting and that the United States should demand a great price for giving it up. He insisted on adding a provision to the Acheson-Lilienthal plan that would prevent any great power from exercising a veto over actions the UN might take to enforce the atomic agreement. (He and Groves actually visualized a UN force with the power to drop atomic bombs on any nation violating the UN accords.) Baruch also insisted that the plan should be offered to Russia and the UN on a take-it-or-leave-it basis. There would be no compromises and no negotiations. Byrnes complained later that the appointment of Baruch had been his greatest mistake.

Debate on the Baruch plan in the UN dragged on until the end of 1946. Finally, as might have been predicted, the Soviets rejected it. Probably they would have spurned any plan and continued to build their own bomb, but the Baruch plan afforded little real chance to assess their intentions. With the failure of the Baruch plan, the United States had committed itself to a strategy that depended on American nuclear superiority to offset Russia's superior conventional forces in Europe. But the full ramifications of such a strategy were not yet clear to most American leaders, military or civilian. The secrets of the atomic program were closely held within the government; even the Joint Chiefs of Staff did not know that, as of 1947, the United States possessed only about a dozen bombs. In fact, those few bombs were unassembled, and the firing mechanism for them had never been tested. The United States was not adding much to this arsenal either, because after the war most of the personnel involved in the project had left the military for civilian life.

Thus ignorant about the United States' atomic arsenal, the Joint Chiefs could make only vague and unrealistic war plans. In early 1947, American planning was still based on the presumption that war with Great Britain was as likely as war with the USSR. If war did break out with the Soviets, the Joint Chiefs of Staff assumed that the United States would use the atomic bomb on some twenty Russian cities and the Russian oil fields in the Caucasus. Yet many of the twenty targeted cities were out of range of American bombers. The Joint Chiefs also had to acknowledge that bombing would do nothing to stop the Russian army from overrunning Europe. They planned to evacuate the American occupation troops in Germany, Austria, and Trieste rather than order them to stand and fight against hopeless odds. Ironically, the military did not have the transportation facilities to carry out the evacuation part of the plan either.

Containment of the Red Army in Europe thus rested essentially on the psychological threat of the bomb rather than any true Western military capacity. Truman and many other Americans were relatively content with this. As long as the United States had its atomic monopoly, even the vague menace of such a powerful weapon seemed a cheap, effective way to counter the Russian threat to Europe. With America's fears of a postwar depression and the desire for reduced taxes, there was strong sentiment for avoiding large military expenditures. Officials like George Kennan, who became director of policy planning for the State Department in mid-1947, regarded the primary Russian threat as political rather than military in any case. Kennan thought the United States should concentrate on bolstering the economic and political systems of the Western European nations as the best defense against political subversion, which he saw as a far more likely Russian tactic than overt military invasion.

George C. Marshall, Byrnes's successor as secretary of state, played a crucial role in promoting American acceptance of Kennan's policy of containment. Marshall no sooner assumed office than he was faced with what seemed to be a major crisis. The British announced that they were no longer financially able to support the Greek government in its civil war against Communist rebels. Both Great Britain and the United States assumed that the rebels were being encouraged by the Soviet Union as part of Russia's expansionist program. Actually, many of the rebels were motivated by opposition to the foreign-born King Paul I, who was supported by Greek right-wing forces and the British. Other rebels were simply involved in a traditional Greek vendetta, based on old family and regional feuds and exacerbated by the brutalities of all sides during and after the war.[3] In fact, although the West did not understand at the time, Stalin was urging Yugoslavia to stop giving sanctuary and arms to the rebels.

Nevertheless, Truman and Marshall saw the British withdrawal from Greece as a serious matter. They had known for some time that Britain's financial weakness might occasion such a retreat. The United States had already loaned the British $3.75 billion to help them cope with their financial emergency and had also decided to give some aid to Greece. Still, American government leaders were surprised by the abruptness of the British decision and galvanized into action by it.

Truman went before Congress to request $300 million for Greece. While he was at it, he asked $100 million more for Turkey. Fearful of residual isolationism and antitax sentiment in the Republican-controlled Congress, the president defined the issue in stark terms. The struggle in Greece was only part of a global struggle between alternative ways of life, he said. The United States must "support free peoples who are resisting attempted subjugation by armed minorities or by outside pressure." The press quickly dubbed this proclamation the Truman Doctrine.

While Truman announced his doctrine, Secretary of State George Marshall was in Moscow with the other big-power foreign ministers trying to complete the peace treaties for Germany and Austria. He had gone into the conference with the conviction that he could not really negotiate with the Russians—"It is either yield to them or tell them 'no,'" one briefing paper had advised him. Russian conduct at the conference confirmed him in that belief. The Soviets repeatedly insisted upon $10 billion worth of reparations in their usual negotiating style, "the same fruitless arguments about minor matters, the same distortions and the same blaring propaganda," according to Marshall. The secretary and his advisers assumed that the reparations demands actually were an attempt to divert resources from Germany and Western Europe, aimed at keeping both areas weak and preparing the way for a Communist upheaval and Russian takeover.

The Americans said no to reparations. They would continue their course toward a divided Germany. And once it was clear to Stalin that he was not going to receive reparations from the western parts of Germany or aid from the United States, he too was ready to accept a divided Germany. Neither Stalin nor the West could afford to see a unified Germany throw its weight to the wrong side, and neither trusted the other not to make an attempt to win over Germany once unification was an accomplished fact. In the absence of mutual confidence, a divided Germany was safer for both sides. Since both sides assumed, however, that the German people would support whichever nation could guarantee them a reunified country, neither wanted to be seen by the Germans as responsible for a permanent division. Thus the United States later refused recognition of East Germany even when, during the various Berlin crises, it understood that the question threatened to bring Europe to the verge of nuclear war.

Marshall returned from the Moscow Conference with nothing settled except his conviction that the Soviets wanted to bring about the disintegration of Western Europe. That disintegration already seemed well on its way by early 1947. Wheat production was only half what it had been in 1938. The diet of people in some areas of Germany had fallen as low as 900 calories a day. Supplies of coal were dwindling. Inflation had boosted wholesale prices in France some 80 percent. When Great Britain had made its pound sterling convertible to dollars, a rush of investors from pounds to dollars had undermined the British economy. The United States had loaned Britain $3.75 billion and France $600 million, but obviously more was needed. America had an economic as well as a strategic stake in offering aid: the United States had an export surplus of $12.5 billion, and Europe was running out of money to buy American goods.

On June 5, 1947, America's secretary of state, speaking at Harvard University, outlined what would be known as the Marshall Plan. The United States would offer some $20 billion for European relief if the European nations themselves would devise a rational, integrated plan for the recovery of the area as a whole, including West Germany. Surprisingly, Marshall also offered to extend the aid to the Soviet Union and its eastern European satellites. This offer was strictly a ruse designed to avoid the appearance that the United States was responsible for the division of Europe. Marshall and his advisers hoped that the strings America attached to the aid would cause the Soviets to reject it. Marshall was afraid the Soviets would sabotage European negotiations for an integrated plan and that the U.S. Congress would reject the plan if it included large grants to Russia.

The gamble worked. The Soviets were not about to make the economic disclosures necessary to joint planning or permit the Americans to judge the uses to which they would put the aid. Neither would they integrate their economy and that of eastern Europe into the much stronger economy of the West and subject their citizens to the lure of American abundance. When the Americans rejected the Russian proposal that each nation draw up its own plan and request aid individually, the Soviets abandoned the conference and ordered their satellites to do likewise.

The Western European nations went ahead to formulate a plan for the economic recovery of the region as a whole, including West Germany. Congress then demonstrated its support of the Marshall Plan by granting $600 million in interim funds. Once the plan was officially prepared, Congress appropriated $4 billion for the first year of operation in 1948. By 1952 the United States had contributed $13 billion to the near-miraculous revival of the Western European economy.

From the Marshall Plan to the War in Korea: The Hardening of Containment

The Truman Doctrine and the Marshall Plan formed the keystones of what came to be known as the policy of containment. The word "containment" was derived from an article published in the prestigious journal *Foreign Affairs* and signed by Mr. X. Enterprising journalists quickly discovered that Mr. X was George Kennan, director of policy planning for the State Department. Thus the article seemed a semiofficial rationale for the policy embodied in the Truman Doctrine and the Marshall Plan. In this condensed version of his Long Telegram, Kennan reiterated his belief that Russia was driven by its own internal dynamics to conjure up an enemy and expand against it until met by superior force. Since a balance of power in Europe was necessary to America's own security, and since World War II had destroyed the ability of Britain, France, and Germany to maintain that balance against Russia, the United States would have to intervene. If this were done, Kennan continued to hold out hopes that the Soviet regime would either mellow or be overthrown from within.

As Kennan would later admit, the article was carelessly phrased and failed to convey the subtleties of his thought. His article spoke of containing Russia at every point it might seek to expand, making no distinction between areas of vital interest and those of marginal interest to the United States. Yet Kennan believed the United States should limit its concern primarily to the major industrial powers of Europe and Japan. Those nations had the capacity to support a significant military force, while many of the governments outside Europe and Japan were neither stable nor popular with their own people and had little real sympathy for Western democratic and moral values. Kennan had been one of the few in the administration to warn against the Truman Doctrine's portrayal of temporary aid to Greece and Turkey as part of a global commitment to defend against communism everywhere.

Likewise, Kennan's article failed to make clear that he believed containment should emphasize economic and political rather than military measures. Kennan thought that an overt Soviet military invasion was unlikely. The Russians were hurt and cautious. Even though their army might be able to sweep over Europe, they would be unable to digest the Western European nations, and they knew it. Their more likely tactic was political and economic subversion that would prepare Western Europe for a more peaceful takeover.

Finally, Kennan's article portrayed containment as a justifiably hostile policy toward Soviet aggression and tyranny. Certainly it was hostile. But it also was predicated on some assumptions the Russians could have been expected to welcome. Containment implied the concession of the Soviet sphere, which probably had been Stalin's primary goal all along. In later years, Kennan would emphasize this more positive side of containment and regret that it had been hardened into a rigid prescription for fighting a Cold War. On the other hand, he had emphasized the shamefulness of the United States having to abandon the eastern Europeans to Russian tyranny and he supported extensive covert operations behind the Iron Curtain intended to weaken Soviet control of its sphere.[4]

Walter Lippmann, the prominent and respected columnist, wrote a highly publicized critique of the Mr. X article making many of these same points. Kennan writhed privately. He wanted desperately to answer and clarify his essential agreement with many of Lippmann's arguments, but in mid-1947 it did not seem that these subtle distinctions would turn out to be so important. Containment was pursued in a limited, flexible manner. The emphasis was political and economic, rather than military. Marshall's undersecretary of state, Dean Acheson, told a congressional committee that the Truman Doctrine did not mean an automatic American commitment to any nation on the globe resisting communism. Each situation would be evaluated independently, and aid would be primarily economic and political.

Acheson's words were borne out by the generous flow of Marshall Plan dollars to the major industrial powers of Europe, while aid to Chiang Kai-shek in China was severely limited. The State Department was still flexible enough to recognize that Mao Zedong did not represent as great a threat to American interests as Russia did in Europe. It was also flexible enough to extend aid to Tito's Communist regime in Yugoslavia when Tito showed in 1948 that he was resisting Stalin's dictates.

These subtle limitations on containment were fragile, however, and no one is quite sure how clearly Kennan himself held to them, let alone the other members of the government. Such restraint and flexibility could not survive the shocking events of the next two years—the Soviet crackdown on Czechoslovakia, the Berlin blockade, the triumph of Mao in China, the explosion of the first Russian atomic bomb, the exposure of the Soviet spy ring that penetrated the American atomic bomb project, the exploitation of the Communist spy issue by U.S. senator Joseph McCarthy, and the North Korean invasion of South Korea. Steadily the United States moved toward a more militant version of containment that seemed at the time to be a natural extension of Kennan's policy rather than a violation of it. Any doubts Kennan expressed were drowned out by the rising accusations of many Americans, especially Republicans, that containment was an immoral, cowardly policy that was soft on communism.

Kennan and Marshall had expected the Soviets to react strongly against the Marshall Plan, but the extent and violence of that reaction surprised them. First, the Soviets forced the nations they had warned away from the Marshall Plan to sign a series of trade treaties they called the Molotov Plan. These treaties ensured that the satellite economies remained oriented away from the West toward the USSR. Stalin also revived the Communist Information Bureau (Cominform) to coordinate the strategy of the Communist parties of Europe. Through it, he ordered the Italian and French parties to cease collaboration with the bourgeois regimes in power. The French and Italian parties began a series of strikes to disrupt the reviving European economies. Many observers began to fear that the Communists could win the elections to be held in France and Italy in 1948. Truman and Marshall publicly warned that Marshall Plan aid depended on the victory of non-Communist regimes in both nations. As the French and Italian elections loomed with the threat to dismantle the American position in Europe, the United States moved toward a more aggressive political and cultural attack on the Soviet Union.

In a May 1948 memorandum, George Kennan outlined plans for both overt and covert propaganda warfare against Communists on both sides of the Iron Curtain. The Central Intelligence Agency (CIA) and the State Department would secretly fund anti-Communist labor movements and political parties in Western Europe, organize political exiles from eastern Europe and the Soviet Union to propagandize against communism, spread that propaganda with radio and films, and even support active guerrilla forces in eastern Europe in violation of Kennan's own advocacy for mere containment as opposed to rollback of the Soviet sphere.

Many of these projects came to grief. A CIA operation to air-drop antigovernment agents into Albania was betrayed to the Soviets by the British spy Kim Philby to deadly effect. CIA-subsidized attempts by the American Federation of Labor (AFL) and the Congress of Industrial Organizations (CIO) to support anti-Communist unions in Europe failed to dislodge the Communists from fairly complete control of the unions in France and Italy. But massive CIA subsidies to French and Italian non-Communist parties did succeed in helping them defeat the Communist parties in the elections of 1948, the elections Truman and Marshall had warned would decide the fate of the Marshall Plan.

American culture, as represented by Hollywood, played an important part in the 1948 electoral defeats of the Communists in France and Italy. American films were immensely popular in Europe. Italians bought 1.6 million movie tickets per day in 1948, and most of those were for American films. The United States Information Service had five offices in Italy, each with at least 100 film titles that were shown on mobile American equipment to 100,000 Italians each month. The most successful of these films was *Ninotchka*, in which Greta Garbo played a Russian who discovers that the West means love, freedom, and prosperity while the Soviet Union is humorously lampooned as drab, dictatorial, and fear-ridden. Although the Roman Catholic Church probably played a greater role in the defeat of the Italian Communists than anything the United States did, an Italian Communist functionary was heard to lament, "What licked us was Ninotchka." (Later, in 1953, Italian laborers in France accepted the Communist Party's suggestion that they take a day off in honor of the death of Stalin, but also they defied the party's wishes by similarly commemorating the death of Hollywood actor Humphrey Bogart.)[5]

Perhaps, however, the most important factor in the defeat of the French and Italian Communist parties in 1948 was not the Vatican, the CIA, or Hollywood, but Stalin's brutal suppression of the relatively independent Czechoslovakian regime. The Western-oriented foreign minister, Jan Masaryk, fell to his death from a small bathroom window in a high building while in custody of the Russians. The Soviets proclaimed the death a suicide, but the most thorough investigation to date concludes that Masaryk was murdered. Masaryk's death was just the beginning of a series of purges, show trials, and mass executions in eastern Europe that continued until Stalin's death in 1953. These, along with the Western Communist parties' opposition to Marshall Plan aid, did a great deal to discredit communism in Western Europe.

They also did a great deal to frighten the West. With American encouragement, Great Britain organized a mutual defense pact that included itself, France, Belgium, the Netherlands, and Luxembourg. This Brussels Pact of March 17, 1948, proclaimed that an attack on one member would be an attack on all. It anticipated that both western Germany and the United States would be incorporated into the arrangement, and the American Senate quickly expressed its approval by passing the Vandenberg Resolution. America's revolutionary decision to sign an entangling alliance with European powers paved the way for the expansion of the Brussels Pact into the North Atlantic Treaty Organization (NATO) in April 1949. NATO incorporated the United States, Canada, Turkey, and Greece along with the original Brussels Pact members.

The original purpose of the Brussels Pact and NATO, however, was not a significant military buildup, but rather a political and spiritual rallying against the possibility of Soviet aggression. The Soviet army, which reversed its decline in 1948 and began a major rebuilding, was vastly superior to the combined American, British, and French forces, and Western intelligence reports assumed that Russia could sweep through all of Western Europe in a few weeks. Yet for the time being, the United States and its allies did little to build up their conventional capacity to resist. It was clear that beyond the spiritual rallying of the NATO alliance and the economic and political revival brought about by the Marshall Plan, the military defense of Europe rested with America's atomic deterrent.

Yet the United States had little capacity to carry out its assigned part. The Czech crisis caught the United States still without an operational war plan, an adequate supply of bombs, or bombers capable of reaching their targets in the Soviet Union. A breakthrough in technology in early 1948 increased the supply of bombs, so that at the end of the year the United States could plan to retaliate against a Russian attack by obliterating seventy

Russian cities with 133 bombs. But the delivery capability was still in doubt. In a mock raid on Dayton, Ohio, in 1948, not a single bomber got through.

The navy and air force urged Truman to undertake massive rearmament programs to correct this deficiency. The air force wanted to build some seventy air groups shaped around the new B-36 bomber. These bombing groups would be stationed on bases the United States would acquire from its allies around the periphery of the Soviet Union. The navy wanted to build supercarriers that would carry smaller atomic bombers within striking range of Russia.

Truman resisted all these rearmament programs. He was not certain atomic bombs could actually be used in warfare. If they were dropped on the Russians, they would not stop a Red Army invasion of Europe, and the horror they inflicted would make the Russians too angry ever to accept a compromise settlement short of total victory or defeat. An atomic bomb could not be dropped on the invading force because it would destroy the very nations America was trying to protect. The cost of building a conventional force that might oppose the Russians without use of the atomic alternative seemed astronomical, especially when added to the navy and air force plans to make the atomic alternative workable in the first place. Finally, Truman was determined to hold the defense budget under $15 billion in order to maintain a healthy domestic economy during the difficult postwar adjustment.

Thus, more by default than by careful planning, the United States and its European allies continued to depend on economic and political measures to contain Russia. As late as April 1949, when the NATO Pact was signed, there was no specific provision to incorporate the American atomic umbrella in the defense of Western Europe.

The Soviet blockade of Berlin that began on June 24, 1948, highlighted the significance and vagueness of that atomic umbrella. The Western occupying powers had given up any real attempt to establish a cooperative four-power rule in Germany by the end of 1946. They were convinced the Soviets would simply stall discussion and action until either the German economy crumbled or the Russians were given $10 billion in reparations. The United States was not about to pour Marshall Plan aid into Germany so Russia could drain it out either in reparations or by buying aid products with inflated occupation currency that the Soviets could print without limit. Instead, the Americans, British, and French combined their zones and established a separate currency to stop the inflation, hoarding, and Soviet purchases of goods going to western Germany. They further incorporated the German economy into the Marshall Plan for all of Western Europe and permitted a German assembly to begin work on a constitution for a separate West Germany. To assuage French fears of this revived Germany, the United States promised to keep occupation troops in Germany indefinitely.

The Soviet Union responded that if Germany was indeed going to be divided, then the rationale for four-power occupation in West Berlin no longer existed. Since the city was deep in the Russian zone, the Soviets announced they would no longer permit overland travel to Berlin from the West. They also cut off West Berlin's electricity. Truman considered this a direct violation of American rights, but was chagrined to find that there was no written agreement guaranteeing Western access by road or rail. Some military leaders proposed sending an armed column to defend the earlier oral arrangements. Truman decided instead to try to supply Berlin by plane through the air corridors that were guaranteed in writing. With a plane touching down at Tempelhof Airport every ninety seconds, the resulting airlift succeeded in bringing in more supplies than the 2 million inhabitants of West Berlin actually needed.

To reinforce this signal of American determination, Truman negotiated an agreement with Great Britain permitting the United States to station B-29s on its soil within striking distance of Russia's major cities. In a great show of force, Truman sent sixty B-29s to British airfields. It was all bluff. America's atomic bombs were kept at home, disassembled and under civilian control. Besides, most of the planes had not been modified to carry atomic bombs, despite Truman's statement that they were "atomic capable."

Some historians have believed that this atomic threat was the primary factor in Stalin's ultimate decision to lift the Berlin blockade. But it is now clear that Russian spies, like the British diplomat Donald MacLean, were in a position to know that Truman was bluffing. Stalin seems to have lifted the blockade instead because it was costing him more than he was gaining. The blockade frightened Western Europe into greater unity, added to the discredit the Western Communist parties had suffered from the Czech crisis, and led to a counterblockade that denied East Germany supplies from the West. It also helped drive American occupation in Japan to concentrate on recovery rather than reform so Japan could contribute to the anti-Soviet economic bloc. In May 1949, almost a year after Stalin had announced the Berlin blockade, he gave it up. Meanwhile, the blockade had solidified German public opinion on the side of the Allies, so that any free election held in a united Germany would be sure to favor the Western powers.

American relief at the end of the Berlin blockade was short-lived. In September 1949, an American plane detected traces of radioactivity from a Russian atomic explosion. America's atomic monopoly had ended. How would the U.S. atomic umbrella defend Europe against superior Russian conventional forces if the Soviets acquired an equal atomic capacity to retaliate? American scientists like Edward Teller and Ernest Lawrence proposed an answer. The United States could maintain its nuclear superiority by building a hydrogen bomb, a bomb so powerful that the atomic bomb would be a mere trigger to set it off.

Other scientists, including J. Robert Oppenheimer, objected. They argued not that a hydrogen bomb was impossible to build, but that it would wipe out humanity. George Kennan wrote an eighty-page paper and numerous memos for the administration incorporating this scientific objection with his political objections. He saw no political use for the hydrogen bomb; it could only annihilate. There were only a couple of targets in all of Russia that could not be obliterated by a single smaller atomic bomb. Kennan argued that the United States would be better off renouncing first use of the atomic bomb and seeking solid international controls. This strategy might leave Western Europe somewhat vulnerable to an invasion by the superior Russian army, but better that than to rely on a weapon that could not be used without endangering the very existence of humankind. Even if the United States built the hydrogen bomb, the USSR would soon have it too. Then America would face the same dilemma, but at an even more ominous level of potential destruction.

The USSR had no intention of invading Western Europe anyway, Kennan argued; containment had succeeded. Now it was time to think of negotiations aimed at a mutual guarantee of European neutrality and withdrawal of most foreign troops from Europe. The Soviet crackdown on Czechoslovakia and the Berlin blockade indeed had been vicious, but they had been defensive attempts to shore up the Russian sphere in the face of the Marshall Plan and the rebuilding of an independent West Germany. A negotiated withdrawal might be possible. If such negotiations failed, the United States could build up a conventional force with NATO to deter a Russian invasion. Prior to negotiations, however, the United States should avoid militarizing containment; it should not build the H-bomb or a powerful NATO army.

Dean Acheson, who had replaced George Marshall as Truman's secretary of state, did not agree. He saw the United States as operating from a position of weakness rather than strength. He did not trust talks with the Russians and thought that the United States should build a superior force before opening any negotiations. America should base its military plans on the Soviet Union's capacity, not its intentions. If the Soviets developed a hydrogen bomb when the United States did not have it, this would be a terrible blow to the courage and morale of America and Western Europe. (In fact, we now know the Russians already had begun work on their H-bomb.) So Acheson withheld Kennan's analytical paper from Truman and other presidential advisers. In a seven-minute meeting, Truman made his decision to go ahead with the H-bomb.

Kennan's paper was unlikely to have changed Truman's mind anyway. The political atmosphere was poisoned by the trial and conviction of diplomat Alger Hiss for lying about his membership in the Communist Party and by the arrest of atomic physicist Klaus Fuchs as a Soviet agent who had revealed secrets of the atomic bomb to Stalin. Shortly afterward, Senator Joseph McCarthy of Wisconsin proclaimed that he had a list of 205 Soviet spies who were working in the State Department with Acheson's knowledge.[6] Truman feared the political consequences if the Soviets exploded a hydrogen bomb and it was revealed that he had decided not to build one.

Truman accompanied his decision to build the H-bomb with an order for a thorough study of America's entire strategic program, a study that was embodied in the National Security Council's (NSC) Memorandum 68. NSC-68 was written by Kennan's successor as head of policy planning for the State Department, Paul Nitze. It conformed to Acheson's insistence that the United States plan to counter the Soviet Union's capabilities rather than its intentions. It defined American national security in global terms. NSC-68 called for U.S. military power capable of responding to any Russian threat anywhere in the world. Finally, NSC-68 urged that the United States build a greater conventional warfare capacity in addition to increasing its nuclear power. NSC-68 would require a defense budget of between $30 billion and $50 billion, double or triple the $15 billion to which Truman was already committed. Truman's economic advisers insisted that America could afford the increase because government spending would boost economic productivity and generate more tax revenue, but Truman withheld approval of NSC-68 pending firmer financial estimates. It would take another foreign policy shock, the North Korean invasion of South Korea, to drive the United States to the fully militarized containment visualized in NSC-68.

The Cold War in East Asia

On October 1, 1949, one month after the United States had detected the Soviet atomic explosion, the Chinese Communists celebrated their victory over the Nationalists by announcing the formation of the People's Republic of China. Although the American State Department had expected Chiang Kai-shek's defeat since mid-1948, the flight of Chiang and his army to the island of Taiwan still came as a shock. But the "fall" of China did not immediately eliminate all flexibility in America's policy toward East Asia. The "old China hands" of the state department, like O. Edmund Clubb, John S. Service, and John Paton Davies, had recognized and reported the corruption and fragility of Chiang's rule and knew his fall was inevitable if he did not reform his regime. His Nationalist government had relied heavily on landowners, military warlords, and the urban commercial community. After 1927 Chiang had alienated the Communist wing of the Nationalist revolution by slaughtering all the Communists he could find. In the 1930s, the Japanese invasion pushed him and his armies into the countryside and forced him to abandon his supporters among the urban bankers and middle classes who stayed behind in the Japanese-occupied cities. Finally, the remnant of the Chinese Communists that had survived the Long March to escape Chiang's purge had won the support of Chinese patriots by a more vigorous prosecution of the war against the Japanese. With land reform and promises of industrial modernization, the Communists gained support among the peasants and the urban population. They kept that support with an efficient government organization.

Stalin had lived up to his Yalta promises to recognize Chiang's government, but he had prevented Nationalist troops from landing at Darien and Port Arthur to occupy Manchuria. Instead he had permitted the Communists to disarm the Japanese in Manchuria, claiming he thought the Communist troops were part of Chiang's army. Then he had reversed himself abruptly and welcomed the Nationalists into the remainder of Manchuria. Obviously he was more interested in keeping China weak and distracted by civil conflict than in aiding Mao Zedong, and the Chinese Communists strongly resented this action. America's "old China hands" knew that Mao would still remain friendlier to the Soviets than to the Americans, but they thought he would retain sufficient distrust of Russia to accept some American support as a check to Soviet influence. They urged that diplomatic channels to the Communists be kept open.

By and large, Truman's State Department followed their advice. In late 1945, shortly after taking office, Truman had sent George Marshall to arrange a coalition government between Chiang and Mao. Marshall had failed. Mao was not about to give up his arms and accept a secondary office under Chiang, as Marshall proposed. Mao remembered too well Chiang's earlier purge of the Communists and his continuing hostility toward the Communists during the war with Japan. Chiang also was adamant against accepting Communists in his government. He rejected Marshall's warning that he was likely to lose a civil war. Ultimately, the Communists withdrew from the talks, Marshall flew home to become secretary of state, and the Chinese civil war resumed.

Despite the disgust of Marshall, Acheson, and most of the State Department with Chiang, they were not willing to abandon him. They still feared Stalin's connection with

Mao, and they believed they still had some leverage over the Communists. Even if Mao defeated Chiang, America's China hands thought Mao would have as many difficulties governing the unwieldy Chinese nation as Chiang and his predecessors. In order to hold China together and maintain some independence from Russia, Mao would need American help. Thus they hoped that America would not have to abandon Chiang or woo Mao in order to have reasonable relations with a victorious Communist regime.

This restrained policy was soon eclipsed by partisan politics. The Truman administration was facing increasing political pressure to do more to fight communism in China. Members of Congress with ties to Chinese missionary and merchant circles—the China Lobby—were urging more aid for Chiang. The Republican Party, stung by its unexpected defeat in the 1948 elections and seeing the loss of China as an attractive campaign issue to use against the Democrats, threatened to hold up aid to Europe unless aid to Nationalist China was included. Many American military leaders also were urging more aid to Chiang. They did not want American troops sent to China, but once Chiang had escaped to Taiwan, they wanted an American fleet stationed off the China coast to prevent a Communist invasion from the mainland. Finally, Senator Joseph McCarthy began to revive Patrick Hurley's old charges that disloyal State Department advisers were responsible for the "loss of China." This particularly hurt Dean Acheson, who had announced after Alger Hiss's conviction for perjury that he would not abandon him.

Under this political pressure, Truman, Marshall, and Acheson walked a tightrope in their policy toward China. Limited aid continued to flow to Chiang. The United States delayed recognition of the Communist regime while quarreling with it about the treatment of American diplomats and property in areas conquered by Mao's troops. But Truman did not station the American fleet off Taiwan, and he agreed that the question of China's admission to the United Nations was a procedural rather than a substantive one, which meant it was not subject to an American veto. Meanwhile, Acheson released a mammoth government report, the *China White Paper*, to demonstrate that Chiang himself rather than the Yalta agreement or supposed later betrayals was responsible for the collapse of his regime.

Some later historians wondered whether there might have been a chance to detach Mao from Stalin if the Truman administration had not been prevented from a more accommodating policy toward the Communist victory in China. Recently published transcripts of letters and conversations between Mao and Stalin, however, make it clear that Mao was fully aligned with the Soviets despite his resentment of Stalin's treatment and that there was no real chance of an accommodation with the United States. Mao genuinely feared U.S. attempts to dislodge him and expected conflict sooner or later over his desire to conquer the remnant of the Nationalists on Taiwan.

Acheson and the State Department tried to rearrange America's policy toward the rest of Asia in the light of the Communist conquest of China. Acheson was fearful that another quick Communist takeover elsewhere in Asia might lead to the collapse of all non-Communist regimes in the area. He and Truman sent John Foster Dulles, the most prominent Republican expert on foreign affairs, to negotiate a peace treaty with Japan that would exclude Soviet participation and leave American troops stationed there for the indefinite future.

The Truman administration also began sending direct aid to the French in Indochina for the first time. Until 1950 the administration had looked askance at the French war to maintain its empire in Vietnam against a Communist and nationalist rebellion led by Ho Chi Minh. But the United States had needed French power and cooperation in Europe to help balance the Soviet threat, and Marshall Plan aid had flowed into France even though the Americans knew that some of it was diverted to the war in Vietnam. Then Mao's victory in China made Truman and Acheson vigorous rather than reluctant supporters of the French effort in Indochina. They had no wish to see another Communist victory in that region. Yet Truman irritated the French by urging them to promise independence for Vietnam, since he believed that a truly nationalist regime would be far more likely to resist the Communist advance than the thinly disguised French colonial regime headed by the puppet emperor Bao Dai. But when pressed, the United States would choose French colonialism over Ho Chi Minh's Vietminh.

Acheson spelled out the Truman administration's overall policy toward Asia in a speech he made to the National Press Club on January 12, 1950. Acheson said that the bulk of America's limited resources had to go to the area of primary interest, Europe. In Asia, the United States would use its preeminent naval and air power to defend a ring of islands around the mainland, including the Aleutians, Japan, and the Philippines. He did not include Korea or Taiwan, but he said that rising nationalism would lead China and the other nations of Asia to resist Soviet attempts to take them over. In the unlikely event of an overt invasion beyond America's defense perimeter, the United Nations undoubtedly would aid "people who are determined to protect their independence." Acheson's confidence was about to be tested in Korea.

The Korean War

The Allies had treated Korea as an afterthought during World War II. Japan had formally annexed Korea in 1910 after expelling Russia in the Russo-Japanese War five years before. The Allies did not make arrangements for Korea's occupation until the Soviet Union entered the Pacific war, only days before Japan's surrender. The Soviets and Americans hastily agreed that Russia would temporarily occupy that portion of Korea north of the thirty-eighth parallel, while the United States occupied the south. The United States assumed that Korea would quickly be united and turned over to an indigenous regime, after which both occupying powers would withdraw their troops.

The American occupation commander, General John R. Hodge, soon found that an acceptable Korean government was not so easy to come by. There simply was no easily legitimated government of Korean nationalists available. A group of Koreans who had taken refuge with the Nationalist Chinese during World War II claimed the status of a provisional government, but it had very shallow roots among the Korean people themselves. Another group of Koreans who had stayed to fight the Japanese during the war formed a People's Republic in Seoul and claimed recognition, but Hodge mistakenly believed it was a puppet regime of Russian and Chinese Communists, so he refused to work with it.

The American occupiers found themselves dependent on individual Koreans who could speak English to communicate between the American occupying government and the Korean people. Most of these English-speaking Koreans were elite conservatives or former police officers and collaborators with the Japanese. Naturally they were not terribly popular with many of their countrymen. The most prominent of these right-wing, English-speaking Koreans was Syngman Rhee, who had spent the war in Washington lobbying for himself as leader of a liberated Korea. Rhee, a clever politician with strong ties to the Korean police forces, managed to divide and rule the various conservative factions in South Korea. He used his position to exclude the centrist politicians Hodge was trying to bring into the new parliamentary system. This caused Hodge to explode that Rhee was a pain in the neck. In the midst of the factional squabbles and popular riots that plagued South Korea, the American occupiers made very little progress toward land or economic reform.

The Russians had better luck in their zone. Their occupying army brought Korean Communist exiles with it and installed them as the government of North Korea. The USSR strictly regulated all contact between North Koreans and the outside world, built a strong North Korean army to aid the Red Army in maintaining control, and established an extensive land reform program that won some local support despite the oppressions of the new regime.

As the Russians and Americans sought to build friendly regimes in their own occupation zones, they naturally had difficulty in agreeing how to unify the peninsula. They did sign an agreement, however, that only Koreans willing to accept the temporary trusteeship of the victors in the Asian theater of World War II, including the Soviet Union and the United States, would be permitted to join a provisional government of a unified Korea. The Soviets therefore insisted on the exclusion of Syngman Rhee and other conservatives in southern Korea who were denouncing any trusteeship that included the Soviet Union. The Americans, on the other hand, ignored their previous agreement with the Soviets and called for peninsula-wide elections that would include Rhee and other anti-Soviet politicians. Because two-thirds of Korea's population was in the south and because Rhee, operating with what General Hodge admitted were "Al Capone" methods, might dominate the balloting in the south, the Soviets refused. They seemed willing to accept a neutralist, left-leaning government, but they were not willing to accept an anti-Soviet, right-wing government that might endanger their access to the resources and industry of northern Korea.

When negotiations between the United States and the Soviet Union for a unified Korea broke down, the United States appealed to the United Nations. At that time, the majority of UN members were favorable to the Western powers, so the United States was able to win a call for unifying elections similar to the American plan. When the Soviets rejected the UN plan, the United States and the UN held elections in the south anyway. Many moderates in the south refused to participate because these separate elections would ratify the division of their country. Taking advantage of their abstention, Syngman Rhee won the leadership of the newly formed Republic of Korea in August 1948. By mid-1949 the United States had followed the Soviet Union in withdrawing the last of its occupation troops. This left Rhee's government dependent on an unpopular constabulary with a reputation for collaborating with the Japanese during the war. Worse yet, the U.S. withdrawal left a small, disorganized army accompanied by a few American military advisers to face a well-trained, well-armed North Korean army of more than 150,000 troops. South Korea's weakness did not keep Rhee from claiming that his government was the legitimate ruler of all of Korea. He began to build his military forces and to send raids north of the thirty-eighth parallel.

American officials were not optimistic about the chances for Rhee's regime. They estimated that 30 percent of the people in South Korea supported leftist policies and were sympathetic to the north. Guerrilla activities were a constant source of concern. The Americans doubted the ability of the fractious, bull-headed Rhee to unify South Korea. They were willing to give him only minimal economic and military aid on the slim hope that he might be able to preserve an independent, Western-oriented South Korea. American troops and economic aid were needed too desperately elsewhere, particularly in the more critical theater of Europe, for the United States to be able to afford a massive commitment to Korea.

American military officials especially wanted American troops out of Korea. They believed that the United States could never win a major conflict on the mainland of Asia. Even General Douglas MacArthur, the commander of the occupation of Japan and a lifelong advocate of a strong American policy in Asia, proclaimed that anyone advocating such a war should have his head examined. MacArthur wanted troops stationed in Japan and in the Philippines, the island periphery of the Asian mainland from which the United States could exert its naval and air power. He was disturbed when the troops withdrawn from Korea during the Berlin blockade crisis were earmarked for European rather than Asian-oriented missions. His disagreement with the Truman administration's Europe First policy would soon cause a public uproar.

If the United States was prepared to tolerate a slow erosion of Rhee's position in South Korea, it was not at all prepared to accept the massive North Korean invasion of South Korea that took place in June 1950. But Truman and Acheson did not make clear to Stalin the limits of their tolerance. Stalin had repeatedly rejected the pleas of the North Korean leader Kim Il Sung to allow the North Koreans to invade the south for fear that such an attack would bring conflict with the Americans. But in mid-1950 Kim promised that his military superiority along with the likely support he would receive in South Korea would allow him to triumph quickly before American troops could arrive.[7] Stalin also considered that Acheson's National Press Club speech exempting South Korea from America's defense perimeter indicated that the Americans would not intervene anyway, so he relented. He told Kim that so long as Mao approved, the Soviets would provide military advice, aid, supplies, and air cover. Mao went along with Stalin even though the attack on South Korea might divert China from conquering Taiwan, and Kim launched his invasion.

Truman regarded the North Korean invasion as a direct challenge to American prestige. In shock, members of Truman's administration speculated that the invasion was a Soviet attempt to skirt the containment line the United States had drawn in Europe. Truman was still smarting from his administration's "loss" of China and could not turn away from what he saw as a direct Communist challenge to American credibility. He was already under attack from Joseph McCarthy's crusade against Communists in government, and Congress had just overridden his veto of the ominous McCarran Internal Security Act. Thus, despite his administration's long avoidance of a major commitment to South Korea, Truman decided without congressional consultation to defend Rhee's regime against the invasion from the north.

The United States first took the issue to the United Nations and received the sanction of the Security Council to defend South Korea. The Americans were fortunate that the Soviets were boycotting the UN at this time to protest the exclusion of the People's Republic of China. The Soviets therefore had no chance to veto the Security Council's action. Truman quickly grasped the opportunity to send supplies and air cover to aid the South Koreans. When that aid proved inadequate to stem the invasion and after it was clear that there were no major uprisings in the south to challenge Rhee's control, Truman decided to commit American troops to the battle. Finally, the combined forces of South Korea and the United States managed to stop the North Koreans at a perimeter around the city of Pusan and cling to a small foothold at the southern tip of the Korean peninsula.

Even while the South Korean and American forces were in headlong retreat toward the Pusan perimeter, Truman was considering a proper punishment for the Soviet and North Korean audacity. On September 11, after the perimeter had been stabilized and plans approved for a counterattack, Truman signed National Security Council Directive 81, which empowered MacArthur to conduct operations north of the thirty-eighth parallel to destroy the North Korean forces and reunify Korea if this could be done without the risk of war with the Soviet Union or China. Truman would have to assess the risk of Soviet and Chinese intervention when American troops approached the thirty-eighth parallel and make the final decision at that time.

Meanwhile, Truman increased arms shipments to aid the French effort in Indochina and sent a portion of the Seventh Fleet from the Philippines to the Taiwan Straits to deter Mao from capturing Taiwan. He still showed some restraint, however, in rejecting the suggestion of MacArthur and others that the United States use the opportunity of the war in Korea to destroy communism in China and all the rest of Asia. He made clear that aid to Taiwan was a temporary military measure to protect the flanks of Korea. When General MacArthur met Chiang Kai-shek and implied a permanent American commitment to the Nationalist regime on Taiwan, Truman sent Averell Harriman to remind MacArthur that he was to avoid such pledges. Then Truman announced publicly that the Seventh Fleet would be withdrawn from the Taiwan Straits after the war in Korea. He even considered demoting MacArthur after the headstrong general released a public statement condemning malicious misrepresentations "by those who invariably in the past have propagandized a policy of defeatism and appeasement in the Pacific."

Any inclinations Truman and Acheson might have had toward restraint were overwhelmed when MacArthur engineered a brilliant amphibious invasion behind the North Korean lines at Inchon. With the North Korean army in frantic retreat, Truman euphorically approved MacArthur's wish to pursue the enemy beyond the thirty-eighth parallel and destroy the Communist regime. MacArthur insisted that the Chinese would never

Conflict in Korea, 1950–1953

intervene and that the American army would defeat them easily if they did. Even the reluctant members of Truman's administration agreed that if the Chinese or the Russians had intended to intervene, they would have done so earlier when American forces were still distant enough to be able to avoid a confrontation.

In fact, Kim and Stalin had already successfully petitioned Mao to intervene. "If war [with the United States] is inevitable, then let it be waged now," they agreed. The Soviets again would provide air cover and matériel, but China would bear the brunt of the fighting and would have to put off its conquest of Taiwan. Chinese troops would fight as "volunteers" in hopes that the United States would avoid a direct attack on China. If that ruse failed and America did declare war on China, Stalin gave a vague promise that he would join the war. But he did not think that the Americans would declare war on China and he told Mao that a "drawn-out war" would be a good thing in that it "gives the possibility to the Chinese troops to study contemporary warfare on the field of battle and in the second place shakes up the Truman regime in America and harms the military prestige of the Anglo-American troops." Stalin was ready to fight to the last Chinese soldier and Mao was willing to go along.

Meanwhile, MacArthur made the most of his authorization to attack north of the thirty-eighth parallel. He ignored orders to send only Koreans, not Americans, close to the Yalu River, which formed Korea's northern border with China. He did not halt even after his troops made contact with Chinese units. He assumed that the 200,000 Chinese troops were in Korea only to protect a cordon sanitaire around their border. Splitting his attacking forces, he dispersed them thinly throughout the broad part of the North Korean peninsula. He was a sitting duck when the Chinese army began its offensive: His forces reeled backward as fast as they had advanced, barely managing to stabilize a defensive line close to the thirty-eighth parallel. MacArthur publicly raged that the United States should carry the war into China, bomb beyond the Yalu, "unleash" Chiang's troops from Taiwan to attack the mainland, and even use the atomic bomb if necessary. The chastened Truman fired MacArthur instead, accepted a limited war, and opened negotiations that dragged on for two years before a tenuous truce could end the conflict.

Truman's acceptance of a limited war opened him to harsh criticism from the Republican right wing. MacArthur returned home after his dismissal to a hero's welcome. His moving farewell to Congress made him a unifying symbol for those who abhorred the Democrats' Europe First strategy. Republicans reminded Americans that Acheson's omission of Korea from the U.S. defense perimeter in his National Press Club speech had invited Communist aggression. Supporting MacArthur's insistence that the object of war was victory, not a stalemate, the Republicans urged that the United States replace the doctrine of limited war with a policy of total war for total victory. They were freer to criticize than they might have been because Truman had refused to ask Congress for an official declaration of war, which the Republicans would have supported fully at the outset of the conflict. In the absence of an official congressional commitment, the Republicans could call Korea "Truman's war."

Truman and Acheson may have been more moderate than MacArthur and many of their Republican critics, but their decision to push beyond the thirty-eighth parallel after the Inchon landings already had escalated the Cold War. Had they stopped at the thirty-eighth parallel and negotiated a peace, the war might have ended after only three months and cost a minimum of casualties, yet would have demonstrated the determination of the United States to resist overt military aggression. The decision to go north extended the war almost three years. It cost America 30,000 lives, and the South Koreans many more. It also cost the United States much of the support of its allies. Great Britain, India, and other nations had supported the United States and the UN decision to resist the North Korean invasion, but they objected strongly to the extension of the war beyond the thirty-eighth parallel.

They objected even more strongly to the increased American commitment to Chiang's Nationalist regime on Taiwan that accompanied the extension. With China now an overt enemy in Korea, all flexibility disappeared on the issues of Taiwan, recognition of Mao's government, and admission of China to the United Nations. America's previously reluctant aid to the French in Indochina became enthusiastic and overt. The United States urged even greater effort than the French themselves were willing to expend, setting the stage for Americans to pick up the war when the French left it. NSC-68 was fully implemented. American defense expenditures tripled from less than $15 billion before Korea to $44 billion in 1952 and $50 billion in 1953. The successive shocks of Czechoslovakia, the Russian atomic bomb, the Communist triumph in China, the Berlin blockade, and finally Korea had brought the Cold War to a dangerous pitch that would continue for another generation.

Controversial Issues

Harry Truman received very favorable treatment from most historians throughout the 1950s and early 1960s. They saw him as a feisty, decisive underdog who had been called upon to fill the gigantic shoes of Franklin Roosevelt and had done a remarkably good job. They praised him especially for overcoming America's historic tendency toward isolationism and rallying the American people to stop the aggressive expansion of Stalinist Russia. They saw the Truman Doctrine, the Marshall Plan, and the formation of NATO as landmarks of American foreign policy, wise decisions that prevented the collapse of Western Europe and restored the world balance of power. They believed American intervention had avoided the tragic results of the appeasement policy of the 1930s. At the same time, they generally argued that Truman's common sense had kept him from overreacting to the Communist threat. His firing of MacArthur had marked his acceptance of the doctrine of limited war in Korea and a sustained, moderate policy of containment. Most historians regarded this as a mature alternative to the natural but simplistic American desire for total war to achieve total victory.[8]

During the 1950s and early 1960s, the primary criticisms of Truman came from the Right. Republicans claimed that Truman and the Democrats were "soft on communism," just as Roosevelt had been.[9] Since most of the attacks on Truman came from the Right, he and his defenders countered by emphasizing their toughness rather than their restraint.[10]

By the mid-1960s, and especially after the escalation in Vietnam in 1965, Truman was under increasing attack from the Left. Moderate revisionists might disagree with radical revisionists over whether Roosevelt had instigated the Cold War, but both could agree that Truman merited blame for his anti-Russian policy. Gar Alperovitz accused Truman of dropping the atomic bombs on Japan long after it was clear that the Japanese could be forced to surrender without such horrors, and he claimed that Truman's purpose had been to make the Soviets more compliant.[11] Gabriel Kolko disputed Alperovitz's contention about the bombs, but only to insist that Truman had pursued his nefarious policy with economic rather than atomic weapons.[12] Other revisionist historians accused Truman of sabotaging the United Nations and blamed him for the division of Germany.[13]

Realists increasingly joined the rising chorus of criticism aimed at Harry Truman's Cold War policies. George Kennan began to clarify his essential agreement with Walter Lippmann's earlier critique of containment as being too global in scope, too ideological, too oriented toward military rather than economic and political measures, and too rigid in avoiding negotiations with the Russians.[14] Other historians also began to move toward this "soft" or "restrained" version of realism. They too contended that Truman had overreacted to communism and should have accorded the Soviets their sphere without so much strife.[15] This trend culminated in several outstanding works, including Melvyn P. Leffler's *The Preponderance of Power: National Security, the Truman Administration, and the Cold War* (1992) and *For the Soul of Mankind: The United States, the Soviet Union, and the Cold War* (2007); and Campbell Craig and Fred Logevall, *America's Cold War: The Politics of Insecurity* (2009).

The end of the Cold War gave historians access to many new documents in the archives of the Soviet Union and the newly independent eastern European nations. Many documents on China's policy in this period also became available. Although these documents did settle some debates, they left plenty of room for a continuing dispute over the wisdom of the Truman administration's foreign policy. It seemed clear from the documents on the Soviet Union that Stalin really did want and expect to cooperate with the Allies after World War II and that his primary concern was obtaining a security sphere in eastern Europe and Asia without any immediate intention to subvert or conquer the West in some sort of communist ideological crusade. But also it was clear that he was determined to act in that security sphere with whatever brutality was necessary and that in the long term he regarded conflict and perhaps even world war with the West as inevitable.[16] This left open the question whether Truman was wise to try to contain the Soviets, given Stalin's ruthless nature and long-term hostility to the West, or whether a policy more respectful of Stalin's realpolitik concern for his security sphere might have moderated the adversarial relationship between the West and Stalin and his successors. Among the books that placed the primary blame for the Cold War on Stalin and argued that at least some form of containment was necessary were Wilson D. Miscamble, *From Roosevelt to Truman: Potsdam, Hiroshima, and the Cold War* (2007); John Lewis Gaddis, *We Now Know: Rethinking Cold War History* (1997); and Marc Trachtenberg, *A Constructed Peace: The Making of the European Settlement, 1945–1963* (1999). A far more critical view of Truman's policy was Arnold A. Offner, *Another Such Victory: President Truman and the Cold War, 1945–1953* (2002). Somewhere in between was Melvin Leffler, *The Specter of Communism: The United States and the Origins of the Cold War, 1917–1953* (1994), a condensed revision of his earlier comprehensive history, *A Preponderance of Power*, mentioned above. For a fascinating glimpse of the state of historiography in incorporating the new documentation from behind the Iron Curtain into an overall view of the early Cold War in Europe, see Geoffrey Roberts, *Stalin's Wars: From World War to Cold War, 1939–1953* (2007), and the roundtable of reviews of that book on line at h-net.org~diplo/roundtables. See also the essays in the first of a projected multivolume work, Melvyn P. Leffler and Odd Arne Westad, eds., *The Cambridge History of the Cold War*, vol. 1, *Origins* (2010).

Further Reading

For outstanding overviews of the role of the atomic bomb in the war on Japan and foreign policy toward the Soviet Union, see Tsuyoshi Hasegawa, *Racing the Enemy: Stalin, Truman, and the Surrender of Japan* (2005), who argues that Truman purposely delayed the surrender of Japan so he could use the bomb to deter Stalin from acquiring territory in Asia, but also argues that the bomb, in conjunction with the Soviet entry into the war against Japan, was necessary to force Japan's surrender; Richard B. Frank, *Downfall: The End of the Imperial Japanese Empire* (1999), who argues that the use of the bomb was justified and necessary to force Japan's surrender; Martin J. Sherwin, *A World Destroyed: Hiroshima and Its Legacies* (2nd ed., 2000), who believes the use of the bomb was unnecessary; and J. Samuel Walker, *Prompt and Utter Destruction: Truman and the Use of the Atomic Bombs Against Japan* (1997). See also J. Samuel Walker, "The Decision to Use the Bomb: A Historiographical Update," *Diplomatic History* (Winter 1990), along with Michael J. Hogan, ed., *Hiroshima in History and Memory* (1996). For the Soviet reaction to the bomb based on recent documents and interviews in Russia, see David Holloway, *Stalin and the Bomb: The Soviet Union and Atomic Energy, 1939–1956* (1994), and Richard Rhodes, *Dark Sun: The Making of the Hydrogen Bomb* (1995). See also Andrew Rotter, *Hiroshima: The World's Bomb* (2008); Sean Malloy, *Atomic Tragedy: Henry L. Stimson and the Decision to Use the Bomb against Japan* (2008); Campbell Craig and Sergey Radchenko, *The Atomic Bomb and the Origins of the Cold War* (2008); and Michael D. Gordin, *Red Cloud at Dawn: Truman, Stalin, and the End of the Atomic Monopoly* (2009).

For U.S. strategic policy and the role of the bomb in this era, see Greg Herken, *The Winning Weapon: The Atomic Bomb in the Cold War, 1945–1950* (1981); Alexander George and Richard Smoke, *Deterrence in American Foreign Policy* (1975); McGeorge Bundy, *Danger and Survival: Choices About the Bomb in the First Fifty Years* (1988); Fred Kaplan, *The Wizards of Armageddon* (1983); Michael S. Sherry, *The Rise of American Air Power: The Creation of Armageddon* (1987); Leon V. Sigal, *Fighting to a Finish: The Politics of War Termination in the United States and Japan* (1988); Stephen C. Rearden, *History of the Office of Secretary of Defense: The Formative Years, 1947–1950* (1984); and Chester J. Pach, *Arming the Free World: The Origins of the United States Military Assistance Program, 1945–1950* (1991).

For analyses of some of the personalities involved in the Cold War, see Walter Isaacson and Evan Thomas, *The Wise Men: Six Friends and the World They Made* (1986); Richard Barnet, *The Roots of War* (1972); John C. Donovan, *The Cold Warriors* (1974); Richard K. Betts, *Soldiers, Statesmen and Cold War Crises* (1977); Hugh DeSantis, *The Diplomacy of Silence: The American Foreign Service, the Soviet Union, and the Cold War, 1933–1947* (1980); and Bruce Kuklick, *Blind Oracles: Intellectuals and War from Kennan to Kissinger* (2006).

Good biographies of Truman are Robert H. Farrell, *Harry S. Truman: A Life* (1994); Alonzo Hamby, *Man of the People: The Life of Harry S. Truman* (1995); and David McCullough, *Truman* (1992). All these biographies are far more favorable to Truman's foreign policy than Arnold Offner's *Another Such Victory*, mentioned above. On Secretary of State James Byrnes, see David Robertson, *Sly and Able: A Political Biography of James F. Byrnes* (1994); Robert L. Messer, *The End of an Alliance: James F. Byrnes, Roosevelt, Truman and the Origins of the Cold War* (1982); and Patricia Dawson Ward, *The Threat of Peace: James F. Byrnes and the Council of Foreign Ministers, 1945–1946* (1979). For Byrnes's successor, George Marshall, see Forrest Pogue, *Marshall: States-*

man, 1945–1959 (1989); Mark A. Stoler, *George C. Marshall: Soldier-Statesman of the American Century* (1989); and Robert H. Ferrell, *George C. Marshall* (1966). And for Dean Acheson, see Robert J. McMahon, *Dean Acheson and the Creation of an American World Order* (2008); Robert Beisner, *Dean Acheson: A Life in the Cold War* (2006); Douglas Brinkley, *Dean Acheson: The Cold War Years, 1953–71* (1992); James Chace, *Acheson: The Secretary of State Who Created the American World* (1998); Gaddis Smith, *Dean Acheson* (1972); and David S. McClellan, *Dean Acheson* (1976).

Excellent biographies of George Kennan are Wilson D. Miscamble, *George F. Kennan and the Making of American Foreign Policy, 1947–1950* (1992); David Allan Mayers, *George Kennan and the Dilemmas of U.S. Foreign Policy* (1989); Walter Hixon, *George F. Kennan: Cold War Iconoclast* (1989); and Anders Stephanson, *Kennan and the Art of Foreign Policy* (1989). Two other figures in the foreign policy bureaucracy who opposed Kennan's increasingly soft line are covered in Strobe Talbott, *The Master of the Game: Paul Nitze and the Nuclear Peace* (1988); Joseph M. Siracusa, *Rearming the Cold War: Paul H. Nitze, the H-Bomb and the Origins of a Soviet First Strike* (1983); and H.W. Brands, *Inside the Cold War: Loy Henderson and the Rise of the American Empire, 1918–1961* (1991). A fascinating joint biography of Kennan and Nitze by Nitze's grandson is Nicholas Thompson, *The Hawk and the Dove: Paul Nitze, George Kennan, and the History of the Cold War* (2009).

For contemporary critics of the Cold War, see Thomas G. Paterson, ed., *Cold War Critics* (1971); Ronald Radosh, *Prophets on the Right: Profiles of Conservative Critics of American Globalism* (1975); James T. Patterson, *Mr. Republican: A Biography of Robert Taft* (1972); and J. Samuel Walker, *Henry A. Wallace and American Foreign Policy* (1976). For the role of the U.S. Congress in the Cold War, see Robert David Johnson, *Congress and the Cold War* (2006). See also David M. Barrett, *The CIA and Congress: The Untold Story from Truman to Kennedy* (2005).

Although published before the end of the Cold War opened many archives behind the Iron Curtain, several books on Soviet-American relations are still valuable, including Adam B. Ulam, *The Rivals* (1971); Milovan Djilas, *Conversations with Stalin* (1962); Vojtech Mastny, *Russia's Road to the Cold War* (1978); William Taubman, *Stalin's American Policy* (1981); and Albert Resis, *Stalin, the Politburo, and the Onset of the Cold War, 1945–1946* (1988).

On Anglo-American relations in this period, see Terry H. Anderson, *The U.S., Great Britain and the Cold War, 1944–1947* (1981); Robert M. Hathaway, *Ambiguous Partnership: Britain and America, 1944–1947* (1981); D. Cameron Watt, *Succeeding John Bull: America in Britain's Place, 1900–1975* (1984); Richard A. Best Jr., *"Cooperation with Like-Minded Peoples": British Influences on American Security Policy, 1945–1949* (1986); Fraser Harbutt, *The Iron Curtain: Churchill, America and the Origins of the Cold War* (1986); and William Roger Louis and Hedley Bull, eds., *The Special Relationship: Anglo-American Relations since 1945* (1986).

A good overview of the Cold War in Europe is James L. Gormly, *The Collapse of the Grand Alliance, 1945–1948* (1987). Two excellent works on the Marshall Plan are Michael Hogan, *The Marshall Plan: America, Britain, and the Reconstruction of Western*

Europe (1987), and Alan S. Milward, *The Reconstruction of Western Europe, 1945–1951* (1984). Still valuable on the topic of the Marshall Plan are Joseph A. Jones, *Fifteen Weeks* (1955), and John Gimbel, *The Origins of the Marshall Plan* (1976). Gimbel also wrote *The American Occupation of Germany* (1968). On Germany, see also Carolyn Woods Eisenberg, *Drawing the Line: The American Decision to Divide Germany, 1944–1949* (1996); Anne Deighton, *The Impossible Peace: Britain, the Division of Germany and the Origins of the Cold War* (1990); and Thomas Alan Schwartz, *America's Germany: John J. McCloy and the Federal Republic of Germany* (1991).

On NATO, see Lawrence S. Kaplan, *A Community of Interest: NATO and the Military Assistance Program, 1948–1951* (1980) and *NATO 1948: The Birth of the Transatlantic Alliance* (2007); Escott Reid, *Time of Fear and Hope: The Making of the North Atlantic Treaty, 1947–1949* (1977); and Timothy P. Ireland, *Creating the Entangling Alliance: The Origins of NATO* (1981). For other aspects of the Cold War in Europe, see Joseph Becker and Franz Knipping, eds., *Power in Europe: Great Britain, France, Italy and Germany in a Postwar World, 1945–1950* (1986); John W. Young, *Britain, France, and the Unity of Europe, 1945–1951* (1984); Charles S. Maier, ed., *The Cold War in Europe: Era of a Divided Continent* (1991); and John Lamberton Harber, *The Reconstruction of Italy, 1945–1948* (1986).

Accounts of the origins of the Cold War in Greece include Robert Frazier, *Anglo-American Relations with Greece: The Coming of the Cold War, 1942–1947* (1991); G.M. Alexander, *The Prelude to the Truman Doctrine: British Policy in Greece, 1944–1947* (1982); Lawrence Wittner, *American Intervention in Greece, 1943–1949* (1982); Theodore A. Couloumbil, *The United States, Greece, and Turkey* (1983); and Howard Jones, *"A New Kind of War": America's Global Strategy and the Truman Doctrine in Greece* (1989). Events in other parts of the eastern Mediterranean are covered in Bruce Kuniholm, *The Origins of the Cold War in the Near East* (1980); Ritchie Ovendale, *Britain, the United States, and the End of the Palestine Mandate, 1942–1948* (1989); Stephen L. Spiegel, *The Other Arab-Israeli Conflict: America's Middle East Policy, From Truman to Reagan* (1985); and Cheryl Rudenbert, *Israel and the American National Interest* (1986).

On Asia, see Akira Iriye, *The Cold War in Asia* (1974); Russell D. Buhite, *Soviet-American Relations in Asia, 1945–1954* (1982); Dorothy Borg and Waldo Heinrichs, eds., *The Uncertain Years: Chinese-American Relations and the Recognition Controversy, 1949–1950* (1983); Nancy B. Tucker, *Patterns in the Dust* (1983); and Robert Blum, *Drawing the Line: The Origins of the American Containment Policy in East Asia* (1982). For a recent attempt to analyze the role of culture in the origins of the Cold War in Asia, see Simei Qing, *From Allies to Enemies: Visions of Modernity, Identity, and U.S.-China Diplomacy* (2007). The Truman administration's occupation policy in Japan is covered in Michael Schaller, *The American Occupation of Japan* (1985); John Dower, *Embracing Defeat: Japan in the Wake of World War II* (1999); Kyoko Inoue, *MacArthur's Japanese Constitution: A Linguistic and Cultural Study of Its Making* (1991); Howard B. Schonberger, *Aftermath of War: Americans and the Remaking of Japan, 1945–1952* (1989); and Toshio Nishi, *Unconditional Democracy: Education and Politics in Occupied Japan, 1945–1952* (1982).

Chinese and Soviet documents released in the 1990s have revealed a great deal about the Communist side of the Korean War. See especially the translations of some of these documents by Katheryn Weathersby in the *Cold War International History Project Bulletin* (Fall 1993, Spring 1995). Books that take account of many of these documents include Sergei N. Goncharov, John W. Lewis, and Xue Litai, *Uncertain Partners: Stalin, Mao, and the Korean War* (1993); Kim Chull Baum and James I. Matray, eds., *Korea and the Cold War* (1993); Chen Jian, *China's Road to the Korean War: The Making of the Sino-American Confrontation* (1994); Michael M. Sheng, *Battling Western Imperialism: Mao, Stalin, and the United States* (1997); Allen R. Millett, *The War for Korea, 1945–1950* (2005) and *The War for Korea, 1950–1951: They Came from the North* (2010); and Gregg Brazinsky, *Nation Building in South Korea: Koreans, Americans, and the Making of Democracy* (2007).

Other books that are still important to the understanding of the Korean war are Bruce Cumings, *The Origins of the Korean War* (2 vols., 1981, 1990); Rosemary Foot, *The Wrong War: American Policy and the Dimensions of the Korean Conflict, 1950–1953* (1985), and *A Substitute for Victory: The Politics of Peacemaking at the Korean Armistice Talks* (1990); James I. Matray, *The Reluctant Crusade: American Foreign Policy in Korea* (1985); John Merrill, *Korea: The Peninsular Origins of the War* (1989); Callum MacDonald, *Korea: The War Before Vietnam* (1986); Burton I. Kaufman, *The Korean War: Challenges in Crisis, Credibility, and Command* (1986); Clay Blair, *The Forgotten War: America in Korea, 1950–1953* (1987); William Whitney Stueck Jr., *The Road to Confrontation: American Policy Toward China and Korea, 1947–1950* (1981); Joseph Goulden, *Korea: The Untold Story of the War* (1982); Charles M. Dobbs, *The Unwanted Symbol: American Foreign Policy, the Cold War, and Korea, 1945–1950* (1981); and Peter Lowe, *The Origins of the Korean War* (1986).

Notes

1. John Lewis Gaddis, *Strategies of Containment: A Critical Appraisal of Postwar American National Security* (1982), p. 15.

2. The firebombing of Tokyo caused more casualties than the atomic bombing of either Hiroshima or Nagasaki.

3. For instance, the leftist guerrilla forces had taken 30,000 hostages in Athens during their flight from the reoccupying British forces and had killed some 4,000 of them. The right-wing Greek government, in turn, arrested and executed thousands when it established control.

4. Works detailing these covert operations behind the Iron Curtain in the early Cold War include Sarah-Jane Corke, *U.S. Covert Operations and Cold War Strategy: Truman, Secret Warfare and the CIA, 1945–53* (2007); Scott Lucas, *Freedom's War: The American Crusade Against the Soviet Union* (1999); Walter Hixson, *Parting the Curtain: Propaganda, Culture and the Cold War, 1945–1961* (1997); Peter Grose, *Operation Rollback: America's Secret War Behind the Iron Curtain* (2000); and Gregory Mitrovich, *Undermining the Kremlin: America's Strategy to Subvert the Soviet Bloc, 1947–1956* (2000).

5. Tony Shaw, *Hollywood's Cold War* (2007); Hugh Wilsford, *The Mighty Wurlitzer: How the CIA Played America* (2008); Laura A. Belmonte, *Selling the American Way: U.S. Propaganda and the Cold War* (2008).

6. McCarthy's charges were wildly exaggerated. But it is now clear that there was an extensive Soviet espionage network in the United States from the 1930s on that successfully penetrated not only the American nuclear bomb effort, but also many industrial and military projects. On the other hand, although high government officials like Alger Hiss, Harry Dexter White, and Laughlin Curry were sending information to the Soviets, it does not seem that they significantly affected U.S. policy making toward the Soviet Union. See John Earl Haynes and Harvey Klehr, *Spies: The Rise and Fall of the KGB in America* (2009) and *Venona: Decoding Soviet Espionage in America* (1999); Allen Weinstein and Alexander Vassiliev, *The Haunted Wood: Soviet Espionage in America: The Stalin Era* (1999); and Katherine A.S. Sibley, *Red Spies in America: Stolen Secrets and the Dawn of the Cold War* (2004).

7. Kim purposely misled Stalin by claiming that the invasion would be aided by a major uprising in the south against Syngman Rhee when, in fact, economic improvements in the south, combined with Rhee's ruthless extermination of leftist guerrilla forces, had made such an uprising very improbable.

8. See, for instance, the earlier editions of surveys like John W. Spanier, *American Foreign Policy since World War II* (1960); John Lukacs, *A History of the Cold War* (1961); Walt Whitman Rostow, *The United States in the World Arena* (1960); Desmond Donnelly, *Struggle for the World: The Cold War, 1917–1965* (1965); William G. Carleton, *The Revolution in American Foreign Policy: Its Global Range* (1963); and Eric F. Goldman, *The Crucial Decade and After* (1960). See also Louis J. Halle, *Civilization and Foreign Policy* (1955); Robert E. Osgood, *NATO: The Entangling Alliance* (1962); Norman Graebner, *The New Isolationism* (1956); Herbert Feis, *Between War and Peace: The Potsdam Conference* (1960); David Rees, *Korea: The Limited War* (1964); John W. Spanier, *The Truman-MacArthur Controversy and the Korean War* (1959); Richard H. Rovere and Arthur M. Schlesinger Jr., *The General and the President* (1951); Trumbull Higgins, *Korea and the Fall of MacArthur* (1960); and Allen Whiting, *China Crosses the Yalu* (1960).

9. See William Henry Chamberlin, *America's Second Crusade* (1950), and James Burnham, *Containment or Liberation? An Inquiry into the Aims of United States Foreign Policy* (1952–1953).

10. See especially Truman's *Memoirs* (2 vols., 1956); James F. Byrnes, *Speaking Frankly* (1947) and *All in One Lifetime* (1958); and Dean Acheson's memoirs, *Present at the Creation* (1969).

11. Gar Alperovitz, *Atomic Diplomacy: Hiroshima and Potsdam* (1965; rev. ed. 1985).

12. Gabriel Kolko, *The Politics of War: The World and United States Foreign Policy, 1943–1945* (1972).

13. Thomas M. Campbell, *Masquerade Peace: America's UN Policy, 1944–1945* (1973); Bruce Kuklick, *American Policy and the Division of Germany* (1972). See also Richard J. Walton, *Henry Wallace, Harry Truman and the Cold War* (1976); Lloyd Gardner, *Architects of Illusion: Men and Ideas in American Foreign Policy, 1941–1949* (1970); and Walter LaFeber, *America, Russia, and the Cold War* (6th ed., 1991). For other revisionist accounts, see the Controversial Issues essay in the previous chapter.

14. Walter Lippmann, *The Cold War* (1947); George Kennan, *Russia, the Atom, and the West* (1958) and *Memoirs* (2 vols., 1967–1972).

15. John Lewis Gaddis, *The United States and the Origins of the Cold War, 1941–1947* (new ed., 2000) and *Strategies of Containment: A Critical Appraisal of Postwar American National Security Policy* (rev. and expanded ed., 2005); Herbert Feis, *The Atomic Bomb and the End of World War II* (1966) and *From Trust to Terror: The Onset of the Cold War, 1945–1950* (1970); Louis Halle, *The Cold War as History* (1967); Lynn Etheridge Davis, *The Cold War Begins: Soviet-American Conflict over Eastern Europe* (1974); Lisle A. Rose, *After Yalta* (1973) and *Dubious Victory: The United States and the End of World War II* (1973); Martin F. Herz, *The Beginnings of the Cold War* (1966); David F. Trask, *Victory Without Peace: American Foreign Relations in the Twentieth Century* (1968); Alonzo L. Hamby, *The Imperial Years: The United States Since 1939* (1976); Norman A. Graebner, Richard D. Burns, and Joseph M. Siracusa, *America and the Cold War, 1941–1991: A Realist Interpretation* (2 vols., 2010).

16. These conclusions are documented in Geoffrey Roberts, *Stalin's Wars: From World War to Cold War, 1939–1953* (2007); Vladislav M. Zubok and Constantine Pleshakov, *Inside the Kremlin's Cold War: From Stalin to Khrushchev* (1996); and Vladislav M. Zubok, *A Failed Empire: The Soviet Union in the Cold War from Stalin to Khrushchev* (2007). For a dissenting view that Stalin was never truly cooperative, see R.C. Raack, *Stalin's Drive to the West, 1938–1945: The Origins of the Cold War* (1995). For an argument that Stalin was weak and wanted cooperation so much that Truman could and should have pushed him harder, see Vojtech Mastny, *The Cold War and Soviet Insecurity: The Stalin Years* (1996). Other important works that use newly opened documents from behind the Iron Curtain to analyze the Soviet side of the origins of the Cold War are Francesca Gori and Silvio Pons, eds., *The Soviet Union and Europe in the Cold War, 1943–1953* (1996); Norman M. Naimark, *The Russians in Germany, 1945–1949: A History of the Soviet Zone of Occupation* (1995); and Laszlo Borhi, *Hungary in the Cold War: Between the United States and the Soviet Union, 1944–1956* (2004).

CHAPTER 10

THE NEW LOOK OF DWIGHT D. EISENHOWER

Although Dwight David Eisenhower ran for president in 1952 as a Republican, he had no quarrel with the interventionist foreign policy of Harry Truman and the Democrats. Eisenhower entered the race for the Republican nomination in part because his concern for collective security clashed with the isolationism of the conservative wing of the Republican Party and its favorite, Senator Robert A. Taft. But Eisenhower shared Taft's fear that the free-spending ways of the Democrats would bring the United States to bankruptcy and weaken its international position. His desire to cut the budget could not help but influence his foreign policy. He was appalled that the defense expenditures Truman projected in accordance with NSC-68 would result in a $44 billion deficit over the next five years. (In expressing his horror at Truman's defense budgets, however, Eisenhower never acknowledged, then or later, that a good portion of the increases in defense expenditures resulted from his own requests as NATO commander.)

In his search for an alternative foreign policy, Eisenhower turned for help to John Foster Dulles. Dulles, the Republican Party's leading foreign affairs expert, had managed to stay in favor with the Taft wing of the party even while espousing an interventionist policy. In a widely read article for *Life* magazine, he suggested that reliance on the threat of strategic nuclear weapons would be a cheaper and more effective way of deterring Soviet aggression than the Democrats' buildup of expensive conventional land forces. Dulles also argued that the United States should seek the liberation of the Soviet satellites and not be content with Truman's "defeatist treadmill policy of containment."

Eisenhower permitted Dulles to write the foreign policy portions of the Republican platform, appointed him secretary of state, and left in his hands the technical implementation of American diplomacy. Pundits of the day came to believe that Dulles actually ran the administration's foreign policy. But the recent availability of Eisenhower's classified and private papers has demonstrated that the president kept the major decisions of the administration in his own hands. He preferred to operate behind the scenes and leave the details, the partisan battles, and much of the blame for any unpopular or unsuccessful maneuvers to his subordinates. He was ready, however, to rein in his advisers if they went off the track.

Eisenhower generally approved of Dulles's policies, but did not see how wholesale threats of nuclear retaliation could be a credible deterrent to low-level Communist nib-

President Dwight D. Eisenhower *(left)* and his secretary of state, John Foster Dulles. *(Courtesy of the Dwight D. Eisenhower Presidential Library)*

bling at neighbor nations. When Dulles nonetheless included the term "retaliatory striking power" in the Republican platform, Eisenhower fumed, "I'll be damned if I run on that." The platform phrase was quickly revised. Likewise, Eisenhower qualified Dulles's platform condemnation of the "negative, futile and immoral policy of 'containment'" by publicly insisting that any liberation of Soviet satellite nations would have to come by "peaceful means." Irked at the rumors that Dulles controlled him, Eisenhower once caustically remarked that there was "only one man I know who has seen *more* of the world and talked with more people and *knows* more than [Dulles] does—and that's me."

Eisenhower used his reputation as a statesman above the party battle to good effect, notably in his campaign pledge to "go to Korea." Such a pledge committed him to no particular policy, yet allowed him to imply that with his authority and experience he would be able to end the war. Thus, he finessed the conservatives' demand that he end the war by winning it and the liberals' insistence that he end it by compromising. After winning the election but before taking office, Eisenhower paid a three-day visit to Korea. On his return, he apparently let the Communists know he was considering the use of atomic weapons if progress toward peace was not made quickly. Abruptly the Chinese dropped the demand that was stalling the truce negotiations, that even unwilling prisoners of war be repatriated. China's policy shift may have been the result of the death of Stalin, who had insisted on continuing the war, rather than Eisenhower's veiled atomic threat, but Eisenhower and Dulles considered the subsequent truce in Korea proof of the effectiveness of their nuclear strategy.

As Dulles explained it, such use of the "deterrent of massive retaliatory power" would enable the United States "to respond vigorously at places and with means of its own choosing." This would be far less expensive than the NSC-68 strategy of trying to defend against every possible type of aggression the Communists were capable of mounting. Instead of reacting to a threat on the enemy's own terms, the United States could shift the nature and location of the confrontation to correspond to America's strengths and its adversary's weaknesses. Dulles and Eisenhower acknowledged that nuclear weapons were inappropriate for minor, low-level conflicts; they would devise supplementary strategies for such "brushfire wars." Nevertheless, the nuclear threat would always lurk in the background.

Eisenhower and Dulles purposely wanted to keep potential aggressors off balance. The Communists would be confronted with the certainty of an American response, but uncertainty as to its nature. Dulles acknowledged the danger of enemy miscalculation inherent in this strategy, but declared, "You have to take chances for peace just as you must take chances in war. The ability to get to the verge without getting into the war is the necessary art. If you cannot master it, you inevitably get into a war. If you try to run from it, if you are scared to go to the brink, you are lost."

Reporters listening to Dulles's explanations dubbed administration diplomacy "massive retaliation" and "brinksmanship." Despite Dulles's objections to this characterization of his policy, the press was not far off the mark. Intercontinental bombers capable of carrying the newly developed hydrogen bomb became operational early in Eisenhower's administration. About the same time, the United States also began to station tactical nuclear weapons in Europe. Despite the rising conventional power of the United States and NATO, Eisenhower considered the West too weak to defend conventionally against a Soviet attack on Europe and he considered it too expensive for America to send troops to fight communism in peripheral areas. Therefore, the president announced firmly that he would use nuclear weapons instantly to prevent a Soviet invasion of Europe, and he implied that he would use them if necessary to combat Communist aggression in peripheral areas as well. He actually did briefly consider using nuclear bombs in Korea and Indochina, and he publicly threatened to use such weapons in the two crises over the Chinese Nationalist–occupied islands of Quemoy and Matsu. But if Eisenhower and Dulles were willing to consider use of nuclear weapons more readily than Truman, they were very cautious in their actual use. They were interested in deterrence, not war. Eisenhower believed that limiting a nuclear war would be nearly impossible. He estimated that 65 percent of the American population would need medical aid in case of a nuclear strike on the United States, and little or none would be available. Nevertheless, he delegated to senior military leaders the authority to use nuclear weapons under certain limited circumstances, so his policy of nuclear retaliation was extremely dangerous, however cautious he tried to be in implementing it.

These defense policies did save money. Eisenhower reduced Truman's 1954 projected defense budget from $41 billion to $36 billion, and to $31 billion for the following year. All the military services took some cuts, but the air force, with its primary responsibility for strategic bombings, suffered only slightly. The army faced the most reductions, from 1.5 million to 1 million men and from twenty to fourteen divisions. In future conflicts, the United States would contribute air and sea power, but would rely on overseas allies for most of the troops.

Reliance on foreign troops sent Dulles in search of more and firmer overseas alliances. He extended America's alliance system to only four more nations than Truman had, but Dulles pushed neutrals harder to abandon their nonaligned status for the Western-oriented alliance system. He condemned neutrality as "immoral" and publicly maintained that nations had to be for America or against it. Privately, Dulles was a bit more flexible, and Eisenhower was even more so. They sent aid to Marshal Tito's Yugoslavia to help it maintain its neutrality against Soviet pressure. Realizing that communism was not monolithic, they considered means to exploit the strains they perceived in the Soviet-Chinese alliance. They felt sympathy for non-Communist independence movements and nationalism in the third world and hoped that gradual independence might produce stability and prosperity in former Western colonies.

But Eisenhower and Dulles failed to pursue this flexibility very far, and thus the United States often found itself on the wrong side of the nationalist and anticolonial conflicts that swept the third world in the postwar era. The administration was unwilling to risk America's relationships with the European mother countries on behalf of third-world colonies because it saw the industrialized nations as vital to the containment of the Soviet Union. Eisenhower did little to support the domestic movement against the racism and segregation in the United States that did so much to discredit America's standing as a free, democratic nation in the eyes of the third world. Most important, Eisenhower and Dulles feared that Communists might exploit nationalist movements or the chaos that often came in the wake of nationalist challenges to existing regimes, and that fear increasingly overwhelmed any sympathy they had for third-world rebels. Thus, the United States generally supported right-wing and colonial regimes against their nationalist revolutionary challengers. After cautious attempts to propitiate neutralists like Indian prime minister Jawaharlal Nehru of India and President Sukarno of Indonesia, the Eisenhower administration turned to portraying them as Communist sympathizers and even went so far as to enlist the Central Intelligence Agency (CIA) on the side of Indonesian rebels in a disastrously failed attempt to overthrow Sukarno. Dulles considered pressure rather than sympathy the best way to keep nations out of the Soviet orbit. Thus, he continued to talk of "rolling back" Soviet control of eastern Europe even when he knew the United States would not risk any major action in Russia's security sphere. (Indeed, the United States stood by while the Russians put down strikes and rebellions in East Germany, Poland, and Hungary.) Dulles also continued to put pressure on the People's Republic of China. He refused it recognition, opposed its admission to the United Nations, and threatened to "unleash" Nationalist leader Chiang Kai-shek for an attack on the mainland. Dulles hoped that this pressure would force China to call upon the Soviets for more economic aid and military support than they were willing to supply, thus breaking up the Sino-Soviet alliance. Perhaps he succeeded. When the Russians refused to provide as much nuclear technology as China wanted, Mao Zedong expelled most Russian technicians.

Dulles aimed his anti-Communist rhetoric at Americans as well as potential foreign enemies. Caving in to Senator Joseph McCarthy's opportunistic, malicious attempts to purge the State Department of its supposedly Communist tendencies, Dulles fired many loyal officers, including the "old China hands" that the right wing had denounced for "losing" China to communism. He even ordered supposedly leftist books removed from American government overseas libraries. Ultimately, Dulles and Eisenhower turned against McCarthy and disowned him, but the political demise of McCarthy owed far more to McCarthy's own overreaching than to anything they did.

Dulles's removal of leftist books from American libraries overseas was a small part of one other aspect of Eisenhower's New Look, an acceleration of the already ongoing cultural and psychological war against communism overseas. Eisenhower believed that "while we can boast of the finest civilization the world has known, the Soviets are convincing many peoples that they are the true exponents of progress, peace and of freedom! What a tragedy!" Eisenhower sought to counter this trend by drastically increasing the funds for the newly created United States Information Agency (USIA) to wage a propaganda war against America's adversaries. The USIA coordinated overseas radio and television programs like those of Voice of America. It established libraries abroad such as those from which Dulles banned leftist books. It sponsored expositions abroad like the Moscow Exposition of 1959. The Moscow Exposition was part of an exchange that permitted the Soviets to mount an exposition in New York, which the Soviets stocked with exhibitions glorifying Sputnik and Soviet achievements in space. America's Moscow Exposition, on the other hand, exhibited the kinds of luxury consumer goods available to ordinary Americans. In an enormous geodesic dome, an overhead screen showed slides of American cities, highways, supermarkets, and college campuses. A model home displayed the modern appliances that accompanied American middle-class life. It was in the kitchen of that model home, with its subversive message of American prosperity, that Eisenhower's vice president, Richard Nixon, and Nikita Khrushchev conducted a highly publicized impromptu debate over the relative merits of the American and Soviet ways of life.

The USIA also promoted American films abroad while pressuring Hollywood to ensure that its films portrayed America in the best light. The USIA's pressure on Hollywood in the 1950s was a continuation of the campaign the American government had conducted since the end of World War II to oppose communism both at home and abroad. The House Un-American Activities Committee, investigating Communist influence in Hollywood, helped produce an unofficial blacklist that denied employment to hundreds of suspected leftists. The head of the Motion Picture Association warned screenwriters: "We'll have no more *Grapes of Wrath*, we'll have no more *Tobacco Roads*, we'll have no more films that treat the banker as a villain." Consequently, the films the United States sent abroad in the late 1940s and 1950s not only promoted the "American way of life" but also often explicitly condemned Communist ideology. For instance, the USIA had a significant role in promoting and even financing movie versions of George Orwell's famous antitotalitarian novels, *Animal Farm* and *1984*.

Religion played a significant role in American propaganda abroad, including Hollywood films. There was a strong resurgence of organized Christianity in the United States during the Eisenhower administration, at which time Congress added "under God" to the Pledge of Allegiance and made "In God We Trust" the national motto. Eisenhower proclaimed: "It is only through religion that we can lick this thing called Communism." American propaganda inevitably contrasted "Godless atheistic communism" with the religious devotion and freedom that existed in the United States. Hollywood reinforced this message in the 1950s with Biblical sagas like *Ben-Hur*, *Quo-Vadis*, and *The Ten Commandments*. *The Ten Commandments* was the most expensive movie made to that date and a box office blockbuster. Cecil B. DeMille, the chief film consultant to the USIA and the director of the picture, said that because the movie depicted the story of Moses, a man sacred to Christians, Jews, and Muslims alike, it would be "a means of welding together all faiths against the common enemy of all faiths, atheistic Communism."

Unfortunately, many critics abroad condemned American cultural exports, such as American films, as a reflection of the shallow, materialistic, and vulgar anti-intellectualism of American culture itself. America, they said, was a giant with the head of a child. Eisenhower bemoaned Europe's depiction of the United States as "a race of materialists" whose "successes are described in terms of automobiles and not in terms of worthwhile culture of any kind." The Eisenhower administration tried to counter this image by arranging tours for American intellectuals and classical musicians. It even worked out a cultural exchange with the Soviet Union that permitted American artists to perform behind the Iron Curtain. As one wag put it:

> No commodity is quite so strange
> As this thing called cultural exchange.
> Say that our prestige needs a tonic:
> Export the Philharmonic.
> That what we call cultural exchange!
> . . . And when our neighbors call us vermin,
> We sent out Woody Herman.

The wag quoted above was Iola Brubeck, wife of jazz musician Dave Brubeck, who collaborated with him in composing a musical satirizing their own participation in government-sponsored cultural exchange tours. As the lyrics imply, the USIA discovered that attempts to project a highbrow image abroad foundered to some extent on the fact that foreign audiences seemed to prefer American pop culture, especially jazz. The audiences for Voice of America broadcasts skyrocketed when jazz came on the air. The bands of musicians like Louis Armstrong regularly toured abroad, where they often found more enthusiastic audiences and more lucrative fees than in the United States. Consequently, in 1955 the Eisenhower administration decided to begin direct sponsorship and funding of overseas jazz tours.

Not only were American jazz bands popular, they were also racially integrated and often led by black musicians. This was a major benefit in the Eisenhower administration's attempt to overcome America's racist image. Racism was as big an obstacle to foreign acceptance of American culture and propaganda as the nation's reputation for vulgar materialism. Foreign audiences saw pictures of the riots greeting the Supreme Court's 1954 decision in *Brown v. Board of Education* to desegregate public schools. They read of the lynching of Emmett Till and the Montgomery bus boycott in 1955. The American government tried to counter such images by helping to finance a four-year tour of the musical *Porgy and Bess* through Europe, South America, and the Middle East. Eisenhower, despite his own discomfort with the race issue and dislike of the Supreme Court's desegregation decision, adopted the jazz tours as his own. He invited trumpeter Dizzy Gillespie to play at the White House in 1956 after Gillespie's successful tour of the Middle East. When Eisenhower called out, "Dizzy, Dizzy" to try to get Gillespie to leave his conversation with Senator Hubert Humphrey and come to the stage to receive an honorary plaque, Dizzy replied casually, "Right over here, Pops."

The jazz tours did not always go smoothly for the bands or for America's racist reputation. Dizzy Gillespie publicly stated that he had no intention of using his State Department–sponsored tour to apologize "for the racist policies of America." He refused to accept briefings about desired conduct from his State Department minders. Nonetheless, he overlooked such incidents as the U.S. cultural attaché in Athens warning his female staff that "respectable girls did not mix with black jazz musicians," and answered his audience's questions about race by saying that although "a hundred years ago, our ancestors were slaves, I'm sure it's gonna be straightened out some day. I probably won't see it, completely, the eradication of racial prejudice in the United States, but it will be eliminated." In the wake of Gillespie's triumphal and profitable tour, trumpeter Louis Armstrong agreed to a government-sponsored tour of the Soviet Union, but he was so outraged by the federal government's failure to intervene when Governor Orval Faubus of Arkansas stood in the doorway to prevent the integration of Little Rock's Central High School in 1957 that he canceled it, proclaiming that "the way they treat my people in the South, the government can go to hell." He even called Eisenhower an "uneducated plowboy" who allowed Faubus to "run the country." But Armstrong relented when Eisenhower belatedly sent troops to protect the black students in Little Rock, praised the president, and undertook a tour of Africa in 1960 that was jointly sponsored by the U.S. government and Pepsi Cola. (Ironically, Armstrong was playing in the Congo at the very time Patrice Lumumba, the leftist prime minister of the Congo, was being arrested, tortured, and executed with the connivance of the CIA, as described later in this chapter.)[1]

Thus, the New Look of Eisenhower and Dulles relied on cultural propaganda as well as massive retaliation, foreign alliances, indigenous troops, and political pressure to maintain its commitments abroad while reducing defense expenditures on conventional land forces. The New Look also placed increased emphasis on covert activities to deal with low-level threats to American interests. Under Eisenhower and Dulles, the CIA helped overthrow the governments of Iran and Guatemala, planned unsuccessful coups in Indonesia and Cuba, and considered or attempted the assassinations of Chinese premier Zhou Enlai, Cuba's Fidel Castro, Patrice Lumumba of the Congo, and Rafael Trujillo of the Dominican Republic. The extent of Eisenhower's knowledge of the CIA's assassination plots is somewhat uncertain, as is that of his successor, John F. Kennedy, but it is doubtful that the agency would have attempted such things without a broad mandate from the president.

Eisenhower, the Soviet Union, and Western Europe

On March 5, 1953, Joseph Stalin died. Shortly afterward, the apparent victor in the struggle for succession in the Kremlin, Georgy Malenkov, called for peaceful competition and coexistence with the United States. He pointed out that atomic weapons might destroy not just the capitalist world, as Stalin and Mao had maintained, but all of civilization. He called for more investment in consumer goods and less in the heavy industry that underlay Soviet military might. He even spoke of tolerating a unified Germany under a freely elected government so long as it was neutral and disarmed. Eisenhower briefly considered calling a summit meeting and offering some concessions to see if the Cold War might not be moderated. Dulles, however, urged caution. Accepting this advice, Eisenhower asked the Soviets to demonstrate their desire for peace with a few concrete steps, such as allowing free elections throughout Germany (which undoubtedly would result in a pro-Western, unified Germany), signing a peace treaty with Austria, ending the Korean War, or freeing the east European satellites. Before any further progress toward a summit could be made, the more erratic and belligerent Nikita Khrushchev ousted Malenkov by criticizing him for inspiring "anti-Marxist, anti-Leninist, and right-opportunist" policies.

Later critics have wondered what might have happened if Eisenhower had met Malenkov's offer more fully, agreed to a summit conference, and offered to avoid any armament of West Germany in exchange for Soviet concessions. Eisenhower and Dulles, however, believed it was better to press the Soviets than to propitiate them. The United States desperately wanted to build up Western Europe's conventional forces, and West Germany seemed the natural source for more soldiers. In addition, Eisenhower and Dulles were wary of a reunified, neutral, and disarmed Germany, even if it had a freely elected, Western-leaning government. West Germany's potential military and economic contribution to Western Europe was far more critical than East Germany's to the Soviet sphere, and Eisenhower and Dulles feared that a neutral, reunified Germany would cripple Western Europe and make its defense almost impossible.

In the wake of Malenkov's fall, Eisenhower moved quickly to rearm West Germany and tie it irrevocably to Western Europe. But a revived and rearmed Germany was a fearful prospect to France as well as to the Soviets. In order to reassure the French, the Western European allies devised a plan for a European defense community (EDC) that would incorporate small units of German soldiers into an integrated European army. Dulles warned the balky French that if they did not agree, the United States might have to undertake an "agonizing reappraisal" of its policy in Europe. Nevertheless, in August 1954, the French National Assembly voted to table EDC without even debating it.

What seemed like a terrible blow to Western unity was turned around with amazing ease. The British, who had held aloof from the continental army contemplated by EDC, stepped in to mediate. The French quickly consented to the integration of German forces into NATO, where the German troops would be subject to the control of the United States and Great Britain as well as the weaker continental powers. Rapid strides toward the further economic integration of Europe followed, and the Western Europeans institutionalized their sharing of economic and atomic resources by founding the Common Market and Euratom in 1957.

Meanwhile, in 1955, Khrushchev and the Soviets countered the military and economic integration of Western Europe with their own organization in the east, the Warsaw Pact. At the same time, Khrushchev, who actually agreed with many of Malenkov's policies but had opposed them as a means of overthrowing his rival, moved to lessen tensions and draw the United States into a summit meeting. He unexpectedly agreed to a peace treaty with Austria that provided for that nation's neutrality and the mutual withdrawal of Western and Soviet occupation troops. He also recognized West Germany. The Soviets even offered a nuclear disarmament plan that included carefully hedged but significant concessions to the Western point of view. They agreed to discuss the reduction rather than the complete elimination of nuclear weapons and to accept some very limited forms of inspection.

With these hints of Soviet flexibility on the critical Cold War issues of nuclear weapons and a European settlement, Eisenhower finally agreed to meet the new Soviet leadership at Geneva in July 1955. The results of this Geneva summit were disappointingly meager. The participants could agree to little more than a vague formula for continuing discussion on a German settlement. The USSR was adamant against a reunified and rearmed Germany linked to the West, while the United States and its allies rejected a neutral Germany ruled by a coalition of West Germans and the East German Communists. Eisenhower did offer a so-called Open Skies plan to permit aerial inspection of all nuclear powers as a means of inspiring the trust necessary to a nuclear disarmament treaty. But the Soviets, who already had access to most of the details of American nuclear production and deployment, who regarded secrecy as an important enhancement of their own inferior nuclear capability, and who knew of the technologically superior American U-2 spy plane, rejected Eisenhower's proposal as one-sided. About all that came out of the summit was a fragile atmosphere of goodwill briefly hailed as the "spirit of Geneva."

The Suez crisis and the contemporaneous Soviet suppression of the Hungarian rebellion of 1956 shattered that spirit. Egypt's Gamal Abdel Nasser triggered the Suez crisis by taking control of the Suez Canal. Nasser and his fellow Egyptian army officers had overthrown King Farouk in 1952 and persuaded Britain to withdraw its troops within four years. The Suez Canal, however, was not to come under Egypt's control but would be run by an international combine dominated by the British and other European users.

Shortly after the last British troops had left, Nasser, to whom the Americans restricted arms sales for fear he would use them in his low-level conflict with Israel, began accepting arms from the Soviets. An outraged Dulles consequently withdrew American offers of financial support for the Aswan High Dam, a project Nasser saw as the key to Egypt's economic development and his own prestige. Nasser responded by seizing the Suez Canal in July,1956, and proclaiming that he would use the revenue generated by the canal to finance the Aswan Dam. Without informing the United States, Great Britain and France immediately began plotting with Israel to retrieve the canal. They agreed that Israel would launch an attack on Egypt. Britain and France would then seize the canal on the pretext that the Israeli-Egyptian fighting endangered navigation there.

The Israeli-British-French military operations succeeded, and a British parachute force actually landed in Egypt to capture a portion of the canal. But Nasser blocked the canal by sinking ships in its navigation channels. Syria backed Nasser by cutting off the oil pipeline that traversed its territory on the way to the Mediterranean. The British Labour Party denounced the invasion and undermined domestic support for Prime Minister Anthony Eden. The Soviets rattled their rockets and threatened nuclear retaliation.

Far more critical than any of these obstacles to the success of the operation, Eisenhower and Dulles, who feared the effect of the British and French role in the Suez crisis on the third world and resented the lack of consultation by their allies, proclaimed the opposition of the United States and took the issue to the United Nations. The United States also began selling off massive amounts of British pounds sterling, which exerted tremendous pressure on the British economy. Finally, Eisenhower refused to ship Western Hemisphere oil to Europe to replace that lost by the closing of the Suez Canal and the disruption of the Syrian pipeline. Such measures finally forced Great Britain and France into a humiliating withdrawal from Suez. The Western alliance lay in tatters, and the United States was left increasingly alone to try to maintain some Western influence in the Middle East and Asia.

At this nadir of Western unity, the Hungarians rose up against Soviet control. The Soviets hesitated briefly and actually withdrew their tanks. Then, at the height of the Suez crisis, Soviet forces surged back into Hungary and crushed the Hungarian freedom fighters. The Eisenhower administration, after talking of "liberation" and encouraging east European resistance to communism in Voice of America broadcasts, stood by and watched with its disillusioned, fractious European allies rather than risk World War III by intervening.

A year later, in October 1957, the Soviet Union launched the first space satellite, *Sputnik*. The missile that carried *Sputnik* into space obviously was capable of carrying a nuclear warhead from Europe to North America. This first potential intercontinental ballistic missile (ICBM) frightened many Americans and led to calls for crash programs to catch up to the Russians. Eisenhower agreed to expand America's ICBM production slightly and to station intermediate-range missiles in Europe. But he resisted the panic calls for a crash program that emanated even from within his own administration. He was convinced that the United States had sufficient power to deter a Soviet nuclear attack and that it would be foolish and outrageously expensive to build beyond that. He even offered to suspend nuclear testing if the Soviets would agree to a mutual moratorium and enter negotiations at Geneva for a formal test ban treaty. The Soviets accepted and announced a moratorium on March 31, 1958. Eisenhower followed suit five months later against heavy opposition from some of his advisers.

Eisenhower was able to make these decisions because of a top-secret program of U-2 flights over the Soviet Union that began in 1956. Those flights could pick up any evidence of a major Soviet nuclear test that violated the moratorium. The U-2 also sent back information that the Soviets were not deploying large numbers of ICBM missiles (in fact, Khrushchev had only four operational ICBMs until after 1960). Khrushchev had decided to wait for the second generation of missiles before installing a full-fledged intercontinental nuclear strike force. Meanwhile, Eisenhower knew that the Soviet air force had few planes capable of delivering nuclear weapons to the United States and that Khrushchev had begun to cut Soviet conventional forces.

Nevertheless, Khrushchev tried to capitalize on *Sputnik* and the supposed Soviet strategic lead. He actually believed that his nuclear threats were the primary reason the British and French had backed down at Suez, and he thought that Eisenhower's ruminations at the Geneva Conference of 1955 about the futility of nuclear war indicated that the U.S. president was weak. Thus, Khrushchev proclaimed to his government underlings that the leader with the strongest nerves would win any Cold War standoff. In November 1958, he announced that the Soviets would sign a peace treaty with East Germany in six months unless there was a negotiated settlement with the West by that time. Since the Soviets already recognized West Germany, recognition of East Germany would complete the process of restoring sovereignty to the conquered Germans. Occupation rights would cease, and foreign troops would have to be withdrawn from West Berlin. Khrushchev offered to make Berlin a free, demilitarized city, but he knew that the expulsion of the Western powers would put an end to German hopes of a unified, rearmed Germany allied with the West. It would also put a stop to the flow of refugees into West Berlin, a drain that had cost East Germany nearly 3 million of its most productive citizens since 1949.

Eisenhower and the West were at an enormous strategic disadvantage in Berlin. They did not have the conventional forces to defend West Berlin against the Russians and East Germans, and the Soviets could wipe out European if not American cities should the United States resort to nuclear weapons. Yet Eisenhower was determined not to abandon Berlin or to negotiate under Khrushchev's six-month ultimatum. He announced that the United States would not try to shoot its way into Berlin or to fight a ground war in Europe, and he made clear his desire for a negotiated settlement. But he implied he would resort to nuclear arms if all other alternatives failed and the Soviets initiated hostilities. He could only hope that Soviet uncertainty would lead Khrushchev to seek a peaceful solution.

After several weeks of growing tension, Khrushchev offered to drop the six-month deadline if Eisenhower would attend a summit meeting. Eisenhower balked at this offer, but invited Khrushchev to an informal tour of the United States and a personal meeting at Camp David. At that meeting, Eisenhower finally agreed to a formal summit, and Khrushchev abandoned his deadline for solving the Berlin issue. They set the summit for May 1960 in Paris, where Eisenhower hoped to sign a formal nuclear test ban agreement.

Just before the Paris meeting convened, the Soviets shot down an American U-2 over their territory. Eisenhower had approved the flight because intelligence sources were reporting that the Russians had begun construction of their first operational ICBM base, and Eisenhower thought U-2 confirmation was worth the risk of endangering the summit. When the Russians announced that they had shot down the U-2, the Americans issued a cover story that it was a weather plane blown off course. But Khrushchev had laid a trap for Eisenhower by concealing the fact that the Soviets had actually recovered the plane's wreckage and its pilot, Francis Gary Powers. Having humiliated Eisenhower, Khrushchev offered him a way out by pretending to believe that Eisenhower had been unaware of these flights. Eisenhower, however, accepted personal responsibility. Khrushchev then demanded that Eisenhower halt all further U-2 flights over the USSR and apologize for past ones. Eisenhower said he had already halted the flights, but he would not apologize for defending American security. Khrushchev stalked out of the summit, proclaiming that he would wait to negotiate with Eisenhower's successor. It was a sad and ignominious way for Eisenhower to end his presidency.

The Dilemma of the Middle East

As the Cold War reached its height in the 1950s and 1960s, the United States found itself increasingly embroiled in what was for it a relatively new arena, the Middle East. Before World War I, the American presence in the Middle East had been limited to a few missionaries and traders who received minimal support from American diplomatic or naval officers. During World War I, Woodrow Wilson briefly asserted an American role in the Middle East by urging Great Britain and France to grant independence to the Arab provinces whose rebellions against the Ottoman Turks the Allies had aided and abetted. Unfortunately, Wilson's influence evaporated in the battle over the Versailles peace terms, and the United States could only watch as the British and French divided the remnants of the Ottoman Empire between them. Great Britain received a League of Nations mandate to legitimate its wartime occupation of Iraq and Palestine. It also used the opportunity to strengthen its control of Egypt and the Sudan. France obtained a League mandate for Syria and Lebanon to go along with its existing North African colonies in Algeria, Tunisia, and Morocco.

American oil industry experts and government officials were especially disturbed when Britain and France announced that they intended to monopolize all oil resources in their Middle Eastern mandates. Experts feared that U.S. oil reserves had been badly depleted by World War I and that the remaining domestic resources would be exhausted within a decade or two. The Wilson and Harding administrations protested loudly that the oil concessions should be open for competition. The British and French adamantly refused such a policy until 1928, when they reluctantly invited some American oil companies to join their international cartel as junior partners. In return these American companies had to abide by the so-called Red Line agreement, formulated by Britain and France at the San Remo Conference of 1920. The Red Line agreement provided that none of the members of the cartel could undertake independent or competitive operations in the mandates.

By the time the American companies were admitted to the cartel, the urgency had passed for the American government. Major oil discoveries in Texas, Oklahoma, and California had produced a petroleum glut in the United States. But some oil companies did not lose interest. Standard Oil of California, which had not joined the cartel and therefore was not bound by the San Remo agreement, acquired independent concessions in Bahrain and Saudi Arabia when those nations managed to throw off some of Britain's control. Shortly before World War II, Standard Oil invited several other American companies to help exploit its concessions by forming their own cartel, the Arabian-American Oil Company (Aramco).

By the end of World War II, the Middle East possessed two-thirds of the world's proved reserves, and American oil companies controlled 40 percent of them. There had been some wartime rivalry between Great Britain and the United States over this oil, but Churchill and Roosevelt had agreed to respect each other's concessions and work together to face what they regarded as the greater threat of Soviet expansion into the area.

Increasingly, the United States found itself bearing the primary responsibility for Western influence in the Middle East. France's defeat by Germany in 1940 had caused it to lose its grip in Syria and Lebanon, and after the war France granted the two nations their independence. France also faced rising nationalist movements in its North African colonies. Meanwhile, Great Britain was forced to turn over its responsibilities for the defense of Greece and Turkey to the United States and its Truman Doctrine in 1947. Britain had its own difficulties with rising nationalism in Egypt, and it faced a nearly insoluble problem of Arab-Jewish rivalry in Palestine.

The United States tried to ease its way into the Middle East by reminding Arab nationalists that Woodrow Wilson and Franklin Roosevelt had favored Arab independence. Arguing that the greatest threat to Arab independence came from the Soviet Union, Truman tried to establish a Middle East Command that would formally ally the Arab countries with the United States, Great Britain, and France to combat Soviet expansionism. The Arabs, however, worried far more about Jewish Zionist ambitions in Palestine than about Soviet Russia, and they regarded the United States and Great Britain as the primary supporters of the Zionists. Arab nationalists thus increasingly ranged themselves against the Western powers.

The Zionist movement to establish a Jewish state in Palestine had crystallized in the late nineteenth century when the rise of nationalism in Europe accentuated the differences between European Jewish communities and the increasingly self-conscious nationalities that surrounded them. Theodore Herzl and the World Zionist Organization led the movement. They encouraged European Jews to immigrate to Palestine and asked that the great powers recognize a Jewish state in the area. The British, who were seeking Palestine as a mandate for themselves during World War I, saw a chance to enlist Jewish support for their position. On November 2, 1917, they issued the Balfour Declaration, proclaiming British support for "the establishment in Palestine of a national home for the Jewish people . . . it being clearly understood that nothing shall be done which may prejudice the civil and religious rights of existing non-Jewish communities in Palestine." Of course, there was no way to establish a Jewish homeland in Palestine without disturbing the rights of the Muslim inhabitants. Nevertheless, the Balfour Declaration and its basic internal contradiction were written into the British mandate for Palestine.

Arab riots against the growing Jewish population in Palestine erupted as early as 1921. They did not become serious until the late 1930s, however, when Nazi persecution provoked a flood of Jewish immigration. The Arabs of the territory called a general strike in 1936 and attacked both Jewish settlements and British authorities. In 1939 the beleaguered British issued a White Paper declaring they would permit only 100,000 more Jews to enter Palestine. The White Paper quota threatened to choke off the flow of Jewish refugees even as the Nazis were beginning their program of genocide.

The United States had never formally endorsed Zionism, although Woodrow Wilson had given a private, reluctant consent to the Balfour Declaration and Congress had passed a joint resolution endorsing a Jewish homeland in Palestine. Throughout the 1930s and 1940s, popular sentiment in America generally favored the Zionist goal, and both the Democrats and Republicans regularly included a Zionist plank in their party platforms. American Jews were the primary financial support of the Jewish communities in Palestine.

But for all the sympathy Americans had toward the Jewish victims of Nazi persecution, the United States did little to provide a refuge for them. The Depression had encouraged a strong anti-immigration sentiment in the American body politic which Roosevelt and the State Department were reluctant to challenge. The State Department additionally feared that Fascist fifth columnists and Communist agitators might slip into the United States in the flow of immigrants. Consequently, while the British requested the United States to absorb more Jewish refugees, the Americans urged the British to open Palestine to further immigration. Neither relented until 1944, when Roosevelt finally formed a War Refugee Board outside the jurisdiction of the State Department. The board vigorously sought to rescue the remaining Jews of Europe, but by then its efforts were too little, too late.

In 1942 the desperate Jews of Palestine began to attack the British and the Arabs in order to force permission for further immigration. They also smuggled their European compatriots into Palestine in violation of the quota. A sympathetic Roosevelt called for a Jewish state in Palestine, but also he promised King Ibn Saud of Saudi Arabia that he would take no action hostile to the Arab people. Ibn Saud and other Arab leaders had made clear to Roosevelt that the Arabs would fight to stop further Jewish immigration or the formation of a Jewish state in Palestine.

Harry Truman was the unfortunate heir of Roosevelt's ambiguous policy toward this insoluble problem. Truman was under pressure from his State and Defense Departments to avoid alienating Arab opinion. They pointed to the potentially disastrous effects of Zionist sympathies upon U.S. interests in Middle Eastern oil and hopes for resistance to Soviet expansion in the area. But Truman sympathized with the plight of the Jews. He also saw political benefits to a pro-Zionist stand. Since Jewish lobbies and votes were critical to elections in several key states while there was no domestic constituency of Arabs, a pro-Jewish stand seemed pure political gain. Thus, he decided in 1945 to urge the British to revise their White Paper quota and permit 100,000 more Jewish refugees into Palestine.

The British, fearful of losing Suez and their oil concessions to angry Arabs, caustically rejected Truman's suggestion. Foreign Minister Ernest Bevin commented that the

Americans were moved less by sympathy than by their desire to avoid more Jews in New York. In 1946 Truman endorsed a Jewish state in Palestine, and the British blamed him for the failure of their already doomed plan for a federated Jewish-Arab state to relieve them of their mandate. Thwarted at every turn, the British handed the issue over to the United Nations.

Meanwhile, tensions rose in Palestine as Jewish settlers, ignoring a new British quota of 1,500 immigrants per month, smuggled increasing numbers of refugees into Palestine. The British captured groups of these illegal immigrants and interned them on the island of Cyprus in concentration camps built by German prisoners of war. In this explosive atmosphere, the United Nations, with the support of a Soviet bloc that wished to see the British out of the Middle East, agreed to partition Palestine between independent Jewish and Arab states. The Arab nations angrily announced they would destroy any independent Jewish state. Syria threatened to cut its oil pipeline. Great Britain, warning that it would not enforce any arrangement that did not have the consent of both Arabs and Jews, insisted that it would abandon the mandate in May 1948.

Truman, fearful of the chaos and war that were impending, suddenly intervened, calling for a truce and a delay in partition. But the Jews insisted that it was now or never for the creation of Israel; the Arabs refused a truce unless there was a unified Arab state in all of Palestine; and no United Nations member offered to help the United States enforce a truce. Partition took place as scheduled, and on May 15, 1948, the Jewish state of Israel was born. Truman regained the support he had lost in the American Jewish community with his truce proposal by recognizing the new nation within minutes after it had been proclaimed. The Arab states, on the other hand, invaded Israel.

The United Nations tried with only sporadic success to impose a cease-fire on the combatants. Finally, in 1949, Israeli troops surrounded much of the Egyptian army and Egypt had to request an end to the fighting. The other belligerent Arab states soon followed suit, but the situation remained volatile. Israel was unhappy with its borders, even though they had been expanded during the war with the Arabs. The Israelis thought their territory was too small to absorb the flood of immigrants they expected. Many Jews claimed the biblical right to restore all of Palestine to Jewish rule by annexing the West Bank area of the Jordan River, the part of Palestine that the United Nations had allotted to the Arabs but that Jews knew as the old biblical provinces of Judea and Samaria. Absorption of the West Bank also would give the Israelis defensible borders. They were particularly worried that if the Arabs attacked Israel at its narrowest point, they would have to drive only nine miles to the sea to split Israel in half.

The Arabs were even more distressed. Some 750,000 people, nearly half the Arab population of Palestine, had fled or been forced from their homes to become refugees in miserable camps in the Arab states bordering Israel. Those who stayed behind became second-class citizens in a Jewish religious state. The displaced Palestinian Arabs posed a prickly problem for the Arab nations of the Middle East, especially for Trans-Jordan, the country that annexed the Arab portion of Palestine. The Palestinians were an energetic and relatively well-educated people. If Israel's neighbors tried to absorb them, the Palestinians might actually displace the indigenous leadership. So, rather than absorb them, most of the Arab border states left Palestinian refugees in temporary camps and encouraged them to devote their energies to restoring Arab rule in Israel. The British abetted the process of Arab-Israeli enmity by discouraging tentative peace moves toward Israel made by King Abdullah of Trans-Jordan and King Farouk of Egypt. The British feared that Israel, which was then neutral and derived substantial support from the Soviet Union, might try to lead the Arab world away from its Western orientation.

The British miscalculated badly. The continuing Arab-Israeli conflict stirred the Arab peoples to rage at the incompetence, venality, and half-heartedness of their leaders' efforts against Israel. Nationalistic army officers overthrew the Syrian regime in 1949. King Hussein, Abdullah's successor in Jordan, barely survived a Palestinian coup. A group of Egyptian army officers overthrew King Farouk in 1952, and one of them, Colonel Gamal Abdel Nasser, soon became the rallying point for the revival of Arab nationalism throughout the Middle East. As such, Nasser threatened not only Israel, but also the British position in Egypt and Suez, the remaining French colonies in North Africa, the vital Western oil holdings in the Middle East, and the large military bases the United States had recently established in Libya and Morocco.

To the still greater discomfort of the West, the rise of Nasser coincided with a change in Soviet policy toward the Middle East. Stalin, regarding the Arab nationalists as bourgeois reactionaries, had done as much as the United States to aid Israel during the Arab-Israel conflict. After Stalin's death, however, Nikita Khrushchev announced Soviet support of Arab wars of national liberation.

To further compound the disturbance of the West, the Middle Eastern oil nations began to realize the strength of their position and to demand greater profits from oil operations. Before World War II, the oil companies had been dominant. They had had the technological expertise and the capital to invest in risky enterprises, while the oil nations had been unable to drive a hard bargain either because they were not free agents (e.g., the British mandates of Iraq and Kuwait) or because they were in desperate need of money (e.g., Saudi Arabia and Iran). Consequently, the oil companies had paid their host nations very low fees and had received exemption from taxation.

The oil countries began to assert their own power in 1948, when Venezuela imposed a 50 percent tax on oil company profits and got away with it. Saudi Arabia and Kuwait quickly demanded similar arrangements. The Truman administration encouraged the oil companies to concede to the demands, for although the United States was still self-sufficient in petroleum, its Western European allies were dependent on imported oil. The State Department proceeded to work out a deal whereby Saudi Arabia and Kuwait would receive 50 percent of the oil companies' profits on operations in their countries, while the United States would compensate the companies by exempting these payments from American taxation. In effect, the $50 million increase in Ibn Saud's profits came from American taxpayers. The State Department had made the oil companies the "paymasters of the Arab states." The Truman administration hoped the subsidies might hold the Arabs in line despite America's support for Israel. It also realized that subsidizing the oil companies to pay the Arabs would circumvent the need to ask a pro-Israeli American Congress for direct appropriations to Israel's enemies.

The British-dominated Anglo-Iranian Oil Company, however, was unwilling to make a similar deal with Iran. The Iranians began to clamor for nationalization of the oil industry. By the time the Anglo-Iranian Company came around to offer a fifty-fifty split in oil revenues, it was too late. In 1951 Mohammad Mosaddeq took over as Iranian prime minister and nationalized Anglo-Iranian's holdings. Great Britain then withdrew its technical personnel and imposed a boycott on Iranian oil with the aid of the American oil companies. The Truman administration tried to find a compromise between the Iranians and the British company and provided some aid to keep the Iranian economy afloat. But Mosaddeq would not compromise on nationalization, the Iranian economy crumbled without its oil revenues, and Iran threatened to turn to the Soviets for help.

Eisenhower and Dulles, despairing of the Mosaddeq regime, decided that nothing the United States could do would successfully prop up the regime to keep it out of the hands of the Communists. Eisenhower and Dulles turned to the CIA to promote a coup that would eliminate Mosaddeq. In 1953, Kermit Roosevelt, the grandson of Theodore Roosevelt, arrived in Iran with $1 million and dispensed $100,000 of it to recruit pro-shah demonstrators from the athletic clubs and slums of Teheran. Unfortunately for the CIA, Mosaddeq anticipated the coup, arrested some of the opposition leaders, and aroused a tremendous demonstration in his favor that sent the frightened shah into headlong flight to Rome.

Still, there was a strong current of discontent with Mosaddeq policies in Iran. Not only did he increase Iran's dependence on the Communist Tudeh Party, but also he dissolved the legislature and personally assumed almost all government power. To control the violent acts of his rioting supporters, Mosaddeq finally had to call out the army and police, who pushed Tudeh Party members off the streets while chanting, "Long live the shah, death to Mosaddeq." Then Kermit Roosevelt's mob put in its appearance. Supported by the soldiers and police, it attracted a cheering throng of thousands of Teheran residents. Mosaddeq went to prison in tears, the shah returned to power, and the legislature installed a retired general as prime minister.

The new government imprisoned or executed hundreds of Tudeh Party members and Mosaddeq supporters. It also worked out a compromise on oil with the Western powers. Iran retained ownership of the oil fields and refineries and shared half the revenues from oil sales with a new Western oil consortium that consisted of five American firms along with Britain's Anglo-Iranian Company. The intrusion of the five American firms into the previously exclusive domain of the Anglo-Iranian Company was yet another sign that the United States was replacing Britain as the dominant Western power throughout the world.

Meanwhile, the Western oil companies believed they had succeeded in making an example of Iran that would deter other oil nations from pushing their advantages too far. The companies even worked out a way to minimize the gains the oil nations had already made. Since the oil cartels in Iran, Saudi Arabia, and elsewhere were selling Middle Eastern oil to the cartels' own parent companies back home, they charged themselves very little. This practice left the oil nations with 50 percent of very low prices, while the oil companies made their big profits on retail sales, which they did not have to share with the producer nations. But the oil companies' victory was far from permanent. The resentful nations formed the Organization of Petroleum Exporting Countries (OPEC) in 1959 to gain a better share of the profits from their oil resources. In the 1970s they would turn the tables on the oil companies and the Western powers.

Like the oil companies, the CIA and the American government also viewed Iran as an object lesson. They saw how easily a handful of CIA operatives with a trunkful of cash had thwarted a dangerous nationalist movement in a third-world country. Eisenhower and the CIA mistakenly assumed that they could repeat this success whenever it seemed necessary. CIA chief Allen Dulles (the brother of Secretary of State John Foster Dulles), for instance, snarled at one State Department official who had defended Nasser's nationalistic conduct, "If that colonel of yours pushes us too far we will break him in half!"

Eisenhower, however, hoped to deal with Nasser and Arab nationalism less drastically. In 1955 he and John Foster Dulles helped organize the Baghdad Pact, which allied Turkey, Iran, Pakistan, Iraq, and Great Britain to block any Soviet advance into the Middle East. Eisenhower continued Truman's policy of indirectly subsidizing the oil-producing nations by offering tax exemptions to the oil companies. He also extended Truman's policy of blocking the Justice Department's attempt to prosecute the oil companies for antitrust activities in the Middle East. Appalled at the potential effect on Arab nationalism of the British-French-Israeli attack on Suez, he compelled the Western nations' retreat.

But once Eisenhower had secured their withdrawal from Suez, he knew he had shattered the prestige of Britain and France in the Arab world. He thought it essential that the United States move dramatically to ensure that the Soviet Union did not take advantage of the power vacuum. In 1957 he secured congressional approval not only for economic and military aid to the Arab nations, but also for the Eisenhower Doctrine. The Eisenhower Doctrine permitted the president to use armed force to protect any Middle Eastern nation that requested aid against "overt armed aggression from any nation controlled by international communism."

Eisenhower made use of that authority quickly. He sent the Sixth Fleet and $10 million to Jordan to help King Hussein and his Bedouin supporters beat back an attempt by Palestinian-led nationalists to dethrone him. When a revolution in Iraq overthrew the westward-leaning monarchy, Eisenhower sought to prevent the spread of the virus by landing more than 10,000 American troops in Lebanon while Great Britain sent equivalent forces to Jordan.[2]

Thus, Eisenhower aligned the United States more and more overtly with the most conservative forces in the Arab world, even though most Arab nationalists were wary of the Soviets and communism. Nasser actually outlawed the Egyptian Communist Party and imprisoned or executed many of its members. The Soviets consequently remained leery of Arab nationalism, despite paying lip service to wars of national liberation. So Eisenhower's excessive interventionism probably pushed Arab nationalism closer to the Soviets than was necessary. Still, the United States had little room to maneuver in the Middle East as it tried to balance its moral commitment to Israel, its need for oil, and the probability that the Soviets would accept whatever influence or territory might be thrown their way by anti-Western Arab nationalists.

Eisenhower and Latin America

Eisenhower ranged the United States against nationalism in Latin America as well as the Middle East, and for the same reason. He feared that Latin American nationalists would invite Soviet influence into another area of strategic and economic importance to the United States. The United States focused most of its attention on Europe and the Far East during the Cold War, but it could not remain oblivious to the continuing strategic value of the Panama Canal, the naval bases of the Caribbean, and the large reserves of oil and copper in Latin America. Besides, after World War II, Latin America's market for U.S. exports came to equal that of Europe and to surpass those of Asia, Africa, and Oceania combined. Thirty-five percent of U.S. imports came from Latin America as well, and the United States had more foreign investments in Latin America than in any other foreign area except Canada.

President Truman had tried to protect the U.S. position in Latin America by extending minor amounts of economic and technological aid through his Point Four program, by giving some military aid ($38 million in 1951), and by signing the Rio Pact of 1947 with the nations of the Western Hemisphere. The Rio Pact promised reciprocal assistance if Soviet intervention threatened any Western Hemisphere nation. These measures, however, did little to cope with the rise of revolutionary nationalism in Latin America. When the Eisenhower administration feared that a nationalist movement in Guatemala might invite Soviet influence into the hemisphere, it turned to the same sort of covert intervention that had been successful in Iran.

Guatemala was a nation and society ripe for revolution. Two percent of its people owned 70 percent of the land. Foreigners, led by the United Fruit Company of the United States, owned most of the big latifundios (plantations) that produced Guatemalan bananas and coffee for export. United Fruit also controlled the nation's railroads and its major Caribbean ports. It made sure that no Pacific port and no other railroads were built to compete with company-controlled facilities. The Maya Indians, who composed two-thirds of Guatemala's population, were left with 15 percent of the least arable land. This was insufficient to provide even a subsistence living for them. With 90 percent of the nation's agricultural production in bananas and coffee intended for export, Guatemala had to import food, which the lower classes, deprived of the ability to produce their own, had to buy at very high prices. Yet half of United Fruit's land lay fallow and unused as the company sought to avoid overproduction of its export crops.

In 1944 a middle-class revolution brought Juan Arévalo Bermej to power. Arévalo was supported mainly by the 30 percent of the Guatemalan population known as Ladinos, those who had adopted European languages and ways. Arévalo forced United Fruit to rent out some of its fallow lands, imposed rent control and a labor code on the latifundios, and eliminated forced labor. United Fruit convinced the Truman administration that Communists influenced the revolution. Consequently, Truman withheld aid and instituted an arms embargo. But he did little else. Arévalo, after surviving twenty-five coup attempts in six years, was succeeded by Jacobo Arbenz Guzmán, who won 60 percent of the vote in the 1950 election.

Arbenz sympathized with the workers' strikes plaguing United Fruit and began ex-propriating and redistributing United Fruit's fallow land, paying the company in com-pensation the low price United Fruit had set on the land for purposes of taxation. United Fruit howled bitterly that Communists had taken over in Guatemala. It had ready allies in the Eisenhower administration, since the Dulles brothers, Secretary of State John Foster Dulles and CIA director Allen Dulles, had been members of the company's law firm. When Arbenz made a deal for Soviet arms, the suspicions of the CIA and the FBI seemed confirmed. The United States secured a reluctant condemnation of the Arbenz regime from the Organization of American States (the Caracas Declaration) and then organized a coup in Guatemala.

The CIA settled on Colonel Carlos Castillo Armas to lead an invasion from neighboring Honduras in 1954. The invasion comprised a total of 150 soldiers, 150 advance agents, a few minor air raids (some bombs were thrown out of planes by hand), a CIA-run radio station that broadcast threats of a huge invasion force, and a great deal of bluff. Arbenz had difficulty calling the bluff, however, because he commanded a disloyal army. He also had little support from the peasants because they had not benefited from his reforms. Arbenz was even afraid to order his planes to scout the invasion force because he feared the pilots would accept the CIA radio invitations to desert. Thus, he could not know how small Castillo Armas's army was or that Castillo Armas had halted it only six miles into Guatemala. Arbenz simply panicked and fled.

Once again the CIA had demonstrated to itself how easily nationalist movements in third-world countries could be manipulated.[3] But others were deriving lessons from Iran and Guatemala as well. In Cuba, rebels Fidel Castro and Che Guevara saw how important it was to rally the peasants and not just the moderate middle class to their revolution. They realized that the CIA-sponsored coups in Iran and Guatemala had been won by luck, bluff, and the weakness of their opponents' leaders, Mosaddeq and Arbenz. When the CIA tried to repeat its Iranian and Guatemalan successes in Cuba, it found the outcome much different.

Meanwhile, the half-secret CIA role in Guatemala further alienated Latin American nationalists from the United States. South Americans picketed, threw rocks, and spit on Vice President Richard Nixon during a highly publicized tour in 1958. Riots broke out in the Panama Canal Zone. Eisenhower tried to win back some non-Communist national-ists by creating the Inter-American Development Bank and subscribing $500 million to it in 1959. But this ploy made little impact on either the problems or the sentiments of Latin Americans.

Eisenhower also tried to appeal to Latin American nationalism and stave off the Cas-tro rebellion in Cuba by demanding that America's longtime client, the corrupt dictator Fulgencio Batista, hold fair elections. When Batista refused, Eisenhower cut off his supply of American arms, and Castro's rebels took over the country on January 1, 1959. Although Eisenhower distrusted Castro's virulent anti-American rhetoric, he recognized that Castro was not close to the Cuban Communist Party and hoped that Castro would moderate his anti-Americanism when he faced the practical issues of governing. Castro, however, refused to moderate his radical plans for Cuba and continued to denounce American control over many aspects of Cuban life. Consequently, Eisenhower ordered the CIA to plan Castro's overthrow, a plan that would ultimately lead to the disastrous Bay of Pigs invasion under Eisenhower's successor.

Eisenhower and Asia

Eisenhower and John Foster Dulles approached revolutionary nationalism in Asia with the same assumptions they did nationalism in the Middle East and Latin America. They were determined that Soviet and Chinese communism should not benefit from turmoil in strategic areas. Once the Korean War ended, Eisenhower was particularly concerned about the French war in Indochina. He believed that a Communist victory in Indochina would mean not only the loss to the West of the area's rice, tin, and rubber, but the fall of Indochina's neighbors like a row of dominoes—Burma, Thailand, Indonesia, and perhaps even Japan, Taiwan, and the Philippines.

Eisenhower thought the French were handling the Indochina war very badly. He thought that their military tactics were foolish and that their refusal to guarantee Vietnamese independence and self-government was destroying the hope of a nationalist alternative to communism. When the Communist Vietminh surrounded and threatened to exterminate a French army at Dienbienphu in 1954, Eisenhower regarded the debacle as the culmination of France's disastrous, expensive strategy.

The French asked for American help, but Eisenhower doubted that any American action could save Dienbienphu. He and Dulles were primarily concerned with saving what would remain of the Western position in Indochina. Eisenhower set several conditions for any help he might give the French and their besieged troops at Dienbienphu. The French would have to make public their request to the United States for aid; America's allies, especially Great Britain, would have to contribute; Congress would have to give its consent; and the French would have to share future control of their political and military operations in Indochina with the United States, grant Vietnam its independence, and prosecute the war more vigorously.

The French refused to share control, Great Britain declined to participate, and Congress proved reluctant. Senator John F. Kennedy proclaimed that an American war in Indochina would be "dangerously futile and self-destructive." Senate Majority Leader Lyndon Johnson warned against "sending American GIs into the mud and muck of Indochina on a bloodletting spree." Eisenhower let the matter drop and permitted Dulles to blame his decision on Britain's refusal to participate.

Nevertheless, Eisenhower warned Communist China that any attempt to expand into Indochina might call forth a nuclear response from the United States. He then sent Dulles to observe as the French, Vietnamese, and British tried to work out a negotiated settlement at Geneva. Russia and China pressed North Vietnam's reluctant leader, Ho Chi Minh, to accept a truce, and the Geneva Conference decided that Vietnam would be divided temporarily at the seventeenth parallel until elections for a unified nation were held two years later in 1956. The United States did not formally accept the Geneva agreement, but "took note" of its provisions, promised not to disturb them by force, and warned that it would intervene if anyone else tried to break them.

After the Geneva Conference of 1954, Eisenhower and Dulles set out to replace French influence in South Vietnam and build a non-Communist regime there capable of winning the 1956 elections (Eisenhower admitted that Ho Chi Minh and the Communists would win 80 percent of the vote if the elections were held in 1954). The United States supported Emperor Bao Dai's appointment of Ngo Dinh Diem as the new prime minister of South Vietnam and funneled American aid through Diem rather than through the French. Diem was a Catholic refugee from North Vietnam who had spent much time in the United States as the guest of several monasteries and other Catholic institutions. Many Americans, including the wealthy, influential family of John F. Kennedy, regarded him as an ideal nationalist alternative to communism or colonialism who could protect Western interests in the third world.

As further protection against Communist expansion, Dulles organized the Southeast Asia Treaty Organization (SEATO). SEATO allied the United States, Great Britain, France, Australia, and New Zealand with the non-Communist Asian nations of Thailand, the Philippines, and Pakistan. Although the Geneva Agreement of 1954 prohibited South Vietnam, Cambodia, and Laos from participating in an alliance, a protocol of SEATO extended the alliance's protection to Indochina. But SEATO was as weak a reed as Ngo Dinh Diem and the South Vietnamese government turned out to be. SEATO included no major Asian power like India or Indonesia, and it had no automatic provisions for collective action against aggression.

One further crisis in Asia bedeviled Eisenhower and Dulles. The Communist Chinese periodically bombarded the offshore islands of Quemoy and Matsu, which were occupied by Chiang Kai-shek's Nationalists as outposts of their refuge on Taiwan. Quemoy and Matsu were not necessary to the defense of Taiwan, and it seemed ridiculous to risk a major war over them. But Chiang was determined to hold them as launching pads for his projected return to the mainland, and Eisenhower and Dulles did not want to demoralize their Nationalist allies or give in to Communist pressure. So when Mao resumed bombardment of the islands in the summer of 1958 (without informing Khrushchev and at least partly as a means to thwart Khrushchev's moves toward détente), Eisenhower announced with studied ambiguity that the United States would defend Quemoy and Matsu if an attack on them seemed to be a prelude to an invasion of Taiwan, and he hinted broadly that this defense would not be limited to conventional weapons. Ultimately the Chinese reduced their pressure and shelling and agreed to informal negotiations. Democrats and other critics roundly condemned Eisenhower for risking World War III over such a trivial issue. The Quemoy-Matsu issue faded, but the Indochina war remained to plague the administrations that succeeded Eisenhower.

Controversial Issues

Until well into the 1970s, historians treated John Foster Dulles as the primary figure behind the foreign policy of the Eisenhower administration. Some praised Dulles for his strong anticommunism, for being a "Patriot, Statesman, and Unflinching Warrior in the Struggle Against Appeasement."[4] Others condemned him for his anti-Communist rigidity.[5]

Indochina, 1953–1954

As hard-line anticommunism started to go out of fashion in the wake of Vietnam, some historians emphasized Dulles's private flexibility and realism.[6] A few right-wingers had thought they detected this flexibility even earlier and condemned it as weakness in the face of Communist aggression.[7] But all agreed that Eisenhower had deferred to Dulles's supposedly greater expertise. Even defenders of Eisenhower admitted this, regretting that Eisenhower had not asserted his own more moderate views over the ideological rigidity of his secretary of state.[8]

In the late 1960s, a few journalists began to revise this view. They asserted that Eisenhower had controlled his own foreign policy and that his restraint in foreign affairs contrasted favorably with the sort of activism that later led Kennedy and Johnson to escalate the Vietnam war.[9] Historians delving into the archives of the Eisenhower Library, which opened in the late 1960s, largely agreed. Like the journalists, most of these "Eisenhower revisionists" praised the president for his restraint, but even those who criticized him as just another Cold War warrior agreed that he had dominated his administration. Debates among historians still rage about the relative worth of Eisenhower's policies, but there is no longer any question that Eisenhower rather than Dulles was the key figure in making American policy in the 1950s.[10]

Further Reading

A good recent biography of Eisenhower is Geoffrey Perret, *Eisenhower* (1999). Generally positive accounts of Eisenhower's foreign policy are Robert R. Bowie and Richard H. Immerman, *Waging Peace: How Eisenhower Shaped an Enduring Cold War Strategy* (1998); Herbert S. Parmet, *Eisenhower and the American Crusades* (1972); and Robert A. Divine, *Eisenhower and the Cold War* (1981). More critical are Chester A. Pach Jr. and Elmo Richardson, *The Presidency of Dwight D. Eisenhower* (1991); H.W. Brands, *Cold Warriors: Eisenhower's Generation and American Foreign Policy* (1988); Piers Brandon, *Ike: His Life and Times* (1986); and Peter Lyon, *Eisenhower: Portrait of a Hero* (1974). A hostile account is Blanche Wiesen Cook, *The Declassified Eisenhower: A Divided Legacy* (1981). A survey of the whole spectrum of Eisenhower revisionism is Richard A. Melanson and David Mayers, *Reevaluating Eisenhower: American Foreign Policy in the 1950s* (1987). The best book on John Foster Dulles and his role in Eisenhower's foreign policy is Richard H. Immerman, *John Foster Dulles: Piety, Pragmatism, and Power in U.S. Foreign Policy* (1999).

On the Eisenhower-Dulles strategy, the New Look, see Saki Dockrill, *Eisenhower's New-Look National Security Policy, 1953–1961* (1996); John Lewis Gaddis, *Strategies of Containment* (rev. and expanded ed., 2005) and *The Long Peace: Inquiries into the History of the Cold War* (1987); Marc Trachtenberg, *History and Strategy* (1991); Charles Alexander, *Holding the Line* (1975); and Douglas Kinnard, *President Eisenhower and Strategy Management* (1977). On nuclear issues, see Craig Campbell, *Destroying the Village: Eisenhower and Thermonuclear War* (1998); George Kistiakowsky, *A Scientist at the White House* (1976); James R. Killian, *Sputnik, Scientists and Eisenhower* (1978); Chalmers M. Roberts, *The Nuclear Years: The Arms Race and Arms Control,*

1945–1970 (1970); George H. Quester, *Nuclear Diplomacy: The First Twenty-Five Years* (1970); Robert A. Divine, *Blowing on the Wind: The Nuclear Test Ban Debate, 1954–1960* (1978); McGeorge Bundy, *Danger and Survival: Choices About the Bomb in the First Fifty Years* (1988); Fred Kaplan, *The Wizards of Armageddon* (1983); Greg Herken, *Counsels of War* (1985); and Richard G. Hewlett and Jack M. Holl, *Atoms for Peace and War, 1953–1961: Eisenhower and the Atomic Energy Commission* (1989). See also Günter Bischof and Saki Dockrill, eds., *Cold War Respite: The Geneva Summit of 1955* (2000) for an excellent series of essays on the arms control negotiating positions of Khrushchev and Eisenhower.

On Khrushchev and the Soviets, two excellent new works make use of recently available Cold War archives: William Taubman, *Khrushchev: The Man and His Era* (2003); and Alexandr Fursenko and Timothy Naftali, *Khrushchev, Cold War: The Inside Story of an American Adversary* (2006). Khrushchev's own memoirs are fascinating but should be read in conjunction with Taubman's biography noted above—Strobe Talbott, trans. and ed., *Khrushchev Remembers* (1970), and a supplement, *The Last Testament* (1974). A good analysis of the contrasting strategic views of the Soviet Union and the United States in this period is William Curti Wohlforth, *The Elusive Balance: Power and Perceptions during the Cold War* (1993).

On Europe, see Marc Trachtenberg, *A Constructed Peace: The Making of the European Settlement, 1945–1963* (1999); Alfred Grosser, *The Western Alliance: European-American Relations Since 1945* (1980); Michael M. Harrison, *The Reluctant Ally: France and Atlantic Security* (1981); Edward Fursdon, *The European Defence Community: A History* (1980); Frank A. Ninkovich, *Germany and the United States: The Transformation of the German Question Since 1945* (1988); and W.W. Rostow, *Europe After Stalin: Eisenhower's Three Decisions of March 11, 1953* (1982).

General histories of the U.S. role in the Middle East include Peter L. Hahn, *Crisis and Crossfire: The United States and the Middle East Since 1945* (2006); Michael B. Oren, *Power, Faith, and Fantasy: America and the Middle East, 1776 to the Present* (2007); Douglas Little, *American Orientalism: The United States and the Middle East Since 1945* (2002); Rashid Khalidi, *Resurrecting Empire: Western Footprints and America's Perilous Path in the Middle East* (2004); Burton I. Kaufman, *The Arab Middle East and the United States: Inter-Arab Rivalry and Superpower Diplomacy* (1996); H.W. Brands, *Into the Labyrinth: The United States and the Middle East, 1945–1993* (1994); Lloyd C. Gardner, *Three Kings: The Rise of an American Empire in the Middle East after World War II* (2009) and *The Long Road to Baghdad: A History of U.S. Foreign Policy from the 1970s to the Present* (2008); and Melani McAlister, *Epic Encounters: Culture, Media, and U.S. Interests in the Middle East, 1945–2000* (2001). On early American relations with the Middle East, see James A. Field, *America and the Mediterranean World, 1776–1882* (1969); Heather Sharkey, *American Evangelicals in Egypt: Missionary Encounters in the Age of Empire* (2008); Ussama Makdisi, *Artillery of Heaven and the Failed Conversion of the Middle East* (2008); and John A. DeNovo, *American Interests and Policies in the Middle East, 1900–1939* (1963). On American interest in the Persian Gulf area and Middle Eastern oil, see Daniel Yergin, *The Prize: The Epic Quest for Oil, Money, and Power*

(1991); Aaron D. Miller, *Search for Security: Saudi Arabian Oil and American Foreign Policy, 1939–1949* (1980); Irvine H. Anderson, *Aramco, the United States, and Saudi Arabia* (1981); Burton I. Kaufman, *The Oil Cartel Case* (1978); Anthony Sampson, *The Seven Sisters: The Great Oil Companies and the World They Shaped* (1975); Benjamin Shwadran, *The Middle East, Oil, and the Great Powers* (1973); Edward A. Chester, *United States Oil Policy and Diplomacy: A Twentieth-Century Overview* (1983); Rachel Bronson, *Thicker than Oil: America's Uneasy Partnership with Saudi Arabia* (2006); Marc J. O'Reilly, *Unexceptional: America's Empire in the Persian Gulf, 1941–2007* (2008); and Robert Vitalis, *America's Kingdom: Mythmaking on the Saudi Oil Frontier* (2007).

On the United States and the Arab-Israeli conflict, see Peter L. Hahn, *Caught in the Middle East: U.S. Policy Toward the Arab-Israeli Conflict, 1945–1961* (2004); Thomas L. Friedman, *From Beirut to Jerusalem* (updated ed., 1995); Isaac Alteras, *Eisenhower and Israel: U.S.-Israeli Relations, 1953–1960* (1993); Michelle Mart, *Eye on Israel: How America Came to View Israel as an Ally* (2006); and Abraham Ben-Zvi, *Decade of Transition: Eisenhower, Kennedy, and the Origins of the American-Israeli Alliance* (1998). On the U.S. reaction to the Jewish refugee problem during World War II, see Yehuda Bauer, *American Jewry and the Holocaust* (1981); Saul S. Freidman, *No Haven for the Oppressed* (1973); and Henry L. Feingold, *Politics of Rescue* (1970). Truman's decision to recognize Israel is analyzed in Michael T. Benson, *Harry S. Truman and the Founding of Israel* (1997); John Snetsinger, *Truman, the Jewish Vote, and the Creation of Israel* (1974); and Evan M. Wilson, *Decision on Palestine: How the U.S. Came to Recognize Israel* (1979).

The best books on Eisenhower's policy toward the Middle East are Salim Yaqub, *Containing Arab Nationalism: The Eisenhower Doctrine and the Middle East* (2004); Nathan J. Citino, *From Arab Nationalism to OPEC: Eisenhower, King Sa'ud, and the Making of U.S.-Saudi Relations* (2002); and Roby C. Barrett, *The Greater Middle East and the Cold War: US Foreign Policy Under Eisenhower and Kennedy* (2007). On the Suez crisis, see Keith Kyle, *Suez* (1991); Steven Z. Freiberger, *Dawn over Suez: The Rise of American Power in the Middle East, 1953–1957* (1992); Donald Neff, *Warriors at Suez: Eisenhower Takes America into the Middle East* (1981); Diane B. Kunz, *The Economic Diplomacy of the Suez Crisis* (1991); Peter Hahn, *The United States, Great Britain, and Egypt* (1991); and Scott Lucas, *Divided We Stand: Britain, the US and the Suez Crisis* (1991). On Iran and the Iranian coup, see Mark J. Gasiorowski, *U.S. Foreign Policy and the Shah: Building a Client State in Iran* (1991); Mary Ann Heiss, *Empire and Nationhood: The United States, Great Britain, and Iranian Oil* (1997); James A. Bill, *The Eagle and the Lion: The Tragedy of American-Iranian Relations* (1988); Mark Hamilton Lytle, *The Origins of the Iranian-American Alliance, 1941–1953* (1987); Barry Rubin, *Paved with Good Intentions: The American Experience in Iran* (1980); and the memoirs of the CIA operative in the coup, Kermit Roosevelt, *Countercoup: Struggle for the Control of Iran* (1980). The latest work summarizing Eisenhower's policy toward third-world nations is a collection of essays edited by Katherine Statler and Andrew Johns, *The Eisenhower Administration, the Third World, and the Globalization of the Cold War* (2006). See also Zachary Karabell, *Architects of Intervention: The United States, the Third World, and the*

Cold War, 1946–1962 (1999); H.W. Brands, *The Specter of Neutralism: The United States and the Emergence of the Third World, 1947–1960* (1989); and the revisionist work by Gabriel Kolko, *Confronting the Third World: United States Foreign Policy, 1945–1980* (1988).

Eisenhower's policy toward Latin America is covered in several critical histories: Michael Grow, *U.S. Presidents and Latin American Intervention: Pursuing Regime Change in the Cold War* (2008); Stephen G. Rabe, *Eisenhower and Latin America: The Foreign Policy of Anti-Communism* (1988); Bryce Wood, *The Dismantling of the Good Neighbor Policy* (1985); Cole Blasier, *The Hovering Giant: U.S. Responses to Revolutionary Change in Latin America* (1976); Samuel L. Bailey, *The United States and the Development of Latin America* (1976); and Walter LaFeber, *Inevitable Revolutions: The United States in Central America* (1983). Emphasizing the agency of Latin Americans in the U.S.–Latin American relationship are Alan McPherson, *Intimate Ties, Bitter Struggle: The United States and Latin America since 1945* (2006); and Kyle Longley, *The Sparrow and the Hawk: Costa Rica and the United States during the Rise of Jose Figueres* (1997). On the Cuban Revolution and Eisenhower's response, see Thomas G. Paterson, *Contesting Castro: The United States and the Triumph of the Cuban Revolution* (1994); Richard E. Welch Jr., *Response to Revolution: The United States and the Cuban Revolution* (1985); and Morris Morley, *Imperial State and Revolution: The United States and Cuba, 1952–1985* (1987). On the coup in Guatemala, see Nick Cullather, *Secret History: The CIA's Classified Account of Its Operations in Guatemala, 1952–1954* (1999); Richard H. Immerman, *The CIA in Guatemala: The Foreign Policy of Intervention* (1982); Stephen Schlesinger and Stephen Kinzer, *Bitter Fruit: The Untold Story of the American Coup in Guatemala* (1982); and Piero Gleijeses, *Shattered Hope: The Guatemalan Revolution and the United States, 1944–1954* (1991).

The best general works dealing with the Vietnam War are George Herring, *America's Longest War* (4th ed., 2002); Robert J. McMahon, *The Limits of Empire: The United States and Southeast Asia Since World War II* (1999); Robert D. Schulzinger, *A Time for War: The United States and Vietnam, 1941–1975* (1997); and Marilyn B. Young, *The Vietnam Wars, 1945–1990* (1991). Outstanding books that concentrate on the early period of the war, including Eisenhower's administration, are David L. Anderson, *Trapped by Success: The Eisenhower Administration and Vietnam, 1953–1961* (1991); Lloyd C. Gardner, *Approaching Vietnam: From World War II Through Dienbienphu* (1988); Andrew J. Rotter, *The Path to Vietnam: Origins of the American Commitment to Southeast Asia* (1987); and Ronald H. Spector, *Advice and Support: The Early Years of the United States Army in Vietnam, 1941–1960* (1985). The best book on the beginnings of the war in Laos is Timothy N. Castle, *At War in the Shadow of Vietnam: U.S. Military Aid to the Royal Lao Government, 1955–1975* (1993). On the Eisenhower administration's relations with China, see Michael Schaller, *The United States and China: Into the Twenty-First Century* (2002); and Chen Jian, *Mao's China and the Cold War* (2001). On policy toward Indonesia, see Robert McMahon, *The Limits of Empire: The United States and Southeast Asia since World War II* (1999); and Andrew Roadnight, *United States Policy Towards Indonesia in the Truman and Eisenhower Years* (2002).

Some special topics are covered in Burton I. Kaufman, *Trade and Aid: Eisenhower's Foreign Economic Policy* (1982); and Stephen Ambrose and Richard H. Immerman, *Ike's Spies: Eisenhower and the Espionage Establishment* (1981).

Notes

1. Kenneth Osgood, *Total Cold War: Eisenhower's Secret Propaganda Battle at Home and Abroad* (2006); Laura A. Belmonte, *Selling the American Way: U.S. Propaganda and the Cold War* (2008); Giles Scott-Smith and Hans Krabbendam, eds., *The Cultural Cold War in Western Europe, 1945–1960* (2003); Tony Shaw, *Hollywood's Cold War* (2007); Penny M. Von Eschen, *Satchmo Blows Up the World: Jazz Ambassadors Play the Cold War* (2004); Lisa E. Davenport, *Jazz Diplomacy: Promoting America in the Cold War Era* (2009).

2. Eisenhower and the British did not try to overthrow the revolutionary regime in Iraq, a failure that Khrushchev attributed to his threats to use nuclear weapons against such aggression. Khrushchev's belief that rattling his rockets had backed the Americans away from intervention in both Iraq and Egypt led him to risk later confrontations with the United States over Berlin and Cuba.

3. Of course, it conveniently ignored its embarrassing failure to overthrow Indonesia's Sukarno.

4. William Henry Chamberlin, *Appeasement: Road to War* (1962). The best book on Dulles from this perspective is Louis Gerson, *John Foster Dulles* (1967).

5. Townsend Hoopes, *The Devil and John Foster Dulles* (1973).

6. Michael Guhin, *John Foster Dulles: A Statesman and His Times* (1972).

7. See George H. Nash, *The Conservative Intellectual Movement Since 1945* (1976).

8. Emmet John Huges, *The Ordeal of Power: A Political Memoir of the Eisenhower Years* (1963); Sherman Adams, *Firsthand Report: The Story of the Eisenhower Administration* (1961).

9. Murray Kempton, "The Underestimation of Dwight D. Eisenhower," *Esquire* (September 1967); Garry Wills, *Nixon Agonistes: The Crisis of the Self-Made Man* (1969).

10. For this emphasis, see the best biography of Eisenhower, Stephen Ambrose's *Eisenhower: The President* (1984). See also Fred I. Greenstein, *The Hidden-Hand Presidency: Eisenhower as Leader* (1982); and Richard H. Immerman, ed., *John Foster Dulles and the Diplomacy of the Cold War* (1990).

CHAPTER 11

JOHN F. KENNEDY, LYNDON B. JOHNSON, AND THE STRATEGY OF FLEXIBLE RESPONSE

John F. Kennedy personified the Democrats' campaign against the supposedly old, tired, and muddled Eisenhower Republicans. Kennedy was young, vigorous, and glamorous. While Eisenhower golfed, Kennedy and his people played touch football. While Eisenhower was balding, Kennedy had a great shock of hair. While Eisenhower seemed to stumble through his answers at press conferences, Kennedy responded sharply with grace, wit, and a touch of irony. When Kennedy and his beautiful wife Jacqueline returned from France, where she had made a hit by speaking French on public occasions, the president wryly introduced himself as the man who had accompanied Jackie to Paris. Asked how he enjoyed being president, he replied, "I have a nice home, the office is close by and the pay is good." What surprised him most, he said, on taking office was that things were just as bad as he and the Democrats had been saying they were.

Kennedy surrounded himself with men whose reputations were similar to his own—young, bright, witty, and well educated. The news media kept count of the number of authors and Rhodes scholars among them. Kennedy quipped that he was holding a reception for the new administration's appointees because he wanted to see some of the names he had been reading about in the papers. Vice President Lyndon Johnson was in some awe of the sophisticated Ivy Leaguers he encountered at the first meeting of the cabinet, but his political mentor, Speaker of the House Sam Rayburn, reassured him: "Well, Lyndon, you may be right and they may be every bit as intelligent as you say, but I'd feel a whole lot better about them if just one of them had run for sheriff once."

Kennedy promised to get the country moving again. He called for a new determination and sense of purpose in the Cold War. He promised in his inaugural address that the United States would "pay any price, bear any burden, meet any hardship, support any friend, oppose any foe in order to assure the survival and the success of liberty."

The price Kennedy thought needed to be paid started with an addition of $2 billion to Eisenhower's defense budget. Kennedy argued that the Republicans had made a serious error by relying on massive retaliation to keep the defense budget down. "We intend to have a wider choice than humiliation or all-out nuclear war," he proclaimed. Bluff and ambiguity were insufficient to deter the Russians. The Soviets had to know they would face a superior force wherever they might probe.

The president proceeded to strengthen America's military and diplomatic positions across the globe. He started with an acceleration of the deployment of Minuteman intercontinental ballistic missiles and submarine-launched Polaris missiles. This he said was to counter a "missile gap" between the post-*Sputnik* Soviet forces and those built under Eisenhower. Kennedy also sought to increase America's capability to fight conventional wars. He doubled the number of combat-ready army divisions, enlarged the Marine Corps, and added fifteen ships to the navy. He particularly emphasized the development of an American capacity to fight irregular guerrilla wars in case Khrushchev followed through with his threat to instigate and support wars of national liberation. The Green Berets became the symbol of Kennedy's concern for these "special forces."

Kennedy promised a more flexible approach to diplomacy as well as to defense. "Let us never negotiate out of fear, but let us never fear to negotiate," he said. So long as the United States was strong, it could afford to be civil. It could seek agreements to reduce arms and deal generously with the third world. Kennedy criticized Eisenhower and Dulles for their hostility toward neutralism. The United States should welcome diversity and nationalism, Kennedy said. America simply should make sure such nationalist movements did not fall into the hands of Communists who might join the Soviet sphere. Kennedy thought that keeping third-world countries nationalist rather than Communist was better done with economic and technical aid, such as that provided by his innovative Peace Corps, than by empty anti-Communist rhetoric, formal alliances, and denunciations of neutrality. As a senator in the 1950s, Kennedy had dramatized this position by criticizing the French empire in Algeria and Vietnam.

The policy of flexible response toward the Soviet Union that Kennedy initiated was never as rational and flexible as Kennedy portrayed it, but after many scares and failures, it did have a measure of success. Kennedy's insistence that nuclear war would inevitably mean mutual suicide and his consequent retreat from the idea of threatening instantaneous massive retaliation for any significant Soviet aggression laid the foundations for détente and the Soviet-American arms control agreements that would be negotiated in succeeding administrations. Unfortunately, the road toward détente was not smooth. The Soviets, under the impulsive, belligerent Nikita Khrushchev, were unpredictable and pardonably skeptical of Kennedy's rhetoric about nuclear détente in the face of America's growing defense budgets and increasing deployments of nuclear weapons. Meanwhile, conservatives were ready to pounce on any evidence that Kennedy and the Democrats were "soft on communism," an opposition Kennedy could not ignore given the razor-thin margin of his victory in the election of 1960. Moreover, Kennedy himself vacillated between harder and softer lines. He often encouraged aggressive planning for military confrontation and then at the last minute accepted a more moderate course of action including a negotiated settlement. The result was a series of frightening confrontations with the Soviets before Kennedy, his successor Lyndon Johnson, and their leading defense adviser Robert McNamara began to move together with the Soviets toward détente.

Kennedy's attempt at a more flexible response toward the third world did not have even the relative success of his flexible response toward the Soviets. His attempt to steer away from equating neutralism with communism and to support nationalist alternatives in developing nations as opposed to either Communists or right-wing dictators was no more successful than Eisenhower's. His policies toward the third world culminated not in détente, but in the tragedy of Vietnam.

The Bay of Pigs and Its Aftermath

In promoting his policy of flexibility and preparedness during the presidential campaign of 1960, Kennedy found himself vulnerable to criticism from both the Left and the Right. On the one hand, Kennedy was calling for a new, more expensive defense policy in the face of testimony from a true military expert, Dwight Eisenhower, that it was not needed. On the other hand, when Kennedy advocated negotiations with the Soviets and tolerance of third-world neutralism, he was open to the even more threatening political perception that he was soft on communism. Consequently, when his presidential opponent, Richard Nixon, declared that Kennedy's campaign opposition to a hard line on Quemoy and Matsu showed he was weak, Kennedy returned the charge by denouncing the Republican administration's inactivity in the face of Fidel Castro's revolution in Cuba.

Actually, Eisenhower was not inactive on Cuba. The Central Intelligence Agency (CIA) was secretly planning an invasion of Cuba by a 1,400-man army of Cuban exiles based in Florida. The initial CIA plan called for the Cuban exiles to establish a beachhead on Cuban soil, create a provisional government, and then have that "government" request a U.S. pacifying force in the expectation that many Cubans would rally to the cause of the rebels. In the worst case, the invaders would slip off to the mountains and inaugurate guerrilla war on the model of Castro himself. Kennedy was reluctant to accept the plan for the exile invasion, but he knew he would pay a high political price if he called off a project developed by the predecessor whom he had accused of inaction against the Cuban revolution. However, he insisted on complete U.S. deniability. Instead of direct U.S. air support, the CIA would use planes disguised as Cuban aircraft supposedly piloted by Cuban deserters. The planned forty sorties would be reduced to eight. At Kennedy's urging, the CIA also moved the landing area away from the town of Trinidad, which was close to the mountains and far from Castro's forces but also populated to the point that a landing would be spectacular rather than quiet. The new landing area would be the remote beach of the Bay of Pigs. While the Bay of Pigs was isolated, quiet, and surrounded by swamps that might impede Castro's defenders, those same swamps would prevent the invaders from escaping to the mountains, which were too distant from the Bay of Pigs in any case.

Many people in Kennedy's administration and the Pentagon recognized the pitfalls in this operation. They understood that Castro had solidified his rule, built and ensured the loyalty of his armed forces, and crushed any hope of effective support from within Cuba for the exile invasion. In the absence of such support, the exile invaders could succeed only if the Americans intervened in force to help them. But Kennedy had made clear his unwillingness to provide such support by insisting on measures that ensured deniability. Unfortunately, the doubters stayed quiet while Kennedy and the CIA plunged ahead in their doomed project.

The invasion at the Bay of Pigs in April 1961 was an absolute disaster. The Cubans quickly surrounded the invasion force and sank the vessel carrying all its reserve ammunition. Recognizing that there was no hope of succeeding or rescuing the force, Kennedy rejected pleas for overt American intervention or air strikes and abandoned the exile army to its fate.

The president took the blame for the invasion himself, much as Eisenhower had done in the U-2 incident. He then ordered an investigation of the operation along with a shake-up of the CIA. (Tragically, distrust of the CIA aroused by the fiasco would lead Kennedy and Johnson to discount the CIA's accurate and pessimistic reports on Vietnam.) The Kennedy administration also continued to try to overthrow Castro by intensifying its economic blockade of the island and ordering the CIA to subvert the regime. This the CIA did by launching Operation Mongoose, under which it organized the sabotage of Cuban targets and attempted the assassination of Castro himself. Meanwhile, the Bay of Pigs loomed over Kennedy's attempts to establish his credentials as the friend of independent nationalism in the third world and especially in Latin America.

Khrushchev Challenges Kennedy

The Bay of Pigs also undercut the image of strength and determination Kennedy thought necessary to project to the Soviet Union before he could negotiate a proper peace. Thus, Kennedy approached his summit meeting with Khrushchev, scheduled for June 1961 in Vienna, with a sense of weakness. He hoped, however, that he might compensate for the effect of the Bay of Pigs with a personal display of competence, confidence, and firmness. He intended to win what Eisenhower had sought at the aborted summit of 1960, a nuclear test ban and the end of Soviet ultimatums on Berlin.

Khrushchev had his own policy imperatives. He desperately wanted to remove the thorn of a high-living West Berlin stuck deep into East Germany by eliminating the Western occupation forces in the city. He knew he had the local conventional military superiority to take West Berlin, but he also knew that his decision to defer deploying intercontinental ballistic missiles (ICBMs) left the Soviets strategically inferior to the United States if Berlin triggered World War III. His solution to this problem was to frighten the Americans by bluster and erratic behavior. Perhaps they would back away despite their strategic superiority if they thought that Khrushchev was irrational enough to launch a suicidal nuclear attack on the United States. Thus, he had broken up the 1960 summit over the U-2 incident. That same year, at a United Nations (UN) meeting, he had banged his shoe on his desk and shouted insults at the British prime minister. He bragged continually that *Sputnik* demonstrated Soviet nuclear superiority over the United States. He announced support for wars of national liberation and threatened to "take the American imperialists by the scruff of their neck [and] give them a good shaking." As one historian put it, Khrushchev was like a person "who seeks to have a friendly chat with a man next door, . . . [but] instead of knocking politely on the door of the apartment, climbs on the window ledge outside, makes ferocious faces through his neighbor's window or loudly bangs at the door, threatening to break it down. In the interval, he explains that all he wants is friendship and neighborly comity."[1]

At the Vienna summit, Khrushchev continued his intimidating behavior, hoping he could rattle his neophyte opponent. He declared he would turn control of West Berlin's access routes over to East Germany in six months, and he followed this ultimatum with a substantial increase in the Soviet defense budget.

Kennedy and the Missile Gap

Kennedy must bear some share of blame for the crises that followed the Vienna summit. The crash missile program he initiated must have seemed ominous to Khrushchev. Kennedy may not have been sure by the time of the Vienna summit that the missile gap was nonexistent, but he had good reason to believe it. The U-2 planes had found no evidence of the deployment of ICBMs until the last two flights Eisenhower ordered. It is unclear how much of the U-2 information Eisenhower revealed to Kennedy before Kennedy's inauguration, but within a month of taking office, Secretary of Defense McNamara hinted that there was no missile gap. Kennedy may still have wished to err on the side of caution because it was possible that the U-2s had missed something. But by September 1961, pictures taken by the newly launched American satellites combined with strategic information offered by the turncoat Soviet colonel Oleg Penkovsky convinced Kennedy that the United States did indeed have strategic superiority. In October, during a particularly tense moment in the Berlin crisis, Kennedy publicly informed Khrushchev he knew there was no missile gap.

Yet America's missile-building program continued. Dropping the missile gap as justification for the acceleration, Kennedy and McNamara argued instead that the United States needed strategic superiority of from 2:1 to 4:1 over Soviet missiles in order to give the United States a flexible, credible response to a nuclear threat. Kennedy and McNamara refused the strategy of "minimum deterrence," advocated by the army and navy, which would have built fewer but invulnerable missiles. Such a force would deter a Soviet first strike because it would permit enough missiles to survive to destroy Russia's major cities. Kennedy and McNamara wanted far more missiles to survive. After absorbing a Soviet first strike, they wanted to be able to destroy all Russia's remaining strategic missiles and then hold Russia's cities hostage. Such a "counterforce" strategy might inspire the USSR to spare American cities and limit the damage involved in a nuclear exchange.

There were a great many problems with this strategy. Could a nuclear war be fought with such control and rationality? And why should the Russians not suspect that America's nuclear superiority implied that the United States itself was contemplating a first strike? American superiority might tempt the United States to presume it could wipe out all Russia's missiles before Russia could retaliate.

Kennedy and McNamara could have avoided this situation by cutting back the missile program once it was clear there was no missile gap. But they reasoned that they had to plan for the worst contingency. After all, the Soviets might intend to build a huge strategic force of missiles even if they were not deploying one at the moment. Neither Kennedy nor Congress was ready to give up America's nuclear superiority and permit Soviet strategic parity. The United States and its European allies depended on this superiority to deter

U.S. president John F. Kennedy *(left)* and Soviet premier Nikita Khrushchev clash at the Vienna Conference. *(Courtesy of the John F. Kennedy Presidential Library)*

an attack by superior Russian conventional forces in Europe. Besides, it would have been politically embarrassing to reverse course after Kennedy had so strongly criticized Eisenhower's strategy.

In any case, Kennedy and McNamara thought a cutback of the missile program might be interpreted as weakness in the face of Khrushchev's continual threats. Consequently, they planned and built a force of more than a thousand Minuteman ICBM missiles to be deployed in hardened silos. They also built hundreds of Polaris missiles for stationing aboard forty-one nuclear submarines. These Minuteman and Polaris missiles carried smaller payloads than the Russian missiles but were designed for greater accuracy and invulnerability, as befitted McNamara's "counterforce, no-city, protracted warfare" strategy.

The Berlin Wall

In this atmosphere of menace, Kennedy gloomily contemplated his options in responding to Khrushchev's Berlin ultimatum. He did not want to make major concessions under the Soviet threat because, with President Charles de Gaulle of France and Chancellor Conrad Adenauer of West Germany urging him to firmness, he thought retreat would destroy the unity of Western Europe and NATO. Yet there was no means to defend Berlin short of general war. With the sinking feeling that the chances of a nuclear exchange were about one in five, in July 1961 Kennedy ordered $3.25 billion added to the defense budget, called up some reserve and National Guard troops, and enlarged civil defense efforts.

Within a month, the world watched astounded as the East Germans began building a wall to seal off East from West Berlin. Khrushchev announced that the wall's purpose was to prevent Western spies from infiltrating East Germany, but he clearly intended it to stop the hemorrhage of refugees to the West.

As Kennedy and his advisers recognized, building the Berlin Wall turned out to be a defensive move by Khrushchev that ultimately allowed him to end the Berlin crisis. But many others in the West feared that it might be an opening move to drive the Western allies out of Berlin. Some commentators even urged Kennedy to knock the wall down. He knew this would mean war, so he limited his action to a show of support that would reassure West Berlin and the other allies. He ordered an American battle group to march from West Germany to the city and sent Vice President Lyndon Johnson to Berlin to meet the American troops. Khrushchev did not try to block access to the battle group, and in October 1961 he defused the crisis by deferring the deadline for a peace treaty indefinitely. He warned one American privately, however, that he regarded West Berlin as the West's exposed foot and planned to stamp on its corns from time to time. He also accompanied his deferral of the deadline with an announcement that the Soviet Union was breaking the moratorium on nuclear tests to begin a series of giant nuclear explosions in the atmosphere. The biggest of these was well over fifty megatons. Kennedy responded by resuming American testing in the atmosphere as well.

The Cuban Missile Crisis and Its Aftermath

As the test of wills between Kennedy and Khrushchev continued, Khrushchev decided to take an immense gamble by secretly installing nuclear missiles in Cuba capable of reaching the eastern United States. Castro, bedeviled by America's increasingly hostile activities against him, had been beseeching the Soviets for protection against another possible American invasion, and that was certainly part of the reason Khrushchev decided to send the missiles. But since Khrushchev could have deterred an American attack with short-range nuclear weapons that would not have threatened the American homeland, it seems clear that his greater motivation was to improve the Soviet standing in the strategic balance of power and improve his bargaining position on such issues as Berlin. The Soviets had hundreds of intermediate-range missiles aimed at Europe, but only forty-four ICBMs capable of reaching the United States. Meanwhile, the United States had some 300 ICBM and Polaris missiles along with thirty intermediate-range ballistic missiles stationed in Turkey and capable of hitting Soviet territory. In fact, Robert McNamara estimated that the United States had a 17:1 advantage in nuclear warheads and bombs capable of hitting the homelands of the two superpowers.

After weeks of rumors about missiles being installed in Cuba, a U-2 flight brought firm confirmation. Kennedy convened an emergency executive committee to survey the possible responses. Some members urged an invasion of Cuba. Others advocated pinpoint bombing to take out the installations. Some, including U.N. ambassador Adlai Stevenson, suggested trading the withdrawal of America's vulnerable and obsolete missiles in Turkey for Soviet removal of missiles in Cuba.

Kennedy was determined to see the Soviet missiles removed before they became operational. Courageously, he resisted the urgings of many of his advisers, including his own brother Attorney General Robert Kennedy, to bomb or invade Cuba. Instead, President Kennedy chose to blockade the island in order to stop Russian ships from delivering any further missiles or warheads, although he left open the possibility of bombing or invading if Khrushchev did not remove the missiles already there. Since it would be a couple of days before any Soviet ships arrived to test the quarantine (the word preferred to "blockade," since under international law a blockade was an act of war), Khrushchev would have time to ponder and negotiate. If at all possible, Kennedy wanted to leave Khrushchev a way to back down gracefully, rather than forcing him into a choice between humiliation and nuclear war.

Tensions mounted as the Soviet ships approached the American naval picket line. If an American ship had to sink a Soviet vessel in order to enforce the quarantine, there seemed little chance that war could be averted. President Kennedy estimated that the chance of nuclear war was somewhere between "one out of three and even." Just before the first Soviet ships carrying missiles and equipment were due to reach the quarantine line, they stopped dead in the water. Secretary of State Dean Rusk remarked, "We're eyeball to eyeball, and the other fellow just blinked." But work continued on the Cuban missile sites. Would the Soviets remove the missiles already in Cuba or seek to make them operational? The tension broke two days later as a letter from Khrushchev arrived in Washington pledging to remove the missiles if the United States promised not to invade Cuba. Kennedy and his advisers were drafting a positive reply when a second Khrushchev letter arrived that raised the stakes. Khrushchev had written his first letter in a mood of despair because Soviet intelligence warned him that the Americans were about to invade Cuba and Khrushchev knew that the invasion would be greeted by Soviet tactical nuclear weapons that would probably trigger all-out nuclear war. When Khrushchev awoke the following morning to find that the Americans had not invaded, he regained some confidence and drafted a new letter proclaiming that the United States would have to remove its Jupiter missiles from Turkey as well as pledge not to invade Cuba.

While Kennedy was willing to accede to this condition, he wanted to avoid a public trade of that sort because he thought it would reward Soviet aggression and deception and also because he feared the political reaction in the United States if he bowed to the Soviet demand. Therefore, at the suggestion of Robert Kennedy, the United States agreed to the first letter as though the second one had never existed. Secretly, however, the Kennedys let the Soviets know that the missiles in Turkey would be removed in due course so long as the Soviets did not reveal this American promise.[2] Khrushchev acquiesced and ordered the missiles in Cuba dismantled. The world had stepped back from the nuclear brink.

Ironically, the Cuban missile crisis pushed the United States and the Soviet Union toward a relaxation of Cold War tensions. Khrushchev abandoned his bullying tactics.

Kennedy emerged from the crisis with the reputation of a hero whose firm but flexible and rational policy had applied the minimum of force, kept open a series of rational options, and provided the Soviets with a graceful means of backing down. Kennedy, having proved his strength and competence, could now afford to negotiate and make concessions without being branded as soft on communism.

Thus, in 1963 Khrushchev and Kennedy signed a formal ban on all but underground nuclear tests. By barring testing only where compliance could be ascertained through satellite surveillance, the test ban treaty circumvented the thorny issue of on-site inspection. The Cold War antagonists also agreed to install a telephone hotline that would allow the leaders of the United States and the Soviet Union to communicate directly in case of a crisis and thus perhaps head off a nuclear exchange.

Kennedy, de Gaulle, and Europe

Unfortunately, there was considerable negative fallout from the Cuban missile crisis as well. Kennedy had not consulted with his NATO allies during the crisis; he had taken on himself the decisions that could have incinerated the world. Charles de Gaulle had loyally supported Kennedy during the crisis, but he saw the lack of consultation as reinforcement of his long-held belief that a revived Western Europe should separate itself somewhat from the Atlantic-oriented Americans and British. Europe should establish itself as a Third Force in world politics under French leadership. De Gaulle recently had managed to withdraw France from a debilitating war with Algerian revolutionaries, and now that it was free of most of its colonial entanglements in Africa and Indochina, de Gaulle was ready to take charge of European affairs. This ambition led to considerable tension with the United States, particularly over the issue of nuclear weapons.

By the 1960s, France and Great Britain both had developed an independent nuclear capacity to support their positions as world powers. Great Britain generally coordinated its nuclear policy with the United States as part of the on-again, off-again pattern of nuclear partnership that had existed since World War II. The United States was anxious that France coordinate its nuclear strike force in the same way. To accomplish this goal, some of Kennedy's advisers were pushing for a multilateral nuclear force (MLF) that would assign several Polaris submarines to NATO to be manned by crews of mixed nationalities. These crews would include not only French and British members, but also West Germans. Advocates of the MLF hoped it would integrate and control the nuclear deterrent of Western Europe, reassure the Western Europeans that the United States would indeed risk its own existence to protect its allies, and sidetrack any thoughts West Germany might have of becoming an independent nuclear power.

De Gaulle disdained such integration. He pointed out that the MLF plan still gave the United States a veto over the use of nuclear weapons assigned to NATO. His disdain increased when the United States offered Great Britain but not France unilateral control over some Polaris missiles as compensation for canceling the Skybolt missile program, which was supposed to have furnished vital launchers for Great Britain's independent nuclear weapons. De Gaulle saw this offer as one more example of the special relationship between the Anglo-Saxons that excluded France from the club of world powers. Consequently, he vetoed Great Britain's belated request for admission to the European Common Market, refused to support a nuclear nonproliferation treaty that the United States and Great Britain were trying to negotiate with the Soviets, and signed a treaty of cooperation with West Germany as the initial building block of his European Third Force. Finally, de Gaulle announced that France would withdraw its troops and facilities from NATO's joint command in 1967.

One other factor in de Gaulle's disillusionment with American policy had been Robert McNamara's attempts to lessen the chances of nuclear war in Europe. McNamara advocated a flexible response policy for Europe as well as the United States. He wanted to build up Europe's conventional forces to deter or fight a Soviet invasion without early recourse to nuclear weapons. McNamara thought this possible because the twelve army divisions West Germany had long promised were now ready and because Khrushchev had been reducing his conventional forces in favor of nuclear arms to the point that Soviet conventional superiority in Europe was less overwhelming than previously thought. De Gaulle, however, saw McNamara's argument as an attempt by the United States to "decouple" its defense from Europe's in order to avoid a nuclear strike that might put the American homeland at risk. For de Gaulle, America's emphasis on conventional defense against a Soviet attack on Europe proved that the United States would not risk New York for Paris. After de Gaulle's withdrawal from NATO in 1967 eliminated French opposition within the organization, the other Western European allies accepted flexible response as official NATO strategy. Nonetheless, they continued to worry about decoupling and they resisted furnishing the number of conventional forces Washington thought necessary to deter a Soviet invasion.

The Soviet Drive Toward Nuclear Parity

The Cuban missile crisis had a significant impact on Soviet as well as Western European affairs. Many Soviet leaders were disillusioned by Khrushchev's reckless gambles and his slowness to deploy the Soviet ICBM force. They overturned Khrushchev in 1964 and began a rapid missile buildup. The new leadership, headed by Leonid Brezhnev and Alexei Kosygin, installed 224 ICBMs by 1966. By 1968 the Soviet arsenal was approaching the equivalent of America's 1,054 land-based ICBMs and included some submarine-launched missiles as well.

The Cuban missile crisis, the disarray in NATO, and the increase in Soviet nuclear power forced Kennedy, McNamara, and ultimately President Lyndon Johnson to rethink their nuclear strategy. Despite the praise Kennedy and McNamara had received after the Cuban missile crisis for a supposedly masterful use of minimum force with options for a gradually escalated response, they realized that they had relied on the threat of a massive strike on the Soviet Union if it came to nuclear warfare, not a limited, controlled attack. The growth of Soviet nuclear power made Kennedy and McNamara even more doubtful that a future nuclear war could be limited or rationally controlled.

Thus, shortly before Kennedy's assassination, McNamara began to advocate not only flexible response in Europe, but also a new strategy premised on Russian nuclear parity rather than American superiority. He called this strategy "mutually assured destruction" (MAD). MAD would deter war because each side knew that the other could absorb a first strike and still devastate its opponent's vulnerable population.

The acceptance of Soviet nuclear parity and the strategy of mutually assured destruction opened the possibility of an arms control treaty between the United States and the Soviet Union. The United States could afford to make concessions because, as McNamara stated publicly in 1967, America's missile force was "both greater than we had originally planned and in fact more than we require." The Soviets, who previously had insisted on total nuclear disarmament and rejected all efforts at arms control because an agreement would have frozen Russia in an inferior strategic position, were now willing to consider a treaty based on parity. In 1968 Johnson and Kosygin signed a nuclear nonproliferation treaty and announced that they would begin negotiations for limitations on strategic weapons.

The Soviet Union short-circuited this progress toward limitation when it invaded Czechoslovakia in the spring of 1968. The Czechs had frightened the Soviets by attempting to liberalize their Communist regime and permit greater freedom of speech and opposition. The Soviets justified their invasion with the Brezhnev Doctrine, which declared that the Soviet Union had a right to intervene in any socialist country to forestall counterrevolution. In the sour atmosphere that followed the crushing of this so-called Prague Spring, Republican presidential candidate Richard Nixon denounced Johnson for considering abandonment of America's nuclear superiority. Johnson already was reeling from opposition to the war in Vietnam, so he deferred the strategic arms negotiations until after the election of a new president. In this way Nixon inherited both the problem of Vietnam and the Soviet drive toward strategic parity.

Kennedy and the Nationalist Alternative in the Third World

While John F. Kennedy devoted most of his attention to the critical issues that threatened to bring a direct confrontation with the other world superpower, his administration did make some halting attempts to break away from what Kennedy saw as the sterile antineutralist policies of the Eisenhower administration toward the third world. Kennedy tried to support nationalist rather than old colonialist or reactionary regimes as counters to Communist movements in developing nations. He extended economic aid to encourage peaceful, democratic reforms as alternatives to the revolutionary socialist model of nation building and modernization. The intent of Kennedy's initiatives, and their failure, can be illustrated in three countries: the Dominican Republic in Latin America, the Congo (later Zaire) in Africa, and Laos in Asia.

The Dominican Crisis

In Latin America, Kennedy faced the prickly problem of appealing to the area's nationalism while also trying to destroy Castro's Cuban regime at the same time. Latin America had become economically more important to the United States after World War II, accounting for 20 percent of U.S. foreign trade and receiving 25 percent of U.S. overseas investments. In March 1961, Kennedy dramatically announced to Latin American diplomats gathered at the White House that the United States was ready to contribute the largest share of $20 billion to encourage development in Latin America. Adopting this Alliance for Progress in August 1961, the members of the Organization of American States (OAS) pledged to carry out internal reforms that would permit equitable distribution of the benefits of the alliance. But the program faltered from the outset.

Even moderate nationalist politicians in Latin America came from families that would be hurt badly by progressive taxation or land redistribution. Yet the only alternative internal source of funds to win over the dispossessed classes would be the confiscation of foreign enterprises. Such nationalization was not likely to win favor in the United States unless the foreign owners were paid so much compensation as to eliminate the net financial gain. In any case, much of the money from the Alliance for Progress went to the military, which the Kennedy administration believed offered one of the few hopes for an efficient nationalizing force in Latin America. The Alliance for Progress also required that most of the aid be spent on U.S. goods, further diminishing the benefits of the program to the poorer Latin American nations. Latin Americans complained that much alliance money went simply to pay their debts to the United States.

Thus, despite the Alliance for Progress, life improved very little for most Latin Americans. Economic growth remained at an anemic 1.5 percent per year in Latin America through the 1960s. An explosive population growth of 3 percent per year, the highest in the world, consumed whatever economic progress was made. Unemployment rose from 18 to 25 million, and wealth remained concentrated in the hands of the top 10 percent or less of the population in most Latin American nations.

The showcase for Kennedy's strategy of the nationalist alternative in Latin America was the Dominican Republic. Dictator Rafael Trujillo, one of the most hated men in Latin America, had taken power in the wake of the U.S. occupation in 1930. At a 1959 OAS meeting, even other authoritarian Latin American regimes urged sanctions against Trujillo. The Eisenhower administration opposed these sanctions and found itself in the unfamiliar position of defending nonintervention in the Caribbean.

Kennedy changed U.S. policy. At an OAS meeting in 1960, the Latin American nations resumed their call for sanctions. Venezuela was especially angry that Trujillo had tried to have its president assassinated. The Kennedy administration at first urged free elections in the Dominican Republic as an alternative to sanctions, but ultimately gave in to the other OAS members. In January 1961, the Kennedy administration even added some new sanctions of its own. Opposition groups within the Dominican Republic, taking heart at this show of U.S. determination, requested help from the CIA in overthrowing Trujillo. The CIA agreed to supply some arms. Three pistols and three rifles reached the rebels before the United States backed away from the plot in the aftermath of the Bay of Pigs. The U.S. withdrawal did not prevent the rebels from assassinating Trujillo in May 1961.

Following Trujillo's assassination, the Kennedy administration used its influence to secure free elections and prevent either a return to military dictatorship or a Castro-like revolution. In December 1962, the Dominican Republic elected a writer, Juan Bosch, as its first constitutional president in thirty-eight years. The United States immediately recognized the new government and increased its aid. Unfortunately, Bosch proved to be "the best short-story writer and the worst politician in the hemisphere," according to Venezuelan ex-president Romulo Betancourt. Within a year, the Dominican military threw him out of office. Kennedy denounced the coup and recalled the U.S. ambassador. Ultimately, however, he recognized a pseudocivilian government set up by the military and restored some Alliance for Progress aid to the beleaguered nation.

The denouement in the Dominican Republic came in April 1965. A group of pro-Bosch officers overthrew the nominally civilian Dominican government. In the ensuing turmoil, Ambassador W. Tapley Bennett reported that American lives were in danger and that Communists were attempting to seize control. President Lyndon Johnson sent in the U.S. Marines. At first he claimed that this move was necessary to protect American lives and property, but a few days later he justified his action with a list of several Communists who were purported to have influence over the rebels. He then proclaimed the Johnson Doctrine: no Communist government would be permitted to take power in the Western Hemisphere. There would be no more Cuba as if the United States could help it.

Johnson's intervention helped secure power for an American-leaning regime of military men headed by a former Trujillo lieutenant, Joaquin Balaguer. Johnson got Balaguer to remove his most reactionary adherents from the government. But the Johnson Doctrine revived Latin American fears of the Monroe Doctrine and the Roosevelt Corollary. When Johnson sought retroactive OAS approval for his actions, he had great difficulty getting the two-thirds vote necessary. Ultimately, however, the OAS sent an inter-American force to join the U.S. Marine contingent in Santo Domingo, both of which were withdrawn in 1966.

The Dominican Republic illustrated the difficulty of trying to find democratic regimes and support gradual, peaceful modernization in the third world. The stark division between the elites and the poor left little room for a moderate center. The United States increasingly faced a choice between reactionary and radical regimes. In the Latin America of the 1960s, reactionaries seemed to be winning. Military coups overthrew governments in Brazil, Argentina, Peru, Guatemala, Ecuador, and Honduras as well as the Dominican Republic between 1962 and 1965. In former times the United States could at least have consoled itself that reactionary regimes tended to be pro-American, but that too was changing. Even military dictatorships began to see their interests aligned with other third-world nations. Latin America joined African, Asian, and Communist countries in the UN to condemn the policies of the United States and the other Western industrialized powers.

Chaos in the Congo

Kennedy's search for democratic nationalist alternatives to radicals and reactionaries was no more successful in Africa than in Latin America. The site of Kennedy's most dramatic African initiative was the former Belgian Congo, soon to be called Zaire. It had significant mineral resources and the largest proportion of wage earners in Africa, but few internal markets for its products. It relied instead on exports and imports, which were managed and consumed by a thin crust of elites while the decaying traditional tribal cultures, deeply divided within themselves, remained unintegrated into the developed part of the society.

The Congo won its independence from Belgium in 1960 and installed a parliamentary government that was a very uneasy alliance of numerous tribes and factions. The new prime minister of the Congo was a leftist nationalist named Patrice Lumumba. The Eisenhower administration initially welcomed Lumumba because he seemed to have the best chance to hold the Congo together. Lumumba's constituency was the urban elite and the most detribalized elements of the interior, tribes so scattered that they would look to a strong national government to protect them against local majorities. Then Eisenhower soured on Lumumba when the prime minister announced to the Belgian representatives at the Independence Day celebration, "From today we are no longer your monkeys." Within five days of independence, several army units mutinied against their Belgian officers and began attacking Europeans. Lumumba at first gave Belgian units permission to help put down the mutinies. But when Moise Tshombe proclaimed the independence of Katanga Province in the midst of the crisis, Lumumba portrayed the whole situation as a Belgian plot to reoccupy the country. He appealed for help from the United Nations and warned he would summon Soviet help if the Belgians were not out of the country in seventy-two hours.

Katanga's secession was an especially sensitive issue because that province's copper, cobalt, diamonds, and tin contributed one-third to one-half of the economy while containing one-third of the Congo's European population. No Congo government could survive without it. Belgium surreptitiously helped Tshombe and Katanga because it feared that Lumumba might disturb Belgian access to the Congo's vital resources. The Eisenhower administration, repelled by Lumumba and wanting to keep support in Europe against Soviet expansionism, leaned toward Belgium and tried to delay UN action to put down the Katanga rebellion. Eisenhower said the United Nations should not be drawn into an internal dispute.

An increasingly desperate Lumumba turned to the Soviets, who sent 125 military technicians to Leopoldville and made plans to fly Lumumba's troops to Katanga to put down the secession. Lumumba's troops attacked four Canadian soldiers with the UN forces that had been sent to Katanga, and Lumumba worried aloud that white UN troops would simply substitute for Belgian colonialists.

At that point, the Congo army, headed by Joseph Mobutu, took over the government and arrested Lumumba. Lumumba's captors took him to Katanga and murdered him. (The American CIA had plans for Lumumba's assassination, but evidently was not responsible for the murder.) Lumumba's ally, Antoine Gizenga, fled to the Congolese city of Stanleyville and established a rival regime that quickly won at least verbal backing from the Soviets, the United Arab Republic, and Guinea.

Kennedy, inaugurated shortly after Lumumba's death, ordered a full reappraisal of American policy in the Congo. "We must ally ourselves with the rising sea of nationalism in Africa," he announced. Colonialists and reactionaries were driving nationalists into

Communist hands. Kennedy shifted to support the bloc of Afro-Asian nations that was urging the United Nations troops to get other foreign and paramilitary personnel out of the Congo, reconcile the Stanleyville and Mobutu governments, and use force as a last resort to prevent civil war with Katanga. Against noisy opposition from conservatives who supported Tshombe as a bulwark against communism, Kennedy furnished American planes to ferry UN troops into Katanga. At the same time, the CIA purchased votes in the Congolese national parliament to ensure that Gizenga and the leftists of Stanleyville would be submerged in a government headed by a liberal labor union politician, Cyrille Adoula. Thus, Kennedy would have his liberal, anticolonial, anti-Communist nationalist alternative.

Adoula's narrow and vulnerable parliamentary majority would not hold, even with CIA bribery, unless he ended the Katanga secession. When the mere presence of UN troops failed to cow Tshombe, Adoula and the UN ordered a march on the Katanga capital of Elizabethville in December 1962. Kennedy balked at sending military aid to Adoula and the UN, however, and the invasion bogged down. Tshombe remained a major irritant to Adoula.

And that was not all of Adoula's troubles. Many Congolese peasants remained disenchanted with the national government. The government confiscated their tribal lands for parks and mines. It relocated the peasants to avoid the tsetse flies that caused sleeping sickness. It forced farmers to grow export crops, such as cotton, thus pushing them into the cash economy under very disadvantageous conditions. Secret societies organized fragmented opposition to the government and the white oppressors. Adoula and liberalism had no answer to this rural radicalism. Adoula could only arrest Gizenga, purge the Lumumbists who might lead the rural disaffection, and become totally reliant on the military to remain in office. And the military of Joseph Mobutu only made matters worse. It lived off the land and exerted its control with great brutality. Eighty-five percent of the government's budget went to pay the salaries of the army and state employees, leaving little for economic development. Corruption and profiteering were rampant.

The rebellion also turned brutal. As fetishes and incantations withered before modern weapons, villagers abandoned the rebels and the rebels resorted to terror tactics. In 1964 they captured Stanleyville and controlled most of the eastern Congo. They also took hundreds of European hostages to deter American and European support for the government, now ironically headed by the former Katanga rebel, Tshombe.

Since the UN had withdrawn its troops from the Congo earlier in 1964, Tshombe, with the support of the CIA, turned to South Africa and various white mercenaries to spearhead his attack on the rebels. Lyndon Johnson contributed American planes and over fifty paratroop advisers. A series of parachute drops and an accompanying ground operation freed 2,000 European hostages and crushed the rebels. But the rebels executed 300 hostages and the Congolese army committed many of its own atrocities. While the operation saved a pro-Western government for the Congo, that government was weak and corrupt, and many African states protested the intervention of Americans, Europeans, and South Africans. Kennedy's hope of associating the United States with the rising nationalist tide in Africa evaporated.

A Flimsy Settlement in Laos

In Laos an unhappy Kennedy accepted a settlement that went beyond his tolerance for nationalist anti-Communist alternatives to colonialism. He consented to a neutralist coalition government that included the Pathet Lao, the Laotian Communist Party. He did so only because anti-Communist alternatives were limited in Laos and, as one Kennedy administration official put it, "Laos was not all that goddamned important."

Laos was a small and divided nation. Its population of only 3 million was split into forty-two tribal clusters and five different language groups. The most powerful tribe, the Lao, comprised 40 to 50 percent of the population. It dominated the southern and lowland areas and used its authority to prohibit minority languages and schools. But poor communications made it impossible for the Lao to extend firm control over the upland and northern areas. Laos had few roads, and even where they were passable, they carried little trade among the inward-looking tribes. Laotians paid so little attention to affairs beyond their own tribal lands that in 1956 fewer than half of the people knew the name of their own nation and only 10 percent knew the name of the prime minister. National politics consisted of a struggle for leadership among twenty families with an active constituency of only about 2,000 people.

When the French began to evacuate Laos and the rest of Indochina following the 1954 Geneva Accords, they left behind three major groups vying for power. The Pathet Lao, headed by Prince Souphanouvong, controlled the northern and upland areas. Although nominally Communist, the Pathet Lao represented the ambitions of minority tribes more than international Marxism, and it permitted minority languages and schools in its territory. A right-wing anti-Communist group, ultimately led by General Phoumi Nosavan and Prince Boun Oum, bitterly opposed the Pathet Lao. Between these two groups stood a neutralist faction led by Prince Souvana Phouma, Souphanouvong's half brother.

Although the French tried to leave Souvana Phouma as their successor, the right wing took over and the Pathet Lao withdrew its cooperation from the central government, effectively partitioning the country. For the time being, however, conflict remained at a low level. The Laotians were a peaceful people and accepted whatever government ruled them, be it colonial or Communist, with considerable passivity. The neutralists even regained power in 1957.

Change was under way, however, as American advisers and money poured into Laos to replace French influence. The American legation in Laos expanded from one person in 1954 to one hundred in 1957. At first this increase did not drastically change conditions in Laos. Much of the growing American mission's effort went merely to maintain its own personnel rather than to influence the Laotians, because conditions in Laos were very difficult for Westerners. One CARE official remarked, "There are only two kinds of Americans in Laos—those who have amoebic dysentery, and those who don't know it." In addition, the American mission was split during most of Eisenhower's administration. Some State Department officials favored the French approach of a restrained policy and support for Souvana Phouma's neutralists. The CIA and many lower-level diplomatic officials in Laos, however, fearing that a coalition between Souvana Phouma and the

Pathet Lao would result in another Czechoslovakia, threw their money and efforts behind the right wing.

Then, in 1959, American congressional conservatives, deciding that Laos was a prime example of the corruption in America's foreign aid program, cut the Laos appropriation drastically. Souvana Phouma's neutralist coalition fell to a right-wing government, and the army of Phoumi Nosovan took the opportunity to conduct an anti-Communist purge. Neutralist troops, led by a young officer, Kong-Le, rebelled against the government and put Souvana Phouma back in power as prime minister. Phoumi Nosavan refused to submit, and the strife escalated into civil war.

After much debate within the administration, Eisenhower threw his weight behind Phoumi and the right wing, to the great consternation of the French, the British, and his own ambassador in Laos. Souvana Phouma, Kong-Le, and the neutralists then began to accept supplies from a Soviet airlift through North Vietnam. When the armies of Phoumi and the Right proved thoroughly incompetent, Eisenhower began to reconsider his policy. But he still insisted to incoming President Kennedy that Laos could not be allowed to fall to the Communists.

As in the Dominican Republic and the Congo, Kennedy reappraised U.S. policy toward Laos. He was slow to accept neutralization, but he quickly saw that the military option was foreclosed when he learned that sending 10,000 troops to Laos would exhaust America's strategic reserve. Finally, he announced he would accept a conference to neutralize Laos if the USSR would end its airlift. He told Averell Harriman, America's roving ambassador charged with negotiations over Laos, "I want a negotiated settlement. I don't want to put troops in."

Negotiations at the Geneva Conference of 1962 dragged on for months. Harriman and Kennedy put pressure on the Communists by sending 3,000 American troops to neighboring Thailand. They pushed Phoumi Nosavan and Boun Oum by withholding American aid payments. Finally, in June, Harriman got his agreement. Souvana Phouma would head a neutralist coalition government with the Pathet Lao and the Right. Foreign troops would withdraw, and Laos would not be used as a base for attacks on other countries.

This agreement kept strife at a relatively low level in Laos for some seven years, but none of the factions lived up to the full terms of the accord. North Vietnam withdrew only forty of its 6,000 troops and continued to use the Ho Chi Minh Trail complex through northern Laos to get supplies to the Vietcong in South Vietnam. The United States withdrew its 666 advisers, but extended aid to Souvana Phouma and to Kong-Le when he fell out with the Communists and fought them. About all that survived of the agreement within months of its negotiation was Souvana's government and a tacit understanding: the Pathet Lao would not challenge Souvana for control of the southern Mekong area, so vital to Laos, Cambodia, and South Vietnam, while America's supporters would not challenge Pathet Lao control of northern Laos.

This fragile agreement simply could not survive the overwhelming events in the rest of Indochina. Laos, as Secretary of State Rusk said, was "only the wart on the hog of Vietnam." The Pathet Lao began to push Kong-Le's troops off the strategic Plain of Jars, and President Lyndon Johnson initiated a secret war in Laos. First, Johnson gave American financial and technical assistance to Laotian air strikes on Pathet Lao territory and the Ho Chi Minh Trail. Then he began secret American bombing raids. Meanwhile, the CIA led the Meo tribes of the mountains in attacks on Communist territory. President Richard Nixon continued this secret war, and by 1972 American aid to Laos was $350 million, ten times the Laotian budget and 75 percent larger than the entire Laotian gross national product. In 1971 Nixon also authorized a South Vietnamese invasion of Laos to eliminate North Vietnamese and Vietcong sanctuaries. This invasion ended in an embarrassing rout of America's allies, and in 1975 Laos fell to the Pathet Lao about the same time Vietnam and Cambodia fell to their Communists. The Pathet Lao then completed the destruction of the country so well begun by North Vietnamese intrusions and American bombing.

Kennedy did not live to see the collapse of his Laotian initiative. He still considered his policy a success in late 1963 and remarked shortly before his death, "Thank God the Bay of Pigs happened when it did. Otherwise we'd be in Laos by now—and that would be a hundred times worse." Unfortunately, he did not say that about Vietnam. Vietnam, like Cuba, showed that his willingness to rely on nationalist alternatives rather than U.S. military intervention to thwart communism had severe limits.

Race and American Foreign Policy in the 1960s: The Civil Rights Movement, the Nationalist Alternative, and the War in Vietnam

Kennedy's attempt to create nationalist alternatives overseas was part of his attempt to come to terms with the racial crisis at home. Civil rights leaders in the United States had long criticized Americans for going to war for democracy abroad while denying basic democratic rights to their own citizens of color. That, however, had not prevented blacks from supporting American foreign policy and even serving valiantly in their nation's segregated armed forces. The black labor and civil rights leader, A. Phillip Randolph, editorialized in 1917 that American blacks were ready to do their bit to further Wilson's war to make the world safe for democracy, but told Wilson also that "this world must be made safe for" blacks because until then "it is not safe for democracy." In the days leading up to World War II, Randolph proclaimed that a German victory would mean that "Negroes would be re-enslaved"—"The Battle of Britain is the Battle of America and the Battle of America is the Battle of the Negro," he argued. But when Franklin Roosevelt hesitated to impose rules barring discrimination in defense industries and the armed forces, Randolph organized a mass march on Washington in 1941. He called the march off when Roosevelt established the President's Committee on Fair Employment Practices, which then prohibited discrimination on the basis of race, creed, color, or national origin in industries holding defense contracts. Even though desegregation of the armed forces would wait until Truman abolished it by executive order in 1948, more than 1 million blacks served in American uniforms during World War II.

They fought again in Korea. Leading black organizations like the National Association for the Advancement of Colored People (NAACP) also supported early Cold War initiatives like the Marshall Plan on the grounds that U.S. support for democracy abroad would push Americans to pay more attention to democracy at home. But civil rights leaders increasingly dissented from U.S. support for its colonialist European allies and supported the rights of people of color abroad to independence from white tyranny. W.E.B. DuBois, one of the founders of the NAACP, had long pushed for such an anticolonialist foreign policy, lobbying both the Paris Peace Conference of 1919 and the authors of the United Nations Charter in 1945 for an end to European colonialism. As the defeat of the European colonialist powers in World War II triggered independence movements throughout the world and as American Cold War policy turned toward the third world after the stabilization of the standoff in Europe, civil rights leaders moved to adopt DuBois' emphasis. The civil rights movement also became more militant domestically in the wake of the 1954 *Brown v. Board of Education* Supreme Court decision and the brutal aftermath. Thus, Kennedy and then Lyndon Johnson came under more pressure to rationalize their racial policies at home with their attempts to thwart communism among colonial peoples fighting for their independence from America's Cold War allies.

Kennedy did not embrace the issues of civil rights and racial justice with great enthusiasm at the beginning of his administration, but the brutal attacks on demonstrators in Birmingham, Alabama, in 1963, an event that would soon be followed by Martin Luther King's March on Washington and "I Have a Dream" speech, brought Kennedy to tell the nation, "We preach freedom around the world, and we mean it. . . . But are we to say to the world—and much more important, to each other—that this is the land of the free, except for Negroes . . . ?" After Kennedy was assassinated later that year, Lyndon Johnson followed Kennedy's call for action by securing passage of the Civil Rights Act of 1964 and the Voting Rights Act of 1965.

Although Kennedy and Johnson progressed on domestic racial issues, they increasingly foundered in their attempts to cultivate nationalist alternatives in nations emerging from colonialism. Moreover, civil rights leaders became more impatient with both American domestic and foreign policy. Malcolm X challenged the whole ethos of the nonviolent integrationist movement of Martin Luther King and was equally militant in his opposition to the foreign policy of Kennedy and Johnson. Speaking of U.S. policy in the Congo in 1965, a few days before he was murdered, Malcolm said:

> They take a man who is a cold-blooded murderer, named [Moise] Tshombe. . . . He murdered the prime minister, the rightful prime minister, [Patrice] Lumumba. . . . Now here's a man who's an international murderer, selected by the State Department and placed over the Congo and propped into position by your tax dollars. . . . And to show the type of hired killer he is, as soon as he's in office, he hires more killers in South Africa to shoot down his own people.

By 1965 the Vietnam War had driven even more American blacks into opposition against U.S. foreign policy. Martin Luther King began in that year to call for an end to the war. By 1967 he was condemning the war not only because it forced blacks to fight for liberties in a foreign land that they did not have in their own, but also because it preserved the "privileges and the pleasures" of the rich from revolutionary movements that threatened foreign investments.[3]

Thus, the Vietnam War both exacerbated the issue of racial justice at home and demonstrated conclusively the bankruptcy of the search for a nationalist alternative by Kennedy and Johnson.

Controversial Issues

Initial assessments of Kennedy's foreign policy emphasized the extent to which he lived up to the tenets of the soft realists in the restraint with which he used power in his relations with both the Soviet Union and the developing world. His early biographers, Arthur Schlesinger Jr. and Theodore Sorenson, both former members of the Kennedy administration, admitted that the Bay of Pigs had been a mistake. But they regarded the Kennedy-McNamara policy of flexible response as far more realistic than the massive retaliation policy of Eisenhower. They saw in flexible response a proper recognition of the inevitability of nuclear parity, the unusability of nuclear weapons, and the preferability of other means of containing the Soviet Union and maintaining a balance of power. They pointed to the Berlin crisis and the Cuban missile crisis as stellar examples of the restrained use of power toward the Soviets and to Kennedy's subsequent American University speech calling for de-escalation of the Cold War, the establishment of the hotline, and the nuclear test ban treaty as the first steps on the road to détente. Schlesinger and other Kennedy advocates praised McNamara and Lyndon Johnson for continuing that process through the extension of flexible response to NATO, the adoption of the mutually assured destruction doctrine with its acceptance of Soviet nuclear parity, and the consequent outline of an acceptable arms control treaty with the Soviet Union. On the other hand, these Kennedy advocates criticized Johnson for what they considered his retreat from Kennedy's tolerance for third-world neutralism in the Dominican Republic, the Congo, and above all Vietnam (a subject whose history and historiography will be covered in the next chapter).[4]

As time passed, the halo effect of Kennedy's martyrdom dimmed, the result not only of revelations about his private conduct toward women and about CIA dirty tricks during his administration, but also of disillusion with the realist views that had led the United States into Vietnam in the first place. Revisionists had already attacked Kennedy and Johnson as hard-line cold warriors.[5] With new documentation available, soft realists joined the revisionists in making more critical reassessments of Kennedy's foreign policy actions.[6] On nuclear strategy and relations with the Soviets, critics pointed out that despite the rhetoric of Kennedy and McNamara about reducing reliance on massive retaliation, they vastly increased both America's strategic and tactical nuclear armaments and went through several worrisome strategic doctrines before arriving at MAD and the recognition of Soviet nuclear parity. Historians also began reassessing Kennedy's performance in the Cuban missile crisis, which earlier pro-Kennedy scholars had found so impressive. A remarkable series of meetings between the Americans and Soviets who were decision makers at the time of the crisis and access to taped recordings of Kennedy's meetings with his emergency executive committee have resulted in revelations emphasizing both the Soviet fear of an American invasion of Cuba as the motive for Soviet action and the lack of control both sides had over the way the crisis played out. Finally, the limits and failures of Kennedy's initiatives in the third world discredited his diplomacy even further in the eyes of both soft realists and revisionists, who found less to distinguish Kennedy's third-world policy from Johnson's or Eisenhower's than had earlier pro-Kennedy analysts.

Hard realists and nationalists, however, welcomed and praised the new evidence that Kennedy had taken a stiffer stand against communism than the soft realists thought proper. The disputes among historians over the evaluation of Kennedy and of American policy in Vietnam, in fact, helped produce the split in the realist school between the soft realists emphasizing restraint and the hard realists seeking a stronger defense against communism. The differing shades of opinion can be found in many of the books cited in the following bibliographical section.

Further Reading

The best biographies of Kennedy as president include Richard Reeves, *President Kennedy: Profile of Power* (1993); Herbert S. Parmet, *JFK: The Presidency of John F. Kennedy* (1983); James N. Giglio, *The Presidency of John F. Kennedy* (1991); and Hugh Brogan, *Kennedy* (1996). The best biography of Lyndon Johnson is Robert Dallek, *Flawed Giant: Johnson and His Times, 1961–1973* (1998). See also Deborah Shapley, *Promise and Power: The Life and Times of Robert McNamara* (1993).

The best and most balanced account of Kennedy's strategy and diplomacy is Lawrence Freedman, *Kennedy's Wars: Berlin, Cuba, Laos, and Vietnam* (2000). Early accounts praising the defense strategy of Kennedy and McNamara are William Kaufman, *The McNamara Strategy* (1964); and Alain C. Enthoven and K. Wayne Smith, *How Much Is Enough?* (1971). Later, more critical accounts are John L. Gaddis, *Strategies of Containment* (1982); Desmond Ball, *Politics and Force Levels: The Strategic Missile Program of the Kennedy Administration* (1981); Michael Mandelbaum, *The Nuclear Question* (1979); Harland B. Moulton, *From Superiority to Parity* (1972); Richard K. Betts, *Soldiers, Statesmen, and Cold War Crises* (1977); McGeorge Bundy, *Danger and Survival: Choices About the Bomb in the First Fifty Years* (1988); Bernard J. Firestone, *The Quest for Nuclear Stability: John F. Kennedy and the Soviet Union* (1982); Morton H. Halperin, *Nuclear Fallacy* (1987); Fred Kaplan, *The Wizards of Armageddon* (1983); Gregg Herkin, *Counsels of War* (1985); Ernest J. Yanarella, *The Missile Defense Controversy* (1977); Ronald A. Powaski, *A March to Armageddon* (1987); Glenn T. Seaborg, *Kennedy, Khrushchev and the Test Ban* (1982) and Seaborg, with Benjamin S. Loeb, *Stemming the Tide: Arms Control in the Johnson Years* (1987); Helga Haftendorn, *NATO and the Nuclear Revolution: A Crisis of Credibility, 1966–1967* (1996); Andreas Wenger, *Living with Peril: Eisenhower, Kennedy, and Nuclear Weapons* (1997); and Robert Weisbrot, *Maximum Danger: Kennedy, the Missiles, and the Crisis of American Confidence* (2001). For the Soviet side of these strategic issues, see William Taubman, *Khrushchev: The Man and His Era* (2003); and Alexandr Fursenko and Timothy Naftali, *Khrushchev's Cold War: The Inside Story of an American Adversary* (2006). For works that take account of some of the recent revelations about the Cuban missile crisis, see Alexandr Fursenko and

Timothy Naftali, *"One Hell of a Gamble": Khrushchev, Castro, and Kennedy, 1958–1964* (1997); Sheldon M. Stern, *Averting the "Final Failure": John F. Kennedy and the Secret Cuban Missile Crisis Meetings* (2003); Philip Nash, *The Other Missiles of October: Eisenhower, Kennedy and the Jupiters, 1957–1963* (1997); Graham T. Allison and Philip D. Zelikow, *Essence of Decision: Explaining the Cuban Missile Crisis* (2nd ed., 1999); James G. Blight and David A. Welch, *On the Brink: Americans and Soviets Reexamine the Cuban Missile Crisis* (1989); and Raymond L. Garthoff, *Reflections on the Cuban Missile Crisis* (2nd ed., 1989). For the Cuban view, see Carlos Lechuga, *In the Eye of the Storm: Castro, Khrushchev, Kennedy and the Missile Crisis* (1995). For Cuba's reaction to the missile crisis and subsequent foreign policy, see the remarkable book by Piero Gleijeses, *Conflicting Missions: Havana, Washington, and Africa, 1959–1976* (2002).

On Lyndon Johnson's general foreign policy, see the Robert Dallek biography listed above. See also H.W. Brands, *The Wages of Globalism: Lyndon Johnson and the Limits of American Power* (1995); Diane B. Kunz, ed., *The Diplomacy of the Crucial Decade: American Foreign Policy During the 1960s* (1994); Robert A. Divine, ed., *Exploring the Johnson Years* (1981); Doris Kearns, *Lyndon Johnson and the American Dream* (1966); Eric Goldman, *The Tragedy of Lyndon Johnson* (1968); and Michael Lumbers, *Piercing the Bamboo Curtain: Tentative Bridge-Building to China during the Johnson Years* (2008).

Kennedy's policy during the Berlin crisis is the subject of Michael Beschloss, *The Crisis Years: Kennedy and Khrushchev, 1960–1963* (1991); Honoré Catudal, *Kennedy and the Berlin Wall Crisis* (1980); Jack M. Schick, *The Berlin Crisis, 1958–1962* (1971); and Curtis Cate, *The Ideas of August: The Berlin Wall Crisis, 1961* (1978). Overall U.S. policy toward Europe is covered in Thomas Alan Schwartz, *Lyndon Johnson and Europe: In the Shadow of Vietnam* (2003); Richard J. Barnet, *The Alliance: America-Europe-Japan, Makers of the Postwar World* (1983); Stanley Hoffman, *Decline or Renewal?* (1974); David P. Calleo, *Beyond American Hegemony* (1987); and Alfred Grosser, *The Western Alliance* (1980). America's problems with trade, the balance of payments, and tariffs can be followed in David P. Calleo, *The Imperious Economy* (1982).

On the CIA in the Kennedy-Johnson years, see John Prados, *Presidents' Secret Wars: CIA and Pentagon Covert Operations Since World War II* (1986); John Ranelagh, *The Agency: The Rise and Decline of the CIA* (1986); Jeffrey T. Richelson, *A Century of Spies: Intelligence in the Twentieth Century* (1995); and Thomas Power, *The Man Who Kept the Secrets* (1979). See especially Bradley R. Simpson, *Economists with Guns: Authoritarian Development and U.S.-Indonesian Relations, 1960–1968* (2008).

On the Bay of Pigs, see Howard Jones, *The Bay of Pigs* (2008); Peter Kornbluh, ed., *Bay of Pigs Declassified: The Secret CIA Report on the Invasion of Cuba* (1998); Peter Wyden, *Bay of Pigs* (1979); and Trumbull Higgins, *The Perfect Failure* (1987). On U.S. policy toward Cuba in general during this period, see Lars Schoultz, *That Infernal Little Cuban Republic: The United States and the Cuban Revolution* (2009); Richard E. Welch, *Response to Revolution* (1985); Maurice Halperin, *The Rise and Decline of Fidel Castro* (1972) and *The Taming of Fidel Castro* (1981); Morris Morely, *Imperial State and Revolution: The United States and Cuba 1952–1987* (1987); and Tad Szulc, *Fidel* (1986). On overall policy toward Latin America in the Kennedy-Johnson years, see Stephen G.

Rabe, *The Most Dangerous Area in the World: John F. Kennedy Confronts Communist Revolution in Latin America* (1999) and *U.S. Intervention in British Guiana: A Cold War Story* (2009); Randall B. Woods, *LBJ: Architect of American Ambition* (2006); Peter H. Smith, *Talons of the Eagle: Dynamics of U.S.–Latin American Relations* (2000); Cole Blasier, *The Hovering Giant* (1976); Gordon Connell-Smith, *The United States and Latin America* (1974); Samuel Bailey, *The U.S. and the Development of Latin America, 1945–1975* (1976); Walter LaFeber, *Inevitable Revolutions: The United States in Central America* (1983); Lester D. Langley, *The United States and the Caribbean in the Twentieth Century* (1985). On the Alliance for Progress specifically, see Jeffrey F. Taffet, *Foreign Aid as Foreign Policy: The Alliance for Progress in Latin America* (2007); and Joseph Levinson and Juan De Onis, *The Alliance That Lost Its Way* (1979). For the Dominican Revolution and intervention, see Piero Gleijeses, *The Dominican Crisis* (1978); Michael R. Hall, *Sugar and Power in the Dominican Republic: Eisenhower, Kennedy and the Trujillos* (2000); G. Pope Atkins and Larman C. Wilson, *The Dominican Republic and the United States: From Imperialism to Transnationalism* (1998).

On Kennedy's policy in Africa, see Thomas J. Noer, *Cold War and Black Liberation: The United States and White Rule in Africa, 1948–1968* (1985); Richard D. Mahoney, *JFK: Ordeal in Africa* (1983); Henry F. Jackson, *From the Congo to Soweto: U.S. Foreign Policy Toward Africa Since 1960* (1982); Edward Chester, *Clash of Titans* (1974); Madeleine Kalb, *The Congo Cables: The Cold War in Africa from Eisenhower to Kennedy* (1982); Sean Kelly, *America's Tyrant* (1993); Ludo de Witte, *The Assassination of Lumumba* (2001); and Stephen R. Weissman, *American Foreign Policy in the Congo, 1960–1964* (1974). The best book on the war in Laos is Timothy N. Castle, *At War in the Shadow of Vietnam: U.S. Military Aid to the Royal Lao Government, 1955–1975* (1993). Other books on U.S. policy toward Asia in these years will be covered in the next chapter.

Notes

1. Adam Ulam, *The Rivals: America and Russia Since World War II* (1971), pp. 285–286.

2. Kennedy did indeed remove the missiles in Turkey, but he covered up his secret deal with the Soviets by allowing a leak to a reporter that Stevenson, in originally suggesting the trade, had "wanted another Munich."

3. Much of the above discussion is based on Jonathan Rosenberg, *How Far the Promised Land? World Affairs and the American Civil Rights Movement from the First World War to Vietnam* (2006).

4. Arthur M. Schlesinger Jr., *A Thousand Days: John F. Kennedy in the White House* (1965), *The Bitter Heritage: Vietnam and American Democracy, 1941–1966* (1967), *Robert Kennedy and His Times* (1978), and *The Cycles of American History* (1968); Theodore Sorenson, *Kennedy* (1965) and *The Kennedy Legacy* (1969); Roger Hilsman, *To Move a Nation: The Politics of Foreign Policy in the Administration of John F. Kennedy* (1967).

5. See, for instance, Bruce Miroff, *Pragmatic Illusions* (1976); and Richard J. Walton, *Cold War and Counterrevolution* (1972).

6. The best summary of this scholarship on Kennedy's foreign policy is Thomas G. Paterson, ed., *Kennedy's Quest for Victory: American Foreign Policy, 1961–1963* (1989).

CHAPTER 12

THE VIETNAM WAR

A few of President Kennedy's advisers, including Averell Harriman and Chester Bowles, argued that Kennedy should follow the same neutralization policy in Vietnam that he had in Laos; but Kennedy refused. The thin margin by which he had defeated Richard Nixon in the 1960 presidential election and the possibility that he would face another Republican hard-liner like Barry Goldwater in 1964 convinced him that he could not afford to look soft on communism. He already had backed away from confrontations at the Bay of Pigs and in the Laotian compromise. He did not believe he could afford another retreat. Besides, a fact-finding commission that included Vice President Lyndon Johnson, chief military adviser Maxwell Taylor, and National Security Council member Walt Whitman Rostow returned from Vietnam to report that the war could be won. Consequently, Kennedy flatly rejected a negotiated settlement. Yet he never established a firm policy of support for Vietnam either. He refused Maxwell Taylor's recommendation to send American troops. He remained as cautious and indecisive as he had been about Laos, improvising from day to day.

Kennedy, Diem, and Ho Chi Minh

The Kennedy administration talked bravely of South Vietnamese prime minister Ngo Dinh Diem as Vietnam's nationalist alternative to communism. Kennedy also reinforced the public image of South Vietnam as a bastion of freedom and progress against the spread of communism from the north. He recalled the exodus of thousands of refugees from North to South Vietnam after the Geneva Conference of 1954 ratified Communist control of North Vietnam. This seemed to most Americans proof of Vietnamese hostility to communism: the Vietnamese had "voted with their feet." American leaders failed to note publicly the reverse flow from the south to the north of 100,000 southerners who had supported the Vietminh rebellion against the French. These American leaders also failed to point out that the vast majority of refugees from the north were Catholics fleeing as much for religious as political reasons.

The Catholic exodus actually made things easier for the North's Communist leader Ho Chi Minh. Not only was he rid of a disruptive minority, but also the exodus made available land for redistribution in his drastic reform program. Perhaps the windfall tempted him to go too far, for he almost destroyed his popularity. Although 98 percent of North

Vietnamese farmers owned their own farm plots, Ho insisted on redistributing them. His Population Classification Decree divided the countryside into five categories, ranging from landlord to agricultural worker. People's Agricultural Reform Tribunals then ordered some 50,000 landlords and rich peasants to be shot, sent twice that many to labor camps, and gave their property to the lower strata. Since property already was relatively equitably distributed, this "reform" sometimes meant that the difference between a friend and an enemy of the revolution was as little as a quarter of an acre or an extra pig. Ho's redistribution program often produced farm plots too small to support families. By late 1955 he backed away from his population classification and land redistribution and moved toward the collectivization of agriculture. Considerable unrest remained in the countryside for several years, but Ho had moved soon enough to avoid the complete destruction of his popularity and to tower over Diem as the symbol of Vietnamese nationalism.

Diem stood little chance of exceeding Ho's popularity and influence anyway. As a northerner and a Catholic, he was an alien to many southerners. He aggravated the situation by choosing northern Catholics as advisers and sending his cronies to replace the traditional elected headmen of local villages. His own land reform program actually undid much of the land redistribution that had taken place in Vietminh-controlled areas prior to the Geneva Conference of 1954. Two percent of the people still owned 45 percent of the land when he was through, while 72 percent of the people had to survive on 15 percent of the land. American aid did little for these villages. It supplied consumer goods that benefited the capital city of Saigon, but were unaffordable or of little benefit to the 90 percent of the population that lived in the countryside. More than 75 percent of American aid was military rather than economic anyway.

Thus, Diem built an army without a political structure to support it. He made up for this lack of political support with bribery and repression. A fierce Catholic and mandarin, he viewed any kind of opposition as subversive. He established a rigid censorship; enacted morality laws against contraception, dancing, prostitution, and occultism; relied heavily on his secret police; and centralized government administration to the point that all forty provinces reported directly to Saigon. Even getting a divorce required a presidential decree.

Eisenhower and Kennedy were aware of Diem's foibles. Eisenhower came close to dumping Diem in 1955, but Diem surprisingly defeated the combination of religious sects, criminal gangs, and private armies that had created chaos in southern Vietnam for years. John Foster Dulles, Eisenhower's secretary of state, and Allen Dulles, John's brother and the head of the Central Intelligence Agency, convinced Eisenhower that this feat proved Diem's potential to establish a viable non-Communist government in the south, so the Eisenhower administration began lavishing aid on Diem. Diem ratified his right to rule by holding an election in which he managed to turn out a 98 percent vote for himself. Then, pointing out that only the French, not South Vietnam, had taken part in the Geneva Conference, Diem refused to participate in the Vietnam-wide election that the Geneva Agreement had set for 1956. Eisenhower and John Foster Dulles supported Diem in that decision although they had hoped that he would cast the blame on Ho Chi Minh by agreeing to the vote while insisting on election procedures that Ho would be bound to reject.

After it became apparent that Diem would not permit reunification of Vietnam through the promised election of 1956, open rebellion broke out in the South Vietnamese countryside in late 1957. Part of this rebellion was a natural reaction to Diem's misrule; part was the product of Vietminh cadres who had buried their arms after the Geneva Conference and remained behind for just such a contingency. North Vietnam gave little support at this stage, since it was preoccupied with the problems of its own revolution. Diem responded to the rebellion with greater repression. He dislodged villagers from their homes, forced them to leave behind the graves of their ancestors, and concentrated them in "agrovilles," where they might be better protected by the army. Forced relocation was bound to backfire in a society where family lands and ancestors were so deeply revered.

By the time Kennedy took office, the Diem government was near collapse. Nevertheless, Kennedy decided Vietnam was more important than Laos and that Soviet premier Nikita Khrushchev was testing him. The United States would have to support Diem whether he was a good ruler or not. Kennedy and his advisers thought that perhaps the problem was Eisenhower's strategy in Vietnam. In the quiet period between the Geneva Conference and the outbreak of rebellion in 1957, Americans had trained and equipped the South Vietnamese army to fight a conventional war such as the one in Korea. Kennedy hoped to redeem the situation by developing antiguerrilla capabilities. He set up the Special Forces unit known as the Green Berets, sent 16,000 military advisers to help lead the South Vietnamese army, urged Diem to reform his government, and tried to get aid directly to the villagers. Kennedy also supported the construction of villages called strategic hamlets, which were reminiscent of Diem's agrovilles except that local militia rather than the army had primary responsibility for protecting the settlements. The Kennedy administration assumed that the peasants would welcome the move to strategic hamlets because they would be protected from the taxes and terror imposed upon them by the guerrillas. In fact, the peasants not only continued to resent their removal from their ancestral lands but, as militia members, they were unwilling to fire upon their brothers and uncles who composed the guerrilla forces.

After a brief surge of success following these new infusions of American aid, the situation began to fall apart again. Not only did the Communist rebels, the Vietcong, regain the initiative, but new resistance to Diem's government sprang up among anticommunist elements in South Vietnam as well. The Buddhists spearheaded this resistance. To protest religious persecution by Diem's Catholic officials, Buddhist monks set themselves afire on the public streets. In the face of spreading antigovernment demonstrations, Diem relied more and more heavily on punitive actions by his secret police under the command of his brother-in-law, Ngo Dinh Nhu. Meanwhile, Nhu's wife callously offered to supply the gasoline and matches for more monkish "barbecues." Finally, in direct violation of Diem's promise to the United States to try to conciliate the Buddhists, Ngo Dinh Nhu launched massive raids on Buddhist temples throughout Vietnam, ransacking the pagodas and arresting some 1,400 people.

Not only did Diem ignore American advice to reform his regime, but also he began talking publicly of American ignorance and arrogance in trying to impose its policies on him. Kennedy also learned that Diem had opened secret contacts with North Vietnam.

Thus, when a group of South Vietnamese generals informed the Americans in August 1963 that they were contemplating a coup, Kennedy did nothing to discourage them and kept the information secret from Diem. The coup fell apart, but it triggered still another reevaluation of American policy in Vietnam. Kennedy sent a two-man team to survey the situation, and it returned with a divided report. One member told Kennedy to seek reconciliation with Diem, the other that there was no chance to defeat the Vietcong as long as Nhu remained in the government and the regime remained unreformed. An exasperated Kennedy exclaimed: "You two did visit the same country, didn't you?"

In the midst of the reevaluation, attorney general Robert Kennedy finally broached the question of whether the United States should withdraw entirely. Perhaps the president considered it; some of his advisers claim he did. Before he was assassinated, he actually approved a plan for removing American advisers by 1965; but probably Kennedy would have been unwilling to quit. His plan to remove the advisers assumed that the South Vietnamese government would be making progress in combating the Vietcong, not disintegrating. He dismissed his brother's suggestion of a withdrawal and reacted angrily to Senator Mike Mansfield's independent, pessimistic report on the situation in South Vietnam. At the very least, Kennedy wanted to put off withdrawal until after he was safely reelected. He told Mansfield that to withdraw earlier would play into the hands of his conservative rival for the presidency, Barry Goldwater, and perhaps set off a new wave of McCarthyism.

Johnson Takes Charge

Kennedy's policy drifted until November 1, 1963, when, with his tacit approval, a revived military junta overthrew Diem's government. The soldiers who captured Diem and Nhu killed them in the back of an armored truck. Three weeks later, John Kennedy himself was assassinated.

Kennedy left to his successor, Lyndon Johnson, a South Vietnam in chaos. The members of the new military junta were squabbling among themselves and proving totally incapable of governing the country. Presidential advisers told Johnson there was a fifty-fifty chance the war would be lost in the next six months unless the South Vietnamese government operated more efficiently. But if there was some question of withdrawal in Kennedy's mind, there was none in Lyndon Johnson's. As vice president he had been part of the mission to Vietnam early in Kennedy's administration that had advocated stronger support for the war effort. He could not stand the thought of being the first American president to lose a war. He remembered the consequences for the Democratic Party of "losing" China in 1949. He also feared that a foreign policy debacle would destroy his ability to push through Congress his treasured Great Society domestic program.

Johnson, like his native state of Texas, was larger than life. His intelligence was as powerful as his physique. Publicly, in his attempt to avoid looking like a hick, he appeared stiff, stilted, and programmed with empty, maudlin slogans. Privately, he was razor-sharp, raucous, and friendly as a St. Bernard trying to crawl into someone's lap. He was fearsomely persuasive in a one-on-one situation, slapping backs, shamelessly

South Vietnam and the Ho Chi Minh Trail, 1968

flattering, horse-trading, and never letting up until he had his commitment. He also could be vulgar and intimidating. He once said of Republican Congressman and future president Gerald Ford that he was so dumb he could not fart and chew gum at the same time. He grabbed a Canadian official who had made statements against the Vietnam War, pinned him against a wall, and shouted in his face, "You pissed on my rug." He said that the Organization of American States "couldn't pour piss out of a boot if the instructions were written on the heel."

Johnson was the last person who would accept defeat in Vietnam. He wanted "the coonskin nailed to the wall." He understood, however, that outright victory was either impossible or too costly, so he resolved at least not to lose. To keep from losing, he began to escalate the American effort in South Vietnam. He threw American backing behind General Nguyen Khanh after Khanh took power in another coup on January 19, 1964. Johnson increased the number of American advisers from 16,000 to 23,000, appointed General William Westmoreland to replace the optimistic and ineffectual Paul Harkins as commander of the advisers, and initiated covert joint commando raids on North Vietnam. He also ordered contingency plans for graduated pressure against North Vietnam, including air strikes. Yet he turned down the recommendation of the Joint Chiefs of Staff for all-out air and ground attacks on the north.

On August 1, 1964, the American destroyer *Maddox* was conducting electronic surveillance of North Vietnam in Tonkin Gulf waters recently vacated by a South Vietnamese squadron that had conducted a covert raid. North Vietnamese torpedo boats attacked the *Maddox*. The destroyer, with the aid of planes from a nearby carrier, drove the torpedo boats away, damaging at least one. An angry Johnson ordered the *Maddox* to return to those same waters the following day accompanied by a second destroyer, the *C. Turner Joy*. Both destroyers reported another attack by torpedo boats, although bad weather conditions made the radar sightings and other evidence of the attack problematical. Johnson ordered retaliatory attacks against North Vietnamese torpedo boat bases and contiguous oil storage dumps. He also got congressional approval of a resolution, drawn up during the earlier contingency planning for air strikes on North Vietnam, which gave the president the power to take "all necessary measures to repel any armed attacks against the forces of the United States and to prevent further aggression."

Johnson did not intend to use this Tonkin Gulf Resolution as a blank check for escalation. He hoped to continue limited warfare and merely retaliate for North Vietnamese actions. After he had safely won the 1964 election, however, the Khanh government fell apart and the South Vietnamese war effort declined still further. The constant changing of ineffectual governments in South Vietnam led one White House aide to comment that the country's national symbol should be a turnstile. Johnson decided to extend his retaliatory policy to include continuous bombing of North Vietnam. He used a February 6 attack on U.S. barracks at Pleiku as the provocation to initiate this bombing program, called Rolling Thunder. Johnson intended Rolling Thunder as a slow squeeze, a gradual escalation of pressure to destroy the north's morale, revive morale in the south, cut off North Vietnamese supplies to the insurgents in the south, and do all this without provoking intervention by the Soviets or the Chinese. With the help of the Kennedy advisers

The Vietnam Quagmire. *Top:* President John Kennedy explains U.S. policy toward Laos and Vietnam in 1961. *Bottom:* President Lyndon Johnson, *(center)* with his key advisers on Vietnam, Secretary of State Dean Rusk *(left)* and Secretary of Defense Robert McNamara. *(Courtesy of the John F. Kennedy and Lyndon B. Johnson Presidential Libraries)*

who had stayed on in his administration, Johnson tried to emulate the realist, flexible strategy of the Cuban missile crisis—using carefully calibrated, limited power to show the Communists that they could not win, while providing them with a face-saving way to retreat. Thus, Johnson would force the enemy to negotiate while he avoided both appeasement and total war.

When Johnson's initial bombing produced no immediate effect, he extended the bombing targets northward. He also approved the use of napalm. Then, in March 1965, he ordered American ground troops to guard the airfields necessary to stage the bombing raids. A month later, he decided to send 40,000 more troops to protect population enclaves, although he rejected the requests of the Joint Chiefs and Westmoreland for still larger infantry contingents.

All the while, Johnson denied that his actions constituted a change of policy, continuing to justify them as retaliatory. His administration issued a white paper blaming the war in the south on North Vietnamese aggression, even though it was clear to policy makers that to this point the revolt was mostly indigenous and fought with captured American weapons far more than with Russian- or Chinese-supplied arms. Johnson also refused to seek a firm mandate from Congress and the country for full-scale war. In this, as in his attempt to fight a limited war, he imitated Harry Truman in Korea. Johnson used the Tonkin Gulf Resolution as authority for his actions. He failed to report that American escalation was designed not so much to win as to improve South Vietnam's morale and prevent that nation's imminent collapse. He refused to risk opposition by raising taxes to support the war. (The combination of increased domestic spending along with the escalation of military expenses produced budgetary deficits that ultimately contributed to devastating inflation in the 1970s.) Johnson consciously emulated Franklin Roosevelt in trying to lead America deeper into what he thought was a necessary war by indirection and disingenuousness.

The president also tried to disarm critics by making dramatic peace initiatives. He ordered several bombing pauses and offered unconditional discussions. He even tried to bribe the enemy with talk of a gigantic economic development program for the Mekong Delta on the scale of the Tennessee Valley Authority. Yet Johnson's final terms remained the preservation of an independent non-Communist South Vietnam. Neither the southern Vietcong rebels, organized as the National Liberation Front (NLF), nor North Vietnam were willing to accept that, so the peace talk of both sides remained hollow public relations efforts.

Johnson's efforts to disarm his critics and his escalated war effort in Vietnam both failed. China and especially the Soviet Union increased the amount and sophistication of the weapons they sent to Vietnam. Coups and countercoups continued to paralyze the South Vietnamese government until the rise of two strongmen, Air Marshal Nguyen Cao Ky and General Nguyen Van Thieu, produced a modicum of stability. Johnson met Ky at Honolulu and, with an exuberant bear hug, threw the weight of the United States behind his government. Then, in July 1965, with confidence that North Vietnam would have to retreat before the might of a superpower, Johnson sent another 100,000 troops to Vietnam and permitted General Westmoreland to change the mission from guarding enclaves to pursuing the enemy in search-and-destroy operations. Johnson refused to permit bombing of North Vietnam's primitive industrial base, the capital of Hanoi, or the main harbor at Haiphong, but he ordered B-52 saturation-bombing raids on suspected enemy territory in South Vietnam.

Yet by 1967, with almost half a million American soldiers fighting in Vietnam, with the U.S. Air Force having dropped more bombs than in all the theaters of World War II, with the expenditure of $2 billion a month, and with the destruction of over half of South Vietnam's timberlands by defoliants, South Vietnam and the United States were no closer to victory than they had been two years before. The United States could not send enough troops to occupy all of South Vietnam, and the South Vietnamese government could not control it either.

Meanwhile, domestic American criticism of the war escalated along with the military effort. University students and faculties held all-night teach-ins. Civil rights leaders like Martin Luther King Jr. denounced the war as not only unjust, but a diversion from domestic racial and economic reform. Newspaper and television reporters challenged administration body counts and reports of progress. Opposition even arose within the administration. Secretary of Defense Robert McNamara, a major architect of Johnson's policy, concluded that most targets in North Vietnam were already destroyed and that no further escalation would be profitable. He advised scaling back America's war effort when he resigned in 1967. The president found himself trapped in the White House, unable to travel or speak without triggering massive antiwar demonstrations.

The crisis came in January 1968. Taking advantage of the holiday laxness during Tet, the Vietnamese lunar new year, the NLF and North Vietnamese regular units launched surprise attacks on thirty-six of South Vietnam's forty-four provincial capitals, five of the six major cities, sixty-four district capitals, and fifty hamlets. One daring team of rebels even penetrated the walls of the American embassy in Saigon and laid siege to it for more than six hours until all of the attackers were killed or captured. The NLF suffered horribly in the attacks. American forces and a surprisingly effective South Vietnamese army repelled most of the attacks within hours or days, although liberation of the old imperial capital of Hue took nearly three weeks. The Communists' NLF suffered some 60,000 casualties, while the United States and South Vietnam lost about 3,500 men. No general uprising took place to overthrow the South Vietnamese government or to welcome the NLF as liberators. Shattered NLF units broke up into smaller groups to resume guerrilla tactics in the villages and jungles. From then on, regular North Vietnamese army units carried the major burden of the Communist war in South Vietnam.

Even though the Tet offensive may have been a tactical defeat for the Communists, it came as a devastating surprise to most Americans that the enemy could launch such a widespread attack at all, especially since the Johnson administration had proclaimed that the war would be won by 1968. Television anchor Walter Cronkite remarked on the air: "What the hell is going on? I thought we were winning the war." The devastation portrayed on the television screens shocked Americans—the Saigon police chief summarily executing a captured guerrilla before news cameras, the Saigon embassy in ruins, an American officer remarking of one liberated village, "We had to destroy the town to save it." Government claims of progress and pacification seemed a mockery in the face of thousands of civilian casualties and nearly 1 million new refugees. Feeding and housing the refugees became impossible. Civilians were all the more reluctant to cooperate with the Americans and the South Vietnamese army after the NLF and North Vietnamese executed thousands of collaborators during the brief time they held Hue and other territories. Promises that the Americans or South Vietnamese could provide protection from guerrilla retribution had proved empty. It was in the aftermath of Tet that American soldiers deliberately massacred 500 civilians at My Lai, the disclosure of which eighteen months later further discredited the war in the eyes of the American people.

Westmoreland blamed the defeatism that followed Tet on media distortions. He prepared to urge Johnson to send reinforcements to exploit the Communist defeat. But Westmoreland permitted himself to be convinced by Army Chief of Staff General Earle Wheeler to ask for reinforcements of 206,000 men not as part of a new offensive strategy, but as necessary to stave off further disaster. Wheeler hoped to push Johnson to declare a state of emergency, mobilize the reserves, and replace his gradualist strategy with an all-out effort to win the war.

Wheeler's strategy backfired. Johnson was not greatly shocked by Wheeler's grimly pessimistic report on the Tet offensive and the state of the war. He was insulated by Westmoreland's earlier portrayal of Tet as an American victory and by full knowledge that the United States had been barely staving off defeat since 1963. But he never communicated his true view of the war to the rest of the country. Johnson calmly turned the request for reinforcements over to Secretary of Defense Clark Clifford. The president was prepared to send the troops necessary to prevent defeat, but expected the number needed to be rather few.

Clifford, under the influence of Pentagon civilians who had been largely responsible for the conversion of Robert McNamara, came to question the entire basis of the war in his report to Johnson. The secretary recommended gradual disengagement. An enraged Johnson refused this recommendation, but decided to send only a few new troops and avoid a major escalation. To counter the demands for disengagement coming from Clifford and a rising chorus outside the government, he also called together an outside commission, dubbed the Wise Men, on the assumption that such hard-nosed elder statesmen as Truman's former secretary of state Dean Acheson and McGeorge Bundy, former special assistant for foreign affairs to both Kennedy and Johnson, would support his determination to continue the war. He was shocked when a substantial majority of the Wise Men reacted as Clifford had to the same briefings and information Johnson had been getting. "Someone poisoned the well," Johnson railed.

Minnesota senator Eugene McCarthy dealt Johnson and the war another blow when he polled 42 percent of the vote in the New Hampshire Democratic primary against the incumbent president. Although many of those voting for McCarthy were hawks who were protesting American defeats rather than demanding withdrawal, they indicated Johnson's weakness. When Robert Kennedy jumped into the race to take advantage of the nation's antiwar sentiment, Johnson realized he was trapped. In a dramatic speech to the nation on March 31, 1968, he ordered an end to bombing in almost all of North Vietnam and named Averell Harriman to undertake a new effort at peace negotiations. To emphasize the sincerity of his move, he announced his withdrawal from the race for reelection.

Johnson, however, did not reduce operations in South Vietnam. He was not ready to compromise much for peace, and he did not think North Vietnam or the NLF was either. He hoped to maintain public support for South Vietnam by proving the insincerity of the Communists in negotiations. South Vietnam feared a sellout, however, and stalled the negotiations in the hope that it would get a better deal from the new president, whom South Vietnamese leaders correctly predicted would be the Republican Party nominee, Richard Nixon. The Nixon campaign secretly encouraged South Vietnam's President Thieu to refuse to participate in negotiations until after the election for fear that a peace agreement would help the presidential campaign of Democrat Hubert Humphrey, Johnson's vice president.

Nixon Takes Over

In 1952 Richard Nixon had watched from his position as Republican vice presidential nominee while Dwight Eisenhower, confronted with an electorate wanting to end the unpopular war in Korea but not wanting to admit defeat, had finessed the issue by promising to go to Korea. Nixon learned the lesson well and devised a comparable finesse to deal with the Vietnam War. He claimed in the campaign of 1968 to have a private plan that, he implied, would permit the United States both to win and to get out of Vietnam. It was enough to help him win a narrow victory over Vice President Humphrey.

Despite Nixon's campaign promises to get out of Vietnam, he did not plan to simply withdraw as liberals urged him to do. Instead he insisted on an "honorable peace," the terms of which were no different from those sought previously by Kennedy and Johnson. The people of South Vietnam had to be free to choose their own government. Americans could not permit North Vietnam or the National Liberation Front to impose a Communist government on an unwilling populace. The United States would make peace and withdraw only if North Vietnam withdrew its troops and permitted internationally supervised elections. Any "honorable" peace agreement had to give South Vietnam at least a reasonable chance to survive as an independent nation.

North Vietnam, however, was not about to honor the wishes even of a majority of southerners to keep Vietnam permanently split. No participants in the war trusted their opponents to hold fair elections even if that were possible in the midst of a civil war. South Vietnamese government officials argued that the elections they had already held (although obviously rigged) demonstrated that they had the support of the people. The NLF insisted that the very survival of the guerrillas demonstrated the majority's support of the NLF movement. In fact, the majority of southerners seem to have disliked both sides. Unlike North Vietnam, South Vietnam was thoroughly divided. Its citizens would not have given majority support to any government, and they were generally reluctant to help or fight for either the existing government or the NLF.

Faced with the intransigence of America's Vietnamese enemies and the reluctance of its Vietnamese friends, Nixon and his chief adviser, Henry Kissinger, devised a three-pronged plan to achieve their goals in Vietnam. First, they would increase military pressure. This would come in the form of accelerated bombing rather than increases in American troops. Nixon and Kissinger would also extend the target list for bombing, removing inhibitions against attacks on the major cities and ports of North Vietnam and on the areas of the Ho Chi Minh trail across the Vietnam border in Laos and Cambodia.

Second, Nixon and Kissinger would withdraw more American troops and turn the ground war over to the South Vietnamese in a program the Americans called Vietnamization. Nixon and Kissinger hoped that this would decrease domestic pressure in the United States against the war and provide more time for their military and diplomatic measures to work. Meanwhile, they expected that greater efficiency in the South Vietnamese army along with the extended bombing would offset the withdrawal of American troops and result in an increase rather than a decrease in military pressure on North Vietnam.

Third, Nixon and Kissinger extended their diplomatic initiatives beyond their Vietnamese enemies to North Vietnam's allies and suppliers. Nixon hoped to deprive North Vietnam of support by manipulating the balance of power. Breaking the long-standing precedent of isolating China, a policy he and his party had long supported, he would go to China, reopen relations, and thereby put pressure on the Soviet Union to try to outbid China for America's favor. As the price for improved relations with the United States, he would demand that the leaders of China and the Soviet Union withdraw their support from North Vietnam. As will be related in the next chapter, both nations refused to do that. But the very fact that they were negotiating with America while the Vietnam War was continuing showed the limits of their support for the Vietnamese revolution and must have put some pressure on North Vietnam to reach a peace agreement.

From Escalation to Withdrawal

Nixon found an early opportunity to escalate military action against the Communist effort in Vietnam. Within a month of his inauguration, North Vietnamese troops began to increase their attacks in South Vietnam. Nixon and Kissinger regarded this increase as a violation of the tacit agreement between Lyndon Johnson and North Vietnam that had led to negotiations—Johnson would halt bombing in the north, and North Vietnam would avoid attacks on major cities or across the demilitarized zone (DMZ). Nixon and Kissinger responded to the activities of the North Vietnamese troops not by resuming the bombing of North Vietnam, but by beginning secret bombing of Communist sanctuaries in Cambodia.

Later, Kissinger justified the secrecy of the Cambodian bombings on the grounds that it demonstrated determination without forcing a public confrontation with Hanoi, China, or the Soviets. The secrecy also aided Cambodian Premier Sihanouk, who Kissinger insisted welcomed attacks on the Vietnamese in his country, but whose weakness and tenuous neutral position would force him to protest if the bombing were acknowledged.[1] When the Communists surprisingly did not make a public protest, Nixon and Kissinger decided to continue both the bombing and the secrecy. With an eye no doubt to avoiding domestic as well as foreign repercussions, they hid the bombing from Congress, the

American people, and much of their own military and government. When inevitably word of the secret bombing began to leak, they put phone taps on suspected government officials and their newspaper contacts. Thus, Nixon added still more to the heritage of distrust and the credibility gap that already existed over Vietnam.

In conjunction with the secret bombing of Cambodia, Nixon announced some clarifications of his negotiating posture and sent an ultimatum to Ho Chi Minh, warning that if peace were not made by November, he would resort to "measures of great force." Then he sent Kissinger to meet secretly with the North Vietnamese to explore the chances for peace outside the limelight of the public negotiations Johnson had initiated.

To the dismay of Nixon and Kissinger, the North Vietnamese continued to scorn the American offer to make peace on the basis of a mutual withdrawal of American and North Vietnamese troops and internationally supervised elections. The North Vietnamese demanded instead that the United States withdraw unconditionally and leave power in the hands of a coalition government composed of Communists and other South Vietnamese who stood for "peace, independence, and neutrality." They made clear that Nguyen Van Thieu and the other top South Vietnamese officials did not fit this definition and would not be part of the coalition. Nixon and Kissinger regarded the North Vietnamese proposal as a demand for outright surrender—the Americans would have to leave South Vietnam and overthrow its government on their way out while leaving the North Vietnamese troops in place.

This left Nixon with the same problem Johnson had faced. American troops were leaving, the South Vietnamese buildup was at least uncertain, and the North Vietnamese would not only continue to fight, but refuse to release American prisoners of war. Nixon and Kissinger furiously surveyed the possibility of inflicting new "savage blows" on the Communists. They even considered using tactical nuclear weapons. They concluded, however, that no such program could work, and Nixon thought that halting the troop withdrawal would destroy his domestic support. He decided to back away from his ultimatum. He would rely on the buildup of South Vietnam, rally America's "silent majority" in support of Vietnamization, and search for new opportunities to use air and sea power to cover and compensate for troop withdrawals.

An opportunity to increase pressure on North Vietnam arrived in March 1970, when General Lon Nol overthrew Cambodia's neutralist Prince Sihanouk and publicly allied himself with the U.S. attempt to eject the North Vietnamese and Vietcong from their Cambodian sanctuaries. Nixon sent American and South Vietnamese troops on a major sweep into Cambodia. The war there now was public. Nixon told the American people that the United States could not stand by like a "pitiful helpless giant." The deposed Sihanouk, however, sided with the Communist Khmer Rouge, a tiny faction that, supported by North Vietnam, steadily increased its size and threat to the weak government of Lon Nol. Fierce American bombing in support of Lon Nol created much resentment in Cambodia and drove many into the arms of Pol Pot and his revolutionary force, the Khmer Rouge, which ultimately would take over Cambodia about the same time Laos and Saigon fell to the Communists.

Meanwhile, the Cambodian invasion jolted American opponents of the war out of the lull produced by Vietnamization and Nixon's appeal to the silent majority. Student strikes and protests broke out across the nation. National Guard troops shot several students at Kent State University in Ohio and Jackson State University in Mississippi. The Senate symbolically withdrew its consent to the Tonkin Gulf Resolution and the Nixon administration barely beat back congressional attempts to cut off funds for the Cambodian incursion. Nixon tried to stay ahead of public opinion at home by speeding troop withdrawals from Vietnam, but also he stepped up bombing of the Laotian and Cambodian sanctuaries. Then, in a test of the progress of Vietnamization, he approved a South Vietnamese invasion into Laos. The United States would supply no troops, only air support. The invasion put a crimp in the North Vietnamese buildup for an offensive, but cost South Vietnam even more dearly. After six weeks of bloody fighting, the South Vietnamese troops had to retreat back across the border, as American television cameras filmed soldiers clinging desperately to the skids of American helicopters in their haste to get out.

With opposition to the war growing, Nixon and Kissinger made a major concession in their secret peace talks with North Vietnam. They no longer demanded that North Vietnam withdraw its troops to match the American withdrawal. Kissinger later argued that the clause in the offer prohibiting North Vietnam from increasing the number of its troops would have left the Communist armies already in the south to wither, although North Vietnam would argue that this clause gave it the right to replace troops to maintain their original number. In any case, the North Vietnamese rejected the settlement unless the United States also abandoned Thieu. Thieu forestalled such a deal by forcing his two major domestic opponents to withdraw from the coming election. Nixon and Kissinger, although enraged by Thieu's maneuver, feared that to remove American support from him would throw South Vietnam into chaos. Negotiations sputtered, and North Vietnam prepared a major offensive for 1972. Nixon and Kissinger prayed that their dramatic initiatives toward China and the Soviets ultimately would force North Vietnam to compromise.

In March 1972, North Vietnam launched its long-awaited offensive across the DMZ and from Laos and Cambodia into the south. Only 95,000 American troops remained in Vietnam, and only 6,000 of them were combat forces. The supposedly revitalized South Vietnamese army would have to stop the Communist forces on its own. It fought surprisingly well, but in the end it failed. Nixon then decided to go all-out to end the war. He ordered B-52 strikes across the DMZ and attacks on the fuel depots around Hanoi and Haiphong harbor. Four Soviet vessels were hit in the raids. Two months later, at the risk of aborting the summit meeting scheduled with the Soviets, Nixon announced a further escalation. Since the North Vietnamese still rejected the American peace offer, he blockaded North Vietnam, mined Haiphong harbor, and increased the bombing. Yet the Soviets did not cancel the summit, and even China advised the North Vietnamese to compromise. Meanwhile, with tremendous losses on both sides, the North Vietnamese offensive ground to a stalemate.

In the face of these military and diplomatic setbacks, the North Vietnamese moved toward some concessions. On October 8, 1972, they dropped their insistence that Thieu resign and agreed that the coalition they had been demanding in South Vietnam would not be an official government, but only a commission to supervise the cease-fire and new elections in which Thieu could take part. Nixon accepted the offer, but Thieu was not mollified. He insisted that the North Vietnamese withdraw their troops before peace could be made. He had not objected when Nixon and Kissinger first had proposed to concede the North Vietnamese presence in the south because he did not think the North Vietnamese would accept any compromise. Now that they had, he threw every roadblock he could in the way of a cease-fire agreement.

Nixon and Kissinger found themselves in a very difficult situation. If they indicated that they had accepted while Thieu rejected the peace agreement, it would disrupt American domestic unity and might lead to a quick South Vietnamese collapse once the United States withdrew. Yet if Nixon and Kissinger themselves reneged on the North Vietnamese terms to protect Thieu, North Vietnam could publish its concessions, and opponents undoubtedly would succeed in getting Congress to cut off further funds for the war. Nixon and Kissinger tried to stall. Kissinger announced just before the American presidential election that "peace was at hand." Then he pressed Thieu to accept the agreement while promising to get some clarifications and modifications from the North Vietnamese. The North Vietnamese, however, knowing that Nixon and Kissinger would be under tremendous pressure to ratify the peace agreement, demanded new concessions of their own. Nixon decided to hold off on the agreement until after the U.S. presidential elections.

After his landslide reelection, Nixon decided to force the issue. He sent new waves of B-52s to attack Hanoi in the so-called Christmas bombing. American ships also reseeded the mines in Haiphong harbor. Following this campaign, the Americans and the North Vietnamese accepted a peace agreement that was essentially the same as the one negotiated in October. Nixon and Kissinger forced Thieu to accept it after they gained a few cosmetic concessions for him. They also secretly promised Thieu that the United States would support him with aid and bombing if North Vietnam violated the accord, although they knew they would have to get congressional consent for such intervention and that Congress would almost certainly refuse.

Nixon and Kissinger proclaimed they had won an honorable peace in Vietnam. They had retrieved American prisoners of war. They had left Thieu in power. They had gained a cease-fire in Laos as well as Vietnam (there was no cease-fire in Cambodia because the North Vietnamese claimed to have no control over the Khmer Rouge, which was probably true). They had established international inspection procedures to prevent infiltration of further men and supplies to the North Vietnamese remaining in the south, presumably leaving those forces to wither away. When the peace collapsed, they insisted it was only because the United States lost its nerve and determination.

When North Vietnam continued to infiltrate through Laos, Cambodia, and the DMZ, the Communist members of the international inspection force prevented action against it. Nixon, weakened and distracted by the investigation into his role in the burglary of a Democratic office in the Watergate Hotel, hesitated to resume bombing the north until all the U.S. prisoners of war were free. He continued bombing in Cambodia, where there never had been a cease-fire, but the inability of Sihanouk and Lon Nol to reconcile prevented a united front against the Khmer Rouge. Finally, Congress took matters out of the hands of Nixon and Kissinger. In May 1973, Congress cut off funds for further bombing in Cambodia. A month later it forced Nixon to cease military activities in all of Indochina as of August 15. It also steadily cut back economic aid to South Vietnam. Then, in November 1973, it passed the War Powers Act. This required the president to notify Congress within forty-eight hours of committing troops abroad and to withdraw those troops in sixty days unless Congress explicitly authorized them to stay.

In 1975 after Nixon had been forced from office for covering up the role of Republican party operatives in the Watergate burglary, the deluge finally hit. The Khmer Rouge, led by Pol Pot, toppled Lon Nol's regime and then killed millions of its own citizens and depopulated its cities in a fanatical back-to-the-soil movement. The North Vietnamese launched preliminary attacks in a projected two-year offensive to defeat South Vietnam, only to have the south collapse in a matter of months. American TV watchers were treated to the horrifying spectacle of American soldiers beating off thousands of South Vietnamese, desperate to escape the triumphant Communists, from the last helicopters evacuating the American embassy. Laos quickly followed Cambodia and South Vietnam, with 40,000 North Vietnamese troops helping the Pathet Lao overthrow the neutralist coalition headed by Souvana Phouma. America's only comfort was that the Communist regimes of Southeast Asia could not unite to expand their influence. The newly unified Vietnam invaded Cambodia, defeated Pol Pot, and set off a continuing guerrilla war that ranged China, Prince Sihanouk, and the Khmer Rouge (with some American support) against Vietnam and its Soviet allies.

Critics of Nixon and Kissinger argued that the Vietnam settlement had never been more than a "decent interval" to permit American withdrawal, and that Nixon and Kissinger knew it. Neither the North nor the South Vietnamese ever abandoned their military campaigns against each other. The south made a grab for territory to strengthen its position immediately after the settlement, which Thieu never formally accepted. The north was a bit more cautious until the Americans were gone, but it never stopped its infiltration into the south. The international inspection commission set up by the agreement was unworkable, unable to agree on its observations, let alone do anything about violations of the peace agreement. The United States simply could not continue to prop up governments that had so little standing with their own people. Nixon and Kissinger had expended vast numbers of lives and enormous resources in their attempt to do so and then had covered their inevitable failure with a paper-thin peace agreement whose inevitable demise they blamed on the media, antiwar activists, congressional spinelessness, and Watergate's sapping of executive power.

The Impact of Vietnam

From the mid-1960s on, as Vietnam destroyed the presidency of Lyndon Johnson and helped to cripple that of Richard Nixon, the Vietnam War began to replace Munich as the most potent symbol of what America should avoid in foreign policy. The charge of "appeasement" or "soft on communism" no longer automatically threw the burden of proof on those who questioned proposals for foreign intervention. Even many conservatives joined those Americans further to the left in arguing that the United States should generally avoid military interventions in third-world countries. One poll taken early in the 1970s showed a majority of Americans unwilling to intervene anywhere abroad except in the case of an invasion of Canada.

Vietnam thus raised powerful challenges to the realist ethos and Kennedy's concept of flexible response. The realist emphasis on containing communism through carefully calibrated programs of diplomatic persuasion and limited wars aimed at circumscribed goals within rationally balanced power systems no longer seemed so realistic. How could any president mobilize popular opinion for limited wars? How many soldiers would die willingly and heroically for such abstractions as the balance of power when principle and morality were not involved? If it were possible to mobilize opinion for such wars, how could they be kept limited as the public became enraged over the inevitable wartime deaths and atrocities? And how could a president retreat when it became apparent that victory required an effort greater than the interests involved were worth?

The most prominent lesson drawn in the immediate aftermath of the Vietnam War was that the United States should not be drawn by dogmatic anticommunism and memories of Munich into military intervention unless the people of the target area clearly welcomed it. Many politicians, journalists, historians, and ordinary Americans concluded from the U.S. experience in Vietnam that the war had been unwinnable from the first because the South Vietnamese government that the United States was trying to preserve was unpopular, undemocratic, and inept. So long as Ho Chi Minh represented Vietnamese nationalism to the majority of his countrymen, foreigners would not be able to win over the Vietnamese people despite extensive economic aid, pacification measures, and other nation-building efforts. Because the South Vietnamese people had been unwilling to support the government and to fight against the revolutionaries, foreign troops could do little to put down the rebellion because they were unable to distinguish between friends and foes.

Inevitably, American bombing and search-and-destroy missions inflicted great suffering on the people of South Vietnam irrespective of their allegiances. Meanwhile, the supposed benefits of American aid merely distorted and corrupted Vietnamese society. Many Americans came to believe that the Vietnamese would have been better off living under the National Liberation Front and the North Vietnamese government than suffering a horrendous war and American intervention on behalf of a South Vietnamese government that was no better and in many ways worse than the Communists.

Radicals, agreeing with this analysis, argued that so long as the United States was a capitalist nation, it would ignore the lessons of Vietnam and inevitably intervene in developing nations as it pursued its anticommunist crusade to maintain its markets and sources of raw materials. Radicals called for revolutionary change in the United States to end the containment policy and prevent any further Vietnams.

Soft realists and other liberals argued that the United States could learn from its Vietnam mistake without revolutionizing America's economy and society. The nation had simply to elect leaders who understood that containment of the Soviet Union did not require military intervention in the developing world. Third-world nationalism would thwart Soviet expansionism just as it had defeated U.S. intervention in Vietnam. Although Laos and Cambodia fell to the Communists at the same time South Vietnam did, the dreaded domino effect did not result in the fall of the remainder of Southeast Asia, let alone Japan, the Philippines, and the other nations that supporters of the war had said were at risk.

For several years the liberal and radical analyses of Vietnam predominated in the books, articles, and other media that dealt with the war. (The historiographical essay at the end of this chapter provides details.) Perhaps as a consequence, the liberal critique of the war also seems to have predominated in the minds of the public and the politicians. The slogan "No More Vietnams" seemed to embody that view and to be almost as powerful as the slogan "No More Munichs" had been in the previous era of American foreign policy. Conservatives therefore worried aloud that the supposed "lessons of Vietnam" would keep the American people from intervening where intervention might be essential to contain communism and maintain the balance of power. Many conservatives were willing to concede that intervention in Vietnam might have been a mistake, but they argued that this should not prejudice the electorate against other interventions that truly might be necessary.

As time wore on, however, conservatives became less defensive about Vietnam. The brutality of the victorious governments in Vietnam, Laos, and especially Cambodia vindicated for many the attempt by the United States to save the people of Southeast Asia from the Communists. And the heating up of the Cold War between the United States and the Soviet Union in the late 1970s and early 1980s reinvigorated the belief of many that Soviet and Communist influence needed to be contained even in peripheral areas. Thus, President Ronald Reagan referred to the Vietnam War as "a noble crusade." Rather than wishing that the lessons of Vietnam would go away, conservatives began to argue that the Left, the historians, and the media had simply learned the wrong lessons from the war. They based their arguments on a wave of new scholarship that challenged the conventional wisdom about Vietnam. These conservative writers and scholars insisted that, except for mistakes in the way the United States fought the war, it could and should have been won.

Among those writing new conservative analyses of Vietnam were Nixon and Kissinger themselves. They argued in their influential memoirs that America had actually won in Vietnam and that a cowardly Congress and Democratic Party had thrown away Nixon's diplomatic victory by refusing to reenter the war when North Vietnam violated the provisions of Kissinger's peace agreement. This argument failed to convince many readers.

But other conservative and military analysts made a more convincing case for a revision of the lessons of Vietnam. (Again, the specific books that promulgated this view are discussed in the historiographical essay at the end of this chapter.) They rejected the contention of Nixon and Kissinger that the war had been won, but thought it could have been won with better political and military tactics. They argued that Kennedy and Johnson had made a political mistake by intervening gradually and halfheartedly in pursuit of limited goals. Instead, Johnson should have gone to Congress for a formal declaration of war, mobilized the American people for all-out conflict, and made a maximum effort for victory.

Militarily, some conservative analysts argued that the United States should have devoted more effort to pacifying the countryside instead of training Vietnamese and

U.S. forces for conventional warfare. But most argued that, ironically, the United States could have won by a more intensive use of conventional warfare tactics. They pointed out that the Tet offensive, which most of the media and early historians had portrayed as a defeat, had actually decimated the National Liberation Front's guerrilla forces. From 1968 on, then, the North Vietnamese regular army rather than guerrillas had carried on the fight. And the United States could have defeated the North Vietnamese army with the same methods that had been successful in World War II and Korea. If the Americans had simply cut off the supplies and reinforcements flowing down the Ho Chi Minh Trail and across the DMZ with a combination of invasion, technological defense lines, and bombing, the North Vietnamese army would have withered and died. (How and whether American forces could have cut off those supplies is still a major issue of debate among military experts.) Instead, the United States pulled its troops out of Vietnam after Tet and left the way open for the North Vietnamese army to invade and defeat South Vietnam by conventional tactics, which it did in 1975.

Thus, conservatives drew lessons from the Vietnam War that were very different from those of previous liberal analysts. Instead of concluding that America should "never again" intervene militarily in the third world, conservatives argued, in the words of Colonel Harry Summers: "Never again must the President commit American men to combat without first fully defining the nation's war aims and then rallying congress and the nation for war."[2] Nixon added that the slogan "No More Vietnams" should mean not that the United States should not try again to contain communism in the third world, but that it should not fail again.

By the late 1970s and 1980s this conservative reading of the lessons of Vietnam had a formidable impact on American foreign policy. It had not entirely displaced the earlier lessons; there was still a notable reluctance in the electorate to intervene militarily in the third world, as exemplified by the bitter debate over American actions in Nicaragua and El Salvador. But the foreign policy and national security officials of the Reagan and first Bush administrations took the conservative lessons to heart.

This was demonstrated in November 1984 in a highly publicized speech by Secretary of Defense Caspar Weinberger on the proper guidelines for U.S. military intervention. Those guidelines were borrowed almost directly from the work of Harry Summers on Vietnam and from the curricula of West Point and the other U.S. service schools that had adopted Summers's view. Weinberger listed six criteria to be fulfilled before the United States committed troops in the developing world:

1. The area should be vital to the national security.
2. The United States should intervene only if it had a clear intention of winning.
3. The United States should have well-defined interests and objectives.
4. The government should be flexible and willing to adjust the size, composition, and disposition of forces.
5. The government should use American troops only as a last resort.
6. The government should send troops only if it had reasonable assurance of popular and congressional support in the United States.

The glaring omission in these principles, however, was any consideration of the people in the country where the United States was going to intervene. Weinberger and the conservatives insisted on the full support of the American people for any such enterprise, but ignored the support of the people who were the object of the intervention. That support, of course, was the single most critical factor in the calculations of more liberal opponents of the Vietnam War, who argued that the lack of such support had made the war unwinnable.

Even if conservatives downplayed this factor, the principles advocated by Weinberger and other conservative analysts did result in some limits on U.S. military intervention in the developing world in the 1980s. Weinberger and the Joint Chiefs of Staff, despite their support of a massive military buildup in the Reagan and Bush years, were at the same time the major voices for restraint in the use of those forces in third-world areas. They might support military aid and covert intervention in Central America, but they were extremely reluctant to send troops to Lebanon in 1983, to invade Grenada and Panama later in the 1980s, and to employ ground troops in Iraq during the Gulf War. They insisted, however, that when intervention did take place, it should be with full force. The Gulf War of 1991 seemed to vindicate this conservative interpretation of Vietnam. When the United States committed overwhelming force to the task of turning back the Iraqi invasion of Kuwait, as recommended by Weinberger and confirmed under the rubric of the Powell Doctrine (after the chair of the Joint Chiefs, Colin Powell), conservatives believed the United States had finally kicked the "Vietnam syndrome."

There was still considerable debate over third-world interventions that, while involving important American or humanitarian issues, did not seem to justify the overwhelming effort dictated by Weinberger and Powell. After the failure of the humanitarian intervention in Somalia under President George H.W. Bush, it was the liberals who supported interventions in Haiti and the former Yugoslavia, while the conservatives disdained interventions that required "nation building" in failed states.

Until 9/11, then, the lessons of Vietnam had become somewhat diluted and confused, only to be resurrected by the invasion of Iraq in 2003. As we will see in a later chapter, the American failures in the Iraqi war revived the debate whether the United States should have avoided intervention entirely or simply managed the invasion better, first by sending more troops, as dictated by the Powell Doctrine, and second by planning properly for the postinvasion occupation.

Controversial Issues

Early histories of the war in Vietnam generally agreed with the Johnson administration that the policy of gradual escalation, limited rather than total war, and offers of unconditional negotiations were proper extensions of the realist containment policy and the doctrine of flexible response. They likened the war in Vietnam to other successful instances of containment—the Marshall Plan, NATO, the Korean War, and the Cuban missile crisis. They accepted the Johnson administration's contention that the war was a product of North Vietnamese aggression rather than internal South Vietnamese dissent. South Vietnam seemed to these historians a testing ground for the Communist attempt to circumvent containment by resorting to wars of national liberation instead of direct conventional attacks.[3]

Ironically, while Secretary of State Dean Rusk, Lyndon Johnson, and their historian defenders relied on the rhetoric of restraint and realism to justify their policies, some of the war's earliest critics were among the primary formulators of the realist perspective on diplomatic history. George Kennan, Hans Morgenthau, and Walter Lippmann opposed the Vietnam War as an excessive commitment to a region that was not essential to the balance of power or to America's vital strategic, economic, or cultural interests. They believed that the nations of Southeast Asia were too culturally and politically diverse to fall like dominoes if the Communists won in Vietnam. These nations were even less likely to be faithful satellites of Russia or China. The realists also doubted that the United States could do much to stave off the Communists even if that were to its interest. The people of South Vietnam were too estranged from their American-backed government. Hans Morgenthau pointed out that a guerrilla war, "supported or at least not opposed by the indigenous population, can only be won by the indiscriminate killing of everybody in sight—by genocide." At first the realists did not advocate immediate withdrawal, since the original intervention had committed American prestige. Instead, they favored the so-called enclave strategy, limiting the war effort to the protection of population enclaves while negotiating for a coalition or even a neutralist Communist government. Then, after the Tet offensive demonstrated that the United States could not even protect enclaves for any length of time, these "restrained" or "soft" realists urged unconditional withdrawal.[4]

While soft realists were among the early opponents of the Vietnam War, their previous advocacy of containment, limited wars, and pragmatic considerations of power and interest over moralism were so much a part of the rationale for American policy toward Vietnam that many historians decided Vietnam was more than a mistaken instance of overzealous and overmilitarized containment. They began to argue that realism and containment were intrinsically flawed and inevitably brutalizing policies. They maintained that moral considerations had to play a greater role in foreign policy. Most of these liberal moralists were journalists rather than scholars, and they did not formulate a full philosophy of foreign relations or place the role of morality in context. They simply recited the numerous horrendous atrocities that resulted from the Vietnam War and showed how realist principles had led to them.[5]

Meanwhile, the very few Western academic experts on the Vietnamese people helped undermine the government position on Vietnam. One of those experts was Joseph Buttinger, who wrote the best history of Vietnam in the English language. Buttinger said all but two authors worthy of inclusion in his bibliography were "critical or firmly opposed to the Vietnamese war."[6]

Works by American government officials also undermined the official American view, sometimes inadvertently. Douglas Pike, a government analyst, published an extensive description of the Vietcong that belied government claims that the Communists in the south were weak and dependent on the north.[7] Chester Cooper, a member of the Central Intelligence Agency, wrote pessimistic assessments of the war from within the government and publicly summarized them in his book, *The Lost Crusade* (1970). But probably *The Pentagon Papers*, a government study leaked to the *New York Times*, did most to discredit the Vietnam War.[8] *The Pentagon Papers* revealed, among other things, the covert operations that had provoked the Tonkin Gulf incident and the contingency planning for bombing the north that Johnson had ordered even while his election campaign in 1964 advocated restraint in Vietnam.

Among opponents of the war, partisans of John F. Kennedy tried to demonstrate that Kennedy had been properly restrained, had understood the limits of America's interests and ability to affect the course of events in Vietnam, and would have withdrawn rather than escalate as Johnson did. They blamed Robert McNamara, Dean Rusk, and the military for presenting Kennedy with a false rosy picture of the progress of the South Vietnamese government and the war effort, thus leading him further into the war than he was inclined to go.[9] Some recent historians with access to far more archives than these earlier scholars also are inclined to believe that Kennedy might have avoided the escalation that took place under Johnson. See the outstanding works by Fred Logevall, *Choosing War: The Lost Chance for Peace and the Escalation of the War in Vietnam* (1999); and David Kaiser, *American Tragedy: Kennedy, Johnson, and the Origins of the Vietnam War* (2000).

Leslie Gelb, who had compiled *The Pentagon Papers* while a member of the government, convinced most historians that neither Kennedy nor Johnson was misled into Vietnam. He argued that both Kennedy and Johnson had good information and that both had escalated the war because politically they could not afford to accept defeat in a war. Gelb argued that Congress should be given a stronger voice in foreign policy to permit American withdrawal when a president was too politically committed to admit defeat.[10] The opening of further archives has confirmed Gelb's argument that Kennedy, Johnson, and Nixon all understood that military victory was highly unlikely and that all three were trying to avoid defeat rather than to win. Meanwhile, the atrocities of Vietnam and the disingenuousness of American leaders made the mild criticisms and prescriptions of the restrained realists and liberal moralists almost laughable to an increasing number of radical historians in the late 1960s and 1970s. These radicals regarded Vietnam as far more than a mistake resulting from understandable misapprehensions about communism or overzealous applications of necessary realistic prescriptions for the Cold War. Revisionists portrayed the war as the inevitable imperialist and interventionist outcome of tragic evils built into the very foundation of America's political and economic capitalist system. They saw Vietnam as the result of America's driving need to dominate the developing world and thus acquire ever-expanding markets and sources of raw materials for itself and its clients and allies. Although the United States itself might not have needed the resources and markets of Southeast Asia, Japan and other American allies in Asia did. The United States had reason to fear losing those allies along with other markets and resources that were critical to America if it did not stop socialist revolutions from closing the developing world to imperialist exploitation.[11]

But if radical explanations gained ground in the 1970s, conservative reinterpretations of Vietnam were more predominant in the 1980s. As already explained, most conservative analysts argued that America could have won the Vietnam War if it had mobilized fully for victory and buckled down to a hard conventional war after Tet.[12] On the other hand, a few conservative analysts argued that while the war could and should have been won, it required more attention to pacification measures and irregular warfare than conventional tactics.[13] These analysts who emphasized pacification were in the minority among the conservatives, but they made at least two excellent points. Gunter Lewy showed that despite the atrocities admittedly committed by the United States and South Vietnam, the Vietnam War was not particularly atrocious compared to other recent wars. The population of both North and South Vietnam increased dramatically during the war and the percentage of civilian casualties was markedly lower than in Korea or World War II. Meanwhile, Andrew Krepinevich showed that the primary tactic recommended by conservative military analysts like Summers and Palmer, cutting the North Vietnamese army off from the supplies necessary for it to carry on the war, would have been almost impossible without a full-scale invasion of North Vietnam that would have risked Chinese or even Soviet intervention. A liberal critic of the war who makes this point even more tellingly is John Prados, *The Blood Road: The Ho Chi Minh Trail and the Vietnam War* (1999).

Two recent works summarize the conservative view that the United States could have won the war. Mark Moyar, *Triumph Forsaken: The Vietnam War, 1954–1965* (2006) is a vehement defense of the war. Lewis Sorley, *A Better War: The Unexamined Victories and Final Tragedy of America's Lost War in Vietnam* (1999) is somewhat milder.

Further Reading

The best of the overall histories of the Vietnam War include George Herring, *America's Longest War* (4th ed., 2002); Robert Schulzinger, *A Time for War: The United States and Vietnam, 1941–1975* (1997); Robert J. McMahon, *The Limits of Empire: The United States and Southeast Asia Since World War II* (1999); Marilyn B. Young, *The Vietnam Wars, 1945–1990* (1991); George McT. Kahin, *Intervention* (1986); and Jeffrey Record, *The Wrong War: Why We Lost in Vietnam* (1998). Stanley Karnow's *Vietnam* (1983) and its accompanying television series of the same name, although somewhat dated, still provide an excellent overview of the subject.

For the Vietcong and North Vietnamese side of the war, see *Vietnam's Southern Revolution: From Peasant Insurrection to Total War* (2008); William Duiker, *The Communist Road to Power in Vietnam* (2nd ed., 1996); Military History Institute of Vietnam, *Victory in Vietnam: The Official History of the People's Army of Vietnam, 1954–1975* (2002); Robert K. Brigham, *Guerrilla Diplomacy: The NLF's Foreign Relations and the Vietnam War* (1999); Wallace J. Thies, *When Governments Collide: Coercion and Diplomacy in the Vietnam Conflict, 1964–1968* (1980); and Truong Nhu Tang, *A Vietcong Memoir* (1985). For the South Vietnamese side and America's failure to build a viable state in South Vietnam, see Seth Jacobs, *Cold War Mandarin: Ngo Dinh Diem and the Origins of America's War in Vietnam* (2006); James M. Carter, *Inventing Vietnam: The United States and State Building, 1954–1968* (2008); and Nguyen Tien Hung and Jerrold Schecter, *The Palace File* (1986), which contains the Nixon-Thieu correspondence.

An excellent book that looks at not only the American and Vietnamese sides of the war but also the policies of the rest of the world toward the conflict is Mark Atwood Lawrence, *The Vietnam War: A Concise International History* (2008).

The best books on Johnson's policies toward Vietnam besides the Logevall book cited above include Larry Berman, *Lyndon Johnson's War: The Road to Stalemate in Vietnam* (1989) and *Planning a Tragedy: The Americanization of the War in Vietnam* (1982); Edwin E. Moïse, *Tonkin Gulf and the Escalation of the Vietnam War* (1996); and Lloyd Gardner, *Pay Any Price: Lyndon Johnson and the Wars for Vietnam* (1995). For Nixon's policies, see Jeffrey Kimball, *Nixon's Vietnam War* (1998); and Larry Berman, *No Peace, No Honor: Nixon, Kissinger, and Betrayal in Vietnam* (2001). See also *America's Rasputin: Walt Rostow and the Vietnam War* (2008). All these books are highly critical of the war.

Memoirs of participants defending the war are Lyndon Johnson, *The Vantage Point* (1971); Walt Whitman Rostow, *The Diffusion of Power* (1972); William C. Westmoreland, *A Soldier Reports* (1976); Richard Nixon, *RN: The Memoirs of Richard Nixon* (1978) and *No More Vietnams* (1985); and Henry Kissinger, *The White House Years* (1979) and *Years of Upheaval* (1982). Other books that argue that the war could and should have been won are H.R. McMaster, *Dereliction of Duty: Johnson, McNamara, the Joint Chiefs of Staff, and the Lies That Led to Vietnam* (1997); Norman Podhoretz, *Why We Were in Vietnam* (1982); Timothy J. Lomperis, *The War Everyone Lost—and Won: America's Intervention in Viet Nam's Twin Struggles* (1984) and *From the People's War to People's Rule: Insurgency, Intervention, and the Lessons of Vietnam* (1996).

An important memoir that apologizes for the war is Robert McNamara, *In Retrospect: The Tragedy and Lessons of Vietnam* (1995). McNamara, who was close to Kennedy as his secretary of defense, believes that Kennedy would have gotten out of Vietnam if he had lived. See also Deborah Shapley, *Promise and Power: The Life and Times of Robert McNamara* (1993).

Two books assess congressional politics during the war and conclude that there was considerable support for restraint in Congress so that neither Kennedy nor Johnson needed to escalate for domestic purposes: Gary Stone, *Elites for Peace: The Senate and the Vietnam War, 1964–1968* (2007); and Andrew Johns, *Vietnam's Second Front: Domestic Politics, the Republican Party, and the War* (2010).

Works that assess the relationship between Vietnam and the American home front include James Miller, *Democracy in the Streets* (1987); Melvin Small, *Johnson, Nixon, and the Doves* (1988); Steven M. Gillon, *Politics and Vision: The ADA and American Liberalism, 1947–1985* (1987); Ole Holsti and James R. Rosenau, *American Leadership in World Affairs: Vietnam and the Breakdown of Consensus* (1984); John Hellmann, *American Myth and the Legacy of Vietnam* (1986); and Loren Baritz, *Backfire: A History of How American Culture Led Us into Vietnam* (1985). On the leading Senate dissenter, see William C. Berman, *William Fulbright and the Vietnam War* (1988); and Eugene Brown, *J. William Fulbright: Advice and Dissent* (1985).

An outstanding book that gives the reader a sense of the war on the ground is Jeffrey Race, *War Comes to Long An: Revolutionary Conflict in a Vietnamese Province* (1972). To get an idea of the impact of the war on the Americans who fought it, see Kyle Longley, *Grunts: The American Combat Soldier in Vietnam* (2008).

For the impact of the war on American memory and politics, see Robert D. Schulzinger, *A Time for Peace: The Legacy of the Vietnam War* (2006); and Patrick Hagopian, *The Vietnam War in American Memory: Vietnam, Memorials, and the Politics of Healing* (2009).

Notes

1. In a press conference, Sihanouk showed his fancy footwork. "I have not protested the bombings of Viet Cong camps because I have not heard of the bombings. I was not in the know, because in certain areas of Cambodia there are no Cambodians. . . . Here it is—the first report about several B-52 bombings. Yet I have not been informed about that at all, because I have not lost any houses, any countrymen, nothing, nothing."

2. Harry G. Summers Jr., "Lessons: A Soldier's View," in Peter Braestrup, *Vietnam as History: Ten Years After the Paris Peace Accords* (1984), p. 114.

3. For official administration positions, see State Department White Paper, publication 7839 (February 1965), and the testimony of Dean Rusk before the Senate Foreign Relations Committee in *The Vietnam Hearings*, introduced by J. William Fulbright (1966). For historical analysis, see Wesley R. Fishel, ed., *Vietnam: Anatomy of a Conflict* (1968). See also Frank N. Trager, *Why Vietnam?* (1966); Chester A. Bain, *Vietnam: The Roots of Conflict* (1967); and Maxwell D. Taylor, *Responsibility and Response* (1967).

4. Hans J. Morgenthau, *Vietnam and the United States* (1965); George F. Kennan, testimony before the Senate Foreign Relations Committee in *The Vietnam Hearings* (1966). Lippmann offered his opinions in numerous syndicated columns, which are best summarized in Ronald Steel, *Walter Lippmann and the American Century* (1980).

5. David Halberstam, *The Best and the Brightest* (1972); J. William Fulbright, *Old Myths and New Realities* (1964), as compared with his *The Crippled Giant* (1972); Frances Fitzgerald, *Fire in the Lake: The Vietnamese and the Americans in Vietnam* (1972).

6. Joseph Buttinger, *Vietnam: The Unforgettable Tragedy* (1977), *The Smaller Dragon: A Political History of Vietnam* (1958), and *Vietnam: A Dragon Embattled* (2 vols., 1967). See also Bernard Fall, *The Two Vietnams* (1963). Before Fall was killed in Vietnam, he also contributed *Vietnam Witness: 1953–1966* (1966) and, with Marcus G. Raskin, *The Vietnam Reader* (1965).

7. Douglas Pike, *Viet Cong: The Organization and Techniques of the National Liberation Front of South Vietnam* (1966).

8. Neil Sheehan et al., *The Pentagon Papers as Published by the* New York Times (1971).

9. Arthur Schlesinger Jr., *The Bitter Heritage: Vietnam and American Democracy, 1941–1966* (1967), and *A Thousand Days: John F. Kennedy in the White House* (1965); Roger Hilsman, *To Move a Nation: The Politics of Foreign Policy in the Administration of John F. Kennedy* (1967); Robert L. Gallucci, *Neither Peace Nor Honor: The Politics of American Military Policy in Vietnam* (1975).

10. Leslie H. Gelb, with Richard K. Betts, *The Irony of Vietnam: The System Worked* (1979). See also Warren I. Cohen, *Dean Rusk* (1980); Larry Berman, *Planning a Tragedy* (1982); David L. Di Leo, *George Ball, Vietnam, and the Rethinking of Containment* (1991); and the two best general surveys of the Vietnam War, George Herring, *America's Longest War: The United States in Vietnam, 1950–1975* (2nd ed., 1986); and George McT. Kahin, *Intervention: How America Became Involved in Vietnam* (1986). Running contrary to the idea that the system worked and kept the president well informed is Neil Sheehan, *A Bright Shining Lie: John Paul Vann and America in Vietnam* (1988). An outstanding historiographical essay on the war that has influenced my own discussion here is Robert A. Divine, "Vietnam Reconsidered," *Diplomatic History* (Winter 1988).

11. Gabriel Kolko provided the most rigorous economic explanation of the war in *Roots of American Foreign Policy* (1969) and *Anatomy of a War: Vietnam, the United States, and the Modern Historical Experience* (1985).

12. Harry G. Summers, *On Strategy: A Critical Analysis of the Vietnam War* (1982); Bruce Palmer Jr., *The 25-Year War: America's Military Role in Vietnam* (1984).

13. Gunter Lewy, *America in Vietnam* (1978); Andrew Krepinevich, *The Army and Vietnam* (1986); William Colby, *Lost Victory* (1989).

CHAPTER 13

RICHARD NIXON
AND HENRY KISSINGER
MANIPULATING THE BALANCE OF POWER

Richard Nixon's "Structure of Peace"

Richard Nixon did not appear presidential. He was shy, unsure of his roots, bland, and unformed in his personality and culture. He compensated for his lack of personal center with forced shows of ebullience and toughness. He tried to emulate the heroic, simple, and forceful good guy of his native West. In public he presented such a carefully cultivated personality that his most sincere protestations often rang false. The smile was too forced, the humor too heavy-handed, the sentiments too maudlin, and the claims to the highest morality too transparently false. He was obsessed with public relations, far more than most other modern presidents, few of whom have been shrinking violets. He always attributed defeats to the better public relations work of his opponents, never to their substance.

The insecurity that drove him and his advisers to be so concerned with his public image took on a more menacing form in private. He had to appear tough, one of the guys. His private conversation, better adapted to the locker room than to the White House, was mean and bitter rather than earthy and expansive in the manner of Harry Truman or Lyndon Johnson. "We floored those liberal sons of bitches," he would gloat. He often gave helter-skelter orders to his aides to play hardball, toughen their positions, and "take care of" his enemies, although sometimes Nixon's violent musings were only a form of thinking out loud or talking for effect. Ironically, for all his tough talk, Nixon could not stand personal confrontations. He usually contrived to agree with everyone face to face, but afterward he would order aides to chastise, deride, fire, or destroy anyone in whom he sensed opposition.

Most of his close advisers learned to discount Nixon's private rhetoric and ignore some of his more brutal or harebrained orders in the confident expectation that the president did not really mean them. Usually, if the advisers delayed long enough, the president would forget or revoke his commands. For instance, Nixon would regularly order his secretary of state, Henry Kissinger, to cut off all aid to Israel until Israel agreed to American policy; then he would renege. But the atmosphere in the White House was like a shark tank.

Some advisers inevitably took Nixon literally, and their obedience led to Watergate and the president's destruction.

Nixon's partner and chief operative in the foreign policy arena was Kissinger, first his national security adviser and later secretary of state. Kissinger, a brilliant Harvard professor and political protégé of the leader of the liberal wing of the Republican Party, Vice President Nelson Rockefeller, represented much of what Nixon hated most. Not only was Kissinger part of the superior, Europe-oriented eastern establishment, but he also was Jewish, and Nixon was anti-Semitic enough to sprinkle his private conversations about Kissinger with slurs such as "Jew boy." Kissinger was in fact a refugee from Nazi Germany who became a major scholarly advocate of the realist, balance-of-power school of thought. He wrote books in praise of the European diplomats who had been early masters of the balance of power: Castlereagh, Metternich, and Bismarck. He studied the uses of tactical nuclear weapons to maintain the balance of power in modern Europe. He had briefly advised the Kennedy administration and he had reported skeptically on the progress of the Vietnam War prior to his acceptance of office under Nixon.

Nixon looked past Kissinger's despised liberal credentials and saw in him a compatible adviser because Nixon and Kissinger shared an especially hard version of the realist outlook. They did not fatalistically accept the balance of power and attempt to work within it; both were ready to take what they considered heroic risks to shape and manipulate it to America's advantage and to drive hard bargains with their adversaries. They shared a disdain for ideological factors or human rights in foreign affairs and were willing to base their policies on power politics almost exclusively.

Besides this policy compatibility, Nixon considered Kissinger a useful presidential tool because Kissinger, a political unknown operating behind the scenes within the White House as national security adviser, would be completely beholden to the president. His status thus differed from that of the secretary of state, William Rogers, who had been approved by the Senate, who ran a large semi-independent agency, and who thus had at least some independent status before Congress and the media. Nixon, by operating through Kissinger as a "back channel" to China, Russia, and Vietnam, could bypass the hated State Department bureaucracy with its "Ivy League liberals," conduct operations efficiently and secretly, and claim all credit for himself while sharing none with Rogers.

Nixon, however, did not anticipate the degree to which he might have to share credit with Kissinger. Kissinger could be deferential and even groveling in the presence of his superiors or those whose good opinion he needed, but he was extremely ambitious. He also was arrogant. He drove his subordinates relentlessly, terrorized them with petulant spells of anger, regaled them with snide stories about "our meatball president," and used their reports masterfully in presenting policy options to Nixon. Some staff members advised newcomers who asked how to get along on the national security adviser's team: "Think of Henry Kissinger as a corkscrew, and think of yourself as a cork." Many nonetheless managed to develop a respect and affection for him. One aide gave him for his office a picture poster of a huge gorilla with the caption, "When I want your opinion, I'll beat it out of you."

Kissinger was even more ruthless with his bureaucratic rivals than with his subordinates, and he quickly eliminated all competition for the ear of Nixon on foreign affairs. Then, as his role in the spectacular back-channel negotiations with China, Russia, and Vietnam became known, Nixon permitted Kissinger to hold public news conferences rather than anonymous backgrounders. Kissinger, with his brilliant analyses and quick wit, became an instant media star. His favorite technique was to poke fun at his own foibles, particularly his megalomania. When asked if he had read Bernard and Marvin Kalb's biography *Kissinger*, he said, "No, but I like the title." After his appointment as secretary of state, one reporter inquired if he preferred to be called Mr. Secretary or Dr. Secretary. Kissinger replied, "I don't stand on protocol. If you will just call me 'Excellency,' it will be okay." When he unveiled the statue of Thomas Jefferson during the opening of the Jefferson room on the eighth floor of the State Department, he quipped with mock disappointment, "Oh, I thought it would be me."

In this way Kissinger established a separate identity from the president. As Watergate eroded Nixon's power and reputation, Kissinger took more and more public responsibility for foreign affairs. Nixon had to move him out of the White House and put him in formal charge of foreign policy as secretary of state in order to protect the administration's diplomatic successes and ongoing negotiations from the taint of the White House scandal, and Kissinger survived to carry the Nixon-Kissinger policies into the administration of Gerald Ford.

At the outset of the administration, Nixon and Kissinger, analyzing the balance of power, believed they had a way to stabilize the Cold War, extricate the United States from Vietnam, and fashion a "structure of peace." First, recognizing the strain between China and the Soviet Union, they would reopen diplomatic relations with China. Cooperation with China would alter the balance of power and give the Soviet Union an incentive to come to its own accommodation with the United States. In order to win such an accommodation, both Russia and China should be willing to withdraw their support from North Vietnam and the Vietcong. The Vietnamese Communists then would have to accept a compromise settlement that would permit Nixon to withdraw American forces.

Once extricated from Vietnam, Nixon and Kissinger had no intention of entangling American troops in any further wars of attrition outside the major arenas of power. In July 1969, President Nixon proclaimed his Nixon Doctrine. The United States would supply money and matériel, but not men, to nations fighting internal or external enemies of the United States. America would intervene with troops only if the enemy were a nuclear power. In line with this strategic doctrine, Nixon announced that the limited uses of American soldiers would permit him to phase out the military draft. He also reluctantly permitted a Congress that was reacting against Vietnam to reduce spending on conventional forces in exchange for continued support of a new generation of strategic weapons—the B-1 bomber, the Trident submarine, and the cruise and MX missiles. As a result, between 1968 and 1974, the number of American air force squadrons fell from 220 to 169, army and marine divisions from 23 to 16, and navy ships from 976 to 495.

Much of this program coincided with the suggestions of moderate and liberal critics of the war in Vietnam. These critics demanded détente, a strategic arms agreement with the Soviet Union, the recognition of China, the end of the draft, withdrawal from Vietnam, and restraint in future interventions. Conservatives, who regarded the long-time anticommunist Nixon if not Harvard professor Kissinger as one of their own, looked on aghast as the grand design unfolded. By the time Nixon resigned in the wake of Watergate and Gerald Ford replaced him, conservatives were denouncing the Nixon-Kissinger policies as near treason. They called the Strategic Arms Limitation agreement a victory for the Soviets. They claimed that negotiations with Moscow merely lowered the West's guard while the Soviets cheated and continued their inexorable march toward world conquest. The conservatives reviled the Vietnam peace agreement as a thinly disguised American surrender that encouraged world communism. They regarded the opening to China with great suspicion and bewailed what they considered the betrayal of the Nationalist government on Taiwan.

Nixon and Kissinger thought these conservative critics lacked a full understanding of the objective world situation and the pragmatism necessary to deal with it. The USSR would achieve nuclear parity regardless of what America did. The best the United States could do was to limit Soviet power and induce it to moderation through continuation of American strength, the manipulation of the balance of power, and hard bargaining for verifiable agreements. To go beyond these goals, to seek to change the Soviet domestic system as well as its external behavior, was to exceed America's capabilities and risk nuclear war.

Nixon and Kissinger regretted the conservative backlash, but were relatively gentle in trying to answer its charges. They considered themselves conservatives who were seeking their goals realistically within the limits of American power. Nixon and Kissinger were less tolerant of criticism from the Left. Radicals and antiwar activists were beyond the pale, fit objects for FBI and CIA surveillance. Nixon also hated the "Ivy League liberals." Kissinger naturally was not so antagonistic, but he still regarded them as deluded and often hypocritical. Liberal critics and soft realists like George Kennan failed to understand the need for strength and toughness. They were not truly realistic.

Liberals and soft realists advocated getting out of Vietnam rapidly because they believed South Vietnam could never form a viable government, win the full support of the people, and effectively resist the Communists of the north and the south. Nixon and Kissinger would stay in Vietnam for four agonizing years at enormous risk and cost in order to win a peace agreement that, while providing little protection for South Vietnam, would give some credibility to Nixon's claim that he had won an honorable peace.

Liberals and soft realists favored minimal deterrence. They emphasized second-strike nuclear weapons on the grounds that Soviet parity made a first strike incredible while the threat of one merely served to destabilize the situation. Nixon and Kissinger insisted that a first-strike capability, tactical nuclear weapons, and some measure of counterforce strategy were necessary, however implausible their actual use might be, in order to offset superior Soviet conventional forces in Europe and the Middle East and to make the American deterrent more credible.

Liberals and soft realists backed away from involvement in third-world revolutions and wars, concerning themselves primarily with the major sources of international power, the industrial democracies of Western Europe and Japan. They believed that third-world nationalism would restrict Russia's ability to exploit revolutions and that the United States could deal with Russia directly if it tried to install military bases in the third world that threatened vital American interests. Nixon and Kissinger seemed to share this view. Not only did they promulgate the Nixon Doctrine, but also they often disparaged the importance of the third world in their private comments. However, they intervened constantly against leftist movements in Africa, Asia, the Middle East, and Latin America. They lavished money, equipment, and covert assistance to prevent the triumph of unfriendly radicals, even if the pro-U.S. regimes they were protecting were feeble, corrupt, and tyrannical.

Nixon encouraged his adversaries to believe he was not only strong, but also somewhat erratic. Like Khrushchev, he hoped this reputation would cow them into submission. Kissinger's hardness was more intellectual. While ignoring Nixon's habitual goading to be tougher, Kissinger used the threat that Nixon might get out of control to browbeat his negotiating partners. Meanwhile, he did his best to educate the American people to accept his version of hard realism. Opposition to Vietnam must not be allowed to drive the United States inward to nurse its wounds and renounce its world leadership, Kissinger warned. Americans must not return to their historical cycle of exuberant overextension and sulking isolationism. The United States needed continuity, confidence, and restraint based on a profound vision of American interest. The United States had to adapt to the limits of its strength without abdicating its responsibility to maintain the balance of power. That meant defending the geopolitical equilibrium even if it was challenged in the guise of human rights and a "progressive tide."

Of course, Kissinger said, "We cannot, and should not, be wedded to a blind defense of every status quo. Justice as well as stability must be a goal of American foreign policy, and indeed they are linked. Yet there are changes in the international balance that can threaten our nation's security and have to be resisted however they come about." Not only must such changes be resisted, Kissinger warned, but they must be resisted early, an inherently ambiguous task:

> For if one waits till the challenge is clear, the cost of resisting grows exponentially; in the nuclear age it may become prohibitive. A nation and its leaders must choose between moral certainty coupled with exorbitant risk, and the willingness to act on improvable assumptions to deal with challenges when they are manageable. . . . The qualities that distinguish a great statesman are prescience and courage, not analytical intelligence. He must have a conception of the future and the courage to move toward it while it is still shrouded to most of his compatriots.[1]

Many of the situations in which Nixon and Kissinger asserted themselves so strongly were indeed ambiguous and shrouded. Nixon and Kissinger gave strong support to reactionary third-world regimes on the grounds that in areas with deep tribal, religious, or racial divisions and with no tradition of democracy, force-fed mass participation was more likely to lead to totalitarianism than to democracy. Friendly authoritarianism was far preferable to hostile totalitarianism. Thus, they supported tyrannical regimes in Iran,

Chile, and elsewhere. They supported white supremacist regimes in Africa until events made that impossible. They adopted extraordinarily harsh measures in Southeast Asia. They made heavy expenditures on obsolescent or ineffective nuclear weapons not because these would be useful in themselves, but because they were needed to drive a hard bargain with the Soviet Union. After all, as Kissinger was so fond of saying, Moscow had never responded to unilateral restraint except with more aggression, and moderation was a virtue only in those thought to have an alternative.

There was some plausibility in the hard bargaining concept of foreign policy followed by Nixon and Kissinger. Yet it was ill adapted to the open and often idealistic society of American democracy. To drive hard bargains and manipulate the balance of power as they wished required harsh, dangerous, and credible threats, often in support of undemocratic and unsympathetic regimes. For those threats to be credible, Nixon and Kissinger needed the support of the American people and Congress. Yet the administration's bombing campaigns in Vietnam, vast appropriations for weapons to force an arms limitation agreement with the Soviets, and military mobilizations on behalf of third-world countries in trouble often seemed out of proportion to the crisis, ineffectual even if carried out, devoted to bad causes, and in danger of drawing the world closer to World War III.

Nixon and Kissinger could not win support by hinting to Americans that administration threats were primarily bargaining chips; other nations would then perceive these moves as mere bluffs. Nixon and Kissinger could not ask Americans simply to trust them. Vietnam had exhausted much of the fund of trust between government and people, and Watergate eliminated the remainder. Kissinger and Nixon relied instead on secrecy in their negotiations, deviousness in securing congressional and public backing for their projects, and Nixon's own reputation for tough, erratic behavior to try to extort better bargains than the objective condition of the balance of power might have allowed. In some areas they performed as virtuosos and succeeded brilliantly; in others they failed abjectly. Nixon and Kissinger blamed most of their failures on the sapping of executive authority by Watergate. Yet many of those failures were inherent in the diplomatic situation and were only made worse by the overreaching of Nixon and Kissinger.

The Opening to China

Nixon regarded China as the key link in his new structure of peace. Kissinger, initially skeptical, remarked to one of his aides about Nixon's desire to meet with Mao, "Fat chance." Kissinger soon came around, however, and lobbied hard to be Nixon's advance man in this revolution in American policy. Nixon and Kissinger hoped that closer relations with China would demoralize North Vietnam and the other Communist forces in Southeast Asia while giving the United States leverage against the Soviet Union as well.

Much of the initiative for improved relations came from China rather than the United States. In 1969 Mao Zedong began sending ambassadors to many nations with which he had broken relations during the Cultural Revolution. He also sent signals to the United States through Pakistan and Rumania that he was ready to resume the contacts America and China had previously conducted through their embassies in Warsaw, talks Mao had broken off in response to the Vietnam War and the Cambodian invasion. On April 6, 1971, China made an even more dramatic gesture to illustrate its intentions: it invited the American ping-pong team, which was playing in a world tournament in Japan, to visit China.

The United States signaled its understanding by steadily reducing its embargo on trade to China. In February 1970, Nixon and Kissinger already had indicated their willingness to take a new tack toward China by abandoning the "two-and-a-half-war doctrine" for a "one-and-a-half-war doctrine." Nixon explained that the United States no longer had to plan and arm for fighting simultaneous wars with the Soviets and the Chinese, along with half a war in the third world, because there was no longer a Sino-Soviet bloc that would coordinate a Soviet invasion of Europe with a Chinese invasion in Asia. Since the United States never had armed sufficiently to implement a two-and-a-half-war doctrine anyway, the announcement cost nothing strategically. It merely brought theory into line with reality. It also signaled to China that the United States no longer considered it an inextricable part of a monolithic Communist conspiracy against American interests.

In July 1971 Nixon and the Chinese arranged for Kissinger to be spirited into Beijing from Pakistan on a secret trip to improve Chinese-American relations and pave the way for a summit meeting between Nixon and Mao in China. Kissinger and Chinese premier Zhou Enlai found they had much in common in their strategic thought. Zhou, obviously reflecting Mao's thought throughout his conversations with Kissinger, was terribly worried by China's 4,000-mile border with the Soviet Union. China had never recognized its border with the Soviets, which actually divided Mongolians from Mongolians and Manchurians from Manchurians, rather than Russians from Chinese. The Soviets, steadily building their forces along the border, had stationed twenty-one army divisions there in 1969, increasing that number to thirty-three by 1971 and to forty-five by 1973. China feared that as Soviet power grew, the USSR would be tempted to use force to prevent the rise of another great enemy. Mao and Zhou wanted to enlist the United States in Beijing's confrontation with Moscow. Zhou urged the United States to organize an anti-Soviet coalition stretching from Japan through China, Pakistan, Iran, and Turkey to Western Europe. China, the most revolutionary of Communist states, was willing to cooperate with capitalists and reactionaries to deter a Soviet attack.

Nixon and Kissinger shared the desire of Mao and Zhou to deter the Soviets. According to Kissinger:

> Should the Soviet Union succeed in reducing China to impotence, the impact on the world balance of power would be scarcely less catastrophic than a Soviet conquest of Europe. Once it was clear that America was unable to prevent major aggression in Asia, Japan would begin to dissociate from us. Faced with a Soviet colossus free to concentrate entirely on the West, Europe would lose confidence and all its neutralist tendencies would accelerate. Southeast Asia, too, would bend to the dominant trend: the radical forces in the Middle East, South Asia, Africa, and even the Americas would gain the upper hand.

The United States would have to resist any Soviet attack on China and educate the American people to understand the necessity for protecting a Communist and potentially hostile nation.

Yet American strategy did not parallel China's in every particular. The United States did not have China's interest in "unremitting, undifferentiated confrontations with the USSR." Unlike China, the United States had the power to match Soviet arms and thwart its ventures. Nixon had the option to play for time, to see what modifications of Soviet policy and conduct could be brought about by deterrence and negotiations. He and Kissinger did not want to become a card China could play against the Soviets, and they did not want to play the China card itself so blatantly as to eliminate chances for leverage, negotiations, and détente with the Soviets. "Complex as it might be to execute such a tactic," Kissinger said, "it was always better for us to be closer to either Moscow or Beijing than either was to the other—except in the limiting case of a Soviet attack on China."[2]

Nixon's dramatic trip to China in 1972 sealed the rapprochement between the United States and China. Aware of the symbolism of his arrival in China, Nixon had burly aides block the aisles of Air Force One after it landed in Beijing. This permitted him to emerge on the tarmac by himself to shake hands ostentatiously with Zhou Enlai, with whom John Foster Dulles had refused to shake hands at the Geneva Conference of 1954. Television cameras recorded the astounding sight of the former Red-baiting Nixon receiving a grand reception in Beijing, conferring with a smiling Mao, who had just put his nation through a horrible revolutionary purge in the Cultural Revolution, waving atop the Great Wall, and talking strategy with Zhou. As a result of the trip, the United States and China established liaison offices in Washington and Beijing that were embassies in all but name. (Jimmy Carter would extend formal recognition to China in January 1979.)

Nixon's China coup was not without cost. Since the Chinese hinted during the summit that they would use only peaceful means to liberate Taiwan, Nixon and Kissinger said the United States would lessen its military presence in Taiwan as tensions in the area decreased and would withdraw entirely if the Chinese reached a peaceful settlement with the island. This meant that even though the United States continued nominally to recognize the Nationalist government on Taiwan as the legal government of China (thus precluding full diplomatic relations with mainland China and the establishment of an embassy in Beijing), Washington significantly reduced its commitment to Taiwan. The fallout was immediate. Western allies broke ranks to eject the Taiwan government from the United Nations and replace it with the Beijing government. The United States opposed the move but none too vigorously.

Nixon's trip also produced a shock in Japan. Secretary of State William Rogers had the unenviable task of informing the Japanese that Nixon would go to China only one hour before Nixon announced his trip publicly on television. Until then, the Japanese had conformed to Washington's wishes and abjured the political and economic profit they might have gained from seeking closer relations with China. Now the United States seemed to be leaving Japan alone as an enemy to China by reversing its policy. Fortunately, the shock did not do lasting damage. The Chinese were so anxious for Western unity against the Soviets that they did not try to play Japan and the United States against each other. China even urged, in a historic reversal of policy, that the United States and Japan maintain close relations.

Nixon's China opening did not have the effect the president expected on the situation in Southeast Asia. Zhou made clear to Nixon and Kissinger that he did not want total victory for North Vietnam or for the Khmer Rouge in Cambodia and that he wanted the United States to stay involved on the continent of Asia. Still, he was not willing to withdraw support from the Communists in Vietnam and Cambodia to help bring this about; he would only urge some compromise. With the American position in Indochina weakening, none of the combatants accepted such mild Chinese advice. Nixon's desperate hope that he could settle the Vietnam War in Beijing or Moscow would prove totally futile.

The Strategic Arms Limitation Talks

Although there was always the possibility that Moscow would react to Nixon's new relationship with China by freezing American relations rather than becoming more amenable, Nixon and Kissinger gambled that the Soviet Union would choose cooperation. They turned out to be correct. The Soviets received Kissinger on a secret trip to Moscow to arrange a summit meeting even though American bombing in North Vietnam had just damaged four Russian ships. The Soviets also went ahead with the Nixon-Brezhnev summit despite the renewed American bombing in May 1972. Like the Chinese leaders, however, the Soviets refused or were unable to force Hanoi out of the Vietnam War as the price of détente. Nixon had wanted Kissinger during his secret preliminary trip to Moscow to make any further discussions dependent on Russian agreement to get North Vietnam to settle, but Kissinger had evaded that dictum so his meeting and the subsequent summit turned primarily to discussions of strategic arms limitations.

Nixon and Kissinger emerged from the Strategic Arms Limitation Talks (SALT) summit of June 1972 with the first SALT agreement. They agreed to a treaty that would limit both the Americans and the Soviets to two antiballistic missile (ABM) sites and 200 interceptors each. Nixon had rammed the American ABM program through Congress primarily as a bargaining chip, and he and Kissinger believed that the program had formed a primary incentive for the Soviets to strike a deal.

While the SALT I negotiators could agree on a formal ABM treaty, they could concur on a temporary limit of only five years for offensive weapons, pending a more permanent treaty arrangement in SALT II. SALT I froze the number of ICBMs already deployed or under construction on each side. This provision left the Soviets with 1,607 land-based missiles and 740 submarine-launched missiles, while the United States had 1,054 land-based ICBMs and 656 missiles on submarines. (The Soviets could raise the number of their submarine missiles to 950 and the United States to 710 if they scrapped a land-based missile for each new submarine missile.) Although the agreement left the Americans with fewer and smaller missiles than the Soviets, Nixon and Kissinger believed they had achieved parity because America's superior bomber force of B-52s was not counted against the American total. Neither were the shorter-range nuclear weapons stationed by the United States, Great Britain, and France in Europe. In addition, if the USSR had

The architects of détente, Richard Nixon *(left)* of the United States and Leonid Brezhnev of the Soviet Union. *(Courtesy of the Richard M. Nixon Presidential Library)*

more launchers, the United States had more warheads, because 700 American missiles were equipped with multiple warheads that were independently targeted (multiple independently targeted reentry vehicles, or MIRVs). SALT I also prohibited interference with spy satellites, the means by which Nixon and Kissinger intended to verify Soviet compliance. Nixon and Kissinger argued that they had gotten a good deal for the United States, because they had in effect frozen missile deployment for five years, and none of the new U.S. weapons—MX, Trident, and cruise missiles—would be ready for deployment within that time.

In fact, however, Kissinger had bungled some aspects of the negotiations by ignoring the administration's arms control experts and initially agreeing to omit submarine-launched missiles from limitation. In order to get the Soviets to bring the submarines back into the negotiations, he had to agree to allow deployment of new submarine missiles at a time when only the Soviets were prepared to do so. In addition, Kissinger ignored warnings from those same experts that omitting MIRVs from the SALT limits might ultimately benefit the Soviets more than the Americans because the Soviets had larger missiles capable of carrying more independent warheads than the United States. It is not clear whether the Soviet Union would have accepted limits on MIRVs, but Nixon and Kissinger assumed they were to America's advantage and did not even try to get an agreement on them.

The Moscow summit and SALT I, combined with the opening to China and the Vietnam peace agreement, brought Nixon and Kissinger to the pinnacle of their popularity. That popularity, however, quickly began to slide downhill. Not only did the bitterness and turmoil of Vietnam survive the peace agreement, not only did Watergate progressively undermine Nixon's credibility, but some of the summit agreements went sour. Nixon and Kissinger at the summit had sought to increase American trade and give the Soviets additional incentives for détente by granting Russia $750 million in credits for the purchase of American wheat. The Americans had not known how desperate Russia's grain crisis was or that there would be a world shortage. After the Russians managed to buy up much of the American crop at bargain prices, many Americans thought the Soviets had snookered Nixon and Kissinger.

The Soviets cast a further pall on détente by cracking down on dissidents shortly after the summit. They also imposed a stiff exit tax on Jewish emigrants from the Soviet Union. The number of Jews leaving the Soviet Union had risen from 400 in 1968 to 35,000 in 1973 after the Soviets increased the Jewish emigration quota in response to an embarrassing attempted hijacking of a civilian aircraft by Jews desperate to leave. By 1973 the Soviets were anxious to reduce this flow of Jewish emigration to Israel in order to please their Arab allies. Many Americans began to claim that détente was serving as a license for Russian violation of human rights. Democratic senator Henry Jackson of Washington, a powerful force in the legislative branch, demanded that the United States refuse to honor Nixon's summit agreement to improve Soviet-American trade unless the Russians lessened domestic oppression. He successfully blocked congressional consent to most-favored-nation status for Soviet trade unless the Soviets changed their emigration policy. When the USSR promised to permit at least 35,000 Jews to emigrate each year, Jackson demanded an increase to 100,000. The Soviets indignantly refused, and emigration fell to 13,220 in 1974. At the same time, Jackson and his allies sought to limit loans to the Soviets from the Export-Import Bank unless Russia eased its persecution of dissidents.

The issue of human rights offered a link between liberal and conservative critics of Nixon and Kissinger. Liberals had long denounced Nixon and Kissinger for supporting violations of human rights in Vietnam and other areas of the third world. Conservatives would disagree with those criticisms, but both could unite in denouncing violations of human rights in Communist nations. Liberals and conservatives also found a way to unite against Nixon and Kissinger on SALT. Critics of SALT I pointed out that the Soviets had profited mightily from that agreement. The Soviets offset the American advantage in MIRVed missiles by deploying their own far more rapidly than Nixon and Kissinger had expected. Not only were the Soviets replacing their 308 monster SS-9 missiles with equally heavy SS-18 missiles that carried ten warheads each, they were replacing their smaller launchers with SS-19 missiles that carried six warheads each. The Americans claimed that these SS-19s should be counted against the SALT I sublimit of 308 heavy launchers Russia was allowed, but the Soviets disagreed. Obviously they were going to deploy far more than 308 MIRVed missiles, and since the throw-weight of these missiles was so much greater than that of America's Minuteman and Polaris missiles, the Soviets potentially could launch far more and larger warheads than the United States.

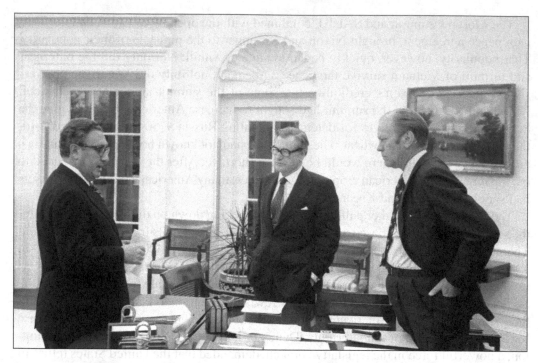

Secretary of State Henry Kissinger *(left)* with Vice President Nelson Rockefeller *(center)* and President Gerald Ford shortly after Nixon's resignation. *(Courtesy of the Gerald R. Ford Presidential Library)*

Kissinger proposed to deal with this problem in the SALT II negotiations by seeking an equal limit on the number of warheads for both sides. Although the Soviet warheads presumably would be larger, American missiles were more accurate, and the limit on warheads would restrict the Russian MIRV program. The Joint Chiefs of Staff, many conservatives, the influential Senator Jackson, and ultimately Secretary of Defense James Schlesinger argued instead that the United States should demand "equal aggregates," meaning equality in launchers and throw-weight rather than warheads. Nixon and his successor, Gerald Ford, chose this equal aggregates approach, which became the foundation of the SALT II agreement.

The SALT II agreement, announced by Ford and Brezhnev at the Vladivostok summit of 1974, allowed the United States and the Soviet Union 2,400 strategic missiles each, 1,320 of which could be MIRVed. To compensate for Russia's advantage in throw-weight, the United States would be allowed 525 strategic bombers to the Soviet Union's 160. Also, SALT II exempted NATO forward-based nuclear systems in Europe, along with the small independent nuclear forces of Great Britain and France, from the American total.

SALT II did not enjoy the wide approbation SALT I had received. Conservatives argued that the compensations for Russia's superior throw-weight offered in SALT II were inadequate. They also argued that the Soviets had proved they were dishonest during SALT I. Conservatives warned that on-site inspection rather than reliance on spy satellites was essential to keep the Russians from future cheating. Liberals claimed that the limit on missiles set by SALT II was too high, since both the United States and the Soviet Union already had sufficient weapons to destroy each other several times over.

Senator Jackson again bridged the gap between liberal and conservative critics by calling for renegotiation of the agreement to force the Soviets to reduce the number of their missiles and bring their throw-weight down to an equality with the United States. The consent of two-thirds of the Senate to a formal SALT II treaty became very uncertain. The Ford administration found it difficult even to put the agreement into final form because America's introduction of the cruise missile and Russian deployment of the Backfire medium-range bomber complicated the issue. Each side claimed that its weapon was a tactical one that did not endanger the other side's homeland and therefore should not be counted against the strategic weapon total. (Actually, under certain conditions, both weapons could reach the opponent's homeland, and neither side trusted the other to avoid those conditions.) Ford and Kissinger, unable to secure final agreement on SALT II in 1976, bequeathed the problem to the new president, Jimmy Carter. Meanwhile, the USSR and the United States agreed to abide by SALT II informally while final negotiations were pending.

Dilemmas in the Developed World: Europe and Japan

The SALT agreements raised serious strategic questions for Europe. NATO strategy since 1949 had relied on the American nuclear umbrella. Kissinger estimated that NATO forces could hold out against a Warsaw Pact invasion only about ninety days without resorting to nuclear weapons. Thus, NATO forces, and particularly American troops stationed in Europe, served as little more than a delaying force to give time for reconsideration before the war went nuclear and as a trip-wire to guarantee that the United States would not abandon Western Europe if war broke out.

Russian nuclear parity undercut this strategic situation. The United States could no longer threaten with relative impunity to launch its nuclear weapons as a response to a Russian conventional invasion. Some conservatives argued that the United States should rebuild its nuclear superiority over the Soviets to restore credibility to its European deterrent, but this seemed impossible technologically and politically. Others urged a buildup of conventional forces in Europe that might deter a Russian invasion without committing the United States to a suicidal nuclear exchange. Kissinger calculated, however, that a conventional defense of Europe would require $12 billion from the United States, along with huge increases in Western European defense budgets. Congress was not about to vote such defense expenditures in the wake of Vietnam. Senator Mike Mansfield was actually gaining support for his proposal to bring home half of the American contingent in Europe. Mansfield argued that Europe should make a greater effort to provide troops so NATO would not have to resort to early first use of nuclear weapons. Yet Europe had no great interest in such conventional increases, since conventional preparedness would give the United States an opening to reduce its nuclear commitment to European defense.

This left NATO relying more and more heavily on tactical nuclear weapons to deter or fight a Russian invasion. Yet this option too seemed problematical. Military theorists admitted that a tactical exchange would probably escalate into general strategic warfare, and even tactical nuclear weapons were so destructive that an attack on Soviet columns advancing into Europe would devastate much of the continent, especially if the USSR responded with its own tactical weapons. Europe naturally preferred a strategy that would lead the Soviet Union and the United States to lob their nuclear weapons at each other over the heads of the Europeans rather than use Europe as the battlefield between superpowers.

Some Europeans advocated another alternative—eliminate Moscow's incentive for an attack by making compromise agreements with the Soviet bloc. Moving very far in this direction, however, might require Europe to become more neutral and to distance itself somewhat from the United States. Nixon and Kissinger were willing to accept a degree of European independence and compromise with the Soviets, but they did not want to see it go so far as European neutralization. They did not denounce French president Charles de Gaulle for his attempt to revive French independence and glory, even though he pulled French forces out of NATO. They tolerated attempts by Germany's first postwar liberal chancellor, Social Democrat Willy Brandt, to soften the antagonism between East and West Germany. But they stopped short of encouraging such movements, and they denounced the rise of so-called Euro-Communist parties, which combined socialist domestic ideology with independence from and sometimes active antagonism to Moscow. Kissinger claimed that the conversion of Euro-Communists to an anti-Moscow stance was too recent to be anything but opportunistic. He threatened to exclude any such regimes from NATO or to withhold secrets from NATO if a Euro-Communist government took its seat with the alliance.

All the conflicting alternatives to cope with Soviet nuclear parity in Europe had serious drawbacks, and none could command full agreement. Attempts to clarify policy only highlighted and exacerbated the differences. The Vietnam War and then Watergate gave the Europeans little incentive to draw closer to the United States or sacrifice anything in order to coordinate policy. As a result, Nixon and Kissinger had to fudge their European strategy. Despite their admission of Russian nuclear parity in the SALT agreements and the consequent irrationality of any first use of nuclear weapons, they felt they could not publicly match Moscow's promise of "no first strike." Despairing of building sufficient conventional forces in Europe, they clung to some vulnerable, land-based strategic weapons, like the prospective MX missiles, which were valuable almost exclusively as first-strike weapons. They continued counterforce planning, relied on tactical nuclear weapons in Europe, and insisted they would abandon such capabilities only in exchange for like concessions on the part of the Soviets.

Meanwhile, West Germany's chancellor Willy Brandt pursued his own answer to the European conundrum—Ostpolitik, or reconciliation with East Germany and eastern Europe. Until Brandt, West Germany had held to the Hallstein Doctrine, under which West Germany would reject formal diplomatic relations with any nation that recognized East Germany. In this way, West Germany could pretend that it represented all of Germany and that Germany would someday be reunited. Unfortunately, the Hallstein Doctrine was increasing West Germany's isolation, for a growing number of third-world nations that were winning their independence were recognizing East Germany. To correct this situation, Brandt extended de facto recognition to East Germany in exchange for East German concessions on trade and visiting privileges between the two halves of Germany. Thus, he tacitly abandoned hopes of reuniting Germany under the West German government.

The West German parliament, however, was not about to accept Ostpolitik and Brandt's deals unless it had firm international recognition of West German rights in divided Berlin. The United States, Great Britain, France, and the Soviet Union technically still occupied Berlin, so final agreement rested with them rather than with East and West Germany. Nixon and Kissinger, with their leverage over a Berlin settlement, could make sure that Brandt did not move too far toward the Soviets. They also ensured that the Soviets gave full recognition to West German control of West Berlin before Moscow could get the agreement on East Germany it so much desired. Nixon and Brezhnev concluded the Berlin agreement at the 1971 summit, finally putting that most dangerous European issue to rest.

The movement toward easing tensions between the eastern and western halves of Europe culminated in 1975 with the Helsinki Final Agreement. This was in effect the formal settlement of World War II, for the United States, the Soviet Union, and the European powers finally accepted one another's boundaries as permanent and "inviolable." Each bloc thus conceded the other's sphere of influence. The Soviets, in exchange for this tacit recognition of their east European sphere, promised to respect a long list of human rights within their bloc. They never did. Not only did they crack down on dissidents, but also they arrested those in the USSR and eastern Europe who presumed to set themselves up as committees to observe compliance with the Helsinki accords. This persecution added to both liberal and conservative disillusionment with détente in the United States.

Although Nixon and Kissinger kept a close eye on Germany's Ostpolitik, Brandt did not take it so far that it caused serious apprehension in the United States. France under de Gaulle's successor, Georges Pompidou, caused more consternation. Pompidou and his foreign minister, Michel Jobert, brusquely tried to exclude the United States from inter-European councils and prevented the full reconsideration of NATO affairs that Soviet parity and French military withdrawal from the alliance seemed to demand. The British, usually supportive of American activism in Europe, did not do much to help Kissinger because they did not want to stir opposition to their renewed request to join the European Common Market. Nixon and Kissinger thus found themselves thwarted in their attempt to refocus attention on NATO affairs by declaring 1973 to be "The Year of Europe."

A dinner given by Kissinger for Jobert in Los Angeles illustrated the decline in goodwill between France and the United States. When Jobert started to give his toast in French, comedian Danny Kaye interrupted to ask if he would give it in English so his audience could better understand him. Jobert frostily replied that he was speaking French for the benefit of his own French delegation. Danny Kaye offered to translate Jobert's toast back into French if Jobert would give it in English. The dumbfounded Jobert complied. It took him and his compatriots several moments to realize that Kaye's translation was French only in inflection and mannerism: Kaye was talking gibberish with a French accent, a routine with which he had convulsed audiences around the world for years. Unfortunately, Jobert and his delegation were not amused.

A far more serious cause of disarray within the Western alliance than Germany's Ostpolitik or French cussedness was what came to be known as the "second Nixon shock" (the first being his visit to China without informing the Japanese). Lyndon Johnson and Richard Nixon had tried to pay for the Vietnam War without increasing taxes. The resulting budget deficit and trade imbalance drove inflation up and undermined the strength of the U.S. dollar abroad. Nixon and his treasury secretary, John Connally, decided on drastic measures. Without consulting their allies abroad, they imposed a ninety-day wage and price freeze, slapped a 10 percent surcharge on imports, cut 10 percent from foreign economic assistance, and suspended the convertibility of dollars to gold. The Europeans and the Japanese were indignant. The 10 percent surcharge on imports hurt their export market in the United States. Abandonment of the gold standard shattered the Bretton Woods system and left Europe and Japan holding vast amounts of dollars that were plunging in value. With considerable bitterness, the United States, Europe, and Japan patched together the Smithsonian Agreement, which fixed new exchange rates. The American dollar would remain off the gold standard and would be devalued in terms of other currencies to help the United States sell more abroad.

Since all nations paid for Middle Eastern oil in dollars, however, the Organization of Petroleum Exporting Countries (OPEC) would not sit still for the devaluation of American currency. To compensate for the loss of revenue due to devaluation, OPEC raised its oil prices. The oil price increases and the even more catastrophic oil embargo that OPEC imposed during the Arab-Israeli War of 1973 split the United States and its allies. Europe and Japan, unlike the United States, were almost totally dependent on OPEC oil. Desperate to avoid offending the Arabs, they publicly dissociated themselves from Washington's pro-Israeli policies. Many NATO allies even permitted Soviet overflights to resupply the Arab armies.

Despite all these symptoms of disintegration in America's relations with Europe and Japan, by 1974 the pendulum began its swing back toward sympathy and cooperation. The Middle East war and oil embargo against the United States ended. The United States proved quite staunch in sharing oil with the Netherlands, which had suffered the embargo along with the United States. Pompidou's death from bone cancer led to changes in French leadership that helped Franco-American relations. Harold Wilson's Labour ministry replaced the conservative government of Edward Heath in England, improving Anglo-American rapport. Nonetheless, the unresolved issues of nuclear strategy, trade, currency, and energy would continue to threaten cooperation and understanding among the Western allies.

The Third World

Theoretically, the Nixon Doctrine should have led to a restrained policy in the third world, since American troops no longer would intervene in third-world crises. When asked about the strategic importance of Latin America, Kissinger had replied disdainfully that South

America "was a dagger pointed straight at the heart of—Antarctica." Yet Nixon, and later Ford, seemed to interpret every third-world crisis during their administrations as involving significant interests or Soviet agitation that had to be countered by the United States. They were unwilling to trust third-world nationalism to limit and ultimately throw off excessive Soviet interference.

Chile

One of the most controversial actions of the Nixon administration took place in Chile. During the Chilean elections of 1964, the CIA, with Lyndon Johnson's approval, had funneled $3 million to Christian Democratic candidate Eduardo Frei to help him defeat the Marxist candidate, Salvador Allende Gossens. In the election of 1968, however, Frei could not succeed himself. In Frei's absence, Allende managed to poll more votes than either of his two opponents, 36 percent of the popular vote, despite $135,000 distributed by the CIA in a spoiling operation against him. (The giant International Telephone and Telegraph Corporation, fearful that Allende might expropriate its operation in Chile, offered $1 million for the CIA to distribute in the election. The administration turned it down, but advised ITT on how best to spend its money to influence the Chilean election.) Furious at Allende's plurality, Nixon demanded that something be done to prevent the Chilean congress from formally voting Allende into office.

Since Allende had won less than 50 percent of the popular vote, under the Chilean constitution the congress had the power to appoint the next president. By tradition, the Chilean congress had always chosen the candidate with the highest vote. Nixon raged to CIA director Richard Helms that he should prevent this outcome even if the cost was $10 million. Nixon and Kissinger were especially sensitive to the possibility of a Marxist regime in Chile because they had just gone through a confrontation with the Soviets over the building of an alleged Russian submarine base at Cienfuegos, Cuba, and feared similar Soviet influence in Chile.

When bribes to the Chilean congress seemed unlikely to prevent Allende's accession, the CIA tried to inspire a military coup. But the Chilean army chief of staff, General René Schneider, insisting that the military support the constitutional process, blocked the coup. Some of the Chilean military decided to kidnap Schneider and take him to Argentina. The CIA backed away from the plot at that point, but a group of Chilean soldiers killed Schneider in a bungled kidnapping attempt. The Chilean military then closed ranks behind the constitution and ensured Allende's confirmation as president.

Allende and the United States inevitably headed toward conflict. Allende moved to nationalize North American copper companies while ignoring the compensation formula worked out by his predecessor. Allende permitted leftist takeovers of newspapers and radio stations. He increased taxes on the middle classes. He encouraged peasant seizures of land. Ultimately, he distributed arms among the populace. The Nixon administration allowed U.S. loans already made to Chile to continue, but efficiently blocked all other economic aid to Chile from the United States or its allies. Meanwhile, the CIA spent over $1 million building domestic opposition to Allende.

In Chile the combination of these American measures and Allende's mismanagement brought chaos. Inflation rose to 350 percent. Strikes spread, especially in the middle-class sector. Shopkeepers struck in August 1972, truck owners in October. Allende had to establish a rationing system. Yet in the legislative election of 1973, Allende increased his plurality from 36 to 43 percent, and he used this win as a mandate to rule by presidential decree. He announced a drastic revision of the educational system, thus throwing the Catholic Church into opposition. Strikes spread to the copper mines and other enterprises. Militants occupied struck businesses in retaliation.

On September 11, 1973, the Chilean military overthrew Allende, who either committed suicide or was killed in his office. The new regime, led by General Augusto Pinochet, took over the universities, disbanded political parties, and suppressed the media. Kissinger and Nixon insisted that Allende had fallen because of his own policies. They claimed that their opposition efforts had been restrained and relatively unimportant and that the United States should be tolerant of the new Chilean government's violations of human rights under the chaotic circumstances that Allende had created. Washington's role in the coup was far greater and more vital, however, than the administration admitted, and critics demanded more than quiet diplomacy to rectify atrocities against the Chilean military government's domestic opponents. With what Kissinger thought was exceptional severity, the U.S. Congress cut off aid to Chile unless the president of the United States certified fundamental progress on human rights.

Pakistan, India, and Bangladesh

The policies of Nixon and Kissinger toward the third world caused another uproar during the 1971 revolution in East Pakistan. When the British had granted India its independence after World War II, they had divided Pakistan from India to separate Muslims from Hindus. Unfortunately, Muslims were concentrated in two widely separated sectors, so the British had created the Pakistani nation out of two provinces separated by the entire width of India that shared nothing but dislike of Hindu India. The differences between East and West Pakistan exploded after a cyclone killed 200,000 people in East Pakistan and the relief efforts of the government in West Pakistan proved inept. East Pakistan demanded autonomy. The West Pakistani leaders decided to suppress the autonomy of 75 million East Pakistanis with an army of 40,000. The atrocities committed by the army raised an outcry throughout the world. Inundated with refugees from East Pakistan, India saw a chance to divide its hated adversary. It intervened and helped establish East Pakistan as the independent state of Bangladesh. West Pakistan then futilely attacked India.

Many Americans recoiled at the Pakistani army's atrocities and sent aid and sympathy to Bangladesh. Nixon and Kissinger, however, decided to "tilt toward Pakistan." Pakistan was their conduit for the opening to China, while India was about to sign a treaty of friendship with the Soviet Union. Besides, Nixon regarded India as the pet of American liberals. Nixon and Kissinger saw no chance that West Pakistan could hold on to Bangladesh, but they wanted to enable Pakistan to retreat with dignity and sufficient remaining morale to deter India from the temptation to grab the disputed West Pakistan province of Kashmir. They sent an aircraft carrier to the Bay of Bengal and threatened to cancel the summit with the Russians unless the Soviet Union got India to accept peace. When India stepped back from the confrontation over Kashmir, Nixon and Kissinger claimed success for their policy, but many American critics denounced their cynicism toward the atrocities in Bangladesh.

Angola

As Watergate sapped Nixon's prestige, Kissinger found the administration less and less able to overcome the American public's revulsion from Vietnam and to gain support for an activist policy in the third world. Thus, when the North Vietnamese launched the attack that finally brought down the South Vietnamese regime, all the pleadings and warnings of Kissinger and President Gerald Ford could not get Congress to authorize a new intervention. The same congressional reluctance short-circuited Kissinger and Ford in their requests for a major American commitment in the newly independent African state of Angola.

Angola and Mozambique were part of the Portuguese empire until mid-1974, when a coup in Portugal engineered by progressive military officers overthrew the Portuguese dictatorship and offered independence to the nation's African provinces. Numerous factions in Angola had been fighting the Portuguese authorities for years, and the CIA actually had given covert aid to a couple of those factions even while officially supporting and subsidizing Portugal. (Portugal permitted important NATO airbases in the Azores.)

Nixon and Kissinger had assigned Africa a low priority in their grandiose foreign policy design, so they had not concerned themselves much with the Angolan issue. They had simply decided to relax the punitive measures against the white minority regimes in the Portuguese empire, South Africa and Rhodesia, on the assumption that the way to constructive racial progress was through friendly persuasion of the whites, not violent revolution by blacks that might open the way for Communists. In pursuit of this so-called tar baby option, enunciated in National Security Memorandum 39, Nixon eased the arms embargo on South Africa, while Congress broke a United Nations boycott of Rhodesia by permitting the United States to purchase chromium from that nation.

As the Angolan independence movement and ultimately the Portuguese revolution confounded the tar baby option, Kissinger and Ford decided to oppose the MPLA revolutionary faction that was receiving support from Cuba and the Soviet Union. They did so by increasing America's ongoing covert aid to two other factions of Angolan guerrillas. One faction was the Front for National Liberation (FMLN) of Holden Roberto. It operated in the north of Angola out of bases in Zaire and received additional advice and support from China, which now regarded the Soviet Union as a rival for influence in the third world. The other faction was the UNITA party of Jonas Savimbi, operating in southern Angola with support from China and South Africa. The State Department officer in charge of African affairs, Nathaniel Davis, resigned when Kissinger ignored his warning that the civil war was an African affair out of the control of the major powers and that the United States should seek a negotiated political settlement. Davis argued that U.S. cooperation with South

Africa in support of the victory of one side would only legitimate Soviet involvement in the eyes of most Africans.

The Soviets more than matched the American and South African effort. Cuba had had advisers (including Che Guevara) in Africa for several years, and Castro successfully urged the Soviets to increase their aid to the People's Movement for the Liberation of Angola (MPLA). The Soviets transported thousands of Cuban soldiers and advisers to Angola. With Soviet aid and Cuban troops, the MPLA demolished Roberto and the FMLN in northern Angola and Savimbi's UNITA along with 3,000 South African troops in the south. Congress refused to counter this escalation, and it cut off the existing covert aid when Davis's resignation and leaks made American intervention a hot public issue. As the MPLA and Moscow's Cuban surrogates emerged victorious in the Angolan civil war in 1976, Kissinger and President Ford disgustedly commented that Congress had been so traumatized by Vietnam and Watergate that it had "lost its guts" and "pulled the plug" on Angola. Ironically, Kissinger also had to mollify China, which condemned America's weakness and indecision in Angola and the rest of the third world.

The Mayaguez and East Timor Incidents

Kissinger and Ford did find two opportunities to circumvent Congress and show that Watergate and Vietnam had not paralyzed the United States totally in the third world. In 1975 Cambodian gunboats captured the American freighter *Mayaguez*. Without seeking Congressional approval, Ford and Kissinger bombed a Cambodian port and sent an amphibious landing force to the island of Koh Tang to rescue the crew. Ironically, the Cambodians were releasing the crew at the same time. Forty-one members of the American amphibious unit were killed in an accident while storming ashore in their useless operation.

Also in 1975 Kissinger had another chance to assert American interests in the third world and exercise the Nixon Doctrine strategy of using surrogates in regional conflicts. A leftist liberation movement in East Timor, a part of the collapsing Portuguese empire, declared its independence in 1975, and Suharto, the Indonesian dictator who had slaughtered the Communists in his country with the help of lists of party members provided by U.S. and British intelligence, asked for American understanding if he moved to incorporate the largely Catholic East Timor into Indonesia's multi-island and predominantly Muslim nation. President Ford said that the United States would not press him on the issue. Kissinger urged Suharto to move quickly so the American government could manage the domestic reaction in the United States and avoid "people talking in an unauthorized way." Suharto's army quickly conquered East Timor and crushed its independence movement.

Cyprus

While all these episodes seemed to indicate the advisability of greater restraint in U.S. foreign policy, there was at least one instance that indicated the dangers of abstention. Greece and Turkey had long been blood enemies despite their common membership in

NATO. A major focus of their rivalry was the island of Cyprus, which lay close to the coast of Turkey but whose population was 80 percent Greek. Greek archbishop Makarios III had maintained a precarious peace and neutrality on Cyprus since Britain had granted the island independence in 1960. In 1974, however, the reactionary colonels who controlled Greece with considerable economic and military aid from the United States supported a coup in Cyprus designed to unite the island with Greece. The United States did little to stop the Greek colonels' adventure, despite receiving warnings of it.

Turkey, with far more military strength than Greece, invaded and conquered the island. Meanwhile, a coup in Greece overthrew the reactionary colonels. Congress, which had previously condemned the Greek coup on Cyprus, then established an arms embargo on Turkey. Both of America's NATO allies condemned the United States. The Greeks blamed the United States for supporting the colonels and failing to prevent the Turkish invasion of Cyprus. The Turks denounced Washington for the arms embargo. To secure their hold, the Turks uprooted the Greek population and separated the Turkish and Greek populations on the island. In November 1983, the Turks on Cyprus declared the part of the island they occupied to be an independent state and received recognition from Turkey, although no other nations accepted that decision. The island is still divided and a source of contention between Greece and Turkey, although there is increasing movement toward a settlement.

Controversial Issues

After leaving office, Richard Nixon and Henry Kissinger both wrote memoirs to defend their policies, which they continued to claim had provided a realistic balance of sticks and carrots that successfully ended the war in Vietnam, contained Soviet aggression, and stifled America's adversaries in the third world.[3] Many early biographers of Nixon and Kissinger joined them in defense of their policies.[4] Raymond Garthoff, a long-time State Department and CIA official who served during Nixon's administration, provided the best and most detailed early critique of the Nixon-Kissinger policies, writing from a restrained realist perspective. While praising the opening to China, the development of détente, and the negotiation of the SALT agreements with the Soviets, Garthoff argued and offered evidence to demonstrate that Nixon and Kissinger made critical mistakes even in negotiating those successes by deceiving their negotiating partners, ignoring the experts in their own bureaucracy (Garthoff among them), and giving up more than they had to. Moreover, Garthoff argued, Nixon and Kissinger were too harsh in their pursuit of a balance of power, particularly in Vietnam, Chile, and Angola.[5]

While Garthoff and others who criticized Nixon and Kissinger from the left had the greatest influence on later academic historical works, criticism of the administration's policies from the right ultimately had a more telling effect on the American political scene. Many Republicans, led by Ronald Reagan, condemned Kissinger, Nixon, and Ford for being weak toward the Russians and the Communist world. Critics on the right argued that SALT I and II gave away too much to the Soviets and permitted them to acquire nuclear superiority. These critics believed that Nixon and Kissinger should have stayed the course in Vietnam and done more to counter Communist activities in the rest of the third world. They even argued that the opening to China was a mistake because it was a sellout of America's Taiwanese friends, a criticism Reagan retracted once he became president.[6] Reagan actually used Nixon and Kissinger as influential informal advisers during his administration, but this role never entirely rehabilitated their reputations in the eyes of most right-wing conservatives.

As noted above, the latest academic histories of Nixon and Kissinger have generally followed the interpretations of Garthoff but added material from recently available tape recordings of Nixon conversations in the White House, phone transcripts of many of Kissinger's calls, and archives in the former Communist world. The most important of those books include Jeremy Suri, *Henry Kissinger and the American Century* (2007); Robert Dallek, *Nixon and Kissinger: Partners in Power* (2007); Elizabeth Drew, *Richard M. Nixon: The 37th President, 1969–1974* (2007); Jussi Hanhimäki, *The Flawed Architect: Henry Kissinger and American Foreign Policy* (2004); and Margaret MacMillan, *Nixon and Mao: The Week That Changed the World* (2007). See also Walter Isaacson, *Kissinger: A Biography* (1992); Robert D. Schulzinger, *Henry Kissinger: Doctor of Diplomacy* (1989); Roger Morris, *Uncertain Greatness: Henry Kissinger and American Foreign Policy* (1977); Mario Del Pero, *The Eccentric Realist: Henry Kissinger and the Shaping of American Foreign Policy* (2010); the three-volume biography of Richard Nixon by Stephen E. Ambrose, *Nixon* (1987–1991); Joan Hoff, *Nixon Reconsidered* (1994); Melvin Small, *The Presidency of Richard Nixon* (1999); William Bundy, *A Tangled Web: The Making of Foreign Policy in the Nixon Presidency* (1998); and more general accounts of the Nixon-Kissinger years, William Hymann, *Rivals: Superpower Relations from Nixon to Reagan* (1987); Franz Schurmann, *The Foreign Politics of Richard Nixon: The Grand Design* (1987); John Robert Greene, *The Limits of Power: The Nixon and Ford Adminis- trations* (1992); Tad Szulc, *The Illusion of Peace* (1978); and Jonathan Schell, *The Time of Illusion* (1976). Especially hostile to Kissinger are Seymour Hersh, *The Price of Power* (1983); and Christopher Hitchens, *The Trial of Henry Kissinger* (2001).

Further Reading

For the Soviet as well as the American side of détente, see Anatoly Dobrynin, *In Con- fidence: Moscow's Ambassador to America's Six Cold War Presidents* (1995); Keith L. Nelson, *The Making of Détente: Soviet-American Relations in the Shadow of Vietnam* (1995); Iliya Gaiduk, *The Soviet Union and the Vietnam War* (1996); Matthew J. Ouimet, *The Rise and Fall of the Brezhnev Doctrine in Soviet Foreign Policy* (2003); Michael J. Sodaro, *Moscow, Germany, and the West from Khrushchev to Gorbachev* (1990); William Curti Wohlforth, *The Elusive Balance: Power and Perceptions During the Cold War* (1993); and the 1994 second edition of Garthoff, *Détente and Confrontation*, mentioned above. On Nixon, Kissinger, and China, in addition to MacMillan's *Nixon and Mao*, mentioned above, see James Mann, *About Face: A History of America's Curious Relationship with China, from Nixon to Clinton* (1999); Yafeng Xia, *Negotiating with the Enemy: U.S.-China Talks During the Cold War, 1949–1972* (2006); Jung Chang and Jon Halliday, *Mao: The*

Unknown Story (2005); Li Zhisui, *The Private Life of Chairman Mao* (1994); and Roderick MacFarquhar and Michael Schoenhals, *Mao's Last Revolution* (2006).

For works specifically on SALT, see in addition to Garthoff's *Détente and Confrontation* the memoirs of one of the SALT negotiators, Gerard Smith, *Doubletalk: The Story of the First Strategic Arms Limitations Talks* (1985); McGeorge Bundy, *Danger and Survival: Choices About the Bomb in the First Fifty Years* (1988); Terry Terriff, *The Nixon Administration and the Making of U.S. Nuclear Strategy* (1995); Michael Mandelbaum, *The Nuclear Question* (1979); and John Newhouse, *Cold Dawn: The Story of SALT* (1973). On the United States and Europe in this era, see William I. Hitchcock, *The Struggle for Europe: The Turbulent History of a Divided Continent, 1945–2002* (2002); Ronald E. Powaski, *The Entangling Alliance: The United States and European Security, 1950–1993* (1994); Lawrence A. Kaplan, *NATO and the United States: The Enduring Alliance* (updated ed., 1994); Tony Judt, *Postwar: A History of Europe Since 1945* (2005); A.W. DePorte, *Europe Between the Superpowers: The Enduring Balance* (1979); Michael M. Harrison, *The Reluctant Ally: France and Atlantic Security* (1981); Catherine McArdle Kelleher, *Germany and the Politics of Nuclear Weapons* (1975); Alfred Grosser, *The Western Alliance* (1980); Richard J. Barnet, *The Alliance* (1983); John J. Maresca, *To Helsinki: The Conference on Security and Cooperation in Europe, 1973–1975* (1985); and James Edward Miller, *The United States and the Making of Modern Greece: History and Power, 1950–1974* (2009).

On the economic problems between the United States, Europe, Japan, and the third world, see Robert Soloman, *The International Monetary System, 1945–1976* (1977); Paul Volcker and Toyoo Gyohten, *Changing Fortunes: The World's Money and the Threat to American Leadership* (1992); Robert K. Olson, *U.S. Foreign Policy and the New International Economic Order* (1981); Richard J. Barnet and Ronald Muller, *The Global Reach: The Power of the Multinational Corporations* (1974); Raymond Vernon, *Storm over the Multinationals* (1977); Alfred E. Eckes, *The United States and the Global Struggle for Minerals* (1977); I.M. Destler, Haruhiro Fukui, and Hideo Sato, *The Textile Wrangle: The Conflict in Japanese-American Relations, 1969–1971* (1979); and Raymond F. Hopkins and Donald J. Puchala, *Global Food Interdependence* (1980).

On the policies of Nixon and Kissinger toward the third world in general, see Odd Arne Westad, *The Global Cold War: Third World Intervention and the Making of Our Times* (2007). On Cambodia, see Kenton J. Clymer, *The United States and Cambodia* (2005); and William Shawcross, *Sideshow: Kissinger, Nixon, and the Destruction of Cambodia* (1979). On Chile and the rest of Latin America, see Peter Kornbluh, ed., *The Pinochet File: A Declassified Dossier on Atrocity and Accountability* (2004); Robert J. Alexander, *The Tragedy of Chile* (1978); Paul E. Sigmund, *The Overthrow of Allende and the Politics of Chile, 1965–1976* (1977); James Petras and Morris Morely, *The United States and Chile: Imperialism and the Overthrow of the Allende Government* (1975); Nathaniel Davis, *The Last Two Years of Salvador Allende* (1985); Kristian Gustafson, *Hostile Intent: U.S. Covert Operations in Chile, 1964–1974* (2007), a full-throated defense of Nixon and Kissinger; Samuel L. Bailey, *The United States and the Development of South America, 1945–1976* (1976); Stephen G. Rabe, *The Road to OPEC: United States Relations with Venezuela* (1982).

On the Nixon-Kissinger-Ford policy toward Africa, in addition to Westad's *The Global Cold War*, mentioned above, see Piero Gleijeses, *Conflicting Missions: Havana, Washington, and Africa, 1959–1976* (2002); Anthony Lake, *The "Tar Baby" Option: American Policy Toward Southern Rhodesia* (1976); Harry M. Joiner, *American Foreign Policy: The Kissinger Era* (1977); Mohamed A. el-Khawas and Barry Cohen, eds., *The Kissinger Study of Southern Africa: National Security Study Memorandum 39 (secret)* (1976); John Marcum, *The Angolan Revolution* (2 vols., 1969–1978); John Stockwell, *In Search of Enemies: A CIA Story* (1978); Arthur Jay Klinghoffer, *The Angolan War: A Study of Soviet Policy in the Third World* (1980); and Charles K. Ebinger, *Foreign Intervention in Civil War: The Politics and Diplomacy of the Angolan Conflict* (1984).

Notes

1. Henry Kissinger, *Years of Upheaval* (1982), pp. 168–169.
2. Kissinger, *Years of Upheaval*, pp. 51–55.
3. Richard Nixon, *RN: The Memoirs of Richard Nixon* (1978); Henry Kissinger, *The White House Years* (1979), *Years of Upheaval* (1982), and *Years of Renewal* (1999).
4. Bernard Kalb and Marvin Kalb, *Kissinger* (1974); Coral Bell, *The Diplomacy of Détente* (1977); Stephen Graubard, *Portrait of a Mind* (1973); C.L. Sulzberger, *The World and Richard Nixon* (1987).
5. Raymond Garthoff, *Détente and Confrontation: American-Soviet Relations from Nixon to Reagan* (1985; 2nd ed. 1994).
6. Norman Podhoretz, *Why We Were in Vietnam* (1982); Richard Pipes, *U.S.-Soviet Relations in the Era of Détente: A Tragedy of Errors* (1981); Aleksandr Solzhenitsyn, *Détente: Prospects for Democracy and Dictatorship* (1976); Robert Conquest, *Present Danger: Towards a Foreign Policy* (1979). Pipes became an adviser to President Ronald Reagan in 1981.

CHAPTER 14

TIME BOMBS IN THE MIDDLE EAST

The Six-Day War, June 1967

As if Nixon and Kissinger were not sufficiently preoccupied with the problems of Vietnam, China, the Soviet Union, and Latin America, they were also confronted with ticking time bombs in the Middle East. The Middle East had remained relatively quiet for a few years after Eisenhower left office in 1960. The pan-Arab nationalism that had seemed so threatening to Western interests under Egyptian president Gamal Abdel Nasser degenerated into a squabbling rivalry between Arab nations. The Soviets, caught between the quarreling Arab nationalist states, were unable to bring Arab radicalism firmly under their wing. Oil continued to flow to the West on beneficial terms. The Arab-Israeli conflict remained a simmering stalemate rather than an all-out war even after Israel diverted much of the water of the Jordan River to a great irrigation project in 1964.

In the last year and a half of Lyndon Johnson's presidency, however, the relative calm exploded. In May 1967, the Soviets warned Nasser that the Israelis were massing armies to attack Syria. Although the report was untrue and Nasser knew it, he used the opportunity to mobilize his armies in the Sinai Desert near the Israeli border. He then requested the United Nations (UN) secretary-general to remove the UN peacekeeping forces that had patrolled the Egyptian side of the Egyptian-Israeli truce line since the Suez war of 1956.

There is evidence that Nasser meant this request primarily as a bluff to apply pressure on Israel, but the secretary-general acquiesced and removed the troops with an alacrity that surprised the Egyptian president. Then, when Nasser thought he detected a note of fear and softness in the Israeli response, he proceeded to escalate the crisis. He blockaded the Straits of Tiran, through which Israel received much of its shipping. Claiming that he would welcome war, Nasser declared that the issue was not just the blockade of Tiran or border adjustments, but also the full restoration of an Arab Palestine. Syria and Jordan joined Nasser in mobilizing. Iraq sent thousands of troops to Jordan, and the Arab oil countries threatened to cut off petroleum to any nations that supported Israel. The Soviets helped by warning the United States not to intervene.

Nasser originally believed that Israel would not fight. But the Israelis had little choice; the smallness of their territory meant they had to mobilize to stop the Egyptians at the border or not at all. Yet mobilization involved so much of their able-bodied labor force that their economy would collapse if they remained mobilized for long. As Nasser came to realize that the Israelis would fight, he hesitated to attack. If he struck the first blow, it would guarantee American aid to the Israeli victim. If Israel struck the first blow, American opinion might rebound against the putative aggressor.

Nasser's hesitation gave the Israelis their chance. When Lyndon Johnson's attempt to mobilize an international effort to end the blockade of the Straits of Tiran faltered, Israel launched a preemptive air strike that caught the Egyptian air force unprepared and virtually destroyed it in one blow. With total air superiority, the Israelis proceeded to capture the Sinai Desert from Egypt, the West Bank of the Jordan River from the Kingdom of Jordan, and the strategic Golan Heights from Syria. These conquered territories were three times the size of Israel itself.

Israel concluded its victorious military operations in only six days, but the basic issues and enmity between the Arabs and Israelis remained. In November 1967, the United Nations got Israel and the Arab states to agree to UN Resolution 242, which called for Israeli withdrawal from conquered territories and the recognition and security of all states in the Middle East. Unfortunately, both sides accepted Resolution 242 solely because they interpreted it to their own benefit. The Israelis argued that Resolution 242's mention of security implied that they could keep enough of the territory they had conquered to give them defensible borders. Thus, they insisted they would hold on to Jerusalem, the Golan Heights, the Gaza Strip, and large portions of the West Bank. (Many Israelis, regarding the West Bank as the biblical provinces of Judea and Samaria, considered it rightfully theirs by biblical prescription.) The Arabs, on the other hand, argued that Resolution 242 required Israel to abandon all conquered territory before negotiations on the security and recognition of Israel could even begin. They also made it clear that they would recognize Israel only if it transformed itself into a secular state and permitted the Palestinians to return.

Lyndon Johnson sided with Israel in this quarrel. He and most other Americans regarded the Arabs as the aggressors who had been deservedly defeated in the Six-Day War. Johnson wanted a settlement in the Middle East, but he agreed that Israel should not give up the conquered territories except in return for a comprehensive peace settlement that guaranteed Israel's independence and security. Johnson's administration sent advanced arms to Israel to counter the Soviets' rebuilding of Arab armies, and Richard Nixon continued that policy when he took office.

Nixon, however, decided he would have to be more evenhanded than Johnson if there was to be a comprehensive peace in the Middle East. The Palestinians had to be accommodated in some way before the Arabs would recognize Israel and grant it security. In October 1969, after thorough consultation with the Soviet Union, Secretary of State William Rogers tried to spell out compromise peace terms. The Rogers plan called for Israel to retreat to its 1967 borders with only "insubstantial" border alterations. Israel and Jordan would negotiate the status of Jerusalem, implying that Israel could not expect full sovereignty over the city. The Palestinians would be repatriated to Palestine or compensated for living elsewhere. In return, the United States and the Soviet Union would guarantee Israel's security.

Israel and Occupied Areas, 1967

The compromise suggested in the Rogers plan managed only to infuriate both Israelis and Arabs. Israel refused to entrust its security to other powers, however friendly they might appear. It had seen the UN withdraw its forces at Nasser's request and leave Israel to Arab mercies. It remembered that the United States and the rest of the world had stood by as Jews were slaughtered in the Holocaust. The Israelis would entrust their security only to "fighting Jews," and they insisted on borders and defense arrangements that would make this possible. Return of the Palestinians to Israel would destroy the Jewish state. The establishment of an independent Palestinian state on the West Bank would threaten Israel with continual guerrilla warfare, for the Palestinians inevitably would attempt to retrieve all of Palestine. Let the Arab states take care of the Palestinians, Israelis said. Jordan already was a Palestinian state. Let the remainder of the Palestinians go there and work something out with Jordan's Hashemite-Bedouin minority.

Of course, for all the insistence on arrangements that would permit it to guarantee its own security, Israel remained dependent on American arms and economic aid. This gave Washington potential leverage to force a compromise. But the Israelis, especially the right-wing and religious parties, were willing to defy excessive American pressure on the gamble that American public opinion, with the help of the Jewish lobby within the United States, would repudiate any administration perceived to be anti-Israel.

The Arabs also denounced the Rogers plan. Nasser called it proof that the United States was the "number one enemy of the Arabs." Since Rogers had issued the plan under his own name, the Soviets quickly backed away in the face of such universal opposition and supported the Arabs. The Arabs insisted on the right of the Palestinians to return to their homeland and to live in a secular, democratic state that reflected the wishes of a proper Arab majority, not a religious Jewish state. They pointed to Israeli expulsions of Arabs and discrimination against those who stayed. The Arabs would do nothing that would lend legitimacy to the state of Israel—neither recognize it nor imply recognition by negotiating directly with it. Some moderate Arab states like King Hussein's Jordan saw promise in the Rogers plan, but they had to be careful in saying so. They wanted neither to disrupt Arab unity nor endanger their own regimes by enraging their resident Palestinians and domestic radicals.

As the Rogers plan fell into the abyss between the Arabs and Israelis, tensions continued to mount. A cease-fire worked out in 1970 did little to stop the sporadic raids of Arab-supported Palestinians into Israel from their refuges in Jordan, Lebanon, Syria, and Egypt. The Soviet Union deployed advanced surface-to-air missiles (SAMs) in Egypt to deprive Israel of the air superiority it had won in 1967. This was the first time Moscow had installed such antiaircraft missiles in a noncommunist country, and the number of Soviet personnel accompanying those missiles continued to increase until it reached some 10,000 soldiers, technicians, and pilots.

Black September

Tensions boiled over into conflict in September 1970 when Palestinian guerrillas hijacked four airliners. They blew up one of the planes in Cairo and the three others in Jordan after stashing the hostage passengers around the Jordanian capital of Amman. King Hussein knew the hijackings would bring Israeli retaliatory bombing raids on his nation. Palestinian guerrilla operations from his territory always did. He himself was under siege from the Palestinians in his country who thought he was too moderate in his attempts to regain the West Bank and destroy Israel; Hussein had barely survived two assassination attempts. Consequently, he decided to use his loyal Bedouin army to expel the guerrillas. He knew the Israelis would approve and intervene to help him if the 17,000 Iraqi soldiers remaining in Jordan from the Six-Day War decided to fight on behalf of the Palestinians. The United States also was prepared to step in if the Soviets intervened.

It was the Syrians, however, who intervened, which no one but Hussein had anticipated. Syria sent hundreds of tanks rumbling into Jordan. The United States offered to recompense Israel for any planes it might lose if it intervened to help Jordan, but this aid did not turn out to be necessary. The Syrian air force commander, later president, Hafez Assad, withheld Syrian air cover. Jordan's own air force quickly knocked out most of Syria's tank columns, Israel mobilized on the Golan Heights, and the Syrians backed away. The Palestinian guerrillas fled Jordan. Most took refuge in Lebanon, where a weak, fractured government could impose few controls on Palestinian enclaves and the continuing Palestinian war against Israel.

The Yom Kippur War, October 1973

With the partial defection of Jordan from the Arab states confronting Israel, Egypt counted on Soviet aid and pressure to get the United States to join in imposing a compromise settlement on Israel. Anwar Sadat, who became Egypt's president after Nasser died in 1970, realized that Israeli strength and American backing made impossible the extreme demands of Palestinians and other Arabs for the total destruction of the Jewish state. But he thought the Palestinians might be accommodated on the West Bank and the Gaza Strip if Israel could be forced to withdraw to its 1967 boundaries. When Nixon and Soviet premier Brezhnev emerged from the summit meeting of 1972 without any new plans for the Middle East, Sadat decided he would have to act himself.

He expelled the 10,000 Soviet advisers in Egypt and freed himself from Soviet demands for full compliance with radical Arab goals. He also circumvented Soviet insistence that any Egyptian action be restrained enough to avoid American intervention and the possibility of a superpower confrontation. On October 6, 1973, the Jewish holy day of Yom Kippur, Egypt and Syria launched a surprise joint attack on Israel. The Israelis and Americans had not expected an attack because the Arabs were militarily inferior to Israel and could not hope to win. They had consequently ignored Sadat's warnings as mere bluff.

Indeed, Sadat did not expect to win a complete victory; he simply hoped he could inflict enough casualties and capture enough territory to puncture Israel's sense of omnipotence and force some movement in Israel's negotiating position. Sadat's armies succeeded better than he had hoped: SAM missiles wreaked havoc with Israel's air force, destroying forty-nine planes. The Israelis lost 500 tanks as well. A portion of these broke down as they dashed from storage depots within Israel across the Sinai Desert. Egypt and Syria destroyed the remainder in combat. The Israelis also suffered more than 2,000 casualties, a large number in such a small, close society.

Meanwhile, the Soviets airlifted planes to Syria and Egypt to help in the fighting. The United States countered by promising to replenish Israeli losses in tanks and planes so Israel could throw in its reserves. There was some debate and delay within the Nixon administration over whether the United States should force Israel to promise to disgorge the conquered territories of 1967 before extending further American aid. But when Israel's precarious military situation became more obvious and the Israelis suggested they might have to resort to nuclear weapons, Nixon decided on a major American airlift. He reconfirmed his decision when the administration learned that the Soviets had put three of their own airborne divisions on alert.

As the perils of the war and the threat of a superpower confrontation grew, the United States proposed a cease-fire in place. After an initial rejection, Israel agreed. Its military difficulties were great, and it could afford to stop in place because, although Egyptian troops had gained territory in the Sinai, Israeli troops had pushed past the Golan Heights to a position within twenty-five miles of Syria's capital, Damascus. The Egyptians, however, insisted they would accept a cease-fire only on the basis of the old 1967 borders. Egypt then launched a new attack on the Sinai. But this one was not nearly as successful as the initial attack. Egypt's tanks by this time were outside the protective range of their antiaircraft missiles and batteries along the Suez Canal. The Israelis chopped up the Egyptian columns from both the air and the land. The Israelis then outflanked the Egyptian attack, crossed the Suez Canal, tore up the SAM missile sites, and trapped the Egyptian Third Army on the Sinai side of the canal.

Throughout the Yom Kippur War, U.S. secretary of state Henry Kissinger maneuvered to keep either side from winning a total victory. He hoped a stalemate would enhance the chances for a compromise settlement of the Arab-Israeli dispute. At first Nixon and Kissinger restricted their support of the Israelis because they expected them to defeat the Arabs handily. Then, when the Israelis trembled on the brink of disaster, Nixon and Kissinger began a massive American airlift. When in turn the Israelis were in a position to destroy a significant portion of the Egyptian army, Kissinger insisted that the Israelis stop short and accept a cease-fire.

In the midst of Kissinger's attempts to arrange the cease-fire, the Arab oil nations added a new dimension to the problem. They announced progressive 5 percent reductions in the production of oil until Israel returned to its 1967 borders. Shortly afterward, the Arab oil nations added to this already potent squeeze a total oil embargo on the United States. In this crisis atmosphere, Kissinger got the embittered Israelis to accept a cease-fire in place on October 22, 1973. The Israelis nonetheless believed they had received tacit permission from Kissinger to complete their encirclement of the Egyptian Third Army, and they cut the last supply road to the trapped force. Facing starvation, the Egyptians tried to break out. Fighting escalated. Egypt asked the Soviets to intervene, and the Soviets sent an ultimatum on October 24 that if the United States did not join them in imposing a cease-fire on the belligerents, the Soviets would do so unilaterally. Nixon refused and alerted American forces to resist the landing of Soviet troops in Egypt. The alert became public; a major confrontation was in the offing.

Fortunately, Sadat defused it by agreeing to an international peacekeeping force with only token U.S. and Soviet participation. The United States then threatened to stop all military supplies to Israel unless it indicated a willingness to negotiate by eight o'clock the following morning. When Sadat, breaking Arab precedent, agreed to direct negotiations with the Israelis on cease-fire arrangements (although at a low level), the Israelis agreed. The Yom Kippur War was over. Nixon and Kissinger, through luck and skill, had managed to prevent the victory or humiliation of either side. Yet the oil embargo still pinched the United States, and the Egyptian Third Army was still trapped. The situation would remain exceedingly precarious until the Arabs and Israelis negotiated a broader settlement.

Kissinger and Step-by-Step Diplomacy

Kissinger believed a broad settlement was within reach. Israel had been shocked enough by its losses and narrow escape to consider a compromise. The Egyptians and other Arabs had avenged the humiliation of the Six-Day War, so they too might be able to retreat from their insistence on the destruction of Israel. Perhaps the Arabs were ready to recognize Israel's sovereignty and accept a state for the Palestinians on the West Bank under Jordanian sovereignty. Perhaps the Israelis would retreat from their 1967 conquests so long as the Arabs recognized their right to exist, the Palestinians were submerged within a moderate Jordan, and the great powers guaranteed Israeli security.

Yet even if Israel and the Arab nations were ready to negotiate, an acceptable settlement would take months of haggling, and Kissinger did not have much time. Egypt would not leave its Third Army trapped for much longer, and the United States would suffer greatly if the Arab oil embargo were extended for a lengthy period. The embargo had already driven a wedge between the United States and its major allies.

Western Europe and Japan had ostentatiously dissociated themselves from American policy in the Middle East in order to escape the oil embargo; having converted most of their industry from coal to oil in the 1960s, they imported two-thirds of their oil from the Middle East. Still, the Arab oil weapon was hurting them badly. Saudi Arabia and the other Arab nations did not embargo oil to Europe and Japan, but did cut production, and panic buying sent prices skyrocketing. The shah of Iran, whose nation was Muslim but not Arab, continued to supply oil to the United States and the West, but also took the opportunity to raise prices and profits as much as he could. By the end of 1973, oil prices had jumped more than 200 percent. To relieve this pressure, the Europeans adopted strongly pro-Arab positions and demanded that the United States join the Soviet Union in imposing peace terms on Israel.

Nixon and Kissinger, however, refused. Kissinger believed instead that he might be able to negotiate a voluntary peace if he mediated one issue at a time in a step-by-step process. He would start with the issues between Egypt and Israel, since these seemed the easiest to settle. There was no strong Palestinian presence in the territories in dispute between Egypt and Israel, and even if disengagement required a measure of Israeli retreat, Israel would still occupy some Sinai territory as a buffer. Progress toward an Israeli-Egyptian peace also seemed to promise some leverage for further Arab compromises, since the Egyptian army was by far the strongest potential force against Israel, and its removal from the Arab side would cripple the Arab military position.

Kissinger personally traveled to the Middle East to negotiate the Egyptian-Israeli disengagement. He and the rest of the players in the Middle East had assumed that the negotiations would take place in Geneva and include the Soviets. Both Israel and Egypt, however, had an incentive to avoid Soviet participation because Moscow would support the most radical Arab demands. Consequently, Sadat and the Israelis invited Kissinger to mediate personally between them. Kissinger shuttled back and forth between them in an exhausting tour de force of diplomacy. He would bounce off the plane in Egypt to effusive embraces and kisses from Sadat, and then take Sadat's proposals back to a suspicious and contentious Israeli cabinet.

Finally, Golda Meir, the Israeli prime minister, decided to take the risk of trusting Sadat and Kissinger. On January 18, 1974, she agreed with Sadat to disengage Israeli and Egyptian forces, limit weapons on the front lines, and permit a UN force to return to supervise the cease-fire. Israel withdrew to the major Sinai passes in its first surrender of territory in twenty years. As Meir announced this momentous step, Kissinger impulsively embraced and kissed her. Remembering Kissinger's many clinches with Sadat, the Israeli prime minister thanked him and told him wryly she had begun to think he kissed only men.

Kissinger then turned to visit Syria; at this gesture of American sincerity, Saudi Arabia and the other Arab oil nations removed their oil embargo on the United States. After much travail, Kissinger got a disengagement agreement in Syria to go along with the Egyptian one. Israel retreated from the Syrian territory it had seized in the Yom Kippur War and from a portion of the territory it had conquered in 1967 as well. It continued, however, to hold most of the strategic Golan Heights, where it had planted more than twenty settlements. Further progress on the Syrian front would be extremely difficult.

Kissinger hoped that the next step would be a Palestinian-Jordanian-West Bank agreement. But here his step-by-step approach bogged down. He had hoped to get Israel to agree to return nominal sovereignty over the West Bank to Jordan in return for a continued Israeli military presence to guarantee security. Palestinian refugees might then accept the West Bank as their homeland and cease their attempts to destroy Israel. Those Palestinians who still wanted to fight would be confronted by both Israeli and Hussein's Bedouin forces. However, despite American urging, the Israelis could not bring themselves to give up the West Bank.

The Israeli Labor ministry held a parliamentary majority of only one, and it was unwilling to oppose the demands of the right-wing and religious parties to settle and hold the area. The Palestinian Liberation Organization (PLO), representing large portions of the Palestinian population, privately informed the United States that its minimum demand for peace was an independent Palestinian state in all of Jordan, meaning that Hussein would have to be overthrown. Kissinger saw no promise in that scheme, for he was sure such a radical state would turn on Israel whatever its promises, and he was unwilling to sacrifice Hussein in any case.

When the Arab states recognized the PLO as the sole legitimate representative of the Palestinian people at an Arab summit meeting in October 1974, Kissinger's Jordanian option seemed doomed. Hussein was not about to press his own claim to rule a Palestinian state on the West Bank and turn the PLO's attention to him rather than to the destruction of Israel. Israel was not about to negotiate with the PLO, whose announced goal was control of all Palestine, especially since the PLO had claimed credit for the massacre of Israeli athletes at the Munich Olympics of 1972 as well as other terrorist raids on Israeli citizens. Israel would not even consider the compromise urged by Europe, the United Nations, and the Soviet Union of an independent Palestinian state ruled by the PLO on the West Bank, separate from both Jordan and Israel.

With a West Bank Palestinian settlement at least temporarily foreclosed, Kissinger saw further progress in Egypt as the only possible chance to keep momentum rolling toward a comprehensive settlement. When Kissinger returned to his Cairo-Jerusalem shuttle, however, he found the gap wider than he expected. Sadat wanted Israel to withdraw beyond the Sinai passes and to return the Sinai oil fields to Egyptian control. He also wanted further progress between Egypt and Israel linked to Israeli concessions on the Palestinian issue. Otherwise, the rest of the Arab states would accuse Sadat of selling out the Palestinian and Arab cause for selfish Egyptian interests.

Israel balked at both demands. It wanted formal peace with Egypt to free its hands to resist unfavorable settlements with the Palestinians and other Arab states, not as a prelude to significant concessions. Kissinger returned to the United States empty-handed after warning the Israelis that excessive quibbling would throw negotiations into the Geneva Conference, where the Soviets would support extreme Arab demands and where hopes for a compromise peace favorable to Israel would be lost. Israeli haggling over issues that "will seem trivial five years from now" could convince Americans that Israel was the true roadblock to peace in the Middle East, isolating the Jews even further, he told them: "It's tragic to see people dooming themselves to a course of unbelievable peril." President Gerald Ford, who by then had taken over from Nixon, was even sterner. He announced a "total reassessment" of American Middle East policy and selectively with-held weapons deliveries to Israel.

Israel finally conceded the Sinai passes and oil fields to Egypt in the Sinai II Agree-ment of September 1975. In exchange for these concessions, Israel obtained an Egyptian promise to use strictly peaceful means in future dealings with the Jewish state. Israel also secured an American commitment to vast weapons supplies and to American military intervention if Israeli security were threatened. The United States was now thoroughly entangled in the Middle East by an all but formal alliance with Israel and serious commit-ments to Egypt and Syria. American personnel even manned the early warning stations separating Israeli and Egyptian troops.

Kissinger's commitments in the Middle East took on ominous dimensions when the other Arab nations exploded in anger at what they considered Sadat's betrayal in making the Sinai II Agreement. In return for Egypt's abandonment of the Arab military confronta-tion with Israel, Sadat had retrieved much of Egypt's own lost territory and resources, but had gotten only the vaguest intimations of further progress on the Palestinian and Syrian issues. Kissinger had promised Sadat to promote a second agreement between Israel and Syria, but also he had committed himself in writing to Israel that Sinai II stood on its own and was not linked to any further agreements. Thus, when Israel refused to consider any but cosmetic changes on the Golan Heights or the West Bank and when Israeli prime minister Yitzhak Rabin gloated in an interview that a separate peace with Egypt would allow Israel to deal "forcefully" with Syria, Syria denounced Egypt's "defection." Syria also began putting together an alliance with Jordan and the PLO forces in Lebanon to compensate for the loss of Egypt's army in the confrontation with Israel.

Civil War in Lebanon, 1975–1976

With Syrian encouragement, Lebanon quickly became the primary focus of the Israeli-Arab confrontation. The PLO had made Lebanon its headquarters because Hussein had expelled the organization from Jordan, Syria would not permit attacks through its tenuous position on the Golan Heights, and Egypt had neutralized itself with the Sinai II Agreement. Only Lebanon was left as a staging ground for continued Palestinian military action against Israel, and its government was too weak to control the Palestinians on its soil. Unfortunately, Lebanese society was as fragile as its government, and it could not survive the Palestinian presence and operations.

Lebanon was an amalgam of ethnic and religious groups whose historic hatreds for one another were barely held in check by the most tenuous of arrangements. Lebanon and Syria had been provinces of Turkey until France acquired them as mandates after World War I. France had made Lebanon a separate entity in the hope of creating a loyal French colony based upon the fierce group of Maronite Christians. The Maronites, followers of a fifth-century monk named St. Maron, had fled the Muslim conquest of Syria in the seventh century and established redoubts in what was then known as Mount Lebanon. Unlike most Christians in the eastern Mediterranean, they had submitted themselves in the twelfth century to the Roman pope rather than to the Orthodox patriarch of Constantinople. As early as 1861, the French had intervened to aid the Maronites against their Muslim enemies, and the Maronites thus regarded the French as their rescuers from a centuries-long Islamic siege.

During World War II, the Allies arranged for the independence of France's eastern Mediterranean mandates. In doing so, they maintained the separation of Lebanon and Syria. This dismayed many Arabs, who regarded Syria, Lebanon, and the British mandates of Palestine and Jordan as components of a Greater Syria, a unified Arab state covering the whole area. Lebanon was left with a population divided into countless factions. The Maronite Christians constituted 55 percent of the population. There were also small numbers of Greek Orthodox and Armenian Christians. Most of the remaining population, however, was divided between Sunni and Shiite Muslims, along with a small, secretive Islamic sect known as the Druze. Despite the hostility among these factions, the near-feudal oligarchs who ruled them managed to agree in 1943 to a National Pact dividing power among them. A Maronite Christian would be president, a Sunni Muslim the prime minister, a Shiite Muslim the speaker of the house, and the Druze would be accorded several minor positions. The Lebanese Parliament would be divided with six Christian members for every five others.

The various factions fought periodically over this distribution of power because the Shiite and Druze offices were mostly ceremonial, and the Christian president wielded substantially more power than the Sunni prime minister. The Muslim oligarchs became increasingly insistent on constitutional reform as the birth rate altered the population ratio in favor of the Muslims. Probably the oligarchs could have worked out a new National Pact with only the usual number of vendettas had not world affairs intruded upon their fragile balance of power. Nasser's dream of a pan-Arabic Middle East stirred many Lebanese Muslims, especially the poor and dispossessed Shiites, to insist on a reformed, secular Lebanon based on absolute majority rule. Since the Muslims had become the majority, they would rule without the hindrance of Maronite Christian domination or the vetoes accorded minority sects by the National Pact. The Palestinians threw their weight behind this radical national movement, a factor of increasing importance after the main body of the PLO arrived from Jordan in 1970.

The operations as well as the presence of the PLO strained relations in Lebanon because PLO raids inevitably drew retaliatory Israeli air attacks. In the early years of Lebanese nationhood, the Maronite Christians had joined the Arab League in opposing the state of Israel, if only to get the Palestinians out of Lebanon and back into their own land. But as the Palestinians joined the Lebanese national movement to overthrow the National Pact, drawing heavier Israeli retaliation, the Maronite leaders pushed for suppression of PLO activities and dispersion of the Palestinians to other countries. As a last resort, the Christians then threatened to secede from Lebanon, perhaps ally their Lebanese enclaves with the West or Israel, and disable one more Arab state on the border of Israel. In this fractious atmosphere, the last bulwark of a united Lebanon, the Lebanese army, became polarized among sects. Independent militias grew, manned often by deserters from the national army.

In 1975 someone fired on a Christian service in Beirut attended by Pierre Gemayal, the leader of the Phalangists, one of the Maronite militias. The Christians retaliated by murdering Palestinians on a passing bus. Lebanon flared into civil war. Syria moved in to prevent disintegration. At first it aided the Muslims against the most intractable of the Maronite factions, but then it turned to fight the PLO to prevent it from inducing the complete secession of the Maronites or inviting a war with Israel before the Arabs were ready. Egypt quickly lined up with the PLO. Iraq, Syria's neighbor and mortal enemy, mobilized troops on the Syrian border. Israel warned it might intervene. Finally, Saudi Arabia and the other Arab states, with quiet support from the United States, succeeded in bringing the Syrian intervention force in Lebanon under the nominal control of the Arab League and imposing a sullen cease-fire. Thirty thousand Lebanese had died and another 600,000 had been forced from their homes, a staggering total in a nation of only 3 million people. By thus exhausting themselves opposing each other in Lebanon, the Arab states gave Israel a breathing space.

The Camp David Process and the Israeli-Egyptian Peace

President Jimmy Carter, who took office in the temporary lull that followed the Lebanese civil war, tried to break out of Kissinger's step-by-step process by offering a plan for a comprehensive settlement. The Carter plan was much like the Rogers plan. It called for a gradual Israeli withdrawal to its 1967 boundaries with only minor (and unspecified) exceptions in exchange for recognition, great power security guarantees, and demilitarized zones on the borders. The Palestinians gradually would receive self-determination in the West Bank and Gaza Strip as an independent state or in federation with Jordan.

Neither the Arabs nor the Israelis were ready for such a compromise, and Carter's own elaborations on the plan gave both sides an excuse to avoid it. Carter first said that Israel should have "defensible borders," the code words in the Middle East for according Israel much of the territory conquered in the Six-Day War of 1967. Carter tried to correct this impression by speaking later of only minor border adjustments and of a Palestinian "homeland," both anathema to the Israelis. The Carter plan bogged down in confusion as the new hard-line Israeli administration, headed by Menachem Begin, insisted on the right to make Jerusalem Israel's capital and to plant new Jewish settlements on the West Bank.

Carter tried to recoup by bringing the Soviets back into the Middle East negotiations. On October 1, 1977, Secretary of State Cyrus Vance and Soviet foreign minister Andrei Gromyko worked out a joint statement that called for reconvening the Geneva Conference within three months. There the Arabs and Israelis would negotiate a comprehensive settlement under the auspices of the United States, the Soviet Union, and the other powers. Immediately Carter ran into criticism. Many Americans denounced him for abandoning Kissinger's policy of excluding the Soviets. Israelis also denounced the Geneva approach even though they had agreed to it under duress. Carter tried to appease his American and Israeli critics by insisting that the United States had no intention of imposing a settlement and by agreeing to alter the U.S.-Soviet understanding to allow the Israelis to veto the participation of the PLO.

As Carter was retreating, Anwar Sadat broke the impending stalemate with another dramatic gesture. On November 19, 1977, he traveled to Jerusalem personally to revive step-by-step diplomacy. This was an unprecedented Arab recognition of Israel's existence and of its rights in Jerusalem. Sadat took the gamble because he feared that when Carter took the U.S. plan to the Geneva Conference, the radical Arabs, with Soviet support, would reject it, the United States would intensify its commitment to Israel, and Egypt would be caught in the middle.

Sadat's emotional appearance before the Israeli Knesset inspired an upwelling of peace sentiment in both Egypt and Israel. Unfortunately, the euphoria quickly dissipated when, after Sadat had returned home, he called his negotiating team back from Israel because Begin had upbraided it for demanding complete Israeli withdrawal to the 1967 borders. Meanwhile, Begin continued to plant Israeli settlements on the West Bank. Then, in March 1978, he sent the Israeli army plunging into Lebanon in response to PLO raids. Under U.S. pressure, he withdrew from Lebanon in favor of a UN peace force in June, but he left a six-mile border strip of Lebanese territory under the control of Phalangist militia forces from several villages in the area. Lebanon was now even more polarized, and Syria again inclined its occupation troops away from the Maronites toward the radical Arab forces.

As the Middle East peace process disintegrated, Jimmy Carter took a desperate risk. He invited Begin and Sadat to the presidential mountain retreat at Camp David, Maryland. The negotiations were long and tense. Carter kept reassuring Sadat while he doggedly cajoled and reasoned with the tenacious Israeli prime minister. Finally, he emerged with the Camp David Accords of September 1978. Begin agreed to withdraw entirely from the Sinai and, if the Knesset consented, to dismantle the Jewish settlements that had been planted there after the Six-Day War. In exchange Egypt would sign a formal peace treaty with Israel incorporating these arrangements in three months. Begin and Sadat also agreed on a vague framework for peace in the rest of the Middle East, particularly the West Bank and Gaza. There would be a "self-governing authority" on the West Bank as a transition regime for five years, after which the final status of the area would be negotiated. There

Anwar Sadat *(left)* of Egypt, Jimmy Carter *(center)* of the United States, and Menachem Begin of Israel. *(Courtesy of the Jimmy Carter Presidential Library)*

was no mention of an independent state or the PLO. Begin and the Israelis naturally took a very restricted view of this agreement, while Sadat and Carter saw it as the prelude to a major compromise.

As it became clear that the Israelis were not going to move toward allowing an independent Palestinian state, the moderate Arab states of Saudi Arabia and Jordan denounced the Camp David Accords and Egypt. Sadat stalled, Israel haggled, and ultimately Carter took an even greater gamble than inviting the leaders to Camp David. He went to Cairo and Jerusalem himself to get agreement to the final peace treaty. He succeeded, and on March 26, 1979, Begin and Sadat traveled to Washington to sign the treaty. They agreed to resume negotiations on the Palestinian issue, but Egyptian recognition of Israel would stand regardless of the outcome of those negotiations.

Negotiations on the Palestinian issue failed. The PLO rejected anything less than an independent Palestinian state under its control. Israel would have nothing to do with the PLO. Carter tried to get the PLO involved behind the scenes, but had to fire his UN ambassador, Andrew Young, when Young publicly admitted he had met with the PLO. Begin exploited the imbroglio by putting new settlements on the West Bank. The United States voted in the UN for condemnation of both the settlements and the Israeli occupation of Jerusalem, and then disavowed its votes, with Secretary of State Cyrus Vance accepting blame for the "mistake." Sadat withdrew from the talks on Palestinian autonomy, and Begin formally annexed East Jerusalem. The Palestinian issue continued to fester and to undermine all hope for peace in the Middle East.

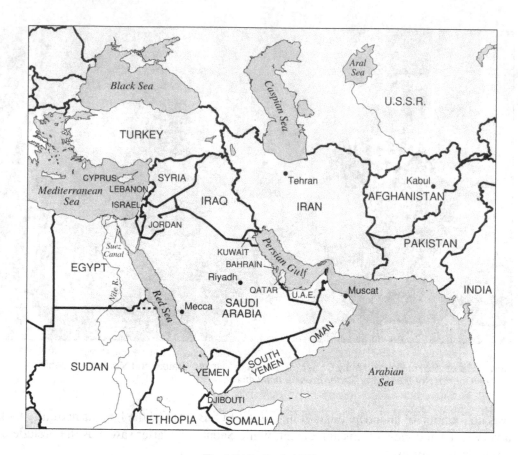

The Middle East, 1979

Eruptions in the Persian Gulf and the Carter Doctrine

In 1979 revolution and war broke out in the Persian Gulf, posing an even greater threat to the flow of oil to the West than the Arab-Israeli conflict. The turmoil began with the overthrow of Mohammad Reza Pahlavi, the shah of Iran.

After the CIA had helped restore the shah to his throne in 1953, the Eisenhower administration had maintained rather restrained relations with Iran. The shah ardently desired to build Iran's military forces, but Eisenhower and his successor, John F. Kennedy, thought it useless to send the shah much military aid. Iran could never match Soviet forces. The United States would have to intervene directly in case of Soviet attack, whatever the level of Iranian armament. Eisenhower and Kennedy urged the shah to spend his oil money on domestic reform and modernization.

By the time Lyndon Johnson acceded to the presidency, the situation had changed. The shah was in a position to do more than just beg for American arms. His oil revenues had increased from $90 million a year in 1955 to $482 million in 1964. He had earned Washington's gratitude by refusing to join the Arab attempt to embargo oil to the West during the Six-Day War of 1967. Besides, the strategic situation seemed more threatening to both Iranian and American interests. The 1958 revolution in Iraq had created a radical regime hostile to both the United States and Iran. The United States was tied up in Vietnam, and while U.S. military support would not equip Iran to fight the Soviet Union on equal terms, it might enable Iran to protect the Persian Gulf against Arab nationalism. In addition, the shah appeared to be making significant progress in the modernization and reform that Eisenhower and Kennedy had urged upon him. In his so-called White Revolution, the shah divided land among the peasants, spent lavishly on buildings and highways in urban centers, protected the rights of religious minorities like the Jews and the Baha'i sect, and increased the rights of women.

The shah used his increased leverage and prestige to press the Johnson administration to buy more Iranian oil and sell Iran more arms. The Defense Department, objecting that increased arms were unnecessary, urged that arms sales to Iran continue to be limited according to whether arms purchases would interfere with social and economic progress. The State Department, however, favored increasing the arms sales, and Johnson agreed. Arms sales to Iran continued to increase in the early Nixon years under the Nixon Doctrine's preference for building up local powers to eliminate the need for direct American intervention. But the tugging and hauling between the State and Defense Departments limited the increases until Nixon ordered the Defense Department in 1972 to stop second-guessing Iranian arms purchases. Nixon declared that the shah could purchase anything he wanted except nuclear arms.

During the Yom Kippur War, the shah supplied the United States with oil in defiance of the Arab embargo. This won him substantial favor in the United States. Since he also used the occasion to triple the price of oil, he gained the wherewithal as well as the political backing in the United States to purchase more arms. Arms purchases soon absorbed 25 percent of Iran's income, outrunning the ability of the Iranians to operate or maintain the equipment. One authority calculated that the shah would have had to conscript the entire high school graduating class every year to have enough technicians to service and operate his sophisticated weaponry. To bridge the gap, the United States supplied thousands of technicians, who alienated much of the local population by living in luxurious enclaves where they were exempt from the jurisdiction of the Iranian courts.

Nixon and Kissinger felt little inclination to challenge the shah's dream of building Iran into the greatest power in the Persian Gulf. Britain was withdrawing from the area by granting independence to the tiny emirates along the gulf—Kuwait, Oman, Bahrain, and Qatar. Nasser and the Soviets naturally would wish to move into the vacuum. The Soviets signed a friendship treaty with Iraq. Marxists took over South Yemen and, with Nasser's encouragement, challenged the government left behind by the British for control of North Yemen. In 1969 Iraq stirred an old quarrel with Iran by claiming the entire Shatt al Arab River that the two nations had jointly administered as their border. By disrupting the Persian Gulf, these events threatened the area that held 75 percent of the noncommunist world's proved oil reserves.

Neither Nixon, Kissinger, nor most other American observers recognized that the shah was building his military power on a foundation of sand. They knew that the shah's modernization program had raised opposition in Iran, but they wrote off that opposition as reactionary religious fundamentalism or as Soviet-inspired agitation stirred by the Communist Tudeh Party. They assumed both would be overwhelmed by the economic and social progress of the shah's modernization program. They did not understand how great a gap between rich and poor the shah's White Revolution had created.

The White Revolution's land reform had given peasants plots of land too small for subsistence. Those farmers who stayed on the land suffered in neglect. Those who escaped to the cities found few jobs in the sophisticated economy that revolved around oil, major construction, and advanced military technology. The transplanted peasants became ardent supporters of the Shiite mullahs whose mosque lands had been confiscated by the shah's reform. Other members of the old middle class began to join the peasants and mullahs as they saw wealth and influence siphoned off by the shah's family and corrupt cronies in the huge building projects and arms purchases that were the pride of the modernization program. The shah accelerated his alienation of the middle class in 1975 when he tried to increase tax revenue by cracking down on bazaar profiteering (but not the higher-level corruption of his family and friends) and ended subsidies to the mullahs. The bazaar merchants helped pay the resultant mosque deficits, cementing a powerful alliance against the shah. This alliance saw the shah as a corrupt, antireligious figure who challenged the deepest beliefs of Islam.

The shah's use of police state tactics and torture contributed further to the opposition building against him. Many other third-world and Communist states exceeded the shah's record of killing 30,000 opponents in thirty years, and the Iranians were accustomed to governments that used such tactics. The cause for which the shah killed and tortured was increasingly suspect, however, and in a country of extended families, one instance of political murder or torture could make a hundred enemies. The CIA-trained secret police, SAVAK, also used thousands of paid informers. SAVAK thus threatened every Iranian, not just activists.

When Jimmy Carter became president in 1977, he spoke out against violations of human rights in Iran and ordered a review of arms sales to the shah for the first time since 1972. But Carter's innovation had little practical effect. His national security adviser, Zbigniew Brzezinski, and the ambassador to Iran, William Sullivan, urged continued support of the shah. Administration policy soon reverted to what it had been under Nixon and Ford. Carter even called Iran an island of stability and praised the shah as an enlightened ruler who justly deserved his people's love and admiration.

Actually, the shah was losing his grip. Unknown to the Americans, the shah had developed cancer. As Iranian disorder and demonstrations increased in the wake of a police attack on protesters in the holy city of Qom in January 1978, the shah vacillated. In the hope of repeating his success of 1953, after each incident he would take a hard line and then soften to win back the moderates. By 1978, however, the moderates were too firmly tied to the bazaar merchants, mullahs, and displaced peasants. In August Iran exploded in fury when a fire rumored to have been set by SAVAK killed 377 people in a theater. With Brzezinski's informal approval, the Iranian army got the shah to impose martial law, and on September 7 the military fired into a crowd in the capital city of Teheran, killing between 700 and 2,000 of the demonstrators. Carter's telephoned support of the shah led to the popular Iranian belief that the American president had ordered the shooting.

Panic buying and strikes, especially a strike by oil workers, threw Iran into chaos. The shah installed a military government and the United States supplied it with antiriot gear. But the Iranian army itself began to disintegrate. Conscripts were unwilling to fire at their own people; officers began to look for a way to make their own deals with the opposition. As the Carter administration belatedly realized that the shah was in serious trouble, it began to draw back from him and urge the formation of a constitutional monarchy.

If there had ever been a chance of a moderate centrist solution in Iran, however, that time was past. The charismatic leader who galvanized the opposition was an uncompromising exiled religious leader, Ayatollah Ruhollah Khomeini, who regarded the shah as a puppet of a satanic United States. Khomeini insisted on a thorough revolution to overthrow the monarchy and set up a rigid, fundamentalist Islamic theocracy. The Carter administration urged the shah to leave his country and tried to set up a moderate government that would incorporate the military. The shah finally left, but moderates withered before the demands of Khomeini, who returned to Iran from exile to the tumultuous cheers of hundreds of thousands. The revolutionary militia acquired over 300,000 weapons as SAVAK and the army fell apart.

Carter tried to salvage the situation by offering cooperation with Khomeini, but Khomeini rejected the attempt. The ayatollah arrested, purged, and executed moderates, Communists, and religious and ethnic dissidents. He portrayed all of them as agents of the United States who stood in the way of a proper Islamic revolution. When the Communists of the Tudeh Party attacked the American embassy on February 14, 1979, and took those within as hostages, Khomeini denounced the takeover and the attackers freed the hostages immediately. Nine months later, however, his own followers captured the embassy when Carter permitted the shah to come to the United States for medical treatment. This time the ayatollah approved. Iran held fifty-three Americans hostage for more than a year with the approval of the official government.

The hostages became a symbol of America's growing peril and impotence in the Persian Gulf. Oil prices once again shot upward in 1979 as Iranian oil became scarce. Then, in June, Iraq exploited the trouble in Iran by breaking its 1975 peace agreement and increasing its control of the disputed border area along the Shatt al Arab. By the fall of 1980, these Iraqi probings exploded into full-scale war. The Iran-Iraq War hindered oil deliveries from those two countries and also endangered all the oil shipments from the Persian Gulf that had to pass through the Strait of Hormuz. France's delivery of Exocet missiles to Iraq in 1983 presaged a growing number of attacks on gulf shipping.

Meanwhile, in December 1979, Russian troops invaded Afghanistan in what seemed at the time a bizarre move to overthrow the already pro-Soviet Marxist regime of Hafizollah Amin. Amin had come to power as the nominal second in command to Nur Mohammed Tarakki in a 1978 coup led by leftist military officers and members of the fractious Afghan Communist parties. The Soviets had welcomed the new Communist government somewhat hesitantly because the previous regime, although noncommunist, had followed a prudent and friendly policy toward the Soviets and had maintained stability along an extensive part of the Soviet border. Tarakki, Amin, and the other members of the new government, on the other hand, squabbled incessantly among themselves and alienated the Afghan people with their vigorous attempts to install secular Marxist laws in place of old Muslim and tribal customs. Since Amin was the driving force behind these disastrous policies and was relegating Tarakki to a figurehead position, the Soviets decided to help Tarakki get rid of Amin and moderate the government's reforms. Tarakki invited Amin to a conference in the palace, the Soviet ambassador assured Amin that it was safe to go, and then an attempt was made to assassinate Amin. The effort went awry, Amin escaped to mount his own coup, and Tarakki himself was the one to die.

Amin demanded and got the recall of the Soviet ambassador who had attempted to carry out the Soviet Union's orders to get rid of Amin, but in the face of a rising tide of Muslim fundamentalist rebellions, Amin still clung to the Soviets' aid and their official if cool friendship. He did not slacken the Marxist reforms that inspired the rebellions in the countryside, however, and he began to sound out possible support from nations like China and Pakistan to lessen his dependence on the Soviets. He even made friendly gestures toward the United States, where he had gone to school and where the Soviets later claimed he had enlisted as a CIA agent. The Soviets probably believed that the only possible outcome to Amin's continuance in office would be either Afghanistan's collapse into chaos and the rise of a fundamentalist Muslim regime or an Afghanistan supported by nations that were Soviet enemies. The Soviets preferred military intervention, with all its drawbacks, to either of those alternatives.

Jimmy Carter and most American observers, however, feared an offensive purpose to the Soviet invasion, the first massive use of Soviet troops outside the Warsaw Pact area since World War II. Afghanistan bordered Iran and put the Soviets in a better position to seize oil resources vital to the West. Afghanistan also bordered Pakistan, a weak dictatorial regime already split by the rebellion of Bangladesh, hated by India, and offering access to warm water ports on the Indian Ocean that Russia had long coveted.

Carter called the Soviet invasion of Afghanistan the greatest threat to peace since World War II. He reversed his pursuit of détente with the Soviets and his restraint in the Middle East by imposing an embargo on grain shipments to the USSR, boycotting the Moscow Olympics, setting aside attempts to secure Senate consent to the SALT II Treaty, and ending restraints on arms supplies to Pakistan (some of which arms American officials knew would go to the rebels in Afghanistan). Most significant, he tossed aside the Nixon Doctrine, which had placed primary responsibility for regional defense on America's allies. With the revolution in Iran and the weakness of Saudi Arabia, Pakistan, and potential supporters in the Persian Gulf area, Carter saw no alternative but to commit American forces directly to the region.

He announced the Carter Doctrine: "An attempt by any outside force to gain control of the Persian Gulf region will be regarded as an assault on the vital interests of the United States of America, and such an assault will be repelled by any means necessary, including military force." To back up this pronouncement, Carter began to assemble a rapid deployment force and set out to acquire staging bases in Kenya, Oman, Somalia, and the British island of Diego Garcia.

Meanwhile, the Iranian hostage crisis continued. When Carter's initial moderate approach failed to get results, he ordered immigration checks of Iranian students in the United States, froze Iranian assets in America, placed a trade embargo on Iran, and then broke relations. Khomeini remained obdurate, so Carter ordered a military rescue attempt. The rescue mission failed humiliatingly when two helicopters broke down in the Iranian desert. Nine months later, as the Iran-Iraq War heated up, Khomeini finally released the hostages in exchange for the unfreezing of Iranian assets. The hostages arrived home on inauguration day in January 1981, when Ronald Reagan was promising never to be so weak in foreign affairs as the Iranian crisis had supposedly shown Jimmy Carter to be.

After 1980 the immediacy of the threat to American interests in the Persian Gulf declined slightly. The Soviets bogged down in Afghanistan and seemed little inclined to extend their military intervention any further, although they continued to support Marxist regimes in Aden, South Yemen, and Ethiopia. Iran's Khomeini proved almost as hostile to the Soviets and communism as he was to the United States. He not only turned aside Russian influence, but systematically exterminated members of the Tudeh Party and other radicals with secular or pro-Soviet leanings. Meanwhile, the Iran-Iraq War, the decline in world oil consumption, and the replacement of Persian Gulf oil by Saudi Arabia and non-OPEC members like Mexico reduced Western dependence on Persian Gulf oil. The volume of oil shipped through the Strait of Hormuz fell 25 percent to only 6 million barrels a day by 1984.

Nevertheless, Ronald Reagan increased the direct American commitment to the Persian Gulf area. His administration planned that by 1988 the rapid deployment force would include 440,000 men, nine divisions, thirty-six tactical air squadrons, two aircraft carriers, and fifty-six other vessels, all at a cost of some $500 billion. Reagan also extended the mission of this force to include possible intervention in other hot spots. One of those spots was Lebanon.

Lebanon and the Injection of American Forces into the Arab-Israeli Conflict

American forces became directly embroiled in the Arab-Israeli conflict as well as in the Persian Gulf in the early 1980s. On October 6, 1981, Muslim fanatics assassinated Anwar Sadat. His successor as president of Egypt, Hosni Mubarak, supported Sadat's peace with Israel. Consequently, in April 1982, Menachem Begin's Israeli government completed its turnover of the Sinai Desert to Egypt by forcibly removing protesting Israeli settlers. Begin, however, was ready to make no such concessions to the rest of his Arab adversaries. In mid-1981, Israel bombed a nuclear reactor Iraq was readying for operations. In December 1981, Israel formally annexed Syria's Golan Heights. Six months later, on June 6, 1982, Israel invaded Lebanon.

Since 1976 Syria and Israel had adhered to a tacit agreement on Lebanon. The Syrian troops in Lebanon would remain behind a "red line" that would keep them away from the Israeli border and the Israeli-backed Maronite militia. Syria also would not deploy ground-to-air missiles in Lebanon. Unfortunately, the agreement crumbled in 1981. Israel shot down two Syrian helicopters that were attacking Maronite strongholds in the Mount Lebanon area outside Beirut. Later, Israel annexed the Golan Heights. Syria brought ground-to-air missiles into Lebanon's Bekaa Valley. The PLO dueled Israeli artillery across the Israeli-Lebanon border and then moved the latest Soviet Katyusha rockets into southern Lebanon.

In early 1982 Israel and the Christian Phalangist militia commander, Bashir Gemayal, discussed plans for a full Israeli invasion of Lebanon, although for months there had been almost no PLO activity across the Israeli-Lebanon border. Israel would wait for a provocative incident, and then send 36,000 troops to link up with the Maronite Christian strongholds in Beirut and central Lebanon. Afterward, the Israelis and Lebanese Christians would strengthen the Christian-dominated Lebanese central government and eject the PLO from the country. With the PLO already out of Egypt and Jordan, its ejection from Lebanon would leave it nowhere to operate on the borders of Israel except Syria, and Israel was confident that it could defend itself against Syria from the Golan Heights. The Israelis hoped that defeat of the PLO would destroy its prestige, reveal it as an obvious creature of Syria, and thus eliminate it as the representative of the West Bank Palestinians.

On June 3, 1982, the inevitable incident occurred. The PLO assassinated the Israeli ambassador in London. Three days later, the Israeli invasion force swept into Lebanon. The Israeli air force mauled the latest Russian jets sent up against it by Syria and then destroyed the ground-to-air missiles in the Bekaa Valley. Israeli ground forces moved quickly to the outskirts of Beirut. A bloody battle for the city was only narrowly averted when Yasir Arafat, the leader of the PLO, agreed to leave Beirut and disperse his followers among nine other Arab countries. In August 1982, the United States sent 10,000 marines to join French and Italian peacekeeping troops in protecting the PLO evacuation.

With the PLO routed, President Ronald Reagan thought the moment propitious to try once again to get a comprehensive peace in the Middle East. He dusted off the old American plans for a Palestinian autonomous entity on the West Bank to be ruled in conjunction with Jordan by King Hussein and for a freeze on Israeli settlements in the area. Although Reagan still offered no solution for control of Jerusalem or the Golan Heights, he called his plan Fresh Start. Israel, which had other plans for exploiting its invasion of Lebanon, immediately rejected it. But there was promising movement on the Arab side. Hussein indicated agreement with Fresh Start. The Arab heads of state, meeting at Fez, Morocco, in September 1982, adopted a Saudi plan that at least implied recognition of Israel, called for an independent Palestinian state under the PLO, and demanded that Israel return to its 1967 borders. For a moment it appeared that there might be some slim hope for a compromise.

Then, on September 14, four days after American marines had completed supervising evacuation of the PLO from Beirut and had left Lebanon, a bomb killed Lebanese president-elect Bashir Gemayal. Vengeful Phalangist militias, whom Israel had authorized to root out any PLO fighters left behind, raged through two Palestinian refugee camps in Beirut and massacred a thousand people. Reagan ordered the marines back into Beirut to join the French and Italians in restoring peace. The Phalangist massacre, however, had destroyed what slim chance there might have been for peace. Embittered rival Muslim and

Christian militias within Lebanon took turns sniping at each other. The European forces, which were seen by the Lebanese and Arab states as props for the Christian-dominated central government, became targets of radical Muslim groups. Fresh Start fell victim to renewed anarchy and civil war.

In April 1983 King Hussein and Yasir Arafat agreed on a memorandum establishing a joint PLO-Jordanian committee to negotiate on the Reagan and Fez plans, but Arafat disowned the effort when his fellow PLO officers refused to support his action. Hussein then disclaimed further involvement in the Reagan initiative. "We leave it to the PLO and the Palestinian people to choose the ways and means for salvation of themselves and their land," he said.

Begin, rejoicing at the demise of the Reagan plan, announced his government's intention to increase the Jewish population on the West Bank from 30,000 to 50,000. Israel also moved to make its Lebanese border more secure. It negotiated an agreement with Amin Gemayal, who succeeded his assassinated brother as Lebanese president, to withdraw Israeli troops from Lebanon on the condition that Syria do likewise and that Israel be permitted to patrol the Lebanese side of Israel's border. Syria rejected this American-supported plan outright. President Assad of Syria insisted that Israel should withdraw unconditionally from its illegal invasion before any negotiations could take place. He supported PLO dissidents against Arafat and his supposed moderation toward Israel. Assad also encouraged Muslim militia resistance to Israeli and European troops in Lebanon. Most ominously, Syria deployed a new supply of Soviet SAM missiles, accompanied by a large number of Russian personnel.

Faced with Syrian intransigence, Israel rejected Lebanese and American pleas and withdrew its troops from the hotbox of Beirut to defensible lines in southern Lebanon. This left the American and European peacekeeping forces in an exposed, dangerous position. Reagan sent a large naval force to protect the peacekeeping troops, but Lebanese snipers, artillery fire, and bombs continued to take a toll of the American, French, and Italian soldiers. In October 1983, these attacks culminated in suicide bombings of the major French and American barracks that killed 230 American marines and more than fifty French paratroopers.

Reagan ordered the giant guns of the battleship *New Jersey* to respond to artillery and sniper attacks on the American marines. He insisted that the American peacekeeping force would not "cut and run" despite Democratic and congressional criticism. He made a new defense arrangement with Israel and refused to press Israel for the modification of the Lebanese-Israeli withdrawal agreement that Syria was demanding. But Reagan and the United States could not stop the deterioration of the situation in Lebanon. Syria backed a successful revolt against Arafat within the PLO forces stationed under Syrian control in the Bekaa Valley. PLO rebels, with Syrian help, trapped Arafat and his decreasing number of loyalists in Tripoli, and once again Arafat had to evacuate his Lebanese base. Syria was left in complete control of the PLO in Lebanon.

Gemayal met in Damascus with Assad and in Geneva with the leaders of the rival Lebanese factions to revise the Lebanese constitution. He offered too little to satisfy the majority Muslim groups, however, and in February 1984 his cabinet resigned. The Shiite

Lebanon, 1983

and Druze militias, with Syrian artillery support, then defeated Gemayal's Lebanese army and took full charge of West Beirut. With the American marines surrounded by hostile Shiite militia in the exposed U.S. base at the Beirut airport, Reagan finally ordered the American peacekeeping force back to its ships. All the other peacekeeping forces except the French left as well.

Syria moved quickly to solidify its influence in Lebanon. Assad helped Gemayal and the other factional leaders patch together a government, and Gemayal in turn renounced his withdrawal agreement with Israel. A new Israeli cabinet, an uneasy coalition of the Labor and Likud parties, besieged by runaway inflation and the burdens of occupation in southern Lebanon, began a staged withdrawal from southern Lebanon after dropping its demand that Syria withdraw simultaneously. The Israelis quickly found that the Amal Shiites of southern Lebanon, who initially had welcomed the Israeli expulsion of the PLO, were now extremely hostile. Shiite snipers and suicide bombers attacked the withdrawing Israeli troops, and Israel responded with raids on Shiite villages to kill or capture the Lebanese attackers and bulldoze the houses of their protectors. The invasion of Lebanon thus seemed only to have exchanged one hostile force for another on Israel's northern border.

Jordan and Egypt also responded to the rising influence of Syria in Lebanon. Jordan resumed diplomatic relations with Egypt, and King Hussein permitted Yasir Arafat to hold a meeting of the Palestinian Council in Amman in defiance of Arafat's Syrian-backed opponents. Arafat, Hussein, and Egyptian president Mubarak agreed on a new peace initiative with Israel and urged the United States to reinvolve itself in the Middle East peace question. But dissension within Arafat's own faction over his agreement with Hussein and Mubarak, combined with the internal paralysis of Israel's divided government, made the Reagan administration extremely cautious. The Palestinian situation seemed as intractable and chaotic as ever.

Controversial Issues

Israelis and Palestinians have argued about their history as strongly as they argued about their territory. Each side naturally regarded the other as the aggressor and for many years saw little ground on which to compromise their differences. Israelis recited a history of Arab enmity and atrocities that would make it impossible to accept or trust a separate Palestinian state in the occupied territories. Israel was sure such a state would simply provide a new launching pad for an Arab invasion to drive the Jews into the Mediterranean Sea.[1] Palestinians, on the other hand, regarded the Jews as having conquered their land with the aid of European imperialists and saw no justification for the continuation of a Jewish state that discriminated against the original Arab inhabitants. They insisted on nothing less than a fully independent Palestinian state and debated only whether they should pragmatically accept the existence of Israel as a Jewish state or insist that it be dismantled.[2] In recent years, as Israelis and Palestinians have been negotiating over a two-state solution, most historians have shifted their discussion to argue over the terms of that compromise. They have also debated Kissinger's policy. Some have endorsed

Kissinger's step-by-step approach.[3] Others thought that Kissinger should have tried harder to get a comprehensive peace by reviving the Geneva negotiating process that included the Soviets and exerting more pressure on Israel.[4]

Further Reading

Among the best histories of the Israeli-Palestinian conflict are Thomas L. Friedman, *From Beirut to Jerusalem* (updated ed., 1995); William B. Quandt, *Peace Process: American Diplomacy and the Arab-Israeli Conflict Since 1967* (1993); Steven L. Spiegel, *The Other Arab-Israeli Conflict: Making America's Middle East Policy From Truman to Reagan* (1985); Mark A. Tessler, *A History of the Israeli-Palestinian Conflict* (1994); Avi Shlaim, *The Iron Wall: Israel and the Arab World* (2000); Charles D. Smith, *Palestine and the Arab-Israeli Conflict* (1988); and Kenneth W. Stein, *Heroic Diplomacy: Sadat, Kissinger, Carter, Begin, and the Quest for Arab Israeli Peace* (1999).

General histories of the U.S. role in the Middle East include Peter L. Hahn, *Crisis and Crossfire: The United States and the Middle East Since 1945* (2006); Michael B. Oren, *Power, Faith, and Fantasy: America and the Middle East, 1776 to the Present* (2007); Douglas Little, *American Orientalism: The United States and the Middle East Since 1945* (2002); Rashid Khalidi, *Resurrecting Empire: Western Footprints and America's Perilous Path in the Middle East* (2004); Burton I. Kaufman, *The Arab Middle East and the United States: Inter-Arab Rivalry and Superpower Diplomacy* (1996); H.W. Brands, *Into the Labyrinth: The United States and the Middle East, 1945–1993* (1994); Barry Rubin, *Cauldron of Turmoil: America in the Middle East* (1992); Lloyd C. Gardner, *Three Kings: The Rise of an American Empire in the Middle East after World War II* (2009) and *The Long Road to Baghdad: A History of U.S. Foreign Policy from the 1970s to the Present* (2008); and Melani McAlister, *Epic Encounters: Culture, Media, and U.S. Interests in the Middle East, 1945–2000* (2001).

On the Iranian revolution and the Iran-Iraq War, see Mark J. Gasiorowski, *U.S. Foreign Policy and the Shah: Building a Client State in Iran* (1991); Barry Rubin, *Paved with Good Intentions: The American Experience and Iran* (1980); Gary Sick, *All Fall Down: America's Tragic Encounter with Iran* (1985); James A. Bill, *The Eagle and the Lion: The Tragedy of American-Iranian Relations* (1988); Richard Cottom, *Iran and the United States: A Cold War Case Study* (1988); Shaul Bakhash, *The Reign of the Ayatollahs: Iran and the Islamic Revolution* (rev. ed., 1990); Hiro Dilip, *The Longest War: The Iran-Iraq Military Conflict* (1990); and Tareq Y. Ismael, *Iraq and Iran: Roots of Conflict* (1982). On Afghanistan and American policy in the Persian Gulf, see Louis Dupree, *Afghanistan* (1978); Gilles Dorronsoro, *Revolution Unending: Afghanistan, 1979 to the Present* (2005); Henry S. Bradsher, *Afghan Communism and Soviet Intervention* (1999); Steve Coll, *Ghost Wars: The Secret History of the CIA, Afghanistan, and Bin Laden, from the Soviet Invasion to September 10, 2001* (2004); and the relevant sections of Odd Arne Westad, *The Global Cold War* (2007). On Lebanon, see Agnes G. Korbani, *U.S. Intervention in Lebanon, 1958 and 1982* (1991); Itamar Rabinovich, *The War for Lebanon, 1970–1985* (1985); Walid Khalidi, *Conflict and Violence in Lebanon* (1980); Jonathan C. Randall,

Going All the Way: Christian Warlords, Israeli Adventurers, and the War in Lebanon (1983); David C. Gordon, *The Republic of Lebanon: A Nation in Jeopardy* (1983); and Marius Deeb, *The Lebanese Civil War* (1980).

Notes

1. See, for example, Chaim Herzog, *The Arab-Israeli Wars* (1982); and Bernard Reich, *Quest for Peace: United States–Israel Relations and the Arab-Israeli Conflict* (1977).

2. See, for instance, Edward Said, *The Question of Palestine* (1979); and Mohammed K. Shadid, *The United States and the Palestinians* (1981).

3. See, for instance, Nadav Safran, *Israel: The Embattled Ally* (1981).

4. A critique of Kissinger for failing to negotiate a comprehensive peace is Edward F. Sheehan, *The Arabs, Israelis, and Kissinger* (1976).

CHAPTER 15

JIMMY CARTER, RONALD REAGAN, AND THE DEMISE OF DÉTENTE, 1976–1984

From Carter to Reagan

In the wake of the Soviet and Cuban intervention in Angola, President Gerald Ford decided that the word "détente" was a political liability, and he instructed his supporters to avoid its use during the 1976 election campaign. In this way he tried to protect himself against the charges of Democratic nominee Jimmy Carter that Ford and Secretary of State Henry Kissinger were "giving up too much and asking for too little" from the Soviets. According to Carter, Kissinger's détente had given the Soviets "an opportunity to continue the process of world revolution without running the threat of nuclear war." Carter endorsed Senator Henry Jackson's claim that SALT (Strategic Arms Limitation Talks) II should have been "broader and more reciprocal."

Yet Carter called for improved relations with the Soviets at the same time that he criticized Ford and Kissinger for conceding too much to them. Declaring that the United States should free itself from an "inordinate fear of communism," he denounced Nixon, Ford, and Kissinger for excessive and immoral intervention against chimerical Soviet and other Communist threats in the third world. Vietnam had taught Americans that "we cannot and should not try to intervene militarily in the internal affairs of other countries unless our own nation is endangered," Carter said. Kissinger should not have interfered in Chile merely because the Chilean government had turned to the left. Only an actual Soviet presence that directly threatened vital American interests would have justified intervention.

Carter's ambiguous campaign did not necessarily guarantee the end of détente or a fractured foreign policy. He was only following the standard gambit of attacking the incumbent administration from the right and the left at the same time. Unfortunately, after he had won the presidential election, he went on to institutionalize the contradictions in his foreign policy by appointing officials who embodied strongly opposing tendencies. Cyrus Vance, Carter's secretary of state, advocated the restrained realist position. He sought to adapt American policy to Russian military parity and the diffusion of power in the third world. Zbigniew Brzezinski, Carter's national security adviser, was a hard realist. He wanted a tougher line on SALT and more active opposition to potential Soviet influence in the third world. As a Pole, he reveled in his chance to "stick it to the Russians." Secretary of Defense Harold Brown generally sided with Brzezinski's harder line, especially on military issues.

Carter did not worry about this ideological split within his administration because he intended to keep control of foreign policy formulation largely in his own hands. "There may have been Presidents in the past, maybe not too distant past, that let their Secretaries of State make foreign policy," he stated. "I don't." Neither would he share much authority with Congress. Carter was a political outsider, a Georgia governor and state politician who had won the Democratic nomination and the presidential election by running against the corruption of Watergate, the errors of Vietnam, and the general incompetence of federal incumbents. He thought he could manage the government without having to rely on the government bureaucracy or the Washington insiders. He intended to serve personally as the bridge between the liberal and conservative tendencies within his administration, the Democratic Party, and the public at large. Personal competence and honesty would create a consensus to replace the ideological contentions and backroom dealings that had plagued recent national politics and American foreign policy.

Carter was confident that he could master the most complex problems. He spent most of his waking hours studying the intricacies of each issue and then personally shaping a decision from the conflicting recommendations of his advisers. He permitted wide-ranging and often semipublic debate on these issues within his administration in the hope that his own competence and the very openness of the policy process, which contrasted so sharply with the secretive, manipulative techniques of Nixon and Kissinger, would generate popular support for whatever course he chose to take.

Carter also counted heavily on his personal morality to contrast with Nixon and attract support for his policies. He made very public his religious commitment. Under the influence of his evangelist, faith-healing sister, Carter had been "born again." He promised never to lie to the American people. He pledged to jettison Kissinger's undiluted power politics and restore a sense of ethics to American foreign policy. He embarked on an international campaign for human rights and, like Senator Henry Jackson, he tried to use it to unite domestic liberals and conservatives. Carter appealed to the Right by emphasizing Soviet and other Communist violations of human rights. He appealed to the Left by denouncing oppression in reactionary third-world regimes, even though many of these nations were friendly to the United States.

Carter also followed Jackson in trying to bridge the gap between Left and Right on the nuclear arms issue. He called for reductions in the SALT II limits on nuclear armaments, a position attractive to the Left, but molded his reduction proposal to bolster the American side of the balance with the Soviet Union, a constant demand of the Right.

Despite Carter's intelligence and good intentions, he failed miserably to master the contradictions within his foreign policy. The gulf was too wide to be bridged by the flimsy materials Carter had at hand. His advisers sniped at one another with increasing rancor. Carter bogged down in the intricate details he insisted on mastering. One of his speechwriters later said that Carter was not a conceptualizer, but had a mind of "the

President Jimmy Carter *(center)* confers with the representatives of the opposing foreign policy viewpoints within his administration, National Security Adviser Zbigniew Brzezinski *(left)* and Secretary of State Cyrus Vance. *(Courtesy of the Jimmy Carter Presidential Library)*

item-by-item engineering variety." Carter was "the first person I would want to look over the plans for a new submarine," but "practically the last person whose thoughts I would want to hear . . . on 'Relations Between the Soviet Union and the United States.' His mind does not work that way." His inability to delegate responsibility deprived him of the time to formulate a coherent foreign policy. Even if he had developed a consistent policy, he lacked the ability to explain and inspire enthusiasm for it. His flat and often whiny speaking style gave less the appearance of calm competence than of resigned passivity in the face of world events spinning out of control.

Perhaps they would have spun out of control no matter who had been president, for the events of the late 1970s were overwhelming. As described in the previous chapter, the intransigence of the Israelis and Palestinians gave little hope for a comprehensive settlement between them, however able and assertive the American president might have been. The Soviet invasion of Afghanistan also was beyond the influence of the president. It is doubtful that any response to the Iranian revolution could have improved the U.S. position with the Ayatollah Khomeini, and the Iranian hostage situation offered even fewer opportunities for successful American initiatives. The oil shortage and price increases that resulted from the Iranian crisis accelerated inflation in the United States and did immense damage to an already weak American economy. Moscow defied Carter's call for human rights, continued its military buildup, adopted hard positions in arms negotiations, increased its support for what it saw as the gathering socialist revolutions in the third world, and sacrificed very little to help Carter maintain the spirit of détente. Carter's attempt to decouple the Cold War from Latin America and Africa by accommodating some third-world desires and tolerating independent leftist regimes backfired politically. Cuba's Fidel Castro kept his troops in Angola, sent others to Ethiopia, and dumped hardened criminals into the stream of Cuban refugees he finally allowed to leave for the United States.

As a result of these disappointments in world affairs, a profound pessimism and sense of national decline permeated the electorate. America's defeat in Vietnam, the Soviet achievement of nuclear parity, the defiance of the United States by Iran's revolutionaries, and the shock of finding America dependent for vital oil supplies on a hostile Middle East undermined the American self-image. Events at home reinforced that sense of decline. A serious economic recession seemed to defy government action or control. Formerly, government deficit spending based on the principles of economist John Maynard Keynes had seemed to reduce unemployment even if it brought a measure of inflation. But Carter found himself faced with an economy in which inflation and unemployment increased at the same time, undermining confidence that government could do anything to control the economy. The hostage crisis then drove home the sense of government helplessness and reinforced the image of Carter's United States as "the pitiful, helpless giant" that Nixon had worried the nation would become.

Domestic cultural and social trends also contributed to the shattering of America's self-image in the 1970s. The nuclear family, long the bedrock of America's sense of itself, seemed under threat from multiple directions. For many, the traditional family, consisting of a powerful father, loving domestic mother, and ambitious but obedient children, had furnished the backbone of the country, producing the moral character, military virtues, and psychological reserves necessary for world leadership. Unfortunately, it seemed, mass consumption was undermining the moral character of families. Fathers were working so hard to produce the standard of living expected by their families that they were largely absent from their duties to mold and discipline the children. In one psychological experiment, a microphone affixed to babies of middle-class families picked up the father's voice an average of only forty seconds per day. The absence of the father in middle-class families in the 1970s echoed the problems that sociologists saw in lower-class and African-American families, where absent fathers had left single women to both care for their children and earn the family living. A famous study of African-American families by Daniel Moynihan in 1965 had argued that the absence of fathers in those families had created a pathology of low expectations, illegitimacy, crime, and a sense of inferiority in black communities. Now, in the 1970s, those conditions seemed to be gaining ground in middle-class families as well.

Moreover, absent fathers meant more powerful mothers, and many worried that this would lead to the feminization of boys along with the decline of the manly virtues necessary for world leadership. The women's liberation movement accelerated those worries as the push for women's rights to work, hold public office, and even choose to have an abortion threatened the convention that women should stay home and care for the children while men earned the family's living. The supremacy of the nuclear family came under even greater threat with the gay rights movement, which began with the 1969 Stonewall riots against police raids on gay bars in New York City. Thus cultural, economic, and international events and trends conspired to create a miasma of doubt and anxiety in the United States during Carter's administration.[1]

Carter responded to this miasma with a speech on July 15, 1979, which came to be known as his "crisis of confidence" speech. "All the legislation in the world can't fix what's wrong with America," he said. "The erosion of our confidence in the future is threatening to destroy the social and the political fabric of America. . . . In a nation that was proud of hard work, strong families, close-knit communities, and our faith in God, too many of us now tend to worship self-indulgence and consumerism." As a remedy, Carter did not embrace the demands for greater equality represented by the women's and gay rights movements but instead tried to counter America's perceived loss of discipline and self-sacrifice by embarking on a campaign to make the United States self-sufficient in energy. He called for a moral equivalent to war, individual sacrifices to conserve energy and render America less dependent on Middle Eastern oil.

While Carter tried to reinvigorate American policy on the domestic front, he did the same in foreign affairs. He saw the Soviet military intervention in Afghanistan in December 1979 as the final blow to his attempts to maintain a moderate détente policy. He told a television interviewer that it had made "a dramatic change" in his opinions about the ultimate goals of the Soviet Union. He and Brzezinski declared that there was an "arc of crisis" extending eastward from Angola in West Africa through Ethiopia, North and South Yemen (where Soviet sympathizers seemed increasingly powerful), Iran, and finally Afghanistan. Assuming that these crises not only benefited but also to a large extent had been instigated by the Soviets, Carter abandoned détente. He began covert aid for rebels in Afghanistan, declared the Carter Doctrine for the Persian Gulf, postponed further Senate consideration of the SALT II Treaty, embargoed grain shipments to the Soviet Union, boycotted the Moscow Olympics of 1980, and announced an increase in the defense budget he would submit to Congress of 5 percent above inflation. Vance went along with much of this retaliation but still wanted to maintain the framework of détente. That and his previous posture of restraint led to a decline of his influence to the point that he was not even consulted on the final decision to try to rescue the Iran hostages. His resignation as secretary of state left the harder-line Brzezinski as Carter's dominant foreign policy adviser during the last year of Carter's presidency.

While Carter had clearly abandoned détente by the beginning of 1980, he had not gone far enough for Ronald Reagan, whom the Republicans nominated in that year to run against him. "Jimmy Carter said we should give back the Panama Canal because nobody would like us if we didn't," Reagan told his campaign audiences. "Jimmy Carter says we should sign the SALT II treaty because nobody will like us if we don't. . . . Well, I say, isn't it about time we stopped worrying about whether people like us and say, 'We want to be respected again!'" Reagan combined these attacks on Carter's foreign policy with denunciations of the president's economic and social policies. "Our problem isn't a shortage of oil, it's a surplus of government," he declared. He insisted that the way to revive the economy was not through government spending but tax cuts and fewer government regulations. In what his Republican primary opponent, George H.W. Bush, called "voodoo economics," Reagan argued that tax cuts would increase rather than decrease tax revenues because tax cuts would increase the production on which taxes were charged. He also appealed to social conservatives and Christian evangelicals who denounced the government and liberals for tearing apart American culture by encouraging women's and gay rights, abortion, busing students to integrate schools, and denying federal tax deductions to racially segregated private schools. He told a convention of Christian fundamentalist ministers not only that he supported their social and cultural agenda but also that he was "born again" and that the Bible was the answer to the entire world's problems. Above all, Reagan radiated an optimism and good nature that contrasted with Carter's downcast insistence that the United States had to learn to live within its means. Reagan declared that America's best days lay ahead; the United States had not "had its day in the sun."[2] Reagan defeated Carter in the election and set out to regain respect for the United States with both a more conservative domestic policy and a more vigorous anti-Communist foreign policy.

Reagan was not experienced in foreign affairs. Carter jibed during the campaign that if the Republicans were elected and Reagan held a summit meeting with the Soviets, all the participants would have to wear nametags. As president, Reagan often made gaffes in extemporaneous remarks that his aides had to explain away the following day. Nevertheless, Reagan was an extremely effective advocate for his foreign policy when he relied on prepared rather than extemporaneous presentations. He had the benefit of experience as a movie actor, television host for *General Electric Theater*, and popular after-dinner speaker for General Electric at various conventions and meetings. He had been fairly liberal during his film acting days, but became more and more conservative during his time with General Electric. He emerged in the 1960s as a spokesman for the Goldwater wing of the Republican Party, served two terms as governor of California, and ultimately won the Republican presidential nomination on a highly conservative platform in 1980. Symbolically, when he became president he replaced the picture of Harry Truman in the cabinet room with one of Calvin Coolidge.

Reagan and the Republicans seemed to disdain nuclear parity and détente with the Soviets. The Republican platform pledged "to achieve military and technological superiority over the Soviet Union." Reagan told the *Wall Street Journal* in 1980, "The Soviet Union underlies all that is going on. If they weren't engaged in this game of dominoes, there wouldn't be any hot spots in the world." He expressed doubts about agreements with the Soviets because they did not keep their word, but reserved "unto themselves the right to commit any crime, to lie, to cheat, in order to obtain" their objective. He told the National Association of Evangelicals in 1983 that the Soviet Union was the "focus of evil in the modern world." He referred to the Vietnam War as "a noble cause."

Presidential rhetoric must never be taken at face value; Reagan's ideological outbursts did not guarantee an unambiguously hard-line policy. As governor of California, he often had taken strong positions and then at the last minute heeded pragmatic arguments to compromise. Much of Reagan's policy would depend on his advisers, for in contrast to

Jimmy Carter, he delegated a great deal of authority to his subordinates. He insulated himself against too much detail, ignored as best he could the bureaucratic infighting in his administration, and tried to save his energy for the big decisions. At times this insulation had rather bizarre consequences, as when his aides failed to wake him after American planes shot down two Libyan fighters that were flying toward an American aircraft carrier in the Gulf of Sidra.

Reagan's first secretary of state, Alexander Haig, represented the pragmatic side of Reagan's foreign policy. He had been Henry Kissinger's executive assistant on the National Security Council before taking on the same administrative duties for Richard Nixon at the White House during Watergate. While serving in the government, Haig advanced in military rank over the heads of his fellow officers. After Haig's stint in the White House, Gerald Ford appointed him commander of NATO.

Haig brought to the State Department the European orientation and hard-bargaining realpolitik outlook of Kissinger. Like Kissinger, he agreed with conservative ideologues on the need for an active anticommunist policy in the third world, but he was willing to accede to Western European desires for a moderate policy toward the Soviet Union. For instance, Haig wanted careful coordination with NATO on such issues as the neutron bomb and the deployment of intermediate-range missiles in Europe. Caspar Weinberger, Reagan's secretary of defense, who represented the administration's hard-liners, referred to Haig's positions as State Department "squish" and said the United States should not be deterred by such matters as German internal politics. Haig sarcastically characterized the "Weinberger line" as the belief that "anything Marxist is evil and must be destroyed. The Soviet Union is ready to collapse and if we just apply a few more sanctions, it will. On the one hand we can insist that we're too weak to negotiate with them, and on the other hand, we're strong enough to conduct brittle confrontational policies the outcome of which we might not be prepared to face."[3]

Pragmatists clashed with hard-liners over several issues involving Europe and the Soviet Union in Reagan's first years. In 1982 Reagan ordered American companies to cease supplying equipment for the gas pipeline the Soviet Union was building toward Europe. He also asked the European nations to abandon the project. When the Europeans balked, Weinberger and other hard-liners wanted to penalize the European subsidiaries of American companies as well as the American companies themselves if they continued to participate in the pipeline project. Haig objected. After all, the Reagan administration had lifted Carter's embargo on wheat shipments to the Soviet Union. How could the United States penalize Europe for seeking comparable trade relations with Russia? Reagan sided with Weinberger and the hard-liners. His decision greatly strained relations with Europe while failing to stop the pipeline.

Haig also clashed with the hard-liners over the 1982 Argentine invasion of the British-ruled Falkland Islands. Haig tried to deter Argentina by warning that the United States would use its influence on the British side. United Nations (UN) ambassador Jeane J. Kirkpatrick, one of the conservative leaders within the administration, objected and said the United States should remain completely neutral. To back the British would violate the Rio Pact's guarantees against threats from outside the hemisphere and diminish U.S. influence in Latin America. She called Haig and his chief aides "Brits in American clothes." Some members of the administration who agreed with Kirkpatrick evidently contacted the Argentines and softened Haig's warning. Haig raged that this had encouraged the invasion. He said that the nation's Atlantic ties were far more important than those with Latin America, and he especially disliked giving any encouragement to aggressive actions on the part of a fragile and brutal Argentine regime that was on the brink of acquiring nuclear weapons. (As it happened, the British retook the Falklands in a masterful operation, the Argentine dictatorship fell, and in 1984 a new centrist democratic government opened conversations with Great Britain to resolve the Falklands issue.)

The struggle for Reagan's ear became so cacophonous that even he could not ignore it. His ire fell primarily on Haig. Haig was a loner and a political infighter trained in the arena of the Nixon-Kissinger administration. His constant public maneuvers to assert his primacy within the administration alienated even his fellow pragmatists. Haig expected to be Reagan's "vicar" on foreign policy, and he resented any intrusions on his territory or slights to his prerogatives. He bridled, for instance, when he was shunted to a compartment in Air Force One too far from the president and then had to ride in a separate helicopter. "What am I, a pariah?" he asked.

Unfortunately for Haig, Reagan liked team players and hated to choose between his advisers. To smooth out the diplomatic process and end the bickering over foreign policy, Reagan removed one of Haig's chief antagonists, national security adviser Richard Allen, who had been a rather weak and ineffectual member of the ideological right-wing group. But Reagan replaced Allen with another hard-liner, William Clark. Clark was embarrassingly uninformed on foreign affairs. When quizzed by the Senate committee considering his appointment, he could not name the leaders of some of the most important nations with which the United States would have to deal. Nevertheless, Clark was an old Reagan crony and a good organizer. When Haig continued his public complaining, it was Haig whom Reagan asked to resign.

While it seemed at first that the conservative ideologues had won, Reagan appointed another relative moderate, former secretary of the treasury George Shultz, to replace Haig as secretary of state. Shultz was a team player, and the quarrels within the administration over foreign policy became less pronounced or at least less public. In addition, the focus of foreign policy shifted from Europe to the Middle East and Central America after the United States began to deploy new missiles in Europe and the Soviets broke off all arms talks. With regard to those third-world areas, a strange metamorphosis took place in the lineup of pragmatists and hard-liners.

Shultz, the supposed pragmatist, advocated sending the marines to Lebanon and then opposed withdrawing them after their position became intolerable. The military chiefs, and Weinberger as their civilian spokesman, took the more cautious line. Vietnam had made the Joint Chiefs reticent in the use of American troops for political purposes unless there were clear-cut military objectives, sufficient strength available, and wide public support. The Joint Chiefs were much more reluctant than Shultz to commit the marines in Lebanon. Similarly, the Joint Chiefs and Weinberger were the last in the administration to support military intervention in the Caribbean nation of Grenada.

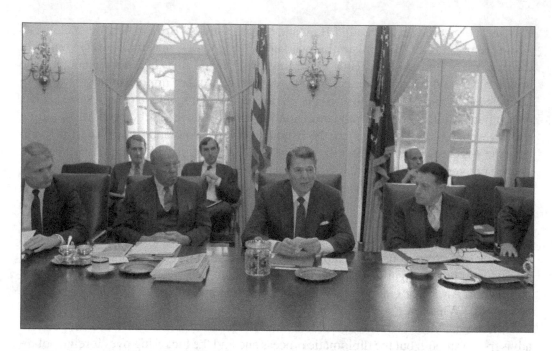

President Ronald Reagan *(center)* confers with the representatives of opposing foreign policy tendencies within his administration: Secretary of State George Shultz *(left)* and Secretary of Defense Caspar Weinberger. *(Courtesy of the Ronald Reagan Presidential Library)*

Until 1985 President Reagan generally took the side of the hard-liners in all these conflicts. He went beyond the advice of the Joint Chiefs in both Lebanon and Grenada. He selected the hardest available options in formulating negotiating positions on nuclear arms talks with the Soviets. He defied the congressional consensus by insisting on major increases in military spending while cutting domestic social programs and incurring huge budget deficits. He rejected Haig's suggestion of a blockade of Cuba and Nicaragua, but he initiated a semisecret Central Intelligence Agency (CIA) war against the Sandinista government of Nicaragua and rejected any serious measures to stop the terrorist campaign of El Salvador's death squads against leftist rebels.

Reagan's hard-line policy culminated in 1985 with his enunciation of what came to be called the Reagan Doctrine. Summarizing the policy he had followed throughout his first term in office, Reagan announced that the United States would defend freedom and democracy against "Soviet supported aggression" on every continent. That required not only confrontation with the Soviet Union itself, but also aid to rebels against pro-Soviet regimes "from Afghanistan to Nicaragua." "Support for freedom fighters is self-defense," he proclaimed. Détente seemed well and truly dead.

The demise of détente can best be traced in the policies of Carter and Reagan toward China, Africa, Latin America, the international economy, and, most important, the Soviet Union and the issue of arms control.

Carter, Reagan, China, and Africa

China

Carter believed the time was ripe to improve American relations with China. The death of Zhou Enlai in early 1976 ushered in a brief revival of radical purges and anti-American rhetoric, but the death of Mao Zedong in September reversed the trend. Protégés of Zhou purged the radical Gang of Four, including Mao's widow, and then deemphasized class strife in favor of more pragmatic approaches to economic growth.

As China moved toward a more pragmatic policy, Carter and Vance proposed that the United States and China open full, normal relations. The sticky problem of Taiwan had prevented this possibility in the Kissinger years, but Carter and Vance offered to circumvent the issue. They would raise the liaison offices of China and the United States to full-fledged embassies while reducing the United States and Taiwan embassies to liaison offices. Vance also urged China to state publicly that it would not use force to settle the Taiwan problem. To Carter's dismay, both China and Taiwan rejected the proposal, and since Carter and Vance had reopened the Taiwan issue, China demanded that the United States sever relations with Taiwan completely.

As part of Carter's later swing toward a harder anti-Soviet foreign policy, Brzezinski indicated during a trip to China in 1978 that even if the United States could not abandon Taiwan as the price of normalized relations with China, his government might pay in other coin. The United States would fall in with China's desire for a stronger policy against the Soviet Union. At a banquet in Beijing, Brzezinski publicly denounced Soviet "hegemony" and won from the Chinese the appellation "bear tamer." The Carter administration also arranged to help China with technology that the United States had denied to the Soviet Union.

On January 1, 1979, the United States and China opened full, normal diplomatic relations. Carter announced that the United States would break its ties with Taiwan, withdraw from the U.S.-Taiwan defense treaty, and remove all American troops from the island. Carter relegated relations with Taiwan to private trade offices. China in turn indicated that it would not try to take Taiwan by force, although it would give no formal commitment. Conservatives protested at the cavalier treatment of America's Taiwanese ally, but Carter pushed ahead to give China increased military support and most-favored-nation trade status.

Ronald Reagan came to the presidency pledged to restore official ties to Taiwan. Yet he and many in his administration saw China as a valuable asset in their tough policy toward the Soviet Union. Reagan consequently refused to raise the status of the informal trade offices that handled U.S.-Taiwan relations. But he did sell advanced planes and arms to Taiwan, which raised a bitter protest from China. Washington and Beijing barely papered over the dispute. The United States agreed to limit arms sales to Taiwan; China reasserted its fundamental policy to seek peaceful resolution of the Taiwan issue. Beijing declared, however, that it would not forswear the use of force permanently, and it opened a series of talks with the Soviets aimed at reducing tensions. Not much seemed to come of these discussions, but Reagan was on notice that China might play a Soviet card as readily as the United States was playing the China card.

Africa

Since Carter expected to improve relations with the Soviet Union in the early years of his administration, he thought he could deemphasize great power competition in third-world areas such as Africa. He treated the Soviet-supported Cuban troops in Angola as a local affair and called for restraint in the American response. He would substitute a concern for human rights, especially the rights of blacks in white-dominated nations, for fear of communism. He appointed Andrew Young, a black Georgia congressman and former aide to Martin Luther King, as ambassador to the United Nations to enlist the United States more firmly on the side of emerging colonial nations. Young and Carter vigorously promoted negotiations to end the white minority rule of Ian Smith's government in Rhodesia. They also induced Congress to repeal the Byrd Amendment, which had allowed the United States to import chromium from Rhodesia in defiance of a UN boycott. Vice President Walter Mondale even had the temerity to suggest to whites in rigidly segregated South Africa that they adopt the "one man, one vote" principle. Meanwhile, Young opened contact with the Marxist leadership of Angola and Mozambique.

Carter's efforts to revise American policy in Africa bore little fruit. South Africa resented the human rights agitation and stalled U.S. initiatives that sought independence for Namibia. Ian Smith of Rhodesia also sidetracked the American-sponsored negotiations on his regime. (Ultimately, Great Britain, the nation from which Rhodesia had declared its independence, did negotiate a settlement that brought black majority rule to the new nation of Zimbabwe.) African states, on the other hand, criticized Carter for not going far enough to reduce American economic connections with South Africa and Rhodesia.

Meanwhile, Soviet intervention into Ethiopia's war with Somalia made it more difficult for Carter to accommodate leftist third-world regimes and avoid injecting Cold War issues into Africa. When the leftist military leader Mengistu Haile Mariam overthrew the American-backed regime of Emperor Haile Selassie in 1977 and expelled his American advisers, the Soviet Union and especially Cuba sent economic, political, and military support. But this alienated Ethiopia's rival Somalia, whose brutal dictator, Siad Barre, also enjoyed Soviet and Cuban backing and who coveted the Ogaden desert area on the Somalian-Ethiopian border. When the Soviets discouraged Siad from his incursions into Ethiopia, he began sounding out the United States for help. The Carter administration made some ambiguous statements about supplying defensive arms, which Siad apparently took as a green light to launch a serious and temporarily successful invasion of the Ogaden desert. The Soviet Union abruptly cut off its aid to Somalia and transported Cuban troops, along with Soviet advisers and tons of equipment, to Ethiopia to help defeat the Somali invasion. Carter refused to supply arms to Somalia because Siad's action was not defensive, but he warned the Soviets that the Cuban presence in Ethiopia and Angola was testing the limits of his tolerance. He then abandoned his attempts to restrict arms sales to Africa and sent weapons to Ethiopia's nervous neighbors, Chad,

Sudan, and Kenya. He also increased aid to Zaire and Morocco for their battles against leftist rebels.

Ronald Reagan accelerated these trends. He criticized Carter's human rights policy and let South Africa know that he regarded its internal racial affairs as its own business. When negotiations over the independence of Namibia broke down, he had the United States join Britain and France in the UN Security Council to veto mandatory economic sanctions against South Africa. He also cut by half American aid to the leftist regime in Zimbabwe. He emphasized Africa as an arena of competition with the Soviet Union and made clear that he would favor any nation that lined up with the United States, regardless of its domestic policies. He and his ambassador to the United Nations, Jeane Kirkpatrick, had no patience with the African and other third-world leftist nations that portrayed the United States as an imperialist obstacle to world justice. Reagan, like the Ford administration before him, punished countries for hostile UN votes by reducing U.S. aid. He also risked American involvement in the war between Ethiopia and Somalia by securing a base for the rapid deployment force at the Somali port of Berbera.

Carter, Reagan, and Latin America

President Carter tried to accommodate some of the needs of Latin America and to use his human rights campaign to encourage gradual reform and centrist regimes in the Western Hemisphere. He believed that improving social and economic conditions in the region was the best way to eliminate opportunities for the Soviet Union and Cuba to extend their influence. Nevertheless, his support for centrist alternatives to communism and revolution was no more successful than John Kennedy's had been. As in Kennedy's day, democratic moderates were too few and the middle classes too weak in Latin America to offer a viable centrist alternative. Instead, reactionary regimes produced harsh revolutionaries, and between them they squeezed most moderates out of power or influence. This left the United States with the choice between reactionaries and revolutionaries, both of which espoused values and tactics difficult for Americans to accept.

The Panama Canal Treaties

Carter's most significant and successful act of accommodation toward Latin America was his negotiation of the Panama Canal treaties. Panamanians had long resented U.S. control of the canal and the arrogant exclusiveness with which the United States ran the surrounding Canal Zone. Serious riots in the Canal Zone had driven Lyndon Johnson to begin negotiations with Panama on the status of the canal, and these talks had continued through the Nixon and Ford years. Carter pledged faster progress and personally intervened when the talks bogged down in 1977. On September 7, 1977, Carter and Panama's General Omar Torrijos signed the two Panama Canal treaties. The first treaty gave Panama immediate jurisdiction over the Canal Zone, placed operation of the canal itself in the hands of a new agency composed of five U.S. citizens and four Panamanians, and assigned Panama a greater percentage of the canal's revenues. The United States would manage and defend the canal under this new agency until the end of the century, and it would continue to control certain military bases and other installations necessary to this task. The second treaty provided that at the end of the century Panama would take over both management and control of the canal.

Despite some vocal opposition in Panama to any continuance of the U.S. presence, 66 percent of the Panamanians who voted in a national referendum approved the treaties. The fight over the treaties was much more difficult in the United States. Opponents, including Ronald Reagan, called the treaties a sellout and warned that they would endanger American security. Senator S.I. Hayakawa of California only half facetiously complained that the canal was ours since we had stolen it fair and square. Proponents of the treaties responded that the canal would be far less secure if Panamanian resentment inspired a campaign of sabotage than if the canal reverted to Panama with U.S. guarantees of its neutrality. Besides, they pointed out, the canal had declined in both strategic and economic importance. Less than 10 percent of U.S. trade flowed through the canal. It was too small to permit the passage of large modern ships such as aircraft carriers, supertankers, and some container ships.

Staking his prestige on the treaties, Carter spared no effort to secure their ratification. When opposition threatened to overwhelm them, he negotiated with Panama a new memorandum of understanding spelling out more definitively the right of the United States to intervene to defend against any threats to peaceful transit through the waterway in time of crisis. Finally, in the spring of 1978, the Senate consented to the treaties with only one vote to spare. In the process, the Senate added an amendment spelling out U.S. rights of intervention within Panama in almost humiliating detail. Nonetheless, the Panama treaties were a considerable triumph for Carter's accommodationist policy.

Cuba

Carter was not so successful in his attempt to accommodate Cuba. At the outset of his administration, he resumed the quiet talks Gerald Ford had broken off after the dispatch of Cuban troops to Angola. Carter suggested that U.S.-Cuban relations would improve if Castro withdrew his troops from Angola and improved human rights conditions in Cuba. Castro responded angrily that it was much more important for the United States to lift its boycott of the island and get out of Guantánamo. From this inauspicious beginning, relations gradually improved. The United States removed travel restrictions to Cuba and ended the blacklist of foreign ships trading with Castro. Both nations expended the interest sections (as opposed to formal embassies) that represented them in the other's capital. Then, in 1978, Castro offered to release 1,500 people for emigration to the United States. He promised further to release 3,600 political prisoners and 7,000 former political prisoners if the United States would accept them as immigrants.

While negotiations continued on this question, Carter suddenly protested the presence of some 2,500 Soviet combat troops in Cuba. Those troops had been there since the Cuban missile crisis and the U.S. government had known it, but the fact that those troops were organized as a combat brigade rather than independent military advisers had been forgotten and lost within the bureaucracy. Then, in 1979, as Carter was growing increasingly sensitive to Soviet and Cuban military activities in the third world, Brzezinski ordered U.S. intelligence agencies to take another look at Soviet activities in Cuba. The agencies "discovered" that the Soviet advisers were organized as a combat brigade, and, without checking the history of the issue in State Department, CIA, or Pentagon files, Carter protested this supposedly new sign of Soviet aggression. Carter's protest opened a Pandora's box. Frank Church, a liberal senator up for reelection in conservative Idaho, abruptly postponed his Foreign Relations Committee's consideration of the SALT II agreement until the Soviet troops were withdrawn. Relations between Cuba and the United States soured.

Then, in April 1980, Cubans who had been heartened by Castro's relenting on emigration policy crowded into the Peruvian embassy because they heard that Cuba and Peru were working out an emigration agreement. Castro withdrew his guards from the Peruvian embassy during the imbroglio, and the number of refugees soared to 10,000. An embarrassed Castro promised that he would permit them to leave Cuba, and Carter offered an open arms policy to those who wished to come to the United States. In the next few months a makeshift flotilla of private boats and rafts, many from Florida, ferried 120,000 Cubans to the United States. Most were political refugees, but Castro vengefully emptied his prisons of hardened criminals and dumped them into the stream of emigrants.

The flow of Cubans overwhelmed the U.S. border patrol, and the Immigration Service confined many of the refugees to prison camps while it tried rather unsuccessfully to screen them. The innocents naturally chafed at their inhospitable welcome to the "land of the free." Carter reaped a bitter political harvest from the refugee fiasco, and U.S.-Cuban relations returned to their previous hostile level.

Reform in Latin America

Carter's attempt to encourage gradual reform in Latin America through the promotion of human rights had little more success than his policy toward Cuba. In the last year of the Ford administration, Congress had responded to the lessons of Vietnam by passing the Foreign Military Assistance Act of 1976. This act denied credits for military sales to nations committing gross violations of human rights unless the president believed extraordinary circumstances warranted an exception. It also instructed the State Department to report regularly on the status of human rights in nations receiving military aid.

Ford opposed this measure, but Carter welcomed and quickly made use of it. He reduced aid to Argentina, Uruguay, and Brazil and withheld weapons sales to other Latin American regimes. Many nations, including Argentina, Uruguay, and Guatemala, refused aid to which human rights conditions were attached. Brazil canceled its twenty-five-year-old military aid treaty with United States. Some democratic countries like Venezuela praised the president's initiative, but others on both the left and right opposed or abstained when called upon to endorse the concept in the Organization of American States (OAS) or the UN. They saw it as another potential opening for U.S. intervention.

Nicaragua and El Salvador

One of the nations Carter tried to influence on human rights was Nicaragua, long ruled by the dictatorial and corrupt Somoza family. Anastasio Somoza Garcia through his control of the National Guard, had taken charge of Nicaragua four years after the U.S. Marines had withdrawn in 1932. In 1934 he engineered the assassination of the popular guerrilla leader who had led the fight against the American marines, Augusto César Sandino. Afterward, he consolidated his rule by permitting only a modicum of ineffectual opposition. By 1944, through plunder and extortion, Somoza owned fifty-one cattle ranches and forty-six coffee plantations. He earned $400,000 a year from U.S. companies he exempted from taxation. When he was assassinated in 1956, his son Luís Somoza Debayle succeeded him, and in 1963 he in turn was succeeded by his brother, Anastasio Somoza Debayle. By 1979 the Somoza family's fortune had grown to $150 million, not including assets abroad. Anastasio Somoza Debayle had even raked off much of the charity aid that had flooded into Nicaragua after an earthquake devastated the capital city of Managua in 1972.

Anastasio Somoza Debayle was not so nimble a ruler as his father or brother. Even the middle classes balked at his blatant plundering of the earthquake charity after 1972. Somoza made no attempt to divide the bourgeois from the peasant opposition, but brutally suppressed them both. Declaring a state of emergency, he used his 7,500-member National Guard to enforce martial law.

Nicaragua was of no particular economic interest to the United States or its major corporations. President Carter worried only that revolution in Nicaragua might open the way for Soviet or Cuban influence. He sought to forestall this by encouraging moderate reform. In 1977 he demanded that Somoza lift his state of emergency. When Somoza complied, opposition immediately broke out again. In 1978, Petro Joaquin Chamorro, a liberal editor who led Nicaragua's moderates, was assassinated, inspiring increased strikes and riots. Somoza finally tried to compromise with the moderates, but it was too late. The moderates had already formed a broad but uneasy national front with the guerrilla forces that had taken on the name of the heroic Sandino. The Sandinistas then drew international attention in August 1978 when they took over the national palace in Managua and held 500 hostages. They ultimately exchanged their hostages for political prisoners, $5 million, and refuge in Panama.

Such radical actions split the opposition front, and the United States, Guatemala, and the Dominican Republic tried to mediate the civil war by getting Somoza to abandon Nicaragua and leave behind a moderate successor regime. A massive uprising in January 1979 brought Somoza to reject this mediation attempt. Once again the opposition united, and Carter cut off aid to Nicaragua.

Carter, however, was hesitant and inconsistent in his attempt to secure a moderate regime to replace Somoza and forestall a radical revolution. Even while the United States cut aid to Nicaragua, the U.S. representative to the International Monetary Fund voted to loan Somoza $65 million. Then, in June 1979, Secretary of State Cyrus Vance proposed that the OAS send a peacekeeping force to Nicaragua. Latin American regimes on both the right and left rejected the call. The OAS instead warned against any outside intervention and demanded that Somoza resign. The United States reluctantly agreed, and the U.S. ambassador in Managua told Somoza flatly he should go. Somoza fled on July 17, 1979; the government he left behind collapsed in twenty-four hours. The revolution had cost the lives of 50,000 people. The Somoza loyalists added to this misery by destroying many of Nicaragua's factories as they fled.

The Sandinistas immediately nationalized all of Somoza's industries, 25 percent of the nation's factories. The Sandinistas later nationalized many other factories, banks, and mines, along with about 50 percent of the agricultural land. They also developed an internal security organization similar to Cuba's. A separate police and security force replaced the National Guard, while local Sandinista defense committees formed neighborhood political units to organize the countryside and expose counterrevolutionaries. The more militant Sandinista ex-guerrillas confined the moderate members of their front to token roles. They launched a campaign of education, characterized by sloganeering and political "reeducation" for the peasants, many of whom had never seen a school or a teacher under the Somoza regime. The Sandinistas passed a law imposing a two-year prison sentence on those whose declarations harmed the "people's interest," and they repeatedly closed down the chief opposition paper, *La Prensa*. They also persecuted the Miskito Indians, many of whom opposed the Sandinistas' integrationist programs. Finally, they readily accepted aid from the Soviet Union and several thousand advisers from Cuba.

On the other hand, the Sandinistas permitted some freedom for opposition parties, newspapers, and unions. They maintained a mixed economy rather than a rigidly centralized one. They did not prohibit movement within the country or emigration from it, and they did not launch a terror campaign.

Carter and his leading aides approached the Sandinistas with considerable wariness. The United States recognized the Sandinista regime quickly, but also it began considering military aid to Nicaragua's neighbors, Guatemala and El Salvador. After considerable debate and expressed hostility toward the leftist regime, Carter finally decided to try to accommodate the Sandinistas and in late 1979 recommended an emergency aid program of $75 million. Congress was even more doubtful than Carter, but after delaying passage for several months, it appropriated the money. The United States sent some $60 million of this appropriation to Nicaragua until Carter suspended payments at the end of his administration because he disliked Sandinista support for the increasing guerrilla warfare in neighboring El Salvador.

Carter was very anxious that El Salvador not become another Nicaragua. As in Nicaragua, El Salvador's elite had confiscated peasant communal lands to establish coffee plantations in the 1870s. In the 1880s it built an army to force the peasants to work on the coffee plantations for low wages. The poor lands left in the hands of the peasants were inadequate to feed them, so food had to be imported. The Depression of the 1930s and rapid population growth in El Salvador squeezed the nation's resources and brought revolution in 1932, led by the founder of El Salvador's Communist Party, Augustén Farabundo Martí. The army, directed by the minister of war Maximiliano Hernández Martínez, suppressed the revolt. In the process it executed Martí and killed between 10,000 and 30,000 people. (Martínez was a theosophist who believed in reincarnation and therefore thought it was worse to kill an ant than a person, because people returned to life.) For the next fifty years, the army was the senior partner in a government coalition with the economic oligarchy. The oligarchy deferred to the army because the military outlawed unions and enforced the vagrancy laws that supplied the plantation owners with cheap labor.

The army, however, was not always completely unified. Some factions occasionally reached out toward moderate reformists, although they always drew back rather quickly. Other army leaders encouraged the operation of security forces and death squads to deal out summary justice to dissidents. By 1944, after a coup and a countercoup, these security forces were operating beyond the control of the government.

In the 1960s Kennedy's Alliance for Progress and the rise of the opposition Christian Democratic party in El Salvador gave some hope for moderate reform. But in the 1972 Salvadoran elections, the army rigged the vote to defeat the Christian Democratic nominee for president, San Salvador mayor José Napoléon Duarte, and then imprisoned, tortured, and exiled him. Opposition agitation continued, however, when rural unemployment reached 57 percent the following year. Catholic clergy supporting a "theology of liberation" encouraged resistance. El Salvador's president tried to restore calm by offering a timid land reform program in 1975, but frantic opposition from the oligarchy and army thwarted even that. General Carlos Humberto Romero took over the government and ended all reformist pretenses.

In 1977 as hopes for moderate reform faded, the radical Left, organized as the Farabundo Martí Front for National Liberation (FMLN) increased its guerrilla activities. The right wing retaliated with death squads, often composed of army and security forces, which murdered rebels, suspected sympathizers, and even opposition priests. By 1979 strikes and violence racked the country. In March 1979 electrical workers cut power to the entire nation for nearly twenty-four hours. In May police fired on the occupiers of San Salvador's cathedral, killing twenty-three and wounding thirty-seven in front of the world's television cameras.

As in Nicaragua, the United States had few investments in El Salvador, but Carter did not want to see another Central American nation become a hostile Marxist outpost. He pressed the government for reform. Gerald Ford already had suspended aid when El Salvador's chief of staff was convicted in New York of selling machine guns to the Mafia. Carter increased the pressure in 1977 by cutting the amount of aid El Salvador would get the following fiscal year if the suspension were lifted. He said the aid would not be increased unless El Salvador improved human rights inside its borders. El Salvador's government then announced it would reject any aid tied to such conditions.

When the Somoza government of Nicaragua fell to the Sandinistas in 1979, Carter stepped up his pressure for moderate reform in El Salvador. In October a group of progressive young army officers responded by staging a bloodless coup. They invited three civilians to join two military men in a junta pledged to disband the largest of the death squads, investigate the rampant killings and disappearances, and establish a minimum wage for agricultural workers. The civilians who accepted, however, soon found that the army had retained its power and would thwart all attempts at reform. The radical Left refused any cooperation with the new government so long as it left the army intact. The civilians soon resigned. One of them, Guillermo Ungo, who had been the vice presidential candidate on the Christian Democratic ticket of 1972 with Duarte, ultimately joined the guerrillas.

Still Carter did not give up. His aides called the Salvadoran civilians who left the government "quitters" and backed the few Christian Democrats who were willing to negotiate a new government with the military. These new civilian members of the junta remained powerless to control the army or the death squads. In January 1980, army sharpshooters fired from rooftops into a demonstration of 80,000 people, killing twenty. Archbishop Oscar Romero of San Salvador, formerly known as a conservative, condemned the government and the cooperation of the Christian Democrats with it. In desperation Carter appointed an outspoken liberal, Robert White, as ambassador to El Salvador. White, who as U.S. minister to Paraguay had openly criticized that nation for human rights violations, set out to encourage reform but also to prevent revolution. As he said privately on his departure for El Salvador, "Washington wants something to the right of Nicaragua. My job is to make that happen."

The government of Christian Democrats and military representatives responded by announcing a sweeping land reform program. It would confiscate the coffee haciendas, compensate the owners in cash and bonds, and turn the lands over to peasant cooperatives. Later, a "land to the tiller" program would give sharecroppers the plots of land they worked. The United States government and the AFL-CIO sent agricultural and labor advisers to aid the program. In addition, the United States promised to help reform the army for a "clean counterinsurgency" program against the radical guerrillas. Carter requested $5.7 million for "nonlethal" military aid to El Salvador in the form of jeeps, trucks, and communications equipment.

Despite these efforts at reform, Carter's hopes for a centrist solution in El Salvador collapsed. The reformers had no real power, and the land reform program remained mostly paper promises. On March 24, 1980, a death squad assassinated Archbishop Romero before the altar of his cathedral. One of the right-wing leaders, Roberto D'Aubuisson, was subsequently arrested in a coup attempt and found to have papers that implicated him in the assassination plot. The Christian Democrats in the government threatened to resign unless D'Aubuisson was punished. The army refused and freed him. Conservative military leaders stripped moderate officers of their power within the army and government, while the right wing accelerated its war on suspected rebels. A death squad killed six leftist leaders meeting in a San Salvador school in November 1980. On December 2 Salvadoran soldiers killed three nuns and a lay missionary, all of them Americans. In January 1981 assassins walked into the Hilton Hotel coffee shop in San Salvador and gunned down a Salvadoran administrator and two American labor advisers from the land reform program.

In the midst of all this violence, the army and the Christian Democrats formed a new government. They made Duarte the first civilian president El Salvador had known in years. His vice president and the real power behind the government, however, was Colonel Jaime Gutiérrez, the army commander in chief. Despite this indication that there was no viable center in El Salvador, the Carter administration continued to support the Salvadoran junta and to hold out hopes for reform. A U.S. investigating team concluded that only low-level figures were involved in the killing of the American nuns. When guerrillas increased their activities in late 1980 in hopes of winning the war before Ronald Reagan took over the American government, Carter renewed military aid to the regime, sent twenty military instructors, and accused the rebels of receiving arms and support from abroad.

Ronald Reagan greatly accelerated Carter's move toward a military solution in Central America, and he did so with far fewer gestures toward centrist reform and human rights. During his campaign he warned that "in El Salvador, Marxist totalitarian revolutionaries, supported by Havana and Moscow, are preventing the construction of a democratic government." Why, he asked, should the United States let "Grenada, Nicaragua, El Salvador, all become additional 'Cubas,' new outposts for Soviet combat brigades? . . . These humiliations and symbols of weakness add up." Secretary of State Alexander Haig announced that the administration considered what was happening in El Salvador as "part of the global Communist campaign coordinated by Havana and Moscow to support the Marxist insurgency." The State Department produced a white paper in a rather flimsy attempt to demonstrate that large amounts of arms supplied by the Soviet Union and Cuba were flowing through Nicaragua to the rebels in El Salvador. The Soviets did increase aid to the El Salvadoran rebels through Nicaragua briefly in 1981 preparatory to what the FMLN announced would be its "final offensive" of that year. But when that offensive failed, Soviet and Cuban military aid dwindled once again to a trickle.

Reagan argued that the strategic situation in Latin America was too serious to be hampered by excessive concerns for human rights. In February 1981 he stated that the discovery and punishment of the murderers of the American nuns were no longer conditions for aid to El Salvador. In July he ordered the United States representatives to the World Bank to support loans to Chile, Argentina, Paraguay, and Uruguay, all of which the Carter administration had boycotted because of human rights violations. Congress tried to stop his jettisoning of human rights considerations by attaching an amendment to the foreign aid bill that required the president to certify progress on democracy and human rights before military aid could be disbursed to suspect regimes. Reagan simply circumvented the requirement. He blithely certified progress by such brutal governments as those of Chile and El Salvador. He reclassified helicopter parts intended for Guatemala as nonmilitary. In November 1983 he pocket-vetoed a congressional extension of the certification requirement.

Reagan increased the amount of aid to Latin America at the same time that he reduced the human rights conditions attached to it. In early 1982 he proposed a Caribbean Basin initiative. The United States would join the wealthy nations of the hemisphere, such as Canada, Mexico, and Venezuela, in offering Central America and the Caribbean trade preferences, incentives for private investment, help in overcoming balance of payments deficits, and direct military and economic aid. The Caribbean Basin initiative immediately ran into trouble. Many Latin American nations complained that Reagan's emphasis on private investment ignored the major needs of their countries—the roads, electrical power, and water systems that only governments could provide. Canada, Mexico, and Venezuela were reluctant to contribute to an economic program so blatantly directed toward support of the fragile military dictatorships in the region. Congress balked at the lack of concern for human rights. Congress also was reluctant to increase Latin American aid while the Reagan administration was drastically cutting domestic social programs. Congressional opposition to Reagan's policies for Latin America, however, remained timid and erratic. Democrats did not want to be blamed for losing Latin America to the Communists. Aid to Honduras tripled to $31 million in 1982. Aid to El Salvador went from $140 million in 1981 to $200 million in 1982.

Meanwhile, in March 1982, Reagan authorized the CIA to organize and support anti-Sandinista guerrilla activities by rebels known as contras, operating out of Honduras. Many contra leaders were former members of Somoza's hated National Guard. As word of this supposedly secret CIA operation leaked out, the Reagan administration assured Congress and the press that his intention was only to stop arms from flowing to the rebels in El Salvador and perhaps to push the Sandinista government toward greater pluralism and democracy. Privately, however, many administration officials admitted that they would not object to the overturning of the Sandinista government. The contras were supposed to hit only military targets, but neutral witnesses observed burned farms and many dead animals and civilians in the region of contra activities. The CIA even helped the contras lay mines in Nicaragua's main harbors and published a manual for the contras outlining guerrilla tactics, including assassination. The contras' brutal tactics seemed merely to strengthen sympathies for the Sandinista regime within Nicaragua.

The Sandinistas restrained themselves from "hot pursuit" of the contras into Honduras because they did not want to provide an occasion for all-out war with Honduras and the United States. The Sandinistas had good reason to fear such a war. The United States carried on large-scale joint training maneuvers in Honduras, built "temporary bases" to house the participants in these maneuvers, and stationed naval task forces off the coast of Nicaragua. U.S. military aid also strengthened the Honduran army against its fragile civilian government.

In April 1982 Reagan's National Security Council issued a secret memo, later leaked to the press, which outlined other aspects of the administration's policy toward Central America. The memo declared it a "vital interest" of the United States to prevent the emergence of Latin American states on the Cuban model, "vital interest" being a diplomatic code phrase usually meaning an interest for which a nation will go to war. Contrary to the public statements of the administration, the memo said the United States would send aid to Guatemala without human rights conditions. In another contradiction to administration statements, the memo stated that the United States would work to isolate Mexico and sidetrack its attempts to mediate a negotiated settlement in Nicaragua and El Salvador.

Reagan's policy in El Salvador soon ran into serious trouble. The rebels boycotted the elections of 1982, and although Duarte and his Christian Democrats won a plurality of votes, the right-wing parties combined in the legislature and used their consequent majority to deny Duarte and his followers a single office in the government. Only Reagan's warnings prevented the right-wingers from making D'Aubuisson president. At the end of the year, 30,000 Salvadorans were dead in the revolutionary war and 600,000 were refugees, 13 percent of the Salvadoran population.

Many Democrats and liberal Republicans urged that Reagan abandon his efforts for a military solution and give more support to the efforts of the Contadora group—Mexico, Venezuela, Panama, and Colombia—to mediate a negotiated settlement in all of Central America. (The Contadora group took its name from a Panamanian island where it first met.) In April, the House appropriations subcommittee cut in half Reagan's request for $60 million in emergency aid to El Salvador and was ready to block the additional $136 million he wanted for the following fiscal year.

Reagan embarked on a major effort to win public and congressional support for his program. In a dramatic televised address to a joint session of Congress, he asked for $600 million in aid to Latin America for 1984. He warned that "the national security of all the Americas is at stake in Central America. If we cannot defend ourselves there, we cannot expect to prevail elsewhere. Our credibility would collapse, our alliances would crumble, and the safety of our homeland would be put at jeopardy." When Congress still balked, Reagan appointed a bipartisan commission on Latin America and asked Henry Kissinger to chair it. Kissinger might be too soft for Reagan on Soviet and European affairs, but he could be expected to support him on Latin America.

The Kissinger report endorsed Reagan's Caribbean Basin initiative and requested $8 billion in aid for Latin America over five years. Although two members of the commission opposed aid to the contras in Nicaragua, the remainder supported continued pressure on the Sandinistas. Defying Reagan, the majority recommended that aid be tied to progress on human rights in El Salvador and the rest of Central America, but Kissinger personally warned that the linkage should not be carried to the length that it would allow the success of Marxist revolutionaries. Marxists would kill more people than the government they replaced in El Salvador, Kissinger warned. The commission itself stated: "Regimes created by the victory of Marxist-Leninist revolution become totalitarian. That is their purpose, their nature, their doctrine and their record." Reagan endorsed the report with Kissinger's caveat on human rights. He announced in the classical Kissinger language of the report that there might be an argument for doing nothing for El Salvador or for doing a great deal more, but there was no logical argument for doing too little. Reagan said he chose to do enough.

A ray of hope emerged in El Salvador when Duarte, with help from American poll watchers and organizers, won control of the Salvadoran legislature in the elections of 1984. Surprisingly, the military extended some cooperation to his policy of moderation. Salvadoran courts convicted several enlisted soldiers of the murder of the American nuns, and Duarte pledged to investigate other instances of army misconduct. He actually removed some of the worst offenders, but did not have the strength to bring them to trial. Murders by death squads fell to 185 in the first nine months of 1984 compared to more than 1,000 in the same period of 1983. Most hopeful of all, Duarte met the rebel leadership and began to seek a negotiated settlement. In the spring elections of 1985, Duarte's Christian Democrats defeated the right-wing parties and won an absolute majority in the legislature.

Congress showed renewed willingness to aid Duarte and El Salvador, but it turned down Reagan's repeated requests for military aid to the contras. Instead, it passed the Boland amendment, which prohibited lethal aid to the contras and specifically prohibited the CIA from dispensing any of the nonlethal aid that was permitted. To circumvent the congressional prohibition, CIA director William Casey and national security adviser John Poindexter arranged to dispense military aid to the contras through one of Poindexter's subordinates, Lieutenant Colonel Oliver North. The money for the operation would come from "donations" by conservative American citizens and by foreign heads of state dependent on U.S. goodwill, such as the sultan of Brunei and the king of Saudi Arabia. Ultimately, North and his superiors derived additional monies for the contras from the profits on the secret sale of arms to Iran after laundering it through the shady Bank of Credit and Commerce International (BCCI). When these operations came to light, they came very close to destroying the Reagan administration.

Meanwhile, Reagan took another chance to circumvent the frustrations of congressional interference and achieve a military solution to radical activities in the Caribbean. In 1979 a leftist coup in Grenada led by Maurice Bishop and his New Jewel movement overthrew the corrupt, repressive anti-Communist Eric Gairy, who had been prime minister since Grenada had secured its independence from Great Britain in 1974. Bishop received arms and advisers from Cuba, started work on a 10,000-foot airstrip, and signed a treaty giving the Soviets permission to land their long-range reconnaissance planes when the airport was finished. Carter treated Bishop with hostility, but kept hands off. Reagan, on the other hand, warned that Grenada was becoming a Cuban and Soviet outpost that endangered hemispheric security. Several other small Caribbean island nations agreed and urged the United States to take action.

The opportunity arrived when the deputy prime minister, Bernard Coard, ousted Bishop and placed him under arrest for allegedly softening toward the United States. When a mob came to free Bishop, the army fired into it and then summarily executed Bishop and several other officials who sympathized with him.

On the grounds that the rebellion endangered the lives of the 1,000 American students at St. George's Medical School on Grenada, Reagan sent in U.S. troops. A lightning attack ran into more resistance than expected from the Cubans near the airport runway, but ultimately some 6,000 American troops secured the island. American forces suffered eighteen dead and sixty-seven wounded. The U.S. government did not reveal the number of Cuban, Grenadan, and civilian casualties.

Reagan asserted that captured documents and weapons, along with the number and training of the supposed Cuban construction workers at the airport, showed that indeed Cuba and the Soviet Union had been planning to make Grenada a major military base. Although the evidence the administration produced was far from conclusive, the American public seemed to accept the invasion as a proper and successful use of American military power, a reassertion of American capabilities two days after suicide bomb blasts in Beirut had killed nearly 300 marines. Many European and Latin American leaders protested, however, and critics worried that the Reagan administration might decide that Grenada proved the viability of the military approach to the rest of Central America.

Carter, Reagan, and the International Economy

Jimmy Carter inherited an extraordinarily difficult economic situation when he took office in 1976. Lyndon Johnson had set off an inflationary spiral by his attempt to fight the

Vietnam War and fund his Great Society at the same time without raising taxes. Nixon had continued Johnson's guns-and-butter policy until deficit spending, oil price increases, and the imbalance between American imports and exports pushed him to impose the "second Nixon shock." He took the United States off the gold standard, imposed price and wage controls, and assessed a 10 percent surcharge on imports. The value of the U.S. dollar floated slowly downward after that, although the Smithsonian monetary agreement of 1971 and the Rambouillet economic summit meeting of 1975 managed to stabilize the situation temporarily and keep the decline within bounds.

Pressures on the American economy and the value of the dollar increased during Carter's administration. America's trading partners in the developed world—Europe and Japan—complained bitterly that the decline of the dollar's value forced them to pay higher prices for oil, since petroleum purchases from the Organization of Petroleum Exporting Countries (OPEC) had to be made in dollars. They also grumbled that the lower value of the dollar gave the United States an unfair edge in selling its exports abroad. They insisted that the United States should reduce its imports of oil. They wanted Carter to remove the subsidies that reduced oil prices to American consumers, letting domestic prices rise to the world level. That would lessen America's imbalance of trade, revive the value of the dollar, and reduce the demand for and therefore the world price of oil.

Carter at first treated the situation with considerable equanimity. He did try to reduce American dependence on imported oil, but he suggested that imports were fueling the American economic boom and helping the economies of the nations that were supplying the imports, many of which were poor third-world nations. He suggested that Japan and Germany particularly open their own markets further to imports. This would encourage American exports and reduce the U.S. trade deficit. It also would allow the administration to continue to resist pressures from American manufacturers of cars, steel, footwear, and textiles for protection against cheaper imports.

Carter became more concerned, however, as his mild remedial measures, including slightly elevated interest rates, failed to halt the dollar's downward slide. Concern turned to alarm when the Iranian revolution interrupted some oil exports and OPEC at once tripled its prices, this time to $35 a barrel. Not only did that increase accelerate the decline of the dollar, but also inflation shot up to an annual rate of 18 percent. At the same time, unemployment began to rise. This stagflation, the growth of deficits and unemployment at the same time, violated all the predictions of the Keynesian economic system and left the Carter administration puzzled and in disarray.

Ronald Reagan won the presidency primarily because of Carter's economic failures. Reagan's prescription of less government intrusion into economic affairs had an impact on foreign as well as domestic policy. He took far more drastic action than Carter to reduce inflation and protect the dollar. He tried to reduce deficit spending by cutting domestic social expenditures. At the same time, however, he cut taxes and drastically increased defense expenditures. The deficit approached the frightening level of $200 billion annually. Reagan claimed that his emphasis on increasing American production (supply side economics) would revive the economy and produce more tax revenue to reduce the deficit than would a tax increase. Meanwhile the Federal Reserve Board tried to counter inflation by restricting the supply of money. Interest rates rose to nearly 20 percent and unemployment rose correspondingly.

The resulting recession reduced consumer and business demand, and inflation slowly began to creep downward. Lower world oil consumption aided this process. An oil glut actually developed despite the cut in production caused by the Iran-Iraq War. Oil prices had been a primary factor in the inflation of the Carter years, and their stabilization and reduction helped the Reagan recovery immensely. America's high interest rates and falling inflation attracted foreign capital, especially from the oil countries themselves, and the dollar strengthened to the point that the Europeans and Japanese began to complain about that as vociferously as they had complained earlier about the falling dollar. At the Williamsburg economic summit of 1983, they argued that the United States should strengthen the dollar by reducing its spending deficit rather than resorting to artificially high interest rates that stole away their capital and undermined their economies. Reagan countered with complaints about barriers to American exports in Japan and the European Common Market.

The result was an uncomfortable standoff. Reagan refused to risk his domestic economic program with concessions to foreigners. The recovery of 1983–1984, however, lowered interest rates and thus reduced the European and Japanese complaints, especially since the strong dollar weakened the ability of American exports to compete abroad. The U.S. trade deficit shot upward, along with the budget deficit.

During these financial crises, Carter and Reagan both resisted domestic pressures for further protection against Japanese and European imports. At Geneva in 1979, Carter completed the negotiations on the General Agreement on Trade and Tariffs that had begun in Tokyo in 1973. This Geneva Agreement of 1979, which replaced the so-called Kennedy Round of the 1960s, reduced tariffs approximately 30 percent. Carter pushed this liberal free trade measure through Congress even in the midst of the economic troubles that beset the end of his administration. After Reagan took office, he successfully pressed the Japanese for further voluntary limits on exports of cars and other manufactured goods to the United States. He also got the Japanese to lower some barriers against American exports, especially agricultural produce. He hoped this would deter new congressional restrictions on imports that might undermine Carter's Geneva Agreement.

Carter and Reagan faced economic problems with the developing nations of the world at least as grave as those with Europe and Japan. American trade and investment in the third world were increasing dramatically. By the 1980s developing nations took more American exports than Europe and Japan combined. They also consumed one of every three acres of U.S. farm production. Although 75 percent of American investments remained in the developed world, the share of the developing world was increasing. In addition, the United States imported vital raw materials from the third world, including 100 percent of America's tin, 90 percent of its bauxite, 100 percent of its natural rubber, and nearly 40 percent of its petroleum.

Many developing countries believed they were not receiving an adequate return for their products. They were angry that although they held nearly three-quarters of the population of the world, they had produced only 17 percent of the gross world product before the oil embargo of 1973. Arguing that the world economy was rigged against them, they pressed the United Nations for a new international economic order. Basing their demands on the work of Latin American economist Raul Prebisch, they sought commodity agreements that would peg the prices of their goods to the prices of the manufactured goods they had to import. They wanted developed countries to reduce the tariffs that blocked the importation of processed and manufactured goods from third-world nations. They demanded that developed countries increase their aid to developing nations from 0.3 percent to 0.7 percent of the contributing nations' GNPs to compensate for past exploitation. They claimed full and permanent sovereignty over their natural resources and insisted on the rights of their national courts to decide without outside interference all questions of compensation for expropriated foreign property. After the success of OPEC, the emboldened developing nations used their majority in the United Nations to pass a 1974 General Assembly resolution in favor of this new international economic order. They also began to try to set up organizations like OPEC to control production and increase prices of other commodities.

Though far from favoring such economic revisionism, Carter indicated some willingness to listen to the third-world program and accommodate it where he could within the existing liberal system. He still placed primary emphasis on the role of private investment, free trade under the most-favored-nation system, and increasing production in developing nations rather than redistributing wealth from the developed countries. Nevertheless, he increased the American contribution to the World Bank for loans to developing nations. He worked for the establishment of an international grain reserve to give emergency aid during times of famine. He refused to support a $6 billion commodity fund to support prices of third-world products by purchasing them if their prices fell below a certain level, but he approved an emergency fund of $400 million. Carter thought the best the international system could do was to encourage self-help and provide emergency relief to the poorest of the poor in the third world.

Carter and Ambassador Andrew Young pointed out that much American and international aid to developing countries failed to trickle down to the poor. Seventy percent of the increase in the GNP in developing countries during the 1970s went to the richest 30 percent of the people, while less than 1 percent went to the bottom fifth of the population. Carter also balked at a UN proposal for a Law of the Sea to govern mining on the bottom of the world's oceans. He refused to submit American ocean operations to the commission established by this treaty because it would have a third-world majority. By the end of Carter's administration, all these issues between the developed nations of the Northern Hemisphere and the developing nations of the Southern Hemisphere were deadlocked.

Ronald Reagan rejected the mildly accommodationist policy of Carter. He broke off negotiations on the Law of the Sea. He lectured the developing nations at the North-South summit meeting in Cancun, Mexico, on the benefits of free markets and self-help. He and his administration accepted no guilt over poverty in the third world. They pointed to Taiwan, South Korea, and Singapore as examples of what developing nations could accomplish within the existing world economic system. Reagan's delegate to the World Health Organization cast the only vote in that body against restrictions on the sale of powdered baby formula in the third world on the grounds that such restrictions improperly interfered with private enterprise.[4] In 1984 Reagan announced that the United States would withdraw entirely from the United Nations Educational, Scientific, and Cultural Organization (UNESCO) and end the U.S. contribution to it. UNESCO had been particularly hostile to the United States and was promoting government controls on international news to "correct" the image of conditions in third-world countries.

For the time being, the developing nations accepted the Reagan policy with resignation. Little could be done toward revising the international economic system without the participation of the United States. The unity of the developing nations eroded as the oil-rich members of the community went their own way. The rise in oil prices, with the accompanying expense of petroleum-based fertilizers, wounded third-world countries even more than the developed economies. OPEC itself fell on hard times, undermining the hopes of those seeking parallel third-world cartels to control other basic commodities. The UN estimated that declining commodity prices cost developing nations $21 billion between 1980 and 1982. Nevertheless Reagan rejected any moves toward international commodity price supports and said recovery in the developed world would revive price levels for third-world products.

Some of the developing nations, in their rush to industrialize, incurred enormous debts to the World Bank, the International Monetary Fund, and private banks. In 1983 the total foreign debt of developing countries reached $700 billion. Brazil, Argentina, Mexico, and Venezuela owed most of that, and all came close to defaulting. If they had defaulted, they would have not only hurt their own economies, but also done immense damage to the world economy as well. This was only one example of the developing nations' inability to influence the developed nations and their potential to do infinite harm if their suffering was not alleviated.

Carter, Reagan, the Soviets, and Nuclear Arms

Jimmy Carter demonstrated his determination to restore moral issues to American foreign policy early in his administration. He protested against Soviet violations of human rights far more than Nixon and Kissinger had done. Just before he took office, he initiated contacts with several Soviet dissidents, and he culminated his human rights campaign in March 1977 by ostentatiously receiving one of these dissidents, Vladimir Bukovsky, in the White House.

Carter lamely tried to assure the Soviets that he did not intend to link his agitation for human rights with such issues as arms control. Nevertheless the political climate surrounding détente soured even more than it had in the last year of the Ford administration. Soviet president Leonid Brezhnev not only denounced Carter's human rights campaign, but dramatically defied it by formally charging one of the leading dissidents, Anatoly Scharansky, with treason. In 1978 the Soviets convicted Scharansky and two others of such charges and imprisoned them.

In this contentious atmosphere, Cyrus Vance and arms control director Paul Warnke advised Carter to avoid any major shift in the SALT negotiations with the Soviet Union.

They wanted the president to concentrate on the few manageable issues blocking final agreement to SALT II, to ratify that treaty, and to defer any new initiatives until after the ratification had restored momentum toward better U.S.-Soviet relations. But Carter decided on a bolder move. Although he had promised Brezhnev he would sign SALT II quickly after negotiating the final compromises, Carter changed his mind and accepted the advice of Brzezinski and Secretary of Defense Harold Brown to offer a whole new negotiating plan. To counter liberal criticisms that SALT II merely ratified rather than reversed the arms race, Carter suggested substantial reductions in the missile limits on both sides. At the same time, he structured the suggested reductions to answer conservative criticisms that SALT II would endanger American security.

Conservative critics like Brzezinski, Senator Henry Jackson, and the influential Committee on the Present Danger, led by Paul Nitze, warned that Russia's buildup of huge MIRVed missiles was approaching the ability to destroy 90 percent of America's land-based Minuteman ICBMs in a preemptive strike. Even though the remainder of America's strategic triad, the nuclear-armed bombers and submarines, might survive, they were incapable of destroying Soviet hardened missile silos; they could only retaliate against Russian cities. After a Soviet attack on American ICBMs, the president would be faced with a choice of submitting to Soviet demands or launching attacks on cities that would guarantee a similar Russian response and the destruction of both societies. The Soviets might assume that the president would submit when faced with such a choice. They would then be tempted to take greater risks in world affairs, if not launch a preemptive strike. The critics of SALT II wanted any arms agreement to reduce the number of heavy Soviet ICBMs capable of destroying the hardencd silos of American Minutemen. Such a reduction would preserve the invulnerability of at least a portion of America's ICBM force and eliminate the temptation for either a Soviet preemptive strike or a more adventurous foreign policy.

With a great fanfare of publicity, Carter sent Secretary of State Vance to Moscow with a plan for reducing the missile limits already set in the SALT II negotiations. Instead of 2,400 strategic launchers each, the United States and the Soviet Union would have fewer than 2,000. The plan required that the bulk of Soviet cuts be made in its large land-based MIRVed missiles. In exchange the United States would abandon its intention to deploy a new generation of ICBMs, the MX (Missile Experimental), each of which would carry ten accurate, potentially silo-busting warheads. Vance also offered a deal on the Soviet Backfire bomber and the American cruise missile, the issues that had blocked earlier agreement on SALT II. The Soviets would be able to build their Backfire bomber so long as they restricted its range to prevent it from being used as a strategic bomber against the United States. Those range restrictions would not prevent the Backfire from being used against Europe, however, and the Soviets were deploying new intermediate SS-20 missiles that also could threaten Western Europe. Therefore Vance's proposal entitled the United States to deploy cruise missiles with sufficient range to reach the Soviet Union from Germany.

The Soviets turned Vance away with an uncompromising "nyet." Complaining that Carter had publicized the proposal before he presented it to them, they called his offer a "cheap and shady maneuver." They argued that their advantage in heavy missiles had been compensation for America's forward-based systems in Europe that were not limited by SALT. They said it was inequitable that these forward-based systems and the new cruise missiles would be able to hit Soviet territory, while the Backfire and SS-20s would not be able to reach the United States. They argued that any weapons that could hit the territory of one of the superpowers were strategic and therefore should be limited by the treaty, while weapons that could reach only Europe, such as the Backfire and SS-20, were tactical and therefore should be exempt. They insisted that SALT II, which they pretended was ready for signing without further negotiation, would have to be ratified before any further progress could be made. It is now clear from Soviet sources that the Soviets were not confident of their own rocket and nuclear technology and wanted the limits set at a high level to ensure that their systems would have backup.

After this highly public fiasco, the Americans and Soviets returned to quieter diplomacy. Both sides were extremely wary, however, and it took two years of false starts, hard bargaining, and overoptimistic declarations by Carter that agreement was near before Carter and Brezhnev signed SALT II at the Vienna summit meeting of July 1979. In this final treaty, the Soviets agreed to reduce the launchers on both sides from 2,400 to 2,250 and to limit the number of warheads on their heavy missiles. In exchange the United States set limits on the range and number of cruise missiles it would deploy.

Henry Jackson and the Committee on the Present Danger denounced the SALT II Treaty immediately. General Edward Rowny, one of Carter's negotiating team, boycotted the signing ceremony in protest that the agreement was too soft, and then he resigned. These critics argued that by leaving intact the Russian advantage in heavy missiles, the treaty would still allow the Soviets to destroy 90 percent of America's land-based ICBMs by the early 1980s. They believed that SALT II would prevent the United States from closing this "window of vulnerability" by lulling Americans into thinking they did not need to increase arms expenditures. They demanded an accelerated program for building the MX and also the Trident II missile, a submarine-launched rocket that, unlike previous submarine missiles, was accurate and powerful enough to threaten silos rather than just cities. They condemned Carter for canceling production of the B-1 bomber, which, armed with long-range cruise missiles, might have countered the Soviet advantage in throw-weight. They also warned that the SALT II verification procedures were inadequate to prevent the Soviets from cheating.

These critics insisted that the Soviets were using arms control and détente to disarm the United States while making no sacrifices of Russian power. The Soviets were more interested in the triumph of the world revolution than in peace, they said. Americans might hope for nuclear stability based on mutually assured destruction and the balance of terror (see Chapter 8 in this volume), but the Soviet nuclear strategy was based on fighting and perhaps even winning a nuclear war. Soviet weapons were far larger than necessary to deter war by threatening American cities. The size of Soviet warheads and the recently improved accuracy of Soviet missiles indicated an intention to attack U.S. strategic missiles in hardened silos if war broke out. The USSR's elaborate civil defense program indicated its belief that its population might survive an American retaliatory strike. Soviet military experts wrote as though a nuclear war might be won. The United States had to have a war-fighting strategy like the Russians, not a merely deterrent capacity. America too must possess accurate and survivable counterforce weapons, along with flexible plans for their use. America must deter Russia by having the ability to answer any level of attack with measures that would deny the Soviets victory, but also avoid a suicidal spasm of city attacks.

Cyrus Vance, Paul Warnke, and their liberal allies inside and outside the Carter administration opposed the war-fighting strategy and the arms buildup it would necessitate. They thought it would be far less dangerous to ratify SALT II and seek further reductions in nuclear arms through new SALT III negotiations. They regarded as ludicrous the idea of a prolonged nuclear war in which each stage of escalation could be carefully controlled. Such hopes only made nuclear war more likely. Neither side could deliver a first strike so surgical that it would exempt cities and hold them for ransom. Even if the initial blasts spared some of the civilian population, radiation and a nuclear-induced "winter" would kill millions. The aggressor thus would have to expect retaliation on its own cities.

Even if the Soviet military might talk about surviving a nuclear exchange and fighting an extended nuclear war, Brezhnev and his fellow party leaders had made clear since 1977 that they regarded nuclear war of any sort as mutual suicide. Brezhnev had no illusions that nuclear war could be fought as a prolonged and gradually escalated conflict. For the United States to build counterforce weapons to deter such a possibility only invited disaster. Americans might regard their counterforce weapons as deterrents, but also such weapons could be used in a first strike, and the Russians undoubtedly would regard them as intended for that. As each nation built its potential first-strike capability in the name of a deterrent war-fighting strategy, each might begin to doubt the survivability of its retaliatory capacity and decide to launch on warning—that is, neither side would wait for an enemy's weapons to explode before retaliating, but launch its missiles the moment its electronic warning systems detected the firing of enemy rockets. Since electronic warning systems often malfunctioned, the risk of accidental war would increase enormously.

Carter and Secretary of Defense Harold Brown tried at first to engineer a balance between the nuclear liberals and the nuclear conservatives, but increasingly they sided with the conservatives. Early in his administration, Carter had pleased the liberals by closing the production line of the Minuteman III missile and canceling the program to increase the accuracy of the old Minuteman I missiles. He also canceled the B-1 bomber project. He knew he could not get the appropriation for both the B-1 and the cruise missile through Congress, and he liked the cruise missile because its slow speed and relative invulnerability made it obviously a second-strike weapon despite its accuracy. (Unfortunately, the small size of the cruise allowed it to be hidden easily, raising monumental problems for future verifiable arms control.)

Carter's cancellations made the military and congressional conservatives cling all the more tenaciously to the new weapons programs that were left—the MX, the Trident II, and the cruise missile. After it was clear that the Soviets would not trade a reduction in their heavy missiles for cancellation of the MX, Carter went along with these conservatives and made sure that SALT II would not prohibit development of new counterforce weapons. Thus, SALT II permitted the development of one new missile by each side, which cleared the way for American deployment of the MX. SALT II also permitted the modernization of older missiles, and Carter saw to it that the definition of modernization allowed him to replace the Trident I submarine missile with Trident IIs.

Having protected the right to build the MX, Carter and Brown devised an enormously expensive scheme to make it less vulnerable to a Soviet preemptive strike. They proposed to deploy the MX as a mobile missile to be moved on tracks between thousands of empty silos. Since the Soviets would not know which silos were dummies and which actually contained missiles, they would not be able to risk a first strike.

Despite the protections Carter built into SALT II for his expansion of American strategic power, opposition in the Senate remained strong. Carter tried to assuage opponents by promising Senate majority leader Robert Byrd that he would not bargain away America's new missiles in future negotiations, but actually deploy them. When the Soviet Union invaded Afghanistan in December 1979, however, the resulting American public outrage doomed the attempt to ratify the treaty, and Carter shelved it until a more propitious time.

The debate over SALT II in the United States proceeded in tandem with debates in Europe over nuclear arms in that theater. It was clear early in the SALT II negotiations that whatever limits might be put on the range of Soviet Backfire bombers, they would still be able to deliver nuclear weapons against Western Europe. In addition the talks on strategic arms did not deal with Soviet missiles whose range was short enough to prevent them from reaching the United States. This left the Soviets free to continue the rapid deployment of their SS-20s, each of which was MIRVed with three warheads.

Washington's preferred response was to build NATO's conventional forces and make a nuclear response to conventional invasion less necessary. In 1977 NATO agreed that each member would increase its defense spending at a rate of 3 percent annually above inflation. But the Europeans worried that a conventional buildup, combined with increased Soviet intermediate-range nuclear forces, might lead the United States to decouple its nuclear force from European defense. In October 1977 Chancellor Helmut Schmidt of West Germany gave a widely publicized speech warning that Soviet deployment of the Backfire and SS-20 was lessening the credibility of NATO's threat to resort to nuclear weapons if it found itself unable to stop a Soviet conventional invasion. At first, Carter tried to play down Schmidt's concerns. His administration pointed out that intermediate-range warheads constituted only 5 percent of the warheads in the Soviet and American strategic arsenals. As long as the United States maintained strategic parity with the Soviet Union and kept its own troops in Germany to demonstrate the risk Russia would run if it invaded Western Europe, the SS-20s posed little threat.

Then Carter canceled production of the neutron bomb. The neutron bomb enhanced the radiation of a nuclear explosion and lessened the size of the blast. NATO had thought the neutron bomb would be useful in Europe to kill invading troops and tank crews without destroying the surrounding buildings and countryside. The bomb, however, raised an outcry in both Europe and the United States. Critics, especially those living in the areas that would be the battlefield, pointed out that it killed friendly as well as enemy people.

Delusions about its capability to limit nuclear war would make war more likely. It also would tempt the United States to avoid threatening an all-out strategic strike on the Soviet Union that would put the territory of the United States at risk. In the midst of this political turmoil, none of the NATO leaders wanted to take responsibility for requesting such a bomb. When Helmut Schmidt refused to make a new and public request for the United States to continue the project, Carter abandoned it. Schmidt and many other Western European leaders were angry that Carter had not supported Europe's defense. Carter decided he had to regain the trust and unity of America's Western European allies.

Thus, Carter and the NATO allies agreed in December 1979 to the so-called two-track decision. At NATO's request, the United States would deploy a total of 572 Pershing II and cruise intermediate missiles in Europe. These missiles, unlike previous American rockets stationed in Europe, would be capable of reaching beyond Warsaw Pact territory to the Soviet Union itself, although NATO quickly pointed out that they could not reach as far as Moscow. They would add little to the warheads already aimed at Russia, but since the United States might choose to fire rather than lose them to a conventional Soviet invasion of Europe, NATO hoped they would further couple American and European defense and deter the Soviets. Meanwhile, in the second track of the two-track decision, NATO asked the United States to open separate intermediate-range nuclear arms limitation talks to accompany its strategic nuclear talks with the Soviet Union.

The two-track decision, designed to reassure Western Europe, rebounded against all its authors. It jarred many Europeans into recognition that their homes might become nuclear battlefields in a war between the superpowers. Brezhnev added to this growing antinuclear movement by offering to deploy only 162 of the SS-20s, the exact total of missiles in the independent arsenals of Great Britain and France, if NATO would abandon deployment of the cruise and Pershing II missiles. NATO rejected the offer. Not only would it once again decouple American and European nuclear deterrents, but Brezhnev offered only to move his SS-20s out of range of Western Europe, not destroy then. Since the SS-20s were mobile, they could easily be moved back. In any case, once NATO's two-track decision was firm, Brezhnev withdrew his offer and spent six months denouncing the projected NATO deployment. The invasion of Afghanistan and deferral of the SALT II treaty added to European uneasiness.

In 1980 the Soviets finally agreed to talks in Geneva about intermediate-range nuclear weapons. But the relief to Europe was short-lived. Disagreements at Geneva showed that negotiating a treaty would be a long and bitter struggle. Europeans also were disturbed when Carter issued Presidential Directive 59, which established more flexible targeting for America's modernizing strategic arsenal. Thus, Carter made overt his war-fighting strategy to replace the strictly deterrent strategy of mutually assured destruction (MAD) that supposedly had guided the United States since 1967.[5] Europeans regarded plans for counterforce strikes and gradual escalation as particularly threatening. As European antinuclear activists put it, when the Soviets and Americans talk of limited nuclear war, they mean limited to Europe. Then, to add to European discomfort, Ronald Reagan won election to the presidency.

Before his election, Reagan showed little interest in continuing arms control negotiations. "The argument . . . will be over which weapons [to build], not whether we would forsake weaponry for treaties and agreements," he declared. He called Carter's SALT II Treaty "fatally flawed" and made clear he would never seek its ratification. He appointed critics from the Committee on the Present Danger to key positions in charge of arms control—Eugene V. Rostow as director of the Arms Control and Disarmament Agency, General Edward Rowny as chief strategic arms negotiator, and Paul Nitze as chief negotiator for the theater weapons talks at Geneva. Reagan eventually replaced Rostow, who insisted on appointing aides who were too liberal, with another member of the Committee on the Present Danger, Kenneth Adelman, who had been quoted two years earlier as calling arms control negotiations "a sham." (Adelman denied making the statement.)

Reagan held all arms control negotiations in limbo for the first sixteen months of his administration, but he promised to abide informally by the "fatally flawed" SALT II Treaty so long as the Soviets did likewise. Meanwhile, he pushed through Congress an enormous increase in defense expenditures. Claiming that the Soviets had developed a margin of military superiority rather than parity with the United States, he proposed an increase of $180 billion over five years. This was in addition to the 5 percent increases voted by Congress during Carter's administration for fiscal years 1981 and 1982. Reagan restored the neutron bomb and B-1 bomber projects. Secretary of Defense Caspar Weinberger and Secretary of State Alexander Haig made statements indicating further movement toward a war-fighting nuclear strategy and limited, staged use of nuclear weapons in Europe. Although Weinberger protested that he was misunderstood and that nuclear war was indeed unwinnable, leaks from a secret defense guidance document confirmed that the United States planned a counterforce attack before resorting to nuclear attacks on cities if the USSR launched a first strike. None of this was startlingly new in theory, but the Reagan administration seemed ready to spend billions of dollars to make its strategy practical. In contrast to Reagan's passionate advocacy of defense expenditures, his arms control initiatives seemed perfunctory at best. He abandoned entirely the negotiations for a comprehensive ban on nuclear testing. When he finally announced in November 1981 that he would resume strategic arms negotiations, he insisted that they be called Strategic Arms Reduction Talks (START) rather than SALT. His START proposal called for the reduction of nuclear warheads from 7,000 to 5,000, only 2,500 of which could be placed aboard land-based missiles. This would force the Soviets to abandon much of their ICBM force in favor of submarine weapons. START would reduce the number of ballistic missiles as well as warheads. Each side could have 850 launchers. This would require the United States to destroy half of its missiles, the Soviets to destroy two-thirds of theirs. In the second stage of the agreement, Reagan would require the Soviets to accept equality in throw-weight as well. Yet the Reagan proposal placed no limits on those weapons in which the United States was superior—cruise missiles and bombers. (Cruise missiles were not ballistic missiles because they did not free fall back to earth, so technically they were exempt from the limitations on strategic ballistic missiles.) Reagan invited the Soviets to make a counteroffer by stating that all things were negotiable, but at the same time he was accelerating the construction of the B-1 bombers and naval vessels to launch long-range cruise missiles.

Reagan also took a hard line in the intermediate missile talks. He offered the Soviets a "zero-zero" option, meaning that the United States would not deploy its Pershing II and cruise missiles in Europe if the Soviets would dismantle all their SS-20s. When negotiator Paul Nitze and his Soviet counterpart in the theater talks came close to a private agreement, trading Soviet reductions in SS-20s for a more limited U.S. deployment, Reagan angrily rejected the tentative compromise. The Soviet government rejected it even more angrily. But Reagan's response convinced many critics in Europe and the United States that his administration was insincere in its pursuit of arms control.

Some of these critics charged that Reagan had sided with the right-wing ideologues in his administration who believed that arms control was a sham and that the United States could and should bankrupt the Soviets in an arms race. Amid such criticism, domestic American support for increased defense spending fell from 71 percent in 1980 to 17 percent in October 1982. Many Americans joined a movement for a freeze on all further nuclear deployments, and freeze resolutions won majorities in the 1982 elections in eight out of nine states. Many of the major Democratic contenders for the presidential nomination endorsed the freeze. Influential former foreign policy and defense officials like Robert McNamara, McGeorge Bundy, and George Kennan made powerful cases for minimal deterrence, abandonment of nuclear war-fighting strategies, and a pledge of "no early first use" of nuclear weapons. In Europe hundreds of thousands of people mobilized against the deployment of American cruise and Pershing missiles.

Reagan responded to this agitation skillfully. He insisted that he was sincerely dedicated to arms control, but was simply driving a properly hard bargain. When Congress balked at the appropriations Reagan requested for the MX missile, he accepted the congressional requirement that he demonstrate his dedication to arms control by offering a new compromise in the START negotiations. He proposed to raise the limit on launchers from 850 to about 1,200. All other provisions of his START offer, however, remained the same.

Reagan also moved to accommodate other objections to the MX. Congress would not appropriate the money for the dummy silo deployment of a mobile MX. Neither did Congress want to deploy the MX in existing vulnerable Minuteman silos. Reagan therefore adopted the idea of "densepack." He would deploy the MX in dense clusters, on the assumption that the numerous missiles the Soviets would aim at them would destroy each other. Congress and many technical experts doubted this densepack concept and there was no way to test it, so Reagan turned the problem over to a bipartisan commission headed by former national security adviser General Brent Scowcroft and including luminaries such as Henry Kissinger, Alexander Haig, Harold Brown, and former defense secretaries Melvin Laird and James Schlesinger.

The Scowcroft Commission suggested an alternative that gained acceptance from many people on both sides of the political spectrum. The commission called for a new Midgetman missile. Each of these small missiles would carry a single warhead. They would be widely dispersed to make it impossible for a preemptive strike to be sure of destroying all of them. Since Midgetman would be relatively invulnerable and would clearly be a retaliatory rather than a first-strike weapon, it might lead the United States and the Soviet Union to back away from the destabilizing race for huge, accurate, MIRVed silo-busters.

But the Scowcroft Commission also recommended deployment of the MX in the old Minuteman holes as an interim measure. Although the MX ran directly counter to the philosophy behind Midgetman and aroused far more controversy, this political marriage of convenience at least temporarily rescued Reagan's MX appropriation in Congress.

Not only did Reagan make clear that he was going to deploy the MX missile, but he also opened a new front in the arms race. In March 1983 he dramatically shifted his nuclear strategy to emphasize plans for a space-based antimissile defense system, which he called the Strategic Defense Initiative. He asked Congress to appropriate $26.5 billion over five years to test and build lasers deployed in space to shoot down Soviet intercontinental missiles before they could reach their targets, a system his critics dubbed "Star Wars." Such a plan would put in jeopardy the antiballistic missile treaty that had been the foundation of the SALT agreements and the doctrine of mutual assured destruction.

Soviet intransigence in the arms control negotiations and other aspects of the Cold War helped to promote Reagan's defense strategy in the face of a great deal of opposition at home and abroad. In 1981 the Polish anti-Soviet labor movement Solidarity took advantage of the food shortages and other austerities brought on by Poland's extremely high foreign debt to challenge the Communist Party's hold on government power. The newly selected Polish pope, John Paul II, lent his support to Solidarity, increasing the movement's appeal to the Polish people. In May 1981 a Turk with ties to the Bulgarian secret service attempted to assassinate the pope, and the Soviets seemed implicated by association. So the Soviets could see that they would face fierce Polish resistance, a powerful reaction from the outside world, and unrest even in eastern Europe and within the Soviet Union if they intervened in Poland. Recently available Soviet documents reveal that in the face of these currents of opposition, Brezhnev and the Soviet leadership decided that they would not use military force to prevent Solidarity from taking power in Poland. In effect they abandoned the Brezhnev Doctrine that threatened Soviet intervention to protect friendly governments in eastern Europe. But they kept that decision secret and bluffed, making loud threats that they would intervene to protect socialism. Intimidated by those threats, Poland's military leader General Wojciech Jaruzelski preempted the Soviets, imposed martial law, and replaced the Communist Party with a military government that proclaimed its continuing loyalty to the Warsaw Pact.

Reagan reacted sharply, not only instituting an economic boycott of Poland but also trying to stop U.S. and European firms from cooperating with the Soviets to build a natural gas pipeline from the Soviet Union to Western Europe. Reagan's pressure caused some strain with America's European allies, who pointed out that Reagan had recently lifted Carter's grain embargo on the Soviets.

Soviet intransigence was even more devastating to East-West relations when the Soviet air force shot down a Korean Airlines plane that had strayed over Soviet territory en route from the United States to Korea. All 269 passengers aboard were killed. The Soviets justified the attack by claiming that the airliner was a spy plane that was purposely testing Soviet air defenses. (Reagan and Shultz made matters worse by claiming that the Soviet pilot knew he was firing on a civilian airliner even though the United State had access to transcripts of conversations between the Soviet plane and the ground commanders that proved otherwise.)

Meanwhile Soviet proposals in both the START and intermediate talks remained warmed-over versions of earlier, self-serving propositions. On the one hand, the Soviets reacted rather moderately to the Reagan defense buildup, with Brezhnev and his successor, Yuri Andropov, arguing both internally and publicly that reason would inevitably triumph in the United States over Reagan's confrontational policy because it was obvious that war would be devastating to both sides. Until late 1983 the Soviets continued to adhere to the idea of détente. Nevertheless Brezhnev's illness and death seemed to have paralyzed the already ponderous decision-making machinery in the Soviet Union and prevented any show of flexibility on arms control or other issues in the first world, while the Soviet concept of détente continued to reject any linkage between those issues and policies in the third world. By late 1983, however, Andropov and the Soviet leadership were ready to jettison even their own adumbrated version of détente. Reagan's manipulation of the Korean airliner incident along with his justification of the U.S. intervention in Grenada as necessary to thwart a Soviet plot to establish another foothold in the Western Hemisphere convinced Andropov that Reagan was not going to moderate his military buildup or seriously negotiate on arms control. Andropov and Soviet military leaders worried that Reagan might actually be contemplating a nuclear first strike. The Reagan buildup so worried Soviet intelligence that from May 1981 until late 1984 it maintained a special alert to guard against an American surprise attack. That alarm increased in November 1983, when the United States and NATO conducted a test of command and communication for the use of nuclear weapons called Able Archer, a test that the KGB worried might be used to cover for a surprise first strike.

It was in this atmosphere that the United States and NATO began actual deployment of the Pershing and cruise missiles in Europe in late 1983. The Soviets responded by walking out of all nuclear arms talks. Reagan confidently asserted that the Soviets ultimately would return to the bargaining table, but it seemed to many people in America and the world at large that the Cold War was going to get even colder.

Controversial Issues

Did détente have to die? Was Soviet policy so aggressive, faithless, and threatening to American and Western interests in the late 1970s and early 1980s that Carter and Reagan had to threaten war over the Persian Gulf, vastly expand defense spending, and assist brutal right-wing dictatorships in the third world to prevent Communist expansion? Jimmy Carter, Zbigniew Brzezinski, and Harold Brown all claimed in their memoirs that it was and that Carter acted appropriately to counter that policy in the last year of his administration. They regarded Reagan's campaign against Carter's supposed spinelessness as shameful and inaccurate.[6] Cyrus Vance, of course, believed that Soviet policy could have been countered with far milder measures and said so in his memoirs.[7] The best and most detailed history of this period, by former State Department official Raymond Garthoff, tends to support Vance's perceptions and soft realist prescriptions. But it and other recent books on the Carter administration make clear that the Soviets were themselves rigid and uncooperative and were increasingly aggressive in the third world.[8]

Reagan officials and historians sympathetic to them did not doubt that a harder line against the Soviets than that of Jimmy Carter was necessary. They only debated how hard it had to be. The conflict between hard realist pragmatists and conservative hard-line ideologues within the Reagan administration has been documented not only by former Reagan officials who participated in the conflict, such as Secretaries of State Alexander Haig and George Schultz and Secretary of Defense Caspar Weinberger, but also by several outstanding academic works.[9]

Further Reading

On the Soviet side of the end of détente, see Georgi Arbatov, *The System: An Insider's Life in Soviet Politics* (1992); Matthew J. Ouimet, *The Rise and Fall of the Brezhnev Doctrine* (2003); Robert D. English, *Russia and the Idea of the West: Gorbachev, Intellectuals, and the End of the Cold War* (2000); Christopher Andrew and Vasili Metrokhin, *The World Was Going Our Way: The KGB and the Battle for the Third World* (2005), and *The Sword and the Shield: The Mitrokhin Archive and the Secret History of the KGB* (1999). On China in this period, see Richard Baum, *Burying Mao: Chinese Politics in the Age of Deng Xiaoping* (1994); and Richard Evans, *Deng Xiaoping and the Making of Modern China* (1997).

On the arms race and arms control, see Ronald E. Powaski, *Return to Armageddon: The United States and the Nuclear Arms Race, 1981–1999* (2000); and Daniel Wirls, *Buildup: The Politics of Defense in the Reagan Era* (1992). Strobe Talbott traces the policies of Carter and Reagan toward SALT II in *Endgame: The Inside Story of SALT II* (1979), and *Deadly Gambit: The Reagan Administration and the Stalemate in Nuclear Arms Control* (1984). John F. Lehman and Seymour Weiss, *Beyond the SALT II Failure* (1981), gave the conservative critique of the Carter policies and spelled out the premises the Reagan administration adopted. See also Dan Caldwell, *The Dynamics of Domestic Politics and Arms Control: The Salt II Treaty Ratification Debate* (1991). On the Strategic Defense Initiative, see Donald R. Baucom, *The Origins of SDI: 1944–1983* (1992); and Paul Lettow, *Ronald Reagan and His Quest to Abolish Nuclear Weapons* (2005). David Holloway, *The Soviet Union and the Arms Race* (1983), offers an outstanding analysis of Soviet thought on nuclear warfare, and Lawrence Freedman, *The Evolution of Nuclear Strategy* (1983), an excellent account of changing strategic thought from World War II to Carter.

On the Carter and Reagan policies toward intervention in the developing world, see Odd Arne Westad, *The Global Cold War: Third World Interventions and the Making of Our Times* (2007); Peter W. Rodman, *More Precious Than Peace: The Cold War and the Struggle for the Third World* (1994); James M. Scott, *Deciding to Intervene: The Reagan Doctrine and American Foreign Policy* (1996).

The best book on U.S. policy toward Central America in these years is William M. LeoGrande, *Our Own Backyard: The United States in Central America, 1977–1992* (1998). Highly critical revisionist accounts of U.S. policy toward Latin America in these years are Walter LaFeber, *Inevitable Revolutions: The United States in Central America* (2nd ed., 1993); and John Booth and Thomas Walker, *Understanding Central America*

(3rd ed., 1999). For soft realist critiques, see Robert A. Pastor, *Whirlwind: U.S. Foreign Policy toward Latin America and the Caribbean* (1992); James Chace, *Endless War: How We Got Involved in Central America* (1984); and Lester Langley, *America and the Americas* (1989). A more conservative nationalist view is Mark Falcoff and Robert Royal, *Crisis and Opportunity: U.S. Policy in Central America and the Caribbean* (1984). The best works specifically on Nicaragua are Thomas Walker, *Nicaragua, the Land of the Sandinistas* (1986); and Stephen Kinzer, *Blood of Brothers: Life and War in Nicaragua* (1991); the best on El Salvador is Tommie Sue Montgomery, *Revolution in El Salvador* (2nd ed., 1990). On the Panama Canal Treaties, see Michael L. Conniff, *Panama and the United States: The Forced Alliance* (1992); and Walter LaFeber, *The Panama Canal: The Crisis in Historical Perspective* (updated ed., 1989).

Insider accounts of the Carter administration's policy toward Latin America include Robert A. Pastor, *Not Condemned to Repetition: The United States and Nicaragua* (revised and updated ed., 2002); and Anthony Lake, *Somoza Falling* (1989).

On international finances, see John S. Odell, *U.S. International Monetary Policy* (1982).

Notes

1. The above discussion of the impact of cultural trends on U.S. foreign policy in the 1970s is based on Natasha Zaretsky, *No Direction Home: The American Family and the Fear of National Decline, 1968–1980* (2007).

2. Michael Schaller, *Right Turn: American Life in the Reagan-Bush Era, 1980–1992* (2007).

3. Laurence L. Barrett, *Gambling with History: Ronald Reagan in the White House* (1983), p. 225.

4. Babies in the third world did far better being breast-fed because they often caught infections from unclean bottles. Also many peasants could ill afford to buy the formula and when they did buy it, they often diluted the formula with bad water to increase its volume.

5. Actually Secretary of Defense McNamara's MAD strategy and all succeeding U.S. nuclear plans included options for counterforce and limited stages of escalation.

6. Jimmy Carter, *Keeping Faith* (1982); Zbigniew Brzezinski, *Power and Principle* (1983); Harold Brown, *Thinking About National Security* (1983).

7. Cyrus Vance, *Hard Choices* (1983).

8. Raymond Garthoff, *Détente and Confrontation: American-Soviet Relations from Nixon to Reagan* (rev. ed., 1994). Two excellent new biographies of Carter that emphasize his foreign policy are Betty Glad, *An Outsider in the White House: Jimmy Carter, His Advisors, and the Making of American Foreign Policy* (2009); and Scott Kaufman, *Plans Unraveled: The Foreign Policy of the Carter Administration* (2008). Both are quite critical of Carter. A much more favorable view of Carter as president is Robert A. Strong, *Working in the World: Jimmy Carter and the Making of American Foreign Policy* (2000). See also David Skidmore, *Reversing Course: Carter's Foreign Policy, Domestic Politics, and the Failure of Reform* (1996); Timothy P. Maga, *The World of Jimmy Carter: U.S. Foreign Policy, 1977–1981* (1994); Odd Arne Westad, ed., *The Fall of Détente* (1997); Gaddis Smith, *Morality, Reason, and Power: American Diplomacy in the Carter Years* (1986); and Burton I. Kaufman, *The Presidency of James Earl Carter, Jr.* (1993).

9. George Pratt Shultz, *Turmoil and Triumph: My Years as Secretary of State* (1993); Caspar A. Weinberger, *Fighting for Peace: Seven Critical Years in the Pentagon* (1990); Alexander Haig, *Caveat: Realism, Reagan, and Foreign Policy* (1984); Deborah Hart Strober and Gerald S. Strober, *Reagan: The Man and His Presidency* (1998); Lou Cannon, *President Reagan: The Role of a Lifetime* (reprint, 2000); Don Oberdorfer, *From the Cold War to a New Era: The United States and the Soviet Union, 1983–1991* (updated ed., 1998); Garthoff, *Détente and Confrontation*, cited above, and *The Great Transition: American-Soviet Relations and the End of the Cold War* (1994).

CHAPTER 16

THE END OF THE COLD WAR

Although 1984 and 1985 marked a low point in the Cold War between the United States and the Soviet Union, there were some indications that relations would improve. President Reagan had cooled his anti-Soviet rhetoric before the 1984 election. During the campaign he insisted that his defense buildup was a prerequisite for arms negotiations, not a means to preclude them. That could have been mere political maneuvering, but about that same time Reagan replaced his hard-line national security adviser, William Clark, with the more pragmatic Robert McFarlane. McFarlane advised Reagan that the military power of the United States had probably reached its apex and would soon start to decline because Congress was resistant to further defense budget increases. Therefore, he said, it might be best to negotiate with the Soviets from the existing position of strength. This seemed possible because the Soviets returned to the nuclear arms negotiating table after Andropov died in February 1984 and Konstantin Chernenko replaced him as leader of the Soviet Union. The Soviets demonstrated their continuing displeasure with the Reagan administration, however, by announcing that they would boycott the Los Angeles Olympics.

The Rise of Mikhail Gorbachev

The chances for Soviet-American negotiations increased further when Chernenko himself died in 1985 and Andropov's protégé, Mikhail Gorbachev, replaced him. Gorbachev had presided over a massive series of studies ordered by Andropov to assess all aspects of Soviet policy and life. Those studies convinced Gorbachev that the Soviet economy was destitute and could not continue to spend nearly 25 percent of the Soviet gross national product on defense. Gorbachev kicked hard-line foreign minister Andrey Gromyko upstairs to the ceremonial position of chair of the Presidium and replaced him with another reformer like himself, Eduard Shevardnadze. Just as Shevardnadze took over the position of foreign minister, Gorbachev and Reagan agreed to meet in Geneva in November 1985.

No sooner had they agreed on a summit, however, than the Reagan administration erected a major barrier to possible arms control agreements. State Department lawyers suddenly challenged a provision in the SALT 1 Antiballistic Missile (ABM) Treaty, a provision many assumed stood in the way of Reagan's beloved Strategic Defense Initiative (SDI) because it prohibited development, testing, or deployment in space of ABM systems of components. These government lawyers reinterpreted the provision by arguing first that the prohibition would not apply to new technologies that had not existed at the time of the treaty's ratification. Moreover, they pointed out that the ABM treaty did not prohibit research and that the term "research" could be interpreted broadly enough to include development and testing if not deployment of SDI. Opponents and even some proponents of SDI in the U.S. Senate complained that this interpretation ran directly counter to the Nixon administration's testimony before the Senate during the original hearings on SALT I. In those hearings, at a time when it was feared that the Soviets were ahead in ABM technology, Nixon's negotiators had assured the senators that both the Soviets and the Americans had agreed to be bound by a strict interpretation of the treaty, including the definition of "research." But on the eve of the 1985 summit Reagan announced that he agreed with the State Department's broad interpretation and would adhere only temporarily to the strict one.

Gorbachev and the Soviets naturally assumed that this position was a ruse to allow the United States to build SDI. They considered a space-based ABM system an offensive rather than a defensive weapon. The Soviets argued that there was no way that SDI could create the sort of umbrella Reagan was insisting would stop all incoming missiles from a massive first strike. Inevitably, enough would get through to destroy most of America's cities. The only use for SDI, therefore, was as an offensive weapon to make possible an American first strike. If that first strike destroyed most of the Soviet Union's missiles, Moscow pointed out, SDI might be able to stop the few remaining missiles from being fired in retaliation.

To prevent the beginning of race to build anti-missile shields, Gorbachev publicly offered to negotiate a 50 percent cut in the ICBMs of both sides if Reagan would agree to a ban on SDI. He then met Reagan at the Geneva summit to negotiate this revolutionary offer.

In Geneva, Reagan and Gorbachev agreed that a 50 percent cut of ICBMs would be possible and desirable and that a separate agreement on intermediate-range nuclear forces (INF) might be worked out. But Gorbachev insisted that an agreement on offensive strategic forces would have to be linked to a ban on SDI. Reagan, on the other hand, was adamant against any limits on SDI. Despite this stalemate Reagan and Gorbachev built enough trust between them to agree to two further summits, the first to be held in the United States and the second in Moscow.

The trust between Reagan and Gorbachev was sorely tested during the following year, however. Negotiations for agreements that could be signed at the upcoming summits traveled a very bumpy road.

At the twenty-seventh Soviet Communist Party Congress in the spring of 1986, Gorbachev gave some testimony of his sincere desire for arms control by announcing a significant change in Soviet defense doctrine. He told the assembled delegates that the Soviet Union would no longer seek "military equality," by which doctrine the Soviets had tried to build forces equal to those of any possible coalition that could be ranged against them. Instead Gorbachev would accept a "reasonable sufficiency" of military strength. In addition he proclaimed that the well-being of all humanity should take precedence in international relations over the socialist class struggle to overthrow imperialism. As part of these changes of doctrine, Gorbachev offered to negotiate a total ban on nuclear weapons and nuclear testing so as to eliminate the need for SDI.

Many political experts on the American and Western side doubted Gorbachev's sincerity, however, because of the expansiveness of his disarmament proposal and because the Soviets, at the same time, were trying to hide the extent of the danger posed by the explosion of their nuclear reactor in Chernobyl. Moreover, the Soviets arrested a prominent American journalist, Nicholas Daniloff, in an obvious retaliation for the imprisonment of one of their spies who had been caught red-handed.

Reagan and the Americans gave the Soviet Union plenty of reason to doubt their own sincerity as well. American ships provocatively sailed inside the Soviet twelve-mile limit in the Black Sea. Reagan announced that the United States would no longer adhere even informally to the SALT II limits. He also flatly rejected the Soviet offer for a complete nuclear test ban. He cited the need to test existing nuclear warheads to ensure that they had not deteriorated. Yet many scientists insisted that actual testing was unnecessary for that purpose. It seemed far more likely that Reagan was keeping the way open to test the atomic bombs that would initiate X-ray lasers for his SDI project.

The Reykjavik Summit and the End of the Cold War

As it became less and less likely that the Americans and Soviets could agree to any arms control measure important enough to justify a summit, Gorbachev startled the West by offering to negotiate an intermediate-missile treaty on the basis of America's zero-zero option. Not only would he destroy all his SS-20s (including those in Asia) in exchange for the destruction of America's far fewer cruise and Pershing II missiles deployed in the NATO area, but he would do so without reference to the continued existence of British and French missiles and without any link to SDI. Gorbachev invited Reagan to a preliminary meeting in October 1986 to complete such an INF treaty and prepare the way for the major summits in Washington and Moscow. When Reagan accepted, the two leaders decided to meet in Reykjavik, Iceland.

In Iceland, Gorbachev surprised Reagan with a far more extensive offer than the INF treaty. The Soviet leader again offered a mutual 50 percent cut in all strategic weapons and included for the first time in this cut many of the monster SS-18 missiles that so worried the Americans. Unfortunately, he went back on the INF offer with which he had lured Reagan to Reykjavik. Gorbachev now insisted that both INF and the strategic arms agreements would require the United States to adhere to the strict interpretation of the ABM treaty for ten years. During that ten-year period, work on SDI would be limited to laboratory research. Still, Gorbachev's offer was a generous one, and Reagan feared that if he rejected it in order to save SDI, he would face tremendous criticism at home and abroad.

Reagan and his advisers huddled feverishly in a side room at Reykjavik and decided to counter Gorbachev's proposal for a 50 percent reduction in strategic weapons with an even broader one. They would offer to eliminate all ballistic missiles. They also would offer to adhere to the ABM treaty for ten years, but without specifying how strictly it

President Ronald Reagan *(left)* and Premier Mikhail Gorbachev *(right)* grimly leave the Reykjavik summit meeting after failing to agree on disarmament. *(Courtesy of the Ronald Reagan Presidential Library)*

would be interpreted. They calculated that such a pledge would still allow them to build SDI. Meanwhile the elimination of ballistic missiles would leave the United States superior to the Soviets in nuclear weaponry because America had more nonballistic cruise missiles and bombers.

Recognizing the one-sidedness of the American offer, Gorbachev raised the bid once again. He renewed his earlier proposal to eliminate all nuclear weapons rather than just ballistic missiles. He was shocked to hear Reagan respond that this was just what he had always wanted to do. Reagan's own advisers were even more shocked than Gorbachev. Reagan had mused before about the desirability of dismantling all nuclear weapons, but most of his aides had assumed that this was just a passing thought of a rather weak mind. They, like almost all previous Western security experts, had resisted total nuclear disarmament because it would leave Soviet conventional forces superior on the Eurasian continent.

Despite Reagan's unexpected concession on nuclear disarmament, there remained the problem of SDI. Gorbachev insisted on interpreting the ABM treaty to limit SDI to laboratory research for ten years. Reagan declined. At that Gorbachev refused to agree even to the INF treaty he had offered to sign independent of any agreement on SDI. Having come so close to a historic breakthrough in the Cold War, Reagan and Gorbachev ended the Reykjavik meeting in anger and disappointment. As they grimly emerged from the meeting hall to their waiting cars, Gorbachev mused that he did not know what more he could have done. Reagan replied acidly, "I do. You could have said yes."

While much of the world was dismayed at the failure of the Reykjavik summit, some American and European security experts breathed a sigh of relief. Europeans denounced Reagan for failing to consult them on a nuclear disarmament agreement that would have left them confronted by superior Soviet conventional forces. Reagan's own advisers and conservative supporters agreed that the notoriously ill-informed president had nearly been sandbagged by Gorbachev. But once Gorbachev and the Soviets got over their initial disappointment at the failure of the summit, their memory of Reagan's obviously sincere willingness to eliminate all nuclear weapons made a deep impression on them.

The initial disappointment over the failure at Reykjavik was so great on both sides that Reagan and Gorbachev did not even exchange New Year's greetings in January 1987. Secretary of Defense Caspar Weinberger almost got Reagan to agree to immediate deployment of some elements of SDI; only congressional opposition prevented it. But after conducting a foreign policy review to decide whether to work any further with Reagan, in February Gorbachev renewed his offer to negotiate a separate INF agreement based on Reagan's zero-zero option, an agreement whereby the Soviet Union would destroy 1,846 intermediate-range missiles and the United States only 846.

Meanwhile Reagan moved to reassure his conservative supporters that he was not a dupe for Gorbachev. On a trip to West Berlin in June 1987, he defied the advice of his State Department to go easy with Gorbachev so as not to imperil the Soviet leader's position within his own politburo. Standing in front of the Berlin Wall with the Brandenburg Gate framed behind him, Reagan proclaimed: "Mr. Gorbachev, tear down this wall."

Interestingly his audience was not just in the West, but in eastern Europe as well. East Berliners could see and hear Reagan over West German radio and television that reached well into East Germany. From those broadcasts over the years, East Germans had been able to appreciate the prosperity and freedom in the West that contrasted so vividly with their own drab lives. Prior to Reagan's speech in front of the wall, West Berlin staged three nights of open-air rock concerts in the same general area featuring David Bowie, The Eurythmics, and Phil Collins. Not content to hear those concerts over the air, thousands of East Berliners gathered near their side of the wall to hear them live. When the East German police tried to block access and break up the crowds, the audience threw bottles and stones and chanted "Down with the wall" and "The wall must go." They also shouted "Gorbachev, Gorbachev," an implied rebuke to their leader, Erich Honeker, who was resisting the liberalizing policies emanating from the Soviet Union. Clearly the cultural contrasts between East and West propagated behind the Iron Curtain by Western media for fifty years had undermined much of the popular support for Europe's Communist regimes.[1]

Although Gorbachev and his Soviet colleagues were offended by Reagan's defiant speech, the Soviet leader decided to continue his negotiations with Reagan. By the time he and Reagan met to sign the INF treaty at the Washington summit in December 1987, Gorbachev had already moved beyond the terms of the treaty to reassure the Europeans

Gorbachev *(left)* and Reagan happily sign the INF treaty, a major step in ending the Cold War. *(Courtesy of the Ronald Reagan Presidential Library)*

that the Soviets posed no threat to them. He had offered to destroy all Soviet short-range as well as intermediate-range nuclear missiles. He had agreed to allow inspections on Soviet soil to verify the number and status of NATO and Warsaw Pact forces. At the summit itself, he hinted that the Soviets might no longer insist on linking a strategic arms treaty to restrictions on SDI. Noting that the U.S. Congress had already cut Reagan's request for SDI appropriations by a third and mandated a strict interpretation of the ABM treaty, he told Reagan what many American critics had been saying—that the project was expensive and unworkable and that the Soviets could build offensive missiles to overcome SDI more cheaply and effectively than the United States could expand it to cope with the increased missiles. Therefore, Gorbachev said, he was willing to go ahead with negotiations for a 50 percent cut in strategic arms with the proviso that the Soviets could back out and begin building new offensive missiles if the United States deployed SDI.

As the pace of negotiations on strategic arms reductions picked up, Gorbachev moved to strengthen his position within the Soviet Union to protect his revolutionary shift in policy. He retired Gromyko as ceremonial head of state, placed himself in a newly expanded office of the presidency, and purged Yegor Legachev, the leader of the Politburo faction that refused to accept Gorbachev's argument that universal human values took precedence over class struggle in international relations. Then, in December 1988, Gorbachev suddenly overtrumped the long and fruitless negotiations between NATO and the Warsaw Pact on conventional forces by announcing that he would reduce Soviet forces unilaterally by 500,000 troops. This would include the withdrawal of six tank divisions from East Germany, Czechoslovakia, and Hungary, and 10,000 tanks, 8,500 artillery systems, and

800 combat aircraft from the European portions of the Soviet Union. The reduction of the Soviets' conventional superiority in Europe would make it far easier for the West to give up the nuclear weapons that it had relied on to counter that threat.

Gorbachev, Bush, and the Collapse of the Soviet Empire

Over the next few years, not only did the Cold War wind down, but also first the Soviet empire in eastern Europe and then the Soviet Union itself completely collapsed. The new American president, George H.W. Bush, was soon worrying that Soviet weakness might pose a greater threat to U.S. interests than Soviet strength.

The Bush administration was considerably less conservative than many members of Reagan's administration, some of whom Bush privately referred to as "marginal intellectual thugs." Nevertheless, Bush and his advisers were at first more cautious on relations with the Soviet Union than the Reagan administration had been. Bush had been appalled by Reagan's willingness at Reykjavik to eliminate all nuclear weapons. When Bush became president, he decided to pause on all further nuclear negotiations until the Soviets had proved their sincerity with agreements on substantial conventional arms reductions along with a retraction of Soviet influence in such hot spots as Afghanistan, Angola, Cambodia, and Central America.

Such evidence of Soviet sincerity was quickly forthcoming. In December 1988, even before Bush took office, the Soviets successfully worked with U.S. Assistant Secretary of State Chester Crocker to broker a deal in Angola. Cuba would withdraw its 30,000 troops in Angola. In return South Africa would take the pressure off the Angolan government by permitting the independence of neighboring Namibia, withdrawing its forces from the area, and pushing Jonas Savimbi, the Angolan guerrilla leader it had supported along with the United States, to participate in elections with the Soviet-backed Angolan government. Bush watched as the Soviets faithfully carried out their part of this agreement.

As further evidence of Soviet sincerity, the Soviet-backed Vietnamese government announced in January 1989 that it was withdrawing 50,000 troops from Cambodia. Soon the United Nations was brokering a deal between the remaining Cambodian government and the various Cambodian opposition groups supported by the United States and China (including, unfortunately, the murderous Khmer Rouge).

At the same time the Soviets stopped supplying arms to the Sandinistas of Nicaragua and urged the Cubans to do likewise. Meanwhile the U.S. Congress was cutting aid to the contras and forcing Bush to join the search led by the other Central American states for a compromise peace. By the end of 1989, Bush, Gorbachev, the Sandinistas, and the contras had agreed to accept the results of a Nicaraguan election to be held in 1990.

Moreover in early 1989 Gorbachev made good on his promise to withdraw his 120,000 Soviet troops from Afghanistan. When Bush insisted that the United States would continue supporting the guerrilla forces unless the Soviets stopped all further aid to the government, Gorbachev agreed to disagree. Thus, although the war in Afghanistan continued, it was no longer a major point of contention between the superpowers.

Finally Gorbachev and Shevardnadze offered a conventional arms treaty between NATO and the Warsaw Pact that would provide for equal numbers of troops, tanks, and artillery in Europe. While this goal could be accomplished by a 25 percent reduction of troops on both sides, it required a 50 percent cut in Warsaw Pact tanks and artillery against only a 10 percent cut in equivalent NATO weapons. Not only was Gorbachev willing to accept such differential reductions, but he agreed to specific limits on the number of troops the Soviets could station on the soil of their eastern European allies. At this point Bush was sufficiently convinced of Gorbachev's sincerity that he agreed to include parity in weapons where NATO was superior, such as planes and helicopters. Bush also agreed to start the reductions in 1992 rather than wait five years as Gorbachev had proposed.

Bush was anxious to accelerate conventional cuts because he wanted to lessen the chances that the Soviets would be able to intervene against the growing independence movements in eastern Europe. Already Gorbachev had shown his willingness to tolerate reform movements in Poland and Hungary even though they had an anti-Soviet potential. In spring 1989, General Wojciech Jaruzelski, leader of the martial rule government in Poland, permitted the legalization of the opposition's Solidarity movement and agreed to free elections. Shortly afterward Hungary began to tear down the barbed wire fences that divided it from Austria and the West. Gorbachev did not invoke the Brezhnev Doctrine to put these movements down by force. Instead he gave his permission for each eastern European Communist Party to go its own way. He probably thought that if the Soviets showed a modicum of restraint and tolerance, the outcome would be "lots of little Gorbachevs" establishing reform communism in eastern Europe in imitation of his own actions in the Soviet Union. But it was not clear what he would do if reform got out of the hands of the Communist Party and into the hands of anticommunist and anti-Soviet reformers.

The test came in June 1989 when Solidarity won ninety-nine out of one hundred contested seats in the elections for the Polish upper legislative house while thirty-three of thirty-five top Polish Communist leaders lost their seats in the lower house. Communists lost even in elections where they ran unopposed because Polish voters simply crossed out their names.

Only a few days before this Polish rejection of communism, Chinese troops had slaughtered democratic protesters in Tiananmen Square in Beijing to protect the authority of the Chinese Communist Party. In the Soviet Union itself, army troops had brutally attacked protesters in the province of Georgia, using shovels as well as bullets to kill nineteen and injure some 200 of them. Would Gorbachev turn to similar measures to thwart an anti-Soviet, anticommunist government in Poland, a government that would threaten Soviet access to the even more strategic nation of East Germany?

The answer came on August 22, 1989, when Gorbachev ordered the Polish Communists to accept the election results and yield power to a coalition noncommunist government. The death of the Brezhnev Doctrine was now public and all of eastern Europe took heed. Hungary, which was already permitting Hungarian citizens to pass freely into the West across its recently demilitarized border with Austria, began allowing East German vacationers in Hungary to join the exodus. In three days 13,000 East Germans fled. East Germany then asked Czechoslovakia to prevent Germans from crossing its territory to get to Hungary and the West. Tens of thousands of East Germans immediately took refuge in the West German embassy in Prague, and they also were soon given permission to leave for the West.

In the midst of this East German hemorrhage, Gorbachev visited East Berlin and received far more enthusiastic cheers from the German crowds than did Erich Honecker, their own leader. After Gorbachev departed Honecker ordered his army to fire on the demonstrations that were continuing in Leipzig. The army refused. Party leaders then ousted Honecker and his entire cabinet, whereupon Gorbachev encouraged the new East German government to relieve the pressure on itself by opening its borders to the West. On November 9, 1989, ecstatic Germans not only surged through that most hated symbol of the Cold War, the Berlin Wall, but began dancing on top of it and hacking it down with whatever tools were handy.

If the domino effect had not taken place in Vietnam, it certainly did in eastern Europe. Shortly before the Berlin Wall began coming down, the Hungarian Communist Party tried to save itself by renouncing Leninism and declaring the nation a republic rather than a "people's republic." But in elections held the following year, the Communists garnered only 8 percent of the vote. In Czechoslovakia a peaceful "Velvet Revolution" brought the replacement of the Communist government by the playwright and former political prisoner Václav Havel. Even in Bulgaria, the most pro-Soviet of all the Warsaw Pact members, the Communist leader Todor Zhikov lost control of the nation he had commanded since 1954.

As the Soviet empire crumbled, George Bush began to take the initiative in seeking Soviet-American accords rather than waiting for Gorbachev to make all the concessions. Bush wanted to bolster Gorbachev's increasingly precarious position within his own country and to nail down agreements that would make it difficult for the Soviets to renege in case Gorbachev was overturned. In December 1989 Bush met Gorbachev aboard ships in the storm-tossed harbor of Malta. On his way to the Malta summit, Gorbachev had stopped off in Italy to see Pope John Paul II and to announce that henceforth the Soviet Union would recognize freedom of religion within its boundaries. This claim reinforced the freedom Gorbachev had already granted to Soviet Jews to emigrate. In response Bush told Gorbachev at the Malta summit that he would lift the Jackson-Vanik restrictions on Soviet-American trade and negotiate a commercial treaty that would grant the Soviet Union most-favored-nation status. He and Gorbachev also agreed to destroy all chemical and biological weapons, to accelerate conventional arms reductions, and to speed up the START negotiations on strategic arms. Gorbachev even told Bush that he wanted U.S. troops to remain in Europe and NATO to keep an eye on the Germans, who he said were headed for unification.

Indeed the Germans were, and Gorbachev gave his formal consent to unification in January 1990. The sticking point remained the insistence of Bush and other Western leaders that a reunified Germany remain in NATO rather than become neutral. Finally the West was able to reassure Gorbachev by promising to integrate East German into West German forces and to reduce these new all-German forces to the size of West Germany's existing defense establishment. West Germany also agreed to formally recognize all eastern European borders and to pay for the relocation of the Soviet troops in East Germany back to the Soviet Union. Bush meanwhile promised that the United States would stay in NATO, where it could keep an eye on the Germans. Gorbachev then relented and allowed elections on the issue of reunification in both East and West Germany. In November 1990, West Germany's Chancellor Helmut Kohl won the election in both the East and the West, and the nation unified under his government's leadership. The primary fault line of the Cold War no longer existed.

As Germany progressed toward unification in 1990, the rest of the Soviet empire in eastern Europe fell apart as well. Shortly after the Malta summit, the Warsaw Pact nations met and condemned the raison d'être for their own alliance by denouncing Warsaw Pact intervention in Czechoslovakia during the Prague spring of 1968 and the Brezhnev Doctrine that intervention had spawned. The only dissenter was Nicolae Ceausescu of Rumania, who returned disgruntled to his country only to be overthrown and executed.

Gorbachev, Bush, and the Collapse of the Soviet Union

While Gorbachev was able to accommodate himself to the collapse of the Soviet empire in eastern Europe, he was not so sanguine about independence movements within the Soviet Union itself. The first of these took place in the Baltic countries of Latvia, Lithuania, and Estonia. It culminated in Lithuania's formal declaration of its independence on March 11, 1990. Gorbachev insisted that independence could take place constitutionally only with the consent of the Soviet parliament. To intimidate the Baltic nations, he reduced the supplies of oil from the Soviet Union upon which they were dependent and sent troops and tanks to occupy public buildings that he claimed were the property of the Communist Party and the central government.

Though the United States had never officially recognized the Soviet absorption of the Baltic states during World War II and though the Soviets now admitted that their annexation had come as part of a secret protocol to the Nazi-Soviet Pact of 1939, Bush did not fully support Baltic independence. He recognized and sympathized with Gorbachev's fear that the Baltics might serve as a model for other dissident Soviet republics, that the Russian minorities in the Baltic states might suffer, and that the Soviet army and other conservative opponents of Gorbachev might use his failure to keep the Baltics as further evidence of his weakness and of the need to displace him. So Bush urged the Baltic nations to move slowly while at the same time emphasizing to Gorbachev that the use of force to put down the independence movements in those states would put an abrupt stop to all further progress in U.S.-Soviet relations.

Gorbachev had reason to fear the model of the Baltic separatist movements because he was soon confronted with other provincial rebellions. The Republic of Georgia remained alienated over the massacre of protesters in 1989. The Republic of Azerbaijan began demanding its independence, whereupon its historic enemies in Armenia demanded their own independence to include the Armenian-populated enclave within Azerbaijan, Nagorno-Karabakh. Soon Gorbachev faced outright civil war in those provinces. The demands for independence quickly spread to more strategic portions of the Soviet Union,

U.S. president George Bush *(left)* and Russian president Boris Yeltsin. *(Courtesy of the George Bush Presidential Library)*

especially the Ukraine, Belorussia, Kazakhstan, and Moldavia. Although only the Moldavian movement became violent, the prospective loss of the other three provinces would take with them much of the agricultural and industrial basis of the Soviet economy, not to mention the nuclear weapons stationed on their territory.

Meanwhile, Gorbachev's standing fell within the rest of the Soviet Union as well. Gorbachev had failed to couple his political reforms with sufficient attention to economic reform. The decline of world oil prices upon which so much of the Soviet economy depended, the huge proportion of the nation's resources spent on the military, and the cost of maintaining Soviet clients in the developing world were all exacerbated by the bad planning, rigidity, and corruption of the Soviet state and party bureaucracy. The combination of these evils devastated the Soviet economy. As the economy fell, the free elections that Gorbachev championed began to return politicians who opposed the central government that Gorbachev commanded.

Bush and his advisers began to fear that as the independence movements challenged a weakened Gorbachev, the Soviet central government might lose control of its nuclear armory, derailing all attempts to dampen the arms race. As Gorbachev sent troops and tanks into the dissident areas and harassed independence-minded governments, Bush wanted to bolster Gorbachev and the Soviet economy by signing the trade agreements that made the Soviet Union a most favored nation. But Bush warned Gorbachev that the United States would not be able to sign those agreements if Gorbachev used force to hold the republics against their will.

Gorbachev decided to rely on harassment and a war of nerves against the republics while withholding a full use of force. This policy alienated Soviet liberals by going too far and Soviet conservatives by not going far enough. Bush, however, decided he could continue to cooperate with Gorbachev at least until German reunification within NATO was completed. He continued to urge the Soviet dissident republics to be cautious in asserting their independence and held Gorbachev's liberal rival, Russian president Boris Yeltsin, at arm's length.

As a result Bush and Gorbachev were able to work out the final German settlement at a summit in Washington in June 1990. In addition they were able to cooperate through the United Nations Security Council to oppose the Iraqi invasion of Kuwait in July. The following November they met in Paris to sign a treaty formally ending the Cold War. At the same time they signed a final version of the conventional arms treaty in which the Warsaw Pact agreed to cuts of 50 percent while NATO cut its weapons only about 10 percent.

Ironically conventional reductions on both sides soon outran the treaty. Within a few months, the Warsaw Pact had disbanded entirely and the Soviets had pledged to pull all their troops out of eastern Europe. In the midst of this conventional build-down, in July 1991 in Moscow, Bush and Gorbachev finally signed a START treaty that limited both sides to 6,000 nuclear warheads and 1,600 strategic launchers.

On his way back to the United States from that Moscow summit, Bush performed a final service for Gorbachev by going to Kiev, the capital of Ukraine, and warning against the province's abrupt moves toward independence. (One of Reagan's former conservative speechwriters famously branded this speech "Chicken Kiev.") But it was too late; Gorbachev had lost his grip. In August 1991, on the eve of the signing of a treaty Gorbachev had put forward to regulate the relations between the central government and the republics, members of his own cabinet who feared the loss of central power placed him under house arrest at his vacation dacha in the Crimea. The inept plotters, however, had not secured full control of the armed forces, communications, or rival government bodies. Boris Yeltsin defied the coup by barricading himself inside the Russian Republic's parliamentary building, the White House. Thousands of Muscovites, rallying to his defense, linked hands around the White House to prevent the tanks and troops surrounding the building from entering except over their prostrate bodies.

The plotters' nerve broke as Yeltsin's Russian government moved to arrest them. One fled to Gorbachev's dacha to beg forgiveness; another committed suicide. Gorbachev was released, and he returned to Moscow to try to resume control of the government without even acknowledging Yeltsin's assistance. To regain his stature he blamed the Communist Party for the coup and then resigned from the party and ended its role in government. But Gorbachev's authority was an empty shell. Russia, Ukraine (formerly known as "the Ukraine"), Belarus (formerly Belorussia), and most of the other major Soviet republics declared their outright independence, joining the Baltics, Armenia, and Georgia in defying any sovereignty of the central government. In place of Gorbachev's central government, they formed a loose association they called the Commonwealth of Independent States. Bush contributed to the disintegration of the Soviet Union by recognizing the independence of the republics, starting with the Baltic nations. On December 25, 1991, Gorbachev

Breakup of the Soviet Union, 1991

resigned and went into political retirement. The Cold War was over, but the United States would have a very short breathing space before it faced other major challenges.

Controversial Issues

The end of the Cold War set off an immediate debate as to whose and what policies were responsible for the Western victory. Hard-line nationalists like Caspar Weinberger claimed that the collapse of the Soviet Union vindicated the uncompromising anticommunist policies he and like-minded conservatives had long demanded and finally instituted under Ronald Reagan. In his account of the Reagan administration, Weinberger railed at his adversaries in the State Department who were too ready to negotiate and make concessions to the Soviets. Only unrelenting pressure on the Soviet Union had won the victory, and even as late as 1990 he was not sure that the pressure should be removed and further agreements made.[2]

George Shultz was one of those within the Reagan administration whom Weinberger was criticizing. Shultz agreed with Weinberger that the hard stance Reagan had taken in the early years of his administration had forced the Soviets to give up the Cold War. But Shultz, like other hard realists, believed that there was a point at which to negotiate and reap the rewards of a firm stance by hard bargaining. He credited himself and his like-minded compatriots with defeating the uncompromising stance of the hard-liners by reinforcing Ronald Reagan's desire to come to a true peace agreement with the Soviets and directing Reagan's vague desires into detailed and enforceable treaties. Thus, for instance, he had parlayed Reagan's belief in the Strategic Defense Initiative into "the ultimate bargaining chip."[3]

Softer realists rejected the idea that Reagan's hard stance had been necessary to end the Cold War. George Kennan called claims that such policies had "won" the Cold War "intrinsically silly." Kennan assumed that it had been necessary to contain the Soviet threat to the major Western allies from the outset of the Cold War, but he thought that an adequate balance of power could have been attained by more restrained diplomatic and military measures than Reagan and most of his presidential predecessors had adopted. According to Kennan, both the Soviets and the Americans had weakened and nearly bankrupted themselves by arming against "unreal and exaggerated estimates of the intentions and strength of the other party."[4] The assumption underlying this view and the present chapter of this book is that Gorbachev rather than Reagan had been most responsible for ending the Cold War and that in doing so he had reacted more to long-term internal trends within the Soviet Union than to Reagan's policies and pressures.

Revisionists disputed the idea that any confrontation of the Soviet Union, soft or hard, had been necessary. They argued that the Soviet Union had never been more than a regional power of the second rank and therefore had posed no real threat to the United States or the West. In fact they believed that the Soviets had performed a valuable service for the United States, restraining their third-world clients in order to avoid being dragged into a war with the United States on behalf of their allies. Thus the Cold War had been a "shadow war" that the United States used to justify its intervention in the third world in order to control its resources and shape an American-led capitalist hegemony. Revisionists assumed that this capitalist intervention into the third world, which they saw as the most significant aspect of the Cold War, would continue even without the Soviet Union as a shadow opponent to justify it. Thus, they argued, nobody won the Cold War because it was not over.[5]

Further Reading

The best historical works that give primary credit to Reagan for ending the Cold War are by John Lewis Gaddis, *The Cold War: A New History* (2005) and *Strategies of Containment: A Critical Appraisal of American National Security Policy During the Cold War* (rev. and updated ed., 2005). See also Paul Lettow, *Ronald Reagan and the Quest to Abolish Nuclear Weapons* (2005); Beth A. Fischer, *The Reagan Reversal: Foreign Policy and the End of the Cold War* (1997); and Jack F. Matlock, *Reagan and Gorbachev: How the Cold War Ended* (2002), a memoir and history by Reagan's ambassador to the Soviet Union.

The best and most complete histories of the end of the Cold War are Don Oberdorfer, *From the Cold War to a New Era: The United States and the Soviet Union, 1983–1991* (updated ed., 1998); and Raymond Garthoff, *The Great Transition: American Soviet Relations and the End of the Cold War* (1994). Both give more credit to Gorbachev than to Reagan for ending the Cold War. Garthoff, who is fluent in the Russian language, has made excellent use of Soviet sources and archives. For works on the Soviet side, see Vladislav Zubok, *A Failed Empire: From Stalin to Gorbachev* (2007); Anatoly S. Chernyaev, *My Six Years with Gorbachev* (2000); Ronald Grigor Suny, *The Soviet Experiment: Russia, the USSR, and the Successor States* (1998); Georgi Arbatov, *The System: An Insider's Life in Soviet Politics* (1992); Robert D. English, *Russia and the Idea of the West: Gorbachev, Intellectuals, and the End of the Cold War* (2000); and Christopher Andrew and Vasili Mitrokhin, *The Sword and the Shield: The Mitrokhin Archive and the Secret History of the KGB* (1999), and *The World Was Going Our Way: The KGB and the Battle for the Third World* (2005).

The best works on the collapse of Soviet power in eastern Europe are Timothy Garton Ash, *The Magic Lantern: The Revolution of '89 Witnessed in Warsaw, Budapest, Berlin, and Prague* (1990), and *The Polish Revolution: Solidarity* (1991); Gale Stokes, *The Walls Came Tumbling Down: The Collapse of Communism in Eastern Europe* (1993); and Philip Zelikow and Condoleezza Rice, *Germany Unified and Europe Transformed: A Study in Statecraft* (1995).

Notes

1. James Mann, *The Rebellion of Ronald Reagan: A History of the End of the Cold War* (2009).
2. Caspar Weinberger, *Fighting for Peace: Seven Critical Years in the Pentagon* (1990).
3. George Pratt Shultz, *Turmoil and Triumph: My Years as Secretary of State* (1993).
4. George Kennan, "The G.O.P. Won the Cold War? Ridiculous," *New York Times*, October 28, 1992.
5. See the essays by Bruce Cumings and Walter LaFeber in *The End of the Cold War*, ed. Michael J. Hogan (1992). See also Odd Arne Westad, *The Global Cold War: Third World Interventions and the Making of Our Times* (2005).

CHAPTER 17

AMERICAN FOREIGN POLICY IN THE AFTERMATH OF THE COLD WAR

The Debate Over American Intervention

For more than forty years, the United States had a fairly simple standard by which to judge the advisability of intervention: the need to contain the Soviet Union. That simple standard did not eliminate all controversy over specific cases of intervention. Nationalists like Ronald Reagan argued that the Soviet Union and communism were responsible for all armed insurrections in the world and thereby justified U.S. intervention in places like Nicaragua, while his restrained realist opponents insisted that such instances fell outside the containment doctrine because they posed no real threat to the world balance of power. But only a few revisionists, who believed that the United States had always intervened against economic rather than strategic threats, argued that the United States should not contain the Soviet Union when the challenge to the balance of power was real and serious. Thus, for most Americans, the debate over U.S. interventionism during the Cold War involved specific details rather than basic principles.

The end of the Cold War destroyed the containment standard for American intervention. The disappearance of the Soviet strategic threat, the changing structure of world power, the rising tide of nationalism and ethnic identity, the challenge of Islamic jihadism, the increased importance of world economics, and the prominence of relatively new foreign policy issues like the environment and drugs complicated the judgments that American leaders had to make about when U.S. armed intervention was necessary or justified. The removal of the Soviet threat thus eliminated part of the incentive for American intervention, but also it eliminated a restraint on such intervention because American leaders no longer had to worry about a Soviet reaction to U.S. intervention that might lead to a major conflict. Shaping a coherent American policy approach to intervention in this complicated but more permissive environment proved difficult for George H.W. Bush and even more difficult for his successor, Bill Clinton.

Bush set a standard for American intervention that might best be characterized as "prudent realism" (he used the word "prudent" so often in his speeches and conversations that comedians made it the most predominant part of their caricatures of him). He argued that the United States should forcibly intervene only when important national interests were at stake, when there were no other effective options, and when force was likely to be effective even when limited in scope, time, and costs. He also argued for what became known as the Powell Doctrine, after his chair of the Joint Chiefs of Staff, Colin Powell. According to that doctrine, if the United States did intervene, it would do so with overwhelming power to achieve a quick and therefore less bloody outcome. Bush's policy thus seemed an outgrowth of the old Weinberger Doctrine and a reaction against the gradualist policies of the Vietnam War.

As already detailed, Bush's cautious and "prudent" policy was clearly evident in his approach to Communist leader Mikhail Gorbachev and the Soviet Union. It was also apparent in the initial strategic review his administration conducted in 1989, which called for the rather mundane goal of "status quo plus." He made his approach even clearer privately when he expressed his contempt for "the vision thing."

However, in the wake of the success of the Gulf War of 1991 and with the need to provide a coherent, inspiring policy to rally public opinion now that the organizing principles of the Cold War and containment were gone, Bush proclaimed a new world order in which the United States would lead the United Nations and the world in the collective protection of stability and democracy against aggression. He quickly climbed down from some of the more grandiose goals of the new world order, however, when some of the Defense Planning Guidance documents behind this policy were leaked to the *New York Times* in 1992. The first of these documents was drafted largely by Zalmay Khalilzad, under the supervision of Defense Department aide Paul Wolfowitz and Secretary of Defense Dick Cheney (all later instrumental in the neoconservative push for a new strategy and war in Iraq under George W. Bush). It rejected the alternative policies of isolationism, collective security, and balance of power in favor of a more unilateral interventionist policy it called U.S. global leadership. Under that policy the United States would strive to maintain its military hegemony by blocking the rise of any rival and would continue its economic dominance through trade liberalization by pursuing free trade agreements such as the North American Free Trade Agreement (NAFTA).

Bush rejected some of the more aggressive and unilateralist aspects of this draft in favor of a policy he called collective engagement. Rather than decrying collective security, this policy statement emphasized cooperation with allies in confronting nondemocratic powers that might try to dominate critical regions. Rather than calling for outright military hegemony, it recommended that the United States maintain the military capability to fight two regional wars simultaneously. Bush and Congress did not fund such a military budget, however, and that part of the policy remained declaration rather than reality.

The exemplar of Bush's policy of prudent realistic intervention was the Persian Gulf War of 1991. When Saddam Hussein of Iraq attacked Kuwait, Bush skillfully put together a coalition that included some Middle Eastern nations and Gorbachev's Soviet Union to expel the Iraqis. (The Gulf War will be covered in more detail later in this chapter.) Bush cited both the realistic national interest of ensuring that an anti-American leader like Saddam did not dominate the oil supplies of the Middle East and the idealistic goal of providing collective security against aggression. His mobilization of an overpowering force in line with the Powell Doctrine defeated Iraq with a minimum of American and allied casualties. Afterward Bush rejoiced that the United States had "kicked the Vietnam syndrome" and shown itself willing to intervene where necessary.

Despite the success of the Gulf War and Bush's declared policy of prudent but vigorous intervention where American national interests were involved, the nation and Bush himself remained muddled about just when American intervention was truly necessary. Without the constraint of Soviet opposition, American public opinion could easily be rallied to intervene where suffering and gross violations of human rights appeared graphically on television. Bush resisted such pressures in the case of the breakup of Yugoslavia and the resulting civil war in Bosnia on the grounds that the Europeans should take care of issues in their own backyard and that American interests were not vitally involved (or, as Secretary of State James Baker put it, the United States did not have a dog in that fight). Bush also refused to intervene in Haiti when the military overthrew the elected president, again because he did not think American interests were threatened.

Yet Bush did intervene in two other instances when public pressure was great and American strategic interests were only slightly involved. When a Florida grand jury indicted the dictator of Panama, Manuel Noriega, on charges of drug smuggling and money laundering, Bush sent 25,000 American troops to arrest him and put a new government in place. Bush could use the realist excuse that the Panama Canal was at risk, but the primary reason may well have been embarrassment because Noriega had been a highly rewarded Central Intelligence Agency (CIA) asset and a conduit of aid to the Nicaraguan contras during Bush's tenure as chief of American intelligence. Bush also intervened with some 28,000 troops to forcibly dispense aid to Somalia, certainly not in pursuit of vital American interests but because the humanitarian crisis was so vividly obvious on television and because there was much popular agitation over his refusal to intervene in Bosnia. (The details of these crises will be covered later in this chapter.)

Thus, the incoherence and volatility of post–Cold War American public opinion significantly affected Bush's intervention policy, and it influenced the policy of his successor, Bill Clinton, even more. Clinton was far less experienced and far less interested in foreign policy than Bush. He saw no winning political issues in foreign policy and instructed his aides to handle diplomatic issues quietly so he could concentrate on domestic issues. In the 1992 presidential campaign, he attacked Bush on foreign policy issues mostly for effect without spelling out any broad disagreements or overall diplomatic vision. He argued that Bush was too pragmatic and cautious and paid too little attention to morality and democracy in foreign policy. Clinton criticized Bush for being too conciliatory toward China and for refusing to challenge the thugs in Haiti who had overthrown President Jean-Bertrand Aristide. But Clinton offered no specific plans to confront those issues and was clearly reluctant to intervene militarily in ways that might result in another Vietnam quagmire or cause heavy American casualties. When he did talk about intervention, he insisted that it not be unilateral but involve multiple allies or the United Nations (UN). Thus, at the outset of his administration, he encouraged the formation of an independent UN military force that could intervene with legitimacy to defend democratic principles and human rights against atrocious regimes.

Whatever impulses Clinton might have felt toward active intervention on behalf of democracy and human rights were quickly punctured when eighteen American soldiers died during a raid in Somalia. Thus when genocidal chaos broke out in Rwanda just as the last American troops were withdrawing from Somalia, Clinton had no stomach to intervene. He later issued a presidential directive on multilateral peacekeeping operations that offered no support for the independent UN force he had previously endorsed and called only for multilateral actions that were in line with American national interests.

Despite the setback Somalia presented to the idea of multilateral humanitarian intervention, the impulse toward such intervention remained strong among political liberals and even affected Clinton himself. Ultimately Clinton reversed Bush's policy against intervention in Haiti and allowed American troops to lead a UN force to restore Aristide. He also reversed Bush's policy against intervention in the civil war in the former Yugoslavia, organizing a NATO force against Serbia first to secure the independence of Bosnia and then to remove Serbian military control over Kosovo.

In all these cases, however, Clinton's intervention was hesitant and halfhearted. He wanted to reduce military expenditures in favor of his domestic program. Consequently he rejected the Powell Doctrine and tried to get by with minimal interventionist forces and minimal American casualties, often by resorting to air strikes rather than ground troops. In Haiti he did send in ground troops but only after he had made a deal with the military faction that had overthrown Aristide guaranteeing that the U.S. troops could land without opposition. In return the United States would treat that faction as a legitimate political party once the invasion displaced it and restored the president. That deal allowed the UN force to occupy the island without casualties, but also it destroyed any hope of real reform in Haiti's government. In the civil wars in the former Yugoslavia, Clinton relied on air power rather than ground forces to defeat Serbia. He used no-fly zones and expanded air attacks to punish Saddam Hussein when Saddam defied the terms of his surrender in the Gulf War. Clinton also used cruise missile attacks on Islamic extremist Osama bin Laden's training camps in Afghanistan and on a supposed chemical weapons plant in Sudan as his response to bin Laden's terrorist activities. These tactics certainly minimized American casualties, but many Americans questioned the long-term effect of such halfway interventions. Haiti was still mired in chaos, poverty, and brutality; Bosnia and Kosovo required continuous occupation by UN peacekeepers to maintain a tenuous truce; Saddam remained in power; and Bin Laden was almost completely unaffected by the cruise missile attack. On the other hand, it was debatable whether a larger scale of intervention could have improved those situations. Would large-scale ground interventions make possible real change and nation building, or would they stir nationalist opposition and perhaps guerrilla resistance that would make nation building impossible, however large the occupying force?

If Ronald Reagan had been correct in saying that "there wouldn't be any hot spots in the world" without the Soviet Union engaging in its game of strategic dominoes, then the end of the Cold War should have eliminated many of the regional problems that forced the United States to consider intervention. Unfortunately the end of the Cold War did not resolve all or even most of those problems because many regional problems, such as poverty, the population explosion, ecological crises, and regional conflicts over nationalism, ethnicity, and religion had little to do with the Cold War. The end of the Cold War even exacerbated some of these problems because the division between the superpowers had sometimes submerged or imposed a perverse sort of discipline on them. Nowhere was that clearer than in the Middle East.

The Impact of the End of the Cold War on the Middle East

The End of the Iran-Iraq War

The stalemated Iran-Iraq War dragged on through the mid-1980s, costing hundreds of thousands of lives. Iraq, exploiting the chaos in Iran caused by the Khomeini revolution, had attacked Iran to rectify the historical wrong Iraqis believed Great Britain and France had done to Iraq by imposing new borders on the remnants of the Ottoman Empire after World War I. Iraq's borders deprived it of a viable port on the Persian Gulf, which oil had made the most important waterway in the world. The border between Iran and Iraq ran down the middle of the navigable channel of the Shatt al Arab waterway to the gulf, but it was easily blockaded. Iraq's only strip of land along the gulf waters, the swampy Fao peninsula, could not support a large port. Consequently, Iraq had to depend upon often-hostile neighbors in order to export its oil and to receive vital imports.

When Saddam Hussein attacked Iran in 1980, he abrogated a 1975 border treaty between Iran and Iraq that had made clear the division of the Shatt al Arab. After his initially successful blitzkrieg, he offered to negotiate a new border settlement with the Iranian revolutionary regime that would give Iraq full control of the waterway. But Ayatollah Ruhollah Khomeini refused. By 1982 Iranian human wave assaults had pushed Iraqi forces back into their own territory at a terrible cost in lives to both sides, and Saddam began to sue for peace. Khomeini again refused. But Iranian legions proved unable to breach the massive Iraqi earthworks and water defenses or to overcome Iraq's liberal use of chemical weapons. With a stalemate on the ground, both sides began launching bomb and missile attacks on each other's cities, spreading the agony but deciding nothing. In 1984 Iraq took the war one step further and began attacking foreign tankers trading with Iranian ports. The Iranians responded in kind.

By 1987 this tanker war had drawn the rival Soviet and U.S. navies into an active role in Persian Gulf waters and brought American forces into violent conflict with Iran. The chief concern of the United States and most other Western nations was containing the spread of an Iranian-inspired, fundamentalist Islamic revolution to the vulnerable, oil-rich Persian Gulf States, including Saudi Arabia as well as Kuwait, Oman, Bahrain, Qatar, and the United Arab Emirates. This concern led the United States to join with most Arab states in supporting Iraq even though Baghdad had been a Soviet client. The United States led an international embargo against Iran, reflagged and escorted Kuwaiti vessels carrying Iraqi oil through the gulf, attacked Iranian warships and planes (tragically including an Iranian airliner), and quickly forgave an Iraqi missile attack on the frigate USS *Stark*. Moreover, the Western allies supplemented the aid that Saddam Hussein had already received from the Soviet Union and helped him build the largest military force in the gulf region. Iraq made significant gains in missile and chemical weapons capabilities as well as nuclear research and development. But outside aid was not enough to enable Iraq to win the war, in part because the United States was secretly aiding Iran at the same time.

In 1985 Israeli officials and some of Ronald Reagan's aides convinced the president that there was a moderate faction within the Iranian government with which the West could deal. This Iranian faction claimed that in exchange for some arms and spare parts to help it carry on the war with Iraq, it could arrange the freedom of several American and Western hostages who had been captured by Iranian-backed militants in Lebanon. Against the advice of the secretaries of state and defense and despite a law prohibiting the dispatch of arms to terrorist states, Robert McFarlane and his successor as national security adviser, John Poindexter, along with their aide, Lieutenant Colonel Oliver North, arranged to have Israel sell American antitank and antiaircraft missiles to Iran. (Colonel North then diverted the proceeds from these sales to support the Nicaraguan contras in order to circumvent a congressional prohibition against military aid to that rebel force.)

The last great Iranian offensive came in late 1986 on the Fao peninsula. After a bloody campaign in which Iran took much Iraqi territory, Saddam Hussein's troops reclaimed the Fao in a lightning-quick strike in April 1987. At this point the opposing armies held almost exactly the same ground with which they had begun the war nearly seven years earlier. The Iraqi economy was in shambles. It had expended $300 billion on the war, amassed an $80 billion foreign debt, and suffered some 400,000 casualties. Iran was isolated, strangling, short of war matériel, devastated by 1 million war casualties, and led by a gravely ill Khomeini. When the United Nations Security Council proposed a cease-fire in July, Saddam accepted it. Iran waited a year before agreeing to the cease-fire, and in August 1988 peace negotiations finally began in Geneva. It was not these negotiations that produced a settlement, however; that settlement would come in the crucible of the second Gulf War.

The Gulf War for Kuwait

After the 1988 cease-fire between Iran and Iraq, Saddam Hussein, with the profitable cooperation of scores of Western companies and governments, intensified his drive to build chemical and nuclear weapons along with the missiles to deliver them. Unfortunately for Saddam, his war debt continued to grow along with his arsenal. The ever-widening gap between Iraq's rich and poor, the inconclusive end to the war with the Iran, and the crumbling Iraqi economy created a growing rumble of internal discontent. The oil market was sluggish and OPEC members, especially Kuwait, routinely ignored quotas designed to prop up the oil prices Iraq needed to pay its debt. Moreover Iraq still had not solved its most gnawing strategic problem—access to the Persian Gulf.

Kuwait offered Saddam a perfect opportunity to chasten OPEC quota busters, secure gulf access, and create an external focus for Iraqi unrest. Saddam therefore revived Iraq's long-standing claim on Kuwait's gulf shoreline as well as a claim to the entire Rumaila oil field that Iraq shared with Kuwait. As further leverage he denounced Kuwait as one of the Persian Gulf States that refused to forgive loans made to Iraq during the war with

Iran. In Iraq's view the rich gulf states were shirking their responsibility to share the burden for mutual Arab defense. Baghdad perceived itself as having protected the gulf states from the Islamic revolution at great cost in blood and riches. Now it demanded just compensation. Saddam, lashing out at his gulf neighbors, played on the general Arab sense of injustice that the residents of the gulf states, which were artificial entities created by Western imperialists and contained only 5 percent of the Arab population, controlled most of the Arabian oil wealth and shared only a few crumbs of aid with their poor and more numerous cousins in Egypt, Jordan, Lebanon, and Palestine.

In July 1990 Iraq accused Kuwait of drilling diagonally into the Iraqi portion of the Rumaila oil field. As OPEC negotiations over the issue got under way, Iraqi troops massed on the Kuwaiti border. Saddam demanded that Kuwait forgive Iraq's $20 billion debt while ceding Babbitt Island, an excellent site for an oil installation, and a strip of coastline that would give Iraq an extensive Persian Gulf port. Saddam promised there would be no attack as long as negotiations continued. Here Kuwait, the United States, and much of the rest of the world committed a gross miscalculation. Most analysts agreed that Saddam was merely saber rattling and that he would focus on rebuilding his economy after some give-and-take with Kuwait. The American ambassador thus told Saddam Hussein that the United States would not take sides in a dispute that was limited to Arab states.

Perhaps taking this statement as a green light, Iraqi forces invaded Kuwait on August 2, 1990, shortly after Kuwait rejected the demands Iraq had made during the OPEC negotiations. Iraq consolidated its hold over the emirate in a few days and immediately began building defensive positions on the Saudi border. Saddam could easily have over-run important Saudi oil fields. That he did not and instead adopted a defensive posture suggests that he had no intention of expanding beyond Kuwait. With the annexation of Kuwait, Iraq had already come close to displacing Saudi Arabia as the world's greatest oil producer and would inevitably become a more important force within OPEC.

If Saddam Hussein expected the United States and the world to accept the annexation of Kuwait as a fait accompli, he miscalculated. Many Arabs cheered Saddam on in the belief that he might share the oil wealth more equitably than the gulf sheikhdoms had done and would confront Israel more militantly. But almost all Arab governments denounced his invasion. So did Iraq's former ally, the Soviet Union. That gave George H.W. Bush the chance to organize an international force against Saddam through the UN Security Council without fear of a Soviet veto.

Even with Soviet and UN approval, Bush faced a major problem organizing resistance to Saddam in the Arab world. After all the money Saudi Arabia had spent on American high-tech armaments, it was humiliating for the Saudis to ask for Western aid to protect the Islamic holy places. It was even more humiliating to allow the United States, the protector of Israel, to station troops on Arab land. To deal with this problem, Bush diluted the American presence by skillfully organizing an international force nominally under UN command. This force included not only Western European troops and those of America's Arab clients like Egypt and Saudi Arabia, but also a former Soviet client, Hafez Assad of Syria. Assad even cut off Iraq's access to the pipeline across Syrian territory through which Saddam could export his oil.

Bush and the UN Security Council first tried to force Saddam's retreat by imposing stringent economic and trade sanctions against Iraq. But Saddam defied the bans and received some goods and support from sympathetic Palestinians in Jordan. With King Hussein of Jordan cowed into neutrality by his Palestinian population, Saddam turned to his opposite border and made peace with Iran. He reaffirmed the 1975 agreement over the Shatt al Arab waterway, thus formally ending the Iran-Iraq War without any significant territorial change on either side.

As Saddam showed no signs of relenting on Kuwait, Bush began pushing his allies for military action. His own military was reluctant. Admiral William Crowe, the former chair of Reagan's Joint Chiefs of Staff, wanted to continue relying on bombing and sanctions to force Saddam to settle without risking heavy American and allied casualties. Bush's own Joint Chiefs insisted that if Bush was going to resort to military action, he should use overwhelming force to avoid another Vietnam. Bush did so. At the expiration of an ultimatum Bush had pushed through the UN Security Council, the defensive Operation Desert Shield gave way in early 1991 to Operation Desert Storm. After weeks of heavy bombing failed to move Saddam, allied ground forces attacked and routed Iraqi troops within a few days.

However Bush's UN mandate extended only to dislodging Saddam's forces from Kuwait, not to pushing on to Baghdad itself and ousting the Iraqi leader. So the allies held up their assault in southern Iraq and called for all internal opponents to Saddam Hussein to rise up and overthrow him. Heartened by the cataclysmic defeat Saddam had suffered, Shiite forces in the south and Kurdish forces in the north rebelled. They were promptly defeated by troops still loyal to Saddam and the Sunni minority. Only belatedly, after permitting Saddam's helicopters to fly unimpeded and slaughter the Shiite and Kurdish rebels, did Bush and the allies intervene with no-fly zones and other measures to prevent the complete subjection and persecution of the disaffected groups. Bush and the allies also continued their economic sanctions against Saddam's government. But Saddam defied many of the agreements he had made to end the war. He blocked many of the attempts of inspectors to confirm the destruction of his weapons of mass destruction. He also hedged on recognizing the borders with Kuwait specified in the 1991 cease-fire agreement; and he thumbed his nose at Western attempts to get him overthrown. He remained in power even as George H.W. Bush, his supposed conqueror, found himself ousted by Bill Clinton's victory in the 1992 U.S. presidential election.

Clinton continued Bush's containment policy against Saddam. When Saddam suddenly moved 10,000 of his elite Republican Guard toward the Kuwait border, Clinton sent 36,000 U.S. troops to Kuwait, and Saddam pulled back. But Clinton relied far more on air power than troops to enforce containment of Saddam, just as he did in most of his other interventions. American pilots flew more than 10,000 sorties in the year 2000 to enforce the no-fly zones and punish the Iraqis for firing on allied planes. Clinton also ordered an attack by twenty-three cruises missiles on suspected Iraqi intelligence stations in Baghdad to retaliate for an attempt by Iraqis to assassinate former President Bush in Kuwait. Finally, in response to Saddam's defiance of UN weapons inspectors, Clinton ordered four days of intense bombing of Iraqi military facilities.

President George Bush *(fifth from left)* and his primary foreign policy and national security officials, including *(from left to right)* CIA director Robert Gates, White House Chief of Staff John Sununu, Secretary of Defense Richard Cheney, Vice President Dan Quayle, Secretary of State James Baker, National Security Adviser Brent Scowcroft, and Chair of the Joint Chiefs of Staff Colin Powell. *(Courtesy of the George Bush Presidential Library)*

Nevertheless the containment regime against Saddam continued to deteriorate. Saddam kept the weapons inspectors out. Moreover the very public suffering of Iraqi civilians in the face of international economic sanctions brought the UN to open the way for Iraq to sell enough oil to pay for food and medical supplies. By diverting much of this trade to the strengthening of his own regime, Saddam managed to hang on to power through Clinton's two terms.

The Question of Palestine

The war for Kuwait combined with the end of the Cold War to affect profoundly not only the situation in the Persian Gulf but also the Arab-Israeli conflict. That conflict had already changed dramatically with the rise of the Palestinians' intifada in 1986. The intifada, or "shaking off," began as a result of two factors. One of these was the impotence of Yasser Arafat and the Palestine Liberation Organization (PLO) after their expulsion from Lebanon to Tunis in the Israeli invasion of Lebanon in 1982. The other was the increasing intransigence of the Israelis, who drastically increased Jewish settlements in the West Bank under Prime Minister Yitzhak Shamir and Housing Minister Ariel Sharon of the hard-line Likud Party.

Palestinians in the West Bank could count on neither the declining PLO nor the retreating Soviet Union and its Arab clients for rescue. Moreover they could not hope for the United States to exert much pressure on Israel to stop the settlements so shortly after the Reagan administration had to retreat ignominiously from its intervention in Lebanon. So the Palestinian residents of the West Bank rose up themselves with stones and labor strikes. Israel responded with an "iron fist" policy, killing about 400 Palestinians in the first two years of the uprising. The iron fist policy rebounded against the Israelis because television pictures of Israeli soldiers shooting rock-throwing Palestinians or breaking their legs raised sympathy for the Palestinians in the United States.

Since most Arab West Bank residents sympathized with Yasser Arafat rather than his rivals for Palestinian leadership, the intifada vaulted him back into prominence. It also pushed him toward a settlement that paid less attention to the demands of Palestinian exiles and radicals for the extinction of Israel and more to the calls of West Bank inhabitants for an independent Palestine in the West Bank and Gaza Strip that conceded the existence of Israel. In January 1988 the PLO issued a fourteen-point agenda from Tunis that won the backing of the Palestinian leadership in the territories. That proposal called for an independent Palestinian state, the rescinding of special taxes in the West Bank and Gaza, coexistence with Israel, and an international conference to discuss the details.

In 1988 the stage seemed set for a major advance toward a peace settlement. Jordan's King Hussein renounced any further claim to the West Bank. Arafat specifically recognized Israel's right to exist and renounced terrorism, the two conditions the United States had placed on opening relations with the PLO. American diplomats in Tunis began official conversations with the PLO for the first time. Meanwhile Arafat accepted American sponsorship of peace negotiations even though this meant accepting Israel's condition that the PLO could not be directly involved in those negotiations.

The peace effort nevertheless disintegrated in 1989. A failed PLO raid on Israel prompted the United States to suspend its conversations with Arafat. When the Palestinians and the PLO sided with Saddam Hussein in the Gulf War, U.S.-PLO relations eroded even further. Shamir pushed harder than ever for Jewish settlements in the West Bank on the grounds that the large immigration of Soviet Jews permitted by Gorbachev required a big Israel. Bush and Secretary of State James Baker became so frustrated with Shamir that Baker read out the White House telephone number during a press conference to let Shamir know where to get hold of him when the Israelis got serious about peace.

Despite the strains that the Gulf War put on U.S. relations with Israel and the PLO, prospects for a settlement soon brightened. With both the Soviet Union and Iraq removed from the power equation, the Arab states surrounding Israel had little alternative but to turn toward the United States and Israel to achieve their goals. Only with Israeli and U.S. consent could Syria retrieve the Golan Heights, Lebanon regain control of the Israeli "security zone" within its borders, and Jordan mollify the Palestinian threat to its Hashemite monarchy.

James Baker made use of U.S. leverage to secure Syrian, Lebanese, and Jordanian agreement to direct peace negotiations with Israel if Israel would stop building settlements in the West Bank. Saudi Arabia joined Syria and Jordan in pledging an end to their economic embargo against Israel in exchange for a halt to Jewish settlements in the territories. Arafat agreed to stand aside and let residents of the occupied territories rather than officials of the PLO represent the Palestinians in the negotiations, although the delegation would still take its instructions from the PLO. When Shamir balked, George Bush announced that the United States would cut off $10 billion in housing loan guarantees unless Israel stopped building the settlements that were blocking negotiations.

The Israelis finally consented, and, with the United States and the Soviet Union operating as joint sponsors, negotiations opened in Madrid in October 1991. The participants made little progress in that and subsequent negotiating sessions, but pressures and opportunities for agreement increased in the ensuing two years. Yitzhak Rabin, whose Labor Party defeated Shamir's Likud Party in June 1992, was more flexible on trading territory for peace than his predecessor. In addition the rise in Gaza and the West Bank of an Islamic fundamentalist organization, Hamas, pushed the Israeli and Arab sides toward a settlement. Hamas opposed both the PLO and any compromise with Israel. Israel tried to counter the influence of Hamas with force and expulsions, which led to harsh protests from many Arabs and their governments. But the protests from the Arab governments were only pro forma, because they too sought to reduce the influence of the fundamentalists and thought that an Arab-Israeli settlement would help do that.

At the urging of the United States, Saudi Arabia resumed subsidies to the more moderate PLO to help it compete with Hamas for influence among Palestinians and continue the negotiations with Israel. On September 13, 1993, the breakthrough came during secret negotiations between the Israelis and Palestinians in Oslo, Norway. With Israel finally talking directly to Arafat and the PLO, the Israelis and the Palestinians signed a framework agreement in which the Palestinians renounced terrorism and recognized Israel in return for interim Palestinian rule in Jericho and the Gaza Strip. Negotiations would continue under this framework on a final comprehensive agreement that would settle the issues of borders, return of refugees, and control of Jerusalem.

The implementation of the Oslo agreement and further progress toward peace were destroyed by terrorism, errors of judgment, and failure of nerve. Israeli evacuation of Palestinian territory in Gaza and Jericho was delayed for months when a Jewish settler in the West Bank town of Hebron massacred more than forty Islamic worshippers. Suicide bombers from the militant organizations Hamas and Islamic Jihad, determined to undermine any recognition of Israel, began blowing up Israeli buses and attacking civilians in Tel Aviv and Jerusalem. Most devastating of all, a Jewish extremist seeking to avoid any concessions of holy land to the Palestinians assassinated Rabin. Rabin's successor, Benjamin Netanyahu, distrusted the peace process and undermined it by permitting further Jewish settlements on the West Bank.

As Palestinian suicide attacks increased, Bill Clinton stepped in to rescue the peace effort by inviting Netanyahu and Arafat to a meeting in Wye, Virginia, where he got the two leaders to agree to restart the process. Under the Wye agreement of October 1998, Netanyahu agreed to evacuate more of the West Bank while Arafat promised to crack down on terrorism. After Netanyahu was defeated by the more moderate Ehud Barak, who let Clinton know that he was determined to reach a quick final settlement with the

Secretary of State Madeleine Albright *(left)* and President Bill Clinton at the Wye Conference. *(Courtesy of the William J. Clinton Presidential Library)*

Palestinians, Clinton decided to make a last effort to secure a comprehensive peace before his own beleaguered presidential term ran out. He invited Arafat and Barak to meet at Camp David for final negotiations in July 2000.

Arafat was a reluctant participant. He wanted Barak and Israel to live up to previous commitments so he could trust a final settlement. Barak, on the other hand, did not want to undermine his standing with distrustful Israelis by making preliminary concessions. He even went so far as to use Clinton to make his offers to Arafat at Camp David without personally stating them or putting them in writing. Nevertheless Barak made clear to Arafat that he was willing to give up more than 90 percent of the West Bank and Gaza and to compensate the Palestinians with some Israeli territory for the West Bank settlements that Israel would keep. He offered Arafat Palestinian control of most of Arab Jerusalem, although he said nothing about the Al-Aqsa Mosque on the Temple Mount, the ruins of the old Jewish Temple supported by the Wailing Wall and holy to both religions. Barak also promised a generous settlement on refugees. Many of the elements of this offer were vague and unwritten, but Barak and Clinton made clear there was room for negotiation and Clinton kept urging Arafat at least to make a counteroffer. Unfortunately Arafat never did, since he feared that once he publicly committed himself to something less than the right of all Palestinian refugees to return to Israel or the retrieval of all the lands lost in 1967, he would lose much of the PLO's constituency. In the end Clinton asked Arafat to give a yes or no answer and Arafat said no, insisting that Palestine should have all of the

West Bank and Gaza and the right of all refugees to return to Israel. Camp David broke up with no agreement and with both Clinton and Barak putting the entire blame on Arafat.

Subsequent negotiations demonstrated that a reasonable settlement was actually within reach. On the eve of Clinton's departure from the presidency, he offered specific ideas on a settlement in which the Palestinians would have more than 95 percent of the West Bank, all of Arab Jerusalem, sovereignty over the Al-Aqsa Mosque, and the return of a small percentage of refugees to Israel with compensation for the rest. Shortly afterward, in January 2001, the Israelis and Palestinians met at Taba in Egypt without the Americans present and agreed on similar terms, including arrangements on other critical issues like the sharing of water resources and the security of transportation routes. If there is ever to be a two-state solution of the Israeli-Palestinian issue, it will probably be very close to the terms of the Taba agreement.

Unfortunately the Taba agreement had no chance of implementation because just after the failure of Camp David, Ariel Sharon, the presidential candidate of the conservative Likud Party running against Barak, took a provocative walk on top of the Temple Mount near the Al-Aqsa Mosque, accompanied by Israeli troops and police. Palestinians, reacting with rage, began a second intifada. This time the Palestinians fought with guns rather than rocks. Sharon, having defeated Barak in the subsequent elections, rejected the entire Oslo peace process. The new U.S. president, George W. Bush, backed Sharon and marginalized Arafat. The peace process drowned in blood and mutual recriminations.

Syria and Lebanon

Syria had pushed the Palestinians toward a settlement so it could afford to make its own deal with Israel. Such a deal would permit Syria to regain the Golan Heights and thwart the rise of Islamic fundamentalism on its borders by getting Israel to withdraw from its occupied security zone on the Lebanese side of the Israeli border. By the 1990s Syria's interest in Lebanon had increased. Syria had successfully intervened in Lebanon, with tacit American approval, to stop a civil war and partially disarm the independent militias. Syria had accelerated its intervention because Amin Gemayel, the Maronite Christian president of Lebanon, had turned over power at the end of his term in 1988 to a Maronite extremist, General Michael Aoun. With Aoun relying on his troops rather than parliament to rule, the power-sharing arrangement established by the National Pact of 1943 broke down. The Muslim and some of the Christian parliamentary members and warlords, meeting in October 1989 under the auspices of Saudi Arabia, arranged a new power-sharing agreement that decreased the power of the Christian president while increasing the Muslim share of the parliament to 50 percent.

Rejecting the agreement, Aoun launched a war to maintain his power and oust the Syrians. The United States threw its support to Syria, and Aoun fled in October 1990. A new Lebanese government was formed under the revised power-sharing constitution, and in May 1991 it signed a treaty with Syria establishing a joint Syrian-Lebanese commission to make the major decisions in Lebanon. With the help of the Syrian army, the new government began to disarm the militias. But Hezbollah, the fundamentalist Shiite,

Iranian-backed militia, balked and won the right to keep its arms in the area next to the Israeli security zone in order to continue its fight with Israel. Lebanon then had to accord the PLO similar rights. Thus the only way Syria could disarm the remaining militias and reduce fundamentalist power on its borders was to negotiate an agreement that gained Israeli withdrawal from the security zone as well as the Golan Heights.

The Clinton administration tried to broker an Israeli-Syrian deal between 1993 and 2000. The Israelis were ready to withdraw from the Golan Heights to restore the Syrian border in exchange for security arrangements and the normalization of relations. Clinton held a last-ditch summit for the Syrians and Israelis just before he left office, but the negotiations failed. The Syrian leader, Hafez al-Assad, died shortly afterward. The Israelis then decided to ignore Syria and retreat from their security zone in Lebanon unilaterally. Hezbollah reaped the credit for Israel's retreat and vindicated for many in the Muslim world the efficacy of violent opposition as opposed to the ineffectual peacemaking of Assad and Arafat.

Islamic Jihadism

During the 1980s American concerns about the rise of Islamic fundamentalism focused on the Iran of the ayatollahs. American strategists took some comfort from the fact that Iran was Shiite and therefore might not have much influence on the rest of the Islamic world, which was overwhelmingly Sunni. Unfortunately for U.S. interests, Sunni fundamentalism was on the rise as well.

The unifying theme of both Sunni and Shiite fundamentalism was jihad or holy war. Modern and moderate Islamic thinkers argued that the jihad commended by the Prophet Muhammad referred to the internal struggle of the devout Muslim against sin and unrighteousness. But more radical Muslims insisted that jihad required holy war against Islam's enemies. They also argued that the Islamic world should be ruled by a caliph, who combined religious and secular authority, according to Sharia, Islamic law derived from the Koran. One of the most influential of these Islamic jihadist groups was the Wahhabi movement, which had been allied with the House of Ibn Saud since the 1840s. Another was the Muslim Brotherhood, which was founded in Egypt in 1928 and then branched out to influence many other movements, including Hamas in Palestine and the group in Egypt that assassinated President Anwar Sadat in 1981. The Muslim Brotherhood also had a branch in Syria that Hafez al-Assad wiped out in 1979 by razing its stronghold in the city of Hama and slaughtering most of its inhabitants. The credo of the Muslim Brotherhood was "God is our objective; the Koran is our constitution; the Prophet is our leader; struggle is our way; and death for the sake of God is the highest of our aspirations."

A third Sunni jihadist movement, Jamaat-e-Islami, was founded in India in 1941 and became a powerful presence in Pakistan after the partition of India in 1947. The various military dictatorships in Pakistan allied themselves with the Islamists, brought them into the intelligence service, and used them as guerrilla fighters in the struggle against India for the disputed province of Kashmir. Pakistan, with CIA assistance, also trained and equipped jihadists from around the world to attack the Soviet occupiers across the border in Afghanistan. When the Soviets left, the Pakistani intelligence service sponsored the takeover of Afghanistan by the radical Islamist Taliban organization in order to end the civil war between various factions that had followed the victory of the jihadists. Meanwhile, foreign jihadists who had fought in the war in Afghanistan spread out around the world, inspiring Islamist movements in many nations. Jihadists fought in Bosnia. They destabilized the peripheral Muslim nations of the former Soviet Union. They carried out attacks on Western targets in Indonesia. Islamists actually won an election in Algeria in 1991, only to have the military impose its own rule, resulting in a vicious civil war.

Among the jihadists who joined the fight in Afghanistan was Osama bin Laden. The son of a rich Saudi industrialist, Bin Laden dedicated his fortune and his life to continuing the jihad after the victory in Afghanistan. Exiled from Saudi Arabia because he opposed Saudi reliance on American troops to defeat Iraq in the Gulf War, he took refuge in the Islamist state of Sudan. There he funded and organized the training and dispatch of jihadists throughout the world. After the Gulf War he began to focus his enmity on the United States, the nation whose troops not only remained on the holy soil of Saudi Arabia but also supported the corrupt, secular Islamic regimes that persecuted Islamists, appeased Israel, and joined the coalition to fight fellow Muslims in Iraq.

The United States was the target of other jihadists as well. As conservative and moderate Muslim governments like that of Egypt began to crack down on their own Islamists, many radicals fled, took refuge in the West, and began to concentrate on Western targets. Among them was a blind Egyptian sheikh, Omar Abdel-Rahman, who had famously given religious authority to the assassins of Anwar Sadat. In 1993 Abdel-Rahman invited and authorized a car bombing attack on New York's World Trade Center that killed six people and injured more than 1,000 others. That attack was intended to be only the beginning of a campaign of terror against the United States, but Abdel-Rahman and his co-conspirators were captured and imprisoned when American investigators recovered the registration number of the van carrying the explosives, arrested the renter of the vehicle, and unraveled the plot.

Unfortunately there were far more jihadists ready to attack American targets. In 1996 terrorists blew up an American air force barracks in Saudi Arabia, killing nineteen and wounding hundreds more. The terrorists were never caught, but American investigators concluded that Hezbollah was the primary instigator with perhaps some assistance from Bin Laden. The Clinton administration set up a CIA office dedicated to following Bin Laden, succeeded in pressing Sudan to exile him, and then authorized the CIA to kidnap him from his refuge in Afghanistan. In 1998 Bin Laden's terrorist organization, al-Qaeda, succeeded in bombing the U.S. embassies in both Kenya and Tanzania. That attack killed more than 257 people and wounded more than 5,000, most of them African bystanders. Besides capturing and imprisoning four of the al-Qaeda bombers, the United States retaliated for the embassy bombings by launching cruise missiles against one of Bin Laden's training camps in Afghanistan and a factory in Sudan where the administration thought—but ultimately could not prove—that Bin Laden was manufacturing chemical weapons. But Bin Laden survived Clinton's attempts to kill him. Bin Laden went on to plan a bombing attack on the Los Angeles airport, which the United States thwarted, and then to successfully bomb the U.S. destroyer *Cole* as it was docked in the port of Aden in 2000. It was only a matter of time before jihadists would succeed in attacking targets within the United States itself.

The Impact of the End of the Cold War on Latin America

Even as the Cold War was ending in 1986 and 1987, Ronald Reagan refused to acknowledge that U.S. strategic interests might no longer be threatened by radical regimes in Central America. Thus he and his administration continued to stall on the Contadora Plan because it mandated the end of foreign aid to all rebels in Central America. When it became clear by 1987 that the Contadora Plan was dead, Oscar Arias, the president of Costa Rica, got all the presidents of the Central American republics to agree to a new peace plan. This Arias Plan called for cease-fires and amnesty between all governments and rebels in the area. Outside military aid to rebels was to stop and all regimes would recognize human rights and hold democratic elections.

Although the Sandinistas of Nicaragua accepted the Arias Plan, Reagan considered it flawed. He continued to argue that only military aid to the contras would force the Sandinistas to accept democracy and carry out fair elections. His position on Central America, however, had been weakened by the Iran-contra scandal, the World Court decision that the United States had violated international law in its attempts to sabotage the Sandinista government, and the adherence of all the Central American governments, including staunch U.S. allies, to the Arias Plan. Thus, Congress, rejecting Reagan's pleas, cut off all military aid to the contras.

With the Reagan policy weakened, Sandinista leader Daniel Ortega announced that Nicaragua would hold free elections in February 1990. The Reagan administration denounced the promise as fraudulent and urged the contras and other opposition groups to boycott the elections. But George Bush changed that policy when he took office in 1989. He, Secretary of State Baker, and Jim Wright, the Democratic Speaker of the House who had led the congressional opposition against Reagan's Central American policy, worked out a deal. The United States would supply $49.7 million in humanitarian aid to the contras, but would provide no military aid prior to the elections Ortega had promised. Moreover Bush ended Reagan's policy of urging the Nicaraguan opposition to boycott the elections.

Both Bush and Ortega assumed that the Sandinistas would win the election. Right up to election eve in October 1990, Bush kept insisting the Ortega was sabotaging the electoral process and warning Gorbachev that the Sandinista regime was a major obstacle to improved U.S.-Soviet relations. Ortega, meanwhile, accepted the participation of the United Nations and the Organization of American States (OAS) in the administration and observation of the elections, in full confidence that he would win a fair poll. It came as a shock to almost everyone, then, when the opposition was able to unite behind Violeta Barrios de Chamorro, the widow of the editor whose assassination in 1978 had triggered the ouster of Somoza, and to outpoll Ortega 55 to 41 percent.

The Bush administration rejoiced at the outcome and promised aid to pull Nicaragua out of the depression caused by war, the U.S. boycott, and Sandinista policies. But little of the aid was ultimately forthcoming, especially after Chamorro offended conservatives in the United States and Nicaragua by keeping Humberto Ortega, Daniel's brother, as head of the armed forces. However the attention of the United States turned away from Nicaragua as the direct Soviet threat to U.S. interests in Latin America ended and Soviet subsidies for Cuba were withdrawn, negating Cuba's ability to threaten the Western Hemisphere.

With the end of the Cold War, the isolation of Cuba, and the settlement in Nicaragua, El Salvador also moved toward peace. That had seemed an unlikely outcome in 1989 because Duarte had died and the right-wing Arena Party's Alfredo Christiani won the election to succeed him. But Christiani decided to accept the Arias Plan because it would end foreign aid to the FMLN rebels. In the fall of 1990, after the defeat of the Sandinistas in the Nicaraguan election, the FMLN also decided to accept a cease-fire and UN mediation. Moreover it gave up its planned offensive against the Arena government. But it agreed to disarm and to participate in elections only on the condition that the government would purge the military officers who had committed the worst atrocities, reduce the size of the army, establish a civilian police force, and provide land for the peasants in rebel-held zones. On New Year's Day, 1992, with the United States urging them on, the two sides agreed to peace on that basis.

As part of the agreement the United Nations was to report on human rights in El Salvador and to identify the people who should be purged from government on both sides for committing human rights atrocities. The UN Human Rights Report concluded that 85 percent of the atrocities had been committed by government forces and only 5 percent by the FMLN. It recommended the removal of some forty Salvadoran officers. After much hesitation the military leadership accepted these terms and retired, paving the way for elections in which both sides could participate. The right-wing Arena Party won those elections in 1994 and ruled El Salvador until 2009.

These developments were followed by a tenuous peace in neighboring Guatemala. Over army protests, the rebels and the government there signed a peace accord on March 19, 1994, to end the civil war and permit the UN Human Rights Commission to investigate charges of atrocities.

Nicaragua, El Salvador, and Guatemala were only three instances of Latin America's progress toward peace and some measure of democracy from the mid-1970s on. Although local conditions were most important in producing this trend, there were some instances in which U.S. policy and the end of the Cold War also made a difference. Jimmy Carter's human rights campaign had increased pressure on some of the dictatorial regimes of the area. Even though Reagan backed away from Carter's overt pressure for democracy and human rights in most instances, the Reagan administration decided in 1984 to demonstrate its sincerity in demanding democracy for Nicaragua by pressing for it in Chile. The United States began voting against international loans for Chile, and in part because of those pressures, President Augusto Pinochet consented to hold elections in 1988. To his surprise he lost by a vote of 54 to 43 percent. Thus Chile resumed its long tradition of democracy, but Pinochet protected himself and those who had committed atrocities on his behalf by maintaining control of the armed forces. Only toward the end of his life in 2006 did Pinochet face charges for his human rights abuses, but he escaped the charges brought against him in Spain and died before Chile could try him at home.

The other regimes that joined the ranks of Latin American democracies in this decade also had to make compromises with the leaders and armed forces that had maintained the previous dictatorships. Argentina led the way with elections in 1983. Brazil, Grenada, and Uruguay replaced dictatorships with free elections in 1985. Guatemala followed suit in 1986. In 1989 General Andres Rodrigues overthrew the long-time Paraguayan dictator Alfredo Stroessner and became president shortly thereafter in relatively free elections. In December 1990, five years after Jean-Claude Duvalier had fled Haiti and ended the thirty-year tyranny of the Duvalier family, that nation elected a new president, Father Jean-Bertrand Aristide. Thus, by 1992, according to Latin American expert Robert Pastor, "every country in South and Central America and every nation but Cuba in the Caribbean had elections judged free and fair by opposition leaders and international observers."[1]

However, if democracy, like the end of the Cold War, improved conditions in Latin America, it proved to be neither permanent nor a panacea. In Haiti the military overthrew Aristide within a year of his election. The United States and the OAS imposed economic sanctions and tried to restore Aristide through pressure and compromise with the military regime. Meanwhile thousands of refugees crammed themselves aboard leaky vessels and set out for the United States. The Bush administration intercepted these refugees and returned them to the mercies of the Haitian military regime without even a hearing as to whether they were fleeing political persecution rather than economic deprivation. Bill Clinton, after promising as a presidential candidate to change that refugee policy, reversed himself and continued it instead, although he did increase pressure on the Haitian regime by freezing Haitian assets and promoting an international trade embargo. Under pressure from the United States, in July 1993 the United Nations negotiated the Governor's Island Accord between Aristide and the coup leaders. Aristide would return to the presidency and promise not to punish the military for the coup. But the military government assassinated two of Aristide's projected cabinet members and inspired a mob to turn away an American naval vessel that was landing a UN force to train the Haitian police. Clinton vacillated for several months. But after the UN Security Council authorized the use of force, Clinton issued an ultimatum to the Haitian regime: "Your time is up. Leave now or we will force you from power." At that point former president Jimmy Carter asked to be allowed to go to Haiti and negotiate the removal of the regime. Overcoming Clinton's reluctance, a delegation consisting of Carter, General Colin Powell, and Senator Sam Nunn got the leader of the government, General Raul Cedras, to leave and permit the restoration of Aristide. American troops landed unopposed and fanned out over the country. Unfortunately, however, the agreement with Cedras recognized the paramilitary opposition to Aristide, many of whose members were CIA assets, as a legitimate opposition on a par with Aristide. American troops could only maintain a tenuous truce between armed backers of the two sides before the United States turned over the mission to the UN forces in April 1996. Chaos, poverty, and near civil war have plagued the island ever since. Aristide was reelected president in 2000 but forced out of office by armed rebels in 2004, with George W. Bush's administration urging him to leave. The best that can be said of the U.S. intervention is that perhaps things would have been even worse without it. But it certainly did little to advance the idea of humanitarian intervention.

It also did little to answer the question as to how the United States should handle the problem of refugees. Haitians, like many refugees from Latin America and the Caribbean, were fleeing both tyranny and poverty. The United States hoped that the replacement of dictatorships by democracies in Latin America might reduce the flow of refugees, but legal and illegal immigrants continued to pour in. Between 1981 and 1989, Latin America furnished 47 percent of the immigrants to the United States. Congress passed a new immigration law in 1986 to restrict the flow of illegal immigrants by legitimating those already in the country, while holding employers liable for hiring any new illegal arrivals. That did not stanch the flow. Democratic elections in Latin America only slightly altered the skewed economic and social systems that drove people to the United States. Thus the diplomatic problems posed by such issues as economic development, immigration, and border controls took on more prominence as the strategic problems that had dominated the Cold War era diminished in importance.

The United States sought better control of its border not only to stop the flow of illegal immigrants but also to stop drug smugglers. Like the immigration issue, drugs had assumed a larger place in American diplomacy as Cold War issues receded. No better example of that prominence could be found than in the bizarre case of Panama.

Panama's General Manuel Noriega had been a long-time informant of the CIA when, in 1986, he used his control of the army to overthrow the government. The United States briefly cut off aid to Panama but restored it because Noriega was valuable as a conduit for arms to the contras and as a source of information about Cuba and drug smugglers. He also provided staging areas for U.S. military operations in Central America and the Caribbean. The United States chose to overlook Noriega's own participation in the drug trade until 1987, by which time Noriega had not only become more blatant in his drug profiteering but had refused further support for the contras and drawn closer to Cuba and the Sandinistas. In late 1987 the United States began to squeeze Noriega by cutting off the $26 million he received in aid and reducing Panama's sugar quota. Then, after a Florida grand jury indicted Noriega for drug smuggling, the United States suspended payments for the Panama Canal.

By May 1989 opposition to Noriega within Panama had risen to the point that he faced certain defeat in the elections scheduled for that month. So Noriega aborted the vote. The United States got the OAS to condemn him, but that organization rejected coercion. Thwarted by the OAS, President Bush invited a coup against Noriega and then failed to come to the aid of military officers who staged one in October 1989. Noriega brutally put down the coup and declared a state of war with the United States. Amid this tension, an American serviceman was killed at a Panamanian checkpoint. Using that death as justification, Bush defied the OAS decision against coercion and on December 20, 1989, launched an invasion of Panama using 25,000 troops from the Canal Zone.

The invasion was brief and bloody. American forces captured Noriega and packed him off to Florida for trial on drug charges, where he was convicted and sentenced to thirty years in an American prison. The United States then installed as president Guillermo Endara, the candidate of Panama's economic elite who was on his way to being elected before Noriega canceled the elections. Bush, most Panamanians, and many Americans regarded the invasion as necessary and justified. But the cost in Panamanian lives in the neighborhoods around Noriega's headquarters was very heavy, and Panamanian resentment grew as neither the new president nor the United States did much to revive the Panamanian economy. Meanwhile most Latin American nations, many of which held no brief for Noriega, regarded the U.S. invasion as further evidence of arrogant interventionism by the North American colossus.

Latin American antagonism to such interventionism made Bush's war on drugs all the more difficult. Bush wanted to cut off the supply of cocaine to the United States at its source in Peru, Colombia, and Bolivia. He offered large amounts of aid to those nations if they would cooperate with U.S. drug agents in destroying coca crops and the laboratories that converted the coca leaves into cocaine. American agents and helicopters joined the police and military forces of the Andean countries to try to eradicate drug crops and laboratories.

Unfortunately the indigenous armed forces, police, and courts upon whom the United States depended to help eradicate the drug trade were often co-opted by drug cartels with access to huge amounts of money. These drug cartels were so strong that their members could assassinate hundreds of officials and destabilize governments. Meanwhile the peasants who raised the coca leaves resisted efforts to switch them to less profitable crops and often allied themselves in a marriage of convenience with antigovernment guerrilla forces.

In Peru, for instance, cocaine growers and drug dealers allied with Shining Path guerrillas. Atrocities on both sides mounted until Peruvian president Alberto Fujimori dissolved the legislature and the courts and took dictatorial powers with the justification that it was the only way to eliminate corruption and fight the guerrillas and drug traffickers. Fujimori ultimately captured the leader of Shining Path, defeated the movement, and reduced the drug trade in Peru, but at a terrible cost to both democracy and human life. When his atrocities and corruption caught up with him in November 2000, he fled the country, to be replaced by a more democratic government.

While the growth of coca declined somewhat in Peru at this time, drug dealers simply expanded their operations in neighboring Andean countries. President Clinton tried to combat that growth in Colombia by waiving human rights considerations and giving the Colombian armed forces more than $1 billion in money and assistance to fight drug dealers and their allies among the left-wing guerrillas and right-wing paramilitary groups. This "Plan Colombia" had some success in disarming the right-wing paramilitary, although it did so by offering amnesty to leaders guilty of terrible atrocities. But the left-wing rebels remained in control of large swaths of Colombia, and coca growing remained prevalent both in those territories and in other areas as well.

In Mexico the United States tried to circumvent corrupt drug enforcement officials in 1992 by kidnapping from Mexican soil a doctor allegedly involved in the torture of a U.S. drug enforcement agent. The U.S. Supreme Court then decided that the doctor could be held for trial against the protests of the Mexican government. Such U.S. intrusions into other nations as the Mexican kidnapping, the invasion of Panama, and military operations in the Andes raised resentment among Latin American nationalists and made them reluctant to endorse military intervention even in such a blatant case of tyrannical usurpation as Haiti.

It was clear, then, that even after the passing of the Cold War and the growth of democracy in Latin America, U.S. foreign policy would continue to face major problems in the region. Basic to those problems, whether immigration, drugs, or political instability, was the Latin American economy.

The economies of Latin America had actually grown considerably since the late 1950s. Per capita domestic product had doubled between 1960 and 1988, and life expectancy had increased from fifty-six to sixty-seven years. But the maldistribution of wealth between nations, classes, and ethnic groups in the region undermined that progress, as did the population explosion that doubled the number of people in Latin American after 1960.

Latin American economic progress was further slowed by the $400 billion debt that the major nations of the region ran up in the 1970s and 1980s. It required 44 percent of the region's foreign exchange just to pay the interest on that debt. Thus, in the three years between 1982 and 1985, Latin America transferred more capital to the United States than the United States had transferred to Latin America during the entire period of the Alliance for Progress that had begun in the presidency of John F. Kennedy. As a result, by 1989 Latin America's per capita domestic product had dropped 8 percent below that of 1981 and inflation was rampant in important nations like Brazil and Argentina.

The Reagan and Bush administrations took a laissez-faire attitude toward Latin American economic problems. They offered little aid to nations that were not under direct threat from Soviet or Cuban intervention. They were very reticent about signing treaties or offering aid to develop the Latin American economies in such a way as to preserve the rain forest and other ecological assets of South America. At the Earth Summit of 1992, sponsored by the United Nations in Rio de Janeiro, Bush refused to sign an international biodiversity treaty to preserve the world's plants, animals, and natural resources. He maintained that the United States and the West would have to finance too many conservation efforts in the third world and that the treaty gave insufficient patent protection for any biological inventions by U.S. companies. Bush also refused to sign a global warming treaty until he had watered down the strict timetable for reducing carbon dioxide emissions.

In addition Bush and Reagan did little to limit the population boom that was putting the world ecology under such pressure. In deference to the antiabortion sentiments of their own domestic constituency, they cut off U.S. contributions to any international birth-control programs that tolerated abortion. Neither did Bush mourn the Vatican's insistence that the issue of population growth be taken off the agenda of the Earth Summit.

Reagan extended his laissez-faire attitude to the debt problems of Latin American nations as well as their ecological and population problems. In 1985, however, his administration did help Latin American nations negotiate a refinancing of their debts through the World Bank. The refinancing lowered their interest payments somewhat, but their basic debt predicament remained.

The Bush administration went considerably further than Reagan on Latin American debts. On May 10, 1989, Bush's secretary of the treasury, Nicholas Brady, proposed that private banks, which owned more of the Latin American debt than donor governments did, reduce interest payments and write off some of the capital of that debt. Meanwhile, under this Brady Plan, the United States would cooperate with Japan, the World Bank, and the International Monetary Fund to offer new loans and debt refinancing to Latin American nations in return for market reforms, privatization of inefficient state enterprises, and balanced budgets. Because these international loans would go to the Latin American nations before rather than after they had renegotiated their debts with the private banks, the debtor nations would have leverage to get good terms from their creditors.

The United States also negotiated reductions in the bilateral official debts these nations owed to the American government. The United States wrote off 90 percent of the debts of Guyana, Honduras, and Nicaragua, 70 percent of the debts of Haiti and Bolivia, 25 percent of Jamaica's, and 4 percent of Chile's. Under Brady's subsequent Enterprise for the Americas plan issued the following year, the United States signed agreements with thirty Latin American nations establishing a framework for negotiating reductions in tariff and trade barriers.

The most important of these debt and trade agreements was with Mexico. Mexico's economy had grown an average of 6 percent per year between 1940 and 1982, becoming the tenth largest economy in the world. But the drop in oil prices left it with a foreign debt of over $100 billion, close to 80 percent of its annual gross domestic product. Real wages dropped 40 percent. People flocked to Mexico City from the countryside, looking for work and thus overburdening the city's and the nation's infrastructure.

In 1986 Mexican president Miguel de la Madrid tried to cope with the crisis by turning away from his state-managed protectionist economy and increasing exports. Mexico joined the General Agreement on Tariffs and Trade and lowered barriers especially to trade with the United States. But in the elections of 1988, Madrid's chosen successor, Carlos Salinas de Gortari, found himself challenged by Cuauhtémoc Cárdenas and a coalition of parties and people on the left who argued that more rather than less protection of Mexico's economy and markets was necessary. Cárdenas wanted to stop payment on the debts rather than subject the Mexican poor to the cuts in income and services that government budget austerity would require. Salinas barely and perhaps fraudulently defeated Cárdenas in the first truly contested election since the Mexican revolution.

Despite the thinness of his mandate, Salinas revolutionized his country's economy and its relations with the United States. In February 1990 Mexico became the first nation to negotiate debt relief under the Brady Plan. The settlement still left Mexico with sizable debt payments, but as the economy recovered, the debt declined to 36 percent of gross national product in 1991. Meanwhile, Salinas continued to privatize state industries. He changed the law to permit foreigners to own more than a 49 percent share of any property in Mexico. Most revolutionary of all, he proposed to join the United States and Canada in NAFTA.

Salinas and Bush saw NAFTA as a counter to the growing economic unification of Europe and the increasing solidity of the Asian bloc led by Japan, China, and the Association of Southeast Asia Nations. Other Latin American nations were moving toward trade liberalization as well. After the success of the Arias Plan, the Central American nations were forming a common market. Meanwhile, Brazil, Argentina, Uruguay, and Paraguay signed a common market treaty that was supposed to result in a single trade area by 1995.

Nevertheless the move toward free trade, privatization, and government budget austerity stirred conflict between first-world modernizers and third-world progressives in Latin America. Many Mexicans, for instance, believed with Cárdenas that NAFTA would keep the Mexican economy functioning as a supplier of raw materials and cheap labor to its stronger neighbors. The problems of unemployment, poverty, and disparity between classes would increase rather than decrease. Cárdenas and his followers preferred a state-directed economy that protected Mexico against competition from stronger economies, redistributed wealth within the nation, and allied itself with the attempt of other third-world nations to change the international economic rules. At the same time NAFTA and freer trade also ran into opposition in the United States. Many Americans feared that U.S. companies and jobs would flee to Mexico, where labor was cheaper and ecological standards less strict.

With an enormous expenditure of effort and political capital, President Clinton managed to overcome domestic opposition and squeeze the NAFTA treaty through the Senate in November 1993. No sooner had he done so, however, than a rebellion in the Chiapas area of Mexico against the Mexican government and NAFTA followed by the assassination of President Salinas's handpicked candidate to succeed him cast the Mexican side of the equation into doubt. Thus, even though the Communist world had collapsed, it was not at all clear that U.S. foreign policy in support of free-market solutions to third-world development would succeed.

That issue became even more salient when, within a month after the U.S. Congress had accepted NAFTA, the world took an even more important step toward reducing trade barriers. On December 15, 1993, 117 nations culminated eight years of hard negotiations with the signing of the General Agreement on Tariffs and Trade (GATT). Although they left several disputed issues out of the agreement to be settled at a later date, the GATT nations agreed to reduce tariffs and other important quotas by an average of one-third over six years. Those favoring the measure argued that the stimulation of world trade by GATT would increase world income by $270 billion in the next few years. Proponents also hoped that the economic integration promoted by GATT would work against the ethnic and nationalist forces of disintegration that were tearing apart the post–Cold War world. But a chorus of dissenters warned that free trade could also contribute to contention and disintegration. Opponents in the United States and other parts of the developed world feared that their high labor and environmental standards would be eroded by competition from nations whose costs of production would remain low because of their lack of labor or environmental protections. Less developed nations worried that free trade would leave them perpetually at the mercy of stronger nations and corporations that would plunder them of their cheap labor and resources and prevent their industrial development.

Opposition to globalization exploded in Seattle in 1999 during a meeting of the World Trade Organization (WTO). The protests there and elsewhere, along with the uneven distribution of the benefits of global trade, pushed the WTO to open a new round of negotiations on trade, billed as a "development round," in 2001 in Doha, Qatar. It was supposed to help developing countries by reducing the agricultural subsidies paid by developed countries to their own farmers to the detriment of farmers in the less developed world. It was also supposed to lessen the impact of patents on the prices of medicine and other advanced technology in poor countries and find a way to encourage nascent third-world industries that had difficulty surviving against multinational giants. Unfortunately the Doha round came to very little, and the issue of globalization remained one of the most contentious in world politics.

In Latin America, President Hugo Chávez of Venezuela replaced the ailing Fidel Castro as the leader of the revolt against U.S. economic policies and globalization. Democratic politics generally in Latin America swung to the left after the year 2000, and Chávez found enthusiastic support from the leaders of Bolivia and Ecuador and at least mild support from many other leaders in Latin America, including the presidents of Brazil and Argentina. Nevertheless, most nations in Latin America continued to contemplate trade agreements with the United States. Such agreements hinged not only on those nations' attitudes toward free trade and the United States, but also on the fluctuating sentiments toward free trade in the U.S. Congress and the American electorate.

The Impact of the End of the Cold War on Asia

The end of the Cold War had a major impact on U.S. policy toward Asia as well as toward Latin America and the Middle East. With the collapse of the Soviet threat, the Philippines felt able to ask the United States to leave its military bases in the islands and the United States felt able to agree, however reluctantly. Nevertheless U.S. economic interests, the regional problems that remained in the wake of the Cold War, and the desire of many Asians to have the United States help regulate the balance between the major powers remaining in the area—China, Russia, Japan, India, and Pakistan—all conspired to keep America militarily as well as economically involved in Asia.

Japan was the dominant economic power in Asia in the 1990s. It produced two-thirds of the continent's output and 16 percent of the world's goods (the United States produced 24 percent). It was also one of America's most important trading partners. Unfortunately, in conducting its trade with Japan, the United States ran a consistent deficit of $50 billion a year during the decade. That created great strains on the U.S.-Japanese relationship. The Americans blamed the trade deficit on unfair Japanese business practices; the Japanese blamed it on America's deficit financing that led to the excessive demand for foreign imports.

Another source of strain on the Japanese-American relationship was Japan's refusal to take on military peacekeeping tasks commensurate with its economic influence abroad, a pacifist stance originally forced upon it by the American occupation after World War II but which the United States now wanted to modify in hopes of receiving help in stabilizing Asia and protecting U.S. interests against a rising China. Japan did furnish a great deal of foreign economic aid to developing countries, more than the United States. Japan also used that aid or the threat of withholding it as a means of influencing strategic affairs. Thus it provided substantial financial support for the Gulf War while it refused aid to Russia unless Moscow would agree to return the disputed Kuril Islands to Japanese control. But Japan refused to send troops even for UN peacekeeping missions. It aroused considerable domestic controversy just by contributing a few unarmed civilian police to the UN operation in Cambodia. A potentially assertive Japanese foreign and security policy was also controversial in the rest of Asia, given that region's harsh memories of Japan's conduct before and during World War II. So, although the United States was eager to have Japan take some of the burden of world peacekeeping from America's shoulders, much of the rest of Asia looked to the United States to maintain a presence in the area as a check on renewed Japanese military ambitions.

While Japan tried to remain out of the world strategic equation, China continued to play an important role in that aspect of American foreign policy. The end of the Cold War and the collapse of Soviet power reduced the threat to China as well as to the United States. That lessened the need of both nations for the strategic quasi-alliance between them. Despite the disappearance of the common enemy, however, many Americans prior to 1989 hoped and expected Sino-American relations to continue to improve because China seemed to be following a path similar to the Soviet Union in liberalizing its economy and politics. The apparent convergence of the American and Chinese political economies brought an increase in trade, tourism, and cultural exchanges.

In 1989, however, the Chinese leader Deng Xiaoping and his fellow octogenarians decided that Western influence and the Chinese student democracy movement were threatening the Communist Party's political control of the nation. When students demanding more democracy occupied Tiananmen Square in Beijing, Deng ordered in the troops and crushed the demonstration. The Tiananmen massacre produced a wave of revulsion in the United States that lasted after Deng resumed the economic but not the political liberalization of China.

President George H.W. Bush, who took a particular interest in U.S. relations with China because he had once served as the U.S. representative there, decided to try to maintain normal relations with Beijing despite Tiananmen Square. He renewed annually China's most-favored-nation trade status despite Beijing's rejection of democracy and violations of human rights. Among those human rights offenses were the imprisonment and torture of political dissidents, the suppression of Tibetan nationalism, weapons sales to anti-Western regimes, and the export of products manufactured by prison labor. Bush believed that it was better to count on quiet diplomatic pressure, the liberalizing effect of world trade, and the imminent death of the old generation of Communist leaders to change China's attitude rather than harsh U.S. sanctions that would endanger Chinese cooperation in vital economic and foreign affairs.

Bill Clinton promised to change that policy when he was elected president. Meanwhile, however, China became even more important to America. China's economy was growing 10 percent per year. By some accounting methods, it was the third largest economy in the world, behind the United States and Japan. Even though America had a trade deficit of some $15 billion a year with Beijing, China took many U.S. exports and, with its rapid growth, promised to absorb even more.

China was important not just in itself but also to American interests throughout Asia. Beijing posed a potential threat to the economic as well as the political status of the United States' important trading partners Hong Kong and Taiwan. China was also vital to the peace and stability of Southeast Asia and the Korean Peninsula.

The end of the Cold War had brought a major shift in Southeast Asia. The Soviet Union pulled out of its naval base in Vietnam's Cam Ranh Bay and cut off the $1.5 billion yearly subsidy it had been providing that nation. Without Soviet aid, Vietnam decided that it could no longer support its occupation of Cambodia and withdrew its troops in 1989. That made possible a Vietnamese rapprochement with both China and the United States.

China had been the primary backer of Cambodia's Khmer Rouge government prior to Vietnam's invasion, and the overturning of that government had enraged Beijing to the point it had actually invaded Vietnam in 1979. China had been repulsed in that attack with almost as many casualties in two weeks as the United States had suffered during ten years of the Vietnam War. After that failure China had joined with the United States to support the Khmer Rouge and two smaller Cambodian factions in guerrilla raids against the Vietnamese-backed Cambodian government from refugee camps in Thailand. After Vietnam's withdrawal from Cambodia, China, the United States, Thailand, and the other nations of Southeast Asia had pushed the Cambodian government and the opposition factions into negotiations under the auspices of the United Nations. Faced with Chinese pressure, the Khmer Rouge finally accepted an agreement in August 1991 that provided for a cease-fire, a coalition interim government, and elections to be held in 1993. After those elections—which were held despite Khmer Rouge protests—a coalition government nominally ruled in Cambodia, but real power was in the hands of Hun Sen, a former Khmer Rouge commander who had defected to the Vietnamese. He ruled brutally but cautiously, avoiding conflict with China, Vietnam, and the United States. He also stalled on trying former Khmer Rouge leaders for crimes against humanity.

The United States needed Chinese help in maintaining peace on the Korean Peninsula as well as in Southeast Asia. After the collapse of the Soviet Union, China remained the only ally of North Korea, and North Korea was hostile to both South Korea and the 30,000 troops the United States had stationed there since the Korean War. There seemed to be some progress toward reconciliation between North and South Korea in the early 1990s as South Korean leader Roh Tae Woo moved away from military dominance of the government and toward South Korea's first truly democratic elections in 1992. But progress stalled in 1993 when North Korea refused to permit UN inspections of suspected nuclear bomb-building sites and later announced that it was withdrawing from the Nuclear Nonproliferation Treaty that required such inspections.

With tensions building in Asia, Clinton decided to avoid a confrontation with China. Dropping the connection he had made between human rights and economic relations with China, he renewed China's most-favored-nation status. Then, with China's assistance, Clinton negotiated a compromise with North Korea in which the Koreans would open their nuclear facilities for inspection and abandon any building of nuclear weapons in return for massive aid in constructing safer modern nuclear power plants. That agreement moderated the problem of nuclear site inspections temporarily, but the issue would reemerge as a crisis during the administration of George W. Bush.

Another potential nuclear hot spot in Asia was Kashmir. As violence between Hindus and Muslims raged in India, the Muslim inhabitants of the Indian portion of Kashmir rose up in rebellion. Pakistan, already leaning toward a militant Islamic policy since its participation in the war of the mujahideen against the Soviet-supported government in Afghanistan, trained and dispatched jihadists to aid the Kashmiri rebels. India tried ruthlessly to put the rebellion down, all the while blaming Pakistan for the outbreak in the first place. With both India and Pakistan producing nuclear weapons, the dispute was extremely dangerous.

Asia no doubt was a less dangerous place for the United States after the end of the Cold War with the Soviet Union. But the economic difficulties of the United States with Japan, the balance of economic and human rights issues with China, the civil war in Cambodia, and the nuclear disputes in Korea and Kashmir were problems enough.

The Impact of the End of the Cold War on Africa

The end of the Cold War had a substantial effect on the few areas in Africa where the United States and the Soviet Union had thought their interests sufficiently involved to intervene. But the withdrawal of the superpowers left almost as many problems as the interventions had brought in the first place.

As the Cold War wound down, some of the disputes in southern Africa that had been exacerbated by the Cold War also began to cool. Reagan's assistant secretary of state for African affairs, Chester Crocker, helped mediate a settlement in Angola and its southern neighbor Namibia. South Africa had used Namibia as a staging ground for raids into Angola against the forces of the leftist government and its Cuban allies. Crocker got Angola and South Africa to agree to a cease-fire and the independence of Namibia in exchange for the departure of the Cuban troops. The cease-fire took effect in 1984 and Namibia received its independence in 1990.

But the civil war continued between the Angolan government and rebels led by Jonas Savimbi, who received the backing of the United States and South Africa. With the departure of the Cuban troops, Crocker succeeded in mediating an agreement between Savimbi and the MPLA government of José Eduardo dos Santos that free elections would take place in 1992. Dos Santos lived up to the terms of the truce and disarmed many of the government's troops. But Savimbi did not, and when he discovered he was losing the election, he charged fraud and began the war anew. The Clinton administration consequently abandoned Savimbi and formally recognized the government of dos Santos in 1993. Nevertheless the war continued with devastating consequences for the civilian population of Angola. Only after government soldiers killed Savimbi in 2002 did a tenuous peace finally come to Angola.

The winding down of Cold War enmity in Namibia and Angola was accompanied by historic changes in the most strategic nation of the continent, South Africa. President F.W. de Klerk, who took office in September 1989, immediately began to dismantle apartheid. He opened negotiations for a transition to multiracial democracy with the leading party of black South Africans, the African National Congress (ANC). De Klerk freed ANC leader Nelson Mandela and other long-jailed political prisoners, legalized the opposition parties like the ANC, and repealed many of the laws that undergirded apartheid. The ANC in turn suspended its advocacy of armed struggle to end apartheid and entered the negotiations for a new constitution.

In a special referendum in 1992, de Klerk won a majority of 68.7 percent in favor of negotiations and his liberalized policy. U.S. president George H.W. Bush tried to encourage the reform process by receiving the leaders of both sides at the White House. At the behest of Mandela, however, Bush left most U.S. economic sanctions against South Africa in place. Finally, in February 1993, de Klerk and Mandela agreed on forming a transitional government that would rule for five years before putting into effect a new constitution that would enact black majority rule. The transitional government would be established in April 1994 by elections in which all South Africans could vote regardless of color. Minority white interests would be protected by requiring a two-thirds vote for all important legislation and by leaving many powers in the hands of regional governments, some of which would remain in the control of whites.

However there remained major obstacles in the way of this settlement. Mangosuthu Buthelezi, leader of the Inkatha Freedom Party, which commanded some 10 percent of the votes in South Africa, insisted that the regions, including the Zulu areas he controlled, should have almost full autonomy from the central government. Violence between the followers of Inkatha and the ANC devastated black areas of South Africa, and there was good evidence that Inkatha was spurred on to its attacks by conservative dissidents in the government security agencies. Right-wing white parties rejected all compromise with black rule, while young blacks and small revolutionary parties insisted that armed revolution in pursuit of immediate, full black majority rule should continue.

Miraculously, in the face of all these obstacles, the elections came off because Buthelezi decided at the last minute to join the electoral process and to allow the elections to proceed in the districts where he had formerly prevented them. Mandela's African National Congress won a substantial majority and he became president of South Africa. De Klerk and Buthelezi joined the coalition cabinet, making for a smooth transition to black majority rule.

The end of the Cold War also made an impact on the northern part of the continent. In the Horn of Africa, Ethiopia and Somalia found that their strategic importance to the great powers had dipped to zero. The Cubans withdrew their forces from Ethiopia and they and the Soviets permitted their client state to succumb to the rebel forces operating out of the provinces of Eritrea and Tigre. The new government installed by the revolutionaries permitted Eritrea to secure its independence in 1993 as Ethiopia itself tried to recover economically from years of chaos, civil war, and famine. From 1998 to 2000 Eritrea and Ethiopia fought a vicious war over a few useless square miles of borderland, and they have remained mobilized on the brink of another war ever since. The United States has generally backed Ethiopia because of Eritrea's leaning toward radical Islam, even though it is Ethiopia that is refusing to abide by the decision of the International Border Commission as to the proper boundary.

Next door to Ethiopia, Somalia fared even worse. Warlords using weapons acquired from both the Soviets and the United States during the Cold War overthrew longtime dictator Mohammed Siad Barre. All order collapsed as the warlords fought among themselves, dislocated peasants, ruined harvests, confiscated relief supplies, and induced widespread starvation. In the summer of 1992, when drought added to the despair of Somalia, the United Nations authorized the United States to airdrop food and sent Pakistani troops to guard and distribute that food. When the warlords began to block the Pakistanis from their mission, George H.W. Bush sent 25,000 American troops to restore order. The American troops did not disarm the warlords, but they did force a truce and establish enough order to make it possible for relief supplies to get through. Bush then drew down the American contingent to 4,000 troops and handed over command to the United Nations in June 1993.

Unfortunately the humanitarian intervention ended in tragedy and failure. After Bush left office the UN tried to get the warlords to disarm and begin a process of building a nation. The most powerful of the warlords in the capital city of Mogadishu, a man named Aideed, resisted and ambushed a Pakistani contingent of the UN forces. American admiral Jonathan Howe, under orders from the Security Council, sent American troops to arrest Aideed using American and UN air cover. The air raids killed many Somalis, but the troops failed to get Aideed. In the melee the Somali militia shot down an American helicopter and then attacked the rescue mission, killing eighteen Marines, wounding seventy-five, and dragging some of the American bodies through the streets. Clinton responded by sending 5,000 more American troops to protect the UN forces already in Somalia, but also setting a firm date of March 1994 for the withdrawal of American forces. He then criticized his own policy of multilateral nation building and humanitarian intervention. Arguing that the mission should have been limited to humanitarian aid and that moving to arrest Aideed was an example of "mission creep," he concluded that it was not America's job to "rebuild Somalia society."

The failure in Somalia discouraged Clinton from any further interventions in Africa despite humanitarian disasters in several failed states on the continent. In Zaire America's longtime client Mobuto Sese Seko had plundered the nation and inspired revolts against him. In Liberia descendants of former American slaves were caught up in a devastating civil war. In Sudan civil war between northern Islamic peoples and southern Christians and animists created famine and destitution. Most devastating of all, there was Rwanda, where a revolt of the majority Hutu ethnic group against the minority Tutsis, who dominated the government and army, precipitated a genocidal slaughter of Tutsis. Clinton did nothing but belatedly send 500 American troops to distribute aid. In the United States African-Americans complained that the United States seemed far more willing to sacrifice to stop wars in European areas like the Balkans than in African nations where conditions were even more horrendous. Clinton ultimately acknowledged his failure to intervene in the Rwanda genocide as the greatest failure of his presidency.

The Impact of the End of the Cold War on Europe

Perhaps the primary effect of the end of the Cold War on Western Europe was the rise of nationalism there. Nationalism was far less virulent in most of Western Europe than it was in eastern Europe, but it still limited the march toward Western European unification. In December 1991 twelve Western European nations signed a European Union (EU) treaty at Maastricht, Netherlands. In the Maastricht Treaty they pledged to form a central bank and a common currency by 1999 and to adopt common laws on foreign, defense, and social policies. Great Britain insisted on a special reservation to the treaty excepting itself from a common social policy. British doubts were soon shared by other European Community members as the worldwide recession led to major conflict over trade and financial policies. Germany, which was contributing billions of dollars to restore East Germany, insisted on keeping interest rates high to prevent its heavy government spending from producing inflation. This forced other West European nations whose currencies were coordinated with the mark under European Union rules to keep their own interest rates high in order to prevent the flight of their capital to Germany. High interest rates in turn prevented the recovery of their economies. Great Britain, Italy, and Spain responded by breaking the European Union rules and devaluing their currencies. By the summer of 1993 even France had to follow suit, and the entire European Union agreed that member nations could deviate from their former relationship to the German mark by 15 rather than 2 percent.

By 1999, however, economic conditions had stabilized enough that all the European Union nations except the United Kingdom, Denmark, and ultimately Sweden installed the euro as their currency. After a difficult beginning in which the euro plunged from an equal value with the dollar to about eighty-five cents, the currency rebounded in 2003 to rise above $1.30. The EU was a stunning economic success. Although it was becoming a stronger trade competitor with the United States, the United States generally welcomed the economic unification of the continent and encouraged its movement toward greater political integration as well.

Doubts among the Europeans themselves, however, continued to dog the European Union's ambition to make itself an integrated political and military entity. Many Europeans feared that the bureaucrats in the EU headquarters in Brussels might intrude on national customs. The rise in immigration to Europe also raised fears that European national identities might be submerged if all border controls within the community were dropped. Consequently, when the EU drafted a constitution that provided for a single president and common policies for defense and immigration, opposition was widespread. The EU tried to overcome this opposition by submitting the constitution to referendums in two of the nations most likely to ratify it, France and the Netherlands. In 2005 the people of both countries voted against it. Further political integration stalled for the time being.

The military integration of Europe also stalled. Some European countries, especially France, wanted to build a European Union force independent of NATO to reduce American influence. After the signing of the Maastricht Treaty in 1991, France and Germany agreed to build an EU force of about 32,000 troops. The American government was of two minds about this. On the one hand it wanted the Europeans to take over and pay for more of their own defense. On the other it wanted NATO, of which the United States was the dominant member, to retain its power and coherence and to extend its operations so the Europeans could help the United States in global operations outside the continent.

In the end it took until 1999 before a European Union force finally took shape and even then the EU Rapid Reaction Force of 60,000 troops was a virtual rather than a standing force. The troops remained with their national armies and would be called up only with the consent of the individual nations and presumably in the absence of NATO action.

Two major issues hindered EU military integration. The first was the desire of many of the newly independent eastern European nations to join the European Union and NATO. The European Union was slow to accept these countries for fear of the labor competition that would flow over the newly opened borders. The eastern European countries then pushed all that much harder for membership in NATO. Russia naturally resented the extension of NATO's defense line into the former Soviet security sphere. George H.W. Bush, wishing to support Russia's president, Boris Yeltsin, in his moves toward democracy, tried to split the difference by offering a vague sort of associate membership in NATO to Poland, Hungary, and Czechoslovakia. Clinton followed Bush's halfway policy by offering eastern European nations a Partnership for Peace with future full NATO membership conditioned on their progress in achieving a free economy and political and human rights. By specifying no timeline for full membership, Clinton tried to provide stability to those nations without drawing a line against Russia. Clinton even offered Russia the opportunity to attend NATO meetings, an invitation that Yeltsin accepted.

However in 1994 Clinton reversed himself and adopted an explicit timetable according to which Poland, Hungary, and the newly split western half of Czechoslovakia, the Czech Republic, would achieve full NATO membership within five years. Yeltsin responded fiercely by saying Europe was in danger of plunging into a "cold peace." But Clinton successfully pushed Europe to override Russian objections, and the three nations formally joined NATO in 1999. In 2002 NATO pushed right up to Russia's border by inviting Latvia, Lithuania, Estonia, Slovenia, Slovakia, Rumania, and Bulgaria to join, and those nations became formal members in 2004. President George W. Bush then announced that the United States would station portions of its antimissile defense in Poland and the Czech Republic. This expansion of NATO created enormous tensions with Russia while at the same time bringing into NATO and the EU eastern European nations that regard the military connection with the United States as far more important than the separate integrated European Union force.

Yet another factor that stalled the movement toward a separate and integrated European military force was the failure of the Europeans to deal with the civil war in the former Yugoslavia. The area encompassed by Yugoslavia had been driven by factionalist hatreds for centuries, even though most Yugoslavs shared a common southern Slavic ethnicity and Serbo-Croatian language. The Serbs, who were Eastern Orthodox in religion, had long been allied with Russia. The Croats and Slovenes in the north were Roman Catholics who had been part of the Austro-Hungarian Empire. The Muslims, who lived mixed among Croats and Serbs in the Bosnian portion of Yugoslavia, had taken the religion of the Turkish Empire, which had ruled much of Yugoslavia for four centuries. While those differences seemed small in the cosmopolitan areas where fraternization and intermarriage were common, the villages in the hinterlands consisted almost exclusively of one group or another, and distrust and dislike for outsiders were very high.

The rivalries between these groups had helped produce World War I when a Bosnian Serb had assassinated the Austrian heir-apparent in Sarajevo because Austria had annexed Bosnia-Herzegovina. Amid much debate between the South Slav factions, the victors in World War I had created the state of Yugoslavia during the negotiations that led to the Treaty of Versailles. But the rivalries remained so bitter that Croatians and some Muslims allied themselves with Nazi Germany to form an independent Croatia during World War II and to slaughter hundreds of thousands of Serbs along with Gypsies and Jews in concentration camps.

Josip Tito, who led Communist Yugoslav partisans against the German occupation, imposed an iron hand on Yugoslavia after the war and tried to substitute class for factional loyalties. But his death in 1980 uncapped the volcano. A cumbersome government in which the presidency rotated between the leaders of each constituent republic collapsed when Serbia's leader, Slobodan Milošević, began appealing to Serbian nationalism as a substitute for the collapsing Communist ideology that previously had sustained his position. He agitated for Serbian control of Kosovo Province, formerly the center of Serbian civilization but now populated almost entirely by Muslim Albanians. He also blocked the scheduled rotation of Croatia's representative into the Yugoslav presidency in 1991. As a result of growing Serb militancy, Slovenia, Croatia, and then Bosnia declared their independence. Milošević, with control of the Yugoslav army and its heavy weaponry, launched invasions in support of local Serbian militia to take control of large areas of Bosnia and Croatia in which Serbs lived. The Serbs then expelled all other inhabitants in a program they dubbed "ethnic cleansing" even though ethnicity was not involved. Their purpose was to attach these areas to a "Greater Serbia." The Croats and to a lesser extent the Muslims performed their own acts of ethnic cleansing when they had the opportunity, although in the absence of the heavy weaponry of the Serbs their opportunities did not come as often.

George H.W. Bush left the initiative in dealing with the crisis to the Europeans. The French and other Europeans furnished a few thousand troops to the United Nations to deliver humanitarian aid to besieged areas, especially in Bosnia. The Europeans and the United States also led the UN Security Council to impose an economic blockade of Serbia. Former U.S. secretary of state Cyrus Vance joined Lord Owens of Great Britain as UN representatives to devise a peace plan for the area. The Vance-Owens Plan called for a cease-fire and the division of Bosnia into several semiautonomous provinces. One of the three rival factions would predominate and presumably govern in each of the provinces but would have to guarantee certain rights to the minority.

During his presidential campaign, Bill Clinton denounced Bush's passiveness and the Vance-Owens Plan on the grounds that they rewarded Serbian aggression. He demanded more forceful action to roll back Serbian gains, reverse ethnic cleansing, and prevent the Balkan war from spreading to Kosovo and Macedonia, where it could involve international conflict with Albania, Greece, Bulgaria, and Turkey. His calls for forceful action, however, did not involve the use of American ground troops. He proposed instead to exempt the Bosnian government from the arms embargo imposed on all of Yugoslavia and to use American and NATO airpower to bombard Serbian heavy weapons positions.

His European and UN allies rejected these proposals. The French and British pointed out that their troops rather than the absent Americans would bear the brunt of Serbian retaliation for any bombing or the lifting of the arms embargo. The Russians argued that American policy was discriminatory against their fellow Eastern Orthodox Serbs. Croatia undermined the moral position of the anti-Serb coalition by opportunistically picking off its own areas of Bosnia.

Finally the economic sanctions began to wear down Milošević. In 1994 he deserted the Bosnian Serbs and joined the embargo against them in hopes of getting the sanctions against Serbia lifted. But the Bosnian Serbs refused to quit. In July 1995 they brushed aside a UN force protecting the sanctuary of Srebrenica and massacred several thousand Muslim inhabitants. It was the worst atrocity in Europe since World War II. Outmanned and outgunned, the Europeans operating under UN auspices could only stand by and watch.

This humiliation finally galvanized the UN and the United States into action. UN troops had already begun to consolidate their positions so isolated units would no longer be hostage to the Serbs, and this move freed NATO to increase its bombing of Serb positions beyond the pinpricks of earlier days. Meanwhile the Croats and the improved Muslim army began winning back territory from the Serbs.

With the Bosnian Serbs reeling, the United States stepped in. Defying much of public and congressional opinion, Clinton and Secretary of State Warren Christopher pledged that the United States would furnish one-third of a NATO force or some 20,000 troops to enforce a peace in Bosnia if the parties could come to an agreement. Clinton and Christopher then convened the combatants in Dayton, Ohio, in late 1995, where they hammered out a settlement that essentially divided Bosnia into ethnic enclaves whose borders would be protected for one year by NATO troops.

Clinton took a big chance by deploying U.S. troops to Bosnia against the wishes of the majority of Americans and a Congress dominated by the opposition Republicans. He won his gamble because the NATO deployment went surprisingly smoothly and the cease-fire in the former Yugoslavia held. But it was clear that international forces, including American troops, would have to remain in Bosnia for many years, despite Clinton's pledge to return the American force within one year. Consequently Congress and the American people, not to mention the Europeans, had little stomach for further intervention in the Balkans. Yet the Balkan crisis was not over.

Once Milošević freed himself from the Bosnian imbroglio, he turned his attention back to the unrest in Kosovo, where he had first launched his xenophobic nationalist campaign. The Albanians in Kosovo, with their 90 percent majority, saw the Serbian defeat in Bosnia as their chance for independence. The Kosovo Liberation Army (KLA), a militia pledged to fight for outright independence rather than mere autonomy, began to increase its attacks on Serbian police outposts. It also began to win the loyalty of the Albanian population away from its moderate leader, Ibrahim Rugova, who favored nonviolent measures to achieve independence.

In March 1998 Serbia launched major operations with heavy weapons against KLA strongholds in Kosovo, killing eighty-five people within a week. Although both George H.W. Bush and Clinton had warned Milošević that they would respond with air strikes if he launched an attack on Kosovo, the response of both the United States and its European allies was a vacillating one of delayed and mild economic sanctions. One reason for this ineffective response was the opposition of Russia and the lukewarm attitude of France toward any sanctions, let alone the use of force. Another was the presence of lightly armed European peacekeepers in Bosnia who were vulnerable to Serbian retaliation if the Kosovo crisis brought the breakdown of the Bosnian settlement. Clinton himself was anxious to avoid military measures because he had just threatened force in Iraq against Saddam Hussein's defiance of the UN weapons inspectors and was mired in a sex scandal with one of his aides. Moreover, unless the United States and its allies were willing to see an independent Kosovo, whose presence might destabilize neighboring Macedonia with its large Albanian minority, armed intervention might also involve the forcible disarmament of the KLA.

With the lack of a credible threat of force from the United States or Europe, a political goal of enhanced Kosovar autonomy that pleased neither side, and opposition from Russia that prevented the UN Security Council from authorizing NATO to use force, the crisis dragged on for nearly two years. The Serb offensive forced hundreds of thousands of Albanians to flee their homes for the inhospitable mountains of Kosovo or beyond into Albania and Macedonia. A temporary truce negotiated in the fall of 1998 permitted the 50,000 Kosovars who had taken refuge in the mountains to survive the winter. But everyone expected the war to break out again when the end of winter would allow major military operations. In fact, as one observer put it, "spring came early" for the Serbs; on January 15 they attacked and massacred the inhabitants of the Kosovar village of Racek.

In the wake of the Racek massacre, Clinton finally convinced NATO to threaten a bombing campaign against Serbia. He did so by getting Russia to agree to the threat if not the action itself and by promising the NATO allies that the United States would participate in any ground action that followed the bombing campaign in order to avoid the kind of disaster that had occurred when the Europeans alone sent troops to Bosnia. With this threat in hand, the United States tried negotiations one more time in February 1999. Milošević not only refused a settlement, but also prepared a new offensive against Kosovo by sending five new brigades to the province. Milošević correctly understood that Clinton was very reluctant to use ground forces in Kosovo, especially American ground forces, and that Clinton and NATO planned only a brief bombing campaign of the sort the Clinton administration had just used against Iraq and Osama bin Laden. Milošević also correctly thought that Russia would stridently oppose the bombing, making it difficult for NATO to continue it. Believing he could survive a short bombing campaign until Russia brought it to an end, he launched an all-out attack on Kosovo. In that offensive Serb forces killed 10,000 people, mostly civilians, and forcibly expelled 1.3 million Albanians from their homes. This was nearly three-quarters of the entire population.

In the face of the Serbian atrocities, Clinton and NATO had little choice but to extend the bombing even though they had prepared no real follow-up plans if Milošević defied the short bombing campaign and refused to come back to the negotiating table. Meanwhile Serb nationalists rallied around Milošević, and the Russians denounced the NATO campaign, as Milošević had hoped. The Russian prime minister on his way to Washington turned his plane around when notified of the bombing. President Yeltsin, warning that the bombing would lead to world war, sent Russian ships into the Mediterranean. The United States faced a diplomatic crisis with China as well when a NATO plane aimed a bomb at what the CIA had mistakenly identified as a Serb military communications center and instead destroyed the Chinese embassy in Belgrade, killing three of its employees. Nevertheless, the bombing campaign continued for seventy-eight days. The number of NATO planes engaged increased from 100 to more than 1,000. Not only did the air attacks destroy Serb military units in Kosovo, they also devastated Serb airfields, military headquarters, electrical installations, bridges, and other important parts of Serbia's economic infrastructure. Ultimately even Russia abandoned opposition to the campaign and joined NATO in negotiating peace with Milošević. Serbia surrendered and NATO moved more than 40,000 peacekeeping troops into Kosovo, including 6,000 Americans and 4,000 Russians. In 2008 Kosovo declared its independence, but Serbia, Russia, China, and many other nations have refused to recognize that independence. A residual NATO force of 5,500 troops still remains in Kosovo to maintain the peace between the Albanian Kosovars, the 60,000 Serbs who remain in the north of the country, and Serbia itself.

Controversial Issues

Not only were the Bush and Clinton administrations confused and inconsistent in thinking about the proper use of intervention in American foreign policy, but historians and analysts of the post–Cold War era have been uncertain as well. Hard realists favored aggressive intervention where important national interests were involved but balked at interventions for idealistic humanitarian purposes; their fellow conservatives in the nationalist camp emphasized the importance of promoting democratic ideals in American foreign policy. Liberals of the soft realist persuasion urged restraint in intervening militarily even where strong national interests were involved, but their fellow liberals denounced America's failure to intervene to prevent humanitarian crises.

For an excellent basic overview of the debate over American intervention policy, see Fraser Cameron, *U.S. Foreign Policy After the Cold War: Global Hegemon or Reluctant Sheriff* (2002). For a liberal denunciation of the failures of the Bush and Clinton administrations to intervene in the humanitarian crises of this era, see David Halberstam, *War in a Time of Peace: Bush, Clinton, and the Generals* (2001). For attempts by two liberals to come to terms with the confusion over a proper interventionist policy, see Charles Kupchan, *The End of the American Era: U.S. Foreign Policy After the Cold War* (2002); and Joseph S. Nye Jr., *The Paradox of American Power: Why the World's Only Superpower Can't Go It Alone* (2002). An excellent history of the foreign policy of George H.W. Bush praises him for his restraint: Ryan J. Barilleaux and Mark J. Rozell, *Power and Prudence: The Presidency of George H.W. Bush* (2004). See also one of the best of all presidential memoirs, George Bush and Brent Scowcroft, *A World Transformed* (1998). For more conservative views of proper interventionist policy, see Robert S. Litwak, *Rogue States and U.S. Foreign Policy: Containment After the Cold War* (2000); and William G. Hyland's critique of the Clinton administration, *Clinton's World: Remaking*

American Foreign Policy (2000). An excellent summary of the specific interventions of this period is Karin Von Hippel, *Democracy by Force: U.S. Military Intervention in the Post–Cold War World* (2000).

Further Reading

On the Gulf War, an excellent analysis of both the diplomatic and military aspects is Lawrence Freedman and Efraim Karsh, *The Gulf Conflict, 1990–1991: Diplomacy and War in the New World Order* (1993). For a fascinating, gossipy view behind the scenes, see Bob Woodward, *The Commanders* (1991). On the military aspects of the war, see Anthony H. Cordesman and Abraham R. Wagner, *Lessons of Modern War*, vol. 4, *The Gulf War* (1996); and Michael R. Gordon and Bernard E. Trainor, *The Generals' War: The Inside Story of Conflict in the Gulf* (1995). For a critical Arab view of the war, see Majid Khadduri and Edmund Ghareeb, *War in the Gulf, 1990–1991: The Iraq-Kuwait Conflict and Its Implications* (1997). For an outstanding collection of documents and essays giving all sides of the issues on the Gulf War, see Micah Sifry and Christopher Cerf, eds., *The Gulf War Reader: History, Documents, Opinions* (1991). See also Brian Davis, *Qaddafi, Terrorism, and the Origins of the U.S. Attack on Libya* (1990); and Robert G. Rabil, *Embattled Neighbors: Syria, Israel, and Lebanon* (2003). For histories of the jihadist threat, see Steve Coll, *Ghost Wars: The Secret History of the CIA, Afghanistan, and Bin Laden, from the Soviet Invasion to September 10, 2001* (2004); Jason Burke, *Al Qaeda: The True Story of Radical Islam* (2004); and Daniel Benjamin and Steven Simon, *The Age of Sacred Terror* (2002). See also Tom Lansford, *A Bitter Harvest: U.S. Foreign Policy and Afghanistan* (2003).

The best books on the U.S. intervention in Haiti are Robert Fatton Jr., *Haiti's Predatory Republic: The Unending Transition to Democracy* (2002); Bob Shacochis, *The Immaculate Invasion* (1999), a critical view of the invasion; and John R. Ballard, *Upholding Democracy: The United States Military Campaign in Haiti, 1994–1997* (1998), a far more favorable view of the American action.

On U.S. policy toward Latin America in the period, see William M. LeoGrande, *Our Own Backyard: The United States and Central America, 1977–1992* (1998); Dario Moreno, *U.S. Policy in Central America: The Endless Debate* (1990); Robert Pastor, *Whirlwind: U.S. Foreign Policy Toward Latin America and the Caribbean* (1992); Tom Barry, *Central America Inside Out* (1991); and Clifford Kraus, *Inside Central America* (1991). On Panama, see John Dinges, *Our Man in Panama: The Shrewd Rise and Brutal Fall of Manuel Noriega* (1991); Kevin Buckley, *Panama: The Whole Story* (1991); and John Weeks, *Panama at the Crossroads* (1991). See also Donald J. Mabry, ed., *The Latin American Narcotics Trade and U.S. National Security* (1989). On U.S. foreign policy toward the environment and overpopulation in Latin America, see Kevin P. Gallagher, *Free Trade and the Environment: Mexico, NAFTA, and Beyond* (2004). On NAFTA, see Maxwell A. Cameron and Brian W. Tomlin, *The Making of NAFTA: How the Deal Was Done* (2000); and Edward J. Chambers and Peter H. Smith, eds., *NAFTA in the New Millennium* (2002).

For works that praise America's efforts toward globalization in measures like NAFTA, see Jagdish Bhagwati, *Free Trade Today* (2002); Douglas A. Irwin, *Free Trade Under Fire* (2005); and two works by Thomas L. Friedman, *The Lexus and the Olive Tree: Understanding Globalization* (1999), and *The World Is Flat: A Brief History of the Twenty-First Century* (2005). For two vivid critiques of American globalization policy, see Joseph E. Stiglitz, *Globalization and Its Discontents* (2003), and *Making Globalization Work* (2006).

On U.S. relations with China, see David M. Langston, *Same Bed, Different Dreams: Managing U.S.-China Relations, 1989–2000* (2001); Jim Mann, *About Face: A History of America's Curious Relationship with China from Nixon to Clinton* (1999); and Jonathan Spence, *The Search for Modern China* (1991). On North Korea, see Don Oberdorfer, *The Two Koreas: A Contemporary History* (2001); Jasper Becker, *Rogue Regime: Kim Jong Il and the Looming Threat of North Korea* (2005); and a more favorable view of North Korea's policies, Bruce Cumings, *North Korea: Another Country* (2003). On U.S. policy toward the Philippines, see Raymond Bonner, *Waltzing with a Dictator: The Marcoses and the Making of American Foreign Policy* (1988). On American relations with Japan, see Yoichi Funabashi, *Alliance Adrift* (1999).

For the controversy over NATO expansion, see Lawrence S. Kaplan, *NATO Divided, NATO United: The Evolution of an Alliance* (2004); Ronald D. Asmus, *Opening NATO's Doors: How the Alliance Remade Itself for a New Era* (2002); Barany Zoltan, *The Future of NATO Expansion: Four Case Studies* (2003); and Gale A. Mattox and Arthur R. Rachwald, eds., *Enlarging NATO: The National Debates* (2001), which examines the debates not only in the United States but in the countries seeking admission to NATO.

The intervention into Somalia and its aftermath can be studied in John L. Hirsch and Robert B. Oakley, *Somalia and Operation Restore Hope* (1995); Kenneth Allard, *Somalia Operations: Lessons Learned* (1995); and Mack Bowden, *Black Hawk Down: A Story of Modern War* (1999).

The interventions in Bosnia and Kosovo have generated much debate. See Louis Sell, *Slobodan Milosevic and the Destruction of Yugoslavia* (2002), for a denunciation of Milosevic as a war criminal whose defeat was essential; G.C. Thomas, ed., *Yugoslavia Unraveled: Sovereignty, Self-Determination, and Intervention* (2003), for a more jaundiced view of American and NATO intervention; Norman M. Naimark and Holly Case, eds., *Yugoslavia and Its Historians: Understanding the Balkan Wars of the 1990s* (2003), for a fascinating analysis of the Yugoslav quandary; Ivo H Daalder, *Getting to Dayton: The Making of America's Dayton Policy* (2000), for a description of American policy toward the Bosnian war and peace; and two books on the Kosovo conflict: Tim Judah, *Kosovo: War and Revenge* (2000), and Ivo H. Daalder and Michael E. O'Hanlon, *Winning Ugly: NATO's War to Save Kosovo* (2000).

Note

1. Robert A. Pastor, *Whirlpool: U.S. Foreign Policy Toward Latin America and the Caribbean* (1992).

CHAPTER 18

9/11

During his campaign for president, George W. Bush seemed to endorse a prudent realist policy like that of his father, George H.W. Bush. In the presidential debate of October 11, 2000, he responded to a question about previous U.S. interventions by endorsing Ronald Reagan's interventions in Lebanon and Grenada and his father's in Panama and the Persian Gulf. But he balked at the humanitarian interventions of Bill Clinton. Though acknowledging that Slobodan Milošević needed to be checked in Bosnia and Kosovo, Bush carped that the Europeans should have taken the responsibility, and he implied that the American troops still stationed there should be withdrawn. He agreed with his father's decision to intervene in Somalia, but opposed the mission creep that had made it a nation-building exercise. He denounced Clinton's intervention in Haiti as a nation-building exercise from the outset. "I am worried about overcommitting our military around the world," he proclaimed. "I want to be judicious in its use. I don't think nation-building missions are worthwhile."

Bush's vice presidential and major cabinet appointments seemed to confirm his realist inclinations. Vice President Dick Cheney was a hard and cynical realist concerned strictly with American national interests and contemptuous of ideas such as soft power, but as George H.W. Bush's secretary of defense he had been moderate in the use of American military force and had never renounced his support of the decision to stop the Gulf War invasion short of Baghdad. Secretary of Defense Donald Rumsfeld, who had been Cheney's mentor when Rumsfeld was secretary of defense under Gerald Ford, had hard realist inclinations similar to those of his protégé. He was interested in missile defense and a high-tech army, not interventionist crusades. Secretary of State Colin Powell was also a realist with a doctrine named after him that emphasized a reluctance to commit American armed forces but the use of overwhelming power once a commitment was made. Bush's national security adviser, Condoleezza Rice, while a person of far less experience and reputation than Cheney, Rumsfeld, and Powell, had made her reputation as a realist scholar while writing about the history of the Soviet Union during the Cold War.

But if the first tier of George W. Bush's administration officers seemed to be composed of hard but prudent realists, the second tier was full of more aggressive nationalist idealists often called neoconservatives. The neoconservatives were conservative in that they supported a major buildup of American military power and its use in the pursuit of national security and interests, but they differed from most conservatives by being more willing to use military force to spread American ideals abroad. They also differed somewhat from liberal interventionists by emphasizing unilateral interventions to promote democracy and free markets rather than multilateral interventions to promote broader human rights goals. Citing prominent scholarly literature purporting to prove that democracies historically never have fought one another, they argued that the United States should pursue regime changes in favor of democracy rather than allying with friendly dictators in the name of national security. Among the intellectual leaders of this movement were William Kristol, editor of the *Weekly Standard*, and Robert Kagan, who published regularly in another vehicle of neoconservatism, *Commentary* magazine.

Kristol and Kagan had helped found an organization called the Project for a New American Century to push for this more assertive policy. In early 1998 the organization sent a letter to President Clinton urging regime change in Iraq. If Saddam Hussein achieved the means to deliver chemical, biological, and nuclear weapons of mass destruction (WMD), the letter argued, he would put "the safety of American troops in the region, of our friends and allies like Israel and the moderate Arab states, and a significant portion of the world's supply of oil . . . at hazard." The letter called for a "willingness to undertake military action as diplomacy is clearly failing." Among its signatories were Kagan, Kristol, Rumsfeld, and a whole host of neoconservatives who would staff many of the second-tier offices in the Bush administration: Paul Wolfowitz, who would become Rumsfeld's deputy secretary of defense; Zalmay Khalilzad, author of the 1992 defense policy draft advocating American military hegemony, who would become Bush's ambassador to Afghanistan and later to Iraq; Elliott Abrams, who would be responsible for Middle Eastern policy on Bush's National Security Council; Richard Armitage, who would become deputy secretary of state; and Richard Perle, who became chair of the Pentagon's Defense Policy Board. Perle clearly spoke the sentiments of this group when, after going to the White House with Rumsfeld and Wolfowitz to discuss the project's letter with Clinton's national security adviser, he said he was "appalled at the feebleness of the Clinton administration."

Many of the neoconservatives in the Project for a New American Century supported the overthrow of Saddam Hussein not only as a realist measure to protect the United States from a potential terrorist with weapons of mass destruction, but also as an offensive measure to realign the politics of the entire Middle East. Whereas many liberals believed that a peace settlement in the Israeli-Palestinian conflict would be the best way to stem the anti-American currents in the Islamic world, many neoconservatives despaired of or actually opposed a compromise settlement and supported the Israeli Likud Party's hard line toward the Palestinians. They saw a democratic, prosperous Iraq as a better means than an elusive Palestinian settlement to entice the region away from the corrupt, ineffectual dictatorships that oppressed their citizens and then diverted their resentments by using Israel as a scapegoat.

Neoconservatives found support for their idea of democratizing the Middle East from some of the leading scholars of the Middle East. Bernard Lewis of Princeton University and Fouad Ajami of Johns Hopkins wrote highly influential books on the theme that the Muslim world was a sick civilization because it had failed to go through a Western-style Enlightenment and was now dominated by irrational clergy and corrupt dictators. Neo-

President George W. Bush *(left)* with neoconservative adviser Deputy Secretary of Defense Paul Wolfowitz.

conservatives also received support from some liberal interventionists who, appalled by the atrocities Saddam had committed against the Kurds and Shiites, advocated military action against Iraq for humanitarian reasons.

It is debatable how seriously the hard realists at the top of the Bush administration took the grandiose democratic project of the neoconservatives prior to the terrorist attack of September 11, 2001. Perhaps the realists would have confronted Saddam even if 9/11 had never happened, but they would have done so to eliminate the WMD threat, stabilize America's oil supply, and perhaps to find a place less problematic than Saudi Arabia to station American troops in the Middle East. After 9/11, however, they folded the neoconservative ideas about a democratic transformation of the Middle East into their strategic vision. Dick Cheney even called the scholars Bernard Lewis and Fouad Ajami into his office in mid-2002 to hear them argue that American intervention was required to bring democracy and modernization to the Middle East.

9/11 and the War in Afghanistan

On September 11, 2001, nineteen al-Qaeda fanatics hijacked four jetliners, flew two into the towers of New York's World Trade Center, another into the Pentagon in Washington, and the fourth into a Pennsylvania field when the passengers tried to prevent the plane from flying to its intended target. On being assured by the Central Intelligence Agency

(CIA) that jihadist terrorist Osama bin Laden was behind the attacks, President Bush issued an ultimatum to the Taliban regime in Afghanistan—which had given sanctuary to bin Laden and his terrorist training camps—to turn over Bin Laden and the members of his al-Qaeda organization to the United States or suffer the consequences. Bush told the American people that the nation's response to the 9/11 attack would be a war not just on al-Qaeda and the Taliban, but on terrorism in general. In a speech to Congress nine days after the attack he announced: "Every nation in every region now has a decision to make: Either you are with us or you are with the terrorists." And he added: "From this day forward, any nation that continues to harbor or support terrorism will be regarded by the United States as a hostile regime."

Bush considered immediately involving Iraq as well as Afghanistan in his war on terror, but Colin Powell warned that many of America's partners who were willing to sign on to a coalition against Afghanistan would drop away if Iraq were included. So Bush decided to defer consideration of Iraq unless there was a direct link between Saddam and al-Qaeda's attack, which he considered a distinct possibility. Nevertheless Bush made clear in his conversations with his advisers that Iraq's turn would come sometime during the war on terror.

Powell was certainly right to be concerned about how much help the United States could expect from other nations in the war on terror if he immediately extended military action beyond Afghanistan. But on Afghanistan, America's allies and many other nations rallied to the cause. Russia stood aside while the United States established bases in its former Central Asian republics, Uzbekistan and Tajikistan, to support the war in Afghanistan. The United Nations (UN) Security Council passed a resolution to cut ties with terrorist groups and freeze their assets. It also demanded that the Taliban turn over Bin Laden. The NATO allies agreed to supply troops to pacify Afghanistan, an action endorsed by the UN Security Council.

The Taliban regime defied the ultimatum to turn over Bin Laden, so the United States launched its attack on Afghanistan on October 7, 2001, less than a month after 9/11. It was not an all-out ground invasion of the sort that had brought the Soviets to grief, but a massive air campaign against al-Qaeda targets combined with a ground campaign of 500 CIA and Special Forces troops in conjunction with fighters from the Afghan Northern Alliance, a force that had been battling the Taliban for years. The Taliban collapsed in November, and the United Nations helped the United States broker a new government headed by Hamid Karzai, a member of the majority Pashtun ethnic group, and including leaders of the Northern Alliance who represented rival minority groups. Most Afghans appeared to welcome the end of the fundamentalist and oppressive Taliban regime. It seemed a quick and complete triumph.

Yet there were ominous portents of what was to come in later phases of the war on terror. Bin Laden, his chief lieutenants, and the head of the Taliban were all able to escape, taking refuge in the border regions between Afghanistan and Pakistan, because there were insufficient American troops to block their escape to the east and the Afghan troops to whom that job was delegated were unable or unwilling to stop them. From their border refuge al-Qaeda and the Taliban issued defiant messages, organized renewed Taliban attacks on the occupying forces, and inspired further terrorist attacks abroad.

The Americans also had too few troops to maintain security in the rest of the country once the Taliban was defeated. The Bush administration, averse to taking responsibility for nation building, had made no real plans for the aftermath of the war. Even as the Taliban began fleeing the Afghan capital of Kabul, Bush and his war cabinet were still debating what should follow. Rumsfeld mused, "We'd like three or four countries to go in, not the U.N., not NATO, but a unified command. . . . It might be some sort of coalition of the willing."

Although the United States and Karzai had too few troops to control the nation, Bush quickly began to draw down American forces for redeployment in the next phase of the war on terror. He turned command of Afghan pacification and rebuilding over to a NATO force authorized by the United Nations to which the Americans would contribute some 18,000 troops and the other NATO nations an equivalent number. But this small number of troops and the restrictions various NATO contributors placed on their forces confined NATO operations primarily to Kabul and the areas controlled by the Northern Alliance. The rest of the country fell into the hands of warlords financed by revived opium poppy production and an increasingly active remnant of the Taliban. By 2007 NATO and American forces had increased slightly in size and moved further into the south of the country, but the effort was often too little, too late. Afghanistan was in danger of becoming a failed state.

9/11 and the Bush Doctrine: A Turning Point in American Foreign Policy

George W. Bush saw 9/11 as the beginning of a new era in American foreign policy, a traumatic event like Vietnam, Munich, and World War I that would change how the American people and government reacted to crises abroad for decades ahead. He defined that change as an aggressive war to counter terrorist threats to the United States, which he saw as emerging not just from al-Qaeda, the Taliban, or even Islamic jihadists in general, but from terrorist groups the world over. Bush made evident the geographical expanse of his war on terror in his first State of the Union address after 9/11, when he branded Iraq, Iran, and North Korea as an "axis of evil" that sought weapons of mass destruction with which they were likely to arm terrorists. Later, in a speech to the cadets at West Point on June 1, 2002, and in a formal national security memorandum, he warned that the United States could no longer rely on the Cold War doctrines of deterrence and containment because unbalanced dictators with weapons of mass destruction could not be deterred from either using those weapons or providing them to terrorists against whom there was no easy means of retaliation. Therefore, in what came to be known as the Bush Doctrine, the United States would adopt a policy of preemption rather than containment, launching preemptive attacks on terrorist threats rather than trying to deter them by threatening retaliation.

Preemption

The doctrine of preemption had always been an unspoken part of American strategy. During the Cold War the United States had been prepared to launch its own preemptive strike to reduce the number of weapons that could hit American targets if it became clear that the Soviets were about to launch a nuclear strike against the United States. But it was assumed that America would act only if the threat was truly imminent. Bush, on the other hand, made clear that by preemption he really meant preventive war. In his speech at West Point he declared that "the war on terror will not be won on the defensive. We must take the battle to the enemy, disrupt his plans, and confront the worst threats before they emerge." The national security strategy memo made his intention even clearer. Formerly, it said, states regarded a threat as imminent and justifying preemption if there were menacing movements of troops and weapons. But in an age of terrorism, such signs of imminent threat were no longer obvious: "The greater the threat, the greater is the risk of inaction—and the more compelling the case for taking anticipatory action to defend ourselves, even if uncertainty remains as to the time and place of the enemy's attack. To forestall or prevent such hostile acts by our adversaries, the United States will, if necessary, act preemptively."

Unilateralism

Bush also made clear that in reacting to terrorist threats, the United States would not be bound by the wishes of other states or international organizations such as the United Nations and NATO. The United States was willing to act alone. Such unilateralist inclinations, although an important part of the war on terror and the Bush Doctrine, actually preceded 9/11. A key aspect of Bush's policy from the outset of his administration was missile defense. Two treaties stood in the way of building that defense. The Comprehensive Test Ban Treaty, which the United States had signed but not ratified, prohibited nuclear tests that the United States wanted to conduct to perfect its antimissile as well as other new weapons. The ABM Treaty, which was part of the SALT agreement, prohibited the testing and deployment of antiballistic missile weapons. Both treaties had strong support among America's allies and the United Nations. Bush defied them all. Although he did not formally renounce the ABM Treaty until after 9/11, from the outset of his administration he had stated publicly that he would scrap it if Russia refused to renegotiate the treaty to accommodate American plans for an antimissile system. As for the Test Ban Treaty, he announced his opposition to it and then let it languish in the Senate, where his Republicans could prevent a two-thirds vote to advise and consent to it. As it became apparent that Bush intended to increase America's own nuclear capabilities, the United States seemed to lose the moral authority to argue against the proliferation of the weapons of mass destruction it so feared would fall into the hands of rogue nations or terrorists.

Bush also angered America's allies and friends by refusing to implement the Kyoto Accord, which would require developed nations to reduce their production of the greenhouse gases that cause global warming by 5 percent below the level of 1990. Clinton had signed the accord in 1997, but the Senate had defeated ratification by a vote of ninety-five to zero. There were significant problems with the Kyoto Accord, but rather than negotiating to modify the objectionable terms, Bush simply withdrew from the treaty as 141 other countries signed it. He challenged the science behind the assertion that human activities were largely responsible for global warming, insisting that "scientific uncertainties remain."[1]

Bush further defied the nation's allies and friends by rejecting a treaty Clinton had signed creating an International Court of Criminal Justice to try war crimes, genocide, and crimes against humanity. Bush feared that American troops might be unfairly hauled before the court for war crimes even though the treaty provided many safeguards against that possibility. He even suspended aid to twenty countries that signed the treaty until they agreed to shield Americans from potential prosecution.

Bush's unilateralist actions had made his administration very unpopular abroad even before 9/11. The terrorist attacks on New York and Washington temporarily offset those anti-American sentiments, and Bush found a great deal of support for his war in Afghanistan even though he did little to court allied backing in that war. He would do even less courting in the run-up to the subsequent war in Iraq, and dislike of Bush's unilateralism would explode throughout the world.

The Domestic War on Terror

Bush conducted an aggressive war against terror not only internationally but also domestically. He was determined not to let terrorists block action against them by appealing to the rights of combatants under international or American law. He adopted the position recommended by legal advisers in the Pentagon and the Justice Department (but opposed by Colin Powell, the State Department, and many leaders of the military, who feared retaliation against American diplomats and troops abroad) that captives in Afghanistan were not entitled to protection under the Geneva Conventions because they were terrorists and irregulars who did not fight according to the rules of war and were not members of states that had signed the conventions. While captives were to be treated humanely and not tortured, the definition of "torture" was very broad. The president's legal counsel, Alberto Gonzales, wrote that the war against terrorism placed a high premium on the need to obtain information from captured terrorists quickly, rendering obsolete the Geneva Conventions' limitations on questioning prisoners of war. According to another memo leaked from the offices of Gonzales and the Pentagon, the treatment of captives amounted to torture only if it resulted in "death, organ failure or a permanent impairment of a significant bodily function."

The Bush administration resorted to various tactics to circumvent limits on the treatment of those it deemed terrorists. The president took upon himself the right to deem captives "enemy combatants" who were subject to imprisonment for as long as the war on terror lasted. Enemy combatants were held in places where the American justice system could not reach—Afghanistan, secret CIA prisons in various countries around the world, or Guantánamo Naval Base in Cuba, which was outside the jurisdiction of American courts. In such places prisoners had no right to challenge their imprisonment in a court of law. Alternatively enemy combatants could be turned over to their countries of origin, where they could expect to face tortures even worse than those permitted by the U.S. Justice Department.

The Bush administration sought increased executive powers to combat potential terrorists within as well as outside the United States. One month after 9/11, Congress responded to Bush's appeal to "untie the hands of our law enforcement officials so they can fight and win the war against terror" by passing the Patriot Act. That act made it easier for the government to obtain subpoenas in terrorism investigations, denied bail to terrorism suspects, established the death penalty for terrorism that resulted in death, and allowed the government easier access to people's private medical, financial, educational, and library records through wiretaps and search warrants. The administration also tapped Americans' phone and e-mail conversations without the warrants it was supposed to get from the Foreign Intelligence Surveillance Court.

In the immediate aftermath of 9/11, the American people were willing to tolerate the increasing power of the executive and the limitations on civil liberties that the Patriot Act represented. As time went on, it became clear that these were not merely temporary emergency measures because the war on terror that justified them had no finite duration. It was a war against a tactic rather than a definable enemy, and that tactic was likely to be used for the foreseeable future. As the Iraq War dragged on and the inevitable atrocities and scandals that accompanied the war on terror emerged, opposition grew. But fear of future terrorist attacks prevented any definitive action by Congress. It renewed the Patriot Act in 2007 with only minor modifications.

The War in Iraq

Immediately after the attacks of 9/11, an aide to Donald Rumsfeld made notes of the defense secretary's reactions: "Judge whether good enough to hit S.H [Saddam Hussein] at same time. Not only UBL [Usama bin Laden]. Go massive. Sweep it all up. Things related and not." Rumsfeld was not alone among the leading members of Bush's administration in advocating that the war on terror should target not just al-Qaeda but also other dangers, especially Iraq. The president shared his concern and only temporarily deferred action on Iraq until after the assault on Afghanistan. On November 21, 2001, just as the Taliban began leaving Kabul, Bush ordered Rumsfeld to survey and update his plans for a possible war in Iraq. Only a couple of months later, while the assault on Bin Laden's probable refuge in the mountains of Tora Bora bordering Pakistan still raged, Rumsfeld was already ordering American troops to be moved from Afghanistan to the Persian Gulf.

There were targets more closely connected with al-Qaeda than Iraq, including terrorist groups in the Philippines, Indonesia, and Yemen. Iraq's Saddam, on the other hand, was a secular tyrant who had persecuted his own Islamic fundamentalists and distrusted Bin Laden because bin Laden had included Saddam on his list of corrupt and insufficiently Muslim dictators who should be overthrown. The CIA largely discounted any serious connection between Saddam and al-Qaeda, but Bush and Cheney never fully renounced their early suspicions that Saddam might have been connected with al-Qaeda and the 9/11 attacks. Thanks at least in part to the administration's continued hints about such a connection, on the eve of the war in March 2003 some 45 percent of the American people believed that Saddam was personally involved in 9/11. In any case Bush and Cheney worried that Saddam might put weapons of mass destruction into the hands of terrorists who could not be deterred from using them against the United States. While such fears also pertained to the other members of the "axis of evil," North Korea and Iran, Iraq seemed an easier target, and the Bush administration was convinced that the American troops that accomplished the overthrow would be welcomed as liberators. Such a welcome might make it possible to create an Iraqi democracy friendly to the United States and tolerant of Israel, the neoconservative dream that Bush and Cheney found increasingly attractive.

The Bush administration had some reason to believe that Americans would be welcomed as liberators. Bush, Cheney, and Rumsfeld discussed the possibility with leading Iraqi exiles, who cited scholars like Lewis and Ajami as well as their own experiences to argue that Iraq was more secular and modernized than most other Middle Eastern nations. They also asserted that Iraq's various sects—Kurds, Sunnis, and Shiites—were not necessarily hostile to one another, but mixed easily in urban environments like Baghdad and had fought side by side in the war against Iran. Finally, they argued that while the Iraqi Shiites, whose majority status would make them rulers of a democratic Iraq, might share a religious kinship with Iran, the fact that they were Arabs while the Iranians were Persians would prevent Iraq from allying itself with the anti-American fundamentalist regime of Iran. Thus when Tim Russert of *Meet the Press* asked Vice President Cheney what would happen "if your analysis is not correct and we're not treated as liberators, but as conquerors," Cheney replied:

> I really do believe that we will be greeted as liberators. I've talked with a lot of Iraqis in the last several months myself, had them to the White House. The president and I have met with them, various groups and individuals, people who have devoted their lives from outside to change things inside Iraq. . . . The read we get on the people of Iraq is there is no question but what they want to get rid of Saddam Hussein and they will welcome as liberators the United States when we come to do that.

Unfortunately Bush and his administration were cherry-picking among scholars and Iraqis so that they heard what they wanted to hear. Many Middle East scholars disagreed with the analyses of Lewis and Ajami, and many Iraqis feared that the Iraqi exiles did not really know what Iraq was like after years of Saddam's dictatorship. These dissenters argued that the Middle East had fallen behind the West economically and politically not because of a failure to go through an Enlightenment but because it had been subject first to European colonialism and then to American and Western economic neo-imperialism that supported corrupt local dictatorships. Therefore, they warned, Iraqis and other people of the Islamic world would see an American intervention, even one directed against a hated dictator, as a colonial occupation that should be resisted.

The confidence that the Iraqis would greet the Americans as liberators and quickly be able to provide their own security permeated the Bush administration's war planning. The contingency plan for war with Iraq that Bush had inherited from the previous administration assumed the need for some 500,000 troops and seven months to mobilize and deploy them. But Rumsfeld's primary goal as secretary of defense was to transform the American military into a small, fast-moving, high-tech force with great striking power. He initially declared that the United States should be able to invade Iraq with 125,000 troops. He badgered the prospective Iraq commander, General Tommy Franks, to reduce the planned invasion force until Franks agreed to a force of some 250,000 and also provided points in time at which the deployment should cease short of that number if Saddam fell quickly. Since Saddam did fall quickly, Rumsfeld canceled some of the deployments so the total coalition force that ultimately wound up in Iraq was about 180,000. Meanwhile Rumsfeld and the administration dismissed the doubts of military experts about the small size of the invasion forces. When Army Chief of Staff Eric Shinseki told the Senate Armed Services Committee that, based on his experience in the Balkans, it would require several hundred thousand troops to occupy Iraq, Paul Wolfowitz publicly scoffed that Shinseki was "wildly off the mark." Rumsfeld made public that Shinseki would not be asked to return as chief of staff, thereby leaving him a lame duck, and then did not bother to attend Shinseki's retirement ceremony. Administration hawks dealt out the same sort of public humiliation to Bush's economic adviser, Lawrence Lindsay, who contradicted administration claims that the war and reconstruction would be cheap and mostly paid from Iraqi oil revenues. When Lindsay estimated that the war might well cost $200 billion, he too was publicly reprimanded, and eventually he was fired. (As of 2012, the war had cost some $800 billion in direct costs not including the interest on the money borrowed for the wars or the expense of treating injured veterans. If those expenses are included, the war will cost about $2 trillion.)

The problem with the low number of troops was not the success of the initial invasion, but the postwar occupation. The invasion force could defeat Saddam's army, but it could not secure the porous borders, provide security to dense urban areas, or even guard the number of WMD sites that American intelligence expected to find. But Rumsfeld's model for the occupation was not the Balkans, whose precedent would have suggested the need for a force of 500,000, but Afghanistan, where initially a minimum of American and NATO troops assisted the Afghans themselves in securing order. Rumsfeld assumed that the Americans would turn over security duties to the government and military forces of Iraq once it was shorn of Saddam and the top layer of his Baathist Party supporters. Rumsfeld and Cheney expected to send an Iraqi exile, Ahmed Chalabi, together with 700 members of his armed and uniformed militia, to lead that Iraqi government. Rumsfeld also expected help from American allies and friendly regimes in the area to conduct the occupation and rebuilding of Iraq, even though foreign opposition to a war in Iraq was strong and deep. Certain of his convictions, Rumsfeld elbowed Colin Powell and the State Department out of the planning for the postwar occupation of Iraq and kept that planning in the hands of the Pentagon, where it was largely neglected until the very eve of the war.

Whatever the military shortcomings of Rumsfeld's plan for a minimal invasion and occupation force, his plan had great political strengths. Because the projected force required only the use of the United States' all-volunteer military, there would be no necessity for a draft and no sacrifice of life asked of the general American population. Since the rebuilding would be financed by Iraqi oil, no economic sacrifice would be asked of the general population either, so Bush could promise to continue cutting taxes. The burden of the war would fall on a rather narrow portion of the American populace that was generally supportive of military action.

Nevertheless, as news of the war planning and troop deployments to the Persian Gulf leaked into the press, the momentum toward war with Iraq began to stir opposition both at home and abroad. The most notable domestic opposition came in the form of an August 2002 op-ed piece by Brent Scowcroft, national security adviser in the first Bush administration and a person many assumed to be speaking for the president's father.[2] Scowcroft conceded that Saddam was a threat to American interests because he sought to dominate the Persian Gulf and control the oil from the region. He was also an atrocious dictator to his own people. "We will all be better off when he is gone," Scowcroft said. But Scowcroft denied that Saddam was an imminent threat to the United States. He argued that there was "scant evidence to tie Saddam to terrorist organizations, and even less to the Sept. 11 attacks." Saddam had little incentive to make common cause with the terrorists or provide them with weapons of mass destruction because such a move would open his own regime to a devastating response from the United States. While there might come a time to depose Saddam, an invasion at this time would be a bloody diversion from the global counterterrorism campaign and raise opposition to that campaign among America's friends. It would also destabilize the Middle East, whose people would rage against the United States for turning its back on the Israeli-Palestinian issue to satisfy what they would see as a narrow American interest. Scowcroft advised that the United States press the United Nations to enforce WMD inspections in Iraq, postponing military action until it was clear that Saddam had acquired a nuclear capability or was complicit in the events of 9/11.

As opposition to the war seemed to crystallize around Scowcroft's opinion piece, the Bush administration launched an all-out publicity campaign to counter it. On September 8, Condoleezza Rice joined other Bush officials making the rounds of the Sunday talk shows to argue against a continued policy of inspections and containment of Saddam's regime. Citing dubious evidence of Saddam's nuclear program, a shipment of aluminum tubes that the administration wrongly declared could be used only for centrifuges for the enrichment of uranium, Rice warned, "We don't want the smoking gun to be a mushroom cloud."

Meanwhile Bush faced a degree of opposition from within his own administration. Secretary of State Powell privately agreed with Scowcroft and wanted to slow the rush toward war. Although he never told Bush outright that he opposed war, he arranged a private meeting with the president in which he pointed out the problems that war would bring. Included among those problems was the difficulty of governing Iraq once the United States deposed its government, to which Powell applied a version of what he privately referred to as "the Pottery Barn Rule — you break it, you own it." Powell argued that the United States should seek a resolution of support from the United Nations before embarking on military conflict. Perhaps the issue could be settled peacefully, and if not, at least the United States might have the support of the international community. Bush was skeptical. He agreed with Vice President Cheney that the United Nations would be a trap. The Security Council might support the disarmament of Iraq through a resumption of inspections, but Saddam was skilled at evading such inspections. Between Saddam and the UN, they could easily delay a final decision until after March, when the desert heat would make a military invasion of Iraq impossible. Bush and Cheney believed that nothing short of the elimination of Saddam and a change of regime could make the United States, Israel, and the world safe from Iraqi WMDs. Bush and Cheney were sure that the members of the Security Council—particularly France, Russia, and perhaps Germany, all of whom had expressed opposition to an invasion—would never agree to endorse military action for regime change.

Bush, however, decided to back Powell and consult the United Nations because Britain's prime minister, Tony Blair, Bush's firmest supporter in the international community, said that UN approval was necessary to secure the backing of his Parliament to send troops with the American invasion force. Moreover Bush had a slim hope that if Saddam surrendered to a UN demand to resume inspections, the humiliation might lead to an internal coup. Nevertheless he made clear to his speechwriter that he wanted the outcome to be Saddam's ouster as well as his disarmament and that the United States would act alone if the UN failed to achieve those goals. Bush gave the resulting speech to the United Nations on September 12, 2002. After reciting Iraq's many violations of the UN resolutions that followed the first Gulf War—including the expulsion of UN weapons inspectors, evasions of UN sanctions, and brutality toward Saddam's own people—Bush proclaimed that Saddam's regime was "a grave and gathering danger. To suggest otherwise is to hope against the evidence. To assume this regime's good faith is to bet the lives of millions and the peace of the world in a reckless gamble." Echoing Condoleezza Rice, he declared: "The first time we may be completely certain he has nuclear weapons is when, God forbid, he uses one." Moreover Saddam might supply those weapons "to terrorist allies," in which case "the attacks of September the 11th would be a prelude to far greater horrors." He concluded with an appeal for the UN to join the United States in action against Iraq while making clear that America would act alone if necessary. "We must stand up for our security, and for the permanent rights and the hopes of mankind. By heritage and by choice, the United States of America will make that stand. And, delegates to the United Nations, you have the power to make that stand, as well."

Bush then took his argument to Congress. In October he demanded that Congress authorize him to use force against Iraq. He promised that force would be the last resort, but insisted that he needed the authority as leverage to gain support for a resolution in the UN and to get Iraq to abide by its commitments. Many members of Congress, particularly on the Democratic Party side, were reluctant to grant that authority because they understood the likelihood that they were in effect declaring war. But they faced the political danger that if they voted against the president they would be seen as unwilling to give him the last chance to secure a peaceful settlement through coercive diplomacy. Many also regretted that they had voted against the Gulf War in 1991 and worried that another vote against a successful war would permanently cast their party as weak on national security.

The Democrats, however, wanted some reassurance that Saddam had weapons of mass destruction and was prepared to use them. There was good reason to believe that Saddam had at least some WMD because when he had kicked out the UN weapons inspectors in 1998 there were still many tons of chemical warfare agents unaccounted for. The CIA National Intelligence Estimate (NIE) for the year 2000 said he probably still possessed these chemical agents but had no warheads to deliver them. It also said he was working on biological weapons, but did not say he had any, and it said that he had not abandoned his nuclear ambitions. Thus the NIE did not conclude flatly that Saddam had any battle-ready WMD.

The Bush administration, however, had been making claims far more definite than this. Vice President Cheney claimed flatly on August 26 that "Saddam now has weapons of mass destruction." In a speech on September 26, Bush used discredited British intelligence to back his statement that Saddam had chemical and biological weapons and could launch them with forty-five minutes' notice. Bush also asserted that Saddam could have a nuclear weapon within six months if he could obtain the plutonium from black market sources to build it.[3] Under Democratic pressure, Bush agreed to commission a new NIE to confirm his administration's claims about the status of Iraq's WMD. The CIA delivered that hurried NIE on October 2. It contained all sorts of uncertainties, ambiguities, and caveats, but the summary stated baldly that Baghdad had chemical and biological weapons and was likely to have nuclear weapons sometime between 2007 and 2009. Worried that there was little definite information in the NIE to support those conclusions, Bush asked CIA director George Tenet if the case was solid. Tenet replied that it was a "slam dunk." On October 10 and 11, after congressional leaders were briefed on the new NIE, the House granted the president the authority to use force against Iraq by a vote of 296 to 133 and the Senate by a vote of 77 to 23.

Colin Powell now used the leverage of the congressional vote to try to secure a strong resolution in the United Nations. The first draft of that resolution, influenced by Cheney and Rumsfeld, called not only for Iraq to readmit the UN inspectors but also to allow additional inspectors from the permanent members of the Security Council, including the United States. It also extended the no-fly zones and said that if Saddam were found in "material breach" of any part of the resolution, the United States and other countries would automatically have authorization to use "all necessary means" to achieve compliance. But when Powell floated that draft in the Security Council, not a single member supported it. Finally, with Bush's grudging consent, Powell agreed to UN Security Council Resolution 1441, which required Saddam first to declare all chemical, biological, and nuclear weapons in his possession and then permit inspections to verify the declaration. If Saddam failed to do so, "serious consequences" would follow. The resolution, however, did not specifically authorize the United States or anyone else to use force. The French, Russians, and Germans assumed that the UN would then need to pass a second resolution stipulating that there had been a material breach and authorizing the United States to use force. For the Americans, however, the vagueness of Resolution 1441's promise of serious consequences, especially when added to the previous UN resolutions, would allow Bush international authority to use force if necessary.

Saddam responded to the Security Council by readmitting the weapons inspectors and, on December 7, submitted a declaration numbering some 12,000 pages purporting to prove that he had no WMD. Cheney wanted to go to war immediately on the grounds that the declaration was an obvious lie and therefore a material breach. But because Saddam had permitted inspections, Bush decided to wait. Perhaps the inspectors would find the smoking gun that would either convince the Security Council to explicitly authorize force or at least enlist broader support for American action. Alternatively perhaps the humiliation of Saddam's acquiescence to the UN would trigger a coup. But as the March deadline drew near, after which weather would make an invasion of Iraq almost impossible, neither the coup nor the smoking gun had materialized. By January 2003, Bush seems to have decided finally that he would have to go to war. To justify that action at home and abroad, he would have to offer proof of Saddam's WMD from American intelligence rather than the UN inspectors.

Bush began that process in his State of the Union message of January 28, when he went even beyond the new National Intelligence Estimate to assert that Iraq had sought significant quantities of uranium from Africa, an assertion that the CIA had removed from an earlier Bush speech because it was not well verified. Then the president sent Colin Powell to the Security Council to make the case internationally. Powell discarded many NIE assertions that seemed unverified, including a supposed meeting in Czechoslovakia between an Iraqi official and one of the 9/11 pilots that Cheney and other Bush officials had used to draw a connection between Saddam and al-Qaeda. Powell also insisted that CIA director Tenet sit right behind him during his speech to the Security Council to demonstrate CIA support of his evidence. Nevertheless Powell included many claims in his speech that turned out to have very dubious evidence behind them. Powell's bipartisan reputation for integrity and the public knowledge that he was far less inclined to war than most other officials in the Bush administration gave those claims enormous influence in the United States. When Bush ordered the invasion of Iraq, he had the support of better than 70 percent of the American public.

Powell was not so convincing to people abroad, however. Presidents Jacques Chirac of France and Vladimir Putin of Russia along with Prime Minister Gerhard Schröder of Germany issued a joint statement that the UN should permit more time for inspections and the disarmament of Saddam without war. The head of the UN arms inspection team, Hans Blix, reported that although some of Iraq's weapons from the Gulf War period were unaccounted for, the team still had not found any WMD and that the evidence for some of Powell's statements was ambiguous.

Despite the certainty of Security Council vetoes from at least France and Russia, Bush ordered Powell to seek a second UN resolution specifically authorizing force because Tony Blair of the United Kingdom had promised Parliament to attempt one. Bush and Powell hoped at least to get a majority vote in the Security Council that would give some moral authority to the invasion. Even that attempt failed. On February 17, 2003, Bush withdrew the doomed resolution and issued an ultimatum to Saddam to leave Iraq within forty-eight hours. Bush made plans to send American troops to Iraq even if Saddam did leave in order to prevent revenge killings. He then waited to initiate action until Blair won a vote from Parliament endorsing war. Ominously one-third of Blair's own party voted against him. But the vote passed and Bush was free to invade.

Meanwhile Saddam was making his own plans. The UN had destroyed most of his chemical weapons stores and he had not, in fact, resumed production of WMD after expelling the UN inspectors in 1998. However, even after admitting in his December 2002 declaration to the UN that he had no weapons of mass destruction, he still threw obstacles in the way of the inspectors because he wanted to maintain the illusion that he did have WMD, partly to bluff the United States and his regional enemies, such as Iran and Saudi Arabia, and also to reassure his own army that he could protect it from a superior force. Although a few generals in the top rank of the Iraqi army knew the truth, many Iraqi officers did not learn that there were no WMD to use on their behalf until the invasion was under way. Meanwhile Colin Powell and the rest of the Bush administration were willing to exaggerate the certainty of their own knowledge about Saddam's WMD program because it seemed totally irrational for Saddam to hinder UN inspectors unless he was hiding such weapons. Saddam's WMD bluff was only one of the many disastrous deceptions and miscalculations on both sides.

Saddam drew a red defense line around Baghdad on one of his war-planning maps that fell into the hands of American intelligence. The Americans feared and the Iraqi army expected that such a line indicated that Saddam would use his WMD if the invasion forces threatened to breach that line. Thus the coalition troops that invaded Iraq had endured extensive antibiological vaccinations and carried cumbersome antichemical gear. In fact Saddam believed he could hold Baghdad with his WMD bluff and the conventional resistance he concentrated in that area because the Americans would falter in their approach to the capital out of fear of heavy casualties. And while Saddam concentrated his best troops behind the Baghdad line, he sent contingents of loyal Baathist Party militia, the fedayeen, to the towns and cities along the southern invasion route to Baghdad to stiffen resistance by intimidating the Shiites and others who might be tempted to welcome the invaders. The fedayeen failed miserably to stop the American forces from reaching and taking Baghdad. But they remained behind the coalition lines to spark a highly successful guerrilla rebellion that neither Saddam nor the American planners had foreseen.

Within three weeks of the invasion, American troops were pulling down a giant statue of Saddam in Baghdad. Within another three weeks, Bush was flying in a military jet to the U.S. carrier *Abraham Lincoln* off the coast of San Diego. There, before a giant banner proclaiming "Mission Accomplished," he emerged in full pilot's regalia befitting his status as a former National Guard pilot to announce to the television audience: "The tyrant has fallen. Iraq is free."

Although Saddam's capture was still a year away, the tyrant had indeed fallen and Iraq was indeed free, at least of him. But the promise of a stable, democratic, and self-governing Iraq was already crumbling. The invasion force had too few troops to secure the areas it bypassed on the way to Baghdad. It had troops enough to guard only 130 of the 946 suspected WMD sites. It could not guard the thousands of conventional weapons sites, and many of those weapons disappeared into the hands of rebels along with the thousands of weapons that the 300,000 soldiers of the Iraqi army carried with them as they walked away from the war. The occupation force could guard some of the oil fields, thus preventing the burning of hundreds of oil wells as had occurred in the first Gulf War, but the occupiers could not guard the power plants, water distribution centers, or much of the rest of the infrastructure. Americans could guard the oil ministry in Baghdad, but not the national museum. And what was unguarded was looted mercilessly.

The United States had neither the plans nor the forces to cope with the postwar chaos and guerrilla war. Retired general Jay Garner, appointed to plan and command the immediate pacification effort, did not take office until three months before the invasion. He rejected the offers of service from State Department advisers who had been working on postwar planning for months. Garner concentrated on what he assumed would be the primary problems after the invasion—refugees, humanitarian assistance, and infrastructure damage. He did not plan much for postwar governing and security, which he assumed would quickly be turned over to the Iraqis themselves once the army and police had been purged of the top layer of Baathist criminals. Unfortunately much of the army and police melted away in the invasion. Garner and the Pentagon assumed that Chalabi would head the Iraqi interim government to which they could delegate authority, but at the last minute Bush and Rumsfeld vetoed that idea because they wanted the Iraqis to have a chance to create an interim government consisting of people from inside Iraq rather than former exiles. Thus there was no Iraqi government and no Iraqi army to give an Iraqi face to the occupation. Garner thought he might be able to turn over much of the peacekeeping to allied troops and the UN, thus giving some international legitimacy to the occupation, even though Bush's unilateral decision for war had diminished the willingness of allies and the UN for the occupation, let alone the invasion.

In May, shortly after Bush gave his triumphal speech aboard the USS *Abraham Lincoln*, Bush and Rumsfeld sent L. Paul Bremer, a former State Department official who had served as chief of staff to Henry Kissinger and ambassador to the Netherlands but never in the Middle East, to replace Garner as head of the new and expansive Coalition Provisional Authority. Rumsfeld and the Defense Department rejected the expected appointment of Zalmay Khalilzad, the Beirut-educated State Department official who had been a leading neoconservative advocate of the war and who knew something about the Islamic world, to serve alongside Bremer and organize an Iraqi provisional government. Instead Bremer himself became the provisional government, and his first act was to formally dissolve the remaining units of the Iraqi army and devastate the Iraqi civil service by disqualifying all Baathist Party members, not just the criminal top tier, from serving in it. The United Nations, despite the way the United States had bypassed it in going to war, did agree to help with the occupation, but on August 19, a huge bomb set by insurgents destroyed the UN headquarters in Baghdad, killed the UN director, and undermined UN assistance. By July 2004 the United States had 133,000 troops in Iraq, Britain 8,300, Poland 2,500; the rest of the occupying force consisted of contingents ranging from thirty to a few hundred from Latvia, Lithuania, Estonia, Albania, Georgia, Ukraine, Moldova, Azerbaijan, South Korea, Thailand, and Tonga. The so-called coalition of the willing that occupied Iraq thus had an overwhelmingly American face.

Such a force and such policies brought many of the Iraqis who had initially welcomed the overthrow of Saddam to regard the American presence as a colonial occupation. The Kurds in the north, who had essentially governed themselves under U.S. protection since the Gulf War, continued to embrace the Americans, and the Kurdish militia maintained reasonable stability in their area. The Shiites of the south, who composed 60 percent of the Iraqi population, initially welcomed the American elimination of Saddam and his minority Sunni regime, but they chafed at the slowness of the United States to turn over to them the full control of the nation that they felt should be theirs under a democratic majority-rule government. Unfortunately the Shiites themselves were divided into at least three major factions, each with its own militia and each seeking control of the Shiite majority. Meanwhile the Sunnis, refusing to accept their minority status, increasingly turned to insurgency against the Americans. Moreover foreign fighters encouraged by al-Qaeda began to join the Sunni insurgents and introduce sophisticated, armor-penetrating bombs and suicide bombers into the mix. They also attacked Shiite civilians and mosques in hopes of stirring a civil war that would pin down and bleed the American occupation forces. Their butchery of civilians did push some Iraqis into cooperating with the occupation forces, but not enough to quell the insurgency.

Unfortunately some actions by American forces helped to undermine their appeal to the beleaguered Iraqi people. At the American prison in Abu Ghraib, guards tortured Iraqi prisoners, taking pictures that whirled around the world on the Internet. However much the administration tried to pin the blame on a few misguided American soldiers, even people well disposed toward the United States could not help but connect Abu Ghraib to the policies of the president himself in bypassing the Geneva Conventions, defining torture in such a way that American interrogators could use extremely harsh measures without violating strictures against it, holding prisoners at Guantánamo indefinitely and without appeal, sending prisoners to secret CIA prisons, and deporting prisoners to home countries where they could expect to be tortured. Abu Ghraib did permanent damage to America's attempt to justify its occupation as an attempt to bring democracy and justice to Iraq.

Bremer and the American forces tried desperately to tame the insurgency and nascent civil war and to build support among the population by restoring the infrastructure, providing security, and creating a truly democratic Iraq government. Saddam's capture in December 2003 and his later trial provided some temporary optimism, which was quickly dissipated by the brutality of his execution on December 30, 2006. Political successes were equally temporary. In January 2005 Iraqis elected an assembly to draft a constitution. Although the resulting constitution was incomplete and disputed, Iraqis turned out again a year later to establish an Iraqi government by electing a legislature that would in turn select a president, prime minister, and cabinet officials. Both elections were resounding successes, with huge turnouts defying insurgent threats against those who tried to cast their ballots. Each of the elections, however, offered only short-term relief. The fact that the elections were national rather than local meant that people voted essentially for their own sectarian leaders and that the delegates owed their loyalties to their ethnic and religious factions rather than to local leaders or to the Iraqi nation as a whole. The government distributed cabinet posts according to factions, with each department composed of members of the sectarian group of the cabinet official that headed it. Sunnis were almost entirely excluded from power, in part because they boycotted the elections rather than accept their minority status. The Americans tried to get the factions to work together and compromise on revisions to the constitution so as to establish a strong central government that included more Sunnis, but the compromise largely failed.

The Americans also pushed for an oil law that would distribute fairly the proceeds from Iraq's only real resource. Iraqi oil reserves were concentrated in the Kurdish north and the Shiite south. Sunni regions had little or none. The Americans wanted a strong central government that could distribute oil profits to the Sunni as well as the Kurdish and Shiite areas, but the Kurds and Shiites were reluctant to give up their power and resources. The oil law, like the constitutional revision, stalled.

American attempts to build Iraqi security forces to replace the coalition occupation forces stalled as well. Bush's whole plan to end the war and bring American troops home was to train the Iraqi army and police. To counter demands to bring American troops home, he often proclaimed that as Iraqi forces stood up, American forces would stand down. But the Iraqi army grew slowly, its soldiers insufficiently trained, equipped, or motivated to take over security duties. The police were in even worse shape. They were so infiltrated by militia members that they were totally distrusted by the Iraqi population. The prospect for Iraqis to provide their own security and allow coalition forces to leave faded into the dim future.

The security situation became even grimmer in 2006 when insurgents bombed the Golden Mosque in Samarra, a revered Shiite shrine. The bombing set off a wave of ethnic cleansing and exacerbated an already dangerous low-level civil war between Shiites and Sunnis, especially in the mixed neighborhoods of Baghdad. Rival Shiite militias also clashed in the south. By 2007 American forces had suffered nearly 4,000 deaths and Iraqi civilians perhaps 80,000. In December 2006 a bipartisan commission headed by George H.W. Bush's former secretary of state James Baker and former Democratic congressman Lee Hamilton suggested a mild change of course by engaging Iraq's neighbors diplomatically to help stem the civil war in Iraq and allow the United States and its allies to draw down their own forces. While many Democrats and some Republicans embraced the report as a means of compromising their differences on war policy, Bush largely rejected it. He feared that any diplomacy with Iran over Iraq would help legitimate Iran's nuclear program and support of Hezbollah. Engaging Syria would undermine the international investigations into Syria's role in the assassination of anti-Syrian government officials in Lebanon. The Democrats themselves were divided on how to end the war. They introduced various measures to reduce the numbers of American troops in Iraq and force the Iraqis to take more responsibility for their own security, but the fear that Iraq would descend into all-out civil war if the United States pulled away hung over all attempts to shift policy.

As the war in Iraq dragged on, the prestige of Bush and the United States fell precipitously. While Bush had the support of 70 percent of the American people at the outset of the war, by 2007 his approval rating was hovering around 30 percent. The approval ratings of the United States among people abroad also plummeted. In Germany they went from 78 percent in 1999/2000 to 56 percent in 2006, in France from 62 percent to 39 percent, in Great Britain from 83 percent to 56 percent, in Spain from 50 percent to 23 percent, in Turkey from 52 percent to 12 percent, and in Indonesia from 75 percent to 30 percent.

The Sunni Awakening and the Surge

Ultimately Bush took it upon himself to change policy in Iraq. In November 2006 he replaced Rumsfeld as secretary of defense with a moderate pragmatist, Robert Gates. Together Bush and Gates brought in General David Petraeus as the new commander in Iraq. Petraeus was the leading Pentagon advocate of counterinsurgency doctrine. In his Princeton doctoral dissertation "The American Military and the Lessons of Vietnam," he had argued that if the United States had fully supported the attempts of General Creighton Abrams to institute the counterinsurgency method of warfare following the Tet offensive, America could have won the Vietnam War. He also had just finished writing the new army field manual on counterinsurgency warfare.

The primary focus of counterinsurgency doctrine was the protection of civilians rather than the killing of insurgents. It took large number of troops to carry out counterinsurgency warfare, however. Petraeus calculated that it required a ratio of one soldier or policeman to every fifty civilians to protect the population. This figure, which was in line with the troop request General Shinseki had made at the outset of the planning for the Iraq War, ran directly counter to the strategy Rumsfeld and his commanders had adopted. Therefore Rumsfeld and his generals had sidelined Petraeus as well as Shinseki. But with Petraeus's appointment, Bush and Gates agreed to a surge of some 30,000 troops, bringing the total number of U.S. and allied forces in Iraq to more than 160,000. Since Iraq's population was some 30 million people, the surge was not enough to bring the ratio of troops to population to 1/50, but Bush and Petraeus hoped that the troops could protect critical masses of the population while the accelerated training of Iraqi troops and police would allow them to approach the proper ratio. Meanwhile American troops moved out of their protected bases and into the cities where they set up smaller posts of 35 to 100 troops, partnered with Iraqi units, and began patrolling on foot.

A second aspect of counterinsurgency warfare was to provide the protected population with good governance and win its support. Here Bush and Petraeus were lucky in that their surge coincided with an uprising of Sunni tribesmen against the foreign-led and brutal al-Qaeda in Mesopotamia. The Bush administration's decision early in the Iraqi invasion to purge almost all Baath and Sunni members of the government and army and to elevate the majority Shiites to power had driven many Sunnis into the arms of Saddam loyalists and al-Qaeda terrorists. When al-Qaeda in turn alienated its Sunni tribal allies, it provided an opening to bring those Sunnis to the side of the Shiite-led government. Petraeus put 100,000 Sunni militia on the American payroll at a cost of $30 million per month. This so-called Sunni Awakening did at least as much as the surge to dampen violence in Iraq. Civilian deaths plunged from 34,500 in 2006 and 23,600 in 2007 to 6,400 in 2008 and 3,000 in 2009. The decline in violence provided an opening for the Iraqi government to try to gain legitimacy and begin to take over its own security. The Shiite prime minister, Nouri al-Maliki, even challenged his fellow Shiites by taking back Basra and the Baghdad enclave of Sadr City from the control of Muktada al-Sadr, a viscerally anti-American Shiite cleric. The Sunni Awakening also provided an opening for Bush to begin to withdraw American troops from Iraq. After making a few token withdrawals, he negotiated a Status of Forces Agreement with the Iraqis in November 2008 that provided for the withdrawal of all foreign forces by the end of 2011. Bush assumed that some residual American forces would remain to support the Iraqi government after that date, but that decision was entirely up to the Iraqis.

Controversial Issues

The debate over Bush's national security policy and the invasion of Iraq was one of the most profound in the history of American foreign policy. The best single source on this debate is Micah L. Sifry and Christopher Cerf, eds., *The Iraq War Reader: History, Documents, Opinions* (2003). To understand the view of the history of the Islamic world that influenced the neoconservative push for the democratization of Iraq, see Bernard Lewis, *What Went Wrong: The Western Impact and the Middle Eastern Response* (2002); and Fouad Ajami, *The Dream Palace of the Arabs: A Generation's Odyssey* (1998). For a critique of that historical view, see Zachary Lockman, *Contending Visions of the Middle East: The History and Politics of Orientalism* (2004).

To understand why many liberals as well as conservatives supported the war to overthrow Saddam, see Kanan Makiya, *Republic of Fear: The Politics of Modern Iraq* (1998); and Kenneth Pollack, *The Threatening Storm: The Case for Invading Iraq* (2002). For the conservative argument, see Laurie Mylroie, *The War Against America: Saddam Hussein and the World Trade Center Attacks: A Study of Revenge* (2nd rev. ed., 2001); and Lawrence F. Kaplan and William Kristol, *The War Over Iraq: Saddam's Tyranny and America's Mission* (2003).

The best histories of the war leave little doubt that the planning for the postwar occupation was almost criminally negligent. They also condemn the Bush administration's misuse of the intelligence on Saddam's WMD in its rush to decide on and promote the war without giving the UN inspectors time to determine the issue with some degree of confidence. Even if the authors see virtue in the decision to get rid of Saddam, they are generally very critical of the Bush administration's disdain for the need to secure multilateral support for forcible regime change. See George Packer, *The Assassin's Gate: America in Iraq* (2005); Michael R. Gordon and Bernard E. Trainor, *Cobra II: The Inside Story of the Invasion and Occupation of Iraq* (2006); Thomas E. Ricks, *Fiasco: The American Military Adventure in Iraq* (2006); James Fallows, *Blind into Baghdad: America's War in Iraq* (2006); and Larry Diamond, *Squandered Victory: The American Occupation and the Bungled Effort to Bring Democracy to Iraq* (2005). The best book on the fighting of the Iraq War is Dexter Filkins, *The Forever War* (2008). For a series of books based on remarkable access to the leading figures of the Bush administration as they marched toward war, see Bob Woodward, *Bush at War* (2002), *Plan of Attack* (2004), and *State of Denial* (2006). Two books stand out among the many that denounce the Bush administration's manipulation of intelligence to rouse support for the war: Frank Rich, *The Greatest Story Ever Sold: The Decline and Fall of the Truth from 9/11 to Katrina* (2006); and John Prados, *Hoodwinked: The Documents That Reveal How Bush Sold Us a War* (2004). Another severe condemnation of Bush and the war is Seymour M. Hersh, *Chain of Command: The Road from 9/11 to Abu Ghraib* (2004).

Further Reading

For more complete portraits of the leading figures in the Bush administration to supplement those in the books on the war listed above, see Robert Draper, *Dead Certain: The Presidency of George W. Bush* (2007); James Mann, *Rise of the Vulcans: The History of Bush's War Cabinet* (2004); Elizabeth Bumiller, *Condoleezza Rice: An American Life* (2007); and Glenn Kessler, *The Confidante: Condoleezza Rice and the Creation of the Bush Legacy* (2007).

For an analysis and critique of the Bush Doctrine and the theory behind Bush's foreign policy, see Ivo H. Daalder and James M. Lindsay, *America Unbound: The Bush Revolution in Foreign Policy* (2003). For the effect of Bush's unilateralist inclinations on the war in Iraq, see William Shawcross, *Allies: The U.S., Britain, Europe, and the War in Iraq* (2004).

Important books on Islamic jihadism and America's response are Jonathan Randal, *Osama: The Making of a Terrorist* (2004); and Daniel Benjamin and Steven Simon, *The Age of Sacred Terror* (2002). For an insider's account by the former State Department official in charge of counterterrorism, see Richard Clarke, *Against All Enemies: Inside America's War on Terror* (2004).

Notes

1. Bush also argued that the "jury was still out" on the theory of evolution and appointed people to government regulatory boards who countermanded the conclusions and recommendations of the scientists on those boards. He would later accept the science behind the warnings about global warming but insist that compulsory caps on the production of carbon would undercut the American economy. He advocated only voluntary measures to reduce greenhouse gases and argued that developing countries like China and India would have to join developed countries in making large sacrifices to combat global warming.

2. According to Bob Woodward, an author with access to the leading figures in various administrations, Scowcroft sent a preliminary version of his article to George H.W. Bush and received back no comment, which Scowcroft took as permission to publish in the *New York Times*.

3. After the war began the British press published a leaked July 2 memo recording a conversation in which Richard Dearlove, the chief of the British intelligence agency MI-6, reported to Prime Minister Blair on meetings Dearlove had held with leaders of the Bush administration. The chief concluded: "Military action was now seen as inevitable. Bush wanted to remove Saddam through military action, justified by the conjunction of terrorism and WMD. But the intelligence and facts were being fixed around the policy."

CHAPTER 19

BARACK OBAMA AND THE POST-9/11 WORLD

Obama's Challenge to the Bush Doctrine

Barack Obama promised a foreign policy profoundly different from the Bush Doctrine of unilateralism, preemption, and the massive use of armed force to spread American ideals. In effect he called for a return to the restrained realist containment policy of Bush's father and Bill Clinton.

In October 2002, while still a state senator in Illinois, Obama had declared his opposition to Bush's pending invasion of Iraq on the grounds that Saddam's threat was not direct and immediate and that the invasion of Iraq would involve a U.S. occupation "of undetermined length, at undetermined cost, with undetermined consequences." Obama's early opposition to the Iraq war helped him win the Democratic nomination for president over Hillary Clinton, who had voted for the war in the Senate. As president he went on to elaborate his opposition to both the Iraq War and the Bush Doctrine. With regard to the ready use of armed force and preemption, he told the West Point cadets in May 2010, "I opposed the war in Iraq precisely because I believe that we must exercise restraint in the use of military force and always consider the long-term consequences of our actions." He further defined the conditions that should guide and limit decisions for war in his acceptance speech for the Nobel Peace Prize in September 2009: "War is justified only when certain conditions were met: if it is waged as a last resort or in self-defense; if the force used is proportional, and if, whenever possible, civilians are spared from violence."

While Obama promised restraint, his policy was far from pacifist. As he told his Nobel audience:

> I know there's nothing weak—nothing passive—nothing naïve—in the creed and lives of Gandhi and King. But as a head of state sworn to protect and defend my nation, I cannot be guided by their examples alone. I face the world as it is, and cannot stand idle in the face of threats to the American people. For make no mistake: Evil does exist in the world. A non-violent movement could not have halted Hitler's armies. Negotiations cannot convince al Qaeda's leaders to lay down their arms.

In fact, while Obama pointedly rejected many aspects of the Bush Doctrine, he did not discard all of them. With regard to unilateralism, for instance, Obama acknowledged in his Nobel speech that many nations had reason to believe that "on certain critical issues, America has acted unilaterally, without regard for the interests of others." In his National Security Strategy Paper of May 2010, issued concurrently with his speech at West Point, he spelled out his dedication to internationalism and diplomacy. He reaffirmed "America's commitment to pursue our interests through an international system in which all nations have certain rights and responsibilities" and to use diplomacy to "create opportunities to resolve differences, strengthen the international community's support for our actions, learn about the intentions and nature of closed regimes, and plainly demonstrate to the publics within those nations that their governments are to blame for their isolation." Yet Obama was not ready to abandon unilateralism entirely. "I—like any other head of state—reserve the right to act unilaterally if necessary to defend my nation," he told his Nobel audience. His National Security Strategy Paper also specifically claimed this right, although coupled with a promise to cooperate with allies and the international community whenever possible. As Sandy Berger, the former National Security Adviser to Bill Clinton, pointed out, Obama was returning to the Clinton mantra: "Together when possible, alone when necessary."

Obama was not ready to abandon all of Bush's policies regarding the war on terror either. He did try to narrow the focus of that war by avoiding the term "war on terror." As his National Security Strategy paper pointed out: "This is not a global war against a tactic—terrorism—or a religion—Islam. We are at war with a specific network, al-Qaeda, and its terrorist affiliates." Obama also jettisoned some of the extreme tactics the Bush administration had used in dealing with captured terrorists. "That is why I prohibited torture," he said in his Nobel speech. "That is why I ordered the prison at Guantánamo Bay closed. And that is why I have reaffirmed America's commitment to abide by the Geneva Conventions." In pursuit of these goals Obama issued an executive order on January 22, 2009, in which he directed the closing of Guantánamo within one year, eliminated CIA secret prisons, limited interrogation techniques to those prescribed by the army field manual, and promised to deport prisoners to their home countries only with promises that they would not be tortured.

However, Obama was unable to fulfill these commitments completely. While he did free some of the Guantánamo prisoners, he failed to close the prison in a year as he had promised. He was thwarted from closing it entirely by opposition in Congress and many state governments to moving the prisoners to institutions within the United States, the refusal of foreign nations to accept many of the prisoners, and his own realization that some prisoners were just too dangerous to turn loose. Congressional opposition also forced him to abandon his plans to try some of the Guantánamo prisoners in federal courts. Meanwhile Obama's pledge to abide by the Geneva Conventions was modified by the fact that insurgents and terrorists without uniforms or legitimate authority were not generally covered by the conventions. His order to limit interrogation techniques to those prescribed by the army field manual still permitted sleep deprivation, intimidation, and other coercive techniques. Moreover, his promise to deport prisoners to their home country only if those countries promised not to torture them was really no different from the Bush policy of rendition. While the Obama administration may have held other countries more rigorously to their promises not to torture than the Bush administration did, there are also reports that when the CIA closed its secret prisons, as promised by Obama, it kept at least one such prison open in Somalia.

With regard to the Bush Doctrine's emphasis on preemption, Obama seemed far less likely to resort to preemption against nation states than the Bush administration, although Obama did not take the possible use of force against Iran's nuclear program off the table. Against al-Qaeda and other terrorists lurking in nations with which the United States was not at war, however, Obama increased preemptive strikes by drones and special forces—for example, in Pakistan and Yemen. He also extended the special operations target list to include at least one American citizen abroad, Anwar al-Awlaki in Yemen, who was killed in late 2011.

Finally, while Obama certainly demonstrated his restraint in winding down the Iraq War, he increased Bush's forces in Afghanistan.

Iraq

The relative success of the surge and the Sunni Awakening along with the Status of Forces Agreement Bush had negotiated with the Iraqi government permitted Obama to fulfill his promise to wind down the Iraq War without having to admit defeat or leave behind a totally broken country. Obama had promised during his campaign to have American troops out of Iraq by mid-2010, but he easily accepted the existing agreement that all American forces would leave Iraq by the end of 2011. He even kept Bush's secretary of defense, Robert Gates, along with the Gates policy. Consequently, American troops pulled out of Iraqi cities in mid-2009 and then ended their combat role by December of that same year. Obama had wanted and expected the Iraqis to request that some American troops remain behind to continue training and assisting Iraqi forces after the scheduled withdrawal date, but when the Iraqis refused to continue granting immunity from prosecution to the Americans, Obama withdrew the last combat units in December 2011.

It was not clear that the Iraqi government was capable of maintaining a high level of security without the continued help of those American forces. The Iraqi government was divided, weak, and in danger of alienating the Sunni population all over again. Prime Minister Nouri al- Maliki actually found his Shiite coalition outvoted in the elections of 2010 by a coalition headed by Ayad Alawi that included a good number of Sunnis. Alawi won 91 seats to 89 for al-Maliki. But al-Maliki formed an alliance with an independent Shiite party headed by Muktada al-Sadr, the anti-American cleric with whose Mahdi army militia al-Maliki had just fought an open battle. By promising a great deal of autonomy to the Kurds, al-Maliki won a parliamentary majority, which he then used to bar Alawi and his followers from any major offices. In these rancorous conditions, the Iraqi government was unable to settle critical issues between Shiites, Sunnis, and Kurds such as the sharing of governmental power, the division of oil revenues, and control of the oil-rich cities of Kirkuk and Mosul. After the last American troops left, al-Maliki ordered the arrest of a number of Sunnis as accused Baathists. This included even the nation's vice-president, who promptly took refuge in the Kurdish enclave. Meanwhile Sunni radicals increased their bombing of Shiite targets. The potential for a renewed sectarian civil war rose accordingly.

Afghanistan

At the beginning of the Obama administration, there were 161,000 U.S. troops in Iraq and 38,000 U.S. troops in Afghanistan. Obama had campaigned on the idea that Afghanistan was a necessary war while Iraq was not. Therefore, he promised that, while withdrawing troops from Iraq, he would dispatch two additional brigades to Afghanistan. These two brigades along with the existing NATO forces in Afghanistan would bring the number of U.S. and NATO troops to a level of about 83,000.

Unfortunately there was no plan in place that prescribed the troop level and strategy that would be necessary to stabilize Afghanistan. General David Petraeus wanted to shift the Afghan strategy from counterterrorism to counterinsurgency as he had so success-fully done in Iraq. But the population of Afghanistan was so large that it would have taken more than 500,000 troops to achieve the 1/50 ratio of troops and police to civilians that Petraeus had calculated was necessary for a counterinsurgency strategy to succeed. With only about 80,000 U.S. and NATO troops, that ratio would require the training and mobilization of 450,000 Afghan army and police forces to supplement them, a goal that seemed impossible. Consequently, Petraeus began talking about sending far more than just two new brigades, and he even remarked that it might take ten years to fully train the Afghan forces and to make counterinsurgency work.

Petraeus's hopes for counterinsurgency faced another problem in Afghanistan that was at least as daunting as troop levels: the need to win cooperation and loyalty from Afghanistan's civilian population. In Iraq Petraeus had reaped good fortune from the Sunni Awakening. But there was no comparable opportunity in Afghanistan. The Taliban was closely tied to the majority Pashtun ethnic group that dominated southern Afghani-stan and neighboring areas in Pakistan. Minority ethnic groups in the north, such as the Hazara and Tajiks, opposed both the Pashtuns and the Taliban and could probably prevent a Taliban takeover in their area, but they could not pacify or rule a united Af-ghanistan. The Bush administration had tried to unite the country by installing Hamid Karzai, a Pashtun, as the president of Afghanistan. But Karzai's government turned out to be corrupt, unreliable, and inept. Its bureaucracy was impenetrable. Getting a driver's license in Afghanistan required forty-two steps, each step accompanied by a bribe. The opium trade was out of control. It financed much of the Taliban war effort, but also it financed some of the warlords upon whom Karzai relied for control of the country out-side Kabul, including his own brother. Karzai himself was bipolar and railed as often against the American and NATO war effort as against the Taliban. He rigged elections blatantly to keep power. Some Afghans might support him as the lesser of evils against the Taliban, but it seemed unlikely that he and the Americans could win over so-called moderate Taliban fighters to the government side as the Sunni Awakening had detached large numbers of fighters from the insurgents in Iraq. In fact Karzai seemed more akin to Ngo Dinh Diem and the failed South Vietnamese government in the Vietnam War than to Maliki in the Iraq War.

Yet another daunting obstacle to Petraeus's hope for a successful counterinsurgency strategy also echoed the failed Vietnam War: the Taliban and al-Qaeda found sanctuaries across the border in Pakistan just as North Vietnam and the Vietcong had found sanctuaries in Laos and Cambodia. Pakistan was America's nominal ally, but the Pakistani population was bitterly anti-American. Many Pakistanis had been schooled in Saudi-funded Islamic madrassas that portrayed the United States as a Christian crusader and enemy nation. Pakistanis also felt betrayed and abandoned by the United States when American funding dried up after Pakistan and the CIA had helped the Afghan mujahideen expel the Soviets in the 1980s. Even worse, the United States had moved closer in the past decade to Pakistan's bitter enemy, India. The Bush administration had even agreed to supply civilian nuclear fuel to India's energy industry, a major exception to America's stance on nonproliferation. Meanwhile the United States continued to oppose Pakistan's nuclear efforts and the proliferation of Pakistani nuclear materials and expertise. The Pakistani army and government even worried that the United States was plotting to take over Pakistan's nuclear arsenal if it was in danger of falling into the hands of Islamists.

After 9/11 the Bush administration insisted that the military dictator of Pakistan, Pervez Musharraf, enlist in the war on terror. Musharraf did permit the United States to ship most of its supplies to the Afghan war through Pakistan and he cracked down to some extent on militant Islamic groups and madrassas. But Pakistan's army, and particularly its Inter-Services Intelligence (ISI) branch, supported militant Islamic groups as their major weapon in their guerrilla war against Indian control of Kashmir. Those militant groups also supported the Taliban and their war in Afghanistan. Pakistan, which feared that India was gaining too much influence with the Afghan government, continued to tolerate and even offer some support to the Islamic militants and the Taliban as a hedge against the day when the United States would withdraw from Afghanistan.

In 2006 Musharraf ceded control of much of the tribal region bordering Afghanistan to tribes sympathetic to the Taliban. In 2008 one of those tribal networks, with the support of the ISI, blew up the Indian embassy in Kabul, killing fifty-eight people. Shortly afterward another Pakistani militant group with close ties to the ISI raided the Indian city of Mumbai and killed 160. The United States pressed Musharraf and the weak civilian government that succeeded him in 2008 to crack down on the militants, especially after the Pakistani branch of the Taliban began major attacks within Pakistan itself and even took temporary governmental control over the Swat Valley. But the Taliban and al-Qaeda continued to find sanctuaries in the tribal areas and some large cities of Pakistan, and the Taliban passed across the border easily to conduct attacks within Afghanistan, probably with at least some continuing connivance of the ISI.

Obama ordered a complete strategic review of the Afghan War immediately upon taking office. But Defense Secretary Gates and Petraeus argued that the situation was deteriorating so badly that the president should not wait for the draft review to be fully developed and debated before he dispatched the two brigades he had promised to Afghanistan. Gates and Petraeus were especially worried that the Taliban would disrupt the upcoming Afghan elections unless security was increased. Obama agreed and ordered the two brigades to embark immediately.

On March 27, 2009, the president spoke to the American people to explain his action and to announce "a comprehensive, new strategy for Afghanistan and Pakistan." The goal would be "to disrupt, dismantle, and defeat al Qaeda in Pakistan and Afghanistan, and to prevent their return to either country in the future." He pointed to the al-Qaeda destruction of the twin towers in New York, the subway bombings in London and Madrid, the assault in Bali, and other attacks in Africa to argue that defeating al-Qaeda would benefit not just the United States but the rest of the world as well and thus deserved military support from U.S. allies. He significantly did not say that a parallel goal was to defeat the Taliban, but he did warn that "for the Afghan people, a return to Taliban rule would condemn their country to brutal governance, international isolation, a paralyzed economy, and the denial of basic human rights to the Afghan people—especially women and girls. The return in force of al Qaeda terrorists who would accompany the core Taliban leadership would cast Afghanistan under the shadow of perpetual violence."

The United States would no longer deny resources to the Afghan War because of the Iraq War, Obama proclaimed. He would send the two brigades along with the 4,000 trainers to recruit and equip an Afghan army of 134,000 and an Afghan police force of 82,000 by 2011, at which time NATO and American troops could begin to hand off security duties to the Afghans and come home. The United States and its allies would also send civilians and money to help build the Afghan economy, wean it away from dependence on the production of opium, and reduce corruption. The Afghan government and the United States would reach out to potential moderate Taliban in hopes of splitting them off from the die-hard militants, thus repeating the success of the Sunni Awakening in Iraq. Finally Obama urged Congress to appropriate $1.5 billion per year for five years to Pakistan for economic aid in addition to the billions in military assistance the United States had sent, all to be contingent on Pakistan "rooting out al Qaeda and the violent extremists within its borders." Shortly after this speech Obama replaced the incumbent commander in Afghanistan, General David McKiernan, an advocate of antiterrorism warfare, with General Stanley McChrystal, a devotee of Petraeus's counterinsurgency strategy.

Unfortunately the "comprehensive, new strategy" that Obama announced in this March 27 speech was not yet a full strategy. Even if the United States successfully reformed the Karzai government and eliminated Taliban sanctuaries, Obama would need far more troops than he had already dispatched to Afghanistan to implement a full counterinsurgency strategy. This problem turned the completion of the strategic review into one of the most profound and intense internal strategic debates in any American administration. It required nine lengthy meetings over a period of eight months.

One faction in the review process, led by Vice President Joseph Biden, argued against a full counterinsurgency strategy because it would be far too expensive and require far too many troops to implement. Biden called instead for a "small footprint" counterterrorism effort that would rely on an ink-blot strategy of controlling a few cities and outposts in Afghanistan from which to launch high-tech drone strikes and special operations against al-Qaeda suspects. The United States would abandon its hopeless attempts to defeat the Taliban, reform Karzai's corrupt government, build up the primitive, drug-dependent Afghan economy, and modernize the tribal society. Instead most of America's economic aid would go to Pakistan, where a failure of the government and the acquisition of its nuclear weapons by a terrorist group would pose far greater dangers to the United States than a Taliban victory in Afghanistan. Biden received support from the U.S. ambassador to Afghanistan, former general Karl Eikenberry, who warned in a leaked cable that Karzai was not an adequate strategic partner and that the Afghan forces could not be recruited or trained sufficiently to defend Afghanistan against the Taliban.

Opposing Biden were Gates, Petraeus, and the Pentagon, who insisted that Obama should send more troops to try to save Afghanistan. Admiral Michael Mullen, the chair of the Joint Chiefs of Staff, tried to forbid the Pentagon from even discussing the Biden option. Obama insisted that it be considered, however, and so the generals began taking their case outside the review committee to the public at large. General McChrystal leaked his own request to the president in which he said he would need 85,000 more troops for a robust counterinsurgency effort, 40,000 more troops for a "balanced" counterinsurgency strategy, and 11,000 more troops if the plan was merely to train more Afghans. Clearly this was the old Kissinger gambit of sandwiching one's real goal between two impossible or unattractive options. McChrystal also called for doubling the number of Afghan troops and police to be recruited and trained to a total of 400,000 men at an initial cost of $55 billion plus $8 billion per year to support them after the American troops had withdrawn. (McChrystal obviously had a low opinion of his opponents in the review process; he and his staff made disparaging remarks about Biden, Eikenberry, and even Obama in the hearing of an embedded journalist, a faux pas that eventually got McChrystal fired.)

Obama was chagrined by the military's demands for more troops so soon after he had sent the two new brigades. But he was adamantly against withdrawal and he thought that he might be able to send enough additional troops to conduct a partial counterinsurgency campaign for at least a short time because he would not have to provide a ratio of one soldier or police officer for every fifty civilians in large portions of Afghanistan that were controlled by Tajiks or Hazara rather than Pashtuns. Moreover NATO and U.S. troops would concentrate on cities, populated areas, and lines of communication. They simply would not take what they could not clear, hold, and successfully transfer to Afghan forces. In the end Obama accepted Gates's compromise suggestion of 30,000 additional U.S. troops and 10,000 more NATO troops as sufficient to conduct a limited counterinsurgency campaign. But he set some conditions on that increase. He wanted it to be a surge like that in Iraq, not a long-term commitment. He insisted that the troops be dispatched quickly to make the maximum impact and that U.S. troops should begin withdrawing by the middle of 2011. Meanwhile the United States would continue and even expand some of its existing counterterrorism tactics, including drone and special operations strikes against al-Qaeda and the Taliban in both Afghanistan and Pakistan. The goal would not be to fully defeat the Taliban but to degrade it sufficiently that the newly trained Afghan forces would be able to defend against it. The surge would provide the time and security necessary to allow the adequate training of the Afghan army and police. As one aide said, the ultimate goal was not to make Afghanistan a Jeffersonian democracy but to leave it "not too terrible a place."

Once Obama had made his decision, he called Biden, Hillary Clinton, Gates, Petraeus, Mullen, and the rest of his security team to a special Sunday meeting in which he presented a short written summary of the decisions they had debated and asked them to state flatly whether they agreed with his decision or not. All agreed. Obama then gave a speech at West Point spelling out to the nation his decision to surge in Afghanistan with 30,000 more troops and to begin withdrawing them in July 2011 while turning over security in selected areas to the Afghans themselves. He forbade his speechwriter from inserting any reference to nation building or even counterinsurgency. As he told columnist Thomas Friedman, he was interested in nation building in the United States, not Afghanistan. "I refuse to set goals that go beyond our responsibility, our means, or our interests," Obama insisted.

No sooner had Obama given his West Point speech than many in Congress, especially Republicans, began to ask whether 2011 was a firm deadline to begin withdrawal regardless of conditions in Afghanistan at the time. They pointed out that the Taliban could just wait out the Americans if they knew the troops would leave in a short time. Obama and Gates hedged by saying the withdrawal would begin in 2011 but the pace would be determined by conditions on the ground. This statement seemed to leave no one satisfied. Opponents of the war worried that Afghanistan would become another Vietnam—a quagmire in which the United States would be stuck for years. Proponents of the war, on the other hand, feared that the American troops would leave before they had a chance to win the war. Hamid Karzai inadvertently came to Obama's rescue. In one of his periodic speeches complaining about American and NATO actions, he announced that he wanted all foreign forces out of Afghanistan by 2014. Leaping at the opportunity, the Obama administration adopted 2014 as the date by which the withdrawal that would begin in 2011 would be completed.

Obama had insisted in his West Point speech that the war in Afghanistan should not be compared to the Vietnam War. Vietnam had not threatened the American homeland as al-Qaeda had done. The United States had truly willing allies and international support in Afghanistan, unlike the situation in Vietnam. Moreover the Taliban did not have the same degree of support among Afghans that the Vietcong and Ho Chi Minh had commanded among the South Vietnamese. Despite Obama's dislike of historical analogies, however, he could not escape some other similarities between the Vietnam and Afghan Wars that haunted his strategy. In Afghanistan as in Vietnam, the United States was allied with an unpopular and inept domestic regime while facing a tenacious indigenous enemy that had sanctuaries across neighboring national borders.

Obama found a ray of hope on May 1, 2011, when a team of navy SEALs raided across the Afghan border into Pakistan and killed Osama bin Laden. Further drone strikes in Pakistan killed many other leaders of al-Qaeda as well. Since Obama had declared the goal of the Afghan War to be the defeat of al-Qaeda rather than the Taliban, some aides urged him to follow the advice Senator George Aiken had offered during the Vietnam War: Declare victory and leave. But Obama stuck to his plan. He began the withdrawal

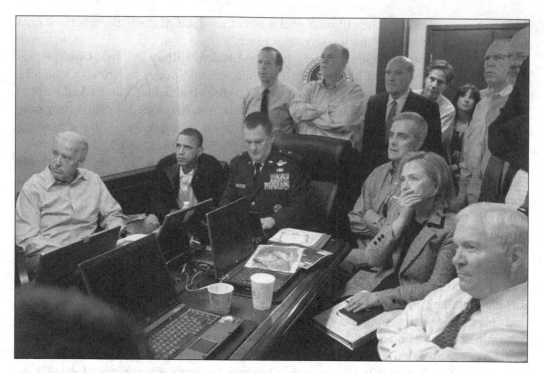

President Barack Obama *(seated second from left)* watches simulcast of the raid that killed Osama bin Laden with Vice President Joe Biden *(seated far left)*, Secretary of State Hillary Clinton *(seated second from right)*, Secretary of Defense Robert Gates *(seated far right)*, and other members of his national security team.

of the 30,000 surge troops in late 2011 to be completed by the summer of 2012, and he insisted he would continue withdrawing troops after that so all troops would be out of Afghanistan by 2014. Meanwhile he did his best to fend off Pakistani resentment and opposition to the cross-border operations that were the key to his antiterrorism strategies. Unfortunately NATO added to the Pakistani resentment already occasioned by the Bin Laden raid when it mistakenly bombed several border guards across the Pakistan border. Pakistan promptly shut down the vital NATO supply corridors through its territory into Afghanistan, while the Pakistani military confronted its own civilian government over a leaked memo requesting American support to prevent a military coup. The chances for a decent outcome to the Afghan War seemed very dim.

The Arab Spring

In January 2011 a young Tunisian street vendor named Mohamed Bouazizi set himself on fire to protest harassment, extortion, and brutality by government officials. His martyr-dom set off a wave of popular protests that brought down the Tunisian president in two weeks. The success of the Tunisian revolution ignited similar protests across the Middle East against the corrupt, brutal, and dictatorial regimes that used the oil riches of the area to enrich themselves, buy off opposition whenever possible, and pay vast military and security systems to destroy any opposition that could not be bought. Most of these regimes also enlisted the support of the West, especially the United States, which valued the stability, the steady flow of oil, and the relatively moderate policy toward Israel that these regimes provided.

The Arab Spring posed a major foreign policy dilemma for the Obama administration. On the one hand, most of the rebellions were initiated not by Islamic radicals who hated the United States, Israel, and Western modernization, but by young idealists who wanted the democracy and economic opportunity they saw in the West. Obama knew that the dictatorships upon which the West had relied for so long were ossified and probably doomed in the relatively near future. Here was a chance that their demise could turn out to benefit rather than derail Western interests in the Middle East. On the other hand, it was highly probable that democratic regimes would be more anti-Israeli than the regimes they overthrew. Moreover there was a good chance that the successor regimes in the Middle East would not be democratic or modernist at all. The young democrats who initiated the Arab Spring demonstrations were not well organized or united. The only well-organized groups in opposition to the Western-leaning dictatorships were either Islamist, tribal, or sectarian. It was at least as likely that the overthrow of the dictators would result in Islamist government, tribal fragmentation, or sectarian civil war as in democratic and inclusive regimes.

Israel, which had reason to be especially worried about the consequences of democratic or Islamist gains in the Middle East, urged Obama to support the old regimes. Saudi Arabia also pushed Obama to oppose the Arab Spring for fear of the sectarian consequences. As the leader of Sunni Islam, Saudi Arabia feared that democratic reforms would incite and empower Shiites in Sunni-ruled nations like Bahrain, where Shiites were 75 percent of the population; Yemen, where they were close to 40 percent; Lebanon, where they were the majority; Kuwait, where they were 25 percent; and even in Saudi Arabia itself, where they were 15 percent of the population. Iran, Saudi Arabia's Shiite rival and nemesis, had already benefited from the American-aided Shiite takeover in Iraq. The Saudis urged Obama not to open the way for further Iranian influence.

Obama decided, however, to take the risk and support the Arab Spring demonstrators against America's previously favored dictators. But he calibrated the degree of his support by taking into account America's own national interests and the nature of the rebellion in each of the affected nations.

The first of the regimes to fall before the torrent of the Arab Spring after Tunisia was that of Egypt. Hosni Mubarak had ruled Egypt with a heavy hand for thirty years and, as part of the deal that accompanied Egypt's peace treaty with Israel, he received American aid in amounts second only to Israel itself. With control of the army and a vast police apparatus, Mubarak brutally suppressed all opposition, especially that of Islamists like the Muslim Brotherhood, and maintained a precarious peace with the Coptic Christian minority in Egypt. Consequently the Obama administration was torn when massive peaceful demonstrations began in Cairo's Tahrir Square and Mubarak sent waves of his security forces, including some mounted on camels, to break up the demonstrations.

On the one hand, the demonstrators were led by young and relatively secular modernists seeking democracy and economic modernization rather than Islamist radicals or anti-Israeli zealots. On the other hand, the Muslim Brotherhood was the best organized political movement in Egypt even if it did not command a majority of the population. In any democratic election, it was likely to win at least a plurality despite its rather late and reluctant participation in the Tahrir Square demonstrations. In Egypt, however, as in no other country affected by the Arab Spring, there was another alternative. Almost all Egyptians still respected the Egyptian army, which had remained aloof from the police and security apparatus that Mubarak had used to jail and torture his opponents. The army could provide the security and organization for a transition to democracy while preventing violence against the Copts, the rise of radical Islam, or a revolution in policy toward Israel. So Obama threw his support behind the demonstrators and called for Mubarak to resign. In only eighteen days the demonstrators forced Mubarak to flee to his villa on the Red Sea and the army assumed control. It scheduled parliamentary elections for the following November and presidential elections shortly afterward but declared that the interim government, under army control, would write the new constitution. Meanwhile the army's interim government sacked thousands of officers in the hated police and put Mubarak himself on trial. The military also indicated it would keep the peace treaty with Israel, but that it would open its border with Gaza and soften its stance toward the militant anti-Israeli Hamas organization that controlled the area.

As the parliamentary elections approached, liberal demonstrators renewed their protests against the army's determination to control the writing of the constitution. The Muslim Brotherhood belatedly joined the protests as it became apparent that it would dominate the new parliament and would want that parliament to write the constitution. Indeed the Muslim Brotherhood won nearly 50 percent of the parliamentary seats while the more conservative Salafist Islamic party won another 25 percent. That pattern of Islamist victory in democratic elections occurred in Tunisia as well, a natural outcome of the fact that the Islamists had formed the only organized opposition to the Middle East dictatorships over the past several decades. Obama and the West could only hope that the Muslim Brotherhood and the Islamist victors in Tunisia would live up to their promises to ally with the liberals rather than the Salafists and create moderate Islamic democratic governments on the model of Turkey.

The third regime after Tunisia and Egypt to face a major challenge from the Arab Spring was that of President Ali Abdullah Saleh of Yemen. Saleh had ruled Yemen for more than thirty years, but outside the capital of Sana he faced continual rebellions from the Houthi tribe of Shiites in the north along the Saudi border and from various separatists in the south. Yemen's branch of al-Qaeda, including the militant American-born cleric Anwar al-Awlaki, found refuge among these dissident tribes. Although Saleh was an unpleasant dictator of a country with almost no important resources and therefore not critical to American economic interests, he did permit the United States to conduct raids and drone strikes against al-Qaeda on his territory and his nation did command strategic coastal areas at the southern end of the Red Sea. So Obama paused until April before endorsing the attempts of the gulf emirates and the United Nations to broker a deal whereby

Saleh would step down in exchange for immunity from prosecution. But Saleh refused to sign the agreement at the last minute and the situation dragged on through June, when a major tribal enemy of Saleh's family, the Ahmar clan, began fighting a civil war in the streets of Sana itself and Saleh was wounded in a rocket attack. Saleh left Yemen for a hospital in Saudi Arabia, where the Saudis supported him and opposed the attempts by the United States and others to oust him. In September 2011 Saleh returned to Yemen and briefly tried to restore himself to power, but in January 2012 he resigned and took refuge in New York for medical treatment. Just what sort of government would follow him remained unclear.

Throughout the remainder of the Arabian Peninsula, the Arab Spring was simply crushed. In Bahrain, the Shiites mounted large demonstrations on behalf of democratic reforms that would empower their 75 percent majority. Saudi Arabia sent its own troops into Bahrain to preempt any rising of the Shiite populations or any increase in Iranian influence in the peninsula. Obama urged the Bahrain monarchy to allow a more inclusive and democratic government but, with the American Fifth Fleet stationed in Bahrain, he stood aside silently when the Saudis intervened. Needless to say, the Saudis also made sure there was no Arab Spring within Saudi Arabia itself.

Outside Tunisia and Egypt, the Arab Spring flared only briefly in two other North African countries. It subsided quickly in Algeria after the government broke up demonstrations without firearms. In Morocco the relatively popular monarch King Mohammed VI co-opted the demonstrations by agreeing to a new constitution. In Libya, however, it was a different story.

Colonel Muammar al-Gadhafi had led a coup to overthrow the king of oil-rich Libya in 1969 during the period of pan-Arab rebellions inspired by Gamal Abdel Nasser of Egypt. For the next forty-two years Gadhafi ruled Libya as an eccentric, volatile, and brutal dictator. He often dressed in animal skins and slept in a tent surrounded by female bodyguards on trips abroad. He created his own political philosophy, which he compiled and printed as *The Green Book: The Solution to the Problems of Democracy; The Social Basis to the Third Universal Theory*. This hodgepodge of anti-imperialism, pan-Arabism, Islam, and non sequiturs was required reading for all citizens of Libya. According to *Green Book* principles, Gadhafi dissolved almost all political and parliamentary institutions in Libya and established instead Peoples' Conferences in which ordinary citizens were supposed to speak directly to him as the Brotherly Leader. By eliminating all intermediary powers and playing local tribes against one another, he created not only a cult of personality but a one-person state. He enforced his rule by imprisoning, torturing, and "disappearing" anyone bold enough to oppose him.

For the first thirty years of his rule, Gadhafi openly challenged the United States and the West by sponsoring revolutionary movements in various African countries, including Chad, Liberia, and Sierra Leone. He supported the Islamic rebellion in the Philippines, helped finance the Irish Republican Army, and sponsored the Palestinian Black September movement that kidnapped and killed Israeli athletes at the 1972 Munich Olympics. In 1986 he ordered a bombing attack on American soldiers in a German disco; Ronald Reagan retaliated with an air raid on Gadhafi's Tripoli compound that killed one of his adopted daughters. In 1988 Gadhafi's agents planted a bomb on Pan American Flight 103 that exploded over Lockerbie, Scotland, killing 270 people. The United States imposed sanctions against Libya as a sponsor of terrorism and aided Chad in its successful border war against Libya.

In 2003, after the United States intercepted a large shipment of nuclear-related equipment headed for Libya, Gadhafi decided to cut his losses and reconcile with the West. He accepted responsibility for the Lockerbie bombing, turned the accused bomber over to Scotland, paid compensation to the victims, and abandoned his nuclear program. The United States and the international community normalized relations with Gadhafi, but his domestic brutality continued and in early 2011 he found himself the target of Libya's own Arab Spring.

The Libyan rebellion began in Benghazi and surrounding areas of eastern Libya, where tribal opposition to Gadhafi had long seethed. The rebels took control of Benghazi and several other eastern cities. Gadhafi responded with full-scale attacks by troops, artillery, tanks, and planes. He made clear that he would show the demonstrators and rebels no mercy. He said he would find them "even in your closets."

As Gadhafi's columns routed the poorly armed and poorly organized rebels in their march toward Benghazi, a massacre of civilians seemed likely. The Arab League passed a resolution calling for the United Nations to establish a no-fly zone such as the West had imposed on Iraq after the Gulf War. French president Nicolas Sarkozy and British prime minister David Cameron called for UN and NATO intervention and found support from the Italians, who were the primary recipients of Libyan oil. In the United States, Secretary of State Clinton, UN ambassador Susan Rice, and Samantha Power—one of Obama's close personal advisers and the Pulitzer Prize–winning author of a book about the failure of the United States to intervene in Rwanda—all urged Obama to intervene on humanitarian grounds. Secretary of Defense Robert Gates, however, warned against overstretching a military already engaged in two wars in the Middle East.

Obama decided that the United States would intervene for humanitarian reasons to stop a slaughter of innocents even though few American interests were involved. But he insisted that such a humanitarian intervention could not be unilateral because that would raise cries of American imperialism. Moreover it would not involve American "boots on the ground" that would add to the burden that American troops already bore in Iraq and Afghanistan. Thus it would be reminiscent of Bill Clinton's intervention in the Balkans.

Indeed the Libyan intervention was multilateral. The United Nations Security Council not only endorsed the Arab League's call for a no-fly zone, but also empowered its members to take all necessary measures to protect Libyan civilians. Although Germany, an important NATO member, had abstained from the vote on the Security Council resolution along with Russia, India, China, and Brazil, NATO agreed to take the leadership of the intervention once the United States had destroyed the Libyan air force and air defense capabilities. America would "lead from behind."

Obama's decision got a very mixed reception from Congress. A majority clearly supported intervention, but many Democrats opposed the intervention outright while many

Republicans objected that it did not go far enough because NATO was incapable of conducting the operation without the United States leading it and the UN authorization stopped short of insisting on Gadhafi's removal. Obama circumvented the opposition in Congress by refusing to submit the intervention to a vote as required by the War Powers Act under the provision that the president had to seek approval within sixty days after he had committed the nation to "hostilities." Obama argued that the Libyan situation did not rise to the level of hostilities and therefore no vote was required. After Obama's criticism of Bush's unilateralism and rationalizations in the Iraq War, this seemed to be a ridiculous play on words and a needless slap in the face of Congress. Obama's aides later implied that they regretted this decision, and it could have come back to haunt him if the Libyan intervention had gone badly.

Fortunately the air intervention succeeded in destroying Gadhafi's superior heavy weaponry. This permitted the rebels to defeat Gadhafi's loyalists and to capture and kill Gadhafi. The interim government was then able to move from Benghazi to Tripoli and assume control of the nation, but several of the local armed militias refused to turn over their weapons and the situation in Libya remained extremely fragile in early 2012.

The Obama administration trumpeted Libya as an example of the virtues of multilateralism. Indeed France and Great Britain flew most of the air sorties after the Americans suppressed Libya's air defenses and their special forces helped to arm and organize the rebels. But the United States still had to provide much of the air surveillance and intelligence, precision weaponry, and refueling capabilities. In fact, despite the leadership the NATO allies had shown in Libya, the shortcomings in their military capabilities were so obvious that Gates proclaimed the alliance was close to becoming irrelevant.

The Arab Spring died rather quickly in most of the Muslim countries north of the Arabian Peninsula. But in Syria it shook the foundations of the nation long ruled by the Assad family. When Hafez al-Assad died in 2000 after thirty years of imposing an iron-fisted rule of his Alawite religious minority over the majority of Sunni Syrians, many hoped that his son and successor, Bashar al-Assad, would reform the regime. Bashar had done his medical residency in London and seemed amenable to Western ideas of modernity and inclusiveness. He began his rule by freeing some political prisoners and withdrawing Syrian troops from Lebanon's capital, Beirut. But he quickly reverted to the ways of his father by imprisoning many members of Parliament and political activists.

Assad also continued a foreign policy hostile to the West and the United States, leading George W. Bush to add Syria to his "axis of evil." Assad continued to give refuge to many Palestinian and other militants and allowed them to cross the Syrian border to fight the American occupation of Iraq. Assad also played a role in the 2004 assassination of the Lebanese prime minister, Rafiq Hariri, a Western-leaning Sunni who was the political rival of the Lebanese Shiites and their Hezbollah militia. The Lebanese mounted mass demonstrations against Syria in the wake of Hariri's assassination, and Assad had to withdraw all of the Syrian troops that had remained in other parts of Lebanon after leaving Beirut at the beginning of Assad's tenure.

However, Assad continued to exercise influence in Lebanon through Hezbollah. Along with Iran, Assad provided weapons and political support to Hezbollah; he abandoned attempts to compromise over Palestinian rights and the Golan Heights as Hezbollah staged a raid across the Israeli border in 2006, killing several Israeli soldiers and capturing two others. When Hezbollah offered to trade the captives for Israeli-held political prisoners, Israel responded with air and rocket attacks along with a limited ground assault. Hezbollah launched hundreds of rockets supplied by Syria and Iran that reached as far south in Israel as Haifa. After a month, the United Nations brokered a cease-fire, and Hezbollah emerged as the defender of Lebanon against Israel and a force powerful enough to prevent any government it disliked from taking power in Lebanon even though Hezbollah too was implicated along with Syria in the assassination of Hariri.

Shortly afterward, in 2006, Israel punished Syria by bombing a suspected nuclear reactor site. The United States agreed that it was a nuclear site and accused North Korea of supplying some of the materials for it. Consequently, in 2010 the Obama administration renewed American sanctions on Syria for supporting terrorism, seeking weapons of mass destruction, and providing Hezbollah with SCUD missiles. Nevertheless the United States, throughout the later stages of the George W. Bush administration and the Obama presidency, made low-level diplomatic contacts in an attempt to improve relations with Assad, draw him away from his alliance with Iran, and maintain some stability in both Syria and Arab-Israeli relations.

The Arab Spring in Syria disrupted this entire scenario. In March 2011, massive peaceful demonstrations began to spread through Syria's major cities. Assad sent waves of police, troops, and tanks against the demonstrators, killing and jailing many but failing to stop the rebellion. Obama and the West were cautious at first, not only because they were worried about the stability of the area in general, but also because a revolt against Assad could easily turn into a sectarian civil war pitting the majority Sunnis against Assad's minority Alawites. As the demonstrations increased and Assad's response became even more brutal, Obama and the West moved from calling upon Assad to listen to his people to insisting that he step down entirely. Even Syria's allies, including Iran, called for him to negotiate reforms with the rebels. But Assad remained obdurate and the crisis continued into 2012.

The Palestinian-Israeli Conflict

President Obama used the Arab Spring as yet another occasion to try to restart serious negotiations for peace between the Palestinians and Israelis. In a speech on May 19, 2011, he called for peace to be based on a return to Israel's 1967 borders, although he also advocated adjustments to that border to account for existing Israeli settlements in the West Bank. This was the first time an American president had specified the 1967 border as a basis for the peace, but the overall proposal was no different from the one that had been on the negotiating table since the Taba negotiations held during the last years of the Clinton administration. Nevertheless Israeli prime minister Benjamin Netanyahu, ignoring Obama's qualification about border adjustments, publicly denounced the 1967 border as indefensible. In a meeting with Obama he adamantly rejected Obama's ideas for compromise and then went before a welcoming Congress to insist that the Palestinians would have to recognize Israel as a Jewish state, give up all right of return, and abandon their claims to any part of Jerusalem. Netanyahu's snub of Obama emphasized both the deadly stalemate in Israeli-Palestinian relations and the impotence of a divided American body politic to break that stalemate.

George W. Bush had regarded Palestinian-Israeli relations as intractable from the outset of his administration. He took office during the Second Intifada, when Palestinian suicide bombers and Israeli raids were killing hundreds on both sides. In June 2002, in the midst of the intifada, Israel began building a barrier between its territory and the West Bank in order to prevent suicide bombers from infiltrating the border. (The Palestinians called the barrier a "wall"; the Israelis insisted it was merely a "fence.") That barrier included many Israeli settlements beyond the 1967 border, and although the Israeli courts forced some rerouting of the barrier in favor of the Palestinians, this unilateral staking out of the potential border made negotiations even more improbable.

Nevertheless Bush made his first major foray into Palestinian-Israeli affairs in 2002 by announcing a plan that he called a road map to peace. Unfortunately it broke no new ground and mortally offended the Palestinians by endorsing the new Israeli barrier. Recognizing that his road map to peace would have little impact on the conflict, Bush hoped instead that the Iraq War and subsequent initiatives elsewhere in the Middle East might bring democratic regimes to the region and make the Arab-Israeli conflict less relevant to America's position in the Arab and Islamic world.

That hope did not materialize either, but Israeli prime minister Ariel Sharon and the Palestinian leadership that had taken office after the death of Yasser Arafat did manage to negotiate a cease-fire in February 2005. A few months later the Israelis decided to cut their losses in Gaza, where there were few Israeli settlements, by evacuating that occupied territory unilaterally. Israel kept control of its border crossings into Gaza, however, and also arranged with Egypt to limit access to Gaza from its border outside Israeli territory. That did not prevent Palestinian militants from smuggling rockets into Gaza and launching them into Israeli territory from this sanctuary. The Palestinian Authority, led by Arafat's Fatah Party, tried but failed to suppress these rocket attacks and then suddenly in 2006 found itself displaced in the Gaza parliament by Hamas, the militant organization that refused to recognize Israel's right to exist and that Israel, the United States, and much of the West categorized as a terrorist organization. A tentative unity agreement between Hamas and Fatah broke down in 2007, and an open battle between the factions in Gaza resulted in total Hamas control. While the Fatah government that controlled the West Bank was still willing to negotiate a two-state solution, it could not speak for all of Palestine as long as Hamas controlled Gaza and insisted that Israel was not a legitimate state with which to negotiate. Israel now looked at the results of its withdrawal from Gaza and wondered if a withdrawal from the West Bank in a two-state solution might not produce the same result. Moreover the Israelis were still smarting from their failure to destroy Hezbollah in the Lebanese border war that had just concluded.

With the Middle East situation spinning out of control, Bush made a last attempt to restart the peace process by convening a conference in Annapolis, Maryland, in November 2007. The conference would bring together the prime minister of the Fatah government in the West Bank, Mahmoud Abbas, and Sharon's successor as Israeli prime minister, Ehud Olmert. Abbas and Olmert had already been meeting for months, along with leaders of many of the Arab and Western nations that had had a role in the Middle East peace process. Abbas was as moderate as any Palestinian leader and had the incentive to achieve a peace agreement that he could use to win support away from his Hamas rivals. Olmert was more accommodating than Sharon and also had the incentive to achieve an agreement to divert attention from a brewing corruption scandal in Israel. Olmert was ready to give up part of Jerusalem for the Palestinian capital, while Abbas also was willing to make considerable border concessions. But Abbas insisted that he would have to submit any agreement to a Palestinian referendum, and Olmert found himself under attack in both Israel and the United States for suggesting concessions on Jerusalem. The conference adjourned without any major agreements and Olmert soon turned to a major ground and air attack in Gaza to eliminate militants who were firing rockets across the border. About 1,400 Gazans died in the three-week assault, the vast majority of them noncombatants. When the Israelis withdrew in January 2009, they imposed severe controls on imports into Gaza, leaving the territory suffering and destitute. The peace process was again at a dead end.

After Obama took office in 2009 he tried to restart the process even under these daunting conditions. In hopes that his renunciation of the Bush policies in Iraq and his modifications of tactics in the war on terror might change the atmosphere surrounding the American position in the Middle East, Obama went to Cairo and made an eloquent speech calling for peace and understanding between the Muslim and the Western worlds. In the course of that speech he called upon Israel to freeze any further building of settlements in the West Bank. The new conservative Israeli prime minister, Benjamin Netanyahu, spurned the request just as he would later break with Obama on the 1967 border issue. Obama backed away rather than confront Netanyahu in both cases.

As the peace process remained frozen in late 2011, Abbas despaired of any meaningful negotiations with the Netanyahu government and decided to circumvent the process by requesting UN recognition of an independent Palestinian state within the pre-1967 borders. It was clear that only an American veto in the Security Council would prevent that recognition, and even then the General Assembly was bound to vote in favor of granting the Palestinians the status of an "observer state" similar to that of the Vatican. This would permit the Palestinians to join UN institutions like UNESCO and the World Court and might even allow them to haul Israel before the court on the charge of illegally occupying the territory of the Palestinian state. Obama vowed to cast the American veto, but tried mightily to divert Abbas in order to avoid the embarrassment of standing almost alone in opposing the Palestinians. The embarrassment would have been doubly acute because Abbas was asking only for a settlement freeze and negotiations based on the 1967 border to reopen talks with Israel, both of which Obama had futilely proposed to Netanyahu. Fortunately for Obama the Europeans refused to cast their votes in the Security Council for Palestine so there was no need for the American veto. Nevertheless UNESCO invited the Palestinians to join its branch of the United Nations and the United States then had to withdraw from that important organization because Congress had mandated withdrawal if Palestine were accepted. The Israeli-Palestinian issue would continue to bedevil the United States, but Israeli policy toward Iran would become even more ominous for the Obama administration.

Iran

Iran made short work of a brief Arab Spring uprising against its Islamic government, even while it encouraged rebellions against its Sunni and Western-leaning rivals in the Middle East. Thus Iran remained one of the most daunting of the foreign policy challenges facing the United States in the post-9/11 era as it defied attempts not only to moderate its opposition to Western and American policies, but also to stop its progress toward a nuclear missile capability.

The shah of Iran had begun Iran's nuclear power program with the encouragement of the United States and had signed the Nuclear Nonproliferation Treaty in 1970. The revolution of the ayatollahs in 1979 made the United States far more wary of the Iranian nuclear effort, but Iran allayed those suspicions somewhat when it agreed in 1992 to allow the UN's International Atomic Energy Agency (IAEA) to inspect its facilities. The West was further encouraged when a wave of reformers elected a moderate, Mohammad Khatami, to the Iranian presidency in 1997. But Khatami's attempts at reform fizzled because the government was firmly under the control of conservative clergy led by Ayatollah Khomeini's hard-line successor, Ayatollah Ali Khamenei. Moreover even Khatami and his reformist constituency united with the hard-liners behind the right of Iran to possess nuclear technology.

The nuclear crisis with Iran began in 2003, when President Khatami, faced with an inspection by the IAEA that he had put off for months, suddenly announced that Iran had a program for enriching uranium that it had not declared, as the nonproliferation treaty required. It turned out that the head of the Pakistani nuclear program, A.Q. Khan, who for years had been supplying nuclear technology and components to rogue regimes like those of North Korea and Libya, had also been supplying uranium enrichment information and equipment to Iran between 1987 and 1996. Iran had also imported uranium from China in 1991 without declaring it. Moreover the IAEA found in one Iranian facility traces of highly enriched uranium of the sort used for nuclear weapons rather than for industrial power production, although it was not clear whether the traces were a result of contamination from equipment supplied by Pakistan or activities within Iran itself.

In response to the IAEA report and condemnation, Iran promised to suspend uranium enrichment "voluntarily and temporarily." Unfortunately the suspension was very temporary. In early 2004 Iran announced that it would resume its enrichment program. The United States, France, and Great Britain offered economic and political incentives if Iran would give up its enrichment program and Russia offered to supply fuel for Iran's nuclear reactors, but the Iranians insisted that they needed to produce their own enriched uranium. They also announced plans to build a heavy water plant to produce plutonium. They insisted that their nuclear program was entirely for peaceful purposes and therefore permitted under the nonproliferation treaty.

The West and especially the United States remained suspicious of the Iranian program, however, especially after Mahmoud Ahmadinejad, an anti-Western firebrand, replaced the moderate Khatami as president. In July 2006 Ahmadinejad defied the UN Security Council's demands to suspend uranium enrichment and the Security Council's sanctions that followed. He said that Israel should cease to exist, denied that the Holocaust had ever happened, and predicted the disappearance of the United States.

From 2008 through 2011 Iran continued to expand its uranium enrichment facilities and to test long-range missiles capable of reaching Israel and U.S. forces in the Persian Gulf area. Obama offered unconditional talks with Iran to try negotiating an agreement, but Iran refused, and the United States and the UN Security Council continued to ratchet up sanctions against it. There was some temporary hope of improving relations when the UN Security Council offered to allow Iran to enrich uranium in Russia if it would give up its domestic enrichment program. The Iranian negotiator accepted this proposal but the government rejected it when the negotiator returned home. The West again saw some hope when massive protests erupted against the blatantly rigged elections of 2009. Khamenei and Ahmadinejad put down those demonstrations with massive force, jailed many of the demonstrators, and tried and executed several of the leaders. The destruction of this so-called Green Revolution demoralized much of the Iranian opposition so that the Arab Spring of 2011 brought only a brief round of street demonstrations that the government easily crushed.

Thus Iran remained on a collision course with the United States, Israel, and the West. Israel pushed the United States to use force if necessary to prevent Iran from acquiring nuclear weapons and warned that Israel might resort to force unilaterally if necessary to counter Iran's threat to its very existence. Obama won a delay from Israel to try increased sanctions against Iran's oil lifeline, but in turn he specifically declared that he would prevent the Iranians from acquiring nuclear weapons rather than contain them afterward. There was still some chance for a negotiated settlement that would limit Iran's uranium enrichment program to a percentage of enrichment below weapons grade in exchange for a tighter international inspection regime to guarantee against the development of a nuclear weapon. But with Iran making threats to close the Strait of Hormuz through which Persian Gulf oil flowed and with both Israel and the leading Republican candidates for the presidential elections of 2012 making very belligerent threats against Iran, it was unclear whether this dispute could be resolved peacefully.

North Korea

Iran was not the only nation whose possession of nuclear weapons frightened the United States and its allies. North Korea, another member of George Bush's "axis of evil," seemed at the outset of the Bush administration even more likely than Iran to acquire nuclear weapons and either use them or smuggle them to terrorists. Therefore, in the wake of 9/11, Bush turned away from Clinton's diplomacy to a confrontational policy toward North Korea just as he did toward Afghanistan, Iraq, and Iran. In October 2002 the Bush administration accused North Korea of embarking on a program to enrich uranium, an alternate means to produce nuclear weapons that would circumvent the prohibition against producing plutonium contained in North Korea's 1994 agreement with Bill Clinton. The Bush administration based its accusation on revelations that Pakistan had sold North Korea some centrifuges capable of enriching uranium. The United States could not prove that North Korea had actually used those as models to build the number of centrifuges necessary to create a bomb, but such activities could be hidden more easily than the large facilities needed to produce forbidden plutonium. In any case Bush cut off oil supplies to North Korea. The North Korean dictator, Kim Jung Il, responded by expelling UN nuclear inspectors and withdrawing from the Nuclear Nonproliferation Treaty. Kim then announced that he already possessed nuclear bombs and he tested intermediate-range missiles capable of carrying such devices. By 2006 North Korea had conducted an underground nuclear explosion and a failed launch of an intercontinental-range missile.

Although North Korea posed a more serious WMD threat than Iraq, Bush, chastened by the failures in Iraq, turned to sanctions and diplomacy rather than military force. North Korea's million-man army blocked the possibility of a land invasion, its secret underground nuclear facilities posed difficulties for a successful bombing campaign, and the proximity of the South Korean capital and 30,000 American troops to the artillery massed across the North Korean border made the military option very unattractive. So Bush pressed North Korea economically by getting a Macao bank to freeze the many North Korean assets it held. He also helped organize Six Party Talks between North Korea, the United States, and North Korea's neighbors, South Korea, Japan, Russia, and China. Under pressure from China, its only ally and major trade partner, North Korea agreed in October 2007 to make a full declaration of its nuclear assets, avoid proliferation of its nuclear technology, and allow inspectors to disable its main nuclear reactors. In exchange North Korea would receive supplies of oil and other energy sources to compensate for the loss of nuclear energy. Also the United States would begin the process of removing economic sanctions and taking North Korea off the list of nations sponsoring terrorism, a process that would parallel North Korean steps toward nuclear disarmament. Meanwhile North and South Korea began talks about economic cooperation and even eventual reunification. The agreement looked promising, but there was still no arrangement regarding North Korea's existing stock of plutonium and nuclear weapons. The United States estimated North Korea's stock of plutonium at about fifty kilograms, enough to make between five and ten bombs.

After some delays North Korea finally made its declaration of nuclear facilities in June 2008, and in response Bush lifted some trade sanctions and notified Congress that he intended to remove North Korea from the sponsor-of-terrorism list in forty-five days, according to U.S. law. But both sides delayed fulfilling the bargain in a quarrel over verification procedures. The United States wanted very intrusive inspections that would include North Korea's existing weapons. North Korea objected and insisted that it should be able to inspect American nuclear weapons in South Korea. The entire negotiation broke apart in April 2009 when North Korea tested a long-range missile capable of carrying a nuclear warhead by firing it directly over Japan. The UN Security Council condemned the launch and began to reapply sanctions on North Korea. North Korea withdrew from the Six Party Talks, expelled the inspectors, and renounced all previous nuclear agreements. It then proceeded to conduct its second underground nuclear test to announce that it was no longer bound by the 1953 armistice that ended the Korean War.

Barack Obama tried to arrest this downward spiral by offering direct bilateral talks with North Korea as a prelude to resuming the Six Party Talks. But when a North Korean torpedo sank a South Korean patrol boat in waters close to the maritime border between the two nations, relations with North Korea again plummeted. North Korea denied involvement in the sinking and revealed to a group of U.S. experts that it had completed a large plant for uranium enrichment. It then shelled the inhabitants of a small island it claimed the South Koreans were illegally occupying. The United States and South Korea continued to conduct joint military exercises that North Korea considered preludes to war.

The Obama administration saw little chance that negotiations with North Korea would be productive. It speculated that North Korea was acting aggressively in part because Kim Jong Il was in poor health and his son and chosen heir, Kim Jong Un was positioning himself as a patron of the army whose support was essential for control of the nation. When Kim Jong Il died in December 2011, and Kim Jong Un replaced him, the belligerence continued so that a nuclear-armed North Korea remained a critical area of instability and uncertainty for U.S. foreign policy.

Russia: The Reset

The Russians, as a participant in the Six Party Talks, played an important role in America's attempt to rein in the North Koreans, just as they played an important role in maintaining sanctions against Iran's nuclear efforts. Moreover the Russians permitted the United States to supply the war in Afghanistan through nations under their influence. Despite Russia's cooperation in these matters, U.S.-Russian relations deteriorated badly during the George W. Bush administration. The Russians resented Bush's support for continued NATO expansion into eastern Europe and especially the role played by American government and nongovernmental organizations in support of democratic revolutions in areas bordering Russia. These so-called color revolutions, modeled on the earlier Velvet Revolution in Czechoslovakia, overthrew authoritarian and corrupt pro-Russian regimes in Georgia (the Rose Revolution), Ukraine (the Orange Revolution), and Kyrgyzstan (the Tulip Revolution). Russian resentment turned to alarm when Bush withdrew the United States from the Antiballistic Missile Treaty and announced plans to install an antimissile system consisting of ten missiles in Poland and a controlling radar system in the Czech Republic aimed at Iran's potential nuclear missiles. Bush argued that such a system was incapable of interfering with Russia's own nuclear deterrent, but the Russians were not mollified.

The deterioration of U.S.-Russian relations plunged to a dangerous level in August 2008 when war broke out between Russia and Georgia, a former Soviet republic. Tensions had been high between Russia and Georgia ever since Georgia had broken from the old Soviet Union and taken with it two border provinces—South Ossetia and

Abkhazia—that contained many nonethnic Georgians who preferred to remain attached to Russia. That dispute escalated after the Rose Revolution of 2003 in Georgia, during which Gorbachev's former foreign minister, Eduard Shevardnadze, found himself and his deteriorating and corrupt regime overthrown by Mikhail Saakashvili, a passionately pro-Western and anti-Russian former protégé of Shevardnadze. Saakashvili had taken a law degree at Columbia University and briefly practiced in New York. He bound himself tightly to the West in both his economic and foreign policies. Not only did he seek membership in NATO but he had the United States train, supply, and even conduct joint exercises with his armed forces.

Russia and Georgia had tried to dampen the dispute over South Ossetia in 1992 by granting considerable autonomy to South Ossetia and agreeing to joint peacekeeping forces in the territory consisting of troops from both countries and from North and South Ossetia. But Russia stirred the pot by granting citizenship and passports to the majority of Abkhazians and South Ossetians who favored Russia. The area became notorious for criminal gangs and smuggling, which the Georgians used as a rationale to send troops into the disputed territories. By 2008 both sides were shelling each other with artillery, conducting military exercises in the region, and mobilizing troops. On August 7, 2008, Saakashvili broke the stalemate by launching a full invasion of South Ossetia only to have the Russians crush the Georgian army and then invade Georgia itself. In the process the Russians destroyed Georgia's ships, planes, and much of its infrastructure. Russia then recognized South Ossetia and Abkhazia as independent nations that it vowed to protect with its own forces.

The Bush administration's UN ambassador denounced the Russian actions as a campaign of terror against the territorial integrity of Georgia, and Bush withdrew the pending Nuclear Cooperation Treaty with Russia from consideration. The Russians responded that the United States had conducted the real campaigns of terror against the national sovereignty of Serbia, Afghanistan, and Iraq. However, the situation cooled as the United States and its Western allies used much less bloody language in their formal complaints that Russia's invasion of Georgia and recognition of the independence of South Ossetia and Abkhazia were "disproportional to the situation," thus implying that resistance within South Ossetia to Saakashvili's invasion might have been proportional. In any case Russia did subsequently withdraw from Georgia and permit European Union inspectors to monitor the Georgian border, but refused to back away from its protection of Abkhazia and South Ossetia as independent states. The United States, meanwhile, dispatched aid to help rebuild Georgia.

With U.S.-Russian relations at a nadir, Obama decided to try to "reset" the relationship. He canceled Bush's plans for deployment of the antimissile system in Poland and the Czech Republic and offered to negotiate with the Russians a smaller-scale system that could cope with the short-range missiles Iran was likely to have in the next few years while being less threatening to the Russian deterrent. Obama also negotiated a new START treaty with the Russians to reduce the number of strategic missiles from about 2,200 apiece to between 1,500 and 1,675 each. But Russia refused to agree to Obama's new antimissile plans and insisted on respect for its sphere of influence. It also remained reluctant to permit the UN Security Council to impose greater sanctions on North Korea and Iran. The reset was only partially successful.

America as a World Power

Obama took to heart the realist dictum that a nation needed to balance its goals with the power available. He recognized the limits of American power to accomplish all that the Bush administration had led the American people to expect. But he found it difficult to achieve even the more modest goals that he set for his own administration. Part of the reason was the obduracy of the foreign leaders with whom he had to work, including Karzai in Afghanistan, al-Maliki and the other factional leaders in Iraq, Putin in Russia, Netanyahu in Israel, and Hamas in Palestine, not to mention the Republicans in his own Congress. Part of the reason may also have been Obama's style of "leading from behind"—that is, sketching broad goals but leaving Congress and others to fill in most of the details. Critics on the Left argued that he should not have backed away from his demand that Netanyahu and Israel stop building settlements, that he conceded too much to the U.S. military's demands for more troops in Afghanistan, and that he failed to follow through consistently in support of the Arab Spring when it came to tyrants who provided favors to the United States. Critics on the Right argued that he planned too rapid a withdrawal from Afghanistan, that he undermined Israeli security by pushing for compromise with the Palestinians and by supporting Arab Spring rebellions that would inevitably be anti-Israeli, and that he gave in to Russian bullying on stationing an antimissile system in eastern Europe. The major reason that Obama found it difficult to accomplish even his most modest goals, however, was the overwhelming nature of the problems he faced and the declining power of the United States to overcome them.

The first of those problems was the weakness of the American economy. Obama recognized that much of the power needed by the United States to accomplish its foreign policy goals stemmed from the strength of its economy. His National Security Strategy made strengthening the American economy the first of his foreign policy goals: "Our strategy starts by recognizing that our strength and influence abroad begins with the steps we take at home. We must grow our economy and reduce our deficit." Unfortunately, he came into office during a recession that threatened to turn into a depression rivaling that of 1929. A boom in real estate prices had induced homeowners to take out large mortgages, which banks and other financial firms packaged into bundles of derivatives that speculators drove to inordinate levels. The ensuing crash devastated the American economy and hurt many other economies abroad.

Obama followed the Keynesian formula of government deficit spending to try to counter the recession on the model of Franklin D. Roosevelt's New Deal. Most of this deficit spending had to go toward rescuing the financial system that was so wounded by the mortgage collapse and preventing banks from succumbing to the point that all credit would freeze up. But Obama also tried to direct much of the deficit spending to rebuild the sort of infrastructure that underlay the economic well-being of all industrial nations. This included not only the physical infrastructure of roads, bridges, railways, ports, airline facilities, and the U.S. auto industry, but also the human infrastructure, such as education and health care, necessary for economic innovation and an effective labor force.

Obama also tried to direct investment toward innovative "green" industries that he hoped would be the next frontier in high-end manufacturing. Such industries would wean America away from dependence on foreign oil while reducing global warming. The American economy had lost much of its industrial base to cheap overseas labor so that 70 percent of the economy was driven by consumer spending rather than the production of goods and services. The housing boom had led to high consumer spending because people had borrowed against the rising value of their homes. When that bubble burst, the housing price collapse prevented consumer spending from returning to drive the economy. Obama's hope was that green energy products might be the next driver of the economy because there was no way the United States could rise to its prerecession level of prosperity by going back to an economy that was 70 percent dependent on consumer spending.

Most economists agreed that the bailout initiated by George W. Bush and accelerated by Obama did keep the economy from collapsing into a depression. But the economy barely revived and unemployment continued to hover around 9 percent through 2011. Green energy products found stiff competition from China, and neither that enterprise nor any other on the horizon managed to revive investment, production, and employment. Meanwhile the federal budget deficit produced by the decline in tax revenues, deficit spending, and even more by the growing obligations of entitlements such as Social Security, Medicare, and Medicaid raised alarms about the path of the American economy.

Obama's proposed solution in mid-2011 was another round of deficit spending to keep the nation from falling into a double-dip recession while promising that once the economy recovered he would raise taxes and lower entitlement and other expenditures to reduce the budget deficit. But the continuing high rate of unemployment undercut Obama's popularity and public confidence in his economic prescriptions. His Republican Party opponents denounced the whole Keynesian economic prescription of deficit spending to counter a recession. They argued that it had been World War II rather than the New Deal that had pulled the United States out of the Great Depression and they insisted that the deficit should be met with immediate budget cuts and no new taxes.

There was a compromise to be made here, a so-called grand bargain in which immediate government spending to create jobs and spur the economy would be followed by cuts to entitlements and other programs. Revenues might be raised by a tax reform that lowered rates while eliminating many deductions rather than by raising taxes on the same system. But this was a hard sell to a body politic reeling from four years of recession and high unemployment. Moreover, neither the Republicans, who argued that government should just get out of the way, nor the Democrats, who hated to see cuts in the social and economic programs they had built during the New Deal and Lyndon Johnson's Great Society, were eager to compromise on the issues of taxes and entitlement cuts. Thus the political opposition was adamant and Obama's leadership was inadequate to overcome it.

Europe's economic situation was even worse than that of the United States, and Europe's economic weakness both threatened America's own economic recovery and reduced the power of the American-European alliance to solve problems in world affairs. Although America's financial crash had triggered the European recession, Europe had already been on the brink of a meltdown anyway. Some of the weaker economies in the European Union (EU) had run up massive debts despite promises by all the eurozone nations to hold government deficits to 3 percent of public debt and to 60 percent of gross domestic product (GDP). But Ireland, Greece, and Portugal far exceeded those limits and the European Union faced a critical decision. The EU could either loan those countries the money to pay their debts in exchange for drastic austerity measures to balance their budgets, or it could watch them default, which would undercut the stability of the major European banks that had purchased the bonds of those nations. The European nations with the strongest economies, especially Germany, objected to subsidizing nations they believed had been profligate in their borrowing. If the European Union failed to rescue Ireland, Greece, and Portugal, however, there was the danger that the banks holding their bonds would fail or freeze credit so that the much larger and troubled economies of Spain and Italy would follow in the wake of the weaker nations. This would mean disaster because the economies of Spain and Italy were too large for the European Union to bail out.

The United States had a great deal at stake in this decision. The American economy relied heavily on trade with Europe. America's banks were closely tied to the European banks that would suffer from any national defaults. And American foreign policy rested heavily on the European alliance. The Obama administration strongly favored measures to hold Europe and the eurozone together and prevent defaults. But when U.S. Treasury Secretary Timothy Geithner met with the European financial ministers in September 2011 and offered this advice, the Austrian finance minister remarked, "I found it peculiar that even though the Americans have significantly worse fundamental data than the eurozone, they tell us what we should do." Obviously, yet another significant issue for America's economy and foreign policy was beyond Obama's control.

While American and European power in the world declined, that of other emerging nations was increasing. China was the greatest beneficiary of this trend. China's economy had grown 10 percent per year since 1990, and its growth remained strong even when the United States and Europe sank into recession after 2007. A large part of China's growth depended on exports to the United States, which China supported by keeping wages low and pegging its currency to the dollar at artificially low rates so its products would be cheap in America and the West. Because the Chinese currency was undervalued, Chinese people could not afford many American imports and the imbalance of trade meant that America's trade deficit with China totaled about $250 billion per year after 2007. China covered that imbalance of trade and kept the value of its currency low by purchasing massive amounts of U.S. treasury bonds with its surplus so that it held more than $1 trillion in U.S. government debt by 2011. Moreover the Chinese government made it difficult for Western and American companies to operate in China by subsidizing its own industries. It required most Western companies to partner with Chinese companies when setting up in China and to share technological data that would enable China to produce certain high-tech goods without Western partners if necessary. China also acquired the means to produce high-tech goods by refusing to enforce the patent rights of Western companies.

The Bush and Obama administrations pushed to rectify this imbalance of trade with some limited success. The Chinese permitted their currency to rise slightly against the dollar and loosened some restrictions on the operations of American businesses. But the real hope of restoring some balance in U.S. trade relations with China rested with China's own determination to develop its internal market and shift its emphasis away from exports. If China succeeded in that goal, it would certainly improve Chinese-American economic relations.

China's explosive economic growth undergirded a rise in military and strategic as well as financial power. China did not seem to have a great appetite for territorial expansion, but there were geographical areas of potential friction between China and the United States. Taiwan was the most dangerous of these areas. China continued to insist that Taiwan was a renegade province and that China would be entitled to take it by force if necessary to prevent its permanent independence. China modernized its military forces, stationed modern rockets within range of Taiwan, and began acquiring submarines and an aircraft carrier that would make it very difficult for America's own fleet to move into the straits between China and Taiwan to thwart a Chinese invasion. When Obama decided to sell $6.4 billion worth of so-called defensive arms to Taiwan in 2010, China broke off scheduled military talks with the United States and threatened to retaliate against American companies doing business in China. Although the quarrel eventually died down, Taiwan remained a cause of friction and even potential war between the two nations.

Besides Taiwan, other islands and potential energy resources in the ocean waters around China also created friction between China and the United States. In the South China Sea, China pressed its claims to the entire set of Spratly Islands, which were also claimed in their entirety by Taiwan and Vietnam and in part by the Philippines, Malaysia, and Brunei. In the East China Sea, China quarreled with Japan about drilling for natural gas around islands known as the Senkaku isles in Japan and Diaoyu in China. China was not pleased when U.S. secretary of state Hillary Clinton offered to mediate between China and the other claimants in the South China Sea. The Chinese were even less pleased when the U.S. Navy conducted joint exercises with South Korea in the Yellow Sea as a response to North Korean provocations. Chinese military leaders sometimes complained that the United States, in supporting Japan, South Korea, and the Southeast Asian nations in these controversies, was trying to surround and contain China.

Along with the imbalance of trade and strategic rivalries, China's treatment of dissidents and political opposition irritated relations between China and the United States. Bush and Obama both protested against Chinese treatment of dissident minorities such as the Tibetans and the Uighurs; Obama's public meeting with Tibet's Dalai Lama in February 2010 was an obvious rebuke to Chinese repression. Denouncing that meeting and other American gestures in favor of Chinese minorities as interference in its internal affairs, China insisted that its treatment of the Tibetans and Uighurs was a matter of national sovereignty. China used the same defense when the United States protested the imprisonment of prominent dissenters like Nobel Peace Prize winner Liu Xiaobo and writer Hu Jia. China's treatment of dissidents raised special problems for America's Internet providers because China insisted that the American companies permit Chinese officials to monitor the transmissions of government opponents. Google moved its Chinese operations to Hong Kong to escape those regulations. But even such a move could not prevent the Chinese from undertaking major cyber-hacking operations against Google, other major corporations, and even U.S. government agencies to get the information they wanted.

Neither Bush nor Obama pushed so hard on these issues as to seriously harm U.S.-China relations. The United States needed China too much in economic matters such as trade and finance and strategic matters such as North Korea, Iran, and Asia in general. China needed the United States as well, so the quarrels remained in the realm of diplomatic rather than economic or military conflict.

Another quarrel between the United States and China that remained in the realm of diplomacy concerned international negotiations over climate change and global warming. George W. Bush had withdrawn the United States from Bill Clinton's commitments under the Kyoto Protocol to reduce greenhouse gases like carbon dioxide that trapped heat in the atmosphere. But Obama pledged to renew America's commitment to reduce global warming. He personally attended the Copenhagen Climate Change Conference in December 2009, along with more than 100 other heads of state and government leaders, to try to conclude a binding treaty to replace the Kyoto Protocol, which was due to expire in 2012. To make it possible for the United States to conclude an agreement, Obama decided to wait no longer for Congress to pass a cap-and-trade bill. The Democratic-controlled House had passed a cap-and-trade bill that was designed to lower carbon emissions 17 percent from the 2005 level by setting a limit on carbon emissions each corporation could emit, but allowing companies to exceed that cap if they purchased emitting rights from companies that got credits for polluting less than they were allowed. The Republicans in the Senate, however, along with some Democrats from coal-producing states, stalled the bill in the upper house. Obama circumvented this stalemate by empowering the Environmental Protection Agency (EPA) to regulate carbon emissions as pollutants under the Clean Air Act.

Despite this maneuver Obama failed to get a treaty on global warming at the Copenhagen Conference. China led a bloc of developing nations, including Brazil, India, and South Africa, that refused to accept binding and verifiable limits on their carbon emissions. They argued that the Western developed nations, who were responsible for the existing high levels of carbon in the atmosphere, should reduce their own levels before asking poorer developing countries to limit theirs. China also objected to any outside verification of carbon emissions. Obama and the West tried to reach a compromise by offering billions of dollars to help developing countries limit their emissions—$30 billion by 2012 and $100 billion by 2020. But the developing countries rejected the offer. On the last day of the conference, Obama negotiated a weak compromise with China and its bloc that provided for goals rather than binding commitments on emissions and aid. But another group of developing nations that included Sudan, Venezuela, and Bolivia prevented the conference from adopting even that compromise. In the end, the conference could only "take note of" this Copenhagen Accord.

Within a few months any sort of cap-and-trade bill or limit on emissions in the United States seemed dead in the water. The economic recession and a Republican surge in the

2010 congressional elections created majorities in both houses that feared the economic impact of greenhouse gas limits. The Republican surge also empowered conservatives who doubted the science of climate change and who wanted to strip the EPA of power to regulate carbon emissions, if not do away with the agency entirely. The worldwide recession dampened enthusiasm for expensive environmental action in other nations as well. Thus when the climate change negotiations resumed in Cancun, Mexico, in December 2010, no heads of state or government attended and the Cancun Conference adjourned with little accomplished. The American quarrel with China and other developing nations over global warming was moot for the time being, but the developing nations had demonstrated their growing influence. Some of them, like India and Brazil, along with Japan and Germany, demanded permanent seats on the UN Security Council in recognition of their increased power in international affairs.

Brazil's rise to world power was part of a general drift in Latin America away from U.S. domination. Brazil even partnered with Turkey to propose alternatives to the U.S. attempt to impose stricter sanctions on the Iranian nuclear program. It was not that all of Latin America was in danger of following the vociferous anti-Americanism of Cuba's Raul Castro, Venezuela's Hugo Chavez, or Chavez's allies in Bolivia, Ecuador, and Nicaragua. U.S. relations with the other major nations of Latin America, such as Argentina, Chile, Colombia, and Mexico, were rather good. But those nations increasingly had economic alternatives to their trade with the United States. China especially was bidding high for the newly discovered oil and other abundant natural resources of Latin America.

Another issue that roiled U.S. relations with Latin America was the illegal drug trade. The market for illegal drugs in the United States has been estimated at more than $50 billion annually. That market provides an irresistible temptation for many people in the poor countries of Latin America. From coca leaf growers and cocaine refiners in the Andean nations of Colombia, Bolivia, and Peru to the Colombian and Dominican traffickers who transport the drugs through the Caribbean and Central America to the Mexican cartels who smuggle the cocaine along with domestically produced heroin and marijuana into the United States, the profits are enormous. But the costs to the nations in which the cartels operate are also enormous. The drug wars between Mexican cartels fighting for control of the access routes to the United States cost 40,000 lives between 2006 and 2011. Seventy percent of the guns recovered in those Mexican drug wars came from the United States. The societies of the Central American and Caribbean nations that serve as conduits for the trade have also been ravaged. The United States negotiated coca leaf eradication programs with some of the Andean nations in South America, including Colombia, Peru, and Bolivia. But those programs were only partially successful and were extremely unpopular with the small farmers who were the primary losers in the campaigns. Cocaine production dropped in Colombia by 58 percent but grew in Peru by 38 percent as traffickers moved their production and refining operations to less populated areas. Meanwhile the indigenous people of Bolivia succeeded in electing a government responsive to them—which terminated the U.S. eradication effort, allied itself with Hugo Chavez, and saw cocaine production rise 112 percent. Some advocates in the United States have argued that the nation should decriminalize drugs, tax them as a means of gaining revenue, use economic rather than legal incentives to reduce drug use, and thus relieve the American prison systems of the 25 percent of all inmates jailed on drug charges. But decriminalization has little support among the public, comes with significant health and moral consequences, and seems unlikely to thwart the gangs who control the production and transportation of those drugs to the United States. With Latin American nations urging the United States to do something about the drug and gun markets that attract trafficking and the United States advocating and subsidizing a war on drugs in Latin America, the problem of drugs continues to fester.

Controversial Issues: The Cultural Divide and American Foreign Policy

The great recession exacerbated an existing cultural divide in the United States that could have a significant effect on U.S. foreign relations in the near future. Unemployment and economic hard times inspired not just dissatisfaction but rage among large numbers of Americans. During the Great Depression, anger had been directed at corporations and the wealthy elite—"the malefactors of great wealth" as Theodore Roosevelt had called them. Such sentiments had resulted in the Democratic Party's dominance of American politics for a generation along with a liberal program of federal intervention to stimulate the economy, control corporate and banking power, elevate the status of workers, and establish progressive rates of taxation. The great recession of 2007 seemed to be repeating that pattern with the defeat of the Republican George W. Bush and the election of the Democrat Barack Obama. But federal intervention to stimulate the economy, regulate banks, and extend greater government protection to consumers and the environment failed to jump-start the economy or bring unemployment much below 9 percent. Obama had good reason to claim that the economic stimulus undertaken by both the Bush and Obama administrations had at least spared the United States another Great Depression. But arguing that things could have been worse is hardly ever a winning position in politics.

The government bailout of banks and corporations, along with the Obama administration's passage of a health-care bill that mandated everyone to purchase health insurance in order to extend protection to all, roused more anger at the government than at the banks and corporations that had played such a big role in creating the speculative bubble. And this rage owed at least as much to the cultural currents in America as to the economic currents.

The Republican Party, the major political beneficiary of the anger at Obama and the federal government, comprised two major constituencies. The first constituency consisted of establishment Republicans. They favored small government because they were traditional laissez-faire Wall Street and Main Street business people. They were mostly well educated, urban, cosmopolitan, prosperous, and moderate on social issues like guns, abortion, immigration, and religion in the public sphere. On foreign policy, they tended to favor strong defense spending and an assertive stance, but such Republicans had supported détente in the Nixon administration and restraint in the

George H.W. Bush administration. Many of them had advised against the Iraq War and favored comprehensive immigration reform in the George W. Bush administration. Such moderate Republicans also had been stronger advocates of Israeli concessions to the Palestinians than most Democrats during the Nixon, Reagan, and George H.W. Bush administrations.

The other wing of the Republican Party consisted of so-called social conservatives. Social conservatives were generally more rural, less prosperous, and less cosmopolitan than establishment Republicans. A great many of them were white Christian evangelicals. They agreed with establishment Republicans on limiting federal power, but they were especially angry at attempts by the government to control guns, protect the right to abortions, prevent prayer in school, recognize gay marriage, or provide any services that encouraged illegal immigration. They valued patriotism and Americanism and they had a somewhat nativist outlook on foreigners and people of other races and religions, especially adherents of Islam. They were highly represented among the 52 percent of Republicans polled in 2010 who believed it was definitely or probably true that Obama "sympathizes with the goals of Islamic fundamentalists who want to impose Islamic law around the world" and the 24 percent of Americans who believed that Obama was himself a Muslim. Social conservatives tended to be populists who detested elites, but not so much the economic elite who had made its money in good capitalist fashion. Instead they detested the cultural elite—the liberal, secular, urban, academic, and cosmopolitan gentry who looked down on social conservatives as uneducated rubes and supported activist government, gay marriage, amnesty for illegal immigrants, gun control, the teaching of evolution rather than creationism in schools, and the establishment of environmental regulations to prevent global warming based on the warnings of a suspect scientific community. This dispute between liberals and social conservatives was nothing less than a culture war, and it had raged at least since the 1960s.

While the Republican establishment, with its emphasis on economics rather than social and moral issues, had been rather moderate and accommodating in its politics, the social conservatives were passionate and uncompromising. Until the recession the two wings of the Republican Party had managed to cooperate and coexist. The establishment controlled economic policy in Congress while conceding judicial appointments to the social conservatives. But economic hard times and the perceived failures of Obama's activist government policies roused a fury among many economic conservatives almost equal to that of the social conservatives. Such angry economic conservatives founded the tea party movement to insist on budget cuts and lower taxes. The tea party movement provided a bridge between economic and social conservatives, allowing them to form a populist alliance that opposed any compromises with Democrats on taxes, government spending, or other liberal aspirations. The conservatives even denounced establishment Republicans as elitists and marginalized all moderation in the party.

The primary impact of this swing to the right was domestic. It made almost impossible any attempt by the establishment Republican congressional leadership to compromise over the means of reducing the long-term federal deficit, which according to most economists and two bipartisan budget study groups required temporary government spending to prevent a double-dip recession and grow the economy to be followed by a combination of increased tax revenue and reductions in entitlement spending on Medicare, Medicaid, and Social Security. But the rightward swing also promised some impact on U.S. foreign policy beyond the possibility that America's weakened financial situation would reduce the power the United States could exercise in the international arena.

The new alliance of economic and social populists tended to be more unilateralist and less concerned with allies or international organizations than either Republican moderates or Democrats. This tendency showed up especially in their attitudes toward Obama's policy in the Middle East. Many social conservatives reacted harshly not just against Islamic terrorism but against Islam itself. They joined almost all other conservatives in giving unwavering support to the hard line taken by Netanyahu and Israel against the Palestinians, and they denounced Obama for pushing Israel to compromise on West Bank settlements, Jerusalem, and other issues. Many of the evangelicals among these conservatives opposed any compromises with the Palestinians because they believed that the second coming of Christ would occur only after the Jews had returned to all of the ancient Jewish Holy Land, including that part of the Palestinian West Bank known in Biblical times as Judea and Samaria. When Obama stood almost alone in the United Nations against Palestinian requests for recognition as a state, they denounced him not for defying international will or for the way this would separate the United States from the democratic majorities gaining power in the Arab Spring, but for appeasing the Palestinians in ways that supposedly led them to appeal to the UN.

The conservative swing will certainly affect other aspects of American foreign relations as well. The United States will no longer participate vigorously in international negotiations to limit global warming. If the Republicans defeat Obama in 2012, they are likely to take a harder line on Russia, China, North Korea, and Iran, although it is not clear just how far that will go. Conservatives will probably affect Latin American relations to some extent by maintaining a harsh policy toward Cuba and by taking stricter stances toward immigration and drugs, although the desire for immigrant labor on the part of Republican business interests and opposition to the war on drugs from the libertarian wing of the tea party movement might moderate policy in those areas to some extent.

Perhaps the most fascinating argument among conservatives will be over military spending, an issue that crosses the lines between and among the various factions in the Republican Party. Although the majority of Republicans have always favored a strong defense, many of them have become disenchanted with the Iraq and Afghan wars and are ready to disengage. Moreover their desire to cut government spending and balance the budget has pushed them in the direction of lower defense allocations. Even though many Republicans have resisted the Democrats' call for cutting defense spending in order to help balance the budget, the most complete long-term budget plans put forward by Republicans have also included significant defense cuts.

It may be that an economic recovery will soften the anger on both sides of the cultural divide. But without that economic recovery the United States will have a difficult time planning and executing a coherent domestic or foreign policy.

Further Reading

On the Obama presidency in general, see Jonathan Alter, *The Promise: President Obama: Year One* (2010); and Ron Suskind, *Confidence Men: Wall Street, Washington, and the Education of a President* (2011). On Obama's foreign policy specifically, see Bob Woodward, *Obama's Wars* (2010); Stephen L. Carter, *The Violence of Peace: America's Wars in the Age of Obama* (2011); and Marvin and Deborah Kalb, *Haunting Legacy: Vietnam and the American Presidency from Ford to Obama* (2011).

For the background and conditions of the war in Afghanistan, see Peter Tomsen, *The Wars of Afghanistan: Messianic Terrorism, Tribal Conflicts, and the Failures of Great Powers* (2011). For the war itself, see Sabastian Junger, *War* (2010). For Obama's policy toward Russia, see Keir Giles, *The NATO-Russia Reset* (2011).

INDEX

Note: Page numbers in italics indicate illustrations.

ABOUT THE AUTHOR

Jerald A. Combs was a professor of history, department chair, and dean of undergraduate studies at San Francisco State from 1964 to 2006 and continues to serve as a consultant to the university on international education. He is the author of *The Jay Treaty: Political Battleground of the Founding Fathers* (University of California Press, 1970) and *American Diplomatic History: Two Centuries of Changing Interpretations* (University of California Press, 1983).